Return on or before the
last date stamped below.

Learning Resources
Centre

Kingston College
Kingston Hall Road
Kingston upon Thames
KT1 2AQ

Frederick the Great

Frederick the Great

A LIFE IN DEED AND LETTERS

GILES MacDONOGH

Weidenfeld & Nicolson
LONDON

First published in Great Britain in 1999
by Weidenfeld & Nicolson

© 1999 Giles MacDonogh

A CIP catalogue record for this book
is available from the British Library.

ISBN 0 297 81777 9

Filmset by Selwood Systems, Midsomer Norton
Printed in Great Britain by
Butler & Tanner Ltd, Frome and London

Weidenfeld & Nicolson

The Orion Publishing Group Ltd
Orion House
5 Upper Saint Martin's Lane
London, WC2H 9EA

For Isolde Alexandra MacDonogh

O Kindheit, o entgleitende Vergleiche.
Wohin? Wohin?

RILKE

Contents

Illustrations

Acknowledgements

This book has had such a long and complicated gestation that it is hard to know how to disentangle those who have helped with this project from those who must have assumed I was working on quite another. Like my previous books on Prussia and Berlin it was written in London and the former Prussian capital, where my friends Stuart Pigott and Ursula Heinzelmann were as generous as ever with their spare room in Wedding, and did much to relieve the stress and strain of working away from my usual desk. Denis Staunton also proved a valuable friend and helping hand. My thanks also to Bernd Buhmann of Berlin Tourismus Marketing GmbH, and the German National Tourist Office in London for arranging my trips to Berlin and Weimar in 1997 and 1998. In Weimar Thomas Kretzer provided me with pictures and information.

Once again I have travelled far and wide in Frederick's former provinces. Potsdam, Rheinsberg and Neuruppin are essential for the understanding of Frederick the Great, but I have particularly warm memories of a day in Kloster Zinna, which afforded insights into both the layout of a Friderician weavers' colony and the fate of Frederick's reputation under the DDR. My thanks to the mayor, Frank Letz, and Oliver Schmidt of the local museum.

Angela Bielenberg was kind enough to drive me round her ancestral stamping ground of the Altmark, which is rich in memories of Prussia's famous king. She also helped unravel the odd knotty bit of German. My friend Andreas Kleber of the Kleber Post in Saulgau effected an introduction with Friedrich Wilhelm Fürst von Hohenzollern, who claims to be the last man to have seen Frederick the Great, when his coffin was repaired in 1952! In Vienna Douglas Graf O'Donell cleared up a point or two about the Wild Geese in Maria Theresa's army.

In London Dr Philip Mansel was a natural source for information on the prince de Ligne; my sister, Katharine MacDonogh, proved an unexpected expert on Sainte Beuve. Dr Lucy Brazil and Dr David James answered some of my questions about Frederick's ill-health and the causes of his death. At the *Financial Times*, Robert Thomson, Jill James and Paul Betts facilitated my trips to Berlin and Potsdam. Charmian Colvin of the Brewers' Association put me in touch with the late Jimmy Young, who turned out to be *the* historical expert on pub signs. With his help I was able to track down a handful of 'Kings of Prussia', which had been renamed at the beginning of the Great War.

In Oxford, my former tutor Dr Colin Lucas, now Master of Balliol and Vice-Chancellor of the University, attempted to shape my thoughts on Frederick and Voltaire over dinner. Dr Nicholas Cronk of Saint Edmund Hall and the Voltaire Foundation introduced me to the French poet's special room at the Taylor Institution, supplied me with books and photocopies, and kindly read the manuscript.

Hugh Lawson-Tancred and Ranjit Bolt were at the mercy of my questions on classical languages, metre and history. Ron Pisakiewicz of the Vienna Philharmonic Orchestra gave me the benefit of his wisdom on J. S. Bach. Jonathon Keates also gave me an ad hoc tutorial on the music at Frederick's court.

The book has been read by Professor T. C. W. Blanning and my agent Peter Robinson, who have both come up with many excellent suggestions for where improvements could be made. Thanks also to Rebecca Wilson and Catherine Hill at Weidenfeld, and to Douglas Matthews for once again consenting to compile my index.

I have to express my eternal gratitude to the staffs of the Staatsbibliothek in Berlin, the British Library, the German Historical Institute and the Goethe Institute in London.

Above all, however, I owe thanks to Candida Brazil, who had to bear the brunt of looking after our daughter Isolde, who was impatient enough to want to come into this world only a couple of weeks after I first put pen to paper.

Giles MacDonogh,
London, 1 January 1998

Frederick the Great

Introduction

There have been many Fredericks: mostly imposters. They started appearing even before his death on 17 August 1786, and they still crop up to this day. The pretenders were quite often abetted by Frederick's own family and circle. Voltaire's scurrilous portrait of the king appeared shortly before Frederick's death. Together with the suspect accounts written by his sister Wilhelmina and by the courtier Pöllnitz, it has succeeded in creating an indelible image that needs to be taken with a handful of salt.

Three years after the death of the Prussian monarch, the French Revolution broke out in France. The ideas of the Enlightenment, which Frederick had pondered, adopted and to some extent enacted, now became part of the armoury of the Revolutionaries. At first the image of the Prussian king stood untarnished: Prussia, after all, showed no signs of that unrest which shook France; but with the fall of Louis XVI and the advent of rule in the people's name, Frederick's progressive ideas began to look very dated.

The real threat to Frederick came from Germany, not France; but it was the French who brought it all about. Before long the Revolution was exporting the idea of nationalism, and Germans began a fruitless search for their non-existent country. Worse still, Bonaparte brought nationalism home to roost when he invaded the Holy Roman Empire and defeated the proud Prussian armies at the battles of Jena and Auerstedt in 1806. Not only did many of the small German states become French puppets, but Prussia was subjected to seven years of savage and thoroughly exploitative occupation. The bitter gall fermented in the Prussian maw. By the time Prussians and other inhabitants of the former Reich were able to throw off the French yoke, many had undergone a transformation: they were no longer just the subjects of so many princes, they were Germans too.

As Germans they wanted Hermanns: strong men who had fought their cause. Frederick was just the thing. The man who spoke, wrote and breathed French; who never mastered what we would call today *Hochdeutsch*; the cosmopolitan intellectual of the Enlightenment, became 'Frederick the champion of the German state'. His image loomed large and everywhere, when German nationalists assembled to call for a united Germany under Prussian leadership. This was the first real imposter, and in many ways the longest lived; for it was at this time that scholars began to put together the first wide-ranging biographies of the Prussian king, and to edit his letters and papers.[1]

This hero, Frederick, needed to be remoulded to fit the desired picture. His suspicious sexuality was swept under the carpet and, with time and translations, the Francophile monarch was rendered into homely German. The peppery macaroni and champagne of his ordinary dinner became a more solid feast of sausages and beer. By the time Germany was indeed unified under a Prussian aegis, the process was nearing completion. Frederick had become a pillar of the new state; he was now an essential part of *Germany*, a land he had never imagined in his wildest dreams.

There was another imposter abroad. In Britain the 'Protestant king' maintained his place in the public imagination until the fashion for German life and culture was wound up by the First World War. Until the British took down the pub signs and turned them over to Kitchener and King George, children were nurtured on images culled from Carlyle's *Frederick the Great*, published between 1858 and 1866. Carlyle added a refinement to the picture of the 'Victor of Rossbach', stamping on an arrogant and impious French serpent: he proclaimed 'Frederick the Hero'. This he undoubtedly was, in as much as his cold and ambiguous nature allowed him to be. For Carlyle, he was the austere prince who took on all comers in the Seven Years War, dodging blow after blow, occasionally settling a punch on one of the chins of his many foes; and he was the snuff-stained 'Old Fritz', sacrificing joy and happiness in retirement, for the sake of his ungrateful people.

There were dissenting voices. Macaulay's sound, good sense provided British readers with another image of 'Frederick the Not So Great'. Frederick the Poet came in for a pasting:

Here and there a manly sentiment, which deserves to be in prose, makes its appearance, in company with Prometheus and Orpheus, Elysium and Acheron, the plaintive Philomel, the poppies of Morpheus, and all the other frippery, which, like the robe tossed by a proud lady to her waiting woman, has long been contemptuously abandoned by genius to mediocrity. We hardly know any instance of the strength and weakness of human nature so striking and so grotesque, as the character of this haughty, vigilant, resolute, sagacious blue-stocking, half Mithridates and half Trissotin,* bearing up against a world in arms, with an ounce of poison in one pocket and a quire of bad verses in the other.[2]

As Germany began to arm, and look about it for conquests, Frederick threw on another mantle, and became the precursor of Prusso-German militarism. The Germans connived at his fate. After the creation of the second German Reich in 1871, historians began more and more to examine the Teutonic navel. They wanted to know how this invincible state had come about, and they settled on the vision of Tacitus: the warlike tribe. Monumental studies were undertaken of Frederick's battles, not least by the Great General Staff. Generals argued the significance of manoeuvres and stratagems, and tried to decide which of Frederick's victories (and they included a few that were virtually defeats) were the greatest. Once Europe sank into war in 1914, all this research served to convince Germany's neighbours that it had all been a long-term plot on the part of the Prussian king, the *philosophe de Sanssouci*, to subjugate Europe to a nasty, brutish, Spartan, Prussian will, and its barking, bureaucratic, bullying, bullet-headed myrmidons.

Nor was Frederick's image helped by the last kaiser, the descendant of his inept brother William, who went so far as to pose for Joseph Uphues' statue of Frederick the Great, which was to be one of the highlights of Berlin's ludicrous *Puppenallee*.[3] This could not help but tarnish the reputation of the prince. The German warlord with the withered arm put on the boots of the philosopher king with a fractured soul.

But if the 'all-highest' warped the picture of Frederick, that was nothing to the effect the National Socialists had on Prussia's king: posters, showing the German Trinity of Frederick, Bismarck and Hitler, and how the little Austrian was now the legitimate heir of the pint-sized Prussian; Goebbels presiding over nostalgia for *der alte Fritz* at the Ufa film studios in Babelsberg; or Hitler, grotesquely ensconced below Anton Graff's portrait of the king, staring beadily around his megalomaniac office. The last macabre image of the Third Reich is equally poignant: it is Hitler, fulminating in impotent fury against those whom he felt were scuttling a

---

* Mithridates was the savage king of Pontus, and one of Rome's most formidable enemies. He is the subject of Racine's tragedy of that name, which Frederick loved. Mithridates and Trissotin both also feature in Molière's *Les Femmes Savantes*.

new 'Miracle of the House of Brandenburg', while Goebbels, the propaganda chief again, read him choice cuts from Carlyle, and encouraged him to do for Göring what Frederick had done for William, in relieving him of his command.

Frederick the Militarist and Frederick the Nazi had been joined by Frederick the Racialist. While Hitler moved his forces across Europe, small armies of intellectuals sat in Whitehall and Washington rewriting the history books and attributing whatever evil they could drag up, to the 'royal highwayman' who had grabbed Silesia from a near defenceless Maria Theresa. Frederick was made the sole author of the partitions that had first eclipsed Poland, lately the ally of Britain and France. Frederick's negative attitude to Poland's aristocratic elite (though it has to be said that he did not think much of the rank and file either) was depicted as the forerunner to Nazi racial policy and the gas ovens of the Final Solution. Some sharp words about the Jews were dragged up too. R. R. Ergang even wrote a book about Frederick's father calling him *The Potsdam Führer*.[4]

When Nazi Germany collapsed, Frederick fell from grace with it. The intellectuals came along behind the advancing soldiers. Their writings formed the basis of the new attitude to the conquered land.[5] They dictated education policy; they decided which of the remaining historical monuments would be blown up; which would be patched up. Most of Prussia was in the east. Neither the Poles nor the Russians had any use for Frederick in the new territories they had carved out of the ruins of Germany. Prussia was virtually reduced to its primitive core, the Mark Brandenburg. Frederick's nightmare of defeat in the Seven Years War had become stark reality. Now the DDR was set up on Prussia's traces and the new regime set about surgically removing 'Prussian militarism' from Germany's past.

Bang went the Berlin palace that had been Frederick's residence during the annual carnival: it was pitilessly dynamited in 1950. In 1968, bang went the palace in Potsdam, where Frederick resided, winter and spring, until it was time to go up the hill to his little jewel at Sanssouci, where he could live in intimacy with his circle of friends and his collection of dogs. That Sanssouci and the Neues Palais survived the expiation is often attributed to the safe keeping of a Russian art historian; true or false, the Russians were happy to plunder the contents of the remaining palaces. The greatest art theft of all time also removed the contents from Frederick's picture gallery, the overdoors and mirrors from Rheinsberg and all other traces of the great king, wherever and whenever they could be found.

Frederick's mounted effigy by Rauch, which had stood a hundred years on Berlin's Unter den Linden was put away. The sight of a king on horseback was not deemed edifying for socialist youth. A similar process took place in the towns and villages of the new state: countless communes had their reasons for venerating Frederick's memory. Now they all had to yield up their statues. That the people were unhappy about this is illustrated by cases in the Oderbruch, which Frederick had rendered inhabitable, and in the little village of Kloster Zinna near Jüterbog, south of Berlin.

The latter weavers' settlement had been created in 1764. A century later the villagers thanked the dead king for creating their most pacific vocation by setting up a statue on the market square. There, every summer, under Frederick's benign, unseeing eye, a school celebration took place which was crowned by a rendition of the choral 'Herr! Mach uns frei'. Even before the Soviet Zone was converted into the Democratic Republic, there came the first request to remove Fritz from his perch. The local council unanimously rejected the demand, they were supported by many of the Russian officers who had moved into the old Prussian bases nearby. After the celebration went ahead in the summer of 1947, there were renewed calls for the destruction of the monument at the local Communist Party session, to demonstrate Kloster Zinna's faith in 'demilitarisation'.

The next year an administrative school was set up in the nearby forest. Plans were laid by members of the FDJ* to take down the statue in the middle of the night. The people of Kloster Zinna mounted guard to protect Frederick's image. When the FDJ arrived at midnight, they decided that the circumstances were not quite right, and drove off again. The FDJ succeeded only by a 'knavish trick'. In the summer of 1949, they invited the *Klosteraner* to a party at the forest school. While the village was absent, the youths succeeded in turning Frederick into a heap of rubble. The people of Kloster Zinna preserved the pieces. Once the regime fell, up again went 'Old Fritz'.[6]

In the middle of all this, the real Frederick was making a series of dramatic journeys followed by at least one reappearance, not in the

---

* Freie Deutsche Jugend, the official youth organisation. It played the same role in the DDR as the Hitler Jugend had in the Third Reich.

socialist east, but in the old Catholic west and south. The Nazis had been as frightened of the Russians as Frederick had been in his lifetime. When it became clear that Berlin and Potsdam were not safe from Russian attack, Göring authorised the removal of the remains of Frederick and his father from their vault in the Garnisonkirche in Potsdam, and the bodies of both kings were concealed in a mine in the Harz Mountains. After the end of the war, they were 'rescued' by the Americans and taken to Marburg in Hesse, where they were lodged in the church of Saint Elisabeth. Somewhere along the way Frederick was taken out of his English tin coffin and put in an oaken one.

In 1952, at the request of the Hohenzollern family, Marburg yielded up the bones of Frederick the Great and the Soldier King, and they were taken to the Burg Hohenzollern, above the town of Hechingen in what had once been the Catholic principality of Hohenzollern and was now part of Baden-Württemberg. After the war, Burg Hohenzollern was the last refuge of the family that had ruled Prussia and finally Germany for half a millennium. In the course of the journey, Frederick's new coffin came apart and a carpenter had to be called in to patch it up.

Friedrich Wilhelm Fürst von Hohenzollern was the head of the old Catholic branch of the family in nearby Sigmaringen. The carpenter respectfully called him to ask if he would like to see Frederick's body before he sealed up the coffin. He still remembers that day and the features of the old king very clearly. There had been virtually no disintegration. The body had been slightly damaged by its transfer, and the lower jaw had fallen in. On the other hand, Frederick was instantly recognisable from his aquiline nose and prominent upper lip. His hair was 'ash grey' and his skin the colour of parchment. He was wearing a faded blue uniform tunic with red facings, black breeches and natural coloured leather boots, which covered his knees. At one point on his chest there was a patch of pure, Prussian blue. Here perhaps had been the star of the Black Eagle, which had probably been pilfered by an American soldier. What Prince Hohenzollern found most remarkable, however, was the corpse's likeness to the drawings and paintings of Adolph Menzel. 'It was as if he had seen the body,' he said.[7]

Frederick was put back to bed, but it took another couple of decades before the real Frederick could be easily picked out from the imposters. Frederick's fate was bound up with that of Prussia, and the former pariah-state was only partially rehabilitated by the retrospective exhibition that took place in the Gropiusbau in West Berlin in the summer and autumn of 1981. In the east, the process had already begun. Rauch's Frederick was riding down the Linden, and the universities had brought out the Marxist-Leninist microscope to perform an autopsy on the man who was considered the most forward-thinking monarch of his time.[8]

The real Frederick may be easier to spot now, but the others are still there. On 17 August 1991, Frederick finally achieved something like the funeral he had intended for himself, when a few members of the Hohenzollern family, together with Chancellor Kohl, reburied him in the vault beneath the terrace at Sanssouci. It proved surprisingly controversial, chiefly because the chancellor insisted on participating, and because a small detachment of soldiers from the Bundeswehr formed a guard of honour. Elements of the press, notably Rudolf Augstein's *Der Spiegel*, mounted a campaign against the ceremony. Surveys in other papers and magazines, however, showed that the danger of militarism, if that is what it was, had largely passed: most of the opinions canvassed had no clear idea in what century Frederick had lived, let alone what he had done to achieve fame.

In historical writing a more recognisable portrait of the Prussian king has emerged since the immediate postwar years. With the return to a punctilious factual approach, however, there has been a concentration on three new Fredericks: the spotlights have been directed at the foreign politician, the general and the administrator; and much has been clarified. The partial approach can never hope to illuminate the whole man, especially not one so complex and multi-talented as Frederick. I have been foolhardy enough to want to look for the real Frederick; and in the following pages I have tried, where possible, to let him speak for himself.

CHAPTER ONE

The Father

[1]

It is tempting to imagine that a long shudder went through Europe in
1740. Three important rulers died, and changed the face of the continent:
Empress Anna of Russia, the Habsburg emperor Charles VI, and Frederick
William I of Brandenburg-Prussia. For the time being, at least, Anna's
death was the least significant of the three. She was eventually succeeded
by her cousin Elizabeth, who resented the outside world and promptly
sent Russia back into a period of Asian isolation. Although Elizabeth's
armies played an important role in the Seven Years War, Russia's
ideological journey westwards was not to start again until the short reign
of the ill-fated Tsar Peter III in 1762. It was continued by his wife and
successor Catherine the Great, with more noticeable *éclat*.

Charles VI was fifty-five when he met his maker. He had allegedly
eaten some poisonous wild mushrooms: 'that plate of toadstools', wrote
Voltaire later, 'changed the destiny of Europe'.[1] The Habsburgs were now
extinct in the male line. His imprudent gourmandise and untimely end
allowed Voltaire's friend and Prussia's new ruler, Frederick II, to begin
his quest for glory at the expense of European peace. Brandenburg-
Prussia was Europe's newest kingdom. The Elector Frederick III of
Brandenburg had been granted the royal title only in January 1701, as a
reward for his continued support for the Habsburg emperors during the
War of the Spanish Succession. The elector of Saxony had scaled those
dizzy heights four years earlier in 1697, when he had had himself elected
king of Poland. In 1713 the elector of Hanover became King George I
of Great Britain. Neither of these purely German princes was allowed to
aspire to a royal crown within the boundaries of the Holy Roman Empire.

Nor was the elector of Brandenburg. He too had to find himself a title
that did not impinge on the imperial dignity. According to his grandson,
King Frederick I, the former Elector Frederick III, first hit on the idea
of calling himself 'king of the Vandals', an allusion to the Slavic Wends

who formed a small part of the population of Brandenburg.[2] Then
his gaze turned towards one of his larger territories in the east. The
Duchy of Prussia lay outside the Imperial Reich; until 1660 it had
paid homage to the kings of Poland, but under the terms of the
Treaty of Wehlau, Frederick I's father, the Great Elector, had extracted
sovereignty from the Poles. Frederick might not be king of Brandenburg,
but he could use the title in his Baltic province. This ruse must have
filled Frederick with glee. He could not even wait for the return of
the good weather before making the arduous journey up to Königsberg,
the capital of the Baltic duchy. He arrived there on 17 December
1700. A month later, on 18 January 1701, he crowned himself king
and instituted the order of the Black Eagle with its legend 'Suum
Quique' as part of his chivalric finery thought appropriate to a king.[3]
Henceforth he was king *in* Prussia, as well as a rather less exclusive
margrave and prince-elector of Brandenburg.

In his own mind, at least, Frederick I was a great deal more. He was
also

Sovereign Prince of Orange, Neufchâtel and Valengin, Gelderland, Magdeburg,
Cleves, Jülich, Berg, Stettin, Pomerania, of the Cassubians and the Wends, of
Mecklenburg, also Duke of Crossen in Silesia, Burgrave of Nuremberg, Prince
(*Fürst*)* of Halberstadt, Minden, Cammin, Wenden, Schwerin, Ratzeburg, East
Friesland and Moers, Count of Hohenzollern, Ruppin, the Mark, Ravensberg,
Hohenstein, Tecklenburg, Lingen, Schwerin, Buhren and Lehrdam, Lord of
Ravenstein, of the Territory of Rostock, Stargard, Lauenburg, Bütow, Arlay and
Breda.[4]

Many of those claims were contested. The Prussians would only ever see
a part of the territories of Principality of Orange and a few hundred
Protestant refugees from the enclave who sought asylum in eastern
Germany at the turn of the century. The Mecklenburg lands were never
to fall to Prussia: the dukes were always wise enough to lay in a provision
of male heirs. Not until Frederick the Great's time did Prussia abandon
its attempts to take over Jülich and Berg. Still, even without the full list,
Frederick I could boast an impressive, large and mixed bag of territories
stretching from the Dutch to the Russian borders.

---

* I.e., a feudal, and not a royal, title.

[II]

History has been hard on Frederick I; so, indeed was nature. He was stunted and deformed. After his death, his most merciless detractors were his own family. His son Frederick William adopted a style of kingship that totally rejected everything his father had stood for. His second wife, Frederick William's mother Sophia-Charlotte of Hanover (the sister of King George I of Great Britain), seems to have preferred her wranglings with the court philosopher Leibniz to any form of congress with her extravagant husband. She is reported to have told a courtier 'That idiot Leibniz, who wants to teach me about the infinitessimally small! Has he therefore forgotten that I am the wife of Frederick the First, how can he imagine that I am unacquainted with my own husband?" As she lay dying in 1705, another asked her if her husband would not miss her: 'Oh! I don't worry about him: he will be preoccupied with the business of arranging some magnificent funeral for me; and providing there is nothing missing from the ceremony, that will be all the consolation he needs.'[6]

Frederick I was new to kingship, and like a *nouveau riche* he sought reassurance in gold and silver as well as all the flashy attributes of baroque monarchy. Berlin, and to some extent Brandenburg-Prussia, had to be made to reflect his new glory. He finished his father's new Schloss at Köpenick; and transformed Oranienburg from a small, moated fortress into an elegant palace. A few miles to the west of the capital, he granted Sophia-Charlotte a smart new palace at Lietzenburg in imitation of the kaiser's new country seat at Schönbrunn near Vienna. The fashionable French gardener Le Nôtre was commissioned to design the park. After her death the palace was renamed Charlottenburg in her honour.

The real magnificence was reserved for Berlin, however. Naturally enough, the focus of Frederick I's attention was on the Schloss, a huge building that had grown up in dribs and drabs since the time when the Elector Frederick Irontooth had chosen to make Berlin his official residence in the mid-fifteenth century. Originally Frederick I had continued the piecemeal rebuilding of his father's time, but after his acquisition of a royal crown he wanted something much more grandiose. Frederick found an architect of vision in the Danziger, Andreas Schlüter. The result was certainly one of the most magnificent palaces north of the Alps; possibly the greatest effusion of north German baroque there was. Pöllnitz believed that the finished Schloss would have surpassed the Louvre in magnificence had it been completed according to Frederick's intentions.

To understand the lavishness of the conception, one has only to think that the famous Amber Room of Tsarskoe Selo was designed for the Schloss. Peter the Great went into raptures when he saw it, and Frederick's austere son promptly had it packed up and dispatched to Russia in exchange for a squad of the tall soldiers he loved so much.[7]

Frederick also opened up the alley of linden trees to the west of the Schloss, thereby creating the first elegant boulevard to be erected outside Berlin's mediaeval walls. At the head of Unter den Linden, as the street was later dubbed, Frederick built the Arsenal, another superb baroque building that owes something to Perrault's Louvre frontage in Paris. To the south of the avenue, the king created the Friedrichstadt, lending the streets names that glorified his spanking new dynasty: Friedrichstrasse, Wilhelmstrasse, Charlottenstrasse and Markgrafenstrasse. Frederick's life-style was as luxurious as its palaces. The rooms buzzed with courtiers as well as a bevy of favoured mountebanks and overmighty ministers. Unlike either his son or grandson, Frederick I maintained a proper court, with a governor for his palace, a court marshal, butler, sixteen chamberlains, thirty-two gentlemen of the bedchamber, seven *Hofjunker* and swarms of lesser noblemen with high-sounding sinecures. The servants were naturally no less numerous, whether they performed their tasks in the palace, stables or kitchens. In the latter alone, Frederick had a court chef with an assistant and no fewer than thirty-six lesser luminaries lending their skills to baking, roasting, stewing and slaughtering animals, fish and fowl.[8]

Perhaps because Sophia-Charlotte had been keen on music (Corelli's *Opus V* set is dedicated to her), the king had a splendid court orchestra composed of thirty-six ordinary musicians, twenty-four trumpeters and two pianists. The court castrato, Antonio Cambiola, was paid a huge fee for the time. Frederick the Great dismissed his grandfather's court as 'One of the most luxurious in Europe ... He crushed the poor in order to line the pockets of the rich; his favourites received huge pensions while his subjects languished in poverty; his stables and apartments resembled an oriental court more than any thing in Europe.'[9]

Frederick I had no charm for his grandson. Modern historians are more sympathetic. They would see the first Prussian king as an underrated figure, who suffered above all from the bad propaganda he received in Frederick the Great's family history: *Mémoire pour servir à l'histoire de la maison de Brandebourg.*[10] In his way, Frederick I was merely re-establishing German kingship after the quasi-total destruction of the Thirty Years War. Frederick the Great himself described in his *Histoire de mon temps* the state of the Empire at the end of the disastrous Thirty Years War: the misery of the people, the poverty of the princes, the general hunger and sterility of the soil. There was no artistic focus 'as there was in Rome or Florence in Italy, Paris or London ... True, there were learned professors at the universities ... [but] no one went to them, because of their rusticity.'[11]

All these problems were addressed by Frederick I, who fostered the arts and made Berlin a showplace of the north German baroque second only to Dresden. At the University of Halle he created a centre of cameralist teaching, which made it the breeding ground of the German civil service until 1945. He acquired territory in Quedlinburg in the Harz, which is normally seen as a positive legacy for a Prussian ruler. Most important of all, he wangled his way on to the board of European rulers, an elevation that augured badly for the Habsburg emperors. It instigated two centuries of Austro-Prussian rivalry that would end up by snuffing out Habsburg power in Germany. Prince Eugene of Savoy is supposed to have complained afterwards: 'The Emperor should have those ministers who gave him such perfidious advice hanged.'[12]

Even his much derided financial policies seem to have been more successful than is generally supposed. He garnered massive subsidies from those who sought his support on the international stage. What is more, the population of his widely scattered lands increased by 50 per cent, which was considered a sign of successful rule in the eighteenth century. Above all, Prussia kept its head above water in a time of immense difficulties on the international stage, and ended up considerably more powerful than it had been before. There was certainly less of an hiatus between his rule and his son's than has generally been supposed.

[III]

It was Frederick I's successor, his son Frederick William I, who established the uniquely Prussian style of kingship.[13] He grew up surly and difficult, his passion fired only by the army. He showed no interest in the magnificence exuded by his father, or the culture so eagerly pursued by his mother. Leibniz's royal pupil tried without success to make her son perform comedies and dance ballets.[14] Naturally she found her son uncouth, and began to give him a wide berth. His tutor, Jean-Philippe Rebeur, had no more luck than his parents. The only way he could instil even the three Rs into the boy was by constantly drawing his metaphors from a battery of military terms. The result, as one recent biographer has expressed it, was to put Frederick William 'on a life-long war-footing with Latin, grammar and spelling'.[15]

The prince grew up short, plump and gouty, his irascibility possibly aggravated by the porphyria that galloped in his mother's family.[16] The only things his Calvinist teachers had been able to drum into the boy were a belief in predestination and an admiration of Holland (a country he visited twice), although the philosophic implications of the Dutch state seem to have left him cold. Frederick I sought to associate his son with the government of the state at the earliest possible opportunity (a privilege not given to Frederick the Great). Frederick William did not have much truck with the king's council and abolished it as soon as he came to power.[17] Both he and his son would later rule without formal ministerial advice. He was made a 'Geheimer Rat' or privy counsellor, which caused him to remark cattily 'privy counsellors are called thus, because they are privy to unimportant decisions only'.[18]

The turning point in young Frederick William's life came when he was granted the manor of Wusterhausen to the south-east of Berlin. From now on this primitive tower house would be his favourite residence, even after he came to the throne and had the palaces of Berlin, Potsdam and Charlottenburg to play with, not to mention a score of other residences of a roomier sort. At Wusterhausen, away from the courtiers he so heartily despised, Frederick William felt he could breathe for the first time. He took an immediate interest in the household accounts, saving every penny to reinvest in his body guard, which he built up into an efficient, well-drilled and superbly kitted private army. He ruled his estate like a state. Later he would rule the state like a manor.[19]

Clearly reacting against his spendthrift father, Frederick William's most noticeable characteristics from his earliest childhood were penny-pinching and meanness. The famous marginalis (government by marginalia was another invention of Frederick William that was continued by his son) non habeo pecunia – 'I don't have any money' (in his distinctly porcine Latin) described his later attitude to kingship.[20]

Apart from being mean and short-tempered, Frederick William was for ever wielding his stick or crutch or dismissing a courtier or subject with a few well-aimed kicks. He had mixed views about the Jews, who settled in increasing numbers in Berlin in the course of his reign. He none the less believed that the state behaved justly towards them and felt that they should acknowledge his generosity in their turn. When one cowered in his presence, Frederick William set about him with his cane, shouting, 'You should love me!, not fear me. Love me!'[21]

His daughter Wilhelmine's *Mémoires* have possibly done more damage to Frederick William's reputation than any other single work, and the bitterness of the princess led her to warp the truth in a dramatic manner. Yet, in places, her judgement rings true:

His temperament [was] lively and volatile which often drove him to violence, which [led] to cruel repentance afterwards. Most of the time he preferred justice to clemency. His excessive fondness for money ... earned him the name of miser. He could only be reproached for that vice in his treatment of his own person or family, as he plied his favourites and all those who showed him devoted service with property.[22]

His first big treat came when his father allowed him to go to war. At the Battle of Malplaquet in 1709, he came into contact with the greatest generals of his day, Prince Eugene of Savoy and Marlborough. In his – Kronprinz – regiment, Frederick William invented the famous Prussian drill, to which his friend, Prince Leopold of Anhalt-Dessau (the 'Alte Dessauer') added the Prussian slow march, better known as the goose-step. This was only finally abolished in the DDR in 1989, because the socialists were under the mistaken impression that it had something to do with Nazism.

[IV]

Frederick William succeeded his father in February 1713, before the Treaty of Utrecht brought the long War of the Spanish Succession to a timely end. He was never crowned. In September 1714 he received the homage of the different orders in Königsberg instead. He 'despised all the trappings of royalty, he was much more attached to the business of carrying out its true duties'.[23] As soon as Frederick William came to power, he displayed a despotic streak that would typify his regimen: 'Gentlemen, our good master is dead,' he told his father's courtiers. 'The new king bids you all go to hell.' The wisest of them took his advice and stayed at home. Frederick William had an inventory drawn up of his father's possessions and placed the court actress Esther Liebmann – scandalous by her very profession – under house arrest.[24]

On 21 April he showed earnest of a new style of government: military ranks achieved precedence over court offices. The field marshal topped the list. At a stroke the Grand Master dropped from fourth to seventh place and had to make way for a lieutenant general. Major-generals counted for more than the governors of His Majesty's palaces. Gentlemen of the bedchamber now weighed in at number 43, while a simple captain ranked 55th. The brightest minds in Prussia chose the army rather than a career in law or administration, something which must have contributed immensely to the efficacy of Frederick the Great's war machine.[25] In 1725 Frederick William established another Prussian tradition by donning military uniform at court. After he had mounted the throne, Frederick the Great generally wore mufti only once a year: on his mother's birthday.[26] It was a far change from the fancy French clothes he wore in his teens, which sent his father into paroxysms of rage. In those days he referred to his uniform as 'Sterbekittel', or a shroud.

The king's simple style of dress affected the whole Prussian elite, and again became one of the hallmarks of *Prussianism*. Pig-tails replaced full-bottomed wigs. The simple *Prussian* blue uniform was from now on more distinguished in the eyes of the nobility and bourgeoisie than the gold and silver braid that predominated at other German courts. The Frankfurter Johann von Loen claimed it was impossible to tell the orders apart: margraves, princes, generals and ministers all dressed down; and they were all both 'genial and polite'.[27]

Frederick William's simplicity extended to his table. His wife, Sophia-Dorothea of Hanover, was particularly appalled to find herself expected to dine on bacon and lentils and mutton tripe with cabbage, dishes which epitomised his earthy tastes. The king drank beer and wine, generally old hock and tokay. The royal cellars also contained stocks of champagne. One day when Frederick William was dining with his minister Grumbkow and was particularly impressed by the ham, he told Grumbkow to send the recipe round to his chef. The chef came to see the king: he wanted the keys to the royal cellars and fifteen bottles of champagne. The king was suspicious, but the chef told him that the ham had to be marinated in champagne for two weeks. Frederick William sent him packing, and wrote to his minister: 'When I want to eat excellent ham I'll come and dine with you. I am not rich enough to make it according to your chef's recipe: my champagne is only for drinking.'[28] Another time the king asked Leibniz's old Academy of Science, largely idle since the philistine king had come to the throne, to explain to him why champagne sparkled. Not unnaturally, the Academy asked for at least forty bottles so that they might carry out the necessary experiments. Frederick William was furious.

'I don't need them to drink my wine, and I would prefer to spend the rest of my life in ignorance of why champagne foamed.'[29]

On occasion the drinking was heavy. At the Tabakscollegium, the normal swill was Ducksteiner beer, from Königslutter am Elm in Brunswick, or hock. As he drank, the king grew 'loud and light-hearted'. Toasts rang out: 'Kaiser and Reich' and against the 'damned French', a 'bunch of rabble'; 'To the German nation, a cur anyone who doesn't mean it from the bottom of his heart.' Anyone who looked as if he did not was as likely as not to be struck on the head by some missile. The great occasions were the anniversaries of Malplaquet on 11 September and the huntsman's feast of Saint Hubert on 3 November. On these days the king was boorish, plates flew and the women made themselves scarce. The men were left to dance – Prussian style – with one another. When the toping finished, Frederick William went to his bed and snored.[30]

Frederick William moved against the pampered court parasites who had oozed around his father. Money lenders were expropriated; the court and ministries were drastically cut; wages were reduced. Courtiers were told to go by foot where possible, so that Frederick William could make economies in the royal stables, cutting the number of horses from 600 to 120. Those privileged to remain suffered greater indignities when the feed destined for the royal mangers was reduced. This meanness had a further advantage for the new king: 'My father gave the horses so much fodder so that everyone could follow him on his trips to the country, I am abolishing it so that they stay in Berlin.' He wanted to be able to choose his own company at Wusterhausen.[31]

Court privileges were abolished and the new king came down heavily on all signs of luxury and corruption. The arts, which had formed such a large percentage of Frederick I's budget, were left high and dry. Frederick William was indifferent to culture. He sold off the silver from all twenty-four royal Schlösser and pleasure pavilions. From now on the royal family and their guests ate off wood and pewter. Only the queen was allowed a little silver. The Lustgarten (or pleasure garden) on the north side of the Schloss was turned into a parade ground; that, after all, was His Majesty's pleasure. This martial role for the garden was later revived by the Nazis. Frederick William finished the exterior walls of his father's superb conception, but had the interiors crudely whitewashed.[32] Schlüter himself wisely fled to Saint Petersburg, where he died.

Frederick I had had a small court theatre installed above the stables opposite the south side of the Schloss. After the king's third marriage to Sophia Louise of Mecklenburg-Schwerin in 1708, there was even an opera – *Roxane et Alexandre* – performed there to add lustre to the occasion. When Frederick William came to the throne, the place was closed down.[33] He did not inherit his mother's love of music: a field marshal called von Brandt was nominally in charge, but the royal huntsman was really interested only in horns. He sacked the costly court orchestra, who must have been relieved to find patronage from the king's cousin, Margrave Christian of Brandenburg-Schwedt, the 'Brandenburg' of Bach's famous concertos.

Frederick William pampered Potsdam, because the Berliners had reacted badly to the idea of a permanent garrison in their city. Now Potsdam received the first new houses of the red-brick Dutch quarter, and the splendid new garrison church, the greatest piece of architecture constructed during his reign. The only evidence that Frederick William took even the slightest interest in the arts as such, however, are the curious paintings he made. Most of these disappeared when the Russians entered Potsdam at the end of the last war, but there is still a small clutch of them in the Jagdschloss Stern, the hunting lodge that was the only 'palace' building – in reality just a small, Dutch-style, red-brick house with a gable – conceived by Frederick William during his reign. The paintings were mostly crude copies of originals in the royal collection. Of the rest, the oddest is a picture of two Jews arguing in a landscape with houses, birds and trees. Then there are the self-portraits: pictures of a soul in agony. On one of them is clearly written in the king's hand 'in tormentis pinxit'.[34]

Frederick William reportedly employed a painter to mix his paints for him, and was not beyond taking it out on him physically if the painting did not go according to his wishes. For all that, he does not seem to have had an unwarrantedly high opinion of his own talents. Once he asked a fawning courtier what he thought one of the paintings was worth: 'You'd be giving it away at a hundred ducats, Sire.' 'Alright, I'll give it to you for fifty because I see you are a connoisseur ...'.[35]

One or two people could see the humour behind the new measures, like this contemporary poet:

> Man setzt nicht mehr so häufig auf Pasteten, Torten, Braten,
> Wer grosse Bissen einige schluckt, dem hilft er von dem Steine,
> Wer sich in Kutschen fahren liess, den bringt er auf die Beine.

Dem, der die Kleider immerdar mit Goldii liess bordieren,
Dem hilft er von der gelben Sucht und lehrt ihn menagieren.[36]

People don't consume so much: pasties, pies and juicy roasts.
There's far less talk of the stone these days, when fellows diet more.
He goes on foot that man who used to loll and glide in coach and four.
Those fine men who used to stroll around in mink and silken shift.
He cures them of the yellow bile and teaches them a sense of thrift.

[v]

The new king's recruiting officers now set off, not just all over Prussia, but all over Europe, to press anyone they could into Frederick William's service, by fair means or foul. 'My father found joy in splendid buildings, huge quantities of jewels, silver, gold and furnishings; in magnificent show. You will allow me to have my own pleasures, and that consists, above all, in having a sizeable body of good troops.'[37] Good and bad were swept away in equal measure. In their place came the expressions now associated with the 'Prussian virtues': discipline, asceticism, strictness and sober-mindedness (*Nüchternheit*). None of his subjects was allowed to remain unaware that there had been a change of pilot.

While Frederick William was no oriental tyrant like Peter the Great, it is hard to deny the charge of despotism. As Frederick William put it himself, 'The only salvation is through God: everything else must obey me.' No one was allowed to know why, no feathers were smoothed by comforting words. Like his son later, Frederick William exhibited a frightening misanthropy at all times. He might have hated luxury and idle debauchery, but he hated the common people too. A nasty temper added substantially to the king's despotic image: 'Incontinent in wrath, and equally incontinent in repentance and remorse, torn this way and that by the most massive emotions which seemed irreconcilable with his sweeping rationalism.' The same intensity governed all: prayer, work and play. As far as the latter was concerned, it consisted almost entirely of hunting to hounds and the turbid sessions of his Tabakscollegium.[38]

He enjoyed his toys too: the tall soldiers called *lange Kerls*, who were brought in from all over Europe like prize specimens for a court menagerie. Some of them were presents from foreign rulers, for, as his daughter Wilhelmina put it, the tall soldiers were a 'canal de grâces' by which you elicited some favour. He did not care much *how* they were recruited, as long as he got them. The Abbé Bastiani was abducted at the altar as he was saying mass,[39] and in the second half of the eighteenth century there was still an Italian innkeeper called Pouzzano in the Poststrasse in Potsdam, who had been kidnapped by recruiting officers in his youth. There was even a move to press-gang the imperial ambassador, von Bentenrieder, when the tall diplomat walked into the Prussian city of Halberstadt after his coach broke down crossing the Harz.[40]

The miserly Frederick William was prepared to pay on occasion. Recruiting officers were authorized to dole out as much as 1500 thalers (5'10 Rhineland: 700 thalers; 6'00: 1000, were the standard rates in 1730), and the best of them received a couple of florins a day in payment.[41] There was one English guard who later became a draper in Berlin, and who lived to nearly a hundred. He was generally regarded as the 'most handsome of the lot', and was paid a ducat a month to keep him in Potsdam. He must have vied for the king's attentions with Jonas, a former Norwegian miner, who was the biggest of the giants. Frederick William even toyed with a genetic experiment: he planned to marry his *lange Kerls* off to particularly tall women to breed lofty children.[42]

The *lange Kerls* were playthings, but Frederick William had a serious army too. From the ideas of his grandfather's field marshal George von Derfflinger, Frederick William introduced the cantonal system of recruitment in 1733, making all men within a geographical area – or canton – liable for service under their own squires. The gentry were certainly not to be spared; the army was seen as a means of preventing them from squandering their money abroad. Frederick William busied himself with the smallest details, from the cut of the uniforms to the length of the men's pig-tails. He was obsessed with the appearance of his troops: if a grenadier had no moustache, he had to paint one on. Where possible he economised. Told that the palisades of the fortress needed repairing, he replied that this was of no interest: 'there is no enemy there'.[43]

Frederick William inherited any army of 40,000. During his 27-year reign, their numbers were increased to 81,000.[44] It was believed at the time that, had the king been less of a miser, he might have doubled its numbers again, for there was enough money languishing in his treasury to pay for a far bigger force.[45] In 1718 he created the Schulenburg Dragoons. In Poland he purchased another regiment of dragoons from the elector of Saxony for twelve Japanese vases. They were called the 'Porcelain Regiment' ever after. He fortified Wesel and Magdeburg according to the advanced principles of the leading French theorist, the marquis de Vauban, and introduced bayonet charges for the first time. The fighting machine that was so effective in the First and Second Silesian Wars was Frederick William's, but his son was soon to discover its drawbacks, chiefly in the cavalry. As Frederick put it: 'Just like the infantry, the cavalry was made up of very tall men mounted on huge horses; giants on elephants who knew neither how to fight nor how to manoeuvre: there was never a revue when some trooper didn't fall clumsily to earth.'[46]

History has associated the word 'militarism' with Prussia's second king. Even in Frederick William's lifetime, travellers came to Berlin and Potsdam just to witness the cities and their ubiquitous soldiers. Loen reported a

royal court that had nothing as splendid as its soldiers. There is no theatre in Berlin whatsoever, diversion is understood to be the handsome troops who parade daily. A special attraction is the great Potsdam Grenadier Regiment ... when they practise drill, when they fire and when they parade up and down, it is as if they form a single body.[47]

Military punishments were draconian – far fiercer than in neighbouring Hanover. Army life consisted of endless, soul-destroying square-bashing, punctuated by beatings or worse. Despite the penalty of hanging, soldiers deserted in droves.[48]

The new militarism needed to be paid for, and this was Frederick William's incentive for putting his economy in order. Mercantilism was the result. It was none the less a tight ship. Like his son, Frederick William saw no good in distant possessions. The little trading counter in Guinea was also sold off. It would be almost two centuries before Prussia took any interest in overseas territories again.

[VI]

Mean and misanthropic, Frederick William none the less had a genuine regard for the well-being of his subjects. His interest in the distant territory of East Prussia went back to his earliest years and his former tutor, Alexander zu Dohna, a member of one of the province's oldest families. A plague had wiped out a large percentage of the East Prussian population in 1709. When Frederick William became king, he set about finding means of restocking the Baltic territory. In 1732 he started using Protestant refugees from the Austrian Salzkammergut. By the mid-century,

3200 villages had been recreated. Royal domains had taken the place of noble seigneuries. The over-mighty Prussian elite, which had been such a bane to Frederick William's grandfather, the Great Elector, was reduced to ninety families.[49] Frederick William showed his more despotic side too: the settlers were forbidden to leave East Prussia. The king's spies were everywhere, and any attempt to get out was officially branded 'desertion' and dealt with appropriately.

It was typical, however, that Frederick William should attempt to kick-start the East Prussian economy at the same time. The far-away Baltic province was Brandenburg's dairy, the home of Tilsit cheese and a sizeable butter-mountain. At first the king obliged the court kitchens to use only East Prussian butter as opposed to the favoured dairy products from Holland. With time Frederick William made the entire population eat East Prussian butter until the surplus disappeared.

Despite his cruelty and austerity, Frederick William was sometimes admired in his time, and has been made into a hero by subsequent generations of Borussomaniacs. Baron Pöllnitz, who knew him well, painted a fairly flattering portrait of the Prussian king:

The prince is informed of everything, and wants to know all that goes on around him. He applies himself to his work which he performs with extraordinary facility, and nothing escapes his mind and he has one of the best memories ... There is no sovereign in the world who is easier to approach: his subjects are even allowed to write to him, with no other formality than addressing the letter to the king.

His ways are simple, he knows nothing of gallantry, and finds it hard to forgive in his officers. Faithful to the queen his wife, he wants everyone to follow his example...'[50]

Loen thought the royal pair more like a normal Christian couple, trying to bring up their children in piety and virtue.[51]

Frederick William wanted a professional civil service, and did not care too much if the bureaucrats came from noble backgrounds: 'open and clever minds' was how he put it.[52] Two out of his three chief ministers, Creuz and Kraut, were originally commoners,[53] and by 1737 there were more than twice as many *Bürgerliche* in the civil service as there were noblemen. Frederick the Great is often given credit for creating the supposedly altruistic Prussian civil service, but in reality it went back to his father's time. So did the idea of codifying and rationalising the legal system. It was Frederick William who appointed the great Cocceji in 1737. Frederick's reputation reaped the rewards.

The Prussian 'socialism' that Oswald Spengler wrote about in *Preussentum und Sozialismus* was the advanced social policy that came into force during Frederick William's reign. Already Brandenburg-Prussia's guilds had their own mutual associations to deal with the sick and the dead. The most important influence on Frederick William's outlook was the Halle theologian August Hermann Francke, who had created a series of educational institutions in the new Prussian university town at the end of the previous century. Although the king was deeply devout, he was suspicious of Francke at first and prejudiced against the movement that Frederick William's son passed off as 'Protestant Jansenists'.[54] Like all the Hohenzollerns, Frederick William had been brought up a Calvinist. Pietism was a synthesis of Lutheranism and Calvinism, which borrowed the universality of grace from the one and combined it with the 'activism' of the other. It was born out of the failure of Lutheran teaching to alleviate the horrors of the Thirty Years War. The Pietists under Francke and the Berlin dean Philipp Jacob Spener did not seek to rebuild the Protestant church, they wanted to reform the world.[55]

These were men of action who took the word out into the stews and slums that abounded in early eighteenth-century Prussia. Like the Jesuits, they were also profoundly interested in education: once a Pietist, always a Pietist. Predestination, which had been at the centre of Calvinist beliefs, was jettisoned: grace was universal. The message was that man should be rid of his 'sin complex'.[56] On the other hand, Pietism was very puritanical: dancing and drinking were forbidden; so were gambling, fine clothes, satisfaction in your trade or aiming for profit as a virtue in itself. They even came down hard on that most German of characteristics, 'simple middle-class respectability and security'. Pietists were taught that they were responsible for the well-being of everyone around them.[57]

In its asceticism, Pietism harked back to the reformed monastic orders. Pupils at the huge Francke Institution in Halle were encouraged to reject the world. For a university-based movement (Francke was actually professor of oriental languages at Halle before he became professor of theology), it was quite anti-intellectual. Clarity and simplicity were encouraged, and foreign languages were shunned. At first the Pietists focused on orphanages and basic schools, but with time they developed an interest in the army which, like all such institutions, was a hotbed of sin. They recruited some important higher officers, such as the Pomeranian field marshal Dubislaw Gneomar von Natzmer, and General von Löben, in their campaign to stamp out drinking, gambling, swearing, whoring and brawling.[58] In this Frederick William was receptive. Already in 1709, he had banned dice and cards in his regiment.[59] The Pietist movement, which had its roots in Saxony, prospered in Prussia, to the degree that its virtues eventually became confused with 'Prussian' virtues, surviving, particularly within the administration, until the last traces of the state were wiped away after 1945.[60]

Frederick I's reign had been fairly tolerant in religious matters. Naturally the Pietists were anxious to influence his successor. In 1711 two officers, Natzmer and Canstein, brought Frederick William together with Francke, who was able to rid the king of the belief in predestination learned from his tutor Rebeur. Frederick William kept quiet about his conversion until after his father's death on 25 February 1713. On 12 April that year he visited Francke's institution in Halle. He was still slightly suspicious: he smelled pacifism. 'What does he think of war?' he asked as he was shown over the premises. 'Your Royal Majesty ... the country needs to be protected; however, I was called to preach. Blessed are the peacemakers.' 'That is good, but his followers, does he counsel them against war?' 'As His Majesty knows well, church and teaching posts are filled by theological students.' 'But the children ... does he not tell them that they will go to hell if they become soldiers?' 'I know many Christian soldiers,' replied the subtle doctor. 'I enjoy more patronage among soldiers than clerics.'[61]

Frederick William must have been aware that the Pietists condemned his press-gangs. Another stumbling block was the opposition of the new king's best friend, the Alte Dessauer, but Francke and his men were able to work on him too; with the result that they succeeded in one of their chief goals: getting Pietists attached to the regiments as padres.[62] Before long Frederick William's last resistance crumbled: 'The man has God's blessing,' he said. 'He can get more done with two thalers than I can with ten. This winter I shall bring him here. He can organise the schools for the soldiers' children.'[63] After his meeting with Francke, Frederick William staffed both the new officer cadet school in Berlin and the military foundling hospital in Potsdam with graduates from Halle. Henceforth all his most trusted aides would be Francke-trained men.

Reaction against his father had made Frederick William mean; his intellectually pretentious mother had bred in him a hatred of theories and abstractions. As he told one expert, 'My friend, I'd like to know what you think about the subject, not what Aristotle or Seneca thought.'[64] He was not opposed to learning, but it had to have practical applications. At the Prussian universities of Frankfurt an der Oder and Halle, state administration, estate management and finance were taught from 1727. Frederick William founded the Charité Medical School in 1725. It soon became the most admired school of its type in Germany. One special feature was the fact that lectures were given in German rather than Latin.

Once you have subtracted the unpleasant sides of his character, the short temper, the violence and the tight-fistedness, two Frederick Williams remain: the one a modern, far-sighted monarch who interested himself in every detail of his kingdom and his subjects; the other the Old Testament king of Jochen Klepper's influential historical novel, *Der Vater* (The Father); a man determined to do the best for his people, yet tormented by the world around him. His successes were legion, but he showed weakness in his foreign policy. His vision of Prussia's role in the outside world was to condition his attitude to his son and lead directly to the tragedy surrounding the coming of age of Frederick the Great.

CHAPTER TWO

The Growing Boy

[1]

Frederick William was initially unlucky with boys: his first two sons died. Frederick Ludwig was born in 1708 and expired the following year. His brother, another Frederick William, made his brief appearance on the world's stage from 1710 to 1711. In the meantime the crown prince's stout bride, Sophia Dorothea of Hanover (she was called 'Olympia' for her imposing stature), had given birth to a healthy girl, Princess Wilhelmina, later to be Frederick the Great's favourite sister.

Frederick the Great himself was delivered sometime between 11 and 12 p.m. on 24 January 1712. His father and grandfather were sitting down to lunch, quite unaware that Sophia Dorothea was going into labour.[1] The court master of ceremonies, von Besser, broke the news. He reported the old king 'beside himself with joy, ... with tears in his eyes, he had himself straightaway carried over to the Crown Princess, [but] could eat nothing thereafter'.[2] The king and crown prince noted the child's jet black hair; Frederick I was particularly pleased to see him 'really fat and fresh'.[3] The king then invested the new-born child with a cumbersome toy in the form of the Order of the Black Eagle. Besser reminded the king that he too had been the third of the Great Elector's sons. 'Ah, so I will give him my name too,' said Frederick. That evening the crown prince's best friend, the Alte Dessauer was present at a little gathering to celebrate the newcomer's arrival. The prince was baptised on the 31st by the bishop, Benjamin Ursinus von Bär.[4]

Naturally, everyone was keeping their fingers crossed: while he continued to thrive, Frederick was the first healthy Prussian prince born since the electorate had been elevated into a monarchy. For a while, he was Prince of Orange too, but his hopes of inheriting the French territory were dashed at the conference table in Utrecht the following year.[5]

[II]

Sophia Dorothea was the very opposite of her austere cousin and husband the king. Like her aunt, Frederick William's mother, she appreciated a show of culture; even more than the late queen, she hankered after a proper court with all its glamour and intrigue. While Frederick I still reigned, all that was possible. After his death her husband introduced a style that was far less palatable, and she was only furtively able to exert her influence and find pastimes that compensated for the dullness of the world around her.

The all-encompassing meanness and the penury of her train must have needled her. She had little or no opportunity to hear the music she loved so much.[6] Loen noted enthusiastically that she had but two 'bad coaches driven by six old horses with a little moor on the side'. The court still spoke French after the death of the first Prussian king, and contrary to some reports, Frederick William spoke it fluently, albeit ungrammatically. He was no match for his wife, who 'might have been confused for a princess of the French royal house'.[7] The other attributes of French life were shunned, however, especially the fashions of the contemporary *petit maître*. One of Loen's friends who had arrived with a suitcase filled with the latest French finery found that he soon had to repack his bags 'in order to escape the displeasure of the king, and the mockery of his courtiers'.[8]

To get her revenge, Sophia Dorothea did what many mothers might be tempted to do in the circumstances: she brought her children over to her side and taught them to hate their father. What he forbad, she allowed; even if it ended up with them being beaten black and blue as a result.[9] To her husband, she played the meek, devoted wife, writing him endless letters when he was away in Potsdam, assuring him of her complete submission to his will;[10] while she further developed her schemes for bringing her Hohenzollern children into line with their Welf cousins on the throne of Britain. Her husband's absences can have troubled her but little: she had her own court in the little baroque palace of Monbijou, outside Berlin's city walls, on the other side of the Spree from the royal Schloss. Here she entertained every night, gambling for small stakes with her coterie,[11] while Frederick William sat it out in Potsdam, living 'more like a [provincial] nobleman than a king'.[12]

Frederick the Great never recorded a criticism of his mother, but Wilhelmina left this scathing description in her posthumous memoirs: 'All the haughtiness and pride of the Hanovers is concentrated in her person. She is excessively ambitious and by nature suspicious and vindictive, never forgiving anyone whom she suspects of having wronged her.'[13] The same would later be said of her eldest surviving son. While Wilhelmina's bile was normally reserved for her father and brother, her mother is generally sympathetically portrayed. Possibly this 'warts and all' thumbnail sketch is one of the more accurate passages in her often untrustworthy account.[14]

[III]

When Frederick was one year old, on 26 February 1713, he was taken to see his grandfather on his deathbed. He was quickly borne away when the child's face turned red and he began to bawl.[15] In those first years of infancy, Frederick spent much of his time with his elder sister, and the two children are captured playing in one of the court painter Antoine Pesne's most successful compositions. Frederick is beating a drum, while his sister is clutching a bunch of flowers. The other players are the court moor and a dog. Wilhelmina is supposed to have told her brother to stop making such a din with his drum, and help her pick flowers. The little boy allegedly replied, 'Beating a drum well is more useful to me than playing, and I prefer it to flowers.' When this exchange was reported to his martial father, the king was delighted and promptly ordered Pesne to record it for posterity.[16]

In 1717 the court received a visit from one of Frederick's godfathers: Tsar Peter the Great of Russia.[17] How much time the five-year-old spent with this oriental despot with western leanings is not clear, but Wilhelmina left a lively description of the tsar's sojourn in Monbijou. He arrived with 400 'so-called ladies in waiting ... almost all of these creatures carried richly clad infants on their arms and when they were asked to whom they belonged, they replied by performing profound Russian bows and adding that the tsar had paid them the honour of fathering their children'.[18] The tsar took a particular shine to Wilhelmina and 'grazed my entire face with his kisses'.[19] The queen's little palace was wrecked by the visitors and, according to Wilhelmina, had to be completely redecorated after their departure.[20] This may, however, have proved a useful way of getting some money out of the miserly king.

Wilhelmina has also left us a portrait of her brother at the time: 'He was clever, but subject to black moods, he reflected for a long time before replying [to questions], but on the other hand, he came up with the right answers.'[21] A similar verdict was delivered by the queen's principal lady in waiting, Frau von Sacertot, who called him a 'little angel': 'he both grasps and learns everything you put before him with the greatest of ease'.[22] From this time dates Frederick's first letter: 27 July 1717. Its blandness is reminiscent of his mother's style, and probably betrays her influence or encouragement. Frederick's worryingly premature sombreness might well have been brought on by his father, who had possibly noticed that the child took physically after his mother, and was determined to banish the devil in him at the earliest opportunity. When he was six, the king decided he was not to see 'operas, comedies and other worldly vanities'.[23]

Frederick William may also have already noticed what he thought to be disagreeable traits in the child. When the boy was seven, he watched him beat his little cane against the palisade outside the Schloss and, referring to the hordes of treasure lodged in the vaults, exclaim 'How happy all these prisoners would be if we could release them.' The king was not best pleased, and attributed the remark to a malign influence.[24] Frederick's education up till then was in the hands of Maturin Veyssière la Croze, an ex-Benedictine monk from the great abbey of Saint Germain des Prés, who had converted to Protestantism in Basle. He was the court librarian. Now the regime became much stricter, according to the reformed Calvinist principles of the day.

Little Frederick was taught French by Madame de Rocoules, as his father had been before him. No one seems to have forced him to learn German properly, not even his father, who communicated in that language rather more willingly (and possibly slightly more fluently) than his son ever did. In 1758, Frederick confessed in ungrammatical German: 'I have not read a German book since my youth and I speak it very badly. Now I'm an old fellow of forty-six and I have no time [to learn it properly] any more.'[25]

Neither Latin nor ancient history was considered at all seemly for the crown prince. This was due to Frederick William's reaction against his own childhood, and the intellectual aspirations of his mother.[26] In 1758, Frederick told Henri de Catt of a disturbing moment in his childhood, when the king had burst in on one of his lessons to find his son declining Latin nouns. Frederick William rounded on the teacher: 'Oh you scoundrel! Latin for my son! Get out of my sight!' At which he kicked and punched the pedant as he threw him out of the room. The terrified boy hid under the table, but the king had not fully worked off his temper on the tutor and dragged the boy out by the hair and beat him too.[27]

Frederick William found his son a new tutor in the person of Jacques Duhan de Jandun, a Huguenot soldier who had come to the king's notice after he had distinguished himself at the Siege of Stralsund; and whose father had been the secretary of the great French general Turenne. Duhan, thought the king, could provide the right tone. He wanted his son to be a great general too, a Prince Eugene or a Marlborough: 'nothing in the world brings a prince honour and glory better than the sword'.[28] Instead of a rocking horse, little Fritz (as his father called him) received a cannon. At the age of six, Frederick had his own company of cadets to drill: 131 boys to command at will. No joke was intended. The little boy had to remember that the army was his vocation in life.[29]

Although Pesne was called in to give the child drawing lessons, and he was allowed to start learning the piano, violin and flute at five and composition under the cathedral organist, Gottlieb Hayne, two years later, Frederick's study plan makes very sad reading indeed. At seven, as soon as he woke on Sunday, Frederick was to fall to his knees. A prayer was provided, and had to be learned by heart. It was to be followed by 'Our Father'. Fifteen minutes was allotted for prayers, washing and application of fresh powder to his hair, then he had precisely seven minutes to accomplish breakfast. At this moment Duhan and the other tutors arrived. Duhan would read him a chapter of the Bible (New Testament only) and together they sang a hymn. It was now 7.45 a.m. Religious instruction continued until 9 a.m. with a reading from and exegesis on the Gospels. Frederick was then taken downstairs where he met the king, and went with him to the Sunday service. After church Frederick ate with his father. The rest of the Sabbath was free. At 9.30 p.m. he said good night to the king, then quickly undressed and washed his hands. He then sank to his knees with Duhan, said a prayer and sang a hymn. By 10.30 he was tucked up in bed.[30]

Sunday was a restful day, and we presume there was time for play after lunch. The rest of the week was rather more serious. On Monday he rose at 6 a.m. After a short prayer he was to wash his hands and face, but he was not allowed to use soap. He put on a tight, wide-sleeved bodice. His hair was combed and tied in a pig-tail, but not powdered. While the servants did his hair, he could drink his tea and eat his breakfast.[31]

It was now 6.30. Duhan and a servant joined him for the 'big prayer', a chapter of the Bible was read, a hymn sung. From 7 to 9 a.m. Duhan taught Frederick history. From nine to 10.45, the theologian Noltenius took over to instil a little Christianity into the boy. Then he had to wash his face and hands with soap, put on white linen and powder, and slip on his coat before going down to the king. He ate with his father and was returned to Duhan at two. It was now the tutor's task to teach him geography. He was to show him maps and explain 'all the European empires, powers and princes, and explain the extent, wealth and poverty of their cities'.[32] From 3 to 4 p.m. was moral instruction; for the next hour came the prince's little bit of German instruction: chiefly letter-writing style. Then at five he had to wash his hands and go to his father. They rode together and Frederick could enjoy the open air. He was free to do whatever he liked 'as long as it was not offensive to God'.[33]

Tuesday was similar to Monday, except that Pantzendorf replaced Noltenius and taught him to fence, and the time given over to German tuition was awarded to arithmetic. On Wednesday Duhan had instruction to test the boy's history, then at 9.30 a.m. he was sent to the king: 'The rest of the day belongs to *Fritzchen*.'[34] French grammar and maths set the tone on Thursday; on Friday it was German's turn. On Saturday lessons in history, writing and maths filled the hours until 10.30 a.m., then Frederick was tested 'to see if he has benefited [from his lessons]. If he has learned something, then the afternoon belongs to *Fritzchen*. If he has learned nothing he must repeat everything that he has forgotten from the previous week from two till six.' Finally the king let it be known that Frederick should learn to dress and undress as quickly as possible, and not be so dirty.[35] When he was fourteen, Frederick was required to do his own accounts too. Frederick William was angry when he discovered that he delegated them to the regimental quartermaster instead. The following year Major Senning was engaged to teach him tactics.[36]

Frederick told Catt that it was his sister, Wilhelmina, who first encouraged his reading. Until then his passion had been running. 'But my dear brother, aren't you ashamed of yourself for running around non-stop? I never see you with a book in your hand. You are neglecting your talents and what sort of role will you play once you are called upon to play one?' Frederick took his sister's lesson to heart. Not only did he begin to read, he became addicted; slipping away from his bed at night, treading carefully past the somnolent figures of his valet or his governor, the East Prussian nobleman, Finck von Finckenstein, in order to plunge his little head into a French novel.[37]

The first book to make a deep impression on Frederick was Fénelon's

Les Aventures de Télémaque of 1699, which he initially read as a boy of nine.[38] The Archbishop of Cambrai had written it for the edification of the duke of Burgundy, grandson of Louis XIV. The untold tale of Odysseus's son Telemachos was conceived from the start as a manual for the future king.* Fénelon felt that the prince should be gently schooled in history, policy and military matters by a series of good stories based on Telemachos's adventures as he went in search of his father.[39] The work was none the less controversial, as it contained an implied criticism of the absolutist policies of the king of France, Louis XIV, which the archbishop countered with a humanitarian, almost pacifistic concern for middle-class well-being;[40] but there was enough in it that would have sounded pleasing to the ears of the fierce king in Prussia, who saw the book as an attack on the wasteful, luxurious court of monarchs such as his father.[41] For example, Mentor tells his charge, 'A young man who likes to dress vainly like a woman, is unworthy of fame or wisdom.'[42]

'Indolence corrupts, pride intoxicates,' says Mentor,[43] whose teaching even encompasses fair dealing in commerce to the benefit of the state.[44] In Crete Telemachos finds a model society that reads a little like an idealised version of Frederick William's Prussia: the citizens eat simple food without sauces; they enjoy modest houses, saving embellishments for their temples alone; they live in good health and have no want; the king acts as father to his people. 'The Gods did not make him king for his own sake,' says Mentor. 'He was intended to be the man of his people: he owes all his time to his people, all his care and all his affection, and he is worthy of royalty only in as much as he forgets his own self and sacrifices himself to the common weal.'[45]

If Telemachos learns the arts of war, he learns that peace has its advantages too. The state needs subjects, and peace allows them to multiply. In peacetime the monarch may propagate good laws and encourage agriculture: 'make the people love you, you will be more powerful and more famous than all the conquerors who ravage so many kingdoms'.[46] At the time, Frederick was probably more impressed by the vivid battle-scenes in *Télémaque*, but many of Fénelon's lessons eventually sunk in, and can be relocated in Frederick's voluminous writings. Some, however, fell on deaf ears: 'A king who sheds the blood of so many men and who causes so much misery to acquire a little glory or to stretch the limits of his kingdom is unworthy of the fame that he seeks and deserves

---

* The duke of Burgundy died in 1711, four years before his grandfather.

to lose all he possesses, for having tried to usurp that which didn't belong to him.'[47]

[IV]

When Frederick achieved the age of twelve, it became clear to his father that something was not quite right with the child: he was not bending to the paternal will. What frightened Frederick William was that his son might seek to overturn his system of government and revert to the costly absolutism of Frederick I's day. In March 1724 the king looked down at his crown prince and wondered what 'went on in that little head: I know he doesn't think like me, and that there are people who plant other ideas in his mind, and make him criticise everything'. Frederick William then added in his inimitable way, 'they are scoundrels',[48] and cuffed the boy for good measure. Then he addressed his son:

Fritz, think about what I have to say to you. Always maintain a good, big army. You will find no better friend ... Our neighbours have no greater desire than to blow us out of the water. I know what they think, and you will get to know them too. Believe me, don't think of vanity, but keep to what is right. Always maintain a good army and have enough money, therein lies the peace of mind and security of a prince.[49]

So far, the problem was chiefly about religion. Since the time of the Elector John Sigismund, the Prussian Hohenzollerns had been Calvinists, while their subjects were chiefly Lutherans. Frederick William had been brought up a strict Calvinist by Rebeur, who had used the idea of predestination as a stick with which to beat his rebellious pupil. Frederick William had spent his childhood in the fear that he had not been chosen for Heaven. The image of a stern Calvinist God had been much softened, however, by the teachings of the Pietist Francke. Out of motives of love, Frederick William had sought to avoid communicating the idea of predestination to his son.[50] The court preacher Andreä, however, had convinced the crown prince that men were preselected for Heaven, and that they could do nothing to change their fate. Frederick William had him sacked in 1725, but he believed the damage had already been done.[51] Frederick's stubborn adherence to this central tenet of Calvinism could be seen as a cynical means to annoy his father, or indeed, he might have been attracted by the faith's greater intellectual rigour.

As a child Frederick had impressed Francke by his piety; he could

quote the New Testament, chapter and verse, and on occasion trip up
his father.[52] By the time he entered his teens, however, he appeared to
have lost interest in religion, and his father's guru was dismissed as a
'Pharisee'.[53] Wilhelmina, who thought his teaching had had a deleterious
influence on her father's health, naturally hated him too. The children
suffered: 'We were not allowed to talk of anything other than the words
of God, all other conversation was banned ... that dog Francke made us
live like Trappist monks.' There was even a suggestion that the children
should wash their own clothes. They got their revenge by giggling during
his sermons,[54] but it was not just Frederick and his sister who sought to
debunk Francke and all he stood for. When the Pietist's son came to stay
at Wusterhausen, the king's two licensed jokers, Fussmann and Gundling,
made his life a misery.*

The rift was growing between Frederick and his father, but it was still
far from the open war that came about in his sixteenth year. When
Frederick fell ill, Frederick William was worried for his son. He wrote to
the Alte Dessauer: 'You don't know [how much] you love your children
when they are healthy.'[55] Frederick and his sister tended to think as one,
but even she was slow to hate Frederick William. Despite the picture she
paints in her memoirs, Wilhelmina's early letters show a young girl who
was delighted by her father.[56] However, the later general Rothenburg
noted that the fourteen-year-old Frederick already 'hated his father with
a vengeance'.[57] Wilhelmina stated that the feeling was mutual, but that
view is hardly justified by the evidence. The truth is probably more that
the severe patriarch thought it inappropriate to show his son affection,
and was ever ready to lash out at him when he committed some fault.
The imperial ambassador, Seckendorff, expressed it reasonably well in a
letter he wrote to Prince Eugene of Savoy in around 1725:

Even though the king loves the crown prince with all his heart, he wears him
out so much with early rising and the strains which carry on all day, that despite
his young years he looks elderly and stiff, as if he is already a veteran of many
campaigns. The king's view is thus: that by experiencing a constant contact with
the soldier's world, he will assume with time the remaining virtues of modesty
and thrift ... What hits you between the eyes, however, is that this way of living

* Little Fritz was not above these little farces himself. Once when he accompanied his
father on a visit to Cleves, he tied General von der Mosel's stirrup so tight that the
officer was unable to mount his horse.

runs counter to the crown prince's inclinations and as a result will, in time, produce precisely the contrary effect...'[58]

In reality, the hard upbringing he was receiving from his father was making the boy furtive and sly. He simply went through the necessary motions.[59] Frederick's real pleasure did not lie in the rigours of a military life, or in the soul searching of Pietism: in a house in the Schlossfreiheit, opposite the royal palace in Berlin, he had installed a library of more than 3000 books complete with librarian, which had been procured for him by his tutor Duhan. There in his limited periods of free time, he could leaf through volumes of Descartes, Bayle, Locke and Voltaire.[60] 'Fritz' became 'Federic' or 'Frédéric le philosophe'. Two months after his confirmation on 4 April 1727, he wrote to Duhan to promise him 2400 thalers a year as soon as he came into some money: 'and I will love you always a little more than I do at the moment, if that is possible'.[61]

Frederick's mind had probably turned against his father's system long before, but it was in Saxony, at Augustus the Strong's splendid royal court of Dresden that it all began to gel. Here, for the first time, the crown prince set eyes on elegance, beauty, luxury and sensuality, and heard music and Johann Hasse's *Cléofide* at the opera. Later he would try to reproduce it in miniature at Rheinsberg.[62] It was a dizzy experience for the sixteen-year-old. The courtiers asked him 'whether he'd like to see theatre and ballet, whether he'd like to dance or hear music, or go to balls or masquerades; to each question he gave the simple answer: "assurément"'. Frederick William noticed that his son was enjoying himself: 'Fritz' he said, 'I am only frightened that you are too happy here.'[63]

Frederick William's particular tolerance towards Augustus the Strong, king of Poland and elector of Saxony, had much to do with Seckendorff's desire to bring Augustus in on the emperor's side and the alliance that was formed the following year. Frederick William was all the more ready to forgive his louche 'cousin' as he was dangling 'Polish Prussia' in his direction in order to let him have a free hand elsewhere.[64] He ran a luxurious, wanton court, squandered his money on the arts, had dozens of mistresses and was reputedly the father of around 300 illegitimate children; worse still, the elector of Saxony – a descendant of the man who had nurtured and protected Martin Luther – had converted to Catholicism in order to have himself elected king of Poland. Dresden was the city that Berlin might have become had Frederick I of Prussia lived, or had Frederick William been more of a chip off the old block. Its position on a wide sweep of the Elbe reminded visitors of Florence, and Augustus had beautified his palaces and churches and stuffed the galleries full of priceless works of art.

Frederick William proved himself to be made of tempered steel; he bent, but he did not break. His daughter noted that he mellowed under the twin influences of Bacchus and Venus; chiefly the former in the form of bumpers of tokay. The famous nude scene, when Frederick William and his son were taken into a room of the palace and shown a naked girl concealed behind a tapestry, was laid on for the king's benefit, not the crown prince's. According to Pöllnitz, Frederick William took it well: he remarked, 'I have to admit she is rather pretty', and turned away.[65] Other accounts have the furious king rudely pushing his son out of the room,[66] or taking his hat off and pulling it over the crown prince's eyes.[67] Perhaps the most significant comment about this farce comes from a letter that Frederick William wrote to the Alte Dessauer, in which he stated, 'I have returned in the same state in which I left':[68] that is, he had remained faithful to the queen.

One wonders if Frederick was even there. Wilhelmina had no doubts, however, and tells us that the prince had time to contemplate this beauty, 'illuminated by so many candles', 'whiter than snow and better formed than the lovely statue of the Medici Venus', and that the effect was to inspire in him an interest in the opposite sex.[69] If we accept Wilhelmina's version, one of Augustus's illegitimate daughters, Countess Orzelska, promptly became Frederick's first mistress. She was allegedly the daughter of a French merchant's wife in Warsaw, and her mother who was already deceiving her father with her half-brother, Count Rudofski, the son of a Turkish woman who was the chambermaid to Gräfin Königsmark, the king's *maîtresse en titre*. Wilhelmina tells us that she was not a classical beauty, but had a 'perfect body'.[70]

Frederick William shows no sign of having been offended by the incident, and asked the king of Poland to visit him in Berlin.[71] An oil sketch by Pesne shows the old roué being presented to the royal princes and princesses, who by now numbered nine: Wilhelmina, Frederick, Frederica, Charlotte, Sophia, Ulrica, Augustus William, Henry and Amalia. The last of the brood, Ferdinand, was not born until 1730, the year of the crown prince's incarceration in the fortress of Küstrin. Like all fathers, Frederick William had his favourites, who did not include Frederick:[72] the boys Augustus William (who was named after the king of Poland, but

called William) and Henry, and his daughter Charlotte, 'Sans Souci' or
'Lotte'. In general he was not overly impressed with girl-children: he was
concerned that they might not all find husbands. He even went so far as
to describe them as weeds, and to suggest that they should be drowned
at birth, like kittens.[73]

Countess Orzelska also visited Berlin. Wilhelmina's account might be
more reliable here, as she was already nineteen and present.[74] The two
monarchs had toping in common, and there was a room in the Schloss
where a table could be brought up on pulleys through the floor, thus
dispensing with the need to have gossiping servants present as the kings
disgraced themselves in their cups. A similar device was later introduced
at Sanssouci.[75]

Frederick himself returned from Dresden in poor health. Wilhelmina
claims it was Countess Orzelska who raised his spirits with the secret
visits she paid him in the Schloss. If Frederick enjoyed the company of
women in his youth, it did not prove an abiding passion. Music was
another matter altogether. Perhaps the most important aspect of the king
of Poland's visit to the Prussian court was that he sent his musicians to
the queen: the lutenist Sylvius Leopold Weiss, who was considered the
best of his day, the violinist Pisendel and the flautists Buffardin and
Quantz, 'whose playing could vie with the singing of the most beautiful
voice'.[76] Quantz's visit was particularly fateful: he was promptly engaged
to give Frederick occasional lessons in his favourite instrument, and his
music has been associated with the Prussian king ever since.[77]

'We had had too much fun in Berlin for it to last long, and from the
Paradise where we were, we plunged into Purgatory.' The antidote to this
revelry and courtly light-heartedness was Wusterhausen, that 'terrible
place',[78] uniformly loathed by the queen and her children, and where the
king felt most at home with his horses, hounds, horns, hunts and the
smoky bacchanals of the Tabakscollegium. Frederick noted tersely at the
time: 'Tomorrow, hunting to hounds, on Sunday, the day after tomorrow,
hunting to hounds, and Monday, hunting to hounds again.'[79] After a brief
glimpse of how the other half lived in Saxony, Frederick was returned to
Prussian reality.

[v]

Despite his halloas, Frederick William was still troubled by his son. It is
just possible that the uxorious prude was a little concerned about his

budding sexuality: rumours about Countess Orzelska, or La Formera, a dancer in the Saxon court theatre, could have come to his ears; or indeed stories about Doris Ritter, the daughter of a Potsdam pedant who was later alleged to be the crown prince's mistress, and who would pay a high price for the rumour. It is just possible, but unlikely: in virtually all of Frederick William's ever more furious utterances against his son, it is the word 'effeminacy' that comes to the fore, which is hardly a charge one would make against a lusty teenager. The king was alarmed by signs of decadence in his boy and thought that his son might give in to 'Sardanapalian luxury' if he were not properly reined in.[80]

Much more important though was his feeling that a crown prince who went against his will was unworthy of the throne. He was 'terribly worried about' his creation, the weird state of Prussia: a middle-sized power wielding the force of a great one, without wealth or tradition, founded on nothing more than his own will, effort and ability.[81] It had many enemies and had somehow to survive. There was also a risk that Frederick would go his own way in foreign policy. The king had no desire to see things go back to what they were in his father's time, when Prussia was a vassal state of the maritime powers, furnishing them with armies when required.[82] In this he must have been aware that his wife was meddling in his business; that his two eldest children were the pawns of a woman determined to bring Prussia closer to Hanover, and to effect a double marriage with their English cousins.

To understand the collapse of the relationship between father and son, it is vital to understand the king's conception of his own state, his creation that he had built since the death of his father. He saw his follower's job as simply to maintain it, not to add to it or alter it, but merely to accommodate himself within its framework, working according to its laws. Frederick was to be the 'ideal successor' and nothing more.[83] His successor would have to fall in with his foreign policy too. If this was timid in comparison to that later associated with his son, it none the less contained clear principles. He wished to continue the expansion of Prussia's borders through the acquisition of small chunks of land within the German Reich. At the Treaty of Utrecht he had made some small gains in Swiss Neufchâtel, Moers and Lingen, which had been territories of the prince of Orange; and Gelderland and the barony of Herstall near Liège as compensation for the rejection of his claims to Orange and some of the principality's other possessions in Franche Comté.[84] Louis XIV had also done him the honour of recognising his 'royalty' as Prussian king, while both the French and the Spanish had accorded him the title of 'majesty', which had not yet been extended to the kings of either Denmark or Sardinia.[85]

There were the enticements of further gains to the north too. The early years of Frederick William's reign were dominated by the northern war against Sweden. In concert with Britain, Russia, Saxony and Denmark, Prussia sought to drive the Swedes out of the last remaining territories they retained in Germany after the end of the Thirty Years War. In a campaign lasting a little over six months, the allies occupied Usedom and Wolgast and the island of Rügen, and successfully besieged the cathedral city of Stralsund on the Baltic coast, sending the Swedish king scuttling back to Stockholm. It was not until a peace was concluded between Great Britain and Sweden four and a half years later that the Prussians took control of their part of the booty – and only then on payment of 2 million thalers. It was a tract of western Pomerania stretching from the Peene to the Oder, including the port of Stettin.[86]

The Prussians had felt cheated of Stettin for decades, ever since Frederick William's grandfather, the Great Elector, had briefly acquired it and been forced to give it back. The port controlled the mouth of the River Oder, so vital to trade in the Baltic. Frederick William made his triumphal entry in 1721. It must have meant a lot to him: Pöllnitz tells us that the tight-fisted monarch scattered money and medals from his carriage to woo the largely German-speaking population of the city.[87] He even went so far as to have two fine baroque gates erected – the Berliner Tor and the Königs Tor – to commemorate his achievement.[88] Perhaps even more extraordinary still, both survived the wartime destruction of the city and the subsequent removal of the traces of German culture that followed the granting of Stettin to the Poles in 1945.[89]

The king wanted his son to understand the importance of the military. Frederick William had built up a superb army, but he was ever reluctant to put it into battle. Its value was to some extent deterrent. He might have hoped to extend his territory by negotiation, treaty and, if possible, finding propitious marriages for his numerous children. After two Hanover marriages in as many generations, many eyes looked beyond the Weser for a bride for the crown prince, and possibly a groom for a princess or two. The Hanovers had become all the better match after they secured the throne of Great Britain.

The double marriage was first mooted in 1725, at the time of the death of George I of Great Britain. The Prussian envoy, Wallenrodt, was asked to sound the British out on a possible alliance, and 'noises were made' about weddings in both Britain and Berlin. Wilhelmina was ear-marked for Frederick Prince of Wales, and Frederick was to wed Anne, the Princess Royal. The issue, however, was vexed. Hanover, with the backing of the powerful maritime state of Great Britain, was not deemed an ideal partner for Prussia as it struggled for supremacy in northern Germany. None the less, Frederick William allowed himself to be talked into the Treaty of Herrenhausen that same year with Britain and France: a defensive alliance directed against Austro-Spanish ambitions in Germany. The idea of a double marriage was aired as earnest of this pact. A marriage or two was just acceptable to Frederick William, but the political settlement desired by the British never was.[90]

Frederick William was by nature better disposed towards the Reich than he was towards non-German powers. In one of his bluntest utterances he said, 'no English people or Frenchmen should [have control] over German territories, and I will put pistols and daggers into the cradles of my children so that they can help keep foreign nations out of Germany'.[91] He was loyal to the Habsburgs – foolishly, as it turned out. He did not challenge the need for a German emperor, and thought the Habsburgs possessed the land and wealth the better to maintain the peace and status quo.[92]

Frederick William's judgement was coloured by considerable ill-will towards his cousins across the Channel. This personal distaste was compounded after 1727 when his cousin and brother-in-law came to the throne as George II. Extraordinary as it may sound, George had bullied Frederick William as a child, and married Caroline of Ansbach, the woman Frederick William had his eyes on at the time.[93] The hatred was mutual. As Frederick William put it himself, 'I shall make no claims for an English princess for my son if they are going to be so high and mighty about it, then my daughter won't be good enough for them [either].' Frederick William was certainly anxious to listen to any foreign policy suggestions that meant turning his back on his hated cousin. These were not slow in coming: the imperial ambassador, Seckendorff, was permanently on call to convince him that Prussia would become a province of Great Britain if he were to strengthen his ties with Westminster.[94]

As far as territory was concerned, Frederick William was determined to gain control of the western duchies of Jülich and Berg, which had been detached from Prussian Cleves a century before. His choice of friends was largely governed by whatever party was likely to advance his suit. He distrusted the non-German powers in this matter, especially as they were likely to back the claims of the Pfalz-Sulzbachs, who were a branch of the Bavarian Wittelsbachs: France's traditional German allies. As the British were then allied to France, they were not likely to give Frederick William much joy either.[95] Seckendorff pressed him to look to Vienna for help. With assurances about Jülich and Berg and the added temptation of the County of Ravenstein and a few handfuls of tall soldiers, he concluded the Treaties of Wusterhausen and Berlin in 1726 and 1728,[96] and relinquished his bond with the western powers that he had made at Herrenhausen.[97] The price was recognition of the Pragmatic Sanction, whereby, despite Salic law (which disallowed female successors to most European crowns), Prussia would agree to accept an archduchess as heir to the Habsburg lands after death of the son-less emperor Charles VI. The bond with Austria removed the political attraction of the English marriages.

In fact, Frederick William cannot be said to have played his hand well at all.[98] Instead of the powerful alliance he might have gained through the double wedding, he pledged support for a Habsburg emperor who treated him with scarcely concealed arrogance and disdain. Vienna's alternative suggestion for the crown prince's bride was a minor German princess whose sole asset was that she happened to be the empress's niece. Nor did the Habsburgs have any intention of taking Prussia's pretensions to Jülich and Berg seriously. As Catholics, they preferred the idea of their co-religionaries, the Pfalz-Sulzbachs. Both in 1734, when Frederick William lent them military support in the War of the Polish Succession, and in 1738, when peace was finally re-established in central Europe, Prussia came away from the negotiating table empty-handed. Too late, Frederick William realised his mistake and negotiated with France to carve up the duchy of Berg between the two of them. Even when he died, he had still not given up on Jülich and Berg, and his Political Testament made it clear that his son Frederick should do all he could to secure the territories.[99]

What was lacking from Frederick William's circle was someone who could give him good, impartial guidance. His best friend was Leopold of Anhalt-Dessau, the 'Alte Dessauer': a man of simple, war-like habits who, despite his position as a minor German prince, had married a *Bürgerliche*, the daughter of an apothecary. His stuff-and-nonsense approach made him suspicious of the crown prince, with his ever more exaggerated French manners. In his youth, he had been of another complexion: 'He loved wine and debauchery . . . but it was notable that neither women nor wine had been able to hold him back when it was a question of acquiring glory.'[100] The Alte Dessauer was a good friend to the Prussian king, but he was not in a position to advise him. Frederick William looked elsewhere.

The key figures in Frederick William's later foreign policy were his minister, Field Marshal Friedrich Wilhelm von Grumbkow, and the imperial ambassador, General, later Field Marshal, Graf Ludwig Heinrich von Seckendorff. Grumbkow was the son of a general. He had fought with distinction at Malplaquet, which surely endeared him to Frederick William. Although he had been a minister to his father, Frederick William confirmed him in office in 1713. He was a rare bird at the king's court: a highly cultured man, who had been brought up in France and married a Mademoiselle de la Chevalerie.[101] He also brought together an elegant circle both at his house in the Königstrasse in Berlin and at his country place, Schloss Niederschönhausen, later more famous as the home of Frederick the Great's spurned wife.

Grumbkow was Frederick William's favourite, but he had his drawbacks. Chief among them was that he was in the pay of the Habsburgs. Frederick William was aware that his minister was two-timing him. He wrote a not altogether convincing justification to the Alte Dessauer: 'I know he is like that, but you need such people to do the business honourable people wouldn't want to soil their hands with. I get more out of him in an hour than I acquit with others in three.'[102] It was a part of Grumbkow's assignment to dissuade Frederick William from marrying his children off to the appropriate Welfs, and persuade him to lend his support to Austria and the Reich.

In this he was eminently successful. Seckendorff was his paymaster. It has been suggested that Frederick William was progressively drawn into the arms of the Habsburgs by the behaviour of his wife and family, but Seckendorff also had particularly good powers of persuasion. He was fully able to govern the choice of marriage partners for the king of Prussia's children.[103] Opposition came from Sophia Dorothea, who had assembled a little party composed of her set at Monbijou: various members of the Schulenburg family[104] (whose estates were on both Prussian and Hanoverian land), and courtiers such as her lady in waiting, Frau von Kameke, and her husband, Wartensleben and Arnim. As a compensation for the possible loss of Jülich and Berg, the queen's party were angling to get their hands on the former Swedish towns of Verden and Bremen on the

River Weser, which lay on the far side of Hanover.[105] Such blandishments were not enough to shake Frederick William's faith in Vienna. Catching up with Seckendorff in Potsdam one day, he told him, 'You believe me to be a good Hanoverian, but my word as an officer, count, I'm more Imperial than Hanoverian.'[106]

The queen could not bear the sight of the Austrian envoy, whom she saw as being responsible for scrapping Frederick William's 1725 alliance with the British.[107] Wilhelmina was naturally a member of the Hanoverian party too: after all, she stood to gain the richest prize of all: the prince of Wales. Both she and her brother also despised Seckendorff, whom they saw as a villain who had turned the king's head.[108] Frederick's verdict was extreme: 'He was sordidly scheming; his manners were crude and rustic; lying had become so much second nature to him that he had lost the use of the truth. He was a usurer who sometimes appeared in the guise of a soldier, and sometimes in that of a diplomat.'[109]

Frederick William met Seckendorff first in the former incarnation at the Siege of Stralsund, and again when he donned his diplomatic coat and arrived in Berlin as imperial envoy in 1726. What brought together all three of the main protagonists in Prussian foreign policy and the marriage affair was drink. Seckendorff was a great toper, and his nephew claims that Grumbkow's consumption was no less 'astonishing', a fact generally recognised at the time, for he was known as 'Biberius' to his friends.[110] Seckendorff had the harder head though, and was able to wheedle secrets out of the Prussian minister in his cups; and better still, remember them the next morning. With a glass in his hand, Grumbkow was much more amenable to Seckendorff's diplomatic logic than he was in his more sober moments.[111]

[VI]

The scene of much of Frederick's calvary was the Tabakscollegium, where Seckendorff endured countless sessions to find the right opportunities to get his own way. Like Pöllnitz and the Alte Dessauer, Seckendorff did not actually smoke, but stuck a pipe in his mouth all the same and occasionally pressed his lips together to give the impression he was puffing on it.[112] One assumes the military men, Generals Schulenburg and Buddenbrock, and the Colonels Derschau and Truchsess, who formed the mainstay of the king's circle, took more pleasure in their pipes. After the serious business was over (Pöllnitz called it a 'tribunal where everything was subjected to examination')[113] Frederick William would deliver war reminiscences.[114] The atmosphere was by now fired by drink, and members of the college and guests had not only to dodge the missiles that shot about the room, but to suffer the practical jokes performed by the jester Gundling. They also had to stomach the effusions of hatred emanating from the person of the king of Prussia, as often as not directed at one or other of his princely neighbours. When he was not growling, he was indulging in his miserly concern for his treasury, or his obsessive interest in the health and well-being of his troops.[115]

It would be wrong to see this mad-hatter's tea party as the general tenor of life at Frederick William's court, but the daily routine was just as onerous for those who had to come into contact with the king. Mornings were taken up with inspecting troops. At midday the king gave audience. This was followed by a family lunch with various invited guests, generally officers. Eighteen places were laid. Then from 1.30 to 6.30 p.m., the king worked in his study. In the evenings, prior to the sessions of the Tabakscollegium, he played cards and gambled with the ladies: piquet, ombre and backgammon.[116] When a stag was sighted, there were hunts in the forest at Stern around the king's modest lodge. The building still exists, its main room of the Tabakscollegium decorated with hunting scenes, the king in person administering the *coup de grâce*. A more unusual decorative feature are the antlers shed each year by the king's pet stag 'Big Hanss', a present from the Alte Dessauer. Given his royal owner, the beast was naturally also a giant: the king appreciated size above all else. Next door is a simple kitchen where the king and his guests washed down after the hunt. The third ground-floor room contained a box bed, where His Majesty could sleep it off.[117]

Stern, of course, was just one place where the jollities could take place. Another was gloomy Wusterhausen, a building which, unlike Jagdhaus Stern, exhibited virtually no pretensions to architecture whatsoever.[118] In the Berlin Schloss there was also a room designed for meetings of the Tabakscollegium. It was at the back, overlooking the tiny garden by the Spree. Meetings started some time after 7 with the drinking and smoking taking place at a long, oak table just like the one preserved at Stern. At one end was a rough armchair where Frederick William sat to preside over the college; at the other end, a similar seat was surmounted by a brace of hare's ears: this was intended for the court buffoon.[119]

Although such heartiness had never been to the crown prince's taste, for the time being he showed willing and went about his military duties. On 14

March 1728, the sixteen-year-old was promoted lieutenant-colonel. A few months later, after the Saxon escapade, Frederick told Augustus's envoy, Ulrich Friedrich von Suhm, of his longing for freedom from his father's tight leash. He was running up debts. Not only had he bought an expensive library, but he was developing a taste for French fashion and clothes, which were a further strain on his modest allowance. He was borrowing money from the bankers Splitgerber and Daun, Verzenobre, and Montolieu, as well as the marquis de Lerrand. The king heard of his debts: 'I will pay them happily', he said, 'as I am not short of money and money is filthy stuff, but only if your conduct and attitude change, and you show an honest heart, and you keep me informed, will you get the money.'[120] Frederick made the mistake of only declaring a part of the sum. The plump Frederick William might even have been slightly jealous of his elegant, teenage son, who had winning looks and was popular with the officer corps. In a fit of rage he burned the boy's gold-embroidered night-gown.[121]

Frederick William had turned to physical violence against his son. Although Wilhelmina and Pöllnitz may have exaggerated this in their memoirs, it would be hard to deny the fact that Frederick was subject to frequent slaps, punches, hair pulling and other humiliations in front of courtiers, officers and diplomats. Frederick William was increasingly annoyed by his son's foppish manners. Where was the future general? Frederick was frightened of gunfire, fell off his horse, did not stand up straight, was dirty and untidy, slept late, was happy on his own or with women.[122] The king wanted his son to go about his business with a smile on his face, but the crown prince was mocking or melancholic.[123] After the Saxon visit, Frederick William let it be known to Colonel von Rochow that all 'effeminate, lewd, womanly concerns were most indecent for a man'.[124] He was never one to mince words: 'He should bear it in mind', he told the sixteen-year-old on 11 September 1728, 'that I can't bear effeminate fellows, who have no [normal] human inclinations, who do shameful things, who can't ride or shoot, whose bodies are thereby unclean, who grow their hair long and curl it like fools, but all is in vain and there is no improvement at all...'[125]

Besides Frederick's 'effeminacy', what hurt Frederick William was his son's apparent mockery of all he stood for. He demanded 'unconditional obedience' from his heir. As he appeared to be laughing up his sleeve at his father's Spartan values, Frederick William sulked, and no longer required his son to say goodnight to him before he went to bed. The king's rage was coming to the boil. He took it out on him not just for his own behaviour, but because of the machinations of his wife.[126] One day he grabbed Frederick by the hair, which being powdered and preened was hateful to him, and threw him to the ground. He wanted Frederick to apologise for his conduct: 'I'll mistreat you as I may my child, but not an officer.'[127]

One day at the Tabakscollegium, Frederick tried to make amends. It was St Hubert's Day, and the pretext for a good cull in the forests. A great, silver-gilt goblet in the form of a mortar encrusted with jewels and containing a second, smaller vessel was brought out. It was filled with wine, twice, and subsequently drained à la ronde. Frederick William forced his son to drink, too much. It went to his head, and the boy told his father that he loved him, leant over the table and began to kiss his hands. He came round the table[128] and kissed the king, then dropped to his knees. Frederick William was pleased: 'Now, that is well done, just be an honest fellow, just be honest,' he said. Frederick was drunk, and had to be put to bed.[129] The king's persecution of his son now abated for a while, although the relief may have lasted a mere fortnight.[130]

The king was determined to have his son more closely superintended. From March 1729 two officers, Rochow and Keyserlingk (who became the prince's personal equerry), were permanently attached to the boy, to prevent him from getting up to mischief. From 21 January the following year, Keyserlingk was also obliged to sleep in his room.[131] Dietrich Freiherr von Keyserlingk would now seem a controversial choice of prefect. Fourteen years older than Frederick, Keyserlingk was a half-Italian, Baltic baron, highly cultured, a linguist and amateur poet; he was later to be the Falstaff of Frederick's Rheinsberg court. Wilhelmina sniffed that he was 'a chatterbox who thought himself a wit and was nothing more than a walking encyclopaedia', adding, for good measure, that he was 'extremely debauched'.[132] As Pesne's portrait of Keyserlingk charmingly displays, the Balt was almost certainly a sensualist, with a fondness for the good things in life, such as wine and food. He may also have been a homosexual, which, given that he was sharing the prince's bedroom, could have confirmed Frederick in certain ideas that were only then half-forming in his mind.[133]

Frederick took a small interest in girls too, principally Doris Ritter. She may well have been courted by any number of officers garrisoned in Potsdam, and it might have seemed appropriate for the crown prince to court her too. Frederick used a Lieutenant von Ingersleben as a go-between in his contacts with the sixteen-year-old. He gave her presents:

a silver tooth-pick box may not sound too romantic to our ears, but there were other things besides, including a pair of 'bad' amber bracelets. She was later said to have been 'a drain on … [Frederick's] resources',[134] but the precise nature of their relationship remains unclear. It is highly doubtful that she in any way merited the savage treatment meted out to her after Frederick's flight.

His new circle of friends was part of the problem. To Borck the seventeen-year-old Frederick wrote of his contentment. 'I am finally learning to be carefree; I am that at this moment, despite what might befall me. I play my flute, I read and I love my friends more than I do myself.'[135] Were they the right people for a sensitive young prince like Frederick? Wilhelmina claims that she thought them a bad lot from the outset. One was the 'minister of his debaucheries', the royal page Peter Keith, the scion of a Scottish family that had settled in Pomerania: 'this young man knew only too well how to insinuate his way into his company, [Frederick] … loved him passionately and gave him his entire confidence … I reproached him several times [for this]'.[136]

There were in fact two Keith brothers, Peter Karl Christoph and Robert. Peter was Frederick's bosom friend. He was banished from court for that very reason, and granted a commission as a lieutenant in the Dossow Regiment garrisoned in Wesel in west Germany. He was still stationed there at the time of the flight.[137]

His other favourite was Hans Hermann von Katte: eight years Frederick's senior and a Francke man.[138] He was an officer in the elite Gensd'armes regiment who had been destined for the law, and had therefore had the chance to travel and study. He was cultured, he painted and played music.[139] According to Pöllnitz, Frederick 'carried on with him like a lover with his mistress'.[140] Pöllnitz and Wilhelmina are the usual sources for Katte, and both tend to run him down. Neither has anything nice to say about his looks, for example. The former calls him 'short and swarthy and extraordinarily defaced by the pox'. Wilhelmina thought him more dangerous than Keith and called him 'more repulsive than likable; a pair of black eyebrows hung almost over his eyes* … A dark,

---

* In Katte's village of Wust in the Brandenburg Mark, the children used to sing a little song about him:

Wer Augenbrauen hat	(If like Katt the nobleman
Wie der Ritter Katt	Your brows are black as sin,
Kommt an den Galgen,	You're fodder for the hangman
Oder auf's Rad.	Or on the wheel you'll spin.)

pockmarked skin added to his ugliness ... he posed as a wit, and a consummate libertine.'[141] The journalist, novelist and Borussomaniac, Theodor Fontane, took neither description at face value, and examined the surviving portraits of the officer at the end of the last century. He wore his hair powdered, divided into three tresses, 'His features were neither handsome nor ugly, betraying his cleverness, energy and a certain aristocratic conceit'.[142]

The new carefree Frederick did not please his father. Frederick William became increasingly brutal, not just towards his eldest son, but to the whole family. Wilhelmina may have doctored her account, again, but it makes lively reading: plates hurled at the heads of the children, because Frederica Louise had the temerity to criticise the 'coarse vegetables' they were obliged to eat; the princes and princesses pursued down the passages by the king in his wheelchair, swinging his crutch in fury; Wilhelmina and Frederick seeking refuge under a bed and in a cupboard to escape their father's wrath, only to discover to their horror that Frederick William had marked the room out for his post-prandial snooze, and having to endure whole hours confined to their hiding places while the king paid his dues to Morpheus and emitted swinish snores. They were his particular bugbears: their father, Wilhelmina tells us (always keen to come first), called her 'English scum', and Frederick, that 'rascal Fritz'.[143]

[VII]

The French were anxious even then to claim the fashion-conscious prince for one of their own. Their consul wrote a memorandum at the time, showing his desire to win the prince over to a French way of thinking. This was considered a wise investment for later. A French 'party' grew up around Frederick, with the backing of the queen.[144] The king scarcely worried about France; England he saw as a more dangerous enemy. Both of Frederick William's elder children had put their hopes in an English match which would liberate them from their father's tyranny. Their plight had become a focus for those who remembered the more liberal regimen of Frederick I, and who gave their support to the queen. Frederick's governor, Finckenstein, was one of these; so was Derschau,[145] who was later to be given the task of interrogating Frederick in Wesel. A new risk was becoming clear to Frederick William: that courtiers might cluster around his son and actually seek to depose him. This thought tortured him all the more. Images of King Philip and Don Carlos must have sprung to mind; of Peter the Great and the Tsarevich Alexander.

In the winter of 1729 in Pomerania, Frederick William distracted himself with hunting, he and his friends bagging 1882 wild boars.[146] It was looking bad for Frederick. The chances of his getting an English bride seemed remote as Seckendorff had been toying with another solution, one more pleasing to Vienna and Prince Eugene. Elisabeth Christine of Brunswick-Bevern was born on 8 November 1715 and named after the empress, her aunt. The Brunswicks were a branch of the Hanoverian Welfs, but one that was no longer politically beholden to them. Her father, the duke of Bevern, heir-apparent to the main Brunswick dukedom, was a respected soldier in the imperial army, and a friend of the Alte Dessauer. At the time when the Treaty of Herrenhausen appeared to have clinched a double marriage for the two eldest Hohenzollern children, Bevern attended a troop revue in Prussian Magdeburg. Seckendorff met him there and the idea seems to have occurred to the Austrian envoy of using a Bevern marriage as a means of annulling the unwelcome new treaty with Hanover.[147]

By 1729, the Treaties of Wusterhausen had been signed, and Prussia's attitude to Britain was hostile. The king of Great Britain was still elector of Hanover, but there were plans to divide the succession. Had the prince of Wales had a second son, it was supposed that he would offer him Hanover and leave his first-born to govern Britain. One idea current at the time was that, if no second son were produced, the electorate would revert to the Brunswick-Wolfenbüttels, which would have considerably enhanced the status of Elisabeth Christine's family, advancing them from the second to the first division of German princes.

Hanover's attitude was seen as threatening some of the smaller German states, Brunswick in particular, and it was hoped that Prussia would take their side. Vienna wanted to pull Prussia into the imperial camp with Saxony to resist the Hanoverians.[148] In the summer of 1729, matters got considerably worse when a major storm blew up on the Prussian–Hanoverian frontier. The Hanoverians locked up one of Frederick William's recruiting officers, who had been gaily removing a consignment of hay which may or may not had the right to be lodged in a barn over the border in Brunswick. This trifling act of larceny led to the mobilisation of 44,000 Prussian troops. Suddenly, Vienna was obliged to re-examine its foreign policy. Did they really want war with Great Britain? The answer was an emphatic no. Frederick William's heels would have to be cooled. The answer was a fraught Anglo-Prussian conference held in Brunswick in the winter of that year. It did little to reconcile the brothers-in-law. As one British observer put it: 'our king's contempt for his brother in law is as great as one man can have for another, and I dread the probable consequences of a rancour so violent and so reciprocal'.[149]

Frederick William was deep in marriage negotiations, which were designed to bring him closer to the Beverns. At first they focused on Frederick's thirteen-year-old sister Charlotte and Bevern's eldest son Charles. Frederick William was keen to divest himself of his 'weeds' as quickly as possible: Frederica was shipped off to the margrave of Ansbach at fourteen. Seckendorff found approval for Charlotte's marriage in Vienna, and an appropriate sum of money went into Grumbkow's purse. Even the queen approved, as she preferred the Bevern boy to Tsar Peter II. A wise hunch, as it turned out: Peter died aged only fifteen in 1730, ending the Romanov dynasty in the male line. Frederick William wrote to the duke to say how happily he consented: 'I know of no better match, that way the alliance with the emperor gets into the blood, which is the greatest honour [for me].'[150]

In October 1729, Prince Eugene had become enthusiastic about Seckendorff's idea of marrying Frederick to the eldest of the duke's daughters, Elisabeth Christine, then aged fourteen and not yet confirmed. The Prussian king was also keen. Seckendorff got to do the dirty work, as usual. On the 22nd he wrote to the duke in his reptilian way:

His Majesty [Frederick William] had the grace to talk to me yesterday. The conversation turned on the subject of the crown prince's marriage to the Princess of Bevern, who was greatly approved. It is now therefore necessary to ask His Highness [i.e., the duke], if I might have a portrait made of the princess. So that I might better conceal my purpose, would His Highness have the goodness to add one of himself and the duchess, as well as one of His Highness, the eldest prince.[151]

Frederick had not given up his hopes of an English marriage for one moment. His mother had taught him to despise everything to do with the empire.[152] The negotiations with Brunswick, and the continuing humiliations Frederick was suffering at the hands of his father, were driving the adolescent to his 'final despair'.[153] On 29 November, he tried to run away for the first time.[154] Sadly, the details of Frederick's attempt at flight have been lost.

The progress of the Bevern marriage and the continuing bellicosity between Britain and Prussia prompted the queen to dabble in a little diplomacy of her own. She wrote to her brother, the king of England, on 17 December 1729 and offered him Wilhelmina for the prince of Wales 'without conditions'. George had his wife answer. Queen Charlotte's reply was luke-warm, haughty, disingenuous and 'vague', but it raised the idea of a double marriage again, with Frederick getting Princess Amalia, as Anne was now reserved for William of Orange.[155] The English were keen to play the queen along, and it was widely assumed in European court circles that the marriages would take place. The Treaty of Seville had created an alliance between Britain, Spain, France and the Netherlands against Austria. Opinion was therefore canvassed among the allies: the Dutch were keen, and the French were in favour as long as the Prussians were not given Jülich and Berg, which had been promised to the Wittelsbachs. There was also the added temptation of trying to detach Frederick William and his crack troops from the emperor and bring them into the allied camp. Jülich and Berg were to remain an insurmountable stumbling block, however.[156]

In January, oblivious of the queen's letter, Grumbkow came to Sophia Dorothea from Frederick William. He had two names to offer her as possible husbands for her eldest daughter: Wilhelmina's cousin, the margrave of Brandenburg-Schwedt, and the prince of Weissenfels. It was a stormy scene. The queen had better things in mind and was furious with Grumbkow, whom she called 'the primary cause of all my sorrows'. Schwedt was a 'worthless wretch', while Weissenfels was not eligible for a king's daughter. Grumbkow got the message. He informed the monarch that neither candidate was suitable. Meanwhile Sophia Dorothea sent her chaplain and Wilhelmina's English teacher, Dr Villa, on a secret mission to the British court.[157] At the end of the month, Frederick made his second attempt to flee to Britain, presumably dejected by the marriage plans.[158]

For the British it was a chance to renew their attempts to wrest Prussia away from Austria and realign it with Britain and Holland. There may indeed have been doubts in Frederick William's mind. On 7 March, the British Resident, Dubourgay, reported that the king was 'tender and affectionate' towards his wife and his two eldest children, and that he had 'slighted' Seckendorff.[159] If Frederick William had indeed considered a change of tack, he was rapidly put to rights by his advisers. Reichenbach, his resident in London, was quick to point out the one-sided deal he could expect from Walpole's Whig ministry: 'The queen of England was weaving a great intrigue around the marriage. The whole project aims to make the king's country [Prussia] dependent, or something like a lackey to the king of England. The only way of effecting this is by means of a match between Amalia and the crown prince.' As it turned out, Reichenbach, as well as being richly subbed by Seckendorff, was also in the pocket of the Tories.[160]

On 2 April an English colonel, Sir Charles Hotham, arrived in Berlin with the job of forming an alliance with Britain. Reichenbach had been able to warn the Prussian court that Hotham had about his person an expensive gift for the queen.[161] All Hotham knew of the marriage question had come from Sophia Dorothea's letter. He now needed to work on the Prussians to find out just how much interest there was in the idea. Hotham was a good choice of minister to Prussia; an old soldier, well connected, a passionate huntsman and with a strong head for drink. He needed the latter, for after the first civilities that took place in the presence of the Prussian ministers, Grumbkow and Seckendorff, on the 4th, 'we all got immoderately drunk'. Later, the men danced together, Prussian-style. In his cups, Frederick William then astonished the assembled company by raising his glass and proposing a toast 'to the marriage'.[162]

He meant Wilhelmina's with the prince of Wales. So far no one had mentioned Frederick at all, except the queen of England in her letter to Sophia Dorothea. This drunken utterance, however, proved a flash in the pan, for the next day 'when he was sober', the king declined to be led out on the subject, and no one else seemed to mention it either, on pain of incurring His Majesty's displeasure. For the time being, Frederick had been left in Potsdam 'for fear that he might be touched by the English wind'.[163] Frederick William's one drunken utterance succeeded in creating some spurious rumours. Pöllnitz tells us that Frederick William sounded positive about Wilhelmina, at least, and that he had even kissed the British envoy. The Prussian courtier (almost a contradiction in terms) even asserts that Frederick William told Hotham that he would get rid of the pro-Austrian elements around him after Wilhelmina's marriage; but this was a sham: 'all these ploys were only to divert the queen; he never had any intention of marrying his children into the House of Hanover: I heard him say as much many times'. There was to be no more Hanoverian blood in the Hohenzollern veins. There was far too much already.[164]

Frederick William continued to avoid the issue of the marriages – single or double – over the next day or two. As the king told General von Borck, he realised now that Hotham was there not just for Wilhelmina's 'beaux yeux', but because he was trying to get him to abandon his allegiance to Austria. On the 10th, Frederick William had an interview with Borck and Friedrich Ernst von Knyphausen during which he asserted that the marriage of Wilhelmina to the prince of Wales was advantageous, but that he would assent to a match between Frederick and Amalia only if the English could bring him the territories of Jülich and Berg: 'If they want to draw me away from the Emperor, why don't they make a few suggestions?'[165]

During the talk Frederick William spoke of his troubled relationship with his eldest son. The idea was raised, in the event of a marriage to an English princess, of dispatching him to Hanover, as Stadtholder, where he would be out of the king's hair. This, it seems, was more sham, for Frederick William was testing his minister Knyphausen, whom he rightly suspected to be an English pawn. The notion was music to Hotham's ears, as his brief was to secure the crown prince as effectively as possible to Great Britain and detach him from father and fatherland.[166] The pro-English Knyphausen was a voice in the wilderness: the 'whole court was in the Emperor's pay'. If Hotham were to make any progress, he knew he would have to have Grumbkow dismissed.[167]

What Frederick William really thought of Hotham's proposals is clear from a letter of 4 April from Seckendorff to the emperor. 'The king swore to me on his honour ... that he would under no condition, as long as he lived, accept an English princess for the crown prince: whatever transpired about the marriage [Wilhelmina's], he would never detract from the engagements entered into with His Imperial Majesty.'[168] Frederick convinced himself that the negotiations were going brilliantly and was naturally overjoyed at the turn of events. He confessed himself 'besotted' with his cousin Amalia. The king sniffed: 'How can you be in love with someone you [have] never seen? What a farce!'[169] When the British court asked for a portrait of the crown prince to show to Amalia, Frederick William replied unkindly that she should be sent a picture of a 'big monkey, that's what he looks like'.[170]

The king avoided direct talks with Hotham. The Englishman lunched at the Schloss in Potsdam on the 22nd and observed Frederick in his 'dejection and melancholy'. 'The more I see of the crown prince, the more success I wish for the alleviation which could come with the conclusion of this affair.' Aware that there was indeed some advantage in the single marriage, Frederick William let it be known that it should remain a simple, 'unpolitical family alliance'. He saw Hotham in Potsdam on 5 May. In the meantime, Walpole had become extremely enthusiastic about the idea of dragging Prussia away from Austria. The Tories, of course, wanted the opposite, and pointed out that the present system of alliances favoured Britain's oldest enemy (France) at the expense of its oldest friend (Austria).[171]

The British were under no illusions, however, and the message was: all or nothing. The British minister made what seemed to him a very generous offer: 'In order to tighten the bond of blood even more, the king of England offered the choice of all his princesses and one specifically for the crown prince ...'[172] Hotham then offered Frederick the stadtholdership that had been aired in the king's conversation with Knyphausen. He also proceeded to demand changes in the Prussian ministries in order to rid them of their heavy, pro-Austrian bias. Reichenbach was singled out, together with an unnamed minister who was preventing due harmony from existing between the two courts. He meant Grumbkow.[173]

Frederick William was not the most patient of men, and his blood was boiling before Hotham had finished his proposals. He informed the British envoy that, although he was prepared to go ahead with the planned union between Wilhelmina and the prince of Wales, he felt Frederick too immature for marriage: 'he was himself of an age and strength when he might with God's will reign for much longer, that he had, thanks be to God, several male heirs, he therefore saw no need to hurry with the eldest ...'[174] From subsequent utterances on the subject, he seems to have thought thirty a decent age. The match was therefore postponed for a dozen years. It was as good as rejecting the proposal outright. Nor was he happy about damaging his relations with the emperor, but he agreed to replace Reichenbach. Frederick William imposed further conditions: that the British should help him win Berg, and they should end their hostility to Austria.[175]

Hotham, who must have felt that the interview had gone badly, begged the king not to reveal the contents of the proposals to his hostile ministers. Frederick William replied that he needed to talk them over with Borck and Thulemeyer. Knyphausen was expressly left out of the list. Of course, it was no time before he poured it all out to Seckendorff, who informed the emperor on 11 May that Frederick William had even gone off the idea of the single marriage; that he considered the offer of a stadtholdership in Hanover 'impertinent'; that Frederick was too young to marry; and that the proposal made it look as if he, Frederick William, did not have the means to 'nourish him himself'. He might possibly consider it if Hanover were to offer him a sweetener or two in the form of land, but clearly did not believe that this would be the case.[176]

The king was furious about Hotham's attempts to rid him of Grumbkow: 'an honourable man who had served him well and loyally'.[177] Perhaps a more serious consideration on his part was that Frederick in Hanover would begin to look like a foreigner to his own people, and would be ignorant of the land he was born to rule. Seckendorff must have been delighted to see the king's niggling and hot-headed opposition to the British offer. However, the king had still not rejected the idea outright, even if the French ambassador, Sauveterre, thought he had.[178] Seckendorff naturally added his own sixpence to the argument: he told the king that any attempt to banish pro-Austrian ministers would mean the beginning of Prussian subjugation to Great Britain, and that a British princess would 'fill his court with intrigues and cabals'. He also used the opportunity to warn the king about Knyphausen.[179]

After his interview with Seckendorff, the king went into lunch. All the Prussian princes were present. Seckendorff was treated to a little show of loyalty. The youngest, Henry,* then aged four, had to drink the health of all 'right-thinking Germans'. Frederick William had recovered his good humour and even appeared to be kindly disposed towards the crown prince. Hotham might have bungled his mission, but the British might have been luke-warm about both marriages: their real purpose was to change the nature of the Prussian king's foreign policy and bend him to their will.[180]

Frederick and the queen's party still believed that salvation was within their grasp. Their strategy was to push the British not to grant one without the other: the double marriage or nothing. Frederick told Hotham not to break off negotiations and wrote to his uncle George in May to say that he would never accept any other bride than Amalia. He also pledged to return the sums lent to him by the king of Great Britain and told Hotham, even then, that it was his greatest wish to come to England.[181] This personal intercession on the part of the eighteen-year-

* Ferdinand was born later that year.

old prince was not kept secret in London, and it came to the ears of General Grumbkow, who took it to the king, occasioning new outbursts of fury against his disobedient son.[182]

On 9 May, Frederick William spent an hour closeted alone with Grumbkow; Knyphausen was excluded again. Hotham had his answer on the 12th, and reported back to his masters in Westminster the following day. He voiced Frederick William's objections to the idea of marrying Frederick to Amalia in the immediate future, while retaining the right to review the situation after a dozen years. The only chance of altering his position on the marriage of the crown prince would be in the unlikely event of the British securing for him Jülich and Berg. Hotham told Borck that he was embarrassed to send this reply back to Britain.[183]

Frederick William did not have far to look for an alternative match. On 14 May the duke of Bevern was in Berlin with his eldest son Charles to celebrate his engagement to Charlotte. Bevern had had cold feet. He had been frightened of the expense of a Hohenzollern (obviously a common complaint for German princes, who lived on little more than their dignities). He had threatened to abandon the marriage plans at precisely the time when there were rumours that Frederick William might be tempted to do a deal with the British. Seckendorff had to warn the duke that he risked losing the bigger prize, Frederick: 'the king said to me only the day before yesterday, "I have made enquiries about the girl. She is apparently pretty and well brought up".'[184]

Later in May, Frederick William and the crown prince were guests of the king of Saxony at a sumptuous, month-long party in a camp above the Elbe at Mühlberg. Once again Frederick was planning his escape. Before he left, he paid a nocturnal visit to his sister, dressed in luxuriant French finery. The princess did not recognise him, and took refuge behind a screen. Frederick laughed out loud, 'He was in the best of moods.' He told Wilhelmina that he could not endure further 'snubs' or the 'hateful yoke' of his father any longer, where he was forbidden to read or play music, and where he was only able to enjoy his pleasures in fear of the king's wrath. He would disappear in Dresden and make for England, where he hoped she would join him in due course; presumably in the guise of princess of Wales.[185]

It was to Mühlberg that the secretary of the British Embassy, Captain Guy Dickens, brought the British response to Frederick William's churlish treatment of the marriage offer: their animosity towards Austria was not germane to the issue; the proposal was for *two* marriages, not one, but

Frederick was not obliged to live in Hanover with his bride if the king did not want him to. Frederick William countered that, as far as he was concerned, the formal request concerned only Wilhelmina. Guy Dickens sent this answer back to London.[186]

According to Hotham, Frederick invited Dickens into his tent before he left, and confessed to him too that he could not take his father's brutality any longer; and that he was planning to flee to Strasbourg (where he seemed to have his eyes on a stay on the Alsatian estate of the French envoy, comte Rothenbourg), to spend a few weeks or months in France, and then to come to England. He believed that his cousins could cover for him, and he did not think that Wilhelmina's marriage hopes would be dashed by his move. His concern for his sister begs an interesting question: was her later bitterness towards her brother caused by the fact that he destroyed her chances of becoming queen of Great Britain? She was certainly a profoundly ambitious woman. Her fate, becoming the wife of an unfaithful Franconian princeling, must have hurt her pride a great deal. The answer is probably yes.

The festivities continued at Mühlberg: no one knew quite how to give a party like the king of Poland. At one stage the men returned from a driven hunt to find that a cake more than 52 feet long had been baked in their absence. Frederick William even gave in to the mood, and presented the Saxon minister Graf Brühl with the Black Eagle.[187] The crown prince was not enjoying himself, but he clearly believed the flamboyant king of Poland was a more sympathetic figure than his own father. When King Augustus was invited to Prussia at the end of June to enjoy, among other things, a splendid hunt in the forest of Lichtenberg (in what is now the edges of west Berlin), Frederick asked the Saxon elector to intercede for him, and let him go to Italy at least. Augustus carried out the commission, but Frederick William's answer was typical of the man: 'Yes, if there's a war on.'[188]

Frederick had Katte's shoulder to cry on. He opened his heart to the older man, telling him much the same story as he had given Wilhelmina and Dickens. Katte later confessed during interrogation that he loved Frederick, and was unable to 'refuse his request' for help.[189] Both Frederick and Katte made the mistake of being too indiscreet:[190] far too many people had an inkling that something was up. Colonel von Rochow began to suspect that some conspiracy was afoot, and warned the prince against doing anything rash. Frederick and Katte now decided that Rochow was an enemy and planned to fall on the officer and gently tie him up, so that he could not prevent their going. In the end, the flight was postponed one more time.

The court returned to Potsdam, where Frederick William sent new word to his British 'cousin': he was prepared to go ahead with Wilhelmina's marriage 'in the not too distant future'. As regards the crown prince, he wanted to postpone the bans, but he gave his royal word that he would not offer his son's hand to any other princess.[191] The British were frustrated by Frederick William's intransigence. They had looked at the king's pro-Austrian advisers and presciently decided that the chief villain was Grumbkow. They had been intercepting the minister's correspondence with Reichenbach, the Prussian resident in London, and discovered that the diplomat had instructions to prevent friendly relations from developing between the two courts.

On 9 July, Frederick had a meeting with Dickens under the south-west portal of the Berlin Schloss, opposite the Steckbahn. He presented the Englishman with a tally of his debts. Dickens endeavoured to talk some sense into the prince, and discourage him from flight; above all to France. Britain did not want him either, and his presence there would be an embarrassment that might lead to a conflagration breaking out in every corner of the continent. Dickens agreed to pay off debts amounting to 15–16,000 thalers,[192] but in return sought an undertaking from the prince that he would abandon his escape plans. Frederick agreed, but only if his father left him behind on his projected tour of south Germany,[193] occasioned by Frederica's forthcoming marriage to her Hohenzollern cousin, the margrave of Ansbach.

On 12 July, Hotham decided to face the Prussian king with the evidence of Grumbkow's duplicity. According to one version, he scattered the minister's letters at the king's feet.[194] However, Frederick William was indifferent and thought it rather underhand to open the minister's dispatches. Pöllnitz has it that he rounded crossly on Hotham, saying 'that no one should lay down the law for him', and gave every impression that he was about to kick him.[195] A more sober version of the interview has the king tell the diplomat: 'Gentlemen, I have had enough of this stuff', and leave the room.[196] It seems hardly likely that the story of the raised foot is true. Pöllnitz, however, maintains that Hotham was so furious that he determined to quit Berlin within the hour. Frederick William is supposed to have swiftly regretted his rashness and asked the Dutch and Danish envoys to tell the Englishman that he had not meant to insult him. He later even sent Borck to apologise,[197] but this would seem to be just yet another of the many misleading stories surrounding Frederick's marriage plans. On the same day as Hotham received his answer from the king, he had the famous letter from Frederick, delivered by a 'person' (Katte), in which Frederick melodramatically affirmed that he would 'rather die' than marry anyone other than his cousin Amalia, although he suspected that his father now had other plans for him.[198]

That night the king told his son that he was not to accompany him on the tour. Frederick toyed with the idea of sending Katte on a mission to George II, but Frederick William changed his mind and decided that Frederick could come after all. In the meantime, Katte had made the necessary arrangements and applied for leave from his regiment to act as a recruiting officer in west Germany for a spell. Frederick and he had a last meeting in the bushes in the garden of the Schloss in Potsdam. Katte promised to meet Frederick in Cannstatt,* and the prince gave him his valuables to keep for him until their next meeting. Frederick proposed doing precisely what he had intimated to Dickens. A promised last interview with Wilhelmina did not take place. Time was clearly very short.[199]

Frederick and his father set off in the dawn light of the 15th, only hours after that last meeting with Katte. They stopped in Leipzig and made an inauspicious halt in Meuselwitz, to collect Frederick's bugbear, Seckendorff, from his estate.[200] He had his uses: his bottomless purse could be made to pay for Frederica's ring and other trifles amounting to 6000 thalers and 2000 guilders which the stingy monarch had refused to stump up.[201] In the meantime, a 'confidant' (almost certainly Katte) had a meeting with the French diplomat Sauveterre, in which he expressed the prince's interest in going to France. Sauveterre informed Versailles, where it was agreed to offer the fugitive prince hospitality.[202] In Bamberg the royal party admired the cathedral on its plateau above the city, then they progressed to Nuremberg for another day of sight-seeing. Ansbach was next. Here a Captain von Katte, a cousin of Frederick's friend, brought him an ominous letter: Hans Hermann had been denied leave.[203]

Despite this setback, Frederick was determined to go ahead. He sent word to Katte to meet up with him and the elder Keith in the Hague, where Frederick would be staying under the incognito of comte d'Alberville. A second letter contained an apology for his action. He

* Now a suburb of Stuttgart.

mentioned the names of those courtiers who had been particularly insensitive: Captain von Hacke and Colonel von Derschau. In the meantime, the cousin, Captain Katte, had talked to Rochow, stating that he found something suspicious about the comings and goings between Hans Hermann and the prince.[204] Seckendorff too might have been alerted by Katte's indiscrete boasting in Berlin.[205]

On the last day of July 1730, the royal tour arrived in Augsburg for the wedding. Frederick William wanted to show his son the imperial capital, and the battlefield at Schellenberg above the River Wörnitz, where Marlborough had been pitted against the Franco-Bavarian forces in the summer of 1704 and had secured a 'notable victory'.[206] They stayed with the Württembergs at Ludwigsburg. Here Frederick had a new, knee-length, red, 'Roquelaure' coat made for him[207] as part of his travelling kit, thereby making Rochow even more suspicious.

After the celebration, the party left the Neckar Valley at Heilbronn and made for Mannheim. On the road to Ginnsheim, the king decided that two good barns in the village of Steinsfurth would make admirable lodgings for the night. The king and his companions would sleep in one, the prince and his lackeys in the other. They were only a few miles from the Rhine and could make an early start the next day. Frederick took the brief literally and was up at 2.30 a.m. on 5 August, even before his father. He put on his new red coat and slipped some gold into his pocket. His servant Gummersbach was watching him. He had been told to keep an eye on the prince by Rochow. When he questioned Frederick, the prince replied, 'But I want to get up. What is it to you?' Gummersbach alerted the colonel. Rochow appeared to reason with Frederick in the village street. At that point Robert Keith arrived with two horses. Rochow asked Keith what they were for. Keith replied he had fetched them for the pages.[208]

Rochow tried to convince Frederick to stop being foolish and to put off the coat, which would merely excite the anger of the king. Buddenbrock and Waldow then emerged on to the street, followed by Seckendorff. Rochow turned to the imperial minister and asked him in a jocular way how he liked the prince's new finery. Frederick took the hint and discarded the coat. For the time being disaster had been narrowly avoided: by the time the king emerged from his slumbers, the crisis had blown over. Frederick William decided that his son's coach should leave first, as it was the heaviest vehicle. In Heidelberg he missed Frederick: 'Where is my son?' he asked. 'He must have driven horribly fast, we couldn't catch up with him; they wouldn't be so mad as to drive to Mannheim before me?'[209]

Frederick William reached Mannheim at around 8 a.m. and was bewildered not to see his son. Frederick did not arrive until 10.30. In his pocket he had a note for the page Keith, instructing him to order post horses. The next day was Sunday, and Frederick William went to church. As he was leaving the building, Robert Keith's conscience bit. He threw himself at the king's feet and confessed that the crown prince had attempted to flee. Keith almost certainly saved his life through his action.[210] Frederick William summoned Rochow and told him that Frederick had tried to desert and that he was amazed that no one had informed him of the fact. Rochow would answer with his 'head, neck and collar'. He was now responsible for getting the prince to Prussian territory 'dead or alive'.[211]

Frederick William was now seriously worried. His fears were heightened by the sight of some French officers riding down the road from Landau; he thought they were in on the plot. He was considerably relieved when he reached the safety of Darmstadt. When he met Frederick again, he said cuttingly that he was astonished to see him: he thought he was already in Paris. Frederick replied arrogantly, in a manner calculated to annoy his father, that that might easily have been the case. On 8 August, the Prussian party reached Frankfurt am Main. The tourism went on despite Frederick's attempted desertion. Frederick saw the 'Römer', the ancient houses around the cathedral, and the Golden Bull, then they took a river boat down the Rhine to Bonn.

When the boat docked in Bonn, Frederick overheard the officers saying that he had to be brought back to Prussia 'dead or alive'. He talked to them, admitting that he had made plans to escape because the king had humiliated him at Mühlberg. Seckendorff promised to speak to the king about him as soon as they got to Moers, the first Prussian-owned town on the lower Rhine. More alarm gripped the party when it was discovered in Gelderland on the 11th that Peter Keith had deserted his regiment in Wesel on 6 August. Frederick William was now made aware that the plans had not only been worked out in detail, but come close to fruition. He saw a major conspiracy afoot involving foreign powers and dispatched his son to the fortress in Wesel. There, on 12 August, Frederick was formally interrogated for the first time.[212]

If we are to believe Pöllnitz and Wilhelmina, it was at this first hearing that Frederick William drew his sword on his son, and was only prevented from killing him by that very same General von der Mosel who had earlier been a victim of one of Frederick's pranks: 'Kill me Sire, but spare your son.'[213] Frederick the Great's most thorough biographer, Reinhold Koser, gives no credence to the story, however. There is no documentary evidence that the scene ever took place.[214] Instead Frederick William called on 'God his Lord and Father' to help him reveal the precise circumstances of the desertion and make his son aware of his 'duty and conscience'.

The hearing got off to a bad start. Frederick asserted that it was his third attempt to flee and that it had been his intention to go to France. From there he intended to write to his father and ask his forgiveness. When he had received assurance that the king would treat him better, he would have returned. Keith, however, had contradicted Frederick. He told his questioners that the prince had told him, 'Once I'm gone I do not ever intend to return.' The king was naturally keen to know who had funded the flight. Frederick, anxious to conceal his negotiations with Guy Dickens, claimed he had picked the diamonds out of the White Eagle order that had been presented to him by the king of Poland.[215] In the course of the hearing, he carelessly implicated Robert Keith, Katte and Lieutenant von Spaen. The last two were arrested as a result.[216]

Frederick William already knew more, and responded by threatening his son with arrest and posting guards on the door. He told Derschau that he did not want to see Frederick and retired from the room. On the 13th Frederick was examined again in the presence of Derschau, who was able to tell his master that Frederick had not told the 'pure truth'. At the third hearing on the 15th, it was already clear that Peter Keith had gone to Amsterdam under the name of Graf Sparre, and that his ultimate destination had to be England rather than France. Frederick had clung to the French story to cover up for his dealings with Dickens. His examiner tested him: 'Why did he not rather choose to go to England, as opposed to France, which in the first place would have been more natural as a result of his relations there?' Because, said Frederick, such a move 'would have strengthened His Majesty's resolve against the [double] marriage'.[217]

Frederick William was clearly in despair. It must have seemed that his worst fears had come true: Frederick was the focus of a British-backed conspiracy to unseat him and introduce a more liberal, dependent regime. He wrote the queen a letter, subsequently lost, which Wilhelmina claims contained the chilling words: 'I have had that rascal Fritz arrested; I shall treat him as his crime and cowardice dictate; I no longer recognise him as my son, he has dishonoured me and my entire house, such a wretch no longer deserves to live.' The queen was reportedly looking pale at a ball given to Monbijou to celebrate her husband's birthday on the 16th.[218] He also wrote to her chief lady-in-waiting, Frau von Kameke. This letter was examined by Koser. It is couched in a rather different language to that used in the letter which he is supposed to have sent his wife: 'my son has tried to desert with the page Keut [sic], I have had him arrested'. The conclusion is comparatively tender: 'I beg you to inform my wife in a manner calculated not to alarm her. And for the rest, have pity on an unhappy father.'[219]

The fourth Wesel hearing took place on the 19th. Once again it hinged on Frederick's ultimate destination. 'No, I wasn't going to England,' said the prince, but no one believed him any more. Once again Frederick failed to make a clean breast of it, and rendered his position more difficult. An appeal for mercy on the part of the prince did no good. The king wrote to General Otto Gustav von Lepel, the governor of the gaunt fortress of Küstrin on the Oder,* to have him prepare a cell for Frederick: two interconnecting rooms with strong doors and bars on the windows.[220]

Frederick William gave in to the wildest fantasies about plots and revolutions. Now it was impossible to alleviate the prince's treatment. General von Buddenbrock was given instruction to take him to Küstrin together with Colonels Waldow and Rochow. The four officers in the coach behind were told that they should be armed with 'good pistols and swords'. The prince's route was clearly mapped out: he was not allowed to touch Hesse, Lüneburg or Hanover, where the king thought an attempt might be made to rescue him,† but was to proceed through the Westerwald instead. After Halle the coaches had to travel north through Dessau, Treuenbrietzen, Mittenwalde and Fürstenwalde to Küstrin. If the convoy were attacked, the general had to make sure that Frederick fell into enemy hands 'nothing other than dead'.[221]

The whole process of transferring him to Küstrin was to be carried out in the strictest secrecy. The two coaches were to travel to Prussian Halle non-stop. If the prince needed to relieve himself, it had to be at

---

* Now Kostrzyn in Poland. The fortress was completely destroyed by the Red Army in 1945, although one can make out part of the glacis to the south of the modern town.
† Wilhelmina claims there was an attempt, but it was foiled by General Dossow.

some distance from any bush or thicket, lest Frederick attempt to escape, or someone try to rescue him. Cold food was taken on board to dispense with the need to stop at an inn.[222] Frederick William took a different route. He stopped to review troops in Lippstadt before proceeding to Anhalt, to pour out his heart to the Alte Dessauer.[223]

CHAPTER THREE

No Two Men Quite Like Them

[1]

Küstrin was a more than usually miserable prospect. The crown prince of Prussia was to be treated as a proper deserter. He was lodged on the second floor and no one was permitted to sleep in his room any more. He was allowed just two servants. His books, flute and sheet music were all to be taken away. In their place Frederick was left to contemplate the Bible, the song-book and Johann Arends' *Wahres Christenthum* (True Christianity). Lepel was told that he was to be stern with him, and let no one into his company. A measure and a half of beer was also prescribed to lighten the load.[1] On 19 September, Lepel received more precise instructions as to how to treat Frederick: the door was to be permanently locked or guarded and only opened three times a day. At 8 p.m. two officers were to bring a ewer and basin. He had seven and a half minutes to wash. Food was brought at twelve noon and 6 p.m. No officers were allowed to converse with Frederick.[2]

In Berlin there had been an attempt to cover up. Katte had burned the prince's letters, and both the queen and Wilhelmina had been feeding the fires to destroy any incriminating evidence that concerned them, and fabricating new letters in their turn. In three days, Wilhelmina claims, they counterfeited over 700.[3] Frederick William was furious when he learned of their chicanery: 'the women have duped us!' he is supposed to have said.[4] Grumbkow could do nothing to calm him down in that mood.[5] Wilhelmina insists that he beat her up and kicked her as she lay unconscious on the ground; but then, Wilhelmina's account is brimming with tales of brutality. Voltaire even claimed that she showed him a scar on her breast inflicted by her father at the time,[6] but that does not seem very likely either: *extremely* haughty princesses do not open their bodices for just anybody, especially not wizened old parvenus like Voltaire. Given her fault, had she refused the hand of the margrave of Bayreuth, she said, she would have been dispatched to fortress detention in Memel.[7]

Frederick William was disgusted with his son. Borrowing fully 17,000 thalers (it was nearer 20,000) when he needed only 9000 particularly troubled the parsimonious sovereign. He wrote to the Alte Dessauer, 'God protect all honest people from wanton children. He is a great worry, but before God and the world I have a clear conscience.'[8] The king ordered Katte's arrest two hours after returning to Berlin on the 27th.[9] Frederick's great friend had told Wilhelmina that he had done nothing to encourage the flight: 'I have written to him and clearly stated that I refuse to follow him. If he undertakes such a move, I shall answer with my head. It will be for a pretty cause, but the crown prince will not abandon me.'[10] In the end he had ample warning, but he wasted valuable time having a French saddle made for himself.[11] He packed and prepared to ride to the king's cousin, the margrave of Schwedt, at Schloss Frie-drichsfelde, then outside Berlin. He was finally arrested by Field Marshal Dubislaw Gneomar von Natzmer (the man who had converted Frederick William to Pietism). Natzmer had told Katte to destroy his papers and tarried three hours to give him time to escape; he 'was very annoyed to find that he was still there'.[12]

Katte sent Frederick's correspondence with Wilhelmina to the queen to prevent it from falling into Frederick William's hands.[13] The king already saw collusion between Wilhelmina and Frederick's friend on 16 August, the day he had ordered the guardsman's arrest.[14] Katte's hearing revealed further details of the plot, but even learning that Guy Dickens had not encouraged Frederick to come to England went no way to assuaging the king's fears or his blood lust. Grumbkow was to leave no stone unturned: 'vous exam[inez] toute la [sic] jourre et nuit', he wrote in his unscholarly French. The prince's friends the subalterns Spaen and Ingersleben were rounded up and thrown into prison. So too was poor Doris Ritter.

When Frederick William discovered about the presents his son had given the schoolmaster's daughter, he suspected that he must have slept with her. He ordered that the girl be examined by a midwife and a doctor to determine whether she were still a virgin. Perhaps she was not, or possibly Frederick William discovered something damning about her morals. Whatever he learned, the king's next move was astonishingly brutal. He ordered that she should be whipped through the streets of Potsdam by the common hangman and then thrown into the spin-house in Spandau for the rest of her born days. Doris Ritter was flogged in front of the town hall, then before her father's house and on every corner of the town. She was finally released from Spandau in 1733, after a petition from her father.[15]

Everyone was under suspicion, even the queen. Christian Otto Mylius (a 'born-again' Pietist), tabled a question for Frederick: 'Whether the queen in his [Frederick's] youth didn't do everything possible to win him over to her way of thinking.' Frederick William did not believe that Katte had revealed all he might. He read through the minutes of his interrogation, and decided there were more names to come out. 'He should be questioned closely and he should be told that if he doesn't confess, he will be tortured´...' Lieutenant von Kalnein, who had done no more than lend Frederick money, was to be shown the instruments in the Hausvogtei prison, the thumbscrew in particular. Frederick William made it clear this was no 'bagatel' (sic). If needs be, torture was to be used to secure statements from both Katte and even Frederick.[16]

Mylius was finding the crown prince a tough nut to crack. To General Lepel, he described him as 'very cunning', and Frederick was particularly sly during the long hearing that took place in Küstrin on 16 September, when 185 questions were tabled by both Mylius and Frederick William. Mylius stressed Frederick William's love for his son: had it been insufficient? Had he not done everything possible to make his son love him? To both questions Frederick said the king's love had been sufficient. Had the prince not been disobedient towards his father? Frederick was forced to admit that he had not followed the king's will in all things, but he had never in all his life had any antipathy towards the king.[17]

Mylius went into Frederick's debts. The intention was clearly to find out how much he had sold out to the British. Why had he not admitted how much he had borrowed? 'Out of fear,' replied Frederick. He had taken no money from the British, he added to his interrogator: the money was a loan. He was able to parry other important questions in the same way: he was not a deserter either. He had decided to take extended leave. He wanted to stay away as long as necessary to make the king treat him differently. He had evidently forgotten that Katte had been given the power to ask Dickens for asylum in Britain. Similarly, the accusation that Frederick had mocked both Grumbkow and Seckendorff caused him to lose some of the coolness he had displayed earlier in the hearing.[18] He had probably already decided that he needed both men if he were going to extricate himself from this mess.

After number 179 came the questions specifically tabled by the king. What sort of punishment did he think he deserved? was the first. Frederick submitted himself to 'the king's mercy'. Later, when he read through the minutes, he added the word 'will'. Mylius was being helpful and decided that this was a winning formula; he altered Frederick's answers elsewhere in the minutes to make them more pleasing to the king.[19] To the question 'Did he deserve to rule his people?' Frederick replied, 'He could not be his own judge.' He was asked whether he was prepared to offer up his life. Frederick returned to the previously established formula: 'he would submit to the king's mercy and will'. Was he ready to give up the succession to the throne? 'His Royal Majesty would not be so unmerciful towards him' was the prince's reply.[20]

The king's mercy was slow in coming. He was still convinced it was an 'English intrigue' and wanted more names; more people to threaten, torture and punish. During the hearing on 11 October, Frederick asked for the right to wear his uniform again. His father minuted in the margin: 'I don't want officers like this in the army, let alone in my [own] regiment.'[21] He toyed with the idea of passing over Frederick and settling the succession on his brother, William, whom he infinitely preferred to his eldest son. William could even work the impossible, and preserve the life of a *lange Kerl* who had deserted.[22] The Prussian envoy in Sweden heard the story that Frederick was to be dispossessed and wrote to the king for clarification: 'this is true', said Frederick William.[23]

Frederick continued defiant. By means of invisible ink (reactivated with lemon juice), he was able to get a letter out to Wilhelmina. 'I'd rather rot in Küstrin', he told her, 'than return to my old position. I have now discovered the bitter truth that an unsympathetic father is the worst thing on earth.' In the same letter Frederick told his sister how much he missed music and how he was looking forward to the days when 'your *Principe* and my *Principessa* will embrace once more'.[24] He meant her lute and his flute.

On 22 October, the minutes of the various interrogations were passed to the court martial sitting in the baroque Schloss of Köpenick, a few miles to the south-east of Berlin. The president was the king's trusted friend, the Pietist[25] Lieutenant-General Achatz von der Schulenburg.[26] Among the four generals, six colonels, three majors and three captains who made up the jury were the Major-Generals Dönhoff and Schwerin (who was later to become Frederick's most stylish field marshal). Derschau too had a vote as one of the colonels. Their job was to try Frederick, Katte, Ingersleben, Spaen and Lieutenant Keith.[27]

The different members of the court martial delivered their verdicts according to rank on 27 and 28 October. Ingersleben's offence of running between Frederick and Doris Ritter was considered minor. Suggestions for Ingersleben's punishment ranged from six weeks' confinement to quarters (major-generals) to six months' fortress detention (majors and colonels).[28] Spaen was privy to certain secrets. He merited a stiffer sentence: to be dismissed from his regiment and incarcerated for anything up to six years.[29] Peter Keith had well and truly deserted. Here the verdicts were consistent with Prussian law. In his garrison the drum should be beaten three times. If Keith did not appear, he should be declared 'unspeakable', his sword broken, and his image hanged in effigy.[30] Keith escaped to serve in the Portuguese army. He returned to Prussia after Frederick came to the throne. He died in 1756 a royal equerry, lieutenant-colonel and member of the Academy of Science, but still complaining that he had not been adequately compensated for his earlier sacrifice.[31]

No one wanted responsibility for judging the crown prince. The officers maintained that, as vassals, it was not their place to judge the son of their king and recommended him to Frederick William's mercy and forgiveness (colonels).[32] Katte's fate divided the court. The captains and generals wanted him confined to Spandau for life. The colonels were anxious that the death sentence be commuted. The majors recommended decapitation on the grounds that he had tried to desert; had given Frederick the advice to flee to Rothenbourg's estate in Alsace; had taken letters to foreign envoys; had arranged loans for Frederick with Berlin bankers and acted as Frederick's treasurer, sending money to Peter Keith on his behalf and his library to safe-keeping in Hamburg; had lied to Colonel Rochow; had lied about his recruiting mission; and had come between the crown prince and the king. The majors none the less humbly recommended that His Majesty think first what effect such a draconian punishment would have on Frederick.[33]

Schulenburg had the job of making sense of all this in his verdict of 29 October. The chief discrepancy surrounded Katte, where despite the appeals to the king's clemency, half the votes had been for the death penalty. The president came out in favour of life-long detention. It was not the answer the king was looking for. He wrote back to Schulenburg: 'You should tell me what the law says and not pass over it with a feather duster [sic] ... the court martial must meet again, and deliver another verdict.'[34]

The court martial, however, refused to be browbeaten and returned the same verdicts. In the meantime Frederick William received a plea for mercy from Katte, in which he compared his life to a tree that would never achieve full maturity. Frederick William was not very impressed with this talk of trees either. On 1 November the king wrote from Wusterhausen to confirm the court's sentences on Spaen and Keith, and pardoned Ingersleben.[35] Others who had simply been close to Frederick were banished: the prince's librarian Jacques, and the brother and sister von Bülow, who had been friends of Frederick. Duhan de Jandun was exiled to Memel.[36] The Freiherr von Montolieu, who had lent Frederick money, wisely fled before he was asked.[37]

On Katte Frederick William proved intransigent. He argued that Katte, an officer of His Majesty's Gensd'armes, was 'directly attached to his Royal Majesty's person and house'. His oath required him to obey the king through thick and thin. Despite the special role given to officers of his regiment, he had entered into negotiations with foreign powers. According to Prussian law, he should have his tongue ripped out with red-hot tongs and be hanged for the crime of *lèse majesté*, but out of consideration for Katte's family (his father was a general, his grandfather Field Marshal von Wartensleben), the king would be satisfied with a simple beheading. For Frederick William it was merely a question of applying the law, and as quickly as possible:

His Royal Majesty also received a little schooling in his youth* and he learned the Latin tag: *fiat justicia et pereat mundus!* (Let justice be done though the world should perish in the act) ... When the court marshal has published the sentence on Katte, let him be told that His Majesty is sorry, but that it is better that he should die than justice be denied the world.[38]

Frederick William now busied himself with the precise details of the execution. The scaffold was set up in the courtyard of the Küstrin fortress, directly under Frederick's window in order to make the strongest impression on the mind of the prince.[39] At 7 a.m. on 6 November, officers from the Gensd'armes were to form a circle around Katte while the sentence was read out. Then he was to be decapitated with a sword. The body was to lie there in the sand until 2 p.m., then be taken away and buried in the pauper's cemetery outside the town.[40] Padre Johann Ernst Müller from the Gensd'armes was to offer the prisoner consolation during his translation from his Berlin cell to the fortress on the Oder.

---

* Very little!

Katte sang hymns and prayed throughout his journey, occasionally refreshing himself with Corsican wine.[41] When he reached Küstrin there was food, tokay and beer. Major von Schack described his 'fearlessness and steadfastness', which he would not forget all his born days. The soldier Lepel reiterated Müller and Schack's statement about Katte's light-heartedness in the face of death. He refused a blindfold, handed over his wig, allowed the soldiers to take off his coat and neckerchief, removed his own shirt, knelt down in the sand and began to pray.[42]

The king had made it clear that Frederick must watch the execution of his friend, a practice that was thought savage even at the time.[43] Years later, Frederick recounted the scene to Catt: 'That hateful citadel, no one spoke to me, dared speak to me, they left me alone with my sad reflections on my friend Katte.' An old officer had come to him in tears. 'Oh my prince, my poor prince,' he said. Frederick thought he had come to take *him* off to the scaffold: 'So, speak, must I die then?' 'No, my poor prince, no, you will not die, but you must allow the grenadier to take you to the window and keep you there.'[44] The soldier was to hold his head to make sure he missed nothing.[45]

Lepel reported the brief exchange of words that took place as the officer was led past Frederick's window to the block: 'I beg of you, a thousand apologies,' cried Frederick. 'Monseigneur, you owe me nothing,' replied Katte. The Gensd'arme and Frankeman then cried 'Lord Jesus, receive my soul.' It was the signal for the executioner Coblentz to wield his sword. Katte's head fell with one stroke. Frederick promptly fainted.[46] The body was left as instructed by the king, but someone had the decency to throw a black cloth over the bloody corpse.[47]

[II]

Frederick was distraught for days; he could neither eat nor sleep. 'The king has taken Katte from me,' he told Lepel, 'but I still see him standing before my eyes.'[48] There was still a chance that Frederick would also be executed. Wilhelmina claims that Colonel Schenk (Schack?) told him as much; that he had refused twice to take on the job, but that the king had insisted: 'May it please God that the king has a change of heart and that I may have the satisfaction of announcing your pardon,' Schenk is supposed to have told the prince.[49] Katte's death, however, announced a slight lightening of the regime in Küstrin, and a minor rehabilitation for Frederick. Frederick William had assuaged his blood-lust. That, and the problems which might beset the succession, convinced him to spare Frederick, rather than the plea for mitigation that he had received from the emperor in Vienna on 1 November.[50]

The crown prince received a royal pardon, delivered by a large party of high-ranking army officers headed by Grumbkow. His sword and the cross of the Black Eagle were returned to him. In return he had to swear an oath of loyalty to his father. It was a formula dreamed up by Seckendorff, who had been worried where it might all end. To have Frederick killed would have meant exceeding his instructions.[51] He had told the king that Frederick belonged to the Empire, and had even made attempts to save Katte.[52] For company Frederick now had Colonel Gerhard Heinrich von Wolden, but the king made it clear that conversation must be limited to certain subjects: if Frederick were to live and succeed, he must learn to rule. They must talk of finance and manufacture, economy and administration, the ordering of the land and the management of money. Examples were to be confined to the Prussian provinces. There were to be no foreign languages, literature or music; and the prince's reading must be limited to the Berlin and Hamburg gazettes or the state archives stored in the vaults at Küstrin.[53]

Frederick's new timetable was reminiscent of the one prescribed for the nursery. On Sundays he was to be up at 4 a.m. From five till seven he was to attend the service in the town church and pay attention to the sermon. His manservant had to make sure he listened, prayed and sang fervently. He was permitted a walk round the walls until the Calvinist service began in the Küstrin Schloss church. He was allowed a little lunch at eleven, but he had to say his prayers first. He had time for a walk in the afternoon, but had to be back at the town church for the Lutheran service from 2 to 4 p.m. Another walk was possible if it were light, then he was to receive his cameralist teachers. He ate again at seven, and after saying his prayers, had to be in bed by 8 or 9 p.m.[54]

During the week, the regime was a little more moderate: he was woken at 5 a.m. in summer and 6 a.m. in winter. After saying his prayers, he repaired to the War and Estates departments in the Schloss to learn the business of statecraft. He was allowed ink and paper. It was a twelve-hour day. At 7 p.m. he 'broke bread' with his teachers. Lights out was at nine. Work began at the later hour of 9 a.m. on Wednesday, but only because he had to attend a two-hour Lutheran service first.[55] From 24 November he was no longer alone. A servant was allowed to sleep at the bottom of his bed and he could dine with him and Wolden. He could even take a stroll round the fortress walls. He still had little contact with the outside world: he was allowed two letters every three months, and they had to come from the king and queen or his immediate family. They also had to be written in German. Frederick William was adamant about this: 'no other language but German should be spoken in the crown prince's presence, no French must be spoken at all.'[56]

The ripples caused by Katte's execution were still spreading into international waters. The Prussian envoy Degenfeld reported from London that the British had not been best pleased by the king's action. Lord Harrington had written on George II's behalf to prevent Frederick William from executing his son. He must have mentioned Katte too, for on 24 November Frederick William answered his international critics in his usual uncompromising way:

[his envoy] should say that if there were still any Kattes I would tell them all that it was enough[,] that he was a perjuring rogue [–] *fiad justiecia aut pereat mundo* [sic –] as long as God gives me life and sustains me as a despotic lord I will have[,] and when I please[,] 1,000 of the grandest heads chopped off[,] and the English should know that I will have no one ruling by my side...[57]

Meanwhile in Küstrin, Frederick was growing a new skin; he was becoming 'a sort of artificial man'.[58] Hille found him cynical and opportunistic. His teachers soon learned he could not be forced. Any attempt to make him a good Christian ended up by leaving him more disillusioned with the church than ever; efforts to render him a model German prince drove him into the arms of the French Enlightenment.[59] There were moments of mental instability. One day he was unexpectedly chirpy. His new teacher, Christoph Werner Hille, wrote to Berlin: 'His Royal Highness is as funny as a chaffinch.'[60] The thought that he might go mad if he were pushed any harder led to a further lightening of the regime. Frederick even pleaded with Grumbkow to permit some 'honourable locals' to eat with him at his table.[61] He was allowed to furnish his own apartment.[62] Once the madness was over, he became very cold. After Katte's death there was only one other occasion in his life when he lost control: after his troops were routed at Kunersdorf, just up the road from Küstrin, in 1759.[63]

The adult Frederick was emerging from his lessons. Hille put him through the drill, and his answers are significant: What was the Oder? The Oder was the only important river flowing through Brandenburg-Prussian territory. Stettin? The port at the mouth of the Oder must never be seen as anything other than Berlin's natural harbour. Silesia? Whoever wins Silesia for Brandenburg-Prussia totally controls the Oder and the Oder trade.[64] With time Frederick's warders took pity on the prince and became more lenient. The wife of President von Münchow, in particular, saw to it that the harshest parts of his punishment were not enacted.[65] Frederick's chief bugbear was the civil servant Hille, who was unimpressed both by the prince's airs and graces, and by his occasional histrionics. Their relationship cannot have been helped, at first at least, by the fact that Frederick refused to conceal his dislike of the middle classes.[66] Hille also could not dislodge Frederick's faith in predestination, 'which he believes with the fatalism of a Turk even now'.[67] Hille's Lutheran, middle-class mind could not countenance Frederick's artistic inclinations either. he wrote to Grumbkow on 18 December:

You think his passion is music, I wish to God it were so! But he has a stronger inclination: he wants to write verse and become a poet. While he hasn't a clue whether his ancestors won Magdeburg in a game of cards or whatever, he can count out Aristotle's poetic rules on his fingers, and for the last two days he has been torturing himself to render into French some German verses that the idiot Wilke* has given him.[68]

Hille blamed Duhan for Frederick's wilfulness. 'The devil with his damned teacher, who knew no more than to allow this shallow stuff to get into his head. He will have to unlearn everything, for although you can say nothing against the quality of his heart, he could one day make people unhappy, just as foolish women turn men into cuckolds.'[69] But Frederick occasionally showed a Hohenzollern interest in territory and the expansion of Brandenburg-Prussia even in those troubled times. He told Hille that he wanted to go on a journey to Brunswick, France and Italy in order to revive his House's claims to Arles and Orange: 'We laughed over his fantasy,' said Hille, 'and then we dropped the curtain on the comedy.'[70]

Evidence that Frederick was already learning to manipulate others comes from a new openness to Grumbkow and Seckendorff. These two men might be seen as the joint authors of his malaise; yet, he realised that, if he was to better his lot, he would have to win them over to his side even if it meant playing the Austrian card. His chances of marrying

---

* The civil servant Samuel Otto Wilke.

Princess Amalia, for the time being at least, were extremely remote.* He was also getting on better with Hille, who admitted that he got nowhere by being strict with the prince, that it was better to be good-humoured and to allow him more freedom. On 30 December, Hille even wrote to Grumbkow to ask if Frederick might have a little party to celebrate his nineteenth birthday on 24 January 1731, but the violins and flutes finally had to be returned to their cases when the king issued stern orders that Frederick might not eat outside the fortress, hear music or dance: 'this is not the place for it', he wrote.[71]

Hille hoped that with time Frederick could learn to be a 'blessed' ruler for his people.[72] The stumbling blocks were predestination and finance. On 27 December 1730, Hille thought he was getting somewhere with Frederick's Calvinism, but a week later he had to admit that he had 'run out of arguments'.[73] Frederick could not be bothered with sums and wanted to leave the business to his ministers while he devoted himself to higher politics. He thought that 'all money remained in the country and always found a natural route back to the monarch's coffers. All detail bores him ...'[74] Trade with Austrian Silesia was another subject that bothered him. He was so crammed full of it that 'When I am asked if I want my beef with mustard, I am only in a state to reply "Look at the new customs arrangements ..." I can't do anything by halves, I have to go in head first.'[75]

Frederick William had given Wolden instructions to 'knock those French and English manners out of his head'.[76] Hille and Karl Dubislaw von Natzmer tried to shake Frederick's faith in French literature by putting it to ridicule, but found that it was an uphill struggle, so ingrained was it from his 'reading of and consorting with Frenchmen'.[77] Nor could they prevent him from writing poetry. Hille advanced a view on his verses that might still hold good today: 'I told him that for a prince they are good, but for an ordinary man, nothing special...'[78]

A little moment of fear permeated the prison when Frederick began to receive fan-mail. A suspiciously named Sophie Sappho from Rougement in Switzerland wrote to the prince to tell him he was a martyr, 'a young, pious[!], shining hero ... all Europe admires you'. The reference to the prince's piety may have indicated that Sophie Sappho was a Swiss Calvinist. The Calvinists thought Frederick a hero because he would not give up his faith in predestination.[79] Wolden thought the letter came from Prussia,

* She eventually married the Prince of Orange.

however, and it naturally gave rise to fears that a party was forming behind the prince.[80]

Frederick was looking for solutions that might bring him back his liberty. On 11 April 1731 he hit on the idea of standing down as crown prince in favour of his brother William, and putting himself forward as a candidate for the Empire. To this end he suggested that one of the two Habsburg archduchesses might be made over to him for a wife.[81] The letter was also signed by a group of men who were forming themselves into the prince's new council: his marshal, Wolden, Natzmer and Rohwedel. Grumbkow was alarmed by this new suggestion from Frederick: 'an archduchess would never marry a prince who wasn't completely Catholic'. He sent the letter back to Hille and told him to burn it in the presence of the prince.[82]

Both Seckendorff and the king none the less heard about the idea, the latter probably after Seckendorff sent word to Prince Eugene in Vienna, who was verging on senility and wanted Frederick William to tell him which archduchess he had in mind. Prince Eugene described the project as 'peculiar'. Frederick William was even less impressed, and he was hurt by the thought that his son might consider converting to Catholicism.[83] Prince Eugene was less senile about one thing, however: he warned Seckendorff against the possible effects of Frederick William's punishing his son. 'The harder the king deals with him, the more stubborn he will become, and in time he will change everything that his father has done.'[84]

Grumbkow thought Natzmer was guilty of putting such ideas as these into the prince's head.[85] From February 1731 dates Frederick's famous letter to Natzmer in which he showed that his mind was already bent on conquering a chunk of neighbouring territory. Prussia's problems were clear: other lands cut into it and it was too small. The army would be fully taken up in its defence and there would not be enough soldiers to mount an offensive. The solution, Frederick told Natzmer, was as follows:

To procure an ever greater expansion of the house ... I believe that the most vital project to bring to fruition is to assemble or tack on to it, those detached parts which [should] naturally belong to the bits we own, such as Polish Prussia, which always belonged to the kingdom [sic], and which was only detached [from it] by the wars between the Poles and the Teutonic Knights who had it at the time...*

* Prussia west of the Vistula and the Nogat was ceded to Poland at the Peace of Thorn

Having acquired this province, we shall have not only created an entirely free passage from Pomerania to the kingdom [sic] of Prussia, but we will hold the Poles in check and be in a position to dictate laws, for the reason that they will not be able to dispose of their goods in any other way than bringing them down the Vistula or the Pregel,* which they would only be able to do with our consent.

A Polish 'corridor' was not all. Frederick's young eyes ranged over western Pomerania, which was still controlled by the Swedes, and Mecklenburg, once the ducal house then in charge had died out. He added Jülich and Berg, no doubt for reasons of filial piety and because he thought that Prussian Cleves could not sit there all alone. Finally, he maintained that Prussia could 'play important roles' in the future, and 'make the Protestant religion blossom in Europe and the Empire'.[86]

A copy of the letter found its way to Prince Eugene in Vienna. If he had not been sufficiently worried by Frederick's proposal to marry an Austrian archduchess, he was definitely alarmed now, and immediately lent his support to reviving the Bevern marriage plans in an attempt to spin Frederick into an Austrian orbit.[87]

Conditions continued to improve in prison. Hille wanted to know if there was any burgundy or champagne to be had in Berlin, perhaps brought up by merchants returning from the fair in Leipzig, as the fortress was dry.[88] The king had given his son permission to write letters to others than his immediate family (if he had any time), which led Hille to suppose that there was a plan to make his life easier.[89] If reconciliation were in the air, it could not come fast enough for Frederick. On 28 April, Hille reported to Grumbkow that he occasionally lost his temper turning into a 'thundering Jove'.[90] Hille was beginning to see qualities in the boy, but he still saw a 'catastrophe for the poor people, if there were to be a sudden change. Good things take time.'[91]

Finally, on 5 May, the crown prince received his first letter from his father, possibly motivated by a bout of sickness that had made him worryingly aware of his own mortality.[92] Frederick William took the chance to rail against those 'cursed people who inspired you to become wise and clever from worldly books'. All this was 'nonsense'.[93] He reminded Frederick, too, that he knew more than his son had revealed in the course of his hearings.[94]

of 1460. *This* Prussia had nothing whatsoever to do with Brandenburg. The connection was only made in 1618.

* The river that bisects the northern part of Prussia, now called the Pregolya in Russian.

The much anticipated liberal regimen did not materialise for another three months, however. Hille had advance warning of the king's arrival. 'The crown prince can be offered [some] consolation; his fate is about to change, [but] only if he [Frederick William] feels that he shows some signs of love.' He told Grumbkow that everyone in Küstrin was well prepared for the royal visit and ready to carry out the king's will. It was Frederick William's first meeting with his son since he walked out of the hearing in Wesel. He arrived on his own birthday, 15 August. Frederick did the right thing and threw himself at his father's feet. The king gave him a severe dressing down, then embraced the boy, by all reports just as moved by the occasion as his son.[95]

It was an important meeting for Frederick in the process of understanding his strange father. Up until then, he wrote, he had not believed that the king possessed a 'spark' of love for him. Now he was convinced that he had 'mistreated him far more for trifles in the past than he had for a great misdeed which he couldn't deny. In short, either the devil is at work, or this peace [between the two of them] will last for ever.'[96] He began to co-operate fully: in a letter to his father written soon afterwards, Frederick came clean and gave him details of his talks with Hotham and his negotiations with the British court. He also confessed that he had led Katte astray, and not vice versa.[97] Frederick William had to spell out what would have been the consequences of a successful flight:

Your mother would have suffered enormously, because I would naturally have suspected her of having [prior] knowledge of the affair; your sister I would have locked up for life in a place where neither sun nor moon would have shone; I would have marched into Hanover with my army and put everything to the torch and sword, I might have had to sacrifice my own life and country. See that [would have been] the fruit of your Godless and unthinking behaviour.[98]

Finally, on 21 August, Frederick William wrote to Wolden to loosen the chains: Frederick might now spend his afternoons outside the fortress. He could go boating, or shoot ducks. The only conditions the king imposed were that Frederick should never be left alone, that he visit no 'maid or female person and that someone must sleep with him at all times'. A tailor and a cobbler arrived at the fortress to see Frederick's shabby physical appearance.[99] He was allowed to have two guests at dinner twice a week. Wolden reassured His Majesty that there were no women for miles around, only men.[100]

[III]

There was already a new cloud on the horizon for the prince: wedding bells had begun to chime. Throughout the months of crisis, Frederick William had been in contact with his friend the duke of Bevern. Like the Alte Dessauer, the duke had offered the king some sympathy, but urged him to forgive his son. While Frederick William's family shunned him, the king longed for a visit from the duke's eldest son, who appealed to him more than his own children in the present circumstances. His correspondence with Bevern shows Frederick William's more human face: 'you can easily imagine', he wrote describing Frederick's desertion, 'how worried this all makes me'.[101] Not for the first time, Frederick William toyed with the idea of abdication. He wanted to retire to Honsdaarsdijk, his estate in Holland. The responsibility of kingship was taxing even him. As he wrote to Frederick: 'If you don't do things right at the beginning, and everything goes topsy-turvy, I shall laugh at you from my grave.'[102]

He sent a letter to Bevern at the same time to tell him, 'You will be pleased to hear that I have made a start on forgiving my eldest son, and I have prescribed a lifestyle [for him] which will serve to improve him by acquainting him with the business of finance and economics.' At the engagement of Charlotte and Charles of Bevern, Wilhelmina threw herself at her father's feet. Frederick William told her that it was not the place for such an emotional effusion: 'You will get everything you have asked for, you shouldn't upset yourself,' he told her.[103]

Frederick was getting fat and irritable, and writing reams of verse. Hille broke the news to him that his father had returned to the business of finding him a wife, and had fixed his gaze on Bevern's eldest daughter. Frederick was obviously alarmed: 'My father himself advised me not to marry young, and [to] a beggar woman like that who will get older and uglier with every year that passes, ... [I] will certainly soon become weary of her ... I will marry only when I am forty, and then with a princess of fifteen whose beauty is still unfolding.'[104]

Frederick was none the less aware that marriage was one way out of prison. He described the daughter of his father's friend as that 'cursed princess of Bevern', but he did not wholly reject the match at that stage. 'I have answered in all submission, and have said that the king should recognise my obedience in everything he decides for me, that I will see this hideous creature, and if I might be able to decide myself whether she is suitable or not, then I would not be found wanting and would obey his commands.'[105] Hille had become more sympathetic towards his charge, whom he thought was losing his offensive *petit maître* airs. He too thought it insensitive and premature to talk of marrying Frederick off: 'Good God,' he wrote to Grumbkow, 'what misfortune could come of it if one sought to ride roughshod over his desires ... To choose what he should have before he has seen [her], to buy the goods without having so much as inspected them, [it will be] just like his sister!'[106]

On 25 May, Wolden had word from the king announcing that he had indeed made up his mind about Wilhelmina. The king's desire to make her happy proved short-lived. The English marriage question was finally laid to rest, leaving Frederick, at least, bitter about his fickle and duplicitous cousins.[107] Instead of marrying the prince of Wales, Great Britain and the stirrings of a mighty empire, Wilhelmina was to help the margrave of Bayreuth rule over a few thousand mortals in his pocket handkerchief-sized state in Franconia. There would be less dowry to pay;[108] there would be the chance that Bayreuth would revert to Prussia; and the margrave was a Hohenzollern, which kept things in the family.[109] Frederick was furious: 'My sister engaged to some idiot and unhappy for [the rest of her] life.' He must have been aware that a similar diktat would be coming his way.[110]

Less than a month later, on 15 June 1730, Grumbkow took a trip to the Oder, and unbeknown to Frederick William, paid a call on the crown prince. He brought a shopping list with him. Frederick could make a choice from one of three possibilities: the princesses of Gotha or Eisenach – both minor Saxon Wettins whose states lay close to Seckendorff's land at Meuselwitz – and Elisabeth Christine of Bevern. What all three had in common was poverty and virtually no political importance. Grumbkow might have been surprised how little sympathy he found among Frederick's gaolers; Wolden told him that Frederick wanted up to a point to be allowed the chance to follow his own inclinations. The rest of Frederick's kitchen cabinet rallied to the prince's side. Frederick clung blindly to his father's previous statements on marriage: that he was not to be allowed to wed until he was thirty; but, as it transpired, Frederick William had returned from his annual tour of inspection in East Prussia with further intimations of mortality. He wanted the succession assured, and quickly.[111]

Grumbkow was playing an odd game. He told Frederick that the Bevern girl was stupid and ugly, and that he still had a lingering affection for the British match. They were having second thoughts in Vienna. Of course, Grumbkow's mission to Küstrin was no secret to Seckendorff, who reported Frederick's choice of three to Prince Eugene on 19 June. 'He is resolved to marry,' said the ambassador, 'because he sees no other way of achieving his freedom. He has decided on the Bevern [match] on condition that she is neither stupid nor unpleasant, but he fears for all that, that the king will not give him enough to live on.'[112]

Frederick still did not understand why he could not have Anne of Mecklenburg, the niece of Anna Ivanovna of Russia and her possible heiress; she at least offered dynastic ties of some consequence. The Russians were keen, and negotiations dribbled on until January the following year.[113] After a year's imprisonment, at the end of August, Frederick was briefly allowed to come to Berlin to see his mother and Wilhelmina before her departure for Bayreuth. He would have found distressing signs of how he had been expunged from his father's heart during the previous twelve months. His regiment – the Crown Prince's Cuirassiers – had been awarded to his brother William. His room in the Berlin Schloss, emptied of his books and papers, which had been promptly burned, had now been redecorated, presumably in his father's taste.[114]

The king was concerned about Frederick's housekeeping; that in the future Frederick should not be so 'sloppy' with his money, 'for a soldier who cannot do his accounts, who cannot manage his money, who saves nothing and runs up debts, is a pretty useless soldier'. Money, the king made it abundantly clear in the same letter, is not there to be frittered away on 'snuff boxes, [silver or gold] cases, amber and other trifles'.[115] The correspondence went this way and that for a few days more, with the prince pleading to be allowed to go back to the army. Frederick William considered giving him a new unit: the Goltz Regiment, based at Ruppin in the Mark Brandenburg, before he packed his son back off to Küstrin at the end of August.[116]

The tone of the letters between father and son was beginning to change. Frederick told his father of a duck shoot on the Oder when he had bagged nothing, and thanked him for horses, a coach and clothes. Frederick William was keen to wean him on to beer, Küstrin beer being apparently rather good.[117] One does not get the impression that Frederick was utterly convinced, and he told his father that he had been drinking champagne, but only under doctors' orders.[118] At the end of September, he received a visit from his mad, bad cousin Charles of Brandenburg-Schwedt. They drank the king's health and, in a suitably hearty gesture, smashed all the glasses afterwards. To his new friend Frau von Wreech, Frederick confessed the extent of the damage: 'We didn't really drink that much, but we made a great deal of noise, we smashed a few windows and reduced a few ovens to rubble.' Hille excused the rowdiness to Grumbkow, blaming it on the margrave's presence in Küstrin. Presumably the minister took a dim view, for Frederick was briefly confined to quarters.[119]

Frederick was calling for his friend Keyserlingk.[120] Another friend, Freiherr Heinrich August de la Motte Fouqué, also came to see him. Frederick William had encouraged his son's relations with the Huguenot officer. He seems to have been allowed to spend the night in Frederick's room, for there is a story that the prince was permitted to stay up later that evening. The rules required Frederick's candle to be blown out at 9 p.m., but they said nothing about Fouqué's.[121]

The prince was also distracting himself with Luise Eleonore von Schöning, the granddaughter and heiress to the estate of one of the Great Elector's greatest generals. She was married to Colonel Adam Friedrich von Wreech and lived at Schloss Tamsel nearby. He might have thought he was showing willing by having a little harmless dalliance with a reportedly good-looking woman, blond, with a complexion of 'lilies and roses'.[122] To Wolden he described Tamsel as 'Calypso's island'.[123] He had had a miniature done of himself, and presented it to her. She did not like grasshoppers, but Frederick had other insects to offer her: 'they are called verses;[124] they have only six feet, sharp teeth, a very long body, and a certain rhythm which ... gives them life'.[125]

She returned the compliment. They went for walks by the Oder. He wrote her satires too, about the crew who held him in check in Küstrin and a fantasy about his ceremonial return to Berlin – how he would be announced by a herd of swine, grunting to their hearts' content, followed by ewes and sheep led by one of his valets; then a troop of Podolian[126] oxen would arrive immediately before the prince himself. The other participants in the procession would be donkeys and peasants. It was presumably a tease about the lowly subject matter of his lessons at the time.[127]

More than a century ago, Theodor Fontane set himself the task of finding out the precise nature of Frederick's relationship with Luise Eleonore. Having read various letters in the family archive at Tamsel, he came to the conclusion that the poems and portrait were no more than a 'homage' from a poetic young prince with a crush. Later Frederick sulked about her for a while, then, in the Rheinsberg years, he expressed his 'curiosity' about seeing her once more.[128] Luise Eleonore, it seems, tolerated his brief passion, but showed no signs of returning it.[129]

When he was not courting at Tamsel, the crown prince told Hille a little of his conception of kingship. Some of his ideas were still childish, but there were also things that he was later to enact.

I assure you I like reading best. I love music, but dancing more by far. I hate hunting, but I like to ride. If I were my own master, I'd do all the things I thoroughly enjoy, but a good part of my time I would devote to my business, which wouldn't really be too much trouble, as I would rely on you. Apart from that I would take care to keep a clean table and have it laid with fine dishes, but not expensive ones. I would retain a few good musicians, but they wouldn't have to play at table; for music is my recreation, and it would disturb me while I ate. I would dine formally and publicly at noon, but in the evening I would surround myself with my friends and look after them properly.[130]

In mid-October, Frederick bit his lip and went hunting with Adolph Friedrich von der Schulenburg. He too reported back to the would-be omniscient Grumbkow. The nobleman had a few things to report on the prince's eating habits: he liked 'strong-tasting foods, he doesn't like fish, even though I had the loveliest trout ... He apparently doesn't like wine. He tastes everything ... but prefers ordinary burgundy cut with water.' He did not like being given advice either. 'He feels that he is surrounded by people who are intellectually inferior to him. He looks for the comical side of everything and likes to mock – a great fault in princes.'[131]

Frederick William showed every sign of enjoying Wilhelmina's wedding. On the third day of the festivities in November, he got up from the table and declared that no one be allowed to leave the room. He had the doors locked and then went up to his room for a siesta. When he returned, refreshed from his slumbers, he called out 'Popolsky'(!) to the musicians and danced with his daughters and some of the other ladies, making a great deal of noise, through the public rooms of the Schloss. Some of the female guests were reported to have been in great discomfort by the time Frederick William had had his fun and allowed the doors to be opened again.[132]

In the course of the wedding, Frederick William told his friend Bevern that he intended marrying Frederick to Bevern's eldest daughter. The next day the king received a delegation from his generals, who pleaded with him to let the crown prince return to the army. This might well have been another of Frederick's ruses to regain his liberty. He was still popular with the officer corps. His father was sceptical. He had decided that Frederick was not cut out for a soldier's life. He had written to him on 28 August to remind his son how much he had been repelled by all those things that he held most dear; that during the hunt, for example, he had sought to get away, finding solace in 'a French book, *bonts mots* [sic], or a play, or playing the flute, [rather than] serving or drill'.[133]

On 27 December, Frederick went to the university town of Frankfurt nearby and dined there with 'a lot of fools'. He enjoyed himself, for all that, especially as he was serenaded by the students.[134] It seems possible that it was on this occasion that he made the acquaintance of Michael Gabriel Fredersdorf, who played the oboe in the regiment garrisoned in the town. Fredersdorf had music in his blood. He was the son of the town musician of Gartz, on the left bank of the Oder, between Schwedt and Stettin. Fredersdorf was three and a half years older than the prince and, of course, a commoner; but this in no way prevented an intimate relationship from growing up between them, and one which lasted until Fredersdorf's death in 1759: Fredersdorf was one of two or three people Frederick referred to as 'tu' or 'Du'.*

Fredersdorf proved useful at that difficult time in Frederick's life. He also played the flute, and clearly extremely well, as he was later to accompany Quantz, deemed to be the greatest virtuoso of his day. Frederick had Fredersdorf brought up to Küstrin, where his flute playing soothed him 'during many troubled hours'. Later he had him released from his regiment, to serve him in his households in Ruppin and Rheinsberg.[135]

Frederick's twentieth birthday was coming up. Once again a request went up to the king to give a party for him. Frederick William was clearly not keen. Wolden had to be more precise in his letter to Grumbkow of 8 January: 'There is no question of an illumination or any other sort of eye-catching festivities, just simply a little concert and a ball after supper.'[136]

Frederick was still being threatened with Elisabeth Christine of Bevern. He made his feelings on the matter abundantly clear in a letter to Grumbkow written on 26 January:

If I am forced to marry her, I will reject her away as soon as I am master, and I don't believe the empress† will be too happy about that. I don't want a goose for a wife. Much more so, I want to be able to talk sense with her, or I shan't

---

* Fredersdorf evidently did not speak French well; Frederick's letters to him are written in a highly idiosyncratic German.

† Her aunt.

talk to her at all. So that is what is going to happen if I am forced, and no man can blame me for it, knowing that I was made to do something that was totally against my inclinations...[137]

Frederick wanted to make himself clear to Grumbkow: 'I feel myself too flighty, and insufficiently attracted to the female sex.'

The family was ganging up on him. His mother gave her approval of the match on 7 February, though presumably tongue in cheek.[138] Assurances of Elisabeth Christine's piety did not help. On 11 February Frederick told Grumbkow that he would prefer 'the greatest whore in Berlin to a bigot'. He told him of the embarrassment he would feel 'playing the *amoroso*', that he had not much 'faith in the taste of Graf Seckendorff'. He then proposed a little reading matter: instead of Arndt (he had had enough of that by then), she should learn Molière's *Ecole des maris* and *Ecole des femmes* by heart; she should learn music,[139] then he might develop a 'penchant' for her; 'but if she is stupid I shall consign her to the devil'.[140]

Frederick was clutching at straws. When a new war broke out with Turkey, he expressed his desire to fight at the side of Prince Eugene.[141] Although Frederick voiced his objections to the Bevern marriage loud and clear within the walls of Küstrin, and in his letters to Grumbkow, he adopted a different tone with his father. Frederick was once again called upon to obey: 'You know, my dear son, that when my children are obedient, I love them very much.' The king had had a chance to look at Elisabeth Christine, and found her 'well brought up ... modest and reserved, as women should be'. He was quite blunt about her appearance: 'The princess is not ugly, but she is not pretty either.' Frederick William then cunningly dangled the carrot before his son's eyes: 'You must tell me what you feel quickly. I've bought the Katsch house, and the Field Marshal will get it as governor [of Berlin], and I am going to have the governor's house* properly restored and furnished, and give you enough [money] so you can entertain, and I will send you off to the army in April.'[142]

Frederick must have been furious with his father, but his reply is couched in that language of submission he knew was most acceptable: 'There is nothing nicer for me than to have the chance to show my most gracious father my blind obedience, and I await in most humble submission

---

* At the top of Unter den Linden.

further orders from my most gracious father.' On the very same day, 19 February, he threatened Grumbkow with suicide:

I have suffered enough for an exaggerated crime ... I still have resources and a bullet could rid me of my frustrations and my life ... Neither the promise of money or land, nor reason can make me change my mind ... [The king] will himself suffer a thousand frustrations when he witnesses the unhappiest marriage in the world and when he hears the mutual acrimony, the loud recriminations which will redound on he who forged our bonds. As a good Christian he might reflect whether it is well done to force two people together [only] in order to lay the foundation for a separation and to provide the cue for every form of sin that is borne out of an unhappy union ... My God, has he not seen enough unhappy marriages?[143]

It is hard to rid oneself of the conclusion that Frederick wrote the two letters expressly to set the cat among the pigeons and cause discord between the king and his minister. Grumbkow promptly took up Frederick's commission and went to the king to raise Frederick's objections. Frederick William had not yet read the letter that his son had sent him. He listened to his minister and agreed that the marriage should be postponed, at least until such time as Frederick had met the girl. Then he read the letter addressed to him. 'With tears in his eyes he told me it was the happiest day of his life; and he went off to see the duke of Bevern in the next room and they kissed one another many times.'[144]

Grumbkow had been made to look a fool. He wrote to Wolden in high dudgeon for his encouragement of Frederick's resistance:

I'm not wise enough to want to have my own head chopped off or have myself cold-bloodedly broken on the wheel. I shall leave this heroism to you others and modestly take my leave from the cloister ... Great God! When I think that a man [Frederick] talks of shooting himself, without having checked or seen the thing [in question], and where the consequences still lie far away in the future! And that, having sent his father an oily, submissive letter, he writes to tell me of his horrible, desperate position, without suggesting a single cure![145]

Grumbkow tried to paint a nicer picture of Elisabeth Christine: 'I tell you she has changed a good deal for the better, and the more you see of her, the more you get used to her, and find her pretty ... and if she puts on a bit of weight and her bust develops, which it is doing already, then she'll be appetising.'[146]

Frederick's little game must eventually have come to the attention of the king, for two days later he was predicting that his son would die an unnatural death: 'let's place our hope in God, that he doesn't fall under the hangman's hand'.[147] The crown prince was still playing Don Carlos. Grumbkow confessed to being beside himself with rage. He told Frederick, 'I am not obliged to lose [my position] and that of my poor family, for your Royal Highness, who is not my master ...'[148] Grumbkow calmed down, eventually, but he refused to intercede for Frederick and his opinion of him had not improved: 'The more I think about the character of the crown prince, the more dangerous I find him.'

Months later, on 4 November 1732, Grumbkow had still not forgotten Frederick's double-dealing. He wrote to his paymaster Seckendorff:

The crown prince has flattered me beyond measure with his attention. I have responded with trust; he seems content that the king will give him 50,000 thalers a year for his outgoings; he is going to have two establishments and plenty of servants. He has said nothing to me of his *belle*, and I have avoided speaking to him on the subject. In short, I think there are on this earth no two men quite like them, father and son.[149]

[IV]

Frederick was finally allowed to leave Küstrin on 26 February 1732. The day after his return to Berlin he met the duke of Bevern and his daughter at Monbijou and the engagement was announced. Frederick could now judge his prize for himself. She was taller than him, with pretty blue eyes and a good complexion, if still showing the scars from a recent bout of smallpox.[150] Even Frederick complimented her eyes, white skin and profile; but he lost heart when he tried to make conversation with her, and pronounced her 'stupid, silly and silent'.[151] Elisabeth Christine was now informed of the identity of her future husband for the first time. She was asked if she liked him. She turned red and said, 'Ja'.[152]

Berlin was on its toes to receive the duke of Lorraine, the fiancé of Maria Theresa of Austria and the man tipped to become the next Holy Roman Emperor. The engagement gave Frederick the chance to represent his father who had fallen ill with a cold. There was a large crowd to witness the publishing of the bans on 10 March. After the ceremony, Frederick kissed the hands of his mother and father, the duchess and Elisabeth Christine. He tried to do the same to the homely duke, but the latter was not having any of it, and promptly kissed his future son-in-law on the cheek instead. Frederick had cried at the exchange of rings. The courtiers assumed they were tears of joy.[154] They may have been duped, but Frederick himself was under no such illusion. He wrote to Wilhelmina that Elisabeth was 'not without wit, but very badly educated, shy and without *savoir vivre* ... Her great service [to me] has been to grant me liberty ... I love you alone.'[155]

Frederick's negative attitude to his future bride was tame compared to other members of his family. The queen conceded her good looks, but had nothing good to say of her mind. Elisabeth replied to every question with a yes or a no, followed by a naive giggle. Charlotte was even nastier: she claimed the duke's daughter 'stank like rotting flesh' and accused her of having a good ten or twelve fistulas. She also claimed she was deformed (which was untrue), with one hip higher than the other. Wilhelmina was not prepared to go so far. She remarked that Elisabeth was fairly graceless, but had a pretty, if infantile face (which is clear from the portraits) and blond curls. However, her teeth were 'black and irregular'.[156] Frederick was capable of remarks every bit as cruel. Wilhelmina accused him of having kissed his fiancée's hands. The crown prince's reply is reminiscent of Oscar Wilde: 'I assure you I haven't kissed them, nor will I kiss them: they are neither pretty nor appetising...'[157]

There might have been a glimmer of hope. Lorraine was supposed to play *Rosenkavalier* and deliver Frederick's proposal of marriage. In the end, however, Francis Stephen wanted nothing to do with it: a new wind was blowing in Europe since the collapse of the Anglo-French alliance, and he did not want to upset the British now that there was a chance of getting them on the Austrian side. The emperor was worried that the British would think that he was behind the marriage.[158] The Austrians even went as far as to make a few trifling moves to have the engagement annulled, and Seckendorff now began to express concern. British diplomats also began attempts to scuttle the match. Frederick was once again offered a British princess, and his sister Ulrica was suggested for the prince of Wales 'sine ulla conditione'. To sweeten the pill, British princes and princesses were scattered before the Beverns too. None of this, however, took into account the stubborn ways, chronic suspicion and unshakable pro-Germanness of the king of Prussia, who liked the duke of Bevern beyond measure and was disinclined to go back on his word. Frederick would simply have to accept it.[159]

The noise from Vienna turned the king into a raging bull. He attacked both his wife and son, who for once, was innocent of the charges. Before a large crowd he declared:

Eh bien, it is suggested I should do things against my honour; if you like, that I should show a little flexibility, if that is the case then the crown prince won't marry at all! I still have three more princes! And even if the house dies out it would be better than we should be blamed for wanting one thing today and another tomorrow.[160]

He took it out on Grumbkow at the Tabacscollegium: 'No, I can't bear it! It hits me right where it hurts! They want me to perform an act of cowardice! Me! Me! No and never! Cursed intrigues! To the devil with them!' Grumbkow tried meekly to suggest that he did not know what the king was talking about. 'What?! Make a knave of me?! I'll say it loud and clear, some damned rogues have sought to betray me! ... people who should know me better want to see me making a mistake! ... I will do such things – that all the world shall ...'[161] The message to the British and the Austrians was coming out very loud and very clear.

On 29 February, Frederick was finally given the right to don his Prussian blue coat again as Colonel of the Regiment von der Goltz. It was split between Nauen, to the west of Berlin, and Ruppin to the north. It was in Ruppin that he could let his hair down properly for the first time. The town had orders from the king to clean itself up, and a new lick of paint was applied to the houses.[162] Frederick himself had been told by his father to find a fitting residence for himself. He moved into a modest house by the red-brick, mediaeval town walls, next door to two other officers of the regiment. He had now to get used to the soldier's life. He wanted his men to look smart: his first act was to change the regimental uniform. He led the officers to a bonfire outside the town and gave them food and drink, telling them it was time to pay their last respects to the Regiment von der Goltz. Stripping off his coat and jacket, he threw them on to the fire, followed by his leggings. After the crown prince's striptease, the regiment followed suit and rode back to town in their new mess-kit.[163]

Frederick was still in regular correspondence with Grumbkow, and despite all that had passed between them, he was able to utter a confidence or two. On 27 August 1732, for example, he groused about Luise Eleonore von Wreech, describing her as 'properly false'.[164] A change of heart in Vienna was slowing things down on the marriage front, but Grumbkow was still anxious to sell Frederick the idea of Elisabeth Christine. He had

had a letter from his daughter, who had met the princess in Quedlinburg in the Harz Mountains. The younger Grumbkow had submitted a full and frank report: Elisabeth did not open her mouth in front of her mother; blushed when addressed; was very strictly governed – she could not even receive women unchaperoned; and she had no idea how to amuse herself. On the more positive side: she lacked neither wit nor judgement (how they were able to tell this if she did not open her mouth is not clear); it had been said that she danced well; and she liked Berlin a lot.[165]

Frederick adopted the mocking tone which had so incensed his father and some of his courtiers. Seckendorff had been writing to him about his 'Dulcinea'. 'People want to beat me into love with a cudgel.' Still, he had learned to play the game. The marriage would ensure his liberty and he would see his 'sposa' as infrequently as he could.[166] He hoped Seckendorff would drop in on him in Ruppin on his way to Denmark. It was the game season and Frederick was looking forward to playing host to the bibulous courtier: 'He'll have lots of all the delicious things I have, I shall spare neither deer nor partridge, and the red champagne will flow ...'* Seckendorff took up the invitation and Frederick was able to report that he had 'feasted him to his best ability'. The duke had written,

thanking me as if I were the man most smitten with the charms of his daughter under the sun ... from the bottom of my heart I wish that the emperor of Morocco would hear of the beauty of this princess and fall in love with her, and that he'd abduct and marry her. Being empress of Morocco takes precedence over the princess royal of Prussia by two degrees.[167]

By playing the game, Frederick had been able to bring together a few of his old friends and some new ones, and enjoy his new-found freedom in little Ruppin. He had good things for his table: oysters and fat capons which allowed him to live like a Hamburger; at one stage he boasted that 200 oysters and a bottle of champagne awaited him: despite his protests, he was always an abstemious man.[168] Writing to Grumbkow, he doctored the account of his daily rounds. He was still receiving exercises from his father, dealing with the minutiae of leases (which he confessed he did not understand);[169] he had the regiment (renamed 'Kronprinz') to look

---

* Frederick reminds us that champagne had not yet made up its mind whether its vocation was to be just white and fizzy. Still white and red champagne were still made in abundance.

after, but then, after lunch, he was able to amuse himself at will – which meant reading and music. At around 7 p.m. he met up with the other officers at one or other of the houses about town and played cards. An hour later he ate dinner before retiring. When the mail coach came from Hamburg there were a few *gourmandises*, and Frederick might give a little party for three or four people in his room. Other than that he went boating on the lake or let off fireworks in the garden outside the town wall.[170]

For all that, he 'had the reputation for being the most debauched man on earth'. Naturally he was not going to come completely clean with Grumbkow, but he admitted, 'I don't think Cato was Cato when he was young.'[171] Much has been said about the 'debauchery' of the Ruppin years in a desire to show Frederick as the gay blade, larking around with his friends, scandalising the townsfolk and cutting a swathe through the local maidens. Some people insist that he caught a venereal infection, that it went untreated and with time rendered him impotent. Frederick clearly took more interest in sex then than he ever showed in his later years. There was even a poem exploring the pleasures of the orgasm, which was sadly, or intentionally, lost by a later generation.[172]

His companions were a group of noble officers, joined after Frederick returned from the Rhine Campaign of 1734 by the French chevalier Isaac François Egmont de Chasot, who was to become one of his closest friends. The king, hearing of the prince's relaxed lifestyle, issued instructions limiting the scope of Frederick's table and regulating his hours of prayer and church attendance. He also rounded on drinking, swearing and gambling.[173] Frederick did not pay too much heed; he was getting on well with the king and finding him lots of tall soldiers for his guard. He even went so far as to take his revenge on a pastor who had attacked his behaviour in a fire-and-brimstone sermon, bombarding his house with missiles and chasing him from his bed.[174]

Aside from scandalising the local population and beautifying his regiment, Frederick took a keen interest in the town. The standard eighteenth-century process had begun, and the Ruppiners were dismantling its largely useless ancient walls. Frederick stopped them. He wanted to preserve the old trees and the nightingales, and create an elegant garden all at once. Until the remodelling of Rheinsberg began to claim his creative attention, his house and garden in Ruppin were the focus of his aesthetic attentions. By all reports, the house was modest, built of wood, but well furnished; in summer the garden provided a little more panache. He called it 'Amalthea', after a nymph whom Jupiter had nourished with goat's milk; it was a play on the more mundane former vocation of the garden, which had been a dairy farm.[175]

On and off, Frederick lived in Ruppin for four years. In the last year of his stay, Amalthea was dignified with a doric temple surmounted by a statue of Apollo, designed by Georg Wenzeslaus von Knobelsdorff,* one of Frederick's intimate friends in the Rheinsberg days, and during the first years of his monarchy. He was thirteen years older than the prince, and had attracted Frederick William's notice by his heroism at the Siege of Stralsund. For all that, his progress in the army was slow. He was still only a second lieutenant in 1729, fourteen years later. It was possibly in this year that Frederick William entrusted him with his wayward son for drawing lessons. Knobelsdorff was being trained in the use of pastels and oils by the court painter Pesne. His painting remained a little hit or miss, but there are good things, especially the delightful little landscape that shows the prince and his friends amusing themselves at Rheinsberg.[176]

The temple was Knobelsdorff's first work of architecture. He flicked through the standard texts: Vignola, Scamozzi and his favourite, Palladio; he might also have been influenced by Voltaire's poem 'Le Temple de l'amitié' of 1732. He had still seen only German models, having spent a few months in Dresden (where he was able to study Pöppelmann's magnificent rococo Zwinger) and made a tour of Franconia, Würzburg and Bamberg in 1734. Frederick packed him off to Italy in 1736, where he was to see more of the sort of architecture he really liked, and come back with ideas that ran counter to the rococo obsessions of his young patron.[177] For the time being, however, Frederick loved his simple temple, and wrote to his sister in August that year that it was all ready for the first sacrifices. In truth its uses were more peaceable. Here he could dine freely with his friends (there was a kitchen downstairs), read or practise his flute. Even after he had moved into Rheinsberg, regimental duties required his presence at Ruppin. He stayed in his modest house, and longed for the cherries, the melons (they wouldn't ripen in Rheinsberg), the grapes from his vineyard, and above all the solitude he was able to find at Amalthea.[178]

---

* In 1787 a fire destroyed much of Ruppin, including Frederick's modest palace. Amalthea, however has survived. The temple roof no longer rests on its free-standing columns: it was turned into an enclosed room later in the century; and in 1830, the local painter Gentz painted the ceiling. The garden has filled up with a lot of nineteenth-century neo-moorish bric-à-brac and other detritus from the DDR years.

He wanted music too, and the best. Frederick was still in contact with Quantz, and through the flautist he heard about the brothers Franz and Johann Benda, who had been in the king of Poland's service. The Bendas, Bohemian Protestants, were among the greatest virtuosi of the day. The violinist Franz arrived in Ruppin in April 1734, and tells in his auto-biography the story of his engagement in Frederick's little orchestra. Benda rented a room in the town. On the 17th he was practising when the king came by with some friends. 'They stopped in their tracks, listened for a while and then sent someone up to ask who I was. I immediately went downstairs and presented myself. His Majesty commanded me to come to him that evening where he graciously accompanied me himself on the piano. With that I entered his service.'[179]

He served Frederick for fifty-three years in all, eventually taking over the job of Konzertmeister from Johann Gottlieb Graun, who had the advantage of having been a pupil of Tartini and Pisendel.[180] Until the composer Carl Heinrich Graun arrived as part of Elisabeth's dowry, Franz Benda had also to sing tenor. Frederick was putting together a proper ensemble with three more violins, two viola players (one was Johann Georg Benda), a cellist, a horn player, a flautist (Fredersdorf), a harpist, a theorbo, a viol and a harpsichord player.

Although musicians all over Europe were getting the message, the king was not to know about Frederick's orchestra. If one of his spies arrived in Ruppin, Frederick sent out the hunt, and the informer naturally went with it. From time to time he was obliged to hear concerts in the woods or in an underground vault. Quantz was still on the scene; he was giving Wilhelmina flute lessons too, and was used as a secret go-between. Frederick found the flautist personally 'insupportable', but he eagerly awaited his biannual visits for all that, and on these occasions an evening concert was performed before invited guests.[181] He may have been arrogant, but Quantz was highly impressed by Frederick's little band. Benda was clearly a wonderful violinist. When Frederick had the chance to hear some others in Heidelberg in 1734, he concluded that none 'comes up to Benda's standard'.[182]

On 4 February 1734 the prince wrote to the ducal field marshal, Johann Matthias Graf von der Schulenburg, in Venice to procure him a castrato for his little court. He had to be 'fourteen or fifteen. I hope you'll find such a thing in one of the Venetian hospitals.' The boy had to have a good ear and an ability to sing scales. Schulenburg was required to get him to Augsburg. From there Frederick could organise transport.

Schulenburg wrote back, confessing he had failed to find a castrato, but he had located a pretty, thirty-year-old woman with 'good morals', who sang divinely. Did the prince want her? He did not. He wanted a boy or nothing.[183]

Such projects required money, and more than Frederick was likely to receive from the king. He had found a means of borrowing, however, by promising his future consideration to foreign courts. At first it was Austria and Seckendorff who came to the rescue. Frederick was careful to conceal the loans in his correspondence. For example, when the Austrian envoy sent him 500 ducats in April 1732, the prince acknowledged receipt of a 'book, that you were kind enough to write for me'. He played the game for all it was worth, even soliciting money for his sister in Bayreuth, promising in return to maintain the Austrian alliance when he came to power. The Habsburgs were cruelly duped.[184]

Frederick now was possessed by two obsessions: the chance of learning the arts of war in the practicum of battle; and the sword of Damocles that hung over his head in the form of Elisabeth Christine of Bevern. He was still cross. He prayed for a streak of lightning to strike his future mother-in-law's arrogant bonnet, and showed he had no more truck with women meddling in government than his father had. 'Women should not be allowed to govern anything on earth. A man who allows himself to be ruled by women is, in my opinion, the greatest knave on earth and doesn't deserve the honourable epithet of man.'[185] He made himself abundantly clear. As soon as the ceremony was over, it would be 'good morning Madam, and goodbye'.

Already then, in September 1732, he was being more positive about his future and telling Grumbkow of his impatience to see the king's beautiful army arrayed in war and his personal desire for glory. 'I can already see myself on the plains of Jülich and Berg; and I seem to see the new subjects prostrate at the feet of their master, and us using our arms to strike terror and fear into the hearts of jealous cowards.'[186] The king was still as infatuated with the emperor as ever. In July he had gone off to meet him in Prague, accompanied by all his cronies, and Seckendorff naturally came too. The ambassador was made responsible for provisions. He seems to have done his job conscientiously and procured crayfish and hock, as well as brown and white beer from the locals along the way. Frederick William met up with Charles at his stud at Kladrup in Bohemia, and proceeded to the Bohemian capital. The emperor fobbed Frederick William off with a few bland assurances on the subject of Jülich, Berg and East Friesland, 'but their talks hinged more on simple assurances of friendship than realities'.[187]

As regards the match, Frederick's days were numbered. The morrow of his twenty-first birthday, he wrote sarcastically to Grumbkow:

I have to say I'm not looking forward to my trip to Brunswick, knowing well in advance what my mute will tell me. It is her best quality for all that, and I agree with you that a ridiculous, stupid wife is a divine blessing. So I'll act out the comedy of Brunswick, which will not be short of laughs, and *il signor Brighella* will mutter sweet nothings to *la bella Angelica*;* but I'm rather frightened that I shall be obliged to do the business, and answer for her.[188]

Two days later he received a present of a snuff box from his fiancée, which he found broken in its box: 'I don't know if it was to show the fragility of her hymen, her virtue or of the universal human countenance.'[189]

* Figures from the *Commedia dell'arte*. Brighella was a plotter.

CHAPTER FOUR

Rheinsberg

[1]

The Beverns' ramshackle palace at Salzdahlum* had to be patched up for the ceremony, but Graun was able to prepare some fine music: an opera of his own making, followed by Handel's *Parthenope*. The occasion was far from lavish: hardly an imperial event. The Prussian party amounted to just thirteen people. Seckendorff came with his own cook; Grumbkow with his personal trumpeter. When the queen arrived with her people, Frederick William, his good humour restored, greeted her with a raucous 'hallo'. The last-minute moves to prevent the marriage had not ceased. Seckendorff had received word from both Prince Eugene and the British.[1] The latter were prepared to offer large sums to stop the ceremony.

Grumbkow flatly refused to beard the king with this business; he had learned his lesson. Seckendorff showed more courage and went up to the king in bed, where he made Frederick William promise to be patient while he spoke. The response was uncharacteristically calm. Seckendorff was told that, had he said as much three months before, there would have been nothing the king would have refused the emperor, even if it lay contrary to his wishes and interests to marry off his eldest son to a British princess. 'But now, when I am already here with the queen, and all Europe knows that the marriage is to take place tomorrow, it is an English ruse to show the whole world that I am a capricious person who has neither honour nor sticks to his word.' If the British still wanted a marriage, he could offer them a daughter. To Seckendorff's enormous surprise, the interview went off in comfort and good humour.[2]

The negotiations were now at an end. The guests watched Destouches's *Le Glorieux* before the marriage took place in the chapel. The king must have heaved a sigh of relief when the trumpeter gave the signal to the musicians in the courtyard that the couple were married. Twenty-four

---

* There is no trace of this today. It was demolished in the nineteenth century.

cannons fired three salvoes and the guests sat down to the wedding breakfast. After the meal, sixteen Brunswick knights performed a torch dance. Then came the fateful moment of the ceremonial undressing of the bride and groom. Before he joined Elisabeth Christine, Frederick jotted down a note to Wilhelmina expressing his joy that it was over and done with.[3] It was Seckendorff who sent the gossip back to Vienna about the wedding night, 'That the king had to parley and threaten the crown prince to get him into the bridal bed, but that he didn't stay there more than an hour and afterwards was clearly to be seen walking in the valley...'[4]

It was a three-day event. The prince had the comfort of music: Graun's sung festive pastoral was performed on the morrow, the next day it was Handel's turn. On 16 June the – one hopes optimistic – guests heard Graun's comedy *Lo Specchio della fedeltà*. Once the festivities were over in Brunswick, the newly-weds travelled back to Prussia with the royal parties. Frederick and Elisabeth stayed in Charlottenburg until the solemn reception by the people of Berlin on 27 June. The crowds began to assemble at 3 a.m. for a parade due to begin at six. The heat was unbearable. A half-hearted Italian comedy was performed that day: a sign that Frederick William was trying to do things more or less as his son would have wished.[5]

Frederick was saved as the king felt that Ruppin was unsuitable for a married couple. Elisabeth would have to remain away from her husband in Berlin. Frederick was delighted to be home after all his traumas and, leaving the 'oriental tyranny' of Wusterhausen, he compared Ruppin to the 'land of Canaan'. The miserly king snapped up Elisabeth's 25,000 thaler dowry and later yielded up a little under a third of it to complete payment on the rude castle at Rheinsberg. The asking price was 75,000, but Frederick William refused to give up more than 50,000 of his own money. Rheinsberg was intended as a home for the royal couple where they might prosper and *multiply*,[6] but Frederick knew he had time in hand before the place could be made ready for them. Meanwhile Sophia Dorothea looked after her son's neglected bride. The scales took a long time falling from Frederick William's eyes. He was constantly looking for signs that a grandchild was on the way. In November that year, however, he reported laconically, 'She's not pregnant.'[7]

The prince received his chance to see action and meet the great Prince Eugene at Philippsburg when Europe flared up again with the War of the Polish Succession, which hissed and spat from 1733 to 1735. Russia, allied to Austria, foisted Augustus III of Saxony on to the Polish nobility, who would almost certainly have preferred one of their own, Stanislas Leszczynski, for their king. Stanislas was the father-in-law of Louis XV of France, and the French naturally entered on his side. Prussia, as Austria's faithful ally, sent troops to fight alongside Prince Eugene.

The great hero proved a disappointment to Frederick: Eugene was now increasingly senile, 'weakened by age and fatigue'. He offered a little good advice, however, telling Frederick to think 'large'. Eugene himself had set some store by the meeting. He wanted to eliminate Frederick's gallic leanings and bring him round to the imperial cause. In the end, however, he found that the French 'poison' had gone too deep.[8] But when the scourge of the Turk and the hero of Oudenaarde and Malplaquet died less than two years later, the crown prince treated the news with undisguised cynicism: 'Prince Eugene has just expired after having played cards the night before his decease; for the love of him I might have wished that he had been killed at Philippsburg, for it is better to lose one's life than one's reason.'[9] Frederick developed a contempt for lesser Austrian generals which would later convince him that he would be able to get away with snatching a rich province like Silesia from them.

In the summer of 1734, Frederick campaigned alongside his father. On the way to Philippsburg he made confused arrangements for a secret meeting with his sister Wilhelmina in Franconia, as the king had tried to prevent the two from getting together.[10] 'It was the last time we met on the old footing. He changed a good deal later', recorded Wilhelmina bitterly.[11]

The campaign was an anti-climax. Frederick found his first brush with active soldiery boring. He might have been over modest: Frederick came under fire in a wood during the campaign, and witnesses observed that he neither flinched nor spurred his horse into a gallop.[12] To the old, one-armed warrior Paul Heinrich de Camas he talked of the confusion of the campaign, which was also 'very unfruitful when it came to laurels'.[13] He wrote to Wilhelmina on 12 July, calling the war 'the most peaceful thing in the world. You don't hear gunfire. The French are reluctant to attack us, and we have just as little desire to have a go at them. The war is being run like the trooping of the colours in Berlin.'[14] When the allies withdrew, '[the French] were polite enough not to disturb us for a moment'.[15] Taking advantage of an opportunity to see south Germany for the first time since the abortive flight, Frederick visited Heidelberg, where he was horrified to see a former Protestant town full of Jesuit seminaries and Catholic convents. To his sister he wrote of his desire to put the whole *galère* to the torch.[16]

The king was moody and ill. One day he was embracing his eldest son, the next rough and rude.[17] Illness was the cause. He had bad gout and was eating just barley broth with a little fish, and drinking wine and water. His physicians had denied him tobacco and he lashed out at everyone with his stick.[18] He was so ill that many predicted that he was approaching his end. That autumn he measured two and a quarter ells* round the midriff and his feet were covered by his grotesquely swollen ankles.[20]

Nine months later, in June 1735, Frederick William had made a complete recovery: he was eating and drinking for three. The crown prince began to believe that his father's sickness was wilful. He was ill when he wanted, and vice versa: 'he has the nature of a Turk'. 'The Good Lord must have a good reason for giving him his life back.' During those ominous times, however, there were further concessions for Frederick. Frederick William placed ever greater trust in his eldest son, giving him authority in matters of justice, but limiting his powers when it came to appointments and promotion, questions of money and mercy, and death sentences. He could now attend meetings with ministers and his style changed: he became more laconic and oracular, and plunged his head into plans for his coming regime.[21]

During the period of the king's illness, the tone of Frederick's correspondence with Wilhelmina took on a sinister, anticipatory air as they waited for the not so old man to die. The letters read like a couple of Hollywood villains planning to murder a rich relative. Frederick wrote from the Rhine on 5 August, for example, 'our fat friend is leaving on the 8th. He was ill and complaining of chest pains, but he's fighting hard against going the way of all flesh ...' A month later he wrote from Heidelberg:

in the end I am completely convinced that I shall enjoy no pleasure in his lifetime. I believe, too, that there are a hundred reasons why you will quickly forget him; for what touches you, my love, comes from the fact you haven't seen him for ages. Have another look at him, I think you would let him rest in peace without too much grief.

Two weeks later he was signing off, 'I am yours, as the pope obeys the

* A French *aune* (Frederick is writing in French) measured 1.2 metres. An English ell was 45 inches.

devil'.[22] Nor was all the wishing on Frederick's side. In February 1735, Wilhelmina wrote to console her brother about the king's recovery: 'He pays so little attention to his health that he'll soon have a relapse.'[23]

Things turned sour between him and his sister when he stopped off in Bayreuth on his return. She must have felt tender. So far Wilhelmina had failed to produce an heir. Her father had commented on the arrival of her daughter in a singularly earthy way: 'Should I congratulate or send my condolences? My daughter should be better fucked.'[24] It was Frederick's first chance to inspect the little court. He was not impressed; he had earlier put it about that the princess of Wales's chambermaids pocketed more money in a year than the margrave of Bayreuth. He surveyed the massed ranks of the local gentry with a mocking air.[25] When they sat down to eat, he sent them up and repeated over and over again the words 'courtlet and princeling'.

Wilhelmina was cut to the quick. Frederick showed his contempt for all that by insisting that a mere subaltern dine at the margrave's table. If Wilhelmina's account of her brother's speech on that occasion is true, Frederick revealed something of his later approach to kingship:

they imagine that I shall squander my treasury and that money will become as common as brick in Berlin, but I shall stop myself from doing that, I shall expand the army and [for the rest] I shall leave it as it was. I shall treat the queen my mother with great consideration, I shall heap honours upon her, but I shan't put up with her meddling in my business, and if she attempts such a thing, she'll have me to deal with.[26]

One wonders how much Wilhelmina tinkered with this speech later.

She records some lines of the physician Superville, who thought the crown prince a thoroughly bad lot (although it was Frederick's idea that he should treat his sister):

The prince is highly intelligent, but he has a bad heart and character; he is false, suspicious, swimming in self-obsession, ungrateful, riddled with vices [and], if I make no mistake, he will become a greater miser than the king is now; he has no faith, and makes up his morality as he goes along. Everything he does is intended to dazzle the world, but despite his sham plenty of people see through him. He has singled me out for the time being to help him learn, as one of his greatest passions is science. Once he has gleaned from me all he lacks, he'll drop me like so many others...

For that reason, Superville added, he had resolved to quit Berlin and head for what Wilhelmina would have us believe was the infinitely more humane court of Bayreuth. It is significant that Wilhelmina ends this account with the words 'I had been cross with my brother for a very long time.'[27]

Frederick was generally better disposed towards his siblings than they were towards him. He lost patience with Wilhelmina later, when she appeared to waver in her support for him during the Silesian Wars, but during the Ruppin and Rheinsberg years, his admiration for her remained undimmed. He was composing, and he sent her the pieces as he finished them. She received a 'solo' in March 1735: 'In the *adagio* I was thinking of the long months since our parting and therefore found the tone of painful lamentation. In the *allegro* I indulged my hope for seeing [you] again, and in the *presto* I translated my warm conception of Bayreuth.'[28] Other letters hardly conform to Wilhelmina's account. In January 1738, the man who had allegedly taunted his sister over her petty *ménage* wrote 'there is nothing prettier than Bayreuth since you began your reign'. Quantz was still running between them ten months later: 'I'd like it if Quantz's flute, which talks infinitely better than he does, could tell you by all the most melodious and touching sounds, by the *adagios* most rich in pathos, everything which my heart thinks and proposes for you.'[29]

As a married man, Frederick could extract even more freedom from his father than he had enjoyed in those first Ruppin days, but he was still not able to turn the clock back as he wished. One thorn in his side was his old tutor Duhan. When Frederick was released from Küstrin, Duhan was still languishing in the fortress at Memel up on the Baltic Coast. Frederick was able to have him let out and sent off to Brunswick as a librarian, but he was unable to bring him back to Berlin. His letters to his tutor are among the most frank he ever wrote. In July 1733, for example, he told him: 'You know that my situation has greatly improved, but what you possibly don't realise is that they have cut deeply into the marble, and that stays for ever.'[30] Nine months later he wrote even more revealingly about how he was obliged to mask his natural inclinations from his father and the court:

I am still the same, but like a mirror that is obliged to reflect all the objects put before it. [What] I want to say [is] that, not daring to be what nature made him, he is sadly bound by the necessity of conforming to the bizarre forms of the objects put before him ...[31] I am talking too much and I will say even more to a faithful friend: if I don't forget the wise precept which says one should hold one's tongue.[32]

[II]

The prince enjoyed new friends when he returned from the phoney war. For the time being, at least, Elisabeth was safely lodged in Berlin; others who were infinitely more welcome could make their way up to Ruppin and later to Rheinsberg. To most of them he awarded a nickname. Ernst-Christoph von Manteuffel, for example, was 'Quinze-vingts'* because he claimed he was 'too blind to illuminate the prince',[33] or sometimes he was 'the Devil', which played on the diabolic part of his name. There was 'Caesarion', an allusion to the diminutive emperor in 'Keyserlingk', who was also the 'Swan of Mitau', in a reference both to his gracefulness and to the Baltic port near his birthplace. Algarotti was another swan, sometimes of Padua, occasionally Mantua, once or twice Venice. His architect was 'Apollodore' or 'le chevalier Bernin'. Jordan was 'Hephaestion' or 'Tindal'.† Grumbkow was referred to as 'Biberius' or 'the Cassubian': he came from Pomerania, like the Slavic tribes of that name. Fouqué was 'Chastity'. The military man was reputed one of the best actors of the court. Lastly, the Saxon envoy Suhm was 'Diaphanes'. Frederick's willing fundraiser was famed for his open-heartedness.[34]

The wits Christoph Ludwig von Stille and the Hofmarshal Wolden seem to have got away with their own names. Major Johann Wilhelm Senning was another feature of the Rheinsberg court. He had been eleven years old when the Great Elector died, had lost a leg in battle and managed to get on with the younger officers for all that. Two other officers who did not indulge in the free thinking of the court were the captains Johann Jobst Heinrich Wilhem von Buddenbrock and the Freiherr von Wylich.[35] They must have valued the proximity of the Calvinist chaplain, Jean Descamps, who was none the less liberal enough to have attended Wolff's lectures at the University of Halle.[36] Not that Frederick

---

* After the hospital for the blind in Paris. Saint Louis's foundation offered beds for 300 blind men and women: fifteen times twenty. The number was associated with the blind ever after. Jacques Hillairet, *Dictionnaire Historique des rues de Paris*, 2 vols and supplement, Paris, 1972, II, 425.

† Which feature or attribute of the Greek god Hephaestus Frederick thought he saw in Jordan is not clear. It could be a reference to anything from artisanship or lameness to illegitimate children. 'Tindal' possibly alludes to the Protestant divine, William Tyndale.

could be accused of atheism: some of his early poems show, there was still a God at the centre of the universe.[37]

This circle formed the basis for Frederick's 'Bayard Order', commemorating the famous French knight. No joke was intended. The order existed for the serious study of the arts of war. It had twelve members, including Frederick's brothers William and Henry and, uncharacteristically, his sister Charlotte. The remainder were close friends. The Grand Master was Fouqué. Deliberations were held in archaic French.[38]

By subtle transformation the light-hearted Ruppin years were about to turn into the hallowed Rheinsberg days, when Frederick was to maintain something akin to a court, albeit a most idiosyncratic one that posed more as a republic of letters. There was no etiquette as such. It was a free society in the Enlightenment sense, a rococo court based on a cult of friendship.[39] Once the Schloss was ready in the spring of 1736, Frederick could no longer forestall Elisabeth, and word was sent for her to join him. His written communications with her during those years are not unpleasant, if a little stiff. He must have left her to her own devices.[40] She had her own, more conventional court with her ladies, which centred on her suite of five rooms, but there were no favourites, and no mistresses were tolerated in Rheinsberg.[41]

The linchpin of Elisabeth's suite was a massive ceremonial bed, a present from the king (she actually slept in a smaller one alongside).[42] Questions were being raised once again as to whether there was any sexual congress between the couple. Someone (almost certainly the king) asked Grumbkow to make enquiries with the crown prince. Frederick teased his old bugbear in his reply:

I am much obliged to you for the interest you take in my procreation, and if I had the same temperament as the stags, which are currently enjoying their rutting season, in nine months the precise thing would happen that you wish upon me. I'm not sure whether it would be a good or a bad thing for our nephews and great nephews; kingdoms are never at a loss for successors, and it is quite without precedent that a throne has been left empty.[43]

To his friend Manteuffel he gave a glimmer of hope. 'But she can hardly complain that I don't love her at all; [but] I really don't know why we haven't had any children.'[44]

Frederick must have desired to be vague. Certain historians have wanted to read into those lines an effort on Frederick's part: he was genuinely trying, and if it was as simple as it was to a stag and a doe, there would be a child. On the other hand, the reference to nephews seems to point to the fact that Frederick was already thinking of his brother, and his brother's children as his successors. He would honour the undertaking he made at the time of his engagement, and have no sexual dealings with his bride.[45]

The thorny subject of Frederick's sexuality needs to be approached even if most German historians either write it off as irrelevant, or satisfy their readers with a bland assurance that it was neither 'abnormal' nor overly pronounced. Thiébault, who knew Frederick only when he was already old, states categorically that Frederick had mistresses at Ruppin and that the accusation of 'Greek or Italian love' was unfounded: no one, not even Pöllnitz, the court gossip, could come up with the smallest shred of evidence.[46] Frederick might indeed have been physically under-developed in his sexual organs. Others cling to the venereal disease theory, or believe that he was impotent, even that he had been castrated.[47] Despite these solutions to the puzzle, one writer (without giving a reference to his sources) goes so far as to quote Frederick giving a graphic anatomical description of Elisabeth of Bevern's genitalia.[48]

Others, notably the French, have gone overboard in accusing Frederick of homosexuality. What makes one reluctant to fall in with this view is that so much of their evidence is culled from one source alone, namely Voltaire; and that Voltaire was definitely seeking revenge for the slights he felt he had suffered at Frederick's hands in Berlin and Frankfurt. Still, Roger Peyrefitte and others are right to point out how much Frederick, and indeed Voltaire, used the language of Greek love in their cor-respondence, and that Frederick made constant allusions to it in his poetry. He even toyed with the idea of writing a tragedy on the subject of Nisus and Euryalis from Virgil's *Aeneid*: 'one of the classic examples of heroic pederasty'.[49]

'Harmony' within the royal family was required, if the crown prince was to be able to continue his train and run up debts as he wished. Frederick William paid a call in September 1736. Manteuffel had instruc-tions to prepare everything in advance 'so that he doesn't repent having made the trip, and to pay special attention to everything which might give him pleasure ...'.[50] The visit seems to have been minutely planned. On the first day, the king could go hunting stags with Keyserlingk, Fouqué and Chasot. Then there was fishing in the lake, and the chance to shoot some ducks or, failing that, pigeons. There was to be a little music, but Frederick William was to have the chance to smoke too. 'I have to say I shall feel a hundred pounds lighter when this glorious act in my neck of the woods has come to a close.'[51]

Frederick discovered that his wife Elisabeth had her uses. For all her faults in Frederick's eyes, she was no party-pooper. After her earlier position in Berlin, she could communicate easily and directly with the queen or king. At the beginning of 1736, for example, Frederick William asked her just what was missing at Rheinsberg: 'I wasn't aware of anything other than mirrors and chairs ... I forgot to mention the ticking for the tableware.' A few days later the king plundered his father's uninhabited palaces and 150 English chairs arrived at Rheinsberg. Frederick, however, had a rather more grandiose conception for his new home, and he put them straight into storage.[52] He did not want any old junk which his father found lying around the royal palaces. Apollodore was to get his first chance to show his real mettle as an architect.

Originally, the king's architect Johann Gottfried Kemmeter had been commissioned to turn the old house into a Schloss more suitable for a crown prince, by refitting the place which consisted of 'only one range of rooms terminated by an old tower'.[53] It was into this building that Frederick and Elisabeth moved in 1736. Frederick disliked Kemmeter's plain-speaking conception, however, presumably because it contained none of the florid rococo detail he favoured. Kemmeter's work survives in the basic form of the town façade. Knobelsdorff's exterior designs considerably changed Kemmeter's workmanlike palace, but Knobelsdorff had to follow the earlier architect's lines more than he liked. What little was left of Kemmeter's interior arrangements were wiped away by Prince Henry, after he was given Rheinsberg in 1744.[54]

By the time Knobelsdorff came back from his Italian journey in April 1737, Frederick was ready to start again. Knobelsdorff had seen Rome, Florence and Venice, and in the latter many of the designs of Palladio. From Rome he had written to Frederick attacking Emperor Constantine for wrecking the temples of the Forum and bringing in the mean little Christian churches, which had slipped on the tatters of former glory: a Gibbon-like sentiment that must have pleased the enlightened prince. On the way back he stopped in Augsburg to see the work of Elias Holl, and Bayreuth. Nearby was Lukas von Hildebrandt's magnificent baroque Schloss Pommersfelden of 1716–17.[55] He brought back sketch books stuffed with drawings, but no opera singers, which had been the other purpose of his mission.[56]

Knobelsdorff's designs envisaged doubling the size of Rheinsberg, adding a second tower to duplicate the effect of the first.* To bind the two halves, and mask some of the infelicities of Kemmeter's conception, Knobelsdorff or Frederick came up with the idea of a colonnade of coupled ionic columns on the waterfront. The feature may have stemmed from Palladio, or indeed from Schloss Oranienburg nearby. Whatever, it proved popular with Frederick, who had his 'Apollodore' design something similar for Sanssouci after Frederick had abandoned Rheinsberg to his brother.[57]

It is sometimes hard to disentangle the two brothers' contributions to the fairy-tale castle on the shores of Lake Grienerick. Pesne arrived on the pretext of handing Frederick a portrait of his mother and stayed to paint the ceilings. The overdoors were by Augustin Dubuisson, one of the court painter's brothers-in-law (another was Frederick's Lyonnais cook, the 'divine Joyard').[58] The presence of the painter inspired Elisabeth to take up her brushes. The decent little self-portrait that still hangs at Rheinsberg is the result. Pesne's work took a long time to complete: the music room, for example, was only ready just before Frederick William's death in the spring of 1740, and some of the work was not completed until 1747.[59] Still, it was in a state to satisfy Frederick in November 1739 when he wrote to his sister and told her of some of the fruits of his borrowing: 'It's all furnished ... there are two rooms full of pictures; the others are in pier glass or gilt or silver panelling. Most of my pictures are by Watteau or Lancret.'[60]

The study, with Pesne's ceiling showing the beautiful Ganymede carried off by Zeus disguised as an eagle, was later redecorated by Henry, destroying its rococo feeling. Pride of place originally went to a portrait of Voltaire, which sat above a case containing the *philosophe*'s collected works, 'opposite the place where I sit, in such a way that I have it always in my gaze'.[61] And the music room, possibly the greatest of Frederick's spaces at Rheinsberg, was swiftly destroyed by his brother.[62] Henry's work is of two distinct periods, but as a general rule it is more sober and forward looking, reflecting a greater accessibility to architectural fashion that Frederick ever had. Frederick was stuck in a rococo time-warp to the end of his days.

Rheinsberg may not have been to Frederick William's taste, but there was a Prussian order about the place despite all the talk of literature and

---

* The towers ended with cornices and balustrades in those days, rather than the pointed roofs that visitors see today.

music. To Suhm, Frederick reported the twofold division of the day: useful and pleasant. Useful things were the study of philosophy, history and languages.

Je prends souvent un livre à la main;	*Often, book in hand, my will pre-scribes*
Du bois touffu cherchant l'om-brage,	*Refuge in some shady bower;*
Ou bien, sur le bord du rivage	*Or, by the lake's wide-ranging shore,*
J'orne mon espirit du butin	*While with the spoils my mind imbibes*
Du quelque auteur Grec ou Latin.[63]	*The outpourings of antique scribes.*

Pleasant things were music, comedies, tragedies and masquerades, all acted out by the members of the court, as well as 'surprises' and present giving. Frederick confessed that rather more time was given over to the useful than the pleasant. The diversions served to refresh the mind and to leaven the moroseness borne of too strong a dose of philosophy.[64]

Even if Frederick left her alone at night, Elisabeth seems to have enjoyed those years and never lost her admiration for the man she married. She wrote to her grandmother to describe the prince's manic programme:

He busies himself from six in the morning until one [in the afternoon] with reading, philosophy, all lovely things. From half past one until three we sit down to eat, afterwards we drink coffee together until four, and then he returns to work and continues until seven. He then writes and comes to the gaming tables. In this way time races by in the variety of activities ... Really, you can say he is the greatest prince of our time...[65]

The king was bought off with food and tall soldiers, but it was a two-way process. In October 1736, Frederick William sent his son pheasants. A few months later Frederick responded with a 'detachment' of pullets and pigeons.[66] In the spring of 1739, Frederick dispatched a lobster and a *lange Kerl* to Potsdam, and later a Dutch cheese. Melons were as yet unavailable.[67] It was not just to fob the older man off; the Hohenzollerns were genuinely interested in what went into their stomachs. Once she had married the duke of Bevern's son, Lotte sent tuck hampers to her brother in Rheinsberg: Harz cheese, Brunswick sausage and 'Mumme', a strong local beer that was mixed with eggs and given to the sick. In her letters she included recipes, including one for a traditional beef roulade.[68]

Frederick's friend Camas sent him cheeses, almonds and coffee.[69]

These provisions no doubt came in useful for feeding Frederick's little gang of friends and the diplomats and others who passed through the Mark to pay their respects. In February 1738, it was the turn of the French ambassador, the marquis de la Chétardie, to spoil their fun.[70] His successor was the marquis de Valory. He impressed the Rheinsbergers even less than de la Chétardie: 'a sot, extremely crude, obsessed with smut [to the degree that] the gentleman is lost from view'.[71] One visitor who came and came and came was the rustic duke of Mecklenburg-Strelitz. It was hoped he would take the hint when he was sent home to Mirow, drunk and filthy, but just a week later he returned with his entire court. 'We lacked only the nanny', Frederick told his father. Frederick William would have approved. He had dismissed the duke's interest in his daughters in his own strong language.[72]

Suhm was one of Frederick's bosom friends. They had talked philosophy deep into the night – presumably in Berlin before Frederick's banishment – and used the emotionally charged language of romantic friendship.[73] The Saxon envoy had the job of translating Christian Wolff into French, because Frederick decided his German was not up to reading the philosopher in the original. Suhm had an exaggerated regard for Wolff, whom he termed 'the greatest philosopher of our century'.[74] Even Frederick's father was coming round to Wolff, and accepting some principles of the Enlightenment at the end of his reign.[75] It was a complete volte-face: it was he who had chased the disseminator of his mother's detested friend, Leibniz, from his chair at the University of Halle. Wolff's real enemies, the Pietists, had an undercover agent at Rheinsberg in the form of Frederick's pet monkey, Mimi:

The faithful companion of my retreat, seeing me deep in the study of Wolff's *Metaphysics*, of which you are the kind interpreter, was impatient to see if I preferred this wholly true and wholly reasonable book to his frivolous chatter and illusory pleasures. The moment came for supper and forced me to abandon my instructive reading in order to pay some attention to my body, which no thinking, reasonable man should neglect. In the meantime, my monkey, the cheekiest of monkeys all, slipped his chain, took up the *Metaphysics*, put a candle to it and clapped to see it burn...

Fortunately, it was only the copy of Suhm's translation. The original was unharmed. Frederick thought such treatment worthy only of Joachim Lange, the Pietist theologian who had had Wolff banished from Halle:

Our wits maintain that the monkey wanted to study the *Metaphysics* and, being unable to construe a word, put it to the flame. Others aver that Lange had corrupted him, and that he played that turn from motives of zeal inspired by the prig. Finally, others said that Mimi was annoyed at the number of prerogatives which Wolff accords to man over beast, and offered up to Vulcan a book which denigrated his race.[76]

In the winter of 1736, Suhm was posted to Saint Petersburg. Frederick's view of the Russians was never charitable. He thought Suhm the wrong man for the job: 'For that barbarous court you need men who can drink like fish and fuck like stoats.' He predicted an early death for his friend.[77] Suhm could be useful to Frederick in Saint Petersburg: in the spring of 1737, Frederick was in debt to the tune of 12,000 thalers ('I am hemmed in on all sides by creditors') and asked the Saxon to borrow the money from the Russians or the Austrians. Twelve days later the devoted Suhm had dispatched a quarter of the sum ('three volumes bound in the English manner').[78] In November that year, Frederick needed another 14,000. Ernest Biron, duke of Courland, was ready to oblige.*

By January 1739, Suhm was able to promise Frederick a fixed loan from the empress of 20,000 thalers a year in peacetime, all carefully laundered by Frederick's bankers in Berlin: Jordan's family bank, and that other Huguenot, Michelet. Frederick made sure that Suhm also had his cut: 3000 thalers here, a commission there, even a ring.[79] It was a dangerous game. Frederick was borrowing money on the collateral of his pliability as the future king of Prussia. The British thought he was their man, Seckendorff had led the Austrian emperor to believe that they had him in the bag, and now he was squeezing further funds out of the Russians. At home, Frederick William had had him locked up for such reckless behaviour, but in this Frederick no longer seemed to fear his father's wrath.

A less controversial source of borrowing was his new brother-in-law. Elisabeth's brother Charles had succeeded his father. Elisabeth ensured her welcome at Rheinsberg by bringing a well-stuffed purse with her.[80] Bevern allowed Frederick to double the size of Rheinsberg. A further 6000 thalers were sunk into the house and garden, bringing his total borrowings from the Brunswicks up to 19,000 thalers. All these matters were arranged by word of mouth, Frederick promising to discharge the

---

* He had been just plain, German, Ernst Bühren, but he had passed through Anna Ivanovna's bed, and she had rewarded him with a dukedom.

debts on his accession. Elisabeth was proving unsurprisingly useful, and it must have been another reason why he insisted that William should marry Elisabeth's sister. He had no desire to fall out with the Brunswicks.[81]

Charles Etienne Jordan came on the scene during the Rheinsberg years. Perhaps he, Fredersdorf and Keyserlingk were the three men who got closest to the misanthropic king. This may have led to a certain amount of carping from the less intellectual members of the court, Chasot in particular.[82] Jordan was a Protestant cleric from a family of Berlin-based Huguenot bankers, but he had lost his vocation after his wife's death and abandoned his cure. He had travelled in Europe, meeting Fontenelle, Voltaire and Pope, and written a *Voyage Littéraire* as a result, but he was most at home in his well-stocked library in Berlin. The sort of deeply cerebral soul whom Frederick longed to have at his court, he was wooed by the prince with desks and bookshelves until he consented to come and help him master written French. Frederick wrote him verse too, calling him 'Plus aimable qu'Erasme, autant ou plus savant.' ('More genial than Erasmus, as learned, or more.')[83]

Such fulsomeness was not rare with Frederick: he compared Duhan to Aristotle.[84] He was still forbidden to see his former tutor, but had not forgotten him. In March 1737 he wrote to him from Rheinsberg: 'We are fifteen friends who have gone into retreat here and sample of the pleasures of friendship and repose. It strikes me that I would [only] be perfectly happy if you could come and join us in our solitude. We know no violent passions, and we apply ourselves to making use of life and that alone.'[85]

There was good hunting to be had around Rheinsberg, but it held no more fascination for Frederick than it had ever done. To his grown-up friend Camas he reported a commission to exterminate 200 'miserable' wild boars which were laying waste to his part of the Mark. 'I performed the task like a tender person; taking pity on their suffering; I made their martyrdom as comfortable as I might. I swear to you I feel no passion for hunting ...'[86] It was none the less important that hunting was seen to be performed at Rheinsberg: it made the king happier about his son, and many of Frederick's friends – Keyserlingk for one – were unrepentant huntsmen.

My sole spheres of activity extend from my hearth to my library; it is not far and I have no time along the way to take in the inclemency of the season. As regards the chase, here I have a whole coterie which hunts for me, and I study for them; everyone does what he likes and no one is restrained in his pleasures. There is little politicking, less speech, and a lot of thought.[87]

While hunting bored him, freemasonry proved much more to Frederick's liking. He was forward-thinking and anti-clerical, and had no truck with court etiquette and outward distinctions of rank. Freemasons, according to Bielfeld, his middle-class friend from Hamburg,

regard the whole world but as one republic of which each nation forms a family and each individual a member; who endeavour by these means to revive the primitive maxims of mankind in the greatest perfection; to unite under the banner men of knowledge; who sacrifice all personal resentment; who banish from their lodges all that can disturb the tranquillity of mind or the purity of manners; and who, in the intervals of their delightful labours, enjoy the innocent pleasures of life...[88]

Bielfeld is a good example of how freemasonry transcended the social divisions of the time. He met Frederick at the latter's reception into the masons in Brunswick in August 1738. The initiation was planned with great secrecy. Frederick had asked Schaumburg-Lippe to manage it all for him, giving him the details of his father's progress so that the arrangements could be made. The count wrote to a certain Baron Albedyll in Hanover, who then set about convening a lodge.[89] Bielfeld received a letter from a Baron * * * in Hamburg inviting him to be present at Frederick's reception. Frederick William was due in Brunswick to attend the fair on his way to Wesel, and it was known that his son was travelling with him. As there would be so many masons in the city at the time, there would be no suspicion aroused. Schaumburg-Lippe was to be his sponsor.[90]

In the middle of August, Barons O and L, together with Bielfeld, arrived in Brunswick worried that the customs men might open their trunks, which contained the 'furniture, insigns and instruments necessary for holding a lodge'. Bielfeld crossed the officer's hand with a ducat. The masons gathered in a 'tolerable good alehouse' and awaited the arrival of Frederick and his father the next day. The investiture was planned for the night of 14–15 August. One of the party had the job of getting the man in the neighbouring room so drunk that he would fail to notice the ceremony. It was well done: 'he would have slept by the side of a battery'. Frederick arrived in the company of Graf Truchsess-Walburg, who wanted to be a mason too. The prince told the others he wished to be treated as a 'private person'. The rites were finished by 4 a.m. and Frederick and his friend returned to the royal palace.[91]

Frederick thanked Schaumburg-Lippe with a ring bearing his portrait. He continued to express himself in letters using the egalitarian language that was then a hallmark of the order. Later he asked Schaumburg-Lippe to stay at Rheinsberg, where he would be treated not only as a friend, but as a 'brother freemason'.[92] In October he was able to report a vast expansion in the number of masons at Rheinsberg.[93] The following spring Bielfeld was to become part of the Rheinsberg lodge. Truchsess-Walburg wrote to ask him if he wished to enter Frederick's service. The Hamburger must have had talents that went beyond mere masonry, for Bielfeld is anxious to stress that Frederick did not favour masons in all things.

Sometime since, a freemason, they say, endeavoured to intrude himself on the king by virtue of his connection, but the monarch finding that the man had no other merit, took no notice of him; he therefore determined to enforce his application by making the king a sign, which he answered, by turning his back on his brother mason, and lifting up the hind flap of his coat.[94]

Bielfeld left one of the best descriptions of the crown prince's court. He first glimpsed Rheinsberg in the autumn light, 'an immense lake bathes almost the foundations; and on the opposite side, a beautiful forest of oaks and beech rises in form of an amphitheatre'.[95] The court came out to meet him: Wolden and his wife, Senning ('an admirable and gay veteran' who had lost a leg in Flanders), the 'gay' Chasot and the 'austere' Knobelsdorff. Jordan was a 'well-made little man', if rather swarthy. Bielfeld was not so impressed by his writing: he had 'infinitely more wit at the end of his tongue, than at the end of his pen'. Fredersdorf was 'tall [and] handsome' and had 'understanding and ingenuity'. He was 'polite, attentive and supple, frugal of his fortune, and yet liberal'. He met Pesne and Dubuisson, the brothers Graun and Benda: 'one of the first violins of Europe'.[96]

If anyone struck Bielfeld, it was the linguist Keyserlingk. This was not so much because his appearance was extraordinary: he was rather ugly, 'short and thick … [with] small eyes, a large nose, a wide mouth, and a sallow complexion', but because he was so odd. He entered the halls like a whirlwind, 'or like Boreas in the Ballet of the Rose'. Bielfeld later encountered the Balt returning from hunting dressed in a nightshirt.

'While he changed, he recited passages from the *Henriade* to me and long chunks of German poetry, he spoke to me about horses and hunting, performed a few pirouettes ... and discoursed all the while on politics, mathematics, architecture and tactics.'[97]

'We see the prince and princess only at table, at play, at the ball, the concert, or other common pleasures of which they participate.' Despite the restricted size of the house, Frederick could elude his courtiers, and concerts were by invitation only. He was generally closeted in his seven-room empire upstairs, but he was occasionally sighted, wearing the uniform of his regiment. Bielfeld regretted his inaccessibility: 'I would freely go some leagues barefooted, at least once a week, to enjoy the delicious pleasure of supping in his company.' There was still a chance to see him amusing himself at the ball: 'The prince dances in a noble and graceful manner. In a word, he loves all rational pleasures, except the chase, the exercise of which he thinks as troublesome, and scarce more useful than chimney-sweeping.'[98]

One day Frederick came down from his ivory tower (it was indeed a tower) and joined in the debauch. Champagne was served and everyone got drunk. Bielfeld had to go out to empty his bladder. When he returned, the crown princess had changed his water for celery wine, which he then, in turn, poured into his wine to dilute it. 'I became joyous.' Frederick made him drink bumper after bumper of Lunel muscat. When Elisabeth broke a glass, it became the signal for a rout: 'in an instant all the glasses flew to the several corners of the room; and all the cristals, porcelain, piers, branches, bowls, vases, etc. were broke into a thousand pieces. In the midst of this universal destruction the prince stood, like the man in Horace, who contemplates the crash of worlds with a look of perfect tranquillity.'[99]

The evening ended badly for Bielfeld: he fell down the grand staircase and passed out. A servant woman mistook him for a dog and kicked him in the guts, calling him by 'an appellation somewhat dishonourable'. The rest of the party had taken to their beds and remained there all day. Such larks were rare at Rheinsberg: 'the prince is very far from being a toper,[100] he sacrifices only to Apollo and the Muses; one day, however, he may perhaps raise an altar to Mars'.[101]

[III]

From the Rheinsberg years began Frederick's correspondence with the leading lights of the European (chiefly French) intelligentsia. As he put it in an early letter to Francesco Algarotti, 'I like to maintain correspondences with superior minds, with people who are completely cerebral, as if they had no bodies [any more]; this is the human elite.'[102] A three-year epistolary flirtation with Bernard Le Bovier Fontenelle began in March 1737 when the Frenchman was eighty (he died in his hundredth year). Fontanelle pretended to be flattered by the prince's attention. He did a little flattering in turn, and assured His Highness that kings made better philosophers than philosophers kings.[103] Charles Rollin, the Jansenist Rector of the University of Paris, was next. Rollin also knew the right tone to please the prince: 'It is rare to find princes who have such a pronounced fondness for all that touches on literature and science ... Princes are born, but great princes are decided by merit alone.' Later, this 'second Livy' told Frederick that he resembled several famous figures of antiquity.[104]

There were richer prizes than these. The philosopher Pierre Louis Moreau de Maupertuis received his first letter from the prince in June 1738 on the recommendation of Voltaire, who was later to vilify Maupertuis so malevolently in the 'Akakia' affair.[105] A year and ten months earlier, on 8 August 1736 Frederick had begun a correspondence with Europe's leading intellectual, Voltaire himself. It was to last nearly forty-two years and fills three entire volumes of Frederick's collected works.[106] Frederick used Suhm's translation of Wolff, 'the most famous philosopher of our time', as a pretext to write to the great man. Voltaire probably thought that epithet belonged to him, but Frederick was also clever enough to flatter the vain Frenchman; speak of the works he admired the most; and launch an attack on intolerant Christianity which was calculated to strike a chord with the man who had taught Europe to cry 'écrasez l'infame'.[107]

Frederick wanted a copy of *La Pucelle*, Voltaire's scurrilous satire on Joan of Arc. He did well: Voltaire was flattered to receive a homage from a prince whose earlier flight and philosophic bent had rendered him famous throughout the continent. It also arrived at a good time: Voltaire was involved in one of his frequent literary squabbles, with libellous pamphlets flying like shuttlecocks across a net. This time he was getting the rough end of the deal. At least Frederick saw him as he wanted to be seen himself. He responded in kind:

In tormentis pinxit. Self-portrait of Frederick's father, Frederick William I.

Frederick William's simple hunting lodge at Stern, in the forest near Potsdam.

Antoine Pesne's portrait of the four-year-old Frederick and his elder sister, Wilhelmina.

Schloss Monbijou in Berlin, where Frederick's mother, Sophia Dorothea held court.

Frederick William's favourite residence, Königs Wusterhausen near Berlin. His children detested staying in the gaunt tower house.

One of the new gates at Stettin, which Frederick's father acquired from the Swedes in 1720.

Frederick's best friend, the officer Hans Hermann von Katte, who was executed before his eyes at Küstrin in 1730.

Schloss Köpenick near Berlin. Here Frederick and his associates were court martialled.

The fortress at Küstrin on the Oder where Frederick was imprisoned. It was blown up at the end of the Second World War.

Frederick as Crown Prince by Pesne.

Amalthea – Frederick's temple of friendship in Neuruppin. Here he held his first intimate dinners as crown prince. The statues were added in the last century.

Rheinsberg, where Frederick and Elisabeth Christine established their court.

Dietrich Freiherr von Keyserlingk, Frederick's Falstaff, as depicted by Pesne.

'Apollodore', Frederick's architect, Georg Wenzeslaus von Knobelsdorff. Painted by Pesne in 1737.

Pesne's portrait of Charles Etienne Jordan, former pastor and intellectual spirit of the Rheinsberg years.

Voltaire by Houdon. Frederick subscribed to the bust after the poet's death in 1778. Voltaire and Frederick had been correspondents and friends since 1736.

Frederick and his
three brothers by
F. Rusch, 1737. From
left to right:
Frederick, Ferdinand,
Augustus William
and Henry.

Graf Kurt Christoph
von Schwerin, who
saved the day at the
Battle of Mollwitz in
1741 and died at the
head of his troops
before Prague in 1757.
Woodcut by Adolph
Menzel.

There is a prince in this world who thinks like a man, a philosophic prince who
will make men happy ... be assured that one day, if the whirlwind of events and
the evilness of man don't alter a so divine character, you will be adored by your
people and cherished by the entire world. Philosophers worthy of the name will
flock to your lands; and, as famous craftsmen arrive *en masse* in a country where
they know their work to be appreciated, thinking men will arrive to surround
your throne.[108]

Already Voltaire was playing with the prince, making promises to come
and see him in Prussia; a useful exit should circumstances once again
become too awkward for him in France: 'You go to Rome to see churches,
paintings, ruins and bas-reliefs. A prince like you is worth a detour ...'[109]
There was already a *lettre de cachet* against him, and Château de Cirey was
conveniently located close to the border with the Austrian Netherlands
in case the French king's police came looking for him.[110] When Frederick
pressed the invitation home, however, Voltaire got cold feet and pointed
to his mistress of the past three years, Gabriel-Emilie Le Tonnelier de
Breteuil, marquise du Châtelet-Laumont, in whose house he was currently
lying low while he waited for the latest scandal to blow over, and who
was not anxious to lose her lover to the crown prince of Prussia. Voltaire
was none the less genuinely flattered by the attentions of the young
prince, and it has been suggested that even if Emilie du Châtelet had not
died when she did, he might still have taken up Frederick's offer to join
him in Potsdam.[111]

Letters flew back and forth, and Frederick sent Voltaire gifts too: a
bust of Socrates and a gold-handled cane for the 'master who educated
Alcibiades':[112] a fairly blunt allusion to Socratic love. As one recent writer
has put it, it was a 'a flirtation which was intellectual and physical all at
once'.[113] This sort of sexual *badinage* came easily to Voltaire too. If the same
authority is to be trusted, he had had plenty of homosexual experiences in
his school days and since. He reciprocated with flattery: 'you think like
Trajan, you write like Pliny, and you speak French like our best writers'. He
referred to Louis XIV: 'I've seen his letters, he didn't know how to spell his
own language.* Under your guiding hand Berlin will become the Athens of
Germany, and possibly of Europe [too].'[114]

Frederick rapidly revealed his deeper purpose: he wanted Voltaire to
be his teacher; to perfect his French style; but if Frederick was showing

* Neither did Frederick, and his French spelling was no better, but others around him
knew how to put it right.

the Frenchman his artistic side, he never intended to fool Voltaire into believing that art came first: he was ultimately more interested in the destiny of Prussia, 'therein lies all the glory I seek'.[115]

Voltaire was still mixing him unctuous compliments. The prince was Alcibiades, Henry IV and Francis I, all rolled into one. He compared his verse to Catullus.

> Les lauriers d'Apollon se fanaient sur la terre,
> Les beaux-arts languissaient ainsi que les vertus;
> La fraude aux yeux menteurs et l'aveugle Plutus
> Entre les mains des rois gouvernaient la tonnerre.
> La Nature indignée élève alors sa voix:
> Je veux former, dit-elle, un règne heureux et juste,
> Je veux qu'un héros naisse, et qu'il joigne à la fois
> Les talents de Virgile et les vertus d'Auguste,
> Pour ornement du monde et l'exemple des rois.
> Elle dit; et du ciel les Vertus descendirent,
> Tout le Nord tressaillit, tout l'Olympe accourut;
> L'olive, les lauriers, les myrtes reverdirent,
>   Et Frédéric parut.[116]

> *Apollo's laurels lay withered across the land,*
> *The arts had languished and also virtue had declined,*
> *Fraud with lying eyes and the Lord Plutus, quite blind*
> *The pawns of kings, bent the thunder to their command.*
> *The voice of outraged nature finally was heard:*
> *I want, said she, to make a land happy and just,*
> *I want to see a hero born who has, in a word*
> *Great Virgil's talents and the virtues of August,*
> *A model for our kings and a jewel for the world.*
> *This she said, and the virtues came down from on high,*
> *The north trembled and from Mount Olympus they sped;*
> *Olive, laurel, myrtle bloomed and why:*
> *   Frederick raised his head.*

Frederick was still more interested in fame than in promoting the *pax borussica* that Voltaire had in mind for him. He was worried that his name would merely 'serve to decorate some family tree, and then to fall into obscurity ...' Voltaire was to receive a signal honour: a portrait of the prince by Knobelsdorff, brought to him by one of his best friends –

Caesarion. Apollodore 'knows that he is working for you; and he is sufficiently pricked to want to surpass himself'. Such pictures were rare. In his life as crown prince of Prussia, Frederick sat only for Pesne and Knobelsdorff. As king he refused the requests of all painters to portray him. Only once, as a special favour to his brother-in-law when he was passing through Brunswick, did he allow his court painter, Johann Georg Ziesenis, to do a rapid oil sketch.[117]

Frederick told Voltaire of his vision of his army and how much it differed from the king his father:

I'd like it to be known for its bravery and not its beauty ... The troops with which Alexander conquered Greece and a large part of Asia were very differently turned out. Iron was their sole embellishment ... They were hardened by the task; they knew how to endure hunger and thirst and all the ills resulting from the bitterness of long drawn out war. A rigid and rigorous discipline bound them intimately, made them all join together to the same end, and cut them out for the job of executing the most wide-reaching plans of their generals with promptitude and vigour.[118]

It was an intimation that Frederick had warlike plans, which were not altogether to Voltaire's liking; but the reply was not wholly bellicose: the Frenchman wanted to know what was this 'Remusberg' that formed Frederick's postal address. Frederick told him that a manuscript had recently been unearthed in the Vatican Library which explained the later fate of Remus after he fell out with his brother Romulus. He escaped his brother's jealous fury and took refuge in north Germany, somewhere near the Elbe, on an island in the middle of a lake. Nearby he built the town of Remusberg, later rendered as Rheinsberg by its German conquerors.[119] Frederick later conceded that the tale might have seemed a little far-fetched, but no more than, say, the anecdote of the Holy Ampulla, or the feats of Merlin the wizard.[120]

Keyserlingk arrived with the portrait. Voltaire described himself surrounded by Frederick's bounty: portrait, part two of Wolff's *Metaphysics* and another dissertation. Tokay was to follow,[121] and a hypochondriac Voltaire celebrated its arrival in verse:

Ma santé serait rétablie,	*Oh what a poor, sick man am I,*
Si je me trouvais quelque jour	*But I could be myself again,*
Près d'un tonneau de vin	*Beside a barrel of tokay.*
d'Hongrie.	

In later utterances, Voltaire declared himself none too enamoured of the presents or his tokay.[122] Frederick would not be put off by Voltaire telling him he was leaving on a trip: 'The Hungarian wine will follow you wherever you go. It is much better for you than hock, which I beg you not to drink, it is extremely bad for you.'[123]

Keyserlingk claimed that he had fallen for Madame du Châtelet: 'when she spoke, I was in love with her mind; and when she didn't, I was [obsessed with] her body'.[124] Voltaire told Frederick what an impression he was making on the French: 'they call you the young Soloman of the North'.[125] Voltaire was getting to grips with the prince's phonetic spelling, which characterised his French as much as his German: 'auser' rather than 'oser', 'tres' instead of 'trait', 'matein' for 'matin', etc. More important, perhaps, his inability to pronounce certain words made it impossible for him to scan his lines: 'amitié' had four syllables instead of three, 'nourricier' three and not four; 'aient' one and not two.[126]

Frederick was trusting Voltaire too much; by telling him his secrets he was providing him with the means to destroy him. Unusually for the sly and secretive Frederick, he walked into a trap. On 19 January 1738, for example, Frederick wrote, 'I know I am not taking a risk in entrusting you with these curious secret documents. Your discretion and prudence put my mind at rest.'[127] He confessed, in that self-pitying style which was to reach its apogee during the Seven Years War, that his life 'has been but a tissue of sorrows, and the school of adversity makes men suspicious, discrete and indulgent[?]. One looks hard at the slightest things when one thinks what possible consequences they might have, and one is happy to save others from the sadness that one has suffered oneself.'[128]

Voltaire also supervised Frederick's reading and recommended writers to the prince, as he would later suggest members for his Academy. Frederick already had his own agent in Paris, Voltaire's childhood friend Nicolas Claude Thiériot, a frivolous, drunken soul who retailed tittle-tattle through the literary salons of Paris, and who seems to have been particularly at home in the homosexual world of the great city.[129] Through Thiériot, Frederick could order the latest works to take Paris by storm. Many of these were by his friend Voltaire himself, although the prince favoured the now largely forgotten tragedies, rather than the *romans* and *contes* still popular today. He also read and corresponded with the poet Gresset and praised Voltaire's rivals: Jean-Baptiste Rousseau, Piron and the younger Crébillon.

His passion remained for the stars of the *grand siècle*: Boileau, Bossuet, Corneille and Racine. Frederick would read and recite these works, even in the times of his greatest despair, substituting the names of the characters for the generals who faced him across the battlefield. Corneille's plays often describe the triumph of Roman virtue, something that Frederick saw enshrined in his very German father, but despite his later popularity with the revolutionaries of 1789, he was no democrat:

> ... quand le peuple est maître, on n'agit qu'en tumulte:
> La voix de la raison jamais ne se consulte;
> Les honneurs sont vendus aux plus ambitieux,
> L'autorité livrée aux plus séditieux...
> Le pire des Etats, c'est l'Etat populaire.[130]

> *When the people rule the land a riot results*
> *And the voice of reason none consults;*
> *Honours are purchased by the most ambitious,*
> *Authority leased to the most seditious...*
> *The worst of governments is by the people.*

Racine was the firm favourite. Frederick could adapt whole scenes to the tragedy of his own existence: Titus denied the chance to marry his beloved in *Bérénice*:

> 'Rome a ses droits Seigneur ...
> Ses intérêts sont-ils plus sacrés que les nôtres."[131]

> *'Rome has its laws, My Lord ...*
> *Are not its rights more sacred than our own?'*

Or Monime lamenting her fate in *Mithridate* recalled the misery of his own forced marriage:

> Ce n'est donc pas assez que ce funeste jour
> A tout ce que j'aimais m'arrache sans retour,
> Et que, de mon devoir esclave infortunée,
> A d'éternels ennuis de me voie enchaînée?[132]

> *Is it not enough that on this fatal day*
> *From that which I have loved I shall be torn away,*
> *That, as the unfortunate slave of my duty,*
> *I shall be harnessed to eternal misery?*

He might have found echoes of his father in tyrants Néron or Mithridate, and his fatalism would have found solace in Phèdre's lines:

> Est-ce un malheur si grand que de cesser de vivre?
> La mort aux malheureux ne cause point d'effroi;
> Je ne crains que le nom que je laisse après moi.[133]

> *Is it such a hardship when you cease to breathe?*
> *For unhappy people death causes no alarm;*
> *I fear only that my name should come to harm.*

Or, in the earlier *Alexandre le Grand*, he might have heeded the criticism of Cléofile:

> Mais qui, Seigneur, toujours guerre sur guerre?
> Cherchez-vous des sujets au-delà de la terre?
> Voulez-vous pour témoins de vos faits éclatants
> Des pays inconnus même à leurs habitants?...
> Pensez-vous y traîner les restes d'une armée
> Vingt fois renouvelée et vingt fois consumée?
> Vos soldats, dont la vue excite la pitié,
> D'eux-mêmes en cent lieux on laissé la moitié,

> *What is it, Lord, just war after war?*
> *Are you looking beyond this earth for subjects more?*
> *Do you want witnesses to your magnificence*
> *In lands strange to their very inhabitants? ...*
> *Will you drag the remains of that great brood*
> *Twenty times dispersed and twenty times renewed?*
> *Your soldiers, whose aspect alone excites pity,*
> *Have left half their number before a hundred cities.*

Later Frederick would be able to reply in kind:

> Ils marcheront, Madame, et je n'ai qu'à paraître:
> Ces coeurs qui dans un camp, d'un vain loisir déçus,
> Comptent en murmurant les coups qu'ils ont reçus,
> Revivront pour me suivre et blâmant leurs murmures
> Brigueront à mes yeux de nouvelles blessures.[134]

> *They will march, Madam, I need only appear:*
> *Those hearts who, in their camp, consume their idle days*
> *Grumbling and counting the wounds they have sustained,*
> *Will brood no more, and live again to follow me,*
> *Will seek to garner fresh wounds for me to see.*

[IV]

Frederick thought the way to get on the right side of Voltaire was to flatter his mistress. From August 1738 began an occasional correspondence with Emilie too, expressing jealousy that she was in possession of the man he wanted most at his court, and admiration for her intellect, which was then coming to grips with higher physics and mathematics. From East Prussia he sent her an amber pen (which she promptly broke), confusing it with the ambergris that is a component of incense, and recommending she burn it at her altars.[135] Voltaire had a little scheme: he wanted to sell Frederick the principality of Beringen, which belonged to Emilie's husband, and which was close to his territory in Cleves.[136] Frederick resisted the usurer-poet by telling him it was best to wait until the death of the last of the Pfaz-Sulzbachs, and then the ownership of Beringen could be reviewed along with Jülich and Berg. Later he told Voltaire there was going to be a war anyway, and that Emilie's principality would be mopped up along with the duchies.[137]

While he wooed Voltaire, he distracted himself with Algarotti, a Venetian from a rich bourgeois family who had studied philosophy and taken up the banner of Newton.[138] He had already captivated society in Paris and London. He was adopted by Voltaire himself and arrived in the English capital with a letter of introduction from him to Lord Hervey. He was 'strikingly good looking ... with large, dark eyes, full sensual lips and high-arched eyebrows'.[139] Both Hervey and the blue-stocking Lady Mary Wortley Montagu promptly fell in love with him. In the summer of 1739 he came to beard the philosopher prince in his Rheinsberg lair in the company of an English friend, Lord Baltimore, whom Frederick liked, despite his bad French and all too rapid English. The rapport was immediate and they sat down and wrote a cantata together. Elisabeth was rather shocked at Algarotti for laughing at religion. It was music to Frederick's ears, however: already in September, he was writing to tell him, 'I shall never forget the week you spent with me.'[140]

It was not just Algarotti's appearance that excited Frederick; it was the charm and knowledge of this cosmopolitan Italian who could expound on Newton, Voltaire and all the great poetic geniuses of his time. When Algarotti returned to London, he sent Frederick books, always the way to his heart: 'At least don't forget the strange productions of Dr Swift. His new, robust and sometimes extravagant ideas amuse me. I quite like this English Rabelais, chiefly when he is properly inspired by satire and he gives in to his imagination.'[141]

Frederick could also send Algarotti a report on his first philosophic project: the refutation of his countryman Machiavelli. On 24 October 1739 he told the 'Swan' (as Algarotti was to be known) that the work was largely finished. 'I didn't need the strength of Hercules to tame the monster Machiavelli, nor the eloquence of Bossuet to prove to right-minded people that unbounded ambition, treason, perfidy and murder are vices which run counter to the commonweal, and that the real politics of kings and all honest men are to be good and just.'[142] To Voltaire earlier that year, he had explained the prince's relationship to his people: he was to be the heart, which garnered the blood from all the other organs: 'He receives the fidelity and obedience of his subjects and he provides peace, prosperity and plenty and everything which might contribute to the growth and good of society.'[143]

It was that interest in the commonweal which led Frederick to oppose the brutal expression of Machiavelli's *Prince*, but he confused the murderous language with the more cogent thought. In some places Frederick's disagreement with the Tuscan is honest enough though: he did not think it right to leave the laws and customs of the conquered land if he could improve them; nor did he agree with a scorched earth policy or the need to take up residence in a conquered land; nor, for the time being at least, did he accept Machiavelli's advocacy of murder or plunder.[144] Frederick proposed the introduction of an enlightened regime that would be more attractive to his new subjects; one that they would instantly recognise as being superior to the one it replaced. On the other hand, Machiavelli knew how powerfully audacity and victory in battle could endear a prince to his people, a lesson Frederick took to his bosom. He was against the use of mercenary troops too. In a passage of *L'Antimachiavel* directed at those German princes, chiefly the Hessians, who hired out their armies to foreign sovereigns, Frederick fulminated:

The institution of the soldier is for the defence of the nation; to rent it out to others to do battle, as one might a mastiff or a bull is, in my opinion, a perversion of both the aims of war and diplomacy. It is said that it is not permitted to sell sacred objects. Well, what could be more sacred than the blood of men?[145]

Machiavelli called for good laws *and* good weapons, and the encouragement of settlements in conquered lands. This would have struck a chord with the German prince, as would Machiavelli's emphasis on the need for instruction in history.[146] It was to some degree the teaching of Frederick's father:

The art of war is all that is expected of a ruler ... we find that princes who have thought more of their pleasures than of arms have lost their states. The first way to lose a state is to neglect the art of war; the first way to win a state is to be skilled in the art of war ... [The prince] must never let his thoughts stray from military exercises, which he must pursue more vigorously in peace than in war.[147]

As one or two German writers have pointed out, the irony was that Machiavelli dreamed of a prince just like Frederick who would have been able to unite Italy and limit the temporal powers of the papacy.[148] But the image that Frederick was anxious to project was of a peaceful prince, cut more in a mould to please his philosophic friends. He painted a picture of the horrors of war and stated his reluctance to use an army for frivolous ends, and despite everything that happened, he continued saying as much to the end of his days.[149] Voltaire had cause to laugh up his sleeve at these pacifistic sentiments, which Frederick so quickly put aside. But his cynicism came after the event. At the time he acted as Frederick's dogsbody, beautifying the prose and carrying the princely manuscript around the publishing houses of Amsterdam. A disillusioned Voltaire wrote at the beginning of Frederick's greatest war: 'If Machiavelli had had a prince for a pupil, the first thing he would have taught him would have been to write against him. But the crown prince would not have understood the subtlety.'[150]

Frederick's writings on political philosophy did not stop there. From this period date the *Considérations sur l'État présent du corps politique de l'Europe*, the *Dissertation sur l'Innocence des erreurs de l'esprit*, and the *Avant propos sur la Henriade de M. de Voltaire*. In the first of the three, the Prussian crown prince examines the political situation in Europe after the various fruitless wars of the 1730s and hints at 'ambitious plans': 'ambition thinks and acts forever in the same way, I shall not say more'. Elsewhere, he expresses mature ideas that crop up in his writings throughout his life.[151] The second is a little off-cut of the Enlightenment. Frederick tells a story he told many times about a lunatic in Les Petites Maisons (the Paris equivalent of Bedlam) who was delighted to think he was in Heaven surrounded by angels. He was bled and woke up to reality, furious to learn he was actually in Hell.[152] In the third, Frederick placed Voltaire's epic poem on equal footing with Homer and Virgil.

Frederick's earlier, pacific voice seems to have genuinely impressed Voltaire. In March 1739 he wrote in some uncertainty as to whether or not Frederick had succeeded to the throne yet:

If you are king, you will make many men happy; if you remain crown prince, you will educate them. If I counted for anything ... I should like you to remain in your happy retirement, and that you might continue to amuse yourself by writing the charming things I love and which I find so enlightening. When you are king you will be taken up with the business of encouraging the arts and making wise and advantageous alliances, establishing manufactures and earning your place among the immortals. I shall hear nothing but talk of your achievements and your glory, but I shall probably receive no more of those charming verses, nor that strong and sublime prose which would certainly give you another sort of immortality if you wanted it ... Never mind; I wish you the throne, because I am honest enough to prefer the happiness of several million people to the satisfaction of myself.[153]

Frederick's poetic output in the Rheinsberg years was not slight. Despite Voltaire's charitable comments, no one was quite safe from his strophes. All his boon companions were awarded a chunk of verse, and the closest of them received two or three apiece: Caesarion, Jordan, Chasot; even Pesne, the harpist Petrini, Emilie du Châtelet and Lord Baltimore. Much of it is dull stuff, a constant reiteration of the principles of the Enlightenment that the prince held so dear, but without the spark of greatness. It was hardly surprising: he was writing in a foreign language, and although he spoke impressive French, the fact that he had mostly heard it spoken by Germans led him to odd stresses and pronunciations. The other problem with much of Frederick's poetry is its formalism: only in very rare instances does he tell us what he feels.[154]

Philosophising and writing verse were not enough for him; he returned to composition too. He set Voltaire's *La Mort de mademoiselle Le Couvreur* to music and sent it to the poet. Voltaire promised that Emilie would perform it.[155] In the winter of 1738 he sent his freemason friend Graf Albrecht Wolfgang zu Schaumburg-Lippe a symphony he wrote in 1736, warning him of a difficult violin part. Schaumburg-Lippe praised the work, and was rewarded with a second: 'I don't use them as often as flute concertos,' said Frederick.[156]

[V]

Frederick was occasionally obliged to quit his idyll and tour his scattered lands at his father's side. In September 1735 the newly gazetted major-general accompanied the king on his annual trip to East Prussia. It was not his favourite place; he thought it only mildly preferable to what he had heard of Siberia: 'It is winter in autumn, the devil knows what it is like in winter.' East Prussia had been none the less a testing place for his father's policies, and in those last years before Frederick assumed the crown, he came to admire the king more and more. In July 1739 he wrote a long letter to Voltaire in which he described the history of East Prussia and the Hohenzollerns, and showed how his father had spared nothing to re-establish the region after the plague. He told the Frenchman there was 'something heroic in the generous and zealous way in which the king has colonised this desert and made it fertile and useful'.[157]

The towns were so swollen that suburbs were growing up, and he predicted that in twenty years the region would be more densely populated than Switzerland or Franconia. Huguenots made up a substantial number of the settlers, and there were whole villages where only French was spoken. The new spirit of the place had been injected by the Salzburgers too, who had just arrived as part of Frederick William's relief package.[158] Frederick's dislike of East Prussia eventually extended to its people, when they cravenly (or so he believed) paid homage to their invaders during the Seven Years War and prepared to become a province of the Russian Empire. One thing in East Prussia came in handy, however, and that was the famous stud at Trakehnen, which the king gave him as a present in the summer of 1739. The prince was 'touched by the return of paternal tenderness'.[159] The income from the stables went some way towards paying off his massive debts.[160] The king, too, was showing that with time he was ready to place his total trust in his wayward son.

Frederick William was unconsciously putting the final flourishes to his reign. In Berlin and Potsdam new *quartiers* were springing up: in the southern Friedrichstadt neat rows of houses with mansards for the lodging of soldiers. In Potsdam it was the Dutch quarter: smart, red-brick houses, like those the king had seen in his favourite Holland, gave the little town a wholly different feel and a modest scale that it was to lose once Frederick changed it again into a stone-built, show-place of the rococo. Bielfeld visited Potsdam at this time, and observed the Dutch quarter, the tall soldiers and the fifes: 'handsome negroes, very finely dressed,

with turbans ornamented with plumes of feathers, and very elegant chains
and earrings of solid silver'. They were better looking by far than the
'ugly' giants, who tended to be 'bow-legged or ill-made in some part of
their bodys; so that we may say in general, that this regiment is more
marvellous than fine.'[161]

Odder still was a visit to a colonel's quarters, where Bielfeld drank
many bottles of hock: 'as they become empty, they are ranged on the
floor in the form of a battalion. The longer the file of these dead men
is, the gayer has been the dinner.' After his meal, the Hamburger went
to a men-only ball with the soldiers. 'God forgive me! but it raised an
odd suspicion in my mind, that these gentlemen who have so much
outward austerity, may not at bottom, be very obdurate.' After his dance
with the bristly squaddies, Bielfeld went to a gathering of local ladies.
'They thought me very cool and sober, in comparison with some of the
champions in our bacchanal combat, who had already got there, one of
whom had set himself down between two chairs, and was absolutely
unable to get up again.'[162]

Bielfeld also went to Berlin, where he observed that the king donated
materials for building. The would-be houseowner had only to pay for the
costs of construction. On Frederick's reluctant visits to the capital (which
he never liked), he noticed the new 'masses of stones' that were growing
up.[163] He came to Berlin to observe form, just as he stocked his regiment
with a few 'six foot arguments' to please the king.[164]

Frederick was building too: on 14 April 1740 a fire in Rheinsberg had
destroyed virtually everything bar the Schloss, the church and rectory,
and twenty-two houses. For some of his courtiers it was a particularly
traumatic time. Benda lost everything he had with the exception of his
violin and a little sheet music; fortunately, he was able to write down a
substantial amount from memory.[165] Frederick had not been in residence
at the time of the blaze. A few weeks later his father died, and there was
no longer anyone to prevent him from dipping into the state's coffers to
repair the damage.[166] Knobelsdorff sat down at the drawing board and
within days new foundations were being laid for the little town we can
still see today.[167] Frederick wrote to his favourite sister to express the
feelings of the townsfolk: 'their misfortune has been great, but almost all
their losses have been made good, and their houses will be better built
than they were'.[168]

Chronic gout and dropsy made Frederick William a capricious companion, ever blowing hot and cold; sometimes a 'benevolent divinity',

sometimes a 'thundering Jove, armed with bolts of lightning',[169] praising or scolding his son. In two letters to Camas written in the second half of December 1738, Frederick records the king going so far as to praise the sciences, then, a week later, the good opinions had disappeared like a dream and he was 'revealing his hatred' for his eldest son 'in manifold forms'.[170] Presumably, Frederick William had already begun the hard labour of trying to read Wolff. To Wilhelmina, Frederick William repeated his earliest fears that his son would squander the fortunes he had amassed on palaces, mistresses and entertainments. He could say nothing about it, for Frederick was already too grown-up.[171]

But these were flashes in the pan: Frederick William was proud of his son, and he had good reason to be. As he told Pöllnitz in those twilight years,

I am not that worried about living, for I leave behind me a son who possesses all the gifts [necessary] for a good ruler. I should not have said that five years ago: he was still too young then; but, thanks be to God, he has changed and I am satisfied. He has promised me to maintain the army and I am reassured that he'll keep his word. I know he loves the soldiers, he has understanding and everything will go well.[172]

Austria's ingratitude towards him riled the king at the end. He must have felt a fool to have placed so much trust in Charles VI. He had not even been informed of the marriage of the Archduchess Maria Theresa to the duke of Lorraine, and despite his willingness to fight for them, they had shown no serious inclination to win him Jülich and Berg. On 2 May 1736 he pointed to the crown prince, that *Fritzchen* who had caused him so much heart- and belly-ache in the past, and with a rare gift of prophecy he said: 'Here stands someone who will avenge me.'[173] He had trained his son better than he might have imagined: the desired strike against the Habsburgs was not to be slow in coming.

CHAPTER FIVE

The New King

Frederick William I of Prussia was only fifty-one, but the light was already flickering behind his eyes. Perhaps because there had been so many false alarms over the past decade, his eldest son paid little heed to each new worsening report from Potsdam. He seems to have been as obsessed with his own health as with his moribund father: he had been ill and Johann Theodor Eller von Brockhausen had put him on a diet. Less than a week before the king's death he was writing to his physician to ask if he might drink milk or lemon tea yet.[1] He was a model hypochondriac.

Indeed, Eller had instructions *not* to disturb Frederick with news of his father's decline. To Voltaire, Frederick had advanced his own diagnosis of the king's illness: a mixture of a wasting disease with dropsy, of which the most obvious symptoms were frequent vomiting. The king was deluding himself if he thought there was a cure. The crown prince had returned to the cold cynicism of 1735. Writing to the doctor on the 13th he summarised: 'One thing is certain, the disease is as extraordinary as the patient ...'[2] He was plainly waiting in the wings 'I can't turn back any more,' he told Voltaire. 'I shall miss my independence and rue the loss of my happy obscurity, I am obliged to mount the world's great stage.'[3]

For all his feigned indifference, Frederick was obliged to witness the deathbed drama. The king groused about having to forgive his enemies – in particular, his cousin George II of Great Britain.[4] He had important business to transact with his son, rehearsing him in the guidelines of his foreign policy: why the Hanoverian Alliance had been jettisoned and why he had backed the Austrian horse in 1728 instead. Finally he revealed to him the secret treaty he had concluded with France in a last ditch effort to salvage a portion of the duchies he had lusted after for so long. The king then summarised his views on the different European courts. Having accomplished this task, he exclaimed, 'Was God not gracious to send me such a splendid and worthy son?' At this Frederick wept, and kissed his father's hand. 'My God, I die in peace, that I have such a worthy son and successor.' Frederick was flattered too, and told Voltaire as much.[5]

The scene continued the next day with more effusions of sentiment. Frederick promised to be 'ever the true son and servant of the king'. At that point Frederick William effectively abdicated, handing over to him the reins of power. From this moment onwards, Frederick was to be addressed as His Royal Majesty. Frederick William's last gesture was to say goodbye to each member of his family in turn. Now the king was evidently content and could go quietly. His last words were uttered in his own dialect: 'Tot, Ick jraule nicht vor Dir!' ['Death, I fear thee not!'] and 'Lord Jesus, I love You, I die in You. You are my reward.'[6] With Frederick at his bedside, Frederick William finally rendered up his ghost at 3 p.m. on 31 May 1740.[7] Frederick over-dramatised his father's passing, making him into a figure from one of the neo-classical tragedies he liked so much. His father had expired, he wrote in the official version of the events, 'with the steadfastness of a philosopher and the resignation of a Christian'; while to Voltaire he said his father 'displayed proof in dying of Catonian stoicism'.[8]

The news reached Frederick's little court in Rheinsberg in the middle of the night. Bielfeld was tucked up in bed when he heard hoofs coming towards the palace and galloping over the wooden bridge below. It was 2 a.m. He poked his head out from the bed hangings, but all was dark and silent again, and he decided to remain under his featherbed. After a few minutes, however, Knobelsdorff tore open the door to his room and cried out, 'Get up quickly Bielfeld, the king is dead!' Downstairs the chief lady in waiting had a large bumper of wine filled and proposed a toast to the new monarch and his queen.[9]

The dead Cato left detailed instructions as to how he was to be treated after his demise. He was not actually buried until 22 June.[10] His corpse was to be washed and dressed in a fresh shirt, laid out on a wooden table, shaved and covered with a clean sheet. The regimental doctor had then to perform his autopsy, but he was forbidden to remove any of the dead king's organs. Knobelsdorff told Bielfeld that Frederick had countermanded his father's orders here and asked Jordan to carry out the operation and embalm the body.* After the examination, the late king was to be dressed in his best hat and uniform. The following day, the

---

* 'and you know well enough that when he is once in his hands he will never come to life again'. Bielfeld remarked, 'I could not forbear from laughing at this sally.'

Life Grenadiers were to parade under black flags with black coverings on their drums. The hymn 'O Haupt voll Blut und Wunden'* was to be sung, and Frederick and his ten-year-old brother Ferdinand were to walk behind the cortège in their uniforms. The two other boys had to remain with their regiments.

Frederick William's body was to be lain under the catalfalque designed for him by Knobelsdorff in the Garrison Church while the organ was played by Ludovici, the court Kapellmeister. He played an elegy composed by Graun to a Latin text written by the cleric Baumgarten.[11] This was surely Frederick's idea. After the service there were to be two salvoes from two dozen cannon. Then the party could begin: beer money was to be handed out to the grenadiers, and officers and generals were to broach the best cask of hock, 'as on this night nothing but good wine may be drunk'. Frederick avoided their boorish company, and dined alone.[12] Two weeks later all the churches in Brandenburg-Prussia were to offer a sermon on the theme of the dead king: 'My obsequies should certainly not render me despicable, but they should not praise me either.'[13]

'The Princess Royal alone seems unconcerned at the death of the king.'[14] She must have had warning that the comparative bliss of Rheinsberg was now to be replaced by another regimen in which she would play only the tiniest of roles. For her, the honeymoon – inadequate as it was – had come to an end.

[II]

With the king's mortal remains safely stowed away in their vault under the Garrison Church, the rule of Frederick II began in earnest. Master in his own house at last, Frederick wanted *all* his friends around him. The Mantuan Swan received a snippet of verse:

> Venez Algarotti, des bords de la Tamise,
> Partager avec nous notre destin heureux
> Hâtez-vous d'arriver en ces aimables lieux;
> Vous y retrouverez *liberté* pour devise.

> *Come Algarotti, run from the Thames' misty shore,*
> *And share with us in our most happy fate.*

* 'Oh Sacred Head Sore Wounded'. It is not clear whether it was the famous J. S. Bach setting in the *St Matthew Passion* of 1729.

Hurry now to join us in our pleasant state;
And find freedom's *our motto once more.*

Algarotti had a note from Caesarion too: 'The king has declared himself a [free]mason, and me too, in the wake of my hero. Consider me a master mason.'[15] Bielfeld had the job of opening the first lodge in the Prussian capital. At the initial meeting, William was admitted along with the duke of Holstein-Beck, Jordan and Fredersdorf.[16]

Algarotti came running. La Motte Fouqué who had left the country, disappointed at his slow promotion in the army, was called back from Denmark. Frederick gave him the Black Eagle and promoted him colonel.[17] Duhan had made polite enquiries. In the hand of a secretary he received the following: 'Monsieur Duhan, I have received your letter and in reply I will tell you that you may come here after you have obtained leave from where you are presently. Your affectionate king, Frederick.' Then in the king's own hand: 'My dear, my destiny has changed. I am looking forward to seeing you. Hurry.'[18]

For Voltaire he wasted three more days, then let the mask slip even further:

I was there at the king's final moments, for his torments and death. I certainly didn't need that lesson to become king, to be disgusted by the vanity of human grandeur.

Please don't see me as anything other than a zealous citizen, a slightly sceptical philosopher, but a truly faithful friend. For God's sake write to me as a man, and despise as I do, titles, names and all outward show.'[19]

To the faithful 'Diaphane' – Suhm – he wrote: 'Your letter went to the wrong address, as I had changed my destiny before it arrived. The wrapping, however, in no way alters what is inside, and the title in no way changes my way of thinking.'[20] Suhm was to sue to leave his Saxon masters, but in the meantime he had a new job. Instead of drumming up loans, he was to recruit for Frederick's Academy. The mathematician Euler was then in Saint Petersburg; Suhm was to offer him tempting sums to come to Berlin.

While his father had been blotchy faced, big headed, short necked, small and fat,[21] Frederick was graceful, small – he was only five foot two – and decently proportioned. His hair was light brown, 'carelessly curled', or tied back in a pig tail. 'His large blue eyes have at once something severe, soft and gracious.' Frederick's diminutive person made little impression: as Bielfeld put it, 'he would not have been chosen to have ruled in the place of Saul ...'[22] What struck people at the time was his alertness, directness and *politesse*.[23] As he grew older, his physical appearance and the state of personal cleanliness grew worse.

The arts and sciences were top priority. Not a month after his father's death Frederick was able to report to Voltaire: 'I have laid the foundations of our new academy. I have *acquired** Wolff, Maupertuis, Algarotti; and I am waiting for replies from s'Gravesande, de Vaucanson and Euler. I have established a new college for the encouragement of industry; I have hired painters and sculptors ...'† Maupertuis was a particular prize, who he thought would give the appropriate form to the revived institution. Frederick met him on his progress to Wesel and packed him off to Berlin: 'I hope that the coming together of so many talented intellectuals will contribute not a little to making a stay in Berlin more pleasant.'[24]

Frederick wanted to see his friends, but many were mistaken in their beliefs that the new king would honour them with wealth and positions of rank. His esteemed Jordan was made head of the national orphanages, hospitals and poorhouses. As for his Falstaff, Keyserlingk, it was not quite 'I know thee not, old man', but high office was not to be within his grasp. He was made adjutant-general, and had to stomach the snub: 'You are a very nice man, you have plenty of wit, you are extremely well-read and you sing and joke wonderfully, but your advice is that of a fool.'[25] Duhan was eventually rewarded with the directorship of the noblemen's academy in Silesian Liegnitz. He wrote to the king to find out what the functions of the post might be: 'They are to peacefully draw your salary, to love me, and to enjoy yourself.'[26] Both Frederick William and Frederick wanted to be loved, but they had very different ways of going about it: for one it was the stick; the other the carrot.

Algarotti's political counsel was not taken seriously either, but he could talk to Frederick about philosophy, art and architecture, and that was enough.[27] During those first few months, Algarotti was perhaps closest to Frederick after Keyserlingk. The queen mother, who had itched to play some sort of role for a generation, was shoved aside too. She would not be needed to intercede with her cousins across the water.[28] Yet she was better off than the queen his wife, who remained chiefly because

---

* My italics.

† Leonhard Euler accepted, Jacques de Vaucanson and Wilhelm Jakob s'Gravesende declined.

Frederick owed it to the Brunswicks, on whom he had depended largely these last few years. His sister Charlotte who had married the new duke of Brunswick was given her own suite in Berlin; not just, one suspects, because she had delivered Frederick's letters to Duhan.[29] Her sister-in-law, Frederick's wife and the duke's sister, had far less to boast about: she might stay in the Schloss in Berlin, but she was to have no access to the king in Charlottenburg or Potsdam.[30]

He had long since made up his mind on these matters: the succession was to go to William, who had been his father's favourite, and who settled matters with the Brunswicks by marrying Elisabeth's sister. After May 1740, Frederick set about educating his younger brother, whose schooling had been more or less cancelled after his father had interpreted Frederick's flight as a product of his fondness for literature and science.[31]

There was to be the bare minimum of a court. Frederick had made it clear, even as crown prince, that he would have no truck with baroque formality or the Spanish etiquette that encumbered the court in Vienna. When the late Field Marshal Grumbkow had written to the crown prince in old age complaining that he had not been addressed as 'your excellency', Frederick had pretended that he was perfectly confused when it came to titles: 'I accord count, marquis, duke, cousin, excellency, brother, etc., to anyone and everyone, without knowing whether I have got it right or not.'[32]

To mirror the other German courts, Frederick begrudgingly filled a few of the offices that had survived his father's broom. There were just nine court charges:[33] first gentleman of the bedchamber, first court marshal, chief equerry, court marshal, grand master of the wardrobe and the royal household, royal steward, marshal of the palace, master of the royal hunt, and the general director of the court theatre. They were not an impressive bunch: Graf Kameke was in charge of the wardrobe, and Fürst Coswaren-Loos held down the functions of grand chamberlain for a while. The office of grand equerry passed from Field Marshal Schwerin to his son at his death at the Battle of Prague. Possibly the most important court officer was the first chamberlain, Baron Pöllnitz, as he was the repository of Prussian tradition, such as it was. He had attended the coronation of the first king in Königsberg and could regale the new king's guests with tales of three reigns. More important, he had a small inkling of protocol.[34]

It was the most rudimentary court in all Europe. Frederick generally made do with a brace of chamberlains to present strangers and travellers,

who appealed greatly to the king. For their part, they generally found
Frederick's establishment tiresome: there was little room for the flirtation
and intrigue that they enjoyed at their home courts.[35] A contemporary
critic (almost certainly Voltaire) mocked the court's lack of pretension:

There is a chancellor, who never speaks, a master of the hunt who wouldn't
dare harm a quail, a grand master who does nothing, a steward who would be
hard pressed to tell you whether there is any wine in the cellars, a grand equerry
who hasn't the power to have a horse saddled, a chamberlain, who has never
handed him a shirt, a grand master of the wardrobe, who doesn't know the
identity of the court tailor; the functions of all these high-faluting offices are
exercised by one man, who is called Fredersdorf.[36]

Fredersdorf was seen by some as the most important man at court.
Voltaire called him the 'grand factotum' and resented him, probably
because of his discretion and his devotion to his master, neither of which
was the Frenchman's long suit. He might have pocketed small sums, but
he was not easy to corrupt. Officially he was the privy chamberlain and
chief treasurer, but his powers went well beyond these trivial offices, and
in today's terms he was head of Frederick's secret service. Whether
Frederick ennobled his humble friend is disputed, but he certainly awarded
him a nobleman's *Rittergut* at Zernikow, in the very year he acceded to
the throne. It has been pointed out that this was possibly even more
extreme than granting him a title, as Frederick was wholly opposed to
the middle classes acquiring the property of nobles.[37]

Fredersdorf was, by all reports, a model landlord. Zernikow was
improved and brick kilns and breweries were built before the great house,
which was erected in 1746.[38] He certainly made money. He had a 'colony'·
in the East Indies and breweries in both Spandau and Köpenick. A
'Fredersdorfer' was for a time a popular brew in Berlin. He built an
alchemical workshop in the Friedrichstrasse. At the age of forty-five he
acquired a rich wife too: Caroline Marie Elisabeth, daughter of the
Potsdam banker Daun. Frederick is supposed to have been greatly
opposed to the union; he was always difficult when his male friends opted
to marry. There were no children. When Fredersdorf died in January 1759
his old cartridge pouch as a simple soldier in the Schwerin Regiment was
laid on his grave. It was still there in 1983. His widow married a nobleman
second time round.[39]

The other important figure of Frederick's court was Maupertuis, who
as President of the Academy held an important office in Prussia. It was

not entirely as Voltaire put it – Frederick did not live 'without church, court or counsel' – but by the standards of his day, his household was remarkably unelaborate.[40] What court there was revolved around poor, stuttering Elisabeth: 'it was to her that they went on the appointed times on the fixed days, ministers, generals, envoys and courtiers; it was to her that foreigners and the like made their presentations: the etiquette was entirely with her court'. It must have been stultifyingly dull. Nothing was said, because no one had anything to report. There was nothing much to eat either: one night the wife of Field Marshal Schmettau had to make do with one preserved cherry. The same source mentions a facetious Frenchman quipping later on in Frederick's reign: 'There is a great gala at the queen's today ... for, as I crossed the Schloss [courtyard] I saw an old lamp lit on the grand staircase.'[41]

After 1740 Frederick's unmarried sisters Ulrica and Amalia were to some degree removed from Sophia Dorothea's power and had their own governess. The queen mother was compensated with a small court complete with marshal and chamberlain. The latter was a dullard called Morien. The marquis d'Argens apparently used to amuse himself by lending him the same book over and over again. He managed to get him to read it seven times in this manner. Finally Morien told him, 'Monsieur, I find it admirable. However, if I might be allowed to say, it seemed to me that the author repeated himself from time to time.'[42]

[III]

Frederick might not have been the builder his grandfather was, but he wanted Berlin and Potsdam to reflect his new glory. His taste was not to be the baroque formality of Frederick I, or the solid, doughty, homely style of his father. The Garrison Church and the Dutch *quartier* in Potsdam, and the Friedrichstadt in Berlin, were about to be upstaged by something more magnificent, and Knobelsdorff was once again selected to order Frederick's visions. Charlottenburg was the first project. Frederick had elected to live there as opposed to the royal Schloss in Berlin, where he would have been too accessible to the indigenous nobility and too close to his wife.[43] Charlottenburg was the building his father had hated, for it represented both the luxury of his own father's court and the onerous intellectual demands of his mother. For Frederick it was too small, and architecturally out of date. Knobelsdorff produced the thin east wing of the Schloss as a pendant to the orangery to the west of the main *corps de logis*. Outwardly it was remarkably plain. The six sets of Tuscan columns that currently provide its unique accent were added almost a century later.

With the interiors at Charlottenburg the rococo style made its first appearance in Berlin. Frederick wanted to continue the rich decorative treatment he had installed at Rheinsberg. The rococo appealed to him not just because its informality summed up his attitudes to courts, but also because of its graceful and jocular musicality. Another advantage in Frederick's eyes was that rococo was to some extent born out of the *obiter dicta* of his favourite painter: Watteau. The engraved edition of Watteau's works was published in 1736, at precisely the time Frederick was beginning his collection at Rheinsberg. At Charlottenburg, Frederick had the benefit of one of the ablest craftsmen of the period: the Berliner Johann August Nahl. Nahl had trained in Sigmaringen, Bern, Strasbourg, Paris and Italy. In Strasbourg, particularly, he had experienced at first hand the *Gesamtkunstwerk* that was the rococo when he worked on the Palais de Rohan-Soubise with Nicolas Pineau. Pineau had been responsible for the decoration of the Hôtel de Roquelaure in Paris.[44]

Nahl worked at Charlottenburg with Johann Michael Hoppenhaupt the elder, who carried out the designs for the Great Gallery.[45] The ceilings were Pesne's work.[46] As a compensation for losing all hope of political power, the queen mother's palace of Monbijou was also to have a complete refit,[47] and Grumbkow's old house, Schloss Niederschönhausen on the River Panke to the north of Berlin, was to be redecorated for Elisabeth. Berlin was rewrought in Frederick's image. In one of the few charitable passages in Voltaire's mean-spirited memoirs, he wrote, 'Now he turned his attention to embellishing the city of Berlin and building one of the loveliest opera houses in Europe and to bringing in artists of every sort ... Sparta became Athens.'[48]

A new suite of rooms and a temporary theatre were designed for the Berlin Schloss, including the inevitable circular study 'come [sic] à Rheinsberg'.[49] Frederick even toyed with the idea of pulling the whole thing down and putting up something with room for a proper garden.[50] The theatre was needed until the completion of Knobelsdorff's project to build a great new opera house on the Linden as part of the Forum Fridericianum. Finally, Frederick had projects for gardens too: the Tiergarten was to be relandscaped and turned into a public park, and he wanted a pleasure garden installed at Schloss Köpenick. Demolition orders were issued for buildings that marred the beauty of Monbijou or the

Academy.⁵¹ All this was already planned in July 1740. In October, Knobelsdorff was packed off on another journey, this time to study the monuments, paintings and sculpture of Paris.⁵²

[IV]

Bielfeld saw Frederick soon after his accession. He came to Charlottenburg on the night of 4 June. All the inns and alehouses were filled with the curious: 'there was not a morsel of black bread, nor a drop of bad beer, to be had for money'. Frederick was 'taking the waters' of Pyrmont (which he did from four till eight every morning)⁵³ in Keyserlingk's room. 'Caesarion' was having a splendid time. As the head of Frederick's 'joyous subjects', he was solicited by everyone who wanted to win the king's favour. The Saxon Johann Ulrich König was particularly well in with Caesarion. Keyserlingk read him snatches of Frederick's poetry ('Which one must without reserve recognise as masterpieces') and briefed him on the 'political catechism' that was *L'Antimachiavel.*⁵⁴ The Baltic baron's moment of glory went to his head: 'He runs about the garden and every part of the palace, with a little amber flageolet at his buttonhole; he plays upon his base viol, he sings, he laughs, he jokes, he rallies. I was fearful at the beginning that so violent an agitation would affect his head...'⁵⁵

And it did. Keyserlingk had a fit, and had to be borne off to his bed. Frederick was inconsolable. If anything, his love for his friend had grown since his father's death, and Keyserlingk even went so far as to proclaim himself the 'all-preferred'. While the Balt sweated in his fever, Frederick visited him every hour. When Caesarion grew iller, Frederick sent for news every fifteen minutes. Frederick recalled the days after Küstrin, when Keyserlingk had had the power to lift him from his depression and claimed he would never recover if he were to die. When the king was told that his friend was on the mend, Frederick's appetite returned: 'Praise be to God!' he said. 'I shall be able to eat my dinner tonight.'⁵⁶

Generally, solicitors got short shrift from Frederick. Bielfeld called 31 May 'the day of dupes', as so many had returned home unrewarded from the hard-hearted new king, grousing about his meanness and ingratitude.⁵⁷ Even his Rheinsberg friend Chasot was dismissed with a flea in his ear when he donned a ring with Frederick's portrait on it, without first seeking permission. On the other hand, there was to be no revenge on those who had had a hand in his misery in 1730. Grumbkow was dead, while Seckendorff had been locked up in the fortress in Graz by a furious

Charles VI for helping to lose a war against the Turks, and was to repay him by leading the Bavarian forces against his old master in the Wars of the Austrian Succession.[58] No one was allowed to mention the Küstrin days, not even Pöllnitz, although König did see a letter to Keyserlingk in which he made it clear that everyone involved would be forgiven.[59]

Katte's father was made a count, on the other hand, and promoted field marshal, but then, so was the more modestly born Algarotti, whose role – past, present or future – remained at best shadowy; and he was given a salary of 2400 thalers to boot.[60] The freemason Bielfeld was created a baron and put in charge of the education of little Ferdinand, Frederick's ten-year-old brother, the 'trouser-trumpeter', a boy of legendary incontinence. Kurt Christoph von Schwerin, who had been a major-general since 1720, was also made a field marshal. But that was enough titles; Frederick created very few in the course of his reign. He liked to give little presents, especially to his brothers and sisters who had lived such an austere life up till then: rings, watches, snuff boxes, fans, canes, porcelain, swords and seals. At Charlottenburg he kept a special cupboard full of such trifles, and the merchant Johann Ernst Gotzkowsky had the job of finding him suitable *objets d'art.*[61]

All Europe's courts scrutinised the behaviour of the young monarch. There was not a moment of idleness. A particularly hard winter had come to a close, and the people were hungry. Frederick had the storehouses opened and sold off the grain at bargain prices. He then issued orders to buy in foreign corn at any price. He was keen to show himself a just man. He abolished the practice of *sacken*: sewing up female child murderers in leather sacks and drowning them in the river.[62] His next move was more revolutionary, as the Hanoverian envoy, Gerlach Adolf von Münchhausen, reported to George II: 'He is not going to tolerate the use of torture in the future.'[63] In fact, Frederick retained torture for use in cases of *lèse majesté*, treason and mass-murder, only scrapping it altogether in 1755; but there is no evidence that it was used during the preceding decade and a half. The abolition of torture was naturally one of the enlightened causes he espoused, but Frederick's aversion may have had something to do with the events of 1730, when his friend Katte and others were threatened with the thumbscrew and the rack. Frederick returned to the subject in his *Dissertation sur les raisons d'établir ou d'abroger les lois* of 1749. Torture was both cruel and useless. By abolishing it, one was certain not to confuse the innocent and the guilty.[64]

There were no signs of pacifism in the new king. Far from it. In those

June days he created seven new regiments by a simple expedient of scrapping the *lange Kerls*, and adding a further 10,000 men to his already swollen ranks. Münchhausen thought this had been a deathbed suggestion from his father, who had pointed out that he might save himself 23,000 thalers a year and raise ten battalions in that way. Frederick, however, was not content to rest there: he added *sixteen* battalions, five squadrons of hussars and a squadron of life guards.[65] Certainly the move was expected of him; the giants had been a standing joke all over Europe. But even with so many new regiments, Frederick was not satisfied. He wanted assurances from his brother-in-law in Brunswick that he would have his men when the shooting started. Charles was reluctant, and Elisabeth had to intercede.[66]

Frederick had already introduced the manic schedule which he was to retain until his dying day: up at four, work till eight, writing till ten, reviewing troops until midday, literary work until five, followed by repose in the company of his friends.[67] To Jordan he wrote at the time: 'Adieu, I'm going to write to the king of France, compose a *solo*, pen some verses for Voltaire, change the rules of the army, and perform another hundred things of that sort.' Elsewhere he wrote to the same: 'You are right to believe that I work hard. I do that to live, for nothing comes closer to death than idleness.'[68]

The verses were suitably high-minded. He contradicted his letter to Jordan, telling Voltaire he would have no time for such frivolity as poetry and music: duty was his supreme God, but then, he confessed, he was not entirely cured of his 'metre-mania'. 'I float between twenty occupations and regret only the brevity of the days ... I assure you that the life of a man who exists only to think and for himself alone, seems to me infinitely preferable to one where the sole task is to make others happy.'[69] Frederick dispatched Camas, his new envoy to France, with some more tokay for the poet:

Hier vinrent, pour mon bonheur,	*Yesterday came, to my great joy,*
Deux bons tonneaux de Germanie;	*Two taut, impressive, bulging butts:*
L'un contient du vin de Hongrie,	*A cask of tokay from the Huns,*
Et l'autre est la panse rebondie	*The other, the gross, distended guts*
De monsieur votre ambassadeur.[70]	*Of Monsieur, your august envoy.*

From Brussels, Voltaire was able to report on French and Belgian opinion. His friend d'Argenson had said, 'He is beginning his reign as he seems to want to continue; everywhere he shows his heart and goodness; he gives justice to the late king, and offers tenderness to his subjects.'

Münchhausen had more to say about Frederick's foreign policy: He intended to do it all himself without taking counsel from any of his father's ministers. He sacked Eckhart, the financial adviser, and temporarily distanced himself from the minister Podewils. He also ostracised the same Schulenburg who had been fawning over him. As the Hanoverian put it, 'No one knows who's cook or who's the waiter.'[71] The Saxon envoy Manteuffel came to the conclusion that Frederick would carry on his father's foreign policy to the letter, which meant pressing for Jülich and Berg, where the Saxons were playing a slimy game. He gave no hope of a favourite or a mistress having any power over the new king; and as for his wife, he told Brühl: 'neither she nor any other woman on earth has up to now exercised a shadow of power over this ruler'.[72]

[v]

On 2 August, Frederick received the homage of his estates in the Berlin Schloss. He sat on a 'sort of throne', which the Danish minister Andreas August von Praetorius thought rather shabby. After the king had acknowledged the princes, diplomats and noblemen, he went out on to the balcony to greet the Berlin bourgeoisie. They shouted 'Es lebe der König' three times, and he tossed 4000 silver thalers into the crowd. He stayed on the balcony for half an hour: 'he appeared lost in observation'. Possibly he was thinking of the waste of money; possibly of the depravity of man. There were 500 at table that day. Once again Algarotti was by his side: 'His conversation must be infinitely pleasant,' said Praetorius.[73]

It was time for the first progress of his reign. He was obliged to go to East Prussia because that was, strictly speaking, where he was king. Voltaire had enquired whether he intended to go through the rigmarole of coronation or not. Enlightened thinking would have rejected such a move outright. Frederick was no more interested than his father had been. He replied that he had opted for the formula of a simple homage again rather than all that nonsensical and superstitious mumbo-jumbo.[74] It must have been a strange and novel sight, that initial journey to the east as king. Frederick went in a coach accompanied by his adjutant-general, Hacke, Algarotti and Keyserlingk, apparently arguing philosophy with the one; and jesting with the other of his friends.[75] Despite all his protests to the contrary, there were few *rendements de compte*: he stopped to review the regiment of the same Graf Schulenburg who had been his father's spy and dismissed the lot of them as 'a bunch of cripples'.[76]

After Königsberg, Frederick went west, stopping to see his sister Wilhelmina. She complained in her memoirs that she had had but one cold letter from him since his accession. Frederick, who had not lost his taste for travelling under assumed names, gave her scant warning of his desire to come to her at her father-in-law's austere retreat of Hermitage, which she was in the process of transforming into the delightful little palace we see today, by commissioning her father's architect Johann Friedrich Grael to build the new wings.[77] He came with William and Algarotti. His conversation with her was about superficial matters: perhaps he suspected her of wanting to meddle in his affairs like their mother; but she approved of Algarotti, as she was separately to pay court to Voltaire. She called him 'one of the greatest minds of the century'.[78]

Frederick was becoming as unpopular with his family as his father had been. To his sister Frederica (who could not abide him), he sent a counsellor in the interests of repairing her faithless marriage. Her husband, the margrave of Ansbach, had taken up with an English woman, Lady Craven. Something from this story was later written into Schiller's drama *Kabale und Liebe* of 1783.[79] Despite the plentiful evidence to the contrary, Wilhelmina decided that Frederick did not care for her any more. She turned once again to her character assassination: the king was losing popularity among his subjects; he was ill-treating his mother; he was failing to reward those who had been faithful to him in the past, and his meanness, 'they said, surpassed that of the late king'. He was angry, suspicious, defiant, haughty and sly.[80]

Frederick had other things on his mind: he wanted to go abroad, and see Paris, if that were possible.[81] Three Germans, an Italian and a dozen servants crossed the Rhine in late August. Frederick and Graf Wartensleben arrived in Strasbourg a day before the others and lodged at the inn called Le Corbeau, having used Frederick's ring to forge a passport to cross the frontier. Prince William and Algarotti spent that night in Kehl on the border, entered the city the next day and found beds at L'Espirit. The men were all in disguise: Frederick was the comte Dufour; William, Graf Schaffgotsch; Wartensleben, Herr von Weinheim; and Algarotti, Graf Pfuhl.[82] On the 26th, Marshal de Broglie made a full report of this curious impromptu visit to his master in Paris, the marquis de Breteuil: 'On arriving at the inn, the king of Prussia advised the landlord to prepare him the best cheer he could, and sent one of his valets to the café in order to bid, in the name of comte Dufour, three or four officers of those present to come sup with him.' Two captains from the Piedmont Regiment took up the challenge.

The next day Algarotti attended mass with the French governor. The others cried off, but William, Wartensleben and Algarotti lunched with Broglie. Frederick made his excuses, saying that he wanted to go out in his coach: to see the sights, climb the tower of the cathedral and inspect the soldiers of the garrison. He also looked over the new rococo interiors of the Palais Rohan-Soubise.[83] The French governor was distinctly suspicious: were these important travellers or a bunch of adventurers? He initially decided that Frederick was Prince William, as he did not believe the king would be so foolhardy as to come to France unannounced. The rest of the party joined Frederick at the comedy later.

Frederick's desire to mingle with the Strasbourgeois proved his undoing. As Broglie reported:

One of the city burghers, whose nephew had been pressed into the *lange Kerls*, and who had been refused permission to return home, and who had seen the king in Berlin, threw himself at [Frederick's] feet and asked for mercy for his nephew. The king of [sic] Prussia said that he was making a fool of him, that he was not the king at all. The burgher replied that he knew him well, and as proof he took out of his pocket one of the medals he had tossed to the people at his coronation [sic], and which he had picked up. The king of Prussia, seeing himself recognised, said that he had caught him out, but that he was to tell no one who he was. [The burgher] immediately went to warn M. de Trélaus, the king's lieutenant at Strasbourg, fearing punishment were he not to inform [on the king]. M. de Trélaus told me.[84]

Broglie dispatched two Prussian soldiers who had enlisted in local regiments. They too recognised the king. He summoned Wartensleben and told him that he knew it was Frederick and that he was prepared to grant him whatever hospitality he desired. 'I could plainly see that I had caused Herr von Weinheim [sic] great embarrassment.' He did not want to admit it was Frederick. Algarotti tried to save the day by telling Broglie that he was indeed a prince of the house of Brandenburg, but not Frederick. When Frederick too paid a call on the governor, Broglie asked him, 'Would Your Majesty prefer me to treat him as the king of [sic]

Prussia or as monsieur le comte Dufour? He only has to say.'[85]

Although Frederick continued to deny his kingship, he agreed to attend the play in Broglie's lodge and to sup with the governor. The news was out, however. A crowd had gathered outside the theatre, anxious to see the king in Prussia. Frederick decided that he did not want to see the comedy after all, but preferred to return to the inn and make his plans to depart. Broglie had been keen to avoid a diplomatic incident by arresting the king. He concluded that Frederick had gravely mismanaged the affair.[86]

Frederick singed his wings in Strasbourg; but he had a further pleasure in store: he was going to meet his idol, Voltaire. However, his anticipation was much tempered by the fact that he was laid low by a dose of quartain fever, which was 'more tenacious than a Jansenist'.[87] The original suggestion was that he should go to Voltaire in Brussels or Antwerp, but Frederick said he was too ill. For whatever reason, they met at Schloss Moyland, Frederick's apparently dilapidated residence in Cleves.

Voltaire left a highly coloured and untrustworthy account of their meeting, which took place between 11 and 14 September. The presence of Maupertuis did not augur well. Professional and personal jealousy (Maupertuis had been a lover of Emilie du Châtelet before Voltaire) led to friction. Voltaire made out that Maupertuis had proposed himself for the presidency of the Berlin Academy, when the truth was the reverse. Maupertuis was there when Voltaire arrived, staying in a barn (the account requires a good imagination) with Algarotti and Keyserlingk. But Voltaire need not have worried: Frederick was not over-impressed by Maupertuis. To Jordan he described him as a 'pretty boy and good company, but greatly inferior to Algarotti...'[88]

At the gate Voltaire found a single soldier mounting guard, while one of Frederick's ministers paced across the courtyard, blowing on his hands to keep them warm. Voltaire was taken into a small, bare room lit by a candle, where a little man dressed in a dressing gown made of coarse blue cloth was lying on a camp bed: 'It was the king, who shivered and sweated under a cheap blanket.' After making a bow, Voltaire began their 38-year relationship by taking Frederick's pulse 'just as if I had been his first physician'. Once the bout was over they sat down to eat and had a jolly supper at which the subjects treated in depth were 'the immortality of the soul, liberty and Plato's androgynes'.[89] Voltaire also recited his play *Mahomet ou le fanatisme*, which was to bring protests from the Sublime Porte when it was represented in Paris the following spring.

Frederick did not feel that the meeting had gone well. He wrote to Jordan, 'with people like that you shouldn't be ill; you should be really well, or better than usual ...' He was still obsessed with his literary hero: 'He is as eloquent as Cicero, as gentle as Pliny, and as wise as Agrippa; in a word he brings together all those admirable talents and virtues of the three greatest men of antiquity.'[90] Frederick was sharply critical of Emilie du Châtelet and her pitiful and, in his view, faulty book on physics. She was lucky to have Voltaire. Such naive hero-worship might lead one to believe that Frederick spent his time in Cleves between his camp bed and swooning in the company of Europe's leading intellectual.

He had other things on his mind, however. The barony of Herstall had been granted to Prussia at Utrecht, but the bishop of Liège had never yielded it up, and he had made matters worse by seizing and incarcerating one of the late king's press gangs in 1738. The tiny barony was believed too insignificant for Frederick William to want to upset the peace of Europe by sending in his troops, but Frederick thought differently. He was aware that any escalation could annoy the emperor, the bishop and possibly the French. Despite all that, he told Jordan he was preparing to frighten the bishop into submission. As early as 16 June he had dismissed his minister's advice on the affair: 'when you talk of war, it sounds like an Iroquois Indian speaking about astronomy'.[91]

Although he was unwell in Cleves, Frederick's mind was engaged: he was there to brief Major-General von Borcke. On 4 September he had sent the bishop an ultimatum accusing him of breaking international agreements and haranguing the people of Herstall (who had shown no inclination to become Prussian) for 'abominable disorder and disobedience'. Ten days later he occupied the town of Maseyck on the Meuse, and released it only after receiving compensation from the bishop amounting 200,000 thalers. The outside world had received its first indication of how Frederick could act with great decisiveness and brutality in his foreign policy. It was all very different to the late king. Some began to ask whether this was how he meant to continue.[92]

[VI]

Herstall was the rehearsal. The opportunity for a full-scale performance was afforded by the Austrian emperor's death. The king in Prussia was still feverish, and had returned to Rheinsberg where he expected a large party of all his favourite people. When Bielfeld turned up with the margraves of Ansbach and Bayreuth, there was no room at the palace, and once again he had to sleep at the inn. On 26 October a delegation from Berlin composed of the freemason Truchsess, Finckenstein and Pöllnitz brought Frederick the news that the emperor had died on the 2nd.[93] Bielfeld permitted himself a few reflections on the extinction of the august house of Habsburg. Finckenstein looked at the charred remains of the town of Rheinsberg: 'Before we have a new emperor, I am certain there will be many lives lost, and many cities reduced to the state we now see this.'[94]

Frederick's thoughts were rather more collected. He summoned Podewils and Schwerin, and he wrote to Voltaire, who was only then preparing to make his second pilgrimage to Prussia, this time to Rheinsberg:

the most unexpected event of all prevents me this once from opening up my soul to you as I usually do, and to chat as I would like. The emperor is dead...

This death disturbs all my pacific ideas, and I believe that come June it will be more about cannon shot, soldiers and trenches than actresses, ballets and theatre ... That business in Liège is all finished [but] those of the present time have far more moment ... it is the occasion for a total overhaul of the old system of politics in Europe...[95]

'Fatal as far as my book [*L'Antimachiavel*] is concerned, but glorious, perhaps, for me in person' was how he described events to Algarotti.[96] Frederick's letter to Voltaire contained some lines of verse describing the bankruptcy of Charles VI's system. These bellicose ideas of his were not so new. He had written to his brother-in-law, Charles of Brunswick, on 13 June in the same dismissive terms, talking of a 'ruined emperor, whose death will plunge Europe into bloody combat'.[97] He had borne a grudge against him for years, one which was fully justified, he felt, by the way his father had been treated over Jülich and Berg. In June he had described the emperor as 'an old ghost of an idol who once had might and potency but is nothing now; he was a strong man but the French and the Turks have given him the pox ...' When the news came, he wrote Charles off with cruel indifference. Officially six weeks' mourning was decreed for Frederick's overlord,[98] but he showed no signs of wanting to observe it himself: 'I'm not going to Berlin. A trifle such as the death of an emperor does not require great upheaval. It was all foreseen, all arranged: so, it is a question only of putting those plans into action which I have been hatching so long in my head.'[99]

He was not going to follow Frederick William's policy of close concert with Austria. He would choose such allies as suited his needs: 'Permanent alliances are chimeras.'[100] He did not feel bound by the Pragmatic Sanction, as Austria had not honoured its promises to win the duchies for Prussia.[101] There was some concern that, if he did not act, others would start helping themselves to the Habsburg Empire before him. Both the Bavarians and the Saxons had strong claims, and the former had been traditionally backed by the French in their desire to break the power of their Austrian rivals. The Bavarians were known to be interested in Upper Austria, the Tirol and possibly even Bohemia. The king of Sardinia was widely seen as having designs on Milan. Praetorious thought Frederick might be interested in the imperial crown, but Silesia was envisaged as a possibility too.[102]

The atmosphere at the house party must have been electric: guests came and went, there were all sorts of fun and games, and in the middle of it all a feverish prince was convening his senior officers to plan bloody war. He joked with Algarotti about the significance of the play they were performing: Voltaire's *Mort de César*: 'here we are gently acting out Caesars and [Mark] Antonys while we wait to imitate them more accurately'.[103] He also chided his friend about a dose of venereal disease he had caught in Berlin:

> Ami, le sexe de Berlin
> Est ou bien prude, ou bien catin,
> Et le sort de tous nos belles
> Est de passer par maintes main.
> Plaire, aimer, paraître fidèles
> Est l'effet de l'amour du
>   gain;
> Mais faites à donner, à prendre,
> Leur générosité sait rendre,
> Le soir, tout l'aquis du matin.
> De Naple un certain dieu mutin,
> Dieu de douleur, de repentence,
> Dit-on, s'assujetit la France,
> Et ravagea comme un lutin
> Tout con friand, tout verge enclin
> Au plaisir de l'intemperence.
> Bientôt du dieu la véhémence
> Le transporta chez le Germain.

> *Berlin's women enjoy high fame*
> *Being either prudes or on the game,*
> *And it can be said of all our belles*
> *Their sires they are ne'er the same.*
> *They'll flog their charms and earn*
> *   huge gains.*
> *By nature made to give and take*
> *All that by morning's toil they make,*
> *Come evening's end they will return.*
> *From Naples the most cheeky faun,*
> *God of misery and remorse,*
> *Has, so they say, conquered all France,*
> *And ravaged by some knavish trick,*
> *Each juicy cunt, each standing prick,*
> *Turned to the pursuit of pleasure.*
> *Now, a God who knows no leisure,*
> *Has slipped on his Teutonic boots,*
> *And it was only from some kindness,*
> *   sure,*

Ce n'est que par reconnaisance	*That some generous prostitute*
Que quelque équitable putain	*Has returned with thanks the soiled*
Vient de restituer son bien	*loot,*
Au gentil cygne de Florence.[104]	*Of a Florentine swan so pure.*

It has been pointed out that the anatomical references to Berlin's female prostitutes and the little presents they bestowed on their suitors were probably a euphemism.[105] Voltaire, on the other hand, felt no need to restrain himself in his more open references to the Italian's affection for men (in this case, the French ambassador's secretary),[106] and sent Frederick some piquant verses on Algarotti:

Mais quand, chez le gros Valori,	*Whenever, with fat Valori*
Je vois le tendre Algarotti	*I see tender Algarotti*
Dresser d'une vive embrassade	*Stiffen, with an electric pass,*
Le beau Lugeac, son jeune ami,	*Lugeac, his young friend so pretty,*
Je crois voir Socrate affermi	*I seem to see Socrates at last*
Sur la croupe d'Alcibiade;	*Clasped to Alcibiades' arse;*
Non pas le Socrate entêté,	*Not that stubborn Socrates whose*
De sophismes faisant parade,	*Sophisms showed a man of class,*
A l'oeil sombre, au nez épaté,	*He of somber eye and snub nose,*
A front large, à mine enfumée;	*With forehead broad and defiant pose;*
Mais Socrate Vénitien,	*But a Venetian Socrates*
Aux grands yeux, au nez aquilin	*With Roman nose and eyes which*
Du bon saint Charles Bor-	*tease*
romée.	*Like Charles Borromeo's, they said.*
Pour moi, très-désintéressé	*For me, quite disinterested*
Dans les affaires de la Grèce.	*In the things that went on in Greece,*
Pour Frédéric seul empressé	*For King Frederick's sake alone*
Je quittais l'étude et maîtresse;	*I quit my love and lost my peace;*
Je m'en étais debarrassé;	*I abandoned all that I own;*
Si je volais dans son empire,	*If I hurried to his empire,*
Ce fut au doux son de sa lyre;	*It was to the soft strains of the lyre;*
Mais la trompette m'a chassé.[107]	*But the trumpet has sent me home.*

Frederick did not seem to care; Algarotti was playing his cards right as far as he was concerned. His disappearance into the homosexual brothels of Berlin merely convinced the king that he needed him all the more. He had hung on for a role in Frederick's Prussia, now he was to be rewarded.

He was invested with the title of 'Graf' at the end of the year, and Frederick offered him the job of doing a little 'shuttle diplomacy' on the side. 'I know few, or, to put it better, no people, who are as universally talented as you are.' He reminded Algarotti of the 'caccia riserbata* ... I shall keep you back for the proper occasion.' The negotiations with Britain were over, but there were other courts, and the possession of a title would give him a little more credence. Tight-fisted Frederick even went so far as to offer him expenses.[108]

The festivities of Rheinsberg continued to conceal their sinister undertone: 'we dance, we rhyme, and my fever is over; in Berlin swans which burn their wings are on the mend'. Frederick had other fish to fry much of the time and was rarely to be seen at the queen's table.[109] Wilhelmina was there and sniffed in her memoirs, 'The time at Rheinsberg seemed to me pleasant only for the good company gathered there. I saw the king but rarely.'[110] Frederick's personal pleasure in his dawning glory was marred by the death of Diaphane. Suhm wrote to him on 3 November, 'My life approaches its end ... adieu, one more tear will wet your feet. Look on it graciously great king, as proof of the tender and unchanging attachment which your Diaphane devoted to you until his dying breath.'[111] He was the first of the Rheinsberg friends to die. Frederick told the Mantuan Swan that 'his memory will persist as long as there remains a drop of blood in my veins'.[112] He would learn to grieve: others would fall thick and fast in the course of the next two campaigns.[113]

Voltaire's arrival should have gone some way to lifting his despondency. Frederick was well, and the Frenchman was 'sparkling with new beauties, and much more sociable', and less hypochondriac (a trait he shared with Frederick), than he had been in Cleves. He might have been expecting Frederick to make him an offer. There was a rumour in France that he would become the new king's chief minister. Voltaire must have been hopeful: he had always fancied playing a political role.[114] Outwardly at least, Frederick could now fully indulge his artistic longings. Even if the Paduan Swan were missing,[115] he had the birds of Mitau and Cirey. 'Cure yourself of the wounds of Cythera, and make sure that we benefit from your wit in Berlin at least, while the whores take advantage of your body.'[116]

To Jordan, Frederick showed signs of impatience towards the great man. Voltaire's famed usury touched a raw nerve, as did his scornful

* The private hunt.

dismissal of some of the pictures in the royal collection – he thought the Watteaus fakes.[117] He had demanded cash to come. The king complained to Jordan, 'Your miser [i.e. Voltaire] will drink the dregs of his insatiable desire to make money; he is going to get 1300 thalers. His six-day appearance is going to cost me 550 thalers per diem. That is a lot to pay a lunatic; no court jester was ever paid such wages.'[118] Two days later, on 30 November, Frederick wrote again: 'The poet's head is as light as his works, and I flatter myself that Berlin will prove seductive enough to make him want to come again, all the more so as the purse of the marquise is not always so well stuffed as my own.'

CHAPTER SIX

Chasing Clouds of Glory

[1]

Nearly a month before, on 2 November 1740, Frederick had been closeted with his field marshal, Graf Schwerin, while the details were worked out for an invasion of Austrian Silesia: 'a rich, fertile country, well populated and buzzing with trade', which paid half the tax bill for Austria and Bohemia, or a quarter of the total for all the Habsburg lands. It was already clear that such a move would mean dropping the hereditary claims to the west German duchies.[1] Frederick started looking around for some dusty claim to the province. As it turned out, there was one, but as one writer has put it recently, it was no more than a 'fig-leaf to cover an act of blatant aggression': the orders to mobilise were given before the diplomats were informed of Frederick's plans.[2] Brandenburg-Prussia had indeed enjoyed rights of succession to Liegnitz, Brieg and Wohlau, which made up about a fifth of Silesia, but these had been renounced during the reign of Frederick's great-grandfather on the death of the last of the Piasts.[3]

Frederick William had suggested Silesia in his 1722 Political Testament. He did not approve the Great Elector's act, or his father's acquiescence in the interests of the royal title. He had built up the army; there was no question that Frederick was to go out and use it.[4] What the new king wrote to his minister was none the less true, 'of all the imperial lands, Silesia is the piece to which we have the most right', and he insisted that his ancestors were in no position to renounce it for their successors: 'his ancestors had repeatedly disclaimed all their pretensions because they were weak; he felt strong, and he revived them'.[5] Podewils was therefore given the job of legitimising the invasion by producing a proper legal claim to be sent to Graf Gotter, Prussia's man in Vienna: 'be my good charlatan, and use the best honey to sweeten the pill'.[6]

Once the province was in the bag, Frederick wrote in the *Histoire de mon temps* in more realpolitikal terms: Silesia was compensation for Berg, allied to a need for him to acquire a reputation and the necessity of rounding off the scattered and disorderly Prussian state.[7] There was naturally a frenzied diplomatic activity to cover Prussia's back. The Bavarians were encouraged to attack, and Austria's allies, the British, were reassured that 'the preservation and true well-being of the House of Austria' was Frederick's sole aim. Algarotti was now in work: the mercury baths would have to cease while he went off to sound out the king of Sardinia on attacking Austria from the rear. Meanwhile, Podewils was informed as early as 12 November that the 'bomb will go off on 1 December'.[8]

Frederick was enjoying scandalising the diplomats. To the Austrian envoy, the marchese de Botta d'Adorno, who had come to Rheinsberg specially to preach reason to the young king, he said, 'You find my troops attractive, I will show you that they are good too.' Frederick made Botta an offer he thought he would refuse: the cession of all Silesia for 2 million thalers and his support in putting Francis Stephen on the imperial throne.[9] The preparations for the campaign were exciting an interest everywhere, but Frederick was away in Rheinsberg, inaccessible to his subjects. Officers were called back to their regiments, and the public speculated on the possible target of Frederick's wrath. Many thought it would be Mecklenburg.[10] He wrote to Jordan, 'Berlin, they say, is like Lady Bellona in labour. I hope she'll give birth to something good and that I shall win the confidence of the public by a few bold and happy enterprises. Well, here I am in the most fortunate circumstances of my life, and in a position which could lay a solid foundation to my reputation.'[11]

He finally arrived in Berlin on 2 December, and amused himself by agreeing with Knobelsdorff the site of the new Opera House on the far side of the old town ditch.[12] Two days later, Berliners witnessed the departure of the troops. Frederick ran into one of his old tutors, Christoph Wilhelm von Kalkstein, who asked him, 'Your Majesty, am I right in thinking there is going to be a war?' 'Who can tell?' replied Frederick. 'The movement seems to be directed on Silesia,' suggested the courtier. Frederick took him by the hand and asked, 'Can you keep a secret?' 'Oh yes, Your Majesty.' 'Well, so can I!' said the king.[13]

Frederick pushed aside the Alte Dessauer too. This was to be his campaign, and the laurels were for him alone. He did not want 'the world to think he had gone to war with his tutor'. The old soldier was probably not too unhappy to be *limogé* in this way. He hated his late friend's son, and remembered his posing as a *petit maître* with contempt.[14] The cockiness was present in the words he wrote to Jordan once he was safely in possession of most of Silesia: 'My age, fiery passion, the lust for glory, curiosity even, [and] if I am to be perfectly frank, a secret instinct, tore me away from the sweet repose I was enjoying, as well as the satisfaction of seeing my name in the gazettes and thereafter in the pages of history, [that] seduced me.'[15] The language sounds shocking to our ears, but it was also the language of Racine and Corneille; of Frederick's favourite reading.

On 14 December, Frederick reached his 24,000-strong army at Crossen in the Brandenburg Neumark. On the 16th they marched into Silesia led by the Gardes du Corps, with their red and gold uniforms emblazoned with the Prussian motto *suum quique* (Frederick already assumed that Silesia was 'his own'). They quickly invested the towns of Glogau, Liegnitz, Schweidnitz and Neisse. Frederick wrote to Podewils: 'I have crossed the Rubicon with flapping flags and beating drums; my troops are full of good will, and the officers ambition; and our generals are thirsty for glory, all will go according to plan ... I shall not return to Berlin until I have made myself worthy of my blood...'[16]

On the 23rd he wrote to his sister, saying that he hoped to have reached Breslau by 10 January. He must have had advance intelligence of his popularity in the city: 'The gates will be opened and we will encounter too little resistance to make any claims to true glory ... If the mountains of Moravia don't stop us, I believe we could soon be before Vienna.'[17] Things went even better than he expected and on New Year's Eve they were camped in front of the Silesian capital, Breslau. The Protestants were jubilant. They even tried to send him a barrel of beer, but the gates were bolted and the cask came back. When he appeared within the walls a day later, the women too were excited at the sight of his soldiers in their fine uniforms. Already the Protestants could be heard telling their children: 'That is our king, our beloved ruler.'[18]

On 14 January 1741, Frederick wrote to Jordan, 'I announce to Your Serenity the conquest of Silesia, and I warn you that Neisse is being bombarded ... Be my Cicero and defend my rights and I shall be Caesar in the act.'[19] With Algarotti the tone was even more self-confident: 'I have begun to improve the shape of Prussia. The contours won't be completely regular ... the whole of Silesia is conquered besides a rundown fort that I'll maintain under siege, possibly until next spring ... In all the sixty thousand I have conquered, I have not found one comparable to the Swan of Padua.'[20] Frederick's glory days had melted even Wilhelmina's heart: 'It has to be said that you have learned the lessons of Maupertuis extremely well. He has circled the earth, and you have rounded off your country.'[21] Both Neisse and Glogau proved tougher nuts than he imagined. Leopold Max of Anhalt-Dessau, the Alte Dessauer's eldest son, took Glogau after a long siege on 9 March.[22]

Voltaire did not approve of the invasion of Silesia. He preferred the character of 'Frédéric le philosophe' to the warrior king. 'He is passionate about glory', he wrote to d'Argenson on 8 January 1741. 'It is true that I have left him; I have sacrificed him, but I love him, and, for the honour of humanity, I would like him to be nearly perfect, or as near as a king can be.' Frederick was, however, still under Voltaire's scrutiny: 'If he behaves badly, I shall break the trumpet with which I sang his praises.' Voltaire was increasingly disillusioned with his fan. He wrote to his friend Cideville in verse from Brussels in March, mocking northern kings who took themselves for Antonines:

J'ai vu s'enfuir leurs bons desseins	*I've seen his good intentions dropped*
Aux premiers sons de la trompette.	*At the first trumpet blast.*
Ils ne sont rien que des rois;	*They are nothing more than kings;*
Ils vont par de sanglants exploits	*And live their lives with bloody things,*
Prendre ou ravager des provinces	*They take or rape a few provinces*
L'ambition les a soumis.	*To suit their ambitious ends.*
Moi, j'y renoncer, adieu les princes;	*I give up, say goodbye princes*
Il me faut que des amis.[23]	*I want no one now but friends.*

Frederick's progress was rapid. Silesia was poorly defended and its people were largely sympathetic to the cause of the Protestant king.[24] The population was then 85 per cent German, with a sizeable Polish-speaking minority only in Upper Silesia. Frederick had problems with the upper classes, who were generally Catholic and loyal to Vienna, and naturally the clergy, to whom he showed a rough and intolerant approach. In Lower Silesia, two-thirds of the people were Protestant and did not believe that Austrians governed them in their interests. As recently as 1738, the law had been shown to be discriminatory towards the Protestant majority.[25] The Jesuit chaplain Rodel, for example, was obliged to admit that 'they always show innate hatred of us'. When he tried to rally the people with a ' "Praised be Jesus Christ!" the people muttered "Praised be the king of Prussia!" ' in reply.[26]

Jordan kept him up to date with the tittle-tattle in Berlin. The Protestant religion was seen by some Prussians – indeed, by Protestants all over Europe – as the only justification for the war. In some cases, commentators ignored the free-thinking reputation of the king of Prussia, and saw him as a religious champion, even ascribing to him the writing of prayers.[27] The confusion must have stemmed from his giving the theme for the sermon to be delivered in the churches of Breslau after the city was delivered up to him: Paul's First Epistle to Timothy, II, 11–12 was meant as a jibe against Maria Theresa: 'Let the woman learn in silence with all subjection. But I suffer not a woman to teach, nor to usurp authority over the man, but to be in silence.'[28]

Frederick would have been a fool wholly to ignore the religious cause where he could make it serve his needs, but it would be erroneous to say that he had launched the strike on behalf of Silesia's Protestants. He was none the less ready to admit that it influenced the fighting zeal of his men, and he made sure that the army was staffed with padres. Jordan wrote to him on 17 January to tell him of the departure of the 'Twelve Apostles': a dozen pastors were leaving for the front. It 'makes everyone happy. We have seen them prepare themselves for the journey with the same joy that people in the old days looked on those who left for the Holy Land.'[29]

Maria Theresa for one was not taken in. She called Frederick the Heretic-king; other epithets were 'the enemy without faith or justice', 'the evil animal' and 'the monster'.[30] Nor was she prepared to cede Silesia: 'Never, never, will the queen renounce an inch of all her hereditary lands, though she perish with all that remains to her. Rather the Turks before Vienna, rather cession of the Netherlands to France, rather any concession to Bavaria and Saxony, than renunciation of Silesia.'[31] It was all music to Frederick's ears. He boasted to Algarotti that in Vienna, 'They say public prayers against me', and soon he would be taken for the Antichrist himself.[32] The accession of an archduchess to the throne had not always been seen with great enthusiasm in the Habsburg lands. Maria Theresa's husband, Francis Stephen, was often perceived as a Frenchman rather than a German. Even in Vienna there were those who complained about the Pragmatic Sanction. Some hoped for better things from the elector of Bavaria. Someone daubed the walls with the following rhyme:

Vivat! Der Kaiser ist tot,	*Hurrah! The Emperor is dead.*
Wir bekommen jetzt grosses Brot.	*We Shall now get better bread,*
Der Lothringer ist uns zu schlecht.	*The Lorraine chap is rather bad.*
Der Bayer ist uns eher recht.[33]	*The Bavarian is our lad.*

She had better luck with the Hungarian nobility, which accepted her for their queen, or rather their king: *moriamur pro rege nostro Maria Theresia*, and agreed to do battle for her.[34]

So far the king of Prussia had skirmished and laid siege, but not fought a pitched battle. The Austrians were proving themselves better at *Kleinkrieg* than the Prussians. In February and March he was nearly captured by Austrian hussars. Frightened of what might happen if he fell into enemy hands,[35] he told William that he was his sole heir, and that he was to look after certain people – including Keyserlingk, Jordan, Fredersdorf and Eichel – after his death.[36] He wrote to Podewils in an overdramatic vein:

I issue you with the strictest orders, and you shall answer with your head, that in my absence [in captivity] you will not respect my commands, you will serve my brother [William] as adviser, and that the state will do no undignified act to secure my freedom. On the contrary, in this case, I wish and order it so that we should hit harder than ever ... I am the king only for as long as I am free. If I die, my corpse must be burned after the Roman manner and the ashes placed in an urn in Rheinsberg. If this happens then Knobelsdorff must design a monument on the model of Horace's at Tusculum.[37]

His chance was to come in the snows at Mollwitz in Upper Silesia on 10 April. Five days before, the Austrians had blocked his communications. Frederick's 22,000-strong force was still in its winter quarters when the Austrian general Graf Wilhelm von Neipperg moved up with a slightly smaller army, more heavily weighted to cavalry than Frederick's. Frederick took them by surprise as they were cooking their dinner. Under the Austrian cavalry charges, however, Prussian morale collapsed. Frederick could not fit all the elements of his army together and 'for a while [they] stood forlornly about like pieces left over from assembling a Christmas bicycle'.[38]

Frederick panicked and fled the battlefield, making for Oppeln where he found the town gates closed. In the process he was once again nearly captured by an Austrian squadron bent on pillage.[39] He eventually found refuge in a mill in the village of Löwen, where he spent the night with a lone ADC.[40] In the meantime, Schwerin rallied the Prussian infantry and turned the tables on the Austrians. Both sides lost about 1500 dead. 'The 20% butcher's bill was hardly unusual for the period.'[41] Frederick did not hear of the victory until the next day: 'I am on top of the world ... I have never experienced a more perfect satisfaction,' he told Jordan, while to his sister he wrote of 'one of the roughest battles fought in the memory of man'.[42] The horse that bore him to safety, the 'Mollwitz Grey', was granted honorary retirement in Potsdam. For the rest of its life it would occasionally take part, unbidden, in the trooping of the colours.[43]

In his own account of the battle, Frederick did not openly mention his ignominious flight. He satisfied himself with an oblique reference to 'young soldiers' suffering from premature despair.[44] To Jordan he was slightly more forthcoming: 'I was terribly alarmed yesterday, hearing the noise of the cannon and seeing the smoke of the powder from the height of the towers.'[45] Frederick or no Frederick, the world was impressed by the Prussian army which had carried the day. The Austrians were hypnotised by the efficiency of the Prussian fire and in their fear created a good deal of noise and smoke, but rarely hit their targets. Frederick learned quickly from his mistakes. The cavalry he had inherited from his father had proved inadequate. He immediately set about reforming it.[46]

[II]

The reputation of the new Marcus Aurelius attracted foreigners to Berlin. One who arrived soon after Mollwitz was Jean-Baptiste de Boyer, marquis d'Argens, a member of the Provençal *robe* eight years older than Frederick. A former diplomat and soldier, he had retired from the army after an accident and devoted himself to scandalising his fellow French nobles with his writing. Frederick was delighted that he sought refuge in Berlin; he awarded him a pension and the office of chamberlain, and put him in charge of court entertainment. D'Argens' pension was agreed as early as May 1741, but the money was a long time in coming, which might have been the reason why the Frenchman was so slow in reaching Berlin. The excise wanted to tax his library, and in June 1742 he wrote to complain to Frederick that 'a king who wins a complete victory every year and conquers two or three provinces has no need to impose a levy on philosophy'. When he did arrive, he found a friend in the duchess of Württemberg, who spent her life in bed. She had two bells on her bedside table: one to call for tokay, the other for champagne. Her company was no less agreeable to the Frenchman for the fact that he himself was horizontal half the time.[47]

D'Argens was lucky to escape for the time being. Frederick had insisted on bringing his other friends to Silesia to witness his feats of arms. Jordan, for one, grew dejected and bored. He wanted to go back to his books in Berlin.

Tout m'attriste en cette contrée;	*Everything's sad in this strange land;*
L'on y boit que du mauvais vin,	*The wine they quaff's as sour as sin,*
L'on n'y voit que fille infectée:	*Their poxy harlots should be banned:*
Que ne puis-je aller à Berlin...	*Can I go back home to Berlin?*
Le bruit du canon me réveille,	*I'm woken by the cannon shot,*
Le cri du soldat inhumain	*And savage soldiers make a din,*
Ne permet pas que je sommeille:	*And sleep here soundly I cannot.*
Que ne puis-je aller à Berlin.[48]	*Can't I go back home to Berlin?*

The First Silesian War was a two-battle conflict; a side-show to the War of the Austrian Succession. Between Mollwitz and the Battle of Chotusitz a year later, there was more diplomatic squabbling than fighting between Prussia and Austria. Having begun the scrap alone, Prussia had collected France with Bavaria as allies and they in turn had launched an attack on Austria from the west, encouraged by Frederick's assurances that he would vote for Charles Albert of Bavaria's candidacy for the imperial throne. Austria was in trouble. The knives were out: France wanted to destroy Habsburg power in Germany, and reduce Austria to Lower Austria, Hungary, Styria, Carinthia and Carniola; Bavaria was hoping for Bohemia, the Breisgau and the Tirol; and Saxony was being encouraged to think of gains in Upper Silesia and Moravia.[49]

Prussian control of part of Silesia was beginning to look like one of the lesser evils. The Austrians' reaction to defeat was to try to buy Frederick off by using their British allies. The British envoy to Vienna, Sir Thomas Robinson, offered him 2 million thalers together with Gelderland and Limburg. Frederick dismissed the offer as an insult and the diplomat as a scoundrel.[50] The king in Prussia, the author of *l'Antimachiavel*, was playing Tartuffe. He talked about the poor Protestants whom he was called upon to protect in Silesia, and whom he could not now abandon to a Catholic ruler.[51] Few of Europe's rulers or their ministers can have believed his sincerity. He was gaining a reputation for untrustworthiness.[52]

With the exception of brave little Neisse on the Oder, Silesia was wholly in Frederick's hands and he could set about consolidating his power by winning friends among the middle classes and the nobility. In July he confirmed the privileges of the burghers of Breslau, shelling out pensions and titles which were ever believed to please the flighty Silesians. Pöllnitz drew up a special list of nobles who might be wooed into Frederick's camp in this way. So much diplomatic and military activity swelled the heads and pockets of the Breslauers.[53] Those Catholic nobles who remained loyal to the queen of Hungary, he determined to make unwelcome in the hope that they would leave. In October the city's officers had to swear an oath to their new master at a lavish banquet. Two-headed Habsburg eagles were cleverly restitched to make Prussian ones. At a dinner of fifty covers, the municipal chef, Rieghe, dressed up chickens to look like Prussian eagles and wrote 'Fridericus Rex' in Breslauer sausages. Two dozen bottles of tokay were drunk and the guests went home with their pockets clinking with gold medals.[54]

Bielfeld came to Breslau too, and was summoned to Neisse to watch the siege. Fredersdorf found him lodgings and he ate at a long table with the king and the princes. After dinner with Schwerin he rode into the body of a deserter hanging from a tree. He told the king, who 'laughed heartily' at his fright. Frederick could now push forward into Moravia, but a phoney war replaced the glory days of earlier that year. He made Schwerin the scapegoat for his own shortcomings. He was already jealous of his laurels at Mollwitz and suspected that the field marshal had wanted to get him out of the way so that he could have the battle to himself: 'You wanted to run with the hare and hunt with the hounds, now you have lost both.' The victor of Mollwitz retired hurt. Frederick blamed his departure on a disagreement with the Alte Dessauer.[55] The Bavarians were now penetrating deeper into Upper Austria and Maria Theresa was facing defeat on all fronts. The need to protect their rear led the Austrians to seek at least a temporary agreement with Frederick. The result was the Treaty of Klein Schnellendorf, signed on 9 October.

This was an informal treaty which was designed to be kept secret from the French and the Bavarians, whom Frederick assured Prussia was still in the fray. Frederick would stop making war, all the while making the bellicose gestures that implied a desire to continue; in return Austria would agree to relinquish Lower Silesia and Neisse, which was to yield after a sham, two-week siege. The advantage of this shady pact was that it left Maria Theresa with two free hands for dealing with the French and the Bavarians. Indeed, Neipperg sent off his very first troops from Silesia the next day, an indication of how badly needed they were elsewhere.[56] Naturally Klein Schnellendorf has had its apologists. Frederick, they maintain, could not have sat back and allowed the French plan to go ahead, whereby the Habsburgs were wholly robbed of their German lands. Klein Schnellendorf was therefore a deliberate attempt to apply a brake to their apparent success.[57]

[III]

It was a pause for breath. The king came home and suffered the carnival in Berlin. He was able to use the new temporary theatre in the Schloss for a performance of Graun's *Rodelinda, regia dei Langobardi*.[58] On 6 January 1742, William was married to Elisabeth's little sister, Louise Amalia. Bielfeld had to present the bride with a crown of flowers in her bridal chamber. William was 'incommoded' by the dirty remarks uttered at the time. After the ceremony Frederick went up to Rheinsberg, hoping for the company of Voltaire and Maupertuis if possible.[59] Voltaire did not materialise, but they kept in contact by letter. Frederick told him that he did not want to leave his idyll again, but that longed-for time of peace and the muses was not to be.

The international stage was busy again. It was all right while Austria had been flat on its back, and Frederick had been living on the fat of a conquered province or two, but the Austrians were recovering quickly. Not so long ago, the Bavarians had been threatening Vienna itself. Now the tables were turned. There was a little side-show on 24 January when Charles Albert of Bavaria was elected Holy Roman Emperor at Frankfurt among a series of glittering balls and banquets. He received the sword of Charlemagne on 12 February, the first non-Habsburg to do so for more than three centuries.[60] The dream was shattered, however, when the new emperor lost his electorate. The Austrians took Munich that same month.

It was time for Frederick to re-enter the war. He travelled down to Dresden, the city looking 'like a magic lantern' in its beauty. He convinced the Saxons to join up with his forces and march into Moravia with him. He settled down in Olmütz, which was in the middle of its carnival, and corresponded with Algarotti who had settled in the Saxon capital, asking for news of La Faustin (Bordogni), the soprano wife of *il caro sassone*: the composer Hasse. He moved west to the southern Moravian town of Znaym, within easy striking distance of Lower Austria and Vienna. From here 15,000 hussars commanded by Hans Joachim von Zieten terrorised the locals in Stockerau and on the slopes of the Bisamberg. They were within four German miles (28 kilometres) of Vienna, and reportedly pulled up vegetables to take back to camp.[61] Wilhelmina wrote to him of the balls in Frankfurt, held to celebrate the accession of the ill-fated Charles VII. Frederick was unable to match her high living, for in Znaym there was only 'drill, bad roads, foraging and hussars'; it was dirty, the men were stupid and the women were ugly. There were too many vines and donkeys: Moravia in a nutshell.[62]

Here he considered annexing parts of Bohemia, rather than persisting in his demands for Upper Silesia. Frederick was bored. He asked Jordan for books: Boileau, Cicero's *Letters*, the *Discussions at Tusculum*, and the *Philippics*, and Caesar's *Commentaries*. In his idleness he was a menace to everyone in Berlin: Knobelsdorff was obliged to write reports on the state of his buildings, furniture and gardens, and the progress of his opera house on the Linden. When the report came back, Frederick found it lacking in detail: he wanted a description of every moulding in Charlottenburg, each one amounting to four pages in quarto. He made several attempts to get the French poet Gresset to accept an invitation to his court, but to no avail.[63]

Voltaire teased him about the slow progress he was making in mustering enough brain-power for his Academy. The royal ballet was another matter: 'Instead of a dozen good academicians, you have amassed, Sire, twelve good dancers. Such things are easier to find and a lot more jolly. From time to time we have seen a hero bored by academicians, where the stars of the opera might amuse him.'[64] Frederick recruited some musicians there and then. He found himself in the vicinity of Benda's parents' home at Neu-Benatek in Bohemia, and had Franz's little brother Joseph come and play the violin for him. He was so pleased with him that he brought the whole family to Berlin.[65] He missed Rheinsberg and his friends. Reports that both Jordan and Keyserlingk were sickening worried him. He found the local people unyielding and unfriendly; firmly committed to their Catholic ruler, they were reluctant to offer him any supplies.[66]

Fortresses continued to fall – Glatz gave in on 26 April – but the opportunity to do battle must have come as a relief. The action at Chotusitz[67] lasted for three hours on 17 May, and once again Frederick secured a bloody victory. This time there were greater losses among the enemy soldiers than in the Prussian ranks. The king was pleased with his victory; although modern commentators have called it closer to a draw, it had wide-ranging political benefits for Prussia.[68] He wrote to Jordan of his second success within thirteen months. 'Who would have believed it a few years back, that your pupil in philosophy, Cicero's in rhetoric and Bayle's in reason would play a military role in the world; who would have credited it that Providence would have chosen a poet to transform the European system.' Jordan reported back on the feeling in Berlin. He had run among the carriages to tell the people of the victory, stopping passers-by. He confessed that happiness had made off with his reason; he felt so elated, it was as if he had drunk too much champagne.[69]

Frederick had stayed to the end this time, and could witness the antics of a martial pastor from Anhalt called Joachim Seegebarth, who rallied both infantry and cavalry when they were on the point of disintegrating. Once again he disliked others hogging the limelight. The Alte Dessauer told him to reward the cleric a good living: 'And if that doesn't happen, I'll give him the best one in Dessau.' Frederick took the hint and granted him a cure in Brandenburg. It has been said that Frederick was so jealous of the pastor that he never uttered his name again, but this is also untrue. Voltaire mentioned him in his account of the war, and Seegebarth crops up in Frederick's correspondence with Jordan.[70]

After the battle Frederick wrote to Podewils to admit how strongly he longed for peace. The treasury, so well stocked at his father's death, was now all but exhausted.[71] He was nervous of committing his thoughts to paper as Austrian hussars had a nasty habit of capturing his couriers and stealing his letters to Algarotti, among others.[72] It was a new form of war, with which Frederick never came to grips: irregulars composed of *Grenzer* and *Pandur* units which moved behind the lines, pillaging at will and harrassing the more conventional forces, and capable of acts of startling brutality. An English woman who set eyes on some Croat irregulars at the time reported:

The men look scarcely human ... the swarthiness of their complexions, their size, their whiskers, the roughness of their dress, without linen, and with bare arms and legs, two or three brace of pistols stuck in their belts, besides other arms, and their habit of turning their heads and eyeballs all the same way to look at their general as they march, all combined together gives them a fierceness not to be described.[73]

Little more than a week later, the French succeeded in winning a battle at Sahay in Bohemia. Frederick sniffed. It was nothing compared to Chotusitz: 'The Battle of Pharsalus made less noise in Rome than this skirmish has done in Paris.' Not long after, Broglie, who had recently been made a duke to honour his military prowess, was routed by Pandurs before Prague. Frederick was moved to verse:

Le jeune Louis l'a fait duc	*Young Louis' made him a duke*
Pour honorer son savoir-faire;	*To honour his part in history;*
S'il eût été par l'archiduc,	*If this title'd come from the Archduke,*
J'entendrais bien le mystère.[74]	*I could fathom the mystery.*

Frederick wanted more news from his friends in Berlin: the progress of everything surrounding the opera house was one thing that absorbed him. Another was the libretto that he had had commissioned for Graun's *César et Cléopatre*. This was performed for the first time in the completed building on 7 December 1742. Algarotti was enjoying himself in Dresden, where he could send Frederick not only news of Hasse and la Faustina, but also sheet music. Frederick particularly wanted the aria *all' onor mio refletti* from the composer's *Lucio Papirio*.[75] His new buildings in Berlin were his 'dolls'.[76] Through Knobelsdorff he was even deep in negotiation with the French to buy Cardinal de Polignac's collection of antique marbles for Charlottenburg.[77]

[IV]

Frederick returned from the First Silesian War in the belief that he had been let down by the Saxons and the French, who had allowed him to bear the brunt of it all. Prussia was not rich enough to fight the long pocket-book of the British, who were backing the Austrians. It would be impossible to expect anything good from drawing the war out longer. He thought his allies guilty of not wanting to get their hands dirty. As he told the Saxon minister Bülow, 'You win crowns with cannons alone.'[78] Victory at Chotusitz also decided Frederick to leave his French allies in the lurch once again: 'we're quits,' he told them. Broglie, who was commanding the French army in Bohemia, remarked, 'he might have used more polite terms, but he didn't understand French'. As Voltaire rejoindered, he knew it only too well.[79]

At the Peace of Breslau in June, and the Treaty of Berlin in July,

Frederick was confirmed in his possession of all Silesia barring a small pocket around Teschen. He explained his conduct to his sister: 'I saw all my allies with their arms crossed, and, not wishing to take on the entire burden of the war, I have left them with the business of getting out of the mess as best they can.'[80] On 8 June 1742, he admitted to Podewils that Upper Silesia was a 'ruined and unsustainable country [and] the subjects will never be loyal to me'. His eyes roamed and settled on richer prizes: Königsgrätz in Bohemia, Mecklenburg or East Friesland.

He had none the less instructed his minister plenipotentiary to obtain *all* Silesia and the county of Glatz, '*Sine qua non* and for the rest anything else you can wring out of them'. The Austrians refused to grant him any greater title to Silesia than duke. Frederick replied in a coarse language that was sometimes his own: 'I don't give a fuck about titles, as long as I have the territory.' His royal title changed too: a few months later the beleaguered emperor returned a few favours by changing him from king *in* Prussia to a more authentic king *of* Prussia. At the time of the Breslau negotiations, he said his intention was a stable peace guaranteed by the maritime powers. This is more or less what he eventually established in 1748 at the Treaty of Aix-la-Chapelle, except that it was not stable at all.[81]

His behaviour towards his French allies drew some wry comments from his friend Voltaire, who was anxious for patronage from the French foreign ministry: 'You are no longer our ally, Sire? But you will become one of the human race ...' Voltaire was increasingly annoyed by the new Frederick. Already the callous 'roi des Bulgares' of his *Candide* was forming in his mind. He charged Frederick and his fellow kings with wanting to destroy mankind, and called him the 'blood-letter of nations'. Voltaire was, however, careful to couch these criticisms in a language that would not offend the king. He wanted to come to Berlin again and see the new Opera House. This was, of course, a pretext: he was hoping to make a little money out of the French state by spying on Frederick. The king took it in good heart. He pointed out that, if Voltaire had an army at his command, he would use it against his multitudinous enemies – real and imagined – in the French literary world.[82]

Reports of the cultural transformation of his capital sustained him. Pesne was finishing the ceiling in the music room at Charlottenburg with a representation of Parnassus and the muses, while Knobelsdorff was creating a suitable setting for the Polignac Collection. The architect was battling with the warrior king over the Opera House. Knobelsdorff had received copies of Inigo Jones designs sent to him by Bielfeld from

England and, ever the Palladian, wanted to adapt them to the site on the Linden. Frederick desired something more frilly and rococo. A compromise was struck in which the fussiness went inside and a cross between La Rotonda and the Villa Foscari rose on Berlin's grandest street.[83]

Potier, the ballet master, had arrived with La Roland and a troop of dancers. They did not stay long, as it turned out, and Frederick rued the departure of La Roland, even if he was heartily fed up with Potier. Later Frederick had to write to Rothenburg in Paris for replacements.[84] Algarotti was charged with the inscriptions for Knobelsdorff's buildings: for the opera house he composed 'Federicus Borussorum Rex Compostis armis Apollini et Musis donum dedit', which was an adaptation of the lines on the obelisk in Rome. It was eventually shortened to the 'Fridericus Rex Apollini et Musis' we still see today. For the Academy of Sciences Algarotti suggested 'Federicum Borussorum Rex Germania pacata Minervae reduci aedes sacravit'. Charlottenburg was to proclaim 'Federicum Borussorum Rex amplificado imperio sibi et urbi'.[85] Frederick was living Berlin life vicariously. He gave Jordan his schedule detailing his route from Silesia and convoked all his friends to be ready for him in Charlottenburg on the day of his return.[86]

Not convinced of his tenure in Silesia, Frederick took up its government with interest, boasting to Jordan that he had achieved more in a week than the Austrians had in eight years.[87] He prudently fortified Glogau, Brieg, Neisse, Glatz and Cosel, and set about rebuilding his armies using the experience of two years of war and the added funds that were available from Silesia.[88] It was an armed peace, but Frederick made the most of it. At the beginning of September, he went to Aachen to take the waters, hoping to see Voltaire there. His fellow hypochondriac tried to cry off again. In his then state he would be 'like an impotent man in the presence of his mistress', which would not do at all.[89] He was *too ill* to submit to a cure, he wailed; but in the end he came. The poet lodged in the king's apartment and they had a four-hour chat, two days running, during which Frederick again tried to convince him to move to Prussia.

Frederick indulged his lust for building and stocked up his academy with famous scientists and his theatre with dancers and 'harmonious capons'.[90] The Polignac marbles arrived undamaged and were arranged in the new wing in Charlottenburg. His circle closed in around him. It contained some new members: the plump 'Chevalier Bernin' (Knobelsdorff) was now flanked by M. des Eguilles (the marquis d'Argens) and the 'Limping Satyr' (Pöllnitz), the permanent butt of his jokes as a result of his frequent changes of religion. Frederick kept Rothenburg informed of the cronies: 'Pöllnitz is ill; Fouqué is drinking tokay and losing at chess; Keyserlingk is drinking water and writing elegies to his beloved...'[91]

D'Argens tried to take his office seriously and write comedies, but he gave up after everyone yawned during a performance of his *L'Embarras de la cour*.[92] Frederick was more excited about the operas he was planning for the carnival and the singers he had engaged: La Molteni, Leonardi, Paolino and Le Porporino.[93] The latter was a male soprano whom he tipped to become one of Europe's great virtuosi and referred to as his 'pupil'. On 6 December there was the first masked ball of the season. The much heralded production of *César et Cléopatre* opened at the Opera House the next day. It was conducted by Graun and Franz Benda, who were dressed in the style of the Paris opera: in red coats and full-bottomed wigs. Frederick entered the *parterre* from the left and seated himself in an armchair.[94]

The king was highly pleased with Graun's music and commissioned a new opera from him in *Artaxerxès*. There were family chores, not least two unmarried sisters, Ulrica and Amalia, who were enjoying what life Berlin and Potsdam had to offer and running up gambling debts. They even had the temerity to ask Frederick to pay them. History does not relate whether he did or not. At the same time, the Austrians were clamouring for compensation and Frederick instructed Podewils to see them off. Money was for the arts alone. In a language worthy of his father, he wrote: 'Le roi de Prusse ne paie rien.'[95]

Another drain on his pocket, Voltaire the secret-agent, reappeared in Berlin. The king had been coaxing him to the capital by stressing the hard time he was having with religious bigots in France, who still contrived to exclude him from his rightful place under the dome of the Académie française. Frederick wooed him with the offer of ample honours in Prussia. In Berlin he would be free of the 'Donkey of Mirepoix',[96] the former bishop who led the opposition to the poet in court circles: 'You won't find any Mirepoix donkeys here. We have a cardinal and a few bishops, some of whom make love in front and some from behind, who are more skilled in the theology of Epicurus than that of Saint Paul, and as a result, people who persecute no one ...' To put a little pressure on Voltaire, Frederick had some of the poet's nasty remarks about the former bishop circulated around Paris. It was a technique he had learned from a master – Voltaire himself.[97]

The Frenchman arrived on 30 August 1743. Although he was as smitten as ever, Frederick was suspicious that he had not been asked for the usual travel expenses and correctly surmised that Voltaire was spying on him. He was therefore hesitant about discussing matters of state with his friend.[98] Voltaire bought off his employers with letters stressing his intimate relationship with the Prussian king, who spent four hours a day closeted in Voltaire's apartment, where he amply revealed his foreign political 'intentions'. The king was disillusioned with the French: their defeat at Dettingen in June 1743, at the hands of his hated uncle George in person, did not inspire him to effusions of respect. He thought it a pitiful performance to be beaten by an army that had not prepared its campaign. He none the less made the right noises about finding a kingdom for the French puppet emperor.[99]

Frederick, William and Voltaire went off to Bayreuth together for two weeks in September to see Wilhelmina, who was doubtless delighted to have the chance to talk to the great mind again and show her brother the many little improvements she had made to her court. She was about to add Voltaire and Maupertuis to a little gallery of philosophers she had at Hermitage, and *Mérope* was performed in Voltaire's honour.[100] However, a new chill was breaking out between Frederick and his favourite sister. He thought she and her husband were taking Maria Theresa's side in the Silesian Wars, and she found him unhelpful in her attempts to deal with her husband's philandering with one of her ladies-in-waiting, Wilhelmine Dorothea von der Marwitz. Voltaire returned to Berlin with Chasot, who complained that the philosopher required two enemas a day.[101] Frederick and William continued their journey without Voltaire and visited their sister Frederica in Anhalt, admiring the work on the new Schloss there. Frederick had a deeper purpose of course: he was anxious to maintain supplies of fresh troops from his cousins.[102]

Voltaire departed on 12 October, promising Frederick that he would return to reside at his court. The king was so pleased that he immediately set about furnishing a house for him. The ambassador described the philosopher's activity as a joke.[103] There had been problems: Voltaire's cupidity ran counter to his own meanness. He also seemed to be getting ideas above his station. Not content with making a pass at the French ambassador's cook (she fought him off!),[104] he was now making cow eyes at Frederick's sister Ulrica. They acted together, and in their congress Voltaire forgot his place. He wrote her some verses as a birthday present, telling her that he had dreamed of her.

Souvent un peu de vérité
Se mêle au plus grossier mensonge.
Cette nuit, dans l'erreur d'un songe,
Au rang des rois j'étais monté;
Je vous aimais, princesse, et j'osais vous le dire.
Les dieux à mon reveil ne m'ont pas tout ôté;
Je n'ai perdu que mon empire.[105]

Often a little of what's true
Is mingled with a monstrous lie.
Last night in a false dream was I,
Risen to royal status like you;
I loved you princess, and dared to tell you straight.
I woke. The gods had not dashed all hope as they do.
I had lost merely my estate.

Frederick took a dim view and replied on Ulrica's behalf, comparing the proud Frenchman to both a dog and a cad:

On remarque pour l'ordinaire
Qu'un songe est analogue à notre caractère:
Un héros peut rêver qu'il a passé le Rhin,
Un marchand qu'il a fait fortune,
Un chien qu'il aboie à la lune.
Mais que Voltaire, en Prusse, à l'aide d'un mensonge,
S'imagine être roi pour faire le faquin
Ma foi, c'est abuser du songe.[106]

It is striking, you will concur,
How a dream is dictated by our character:
A general will dream of investing Baghdad;
A trader imagines a boom;
The dog even barks at the moon.
But Voltaire in Prussia, with the help of a lie,
Puts on a king's great purple robes to play the cad,
It's some outrageous dream, oh my!

One writer has maintained that Voltaire never forgave the slight contained in this lacklustre verse and itched to take his revenge. The stories of Frederick's homosexuality that travelled round Europe were the result.[107] It seems unlikely, however, that Voltaire would have returned in 1750 had he been so offended by Frederick's putting him down over Ulrica.

Theirs was a puzzling relationship. There was a permanent friction between them, and Voltaire never ceased to cause problems for the king by his indiscretions, yet they seemed to nourish one another. Despite the bad blood over Ulrica and Voltaire's ham-fisted espionage, Frederick was soon writing to him offering him all sorts of blandishments to take up residence in Berlin. He could have anything he wanted; the only chains were to consist of 'friendship and well-being'. Voltaire fobbed him off with the need to order his affairs, then teased him about Ulrica. He had reached Lille: 'Your Majesty, the queen mother and Princess Ulrica are irreplaceable. I don't yet possess the army of 300,000 men I'd need to abduct the princess, yet on the other hand, the king of France has more.' He received her portrait along with one of the queen mother. The former he kissed: 'she can blush if she likes'. He wrote another wicked verse:

> Il est fort insolent de baiser sans scrupule
> De votre auguste soeur les modestes appas;
> Mais les voir, les tenir, et ne les baiser pas,
> Cela serait trop ridicule.[108]

> *It is insolent to unscrupulously kiss*
> *Your most royal sister's modest charms: quite bad!*
> *But to see them, hold them, and not do this,*
> *Oh Sire! That would be simply mad.*

Frederick must have been relieved when events came to his rescue: 'My sister Ulrica is seeing part of your dream come true; a king has asked for her hand in marriage ... She is going to a land where her talents will allow her to perform a large and lovely role.'[109] Ulrica had been considered too old for a husband at twenty-two, but she fell on her feet. The heir to the Swedish throne was Duke Adolf Friedrich of Holstein-Gottorp, prince-bishop of Lübeck. The tsarina thought he needed a wife. Frederick was slightly cool about the marriage, possibly because Sweden was a client state of Russia, possibly because it involved his sister converting to Lutheranism, but it went ahead after a dummy ceremony the following July in Berlin, at which the prince-bishop was represented by Count Tessin.

Despite the absence of the groom, there was a lavish ball in the orangery in Charlottenburg and a supper where the guests ate off a gold service. The orange trees were in bloom and Italian opera was performed on a stage set up at the far end. 'The incomparable Solimbini here excelled herself.' Bielfeld found her 'more tender and more pleasing than [Giuseppe] Farinelli ... The one sings to the ear, the other to the heart.'[110] A fresh consignment of 'Italian capons' had arrived in the nick of time, including Pasqualino Bruscolini, Felice Salimbeni, Antonio Romani and Signora Venturini. Salimben or Salimbeni was considered one of the finest singers of his day. 'They are going to hold all Berlin spellbound.'[111]

The music might have gone to the head of Ulrica's sister Amalia, who might indeed have been jealous, and annoyed that she was to be the only girl who satisfied her father's gloomy prognosis that 'they won't all get husbands'. On that day it has been said that she fell for a very tall cadet in Frederick's Garde du Corps, Freiherr Friedrich von der Trenck, who had been robbed of the scarf from his expensive uniform. 'Come tonight and I will compensate you for your loss,' she is supposed to have said. In his account of the affair, he kept her identity secret, calling her 'a woman whom I could only observe with humility'. Trenck claims to have found the time to visit his mistress by pretending to be a passionate huntsman. He was finally betrayed by another officer, who was a 'brazen Ganymede'. Frederick then sought a pretext to have him placed out of harm's way.[112]

It is a good story and thrilled the public when Trenck's memoirs were published soon after Frederick and Amalia's deaths, but it has sadly been shown to be full of holes.[113] Only one thing might lead one to believe that there was indeed something between the baron and the princess, or that it was felt to be so at the time, and that is Voltaire's *Candide*. Cunégonde's father in the celebrated novel is called 'Thunder-ten-*tronkh*, one of the most powerful lords in Westphalia, where Candide was illegitimate. Candide's calvary begins when he 'innocently kissed the hand of the young lady with a vivacity, a sensibility and a quite particular grace; their lips met, their eyes glowed, their knees trembled, and their hands strayed'.[114] The baron promptly had Candide thrown out of the house. Was it a satire on the Trenck affair?[115]

It was four years late, but on 23 June Frederick felt he had enough members to revive the Academy, even if there were no specific building for it yet. As the secretary, Formey, put it, the death of Charles VI 'had distracted His Majesty and prevented him from carrying out at first the projects he had had for the advancement of the sciences'.[116] Assemblies alternated between the houses of Field Marshal Schmettau and Minister Borck. The first committee was largely made up of Frederick's governmental advisers, but Eller, Jordan and Bielfeld also took part. The latter drew up the new rules, which separated the Academy into four classes: mathematics, speculative philosophy, physics and experimental philosophy, and the polite arts.[117]

Frederick was reminded of the need for a good rapport with the Russians. Their appearance on the side of the Austrians would have spelled disaster for Frederick, and the chancellor Bestuzhev would certainly have stepped in on Austria's side had he not had his hands full with the Swedish War.[118] To win a few more friends at the Russian court, Frederick supported the marriage of Catherine, the daughter of one of his former generals, Prince Christian August of Anhalt-Zerbst, to the tsarina's heir, Peter the Great's grandson, Prince Peter Ulrich of Holstein-Gottorp. All the more so because Catherine's mother, who was to accompany her daughter to Russia, was doing a little secret work for Frederick at the time, in return for finding a place for a favourite sister at the head of the Prussian-owned religious foundation at Quedlinburg in the Harz.[119]

Catherine and her mother set out from Zerbst on 10 January 1744. On the way they stopped in Berlin. It was the carnival and ball season. Graun's *Alexandre et Porus* to a libretto by Metastasio had been performed in the new Opera House in the run-up to Christmas.[120] Catherine had to sit next to Frederick at a ball supper and they spoke of opera, comedy, poetry and dancing: 'at first I was very shy with him,' Catherine wrote later, 'but I gradually got into my stride. At the end we were getting on very well, so that the whole company stared to see His Majesty conversing with a child.'[121] It was a peaceful meeting of two minds, later to be seen as the greatest monarchs of their age.

[v]

The Austrians had driven the hapless Charles Albert from his electorate and now he was a pantomime emperor without land or subjects. Concessions would have to be offered, but clearly not at the expense of Silesia, where Maria Theresa was encouraging civil disobedience. Frederick responded by cooling down his earlier policy of driving out elements unsympathetic to Prussia.[122] Austria could have the Breisgau back, and the bishoprics of Salzburg and Passau could be secularised and awarded to them. Frederick began to notice Maria Theresa's son Joseph. His birth on 13 March 1741 had been greeted with 'that's but a trifle here'. Now he was offering him the title of king of the Romans and the succession as Holy Roman Emperor when the time came. France needed to keep him in the war until they could pull something out of it.[123] At the end of May, Frederick picked up a new territory he had coveted: the last prince of East Friesland died, and Frederick quickly moved in to claim his succession. It gave him a useful north sea port in Emden.[124]

On 5 June 1744 Frederick's ambassador in Paris, Graf Friedrich Rudolf Rothenburg, concluded a new alliance with the French. Prussia would go to war again in order to create a kingdom for Charles Albert in Bohemia. At least the path was familiar now. Frederick's armies marched straight into Moravia and Bohemia and stopped before Prague. He taunted the French ambassador, Valory: 'My fat friend, we will take Prague while your Frenchmen simply make mistakes.'[125] After a six-day siege in September 1744, the city commander, General Ogilvy, surrendered. Frederick abandoned the Bohemian capital soon after, but regretted his action, blaming it on too great a consideration for his allies.[126] He was forced, however, to admit that his communications with Silesia were simply not good enough now that Saxony was in the Austrian camp. The Bohemians, one and all, hated him. Food and other supplies could not be procured easily from the population, and long before Bonaparte uttered his famous line, Frederick was categorical: 'the stomach was the foundation stone in the building of an army'.[127]

The Prussian army was starved, frozen and harassed out of Bohemia. Once more Austrian Hussars and irregulars not only destroyed his lines of communication, they also menaced the retreating army's rear, alighting on any poorly guarded baggage train and slaughtering stragglers. It could not be said that Frederick had lost a battle, but in terms of death and desertion, he had suffered more during a humiliating retreat. As much as a third of his army might have been put out of commission during the return march.[128] Also while he had been away in Bohemia, the wolves had broken into his new sheep pen. He wrote to Louis XV to tell him that Upper Silesia and Glatz were 'flooded with twenty or so thousand Hungarians ... I have gathered my troops to tidy up the land and purge it of that infamous race.' Little over a week later he told the duc de Noailles that they were already on their way.[129]

On 20 January 1745, Emperor Charles VII expired, thereby removing the point of this costly exercise. It now looked certain that Francis Stephen would be elected in his stead. No death could have been worse planned. Frederick was as anxious as ever to wriggle out of his commitments to France.[130] Friends were dying on him too. In April 1745 he learned of the fatal illness of Jordan, who was just forty-four: 'Don't upset me with your sickness. You make me sad, as I love you with all my heart.' Césarion was fading too. It was Podewils who broke the bad news. Frederick wrote back: 'I am more dead than alive at the reception of your announcement. In three months I have lost both my most trusted companions. Now I am just a stranger in Berlin without ties or true friends. The news has touched me so deeply that I cannot write any more. Reason and philosophy must fall silent before worldly grief.' To Duhan he wrote that he felt like a widow and an orphan all in one. He told Duhan to look after himself, as he was practically the unique remaining member of his old inner circle.[131]

Frederick had the chance to redeem himself on 4 June. The greatest battle of the Second Silesian War – probably of either – was Hohen-friedberg. Some would say that it stands with Leuthen as Frederick's greatest achievement in the field.[132] Frederick's reforms to the cavalry had paid off, and both the Zieten Hussars and the Bayreuth Dragoons played a disproportionate role in the victory. Together with the Alte Dessauer's son, Leopold, Frederick routed the combined Austrian and Saxon army, capturing over 7000 officers and men and 77 flags and standards, and killing 4000. Austrian and Saxon losses were three times as great as Prussian: 'an unusual proportion in the eighteenth century'.[133]

Frederick was proud not only of his own, but also of his brothers' performances. He told Leopold's father that the 'Prussian army had never distinguished itself in that way.' They 'fought like lions for the Fatherland. The Romans never achieved anything so brilliant.' To Podewils he expressed the vain hope that Hohenfriedberg would bring about lasting peace. He thought that the victory might placate the French and wrote to Louis XV to inform him that he had paid him back in kind for Fontenoy. To his old tutor Duhan, he boasted less: 'passing successes should not bloat the pride of the thinking man'.[134]

Frederick discovered that Trenck, the purported lover of his sister Amalia, was in correspondence with his cousin, the Pandur leader Colonel Franz von der Trenck; the man later suspected of lightening Frederick of his baggage train at Soor. Colonel Trenck had expressed a desire to make his cousin his heir. The king had the Prussian Trenck arrested and taken to his friend La Motte Fouqué in Glatz, where he was locked up in the fortress.[135] The fact that Frederick entrusted Trenck to Fouqué again suggests that the king took the business very seriously indeed; he feared Pandur Trenck *et al.* far more than any conventional Austrian forces. It must have been for this reason that he had the Garde du Corps imprisoned for treason, rather than *lèse majesté*. Fouqué had been given a political role in the very Catholic county of Glatz, where the people were not well disposed towards their new master. He developed a reputation for ruthlessness, especially towards the irregulars, and hanged as many 'brigands' as he could, leaving them swinging from trees on the public highway.[136] Trenck later called Fouqué 'an enemy of mankind', and found the earliest opportunity to slip his chains.[137]

Frederick was ordering art by the yard. In July, Rothenburg had found him a clutch of Watteaus and a huge table in Paris to add to the Lancrets he had bought him in March. He also wanted a big sculpture for his garden, presumably at Sanssouci: 'I don't care about the subject, as long as it is pretty.' Another Lancret was purchased in May. It represented the *commedia dell'arte* and cost 1200 thalers. Attempts were made to interest him in a Le Moine and a Poussin, but the dealer Petit was told that His Majesty was not interested. To use his ambassador in this way was not so strange, when it is known that he had sent one of his 'capons', Porporino, to look for paintings too. It was not just art that Frederick received from his man in Paris. Rothenburg was there to procure pommade, perfumed powders, samphire, vine rootstock (muscat and others) and Spanish 'snow' hams, which were to be sent directly to Joyard.[138] Thiériot was ordered to buy some Shakespeare as well as a *Traité contre le pouvoir de l'imagination des Femmes enceintes sur leurs enfants*.

The Battle of Soor on 30 September did not look so glorious as Hohenfriedberg at first: the Austrians and their allies caught Frederick's army napping 'in their blankets' and their lack of preparedness allowed Hungarian hussars and others to plunder at will. Frederick rallied his men, but not without personal danger to himself. His horse's head was shattered by a bullet. 'You see, I was in the soup right up to my ears, but no shot can touch me!' he boasted to Fredersdorf.[139] Soor proved another victory, although, by Frederick's own admission, not so decisive as Hohenfriedberg: the Austrians were able to make good their escape. Still, Prussian losses were a little over half those sustained by the Austrians and to the Alte Dessauer he claimed the enemy were 'totally defeated once again'. He was still cross with his eldest sister for not offering him whole-hearted support: 'We have just beaten the Austrians, or your Imperial [army] or whatever you please to call it. I think they will have their fill.'[140]

The king's sense of personal loss at Soor was considerable: more macabre irregulars lightened the Philosopher King not only of his books, snuff boxes, flutes and ciphers, but also of his secretary Eichel and some of his favourite dogs. For a while he thought poor Eichel dead. Elisabeth's brother Albert was indeed killed, which came as a shock to Frederick's queen. In her grief she even went so far as to complain of the king's indifference to her in a letter to her surviving brother Ferdinand. Those lost among his favourites included 'the good, brave [Georg Vivigenz von] Wedell', 'our Achilles'. Henry distinguished himself again at the battle, and Frederick always gave him credit for his performances.[141]

Quantz was commissioned to make Frederick two new flutes, one with a strong and another with a gentle tone.[142] He wrote to Podewils to organise a *Te Deum* in Berlin and to Duhan to make good the reading matter at the very least, telling him to look for the works in Jordan's library. The list had grown. He wanted not only the same works by Cicero (plus the *Catalines*), but also Bossuet on history, Lucian, the last edition of Voltaire, including the complete *Henriade*, Horace, Gresset, Chaulieu, Jean-Baptiste Rousseau, the military writer Feuquières, the last two campaigns of Turenne, Voltaire's *Poème de Fontenoy* (which celebrated Marshal Saxe's victory over the British) and Montesquieu's *Lettres Persanes*.

Frederick was wondering if this string of victories was enough. Was the public satisfied? Or did he need to 'box the Austrians' ears again'?[143] He actually set out for home, and was busy giving Fredersdorf instructions as to who was to be invited to a welcoming dinner, but he had to return to the theatre of war when he learned that the Austrians had regrouped.[144] Kesseldorf was the last martial incarnation of the Alte Dessauer, who had stepped in to lend his friend's son a helping hand. Before the battle he expressed his homely religion in a prayer: 'Lord God help me, and if you don't want to, at least don't help those rogues, our enemies, but watch over us while we fight. Amen. In Jesus' name, *march!*'[145] The Austrians and Saxons certainly got the promised drubbing: they lost between a third and a half their army. Frederick took off his hat and embraced the old general 'as a sign of reconciliation'.[146] The enemy was on the run: 'We are routing them everywhere. Nowhere do they hold ranks.'[147] Frederick's armies now headed for the heart of Saxony to press home their victory. Since the time of Charles XII, no one had undertaken such a rapid march through such pitiful conditions. His troops arrived in Leipzig on 1 December 1745.[148]

Frederick had arrived in Dresden at the right time: on 18 December there was a performance of Hasse's most popular opera, *Arminio*, which impressed him deeply. But even going to the opera every night and sending huge consignments of Meissen porcelain back to Berlin was not enough.[149] He was in a gloomy mood again, although that might have had something to do with digestion. He told his faithful Fredersdorf that he was as 'constipated as a Turk' and that his belly was as fat as a barrel.[150] When the peace was signed in Dresden on Christmas Day, he expressed the hope that reason would replace lunacy from now on. He was confirmed in his possession of the whole of Silesia once again, and in turn he gave his *a posteriori* vote for the election of Francis Stephen as Holy Roman Emperor. His new friend, the secretary of the French legation in the Saxon capital, Claude Etienne Darget, congratulated him on bringing peace to Europe. Frederick wrote in reply that he had been made aware of the fickleness of his position: 'Had I been unlucky today I'd be a ruler without a throne and my subjects would be suffering a terrible fate ... My God, shall I never enjoy my life? From now on I shan't hurt a fly, except to defend myself.'[151]

Frederick returned to his capital on 28 December. He stopped for lunch at the hated house of Wusterhausen, which he had given to William. Berlin had experienced moments of uncertainty when it was thought that the city might fall to the enemy.[152] Dawn was announced by a peal of bells and the militia began to assemble before the houses of their captains. Prince Henry went to join his brothers at Wusterhausen, and all three drove into town in an open phaeton. On the heath at Britz to the south of Berlin, they were met by a procession of young mounted merchants from the city, led by the royal postmaster. There were a hundred postillions in blue, the butchers in brown, the master of the forests and the huntsmen in green, followed by volunteers, pages, guards and coaches stuffed with nobles.[153]

At the gates there was a deputation from the municipal magistrates waiting to welcome Frederick to his residence. 'The king of Prussia returned to Berlin to enjoy the fruits of his victory. He was received under triumphal arches. All the people tossed him laurel wreaths crying: "Es lebe Friedrich der Grosse". Others shouted, "Vivat Friedericus Magnus" or "Vivat, vivat Friedericus rex, victor, augustus, magnus, felix, pater patriae!" Whatever the language, the feeling was much the same. The people were overjoyed to see their victorious king: Frederick the Great.[154]

CHAPTER SEVEN

Frederick the Great

[1]

Frederick was not impressed by the effusion of popular joy or the bright lights that had been kindled for his homecoming. He had another death to deal with: in this case his former tutor, Duhan de Jandun. Frederick, with all three of his brothers, rode straight round to Duhan's house. 'It was a noble sight, to see a dying man surrounded by princes, and by a triumphant monarch, who in the midst of the incessant clamour of exultation, sought only to alleviate the sick man's pains.' Frederick was indeed touchingly fond of the man who, despite the most fervent opposition imaginable, had first incited his love of art, poetry and philosophy. Duhan died the next day and Frederick agreed to look after his old teacher's family. His sister was given a pension, married a French nobleman, and lived next door to Princess Amalia on the Linden.[1]

He had missed Christmas, but the carnival was in full swing. Three days after His Majesty's return, there was a Feast of Peace in the new Opera House, followed by a masked ball. It lasted until late into the night. At noon the next day, Bielfeld saw two women come out dressed as shepherdesses, 'who, it seems, after sacrificing liberally to Bacchus, had delivered themselves up to Morpheus ...' They made such a noise that someone let them out on to the street, where they were instantly surrounded by 'a number of boys and rabble, who pursued them with jeers, quite to the next guardhouse, where they took refuge'.[2]

Frederick had little time for frivolity. Prussia was in tatters and 8 million thalers of Frederick William's carefully amassed coin had gone up in smoke, leaving just 15,000. In the last stages of the war, he had melted down the silver in Schloss Charlottenburg and considered selling the port of Emden in East Friesland to the British for a million thalers.[3] It has been calculated that, between 1740 and 1756, Frederick spent 83 per cent of his revenues on arms. The war had another side to it, however: it had been a source of employment and certain members of Prussia's small manufacturing class had been able to line their pockets. The privileged Potsdam firm of Splitgerber and Daun,[4] for example, were now making 300 muskets a week. Nor was the war as unpopular with the peasantry as some have said. Deserters often re-enlisted, and not too many questions were asked. The cantonal system meant that regiments had become like football teams, and there was a fierce loyalty towards them in the villages, and for the squires who led them in the field.[5]

He needed to take stock of his wasted land. He made his progresses, often with members of his own circle rather than the appropriate ministers. Bielfeld, for example, accompanied him to Silesia, Magdeburg and Stettin. It was the first time that a reigning monarch had visited Silesia since 1611. Here Frederick was happy to introduce a new system to replace the one left behind by the Habsburgs. Silesia now became the launching pad for administrative reforms.[6] One of the first steps was to bring it into line with the rest of Prussia by abolishing the power of the local nobility, creating two administrative chambers and appointing a minister, Ludwig Wilhem Graf von Münchow, to oversee the whole. Gradual changes were also made to Silesian law.[7]

Frederick claimed that travelling with a small retinue meant less distress for his people. As his old coach passed through the villages, he received petitions and enquired after grievances. 'He then turns the poison into wholesome food',[8] although some petitions were treated with contempt, especially if they required more money. A civil servant complained that he had had the same job for too long. Frederick replied that he had a pack of old mules in his stables, who had been doing their job for ages; none, however, would become an equerry.[9] A Huguenot pastor who thought his stipend too mean was told to take his mind off earthly things; they were the king's affair, and unfitting for a man of his cloth: 'Remember that the Apostles went barefoot and had no income whatsoever.'[10]

Cynical about the Prussian church, of which he liked to pose as the titular head, being archbishop of Magdeburg, Frederick plundered the sinecures that had survived the reformation in Brandenburg and Silesia as a means of rewarding his ministers and friends. Graf Gotter voiced the habitual complaint that he was unable to live on his salary. Frederick bid him be patient until a canonry worth 8–10,000 thalers fall vacant in Halberstadt. When Gotter left his service, Frederick was quick to reassume the canonry for use elsewhere.[11] Such cynicism, however, had not prevented him from attending Lutheran services in Dresden during the peace negotiations to court the Saxon Protestants, including a Christmas service in the Frauenkirche. Frederick was initially popular in Saxony, where the population disapproved of their own king's mercenary conversion to Catholicism.[12]

It was his father's style: a few words scribbled in the margin settled the issue. Voltaire exaggerated Frederick's omniscience, but little escaped his attention: 'In this way all the affairs of state could be expedited in an hour', wrote the Frenchman. 'It was rare that ministers or secretaries of state met him. There were some who never spoke to him. His father, the king, had put finances in such good order, everything was executed with military precision, [and] obedience was so blind, that a land four hundred leagues long was administered like an abbey.' Frederick's Berlin-based General Directory numbered seventy-three persons in 1747–8, including six ministers. On top of these there were five private secretaries and fifteen more lowly clerks. Three years later the number of civil servants in all Prussia was still around 3000. That was very small.[13]

Manufactures were to be given a boost too. Only a year after the peace, Wilhelmina was writing to her brother to thank him for a Christmas present of cloth manufactured in Berlin. It was almost certainly made by the Pole Gotzkowsky, who had had the sense to cultivate Frederick in his youth. He started a textile factory in Berlin around 1730, and from the time of Frederick's accession imported fancy cloth. Wilhelmina was impressed: 'I am amazed that the manufacture of material in Berlin should have made such progress in this time ...'[14] Silesia was a great financial boon to Frederick. Already for the strife-filled year of 1745/6, the new province yielded 687,000 thalers, of which more than two-thirds derived from the salt monopoly. There was also mining, linen weaving, glass, pottery and the business houses of Breslau, which maintained their contacts with markets in Britain, Spain and South America. Ten years after its annexation, Silesian exports amounted to 10 million thalers: 45 per cent of Prussia's exports and 44 per cent of its imports.[15]

Frederick had also inherited East Friesland, a centre for ship-building and access to the North Sea, which brought him in an additional 48,000 thalers. The province's law was overhauled and many quaint local and inefficient customs went with it in the idea of putting East Friesland's administration on a 'Prussian footing'. Frederick received no homage from the territory until his first visit in June 1751, when he was received with great enthusiasm. He came again four years later on his way to Holland, and launched a ship. By that time East Friesland was exporting to the value of 300,000 thalers a year.[16]

Frederick was also keen to 'acquire provinces in peacetime' by max-
imising land use. Once again it was a reform project that had been first
aired in his father's time. The Oderbruch was the area which chiefly
required attention: the swampy land on the left bank of the Oder between
Frankfurt and Stettin.[17] The first attempts to reclaim it took place in 1746,
as soon as Frederick returned from the Second Silesian War. The engineer
was naturally a Dutchman, Simon Leonhard van Haarlem, an expert on
dykes, who worked in concert with Frederick's mathematician Euler. By
1753 as much as 10,000 hectares of land had been drained and was ready
for the first 1200 or so settlers from all over Germany and Poland. The
work continued unabated throughout the Seven Years War and ended up
creating twenty-one new villages. To make the new settlements more
attractive, the peasants had only to pay a sum in rent, and not carry out
the feudal services that were still incumbent on peasants elsewhere. This
caused widespread resentment. At the end of the decade there were even
a few peasant uprisings in East Prussia.[18]

Frederick William had also had plans for Pomerania. Under Frederick,
forests were cleared for settlement. The new villages commemorated
important officials in the General Directory, so there was even a Cocce-
jidorf and a Moritzfelder named after the Prince of Anhalt Dessau who
was placed in charge of the project; a Schwerinstal and a Möllendorf
named after two important generals; and an Amelienhof named after
Frederick's sister. On the Pomeranian coast, Frederick constructed the
port of Swinemünde at the mouth of the River Swine. Neither Frederick nor his architects appear to have lavished much attention on
the new port, although it grew up and prospered in its own way. Theodor
Fontane, who went to live there in 1827, described it as 'an unlovely
hole'.[19]

The war had killed peasants and destroyed villages. Where possible the
land was to be repopulated by attracting industrious non-Prussians. In
Upper Silesia this had the added advantage of diluting the heavily Catholic
and anti-Prussian blood in the villages. The repopulation took place in
the Electoral Mark too, however. There were as many as 50,000 new
royal subjects created in this way before 1756. One unusual case was the
colony of Bohemian Protestants at Nowawes on the right bank of the
Havel across from Potsdam. This was the creation of Georg Benda, the
father of Frederick's musicians of that name. He had clearly been itching
to shed his Catholicism and reveal his true Protestant self. The houses
were built on the pattern established after the Rheinsberg fire. A number

of these have survived in an altered state. Nowawes is Czech for 'new village'.[20]

There was time now to institute reforms, but there were to be no wide-ranging changes. Frederick was happy enough to continue the system he inherited from his father.[21] Attention might be given in some domains, however. Jordan had been appointed to shake up the universities. At his death the work was allocated to Bielfeld, another member of the Rheinsberg circle. In 1740 there were more *studiosi* in theology than in any other subject, especially in Halle, where Pietism still reigned. Frederick showed his contempt for his father's pet cause by both reinstating and ennobling Wolff in 1745. He wanted more lawyers and cameralists and changed the curriculum appropriately, introducing the system of unpaid *Referendäre*, legal pupils who helped perform the work of the courts. From now on the student would be so regulated by the state that he was the next best thing to a bureaucrat. In his reforms of the judiciary, Frederick allowed himself to be led by his minister, Cocceji.[22]

From 31 May 1746, Prussia opted out of imperial justice with the scrapping of the appeals to Vienna. This liberated it from the constraints imposed by German law. Already in 1738 Frederick William had asked Cocceji to draw up a complete legal code. After the demise of the appellate jurisdiction, Frederick asked him again. The results were the *Codex Fridericianus Pomeranicus* and the *Codex Fridericianus Marchicus* of 1747 to 1748.[23] Appeals went to the king. Voltaire cites the case of a man who had enjoyed a love affair with a she-donkey, which was a capital offence. Frederick minuted that the sentence was annulled: 'in his lands one could enjoy freedom of both conscience and penis'. A similar tale is told of the cavalry trooper who was found to have sodomised his horse. Frederick again refused to enact the punishment deemed due in the circumstances: 'The man is a pig', he wrote. 'Transfer him to the infantry.'[24]

[II]

Three times during the Silesian Wars, Frederick had reneged on his alliances and earned himself the name of an untrustworthy partner. He was still keen to keep in with the great powers – Britain and Russia in particular. He knew that business remained unsettled between him and Maria Theresa even despite the guarantees of his ownership of Silesia meted out at the Conference of Aix-la-Chapelle, but he never descended to personal insult, beyond speculating on who might wear the trousers in that *ménage*. For some of the lesser states he had nothing but contempt. He particularly singled out aristocratic oligarchies such as Poland, Sweden and Holland: 'former great powers', he called them. He was happy to use spies as much as possible, and his espionage network was managed by the super-loyal Fredersdorf, who had infiltrated the Austrian embassy in Berlin by means of the mistress of the ambassador's secretary. Similarly, Frederick had copies of the dispatches which passed through the Saxon court by means of a corrupt official.[25]

Gone was the golden boy, the sensitive, philosophic prince so cruelly suppressed by his paranoid, thuggish father; here, posing as his opposite, was Machiavelli's champion. To mark the change in his image, Frederick wrote a new introduction to *L'Antimachiavel*, in which he made it clear that it was better to break your word – those 'nécessités fâcheuses' – than to let your state be consumed by your enemies.[26]

The diplomats' judgements reflect Frederick's new status as Europe's bugbear. The French ambassador, the marquis Guy de Valory, provided his superiors with a lengthy pen portrait of Frederick.

He is small and of noble comportment. His build is irregular; his hips sit too high and his legs are too fat. He has handsome blue eyes, which bulge out a little too much, but which easily betray his mood; so that their expression changes according to his different states of mind ... His hair is thick, he has a winning mouth and nose, his smile is amiable and spiritual, but often bitter and mocking.

Valory was struck by his maniacal coffee drinking. By his own admission he consumed 'only six or seven cups in the morning now ... and after lunch just one pot'. It had not always been so. He once drank forty cups in an attempt to see if he could do without sleep. His body went through such agonies as a result that it was years before he believed he had fully recovered from the experiment. He was addicted to strong tastes: even at the end of his life he tended to lace his morning cup with mustard.[27]

'The king does everything by extremes...' Valory had noted his tendency to misanthropy and his uncanny knack of preaching against it as a vice in the same breath. He was mean, mistrustful and hypocritical; constantly changing his opinion, and causing endless havoc among his ministers by meddling in everything they did. Valory was prepared to concede Frederick's talents in the field, but not in every other domain where he felt himself gifted. Valory damningly compared Frederick's passion for the arts to his father's for tall soldiers. 'It is impossible to be more intellectual, but it is certainly possible to put your intellect to better use.'[28]

Another diplomat who reported to the French foreign minister was the Jacobite Richard Talbot, Lord Tyrconnell. His interpretation of Frederick's character has less authority than Valory's, the fat marquis had spent many years observing his subject, and had often been the butt of his satire:

The king of Prussia is an extremely contradictory character. He loves greatness, glory and actually everything that improves his fame abroad. Despite this he is the shyest and most indecisive person, without a spark of courage or nerve. He always sees the events in the blackest light and suffers from the greatest fear ... The king is distrustful by nature and generally thinks that mankind is beyond redemption.[29]

Charles Hanbury-Williams had been enjoying life as envoy to the fun-loving court of Saxony before he received the unwelcome posting to Berlin. In Dresden he had been frustrated by his unsuccessful attempts to learn the secrets of the Prussian court. He hated Frederick. He was 'a jealous and suspicious prince who can't bear to have his own actions pry'd into, while at the same time he leaves no stone unturned nor any means (good or bad) unemployed to penetrate into those of other peoples'. His mission was a failure from the start: Frederick scarcely even bothered to observe the protocol required for foreign envoys: 'he looks upon [them] as spies of the most dangerous sort...'[30]

It was Frederick's second nature: he was not the man to allow a dangerous being to come too close. A natural paranoia had been amply supplemented by the trials of his childhood and adolescence. For a man who liked to see himself as a patron of the arts, he was strangely suspicious of portrait painters. As he told Voltaire in no uncertain terms, 'I am not being painted, I never have myself painted; I can therefore only offer you medals.'[31]

Pesne and Knobelsdorff's portraits were seen as sufficient for the medals he handed out to the likes of Voltaire. Chodowiecki or Graff, or anyone else who wanted to draw him, had to make their sketches as well as they might while Frederick was out on parade.[32]

Antoine Pesne was cold-shouldered when Frederick became king and toyed with the idea of going home. Frederick wrote to Jordan in May 1743 to try to calm him down. Money, it seems, was the problem: 'endeavour to dissuade Pesne from emigration. He is a lunatic who will be paid, and who, after thirty years in Berlin, has not been able to cure himself of the inconstancy and frivolity of his nation'.[33] Either lucre or Jordan had its effect: Pesne died in his city of adoption fourteen years later.

Besides medals Frederick ordered snuff boxes in profusion, and dished them out as other monarchs awarded titles. It was the court jeweller, Jordan (the brother of his dead friend), who commissioned the artists concerned. The Danziger Daniel Chodowiecki, the Prussian Hogarth, was responsible for engraving the famous print of Frederick on his horse, but their relationship was fraught. Frederick would have himself depicted in no mythological scenes. He did not want to see himself as Hercules with a lyre or Apollo with a bow. When Chodowiecki made a plate of this type, Frederick told him to destroy it: 'This costume,' he told the artist, 'is only for theatre people.'[34]

Rather than Chodowiecki's realism, Frederick preferred Georg Friedrich Schmidt 'because he engraved in the French manner', or some of the other minor talents of the time, such as Bernhard Rode, who became famous for his hagiographical prints based on popular anecdotes from Frederick's life. It was Schmidt who engraved the *Mémoires pour servir à l'histoire de la maison de Brandebourg.*[35]

[III]

Not only was it important to re-establish his kingdom, but the arts and sciences were also at the forefront of Frederick's mind. Only two weeks after his return Maupertuis, freed from Austrian captivity (they had, in fact, treated him with respect), was pestering Frederick for his patent as president of the Academy: 'that position first made honourable by Leibniz, and rendered ridiculous by Gundling[36] ... will be for me, Sire, what you want it to be'. Frederick responded with uncharacteristic speed for an issue requiring an outlay of funds. Maupertuis had his patent on 1 February, and took up the position on 3 March. He was to discover that Frederick was not so easy to work with.

When Maupertuis asked for money to found a professorship of astronomy, Frederick told him he was 'as poor as a church mouse': 'He is founding a great number of villages for the peasantry. When they have been looked after, some consideration will be given to astronomers.'[37] Maupertuis proved to be one of the few foreigners whom Frederick lured up to Berlin who stuck it out till almost the bitter end (he died in Basel in 1759), but then he was unique in his decision to marry a Prussian: Eleonore von Borck, lady-in-waiting to Princess Amalia. D'Alembert resisted all efforts to get him to settle in Berlin. He thought the idea of being President of the Berlin Academy too dull.[38]

On 1 December 1745 Frederick expressed the view that he might not return to Berlin until he could listen to opera in peace.[39] The Berlin House had adopted the latest Italian architectural fashions, which had been brought to northern Europe by the Galli-Bibiena family, and more specifically to Berlin by Giuseppe Galli-Bibiena. The world on stage was hived off from the audience in the *parterre* and the boxes, separated by the orchestra, which was increasingly relegated to a formal pit.[40] The Berlin Opera was soon up and running, and Frederick had a first-class orchestra to play in it. He had even recruited a few oboists and bassoon players while he was in Dresden in December. There were now the keyboard players: Schale and C. P. E. Bach; twelve violins, including J. G. Graun and the brothers Franz and Joseph Benda; four violas; four cellos; three double basses; four flutes, including Quantz; four oboes; two bassoons; one forest horn; a theorbo; and a harp.

To stress Franz Benda's importance to Frederick, it should be said that his salary had climbed to 800 thalers, which was four-fifths of that paid to the king's personal physician or the marshal of the king's court; and that was before bonuses. On the other hand, it was small compared to Frederick's favourite 'capons', or indeed Alessandro Scarlatti's pupil Quantz. La Gasparini received 1700; Porporino and Quantz (who finally entered Frederick's service in 1742), 2000; and Salimbeni, all of 3000 thalers.[41]

Opera was to be performed in Berlin on Mondays and Fridays in December and January, and on the queen mother's birthday in April. While the king was ordinarily resident in Potsdam, there was a daily concert in the Schloss from 7 to 9 p.m. and an occasional intermezzo in the Schloss theatre. Two operas were commissioned every year, with provision for six performances of each. Whereas the comedy on the Gensdarmenmarkt needed to be paid for, in principle the Opera House was like the contemporary British Museum: free to all those possessing a decent pair of shoes; in reality, however, most of the seats were reserved before the performance.[42]

C. H. Graun was the man about whom the whole edifice turned. He had been summoned to Charlottenburg in 1740. 'Now I have also thought about him,' Frederick told Graun, employing the third person he generally used to speak to his subjects, 'from now on he shall receive an annual stipend of 2000 thalers and every opera [he writes] will be specially remunerated.' Graun was astonished: 'Good grief, Your Majesty. That is a great deal!' Keyserlingk, who was present, laughed: 'You are the first person to say so.' Frederick reportedly smiled in a good-humoured way about this reference to his habitual parsimony and continued, 'I will also let him have money to travel to Italy, where he must go immediately after I set off for [East] Prussia, and find me male and female singers and bring them back.' Graun asked more questions, but Fredersdorf cut him short: 'They must be of the sort that we don't have to return.' Graun was also instructed to obtain a libretto from Metastasio, but not a long one.[43]

Frederick did not realise it, but his greatest catch was C. P. E. Bach, who also enlisted in the royal orchestra at his accession. There was a character clash, and the monarch, who found the younger Bach 'irksome', did not value him as much as some others who are largely forgotten today: Benda, Johann Friedrich Agricola, Johann Philipp Kirnberger (who was Konzertmeister to Amalia), Christoph Nichelmann or Christoph Schaffrath. Yet Frederick and Amalia, who was also a patron of music, managed to hang on to Bach until 1767, before he left for Hamburg. As the king wanted to be centre of attention at the nightly concert, Quantz was more important to him than anyone else. He is thought to have composed most of Frederick's 300-strong repertoire of concertos for flute and orchestra. Monotony was avoided by 'an orderly rotation'.[44]

For a while the fifteen-year-old J. C. Bach was also in Potsdam, joining his brother Emmanuel after Johann Sebastian's death in 1750.[45] Christian would have found himself in his elder brother's 'friendship circle': men of letters and musicians such as Rammler, Lessing, Sulzer, Agricola, Krause and Graun. Emmanuel Bach satirised them in his 'character pieces'. There was 'La Gleim', about the poet Johann Wilhelm Ludwig Gleim, who was secretary first to Prince William of Brandenburg-Schwedt, then to the Alte Dessauer, until he was rewarded with a sinecure as canon and secretary to the chapter in Halberstadt, where he whiled away his time, the champion of German letters, until his death in 1803. Gleim's character was 'urbane and slightly hypochondriac'. 'La Polt' commemorated Johann Heinrich Polt, professor of medicine; while 'La Stahl' referred to another physician whom Bach stayed with in 1741.[46]

It was never easy to work for Frederick, and musicians were no exceptions. While the king hated German singers, comparing the noise they made to a neighing horse, life was scarcely easier for his favourite Italians. The singer Annibali begged him for the chance to rest before he attended an audition before the king. Frederick said no. When Annibali sang unmelodiously, he turned on Graun: 'Can't he [i.e. Graun] hear that he is singing out of tune? Can't he hear that he is dragging [the music], that he has no ear? That he is not keeping to the tempo?' He was reportedly as tough with his performers as he was with his troops. He stood behind the conductor at the opera with his eyes on the score to make sure that no one played a wrong note.[47]

Berlin and Potsdam had been under wraps during the wars, but now the scaffolding was coming down to reveal an architectural conception entirely different from Frederick William's. For a mean man, Frederick built a fair number of palaces. Sanssouci was to be his most representative: a statement about both the man and his informal idea of kingship; a retreat for him and his surviving friends. Because Frederick interfered so much with his artists, few found it tolerable to stay with him for long. After his work was complete at Charlottenburg, Nahl moved to Potsdam, where he worked with Friedrich Christian Glume and the brothers Johann Michael and Johann Christian Hoppenhaupt on transforming the Stadtschloss, where Frederick had elected to have his winter quarters. He had already grown bored with Charlottenburg.[48]

It must have been easier when Frederick's mind was taken up with war, for soon after he returned from Dresden, Nahl fled to Strasbourg and his work was taken over by Johann Christian Hoppenhaupt. Jean-Laurent Legeay was another victim of his tyrannical ways, and he too beat a retreat after Frederick criticised his plans for a new palace in the park at Sanssouci.[49] Nahl had remained long enough to sketch out the Herms for Sanssouci, which were then carried out by Glume. The building history for this little gem is complicated: the first drawing was Frederick's own, made after a picnic on the site in August 1743. Frederick thought his martial capital would benefit from a 'merry pleasure dome'. There is a suggestion that its profile, rising out of the vineyard terraces, was inspired by Johann Lukas von Hildebrandt's Belvedere in Vienna. Frederick was, despite his disillusionment with the old prince Eugene, an admirer of his earlier military feats.[50]

If Knobelsdorff was less a member of the intimate circle than he had been, he was still entrusted with major projects as Superintendent of the Royal Buildings, and had his role in Frederick's counsels as a member of the General Direktorium.[51] He remodelled the Tiergarten, which had lost many of the baroque features that it had received when Frederick I had created the Grosse Stern, as Frederick William turned the vast park over to military uses. Knobelsdorff laid out the Kleine Stern and the famous 'Zelte', the refreshment 'tents' that were a feature of Berlin life until the nineteenth century. In 1743 he had bought the silk manufacturer Jean Belchier Fayé's dairy farm on the Spree, hard by the site of the present Schloss Bellevue. Knobelsdorff built himself a house there and had Pesne do the ceilings.[52]

The Opera House on the Linden had ended up by being quite revolutionary in design, ringing the knell on the old-fashioned court theatres of the Dresden, Darmstadt or Hanover sort. Frederick had even more lavish plans for his Forum. The Opera House should have been flanked by a building for the Academy in the same Palladian style and the whole brought together in a vast square based on the Place Vendôme in Paris. None of that was built *per se*, but Knobelsdorff was able to transform the Potsdam Stadtschloss from the early baroque building that had been handed down from the Great Elector's time by playing with colours: white marble pilasters on red brick, and a blue copper roof. Once again Frederick himself provided a sketch of the building he wanted. A theatre was naturally considered vital, and this was decorated by Glume and Pesne's replacement as court painter, Charles Amédée Philippe van Loo to represent Apollo and the Muses. Van Loo finally arrived in the winter of 1747–8. In the marble hall of the Schloss, he paid tribute to the Great Elector with a huge painting of his apotheosis.[53]

Knobelsdorff was also entrusted with the business of making sense of the king's sketch for the house on the vineyard hill near Potsdam. The detailed designs for this 'Italian palace', which eventually came to be known as Sanssouci, were carried out by Friedrich Wilhelm Diterichs. Diterichs, Knobelsdorff and the elder Boumann then all had a hand in the construction.[54] Building began at Sanssouci on 14 April 1745. The outside was finished on 8 November 1747, too late for the king to use it that year. The interiors were not ready until the end of July 1748. The vineyard theme was maintained for the garden front, with Silenus taking pride of place with his train of nymphs and satyrs. It was inspired by Permoser's work at the Dresden Zwinger, which Knobelsdorff knew from his travels. Under the new house, Frederick arranged the new vineyard, telling his scouts to collect every known European vine.[55]

As was right and fitting for a rococo palace, the interiors surpassed the exterior. Frederick wanted the centre-piece to be round. It was an *idée fixe* of his: visible at Amalthea, the Temple of Apollo at Rheinsberg and the Antikentemple at Sanssouci, and St Hedwig's in Berlin and the French church in Potsdam. Knobelsdorff's vaguely Pantheon-inspired marble hall is a space on a par with the very best of the genre – Amalienburg, Brühl or Benrath – while the concert hall brings together Pesne's ceiling with Charles Sylvain Dubois' overdoors, and the sinewy carving of Johann Michael Hoppenhaupt, Johann Michael Merck and Georg Franz Ebenhech. Another triumph was the circular library, which Frederick had made clear must be an imitation of that in Rheinsberg. Knobelsdorff then lengthened the composition by tacking on the orangery (later the Neue Kammern) to the left.[56] Frederick must have been happy with his residence: he could not wait to get his friends to join him in his Valhalla.

[IV]

War had done little to improve Frederick's tolerance of his fellow man. Not long after Mollwitz he was writing to Voltaire to express his contempt: 'men are not made for truth. I see them as a troop of stags in a great lord's park, they have no other function than to stock and restock the enclosure.' Voltaire tried to correct the king and reproved him for his unkind thoughts, but Frederick was not willing to alter his view: 'Deceit, bad faith and falsehood are sadly the dominant characteristics of most of the men who govern nations and who should be examples to their people. The study of the human heart is a truly humiliating subject...'[57]

At the time, he had longed for Rheinsberg and his friends, but Frederick's world had since been made poorer and sadder for the loss of such companions as Keyserlingk, Jordan and Duhan. Jordan's portrait was hung up in his *cabinet*, and Thiébault tells the story of one of his friends – it is hard to say which – whose coffin was taken into Frederick's apartment, after which it was only with some difficulty that his servants convinced him to relinquish it, for the body had begun to stink.[58] Despite his impossibility on close acquaintance, Frederick felt he could not go on without friends. He took issue with d'Argens' contention in his *Nouveaux mémoires* that a Carthusian might be happy, despite his solitude. 'I should like to say affirmatively that he is not. A man who cultivates the [arts] and sciences and who lives without friends is a lone wolf. In a word, the way I see it, friendship is indispensable to our happiness.'[59] The problem was that after the Silesian Wars he became increasingly misanthropic, and difficult towards the few people whom he allowed to come close.

D'Argens was one of those who made it into that tight little world. D'Argens was as much loved as anyone after 1745, but he was the constant butt of Frederick's mockery for his slowness, sleepiness or hypochondria, which might have exceeded Frederick's own: 'Voltaire is less fertile for malice, or Maupertuis for worry, a brothel is the poorer for cunts ..., and the churches for idiotic sermons, compared to your tally of new-found maladies', he wrote to him in 1752. Boswell, who met d'Argens just after the Seven Years War, confirmed the sickly nature of the marquis: 'He is a miserable being, for he is a hypochondriac and terrified of death. He had worn a flannel under-waistcoat four years and durst not take it off for fear of catching a cold ...' The king, however, convinced him to shed the garment: 'The marquis agreed to quit his waistcoat. But it had so fixed itself upon him that pieces of skin came away with it.'[60]

Eighteen months after the Peace of Dresden, d'Argens went to Paris to drum up a few stars for His Majesty's theatres, as well as craftsmen and writers. He returned for the carnival in 1747, then departed a second time. Frederick added hopefully that he would be 'followed any moment by the entire band of Terpsicore'. The trip was largely unsuccessful. Few of the writers and artists Frederick fancied at his court wanted to abandon Paris for Berlin. The painter van Loo played hard to get at first. Gresset not only had an income of 2000 livres, his mistress was one of the prettiest women in town. Even Voltaire was back in favour and hobnobbing with La Pompadour in Versailles. He wanted to introduce d'Argens to her, 'but business kept me in Paris and I put him off for a few days'. The job was clearly so arduous that d'Argens did not return to Potsdam until the summer of 1751.[61]

In March 1747, Frederick expressed some disappointment with his flighty friend Algarotti, who had now returned after finding every possible excuse to absent himself from his over-demanding master. During the war his attempts to bring Sardinia in on Prussia's side had proved ineffective. The secret diplomat was not thinking enough about his responsibilities to the land that paid him, and which had ennobled him too, and was flirting with the Saxons instead. This sort of taunt often encouraged Algarotti to fall back into line. He was given the formal position of chamberlain. His job was ever loosely defined – 'to procure me all sorts of *agréments* for my person'. The vagueness surrounding his role gave rise to gossip. Frederick assured his sister that it was innocent: 'He is engaged here on the footing of a chamberlain ... I would find it hard to find better than him in all Europe.' Presumably she knew something of the talents which have led him to be described as one of the fathers of modern art criticism. He was advising her on her decorative schemes in Bayreuth. Part of his brief involved the purchase of paintings for the royal collections, but many of those he sent back to Frederick were simply too big to be hung in the rather narrow and unsuccessful picture gallery at Sanssouci. The problem was solved when Knobelsdorff hit on the idea of a free-standing gallery farther along the terrace from the little palace.[62]

A year later Algarotti was reporting on the progress of industry in Prussia and singing for his supper with oily flattery. Without thought or lecture, he now turned to architecture, and he used the digs at Herculaneum as an excuse to disappear to Italy again. He came back in January 1749. Frederick was sceptical: 'He hardly moved from Bologna, where he studied [the excavations] as I believe he might have been able to do here.' Knobelsdorff was already a sick man, and was asking to be relieved of his duties. He had married a *Bürgerliche* in 1746, and Frederick had disapproved, meanly deciding that the children from the marriage could not be noble.[63]

Knobelsdorff had already reshaped the centre of Potsdam, copying designs from Lord Burlington in England and the obelisk from Bernini's Rome. To the Dutch Quarter laid out by Frederick William (and continued in a more grandiose fashion by his son), Frederick added a French and an Italian Quarter.[64] Now that Knobelsdorff was withdrawing from active life, Algarotti's talents proved a boon to Frederick. By August 1749 he was at the drawing board designing houses for the new streets of Potsdam, which were growing up between the old town around the palace, and Sanssouci, as well as the old market place, between the Stadtschloss and the Nikolaikirche. The latter was remodelled to look like Santa Maria Maggiore in Rome, while the French church was built in imitation of the Pantheon in the same city. The Barberini palace on the Alte Markt had nothing to do with La *Barberina*. It was built in imitation of the Palazzo Borghese in Rome in 1772 and was called the Dieckowsche or Schulzische house in Frederick's lifetime. It was one of the most impressive buildings in Potsdam until its destruction in 1945.[65]

The new designs were based on the Palazzo Pitti in Florence, Serlio and the new volume of Palladio, which included the architect's plans for town houses in Vincenza. Algarotti hoped that Frederick would 'naturalise' his countryman Palladio. Still in the same architectural idiom, Algarotti received the 1725 edition of *Vitruvius Britannicus* from Lord Burlington, who had given it to Michel, Frederick's envoy in London. It included Lord Burlington's designs for his house in Chiswick, General Wade's house in Great Burlington Street in London and the Assembly Rooms in York. These he commended to His Majesty. Frederick duly made a few designs for Potsdam, which were then interpreted by Boumann. One or two of these survived the conflagration of 14 April 1945:[66] 'one should tremble giving architectural designs to a Trajan', wrote the unctious Italian, 'who knows how to be his own Apollodorus'.[67]

The old core of the Rheinsberg symposium was disappearing. Frederick's ambassador to Paris expired in 1751: 'Yesterday Rothenburg died in my arms ... I can see nothing for my own pain, all my thoughts are consumed by the loss of a companion with whom I lived in complete friendship these twelve years past ... I believe that in this world the only happy people are those who love no one.'[68] Bielfeld's star was still in the ascendant for the time being at least, but by the 1750s he was out of favour for making the decision to marry, which normally meant banishment from Frederick's intimate circle. He was not lacking in funds and bought the former Russian ambassador's residence in the Wilhelmstrasse in Berlin. It was more of a palace than most things in that city: backing on to the Tiergarten, it had four courts and stabling for twenty horses.[69]

That left only La Motte Fouqué from the old gang. Frederick had inherited his minister August Friedrich Eichel from his father. Like Fredersdorf he was a friend in the shadows, his right-hand man and confidant in those moments when his pampered French wits were still asleep in their cots. He has been described as the 'most influential man in Prussia in the first half of Frederick's reign'.[70] Darget, whom Frederick managed to lure to Potsdam in 1749, to some extent bridged the divide: as a former French diplomat and his reader, he was more socially presentable.

Two more members of Frederick's coterie who emerged after 1745 were the Jacobite brothers James and George Keith. James Keith, who had taken up arms against George I in 1715,[71] had risen to the rank of general in the Russian service, but Frederick had mopped him up and bribed him with a marshal's baton in 1747. His brother George was the last hereditary earl Marischal. He had been in Venice when his brother entered Frederick's employment, but James had written to him to come to Berlin forthwith. He told his brother about Frederick:

I have the honour and sup with him almost every day. He has more wit than I have wit to tell you; speaks solidly and knowingly of all kinds of subjects; and I am much mistaken, with the experience of four campaigns, if he is not the best officer in his army. He has several persons with whom he has almost the familiarity of a friend, but no favourite; and has a natural politeness for everyone who is about him.[72]

The king took an immediate liking to the earl. When Keith confessed that his Scottish estate had been confiscated after his taking part in the revolt of the Old Pretender, Frederick gave him 2000 thalers and the Black Eagle, which he wore in preference to the Garter, although that had been hung on him by the Young Pretender himself.[73]

Frederick was also concerned for his own family, who had been bought off with lavish palaces to keep them at a distance from the affairs of state. On June 28 1744, William received Oranienburg and Henry Rheinsberg. That did not mean the eighteen-year-old Henry was now master of his own destiny; in fact, he does not seem to have visited the house more than twice before 1753.[74] William had been made his successor following the Battle of Mollwitz. He had had a son on 25 September 1744, so Frederick could now sleep in peace.[75] The child, Frederick William, followed Frederick on the throne. All subsequent Hohenzollern rulers of Prussia and Germany descended from William.

William's normality and his ability to produce heirs were also a drawback. He soon found his wife as unappetising as Frederick found his own Elisabeth, and developed crushes on other women he found, chiefly at his mother's court. He fell hopelessly in love with the sixteen-year-old Sophie von Pannewitz. It became so obvious that Frederick had to step in and arrange her marriage to one of her cousins. As the British envoy, Sir Charles Hanbury-Williams summed it up slightly cruelly: 'the prince of Prussia likes every woman better than his wife'.[76] William's wandering eye and lack of political acumen were the cause of a few rough words from his elder brother. Frederick's letters began to sound remarkably like those his ireful father had addressed to him: 'after my death you may use [the state] as you wish, [but] if you deviate from the system my [sic] father introduced into this country, you will be the first person to feel it'.[77]

Henry had been introduced to literature, to curb his natural wildness and brutality,[78] but his new training left him even more a fish out of water than Frederick. He claimed to be incapable of speaking German and struck a strange figure with his boss-eyes and his fantastic garb.[79] It was more of a problem to keep him out of the running of the country than William, for he was brighter, and had already shown that he had the makings of an excellent soldier.[80] Political impotence was particularly hard on Henry. In 1743 Frederick had received a report that the Swedes were clamouring to elect Henry their king. Frederick would not even entertain the idea, dismissing it as 'a chimerical proposal'. Frustrated ambitions might have caused Henry to dislike the king his brother, but there was more. Again, Frederick sought to hold him in check, especially when he wanted to amuse himself. It would seem that Henry preferred to escape from the Potsdam Schloss and the fraternal eye and make for the stews. Frederick complained that only his occasional helping hand in Henry's love affairs softened the young man's attitude towards him.[81]

Frederick was not convinced by Henry's protestations of fraternal love: 'If you love me, it must be a love of the metaphysical sort. I have never seen love of this type where there is no regard, communication, or indeed the slightest sign of affection ... I know your distance only, [and] your coldness.'[82] In a third undated letter written in 1746, Frederick made it plain that Henry was indulging his sexual appetites:

You only trust me when difficulties with your love life oblige you to run back to me, as the only person capable of sorting things out; but on other occasions you don't accord me the slightest confidence ... I am bound to you no less by blood than by inclination. You may not judge my conduct without condemning your own.[83]

Was Henry consuming fruit forbidden to Frederick himself? Despite what Voltaire put about, there is little evidence of Frederick giving in to sexual temptation after 1740. Henry would seem to have shared Frederick's homosexual tastes, but to the king's chagrin, he was determined to enjoy them. Eventually Frederick might have put his foot down, for in April 1750 he was writing to William to find out whether there was still bad blood between him and Henry.[84]

The third brother, Ferdinand, was a sly individual who never showed any fondness for his eldest brother and communicated his black thoughts on that score to his brother Henry alone. He was still only fifteen when the Second Silesian War ended. Jordan had been his governor. After the bibliophile's death, he was granted to Bielfeld. He showed no aptitude for letters either. Frederick treated him politely, but distantly, observing that he had inherited one particular taste from his father: 'My brother Ferdinand hunts for the whole family.'[85]

The months that came immediately after the end of the conflict were also marked by continuing bad relations with Wilhelmina. The issue was complicated by her husband's status: he was an imperial prince and, even as a Hohenzollern, no vassal of his cousin in Berlin. She endeavoured to put her brother right: 'As regards Her Hungarian Majesty, I have never had any predilection or particular attachment to her interests. I give justice to her merits and I believe that I am allowed to offer praise to all those who possess them.' Frederick's reply was begrudging, but he intended to open the door to reconciliation: 'I never suspected your heart of complicity in all the disappointments you have given me these last three years.'[86] Wilhelmina must have worked the gall out of her system by then: she had used it as ink for her memoirs.

[v]

In May 1745, Frederick was back in Potsdam, and Bielfeld, for one, had the chance to see his 'oracle' every night. After the concert, the invited guests sat down to supper: 'the conversation is gay, and the king is frequently surprised, to hear the clock strike two ...'[87] In July, Frederick took his summer break in Rheinsberg, as he continued to do until Sanssouci was ready for him. This time the queen mother and Wilhelmina came too. Relations were better, between brother and sister, they swopped notes on music, and on Hasse and Felice Salimbeni's singing. He wrote to William on 15 July after most of the company had already quit the palace. The sojourn at Rheinsberg had made Frederick nostalgic. He had revisited Ruppin and Nauern, 'and places which had brought back memories of the happy errors and wild moments of my young age. Looking back on the theatre of my clamorous pleasures, I saw all the old townsfolk muttering to themselves.' They were remembering his passion for broken glass: 'Well, we have been able to keep our windows in order since that lunatic went away and broke the queen of Hungary's.'[88]

Frederick was writing. He had taken the temperature of the water with an instruction for the young duke Charles Eugene of Württemberg, which he had penned two years before. It dealt with the duties of a prince; a pendant to L'Antimachiavel: 'Do not believe that the land of Württemberg was created for you; think rather that providence brought you into the world to bring happiness to its people.' He was to pay attention to finances: 'The nervous system of a country; if you understand them you will always be the master of everything else.' He advised his young ward to leave religion well alone; it was the province of the 'supreme being' and not the business of the ruler. On the other hand, 'Tolerance will make the people adore you; persecution will make them abominate you.' Charles Eugene did not learn his lesson. He was hated, to the degree that he became another one of the models for the cruel prince in Schiller's *Kabale und Liebe*.[89]

From 1746 date the first drafts of Frederick's *Mémoires pour servir à l'histoire de la maison de Brandebourg*, in which he looked into the ancestral entrails. It is filled with insights into the monarch himself. For example: 'It is always a mistake to look for the motives behind men's actions, beyond the human heart and human passions.' The work also contains one of Frederick's most famous lines:

A prince is the first servant and first magistrate of the state; it is he who decides to what use taxes should be put; he levies them in order to be able to defend the state by means of the troops he maintains, in order to uphold the dignity with which he is invested, to reward service and merit, to establish some sort of balance between rich and poor, to relieve the unfortunate in every walk of life, in order to breed magnificence in every limb of the body of the state in general. If the sovereign has an enlightened mind and an honest heart, he will direct all expenditure for the commonweal and to the greatest advantage of his subjects.[90]

Despite this high-mindedness, in September he again confided to his successor his thoughts about the recent war. He had not served his people so well; he had taken 'terrible risks for the state; I saw my reputation sink and steady again; finally, after having encountered so many hazards, I cherish the opportunity to catch my breath'. The others were still fighting it out, but excellent news had come from England that there was a possible alliance on the cards and for the time being the British had offered to guarantee his gains in Silesia. He had only 'fought the war to achieve the peace'.[91] A week later he was ensconced in his library with Tacitus, Livy, Plutarch and a small pile of modern writers, making up for the time lost when he could not dedicate himself whole-heartedly to study. The autumn was agreeably lost, therefore, in reading, music, architecture and planning his new gardens.[92]

By the time the carnival came round once again, Frederick had achieved a sort of calm. He wrote to Wilhelmina, to sing the praises of Graun's latest opera, *Cajo Fabricio*: 'his masterpiece'. 'I spend my life extremely pleasantly here: dividing my time between the theatre, good company and study.' To Voltaire he wrote on 18 December, 'The curtain is rising at the Comedy. Barberina, Cochois, Hauteville, are calling; I am going to admire them.'[93] Frederick had first seen the dancer Barberina Campanini in May 1744, just before he went off to war, when she had performed an *intermezzo* in the Alabaster Hall of the Berlin Schloss. He was so struck with her that he commissioned a portrait by Pesne. Later he prevented her from marrying an English 'milord' and had her brought back to Berlin under guard. Such jealous behaviour, and the fact that he hung her picture behind a glass door in his bedroom, gave rise to persistent rumours that she had been Frederick's mistress. It might have suited Frederick to encourage this gossip. Voltaire did his best to prick the speculative bubble: he quipped that he liked her only because she had the legs of a man.[94] In 1749 she married the son of the chancellor Cocceji, with whom she had indeed had an affair.[95]

On 13 February 1747, Frederick had a small stroke which he thought could have been fatal, but bad health did not prevent him from enjoying the arrival of a talented new cook in March, or indeed from celebrating his mother's birthday with the usual two-day event: theatre, opera and an intimate supper to finish.[96] Sanssouci was not ready, but it was not out of mind. He bought a sculptured group of praying boys from Fürst Liechtenstein and had it positioned outside the window of his circular study. In April the death of the Alte Dessauer occasioned a little ribaldry from Fredersdorf. The warrior had sworn to Lucifer with every utterance: 'The old prince will enjoy himself enormously when he sees all those devils that he had always so ardently invoked.'[97]

Potsdam received a distinguished visitor in May: Johann Sebastian Bach. He had come with his son Friedemann to visit Emmanuel, and to try out the Silbermann piano in the Potsdam Schloss as well as the new organ in the Heiliggeistkirche.[98] Frederick learned of his presence by the *Berlinische Nachrichten* and summoned him on the 7th. Frederick might well have wanted to bait the musical patriarch, whose style of music was not one he favoured. He played him an impossible sequence of twenty-two notes on the piano and asked Bach to extemporise. He wanted a six-part fugue from his *thema regium*. The composer excused himself to the king: 'I soon noticed that due to a lack of necessary preparation, the performance would not be such as such an excellent theme required.' He played him a theme out of his own head instead, and transformed that into a six-part fugue.[99]

Bach might have been temporarily stunned by the *thema regium*, but he came round. He performed a concert before a huge audience in the Heiliggeistkirche the next day, and left soon after. Two months later, on 7 July 1747, he dispatched the *Musical Offering* from Leipzig: 'I hereby dedicate to Your Majesty in most profound submissiveness a musical offering, the noblest part of which was touched by His Majesty's hand.' That original delivery contained the first third of the piece, up until the six-part *ricercare*, or long drawn-out elaboration. The following two parts were later delivered by C. P. E. Bach. The text also contained messages for the king. Over the *ricercare* were the words 'Regis jussu cantio et reliqua canonica arte resoluta': 'developed from the theme offered by the king together with another in the canonical style', a possible reference to the fact that he had not liked the *thema regium* at all. In the two canons there was another musical tease: 'Quaerendo invenietis' – 'you'll find it [the king's theme] if you look'.[100]

What Frederick thought of the *Musical Offering* is not recorded. There is no evidence that it was played, or that the king ever thanked Bach for his labours. It is cerebral music, and not the light-hearted and flirtatious rococo that was more popular with the monarch. Frederick might even have been annoyed that Bach managed to untie the musical knots he had made for him. The piece ended up in the hands of Frederick's equally musical – and more forward-thinking – sister Amalia, who made a present of it to the Joachimsthaler Gymnasium in Berlin.

In May there was also a formal consecration of the king's new palace. Frederick had toyed with the names 'Lusthaus', 'La Vigne' and 'Weinberghaus' before settling on Sanssouci.* D'Argens had asked him why he had chosen the name. Frederick pointed to the vault he had dug on the top terrace: 'When I am there, I shall be *without a care.*'[101] There was a concert in the royal chapel and 200 guests were invited, but the queen's name was not on the list. The new retreat had been conceived as a 'monastery' with Frederick as the abbot. Women were made increasingly unwelcome. When Hanbury-Williams was posted to Prussia at the end of the decade, he noted bitchily, 'No female is allowed to approach the court, males wash the linen, nurse the children, make and unmake the beds.' But then, Hanbury-Williams' tactless and snobbish

---

* 'Pleasure House', 'Vineyard House', 'Sanssouci' was incidentally a childhood nickname for his sister, Charlotte. I have used the German form here; naturally in Frederick's day it was written as two words.

approach put the Prussians' backs up. He was, by his own admission, 'shunned and avoided by everybody'. What he knew about Potsdam was merely gossip from fellow diplomats in Berlin.[102]

Frederick was still allotting part of his year to Rheinsberg, until the interiors were ready. In 1747 the house party performed Racine's *Britannicus* with Bielfeld as Nero and Princess Amalia as Agrippina. A fire at Charlottenburg had destroyed a few of the rooms, but Frederick gave orders to rebuild them as they were.[103] In September, Frederick made another journey to Silesia. The process of re-establishing the war-torn lands had continued apace. A good harvest had 'completely healed the wounds made by the incursion of the Austrians'. The forts were ready at Brieg and Neisse and building at Glogau, Cosel, Glatz and Schweidnitz.[104]

Another philosophic work was finished that year, *Des moeurs, des coutumes, de l'industrie*. It allowed Frederick to speak out on several subjects that concerned him. The German language, its lack of rules* and its multitudinous dialects, was one. He had a kind word only for Friedrich Ludwig von Canitz: 'the German Poet'. Frederick dismissed his mother tongue as 'crude and still almost barbaric'. The Huguenots were another subject: Britain and Holland might have received the cream, but the most industrious had settled in Brandenburg after the Revocation of the Edict of Nantes: goldsmiths, jewellers, clockmakers and sculptors; they also added their lustre to the land, planting tobacco, fruit and vegetables, turning the Brandenburgian sandbox into admirable kitchen gardens.[105]

At the beginning of 1748, Frederick's opera company performed an opera by Graun based on Corneille's *Cinna*.[106] In August he could move into Sanssouci at long last. His *petits soupers* were not to have the relative informality of the Rheinsberg years. A new stiffness had crept in and there was, of course, a largely renewed *dramatis personae*. Still our favourite image of this royal 'symposium' is the Menzel painting *Die Tafelrunde*,[107] which depicts the group at its most illustrious: Voltaire, d'Argens, Algarotti, La Mettrie, the Keiths, Rothenburg and Stille. It was a free elite, and not a gathering place for solicitors, favourites or mistresses. There was no room for the home-grown middle classes either: despite his protestations of love for Fredersdorf or Eichel, they did not have a seat at their master's table.[108]

Frederick had no time to attend the wedding of his niece Elisabeth Frederica Sophia to Charles Eugene of Württemberg in Bayreuth that

---

* Perhaps he felt there were no rules because he had never learned any.

autumn, and missed the chance to see Wilhelmina's magnificent new opera house, which was intended, in part at least, for her own creations: *Semiranus* and *Uomo*. She had examined the plans and elevations of Knobelsdorff's building on the Linden, but in the end she had gone her own way. The sober exterior façade by Joseph Saint Pierre gave little inkling of the lavish, but slightly old-fashioned Italian baroque interiors by Giuseppe and Carlo Galli-Bibiena. William attended, and was delighted to receive a present from the hands of a hired quack: a golden pill box containing a powder designed to help him produce heirs.[109]

For the carnival in 1749, Graun produced *Ifigenia in Aulide*, which had been adapted from Racine.[110] His next production, *Angélique et Médée*, was first aired at the queen mother's birthday.[111] It was one of Frederick's most creative years: poetry, music and philosophy tripped off his pen. He was always honest about his abilities. He gave Voltaire licence to correct and criticise his poetry, adding that, as a German, he was never going to be able to rival the best of native talent. As a philosopher he had the shortcomings of having no understanding for geometry or metaphysics. The one he abandoned to the English; the other was no more than an 'air-balloon'.[112]

One of his most sustained poetical works was the satire *Le Palladion*, written in imitation of Voltaire's satire *La Pucelle*, to keep himself amused during the tedium of the carnival. It rather unkindly borrowed the person of his reader, Darget, as its hero and recounted some more-or-less true events in the Silesian Wars. Pandurs had attempted to capture the French ambassador, Valory, and make off with some important papers he was carrying at the time. His secretary Darget was taken for him, and as a good servant, he did not let on until it was too late. He was released as soon as the Pandurs learned their mistake.[113]

It was an opportunity to ridicule a great many of Frederick's enemies: Charles of Lorraine, the general and brother of the new emperor, who was happier sitting down to a lavish meal than fighting; the 'perfumed troop' of Saxons; and his friends too. Chasot is there, for example, with his Norman father, the proud possessor of 'more than a hundred baskets full of apples'.[114] The 'fat marquis' makes his entry in the third canto, kidnapped by Pandurs at Jaromirz. Their leader Franquin dresses himself in the best Prussian clothes, prized from his Aladdin's cave of booty, then enjoys a sumptuous meal at the expense of the Bohemian peasants, the very same people who were so reluctant to share their production with Frederick.

Rien ne coûtait, on faisait
bonne chère,
On s'engraissait des malheurs
de la guerre.
On fait venir le champagne
moussant,
Qui pétilla bientôt dans chaque
verre,
Le port-à-port, le Tokai jau-
nissant,
Vin butiné, volé furtivement.

*They dined in style, as nothing costs
a thing,*
They got fat from war and suffering.
*They popped the bottles of sparkling
champagne,*
*Which foamed in every glass – fit for
a king–*
*The port went round, the yellow tokay
came,*
Booty all, and all most slyly stolen.

The Pandurs are naturally not content with normal pleasures. After a
little rape, they try something new

Rassasiés des délices connues,
Ils enfilaient la route par la
gauche,
Et ils s'enivraient de plaisirs
défendus...[115]

*They were sick and tired of normal
vice,*
And they decided to come from the left,
*Finding sinister sex was twice as
nice...*

If this left-handed sex left one or two things to the imagination, Frederick's
circle were to hear more in the description of Darget's education at the
hands of the Jesuits. Darget had defended himself against the first
schoolmaster, but a second fell on him and disguised his seduction behind
a history lesson:

Vous y verrez des héros pleins
de gloire,
Tantôt actifs et tantôt patients,
A leurs amis souples et com-
plaisants.
Tel pour Socrate était Alcibiade,
Qui, par ma foi, n'était un Grec
maussade;
Et tels étaient Euryale et Nisus.
En [sic] citerais, que sait-je?
Tant et plus;

*You will meet stout heroes heaped
with glory,*
*Most often they are active, sometimes
passive,*
*For their friends supple and content
to give.*
Like Socrates and Alcibiades,
*My God, a grumpy Greek he longed
to please;*
Euryalis and Nisus, also two.
*The list I could cite would fill a
Who's Who;*

Jules César, que des langues obscènes	There's great Caesar, of whom the gossips said,
Disaient mari de tous les Romaines,	He graced many a Roman matron's bed,
Quand il était la femme des maris.	In fact he was the pathic to their sires.
Mais feuilletez un moment Suétone,	Flick through Suetonius when you can,
Et des Césars voyez comme il raisonne.	You'll see that every Caesar had his man.
Sur ce registre ils étaient tous inscrits;	You'll learn they were all a bunch of queers;
Ils servaient tous le beau dieu de Lampsaque.*	They all worshipped at old Priapus's shrine.
Si le profane enfin ne vous suffit,	But if these worldly men aren't proof enough,
Par le sacré dirigeans [sic] notre ataque:	Here are a few names in the sacred line:
Ce bon ... que pensez-vous qu'il fit,	The saintly ..., imagine what stuff,
Pour que ... le couchât sur son lit?	He used to make ... sleep so rough?
Sentez-vous pas qu'il fut son Ganymède?...	Don't you suspect he was his catamite?...
Tous les recteurs crient: il a raison!	All the tutors shouted 'e' Gad he's right!'
Dans ce moment, le grand diable sait comme,	And all at once proud Satan he could see,
Fondent sur moi ces brandons de sodome;	This pack of sodomites jumping on me.
Et pour avoir la paix dans la maison,	And to get some peace on that stormy night,
Necessité fut de n'être pas sévère.	I couldn't be too hard on those poor guys,
Je devins donc leur malheureux plastron,	And I became their unhappy Ganymede,

* Lampsacus in Asia Minor was famous for the cult of Priapus.

Et lorsqu'en rut se sentait quelque père,	*And when some cleric felt his sap to rise*
J'étais, hélas, sa monture ord-inaire.[116]	*I was, alas, awarded for his prize.*

Readings of *Le Palladion* surely raised a few laughs at Frederick's *petits soupers*. One or two of his friends must have been indiscreet. Soon there was talk in Paris and Versailles, where the French king voiced a singular desire to lay his hands on a copy. Wheedling the poem out of Frederick became a diplomatic priority. A year later Valory wrote that he wanted to read Frederick's description of his exploits with the Pandurs for himself. Frederick was not prepared to let it go: 'how the theologians, politicians and purists would scream'. When Valory pushed, Frederick sent him his *Histoire de Brandebourg* instead.[117]

Frederick had given Darget a rough ride in verse: sodomised by so many Jesuit fathers. Perhaps for that reason he wrote him a poem too: 'A Darget, apologie des rois'. In it he admitted that the life of a king's secretary was not always a happy one. Based on Boileau's *Epitre XI, A mon jardinier*, it is one of Frederick's most successful poems.

Tous les jours, par cahier, tu mets ses vers au net,
Et quand tu les lui rends, Dieu sait le bruit qu'il fait:
D'un sévère examen le pointilleux scrupule
S'étend par chaque point et sur chaque virgule;
Là sont les *e* muets qui devraient être ouverts
Ou c'est un mot de moins qui fait clocher un vers;
Puis, en recopiant cet immortel ouvrage,
Tu donnes son auteur au diable à chaque page.

Every day you put whole books of his verse to rights,
God knows, a thankless task which leads to frequent fights:
The meticulous pedant he alights on a
Misplaced colon or full stop, or a missing comma;
Here is a silent e, which should be stressed
And there's a missing word which leaves the line a mess;
Then as you copy out the immortal autograph,
You damn its author with every paragraph.

After satire, Frederick also sought to excel in a more Prussian epic: *l'Art de la Guerre*. 'War from time immemorial was ever the first of the arts.' More interesting, perhaps, than the narrative are the surviving corrections to the manuscript made by Voltaire. They were always heeded. Voltaire corrected Frederick's poor ear for French syllables (examples of two syllable words: *vaurien, chrétien*) and made a few wittier observations, such as 'as Ovid never said, not him or anyone, that the Amors had slept with the Graces, I don't think we should suggest poncing, however pretty the idea'. 'As for the rest, this ode is one of your loveliest works; I love this beat with a passion. I think I am the father, but you have made it better.' The rest sounds like a half-term report: 'It would be a great pity if you were to give up poetry when you are at the peak of your genius and the flower of your age, and after the astonishing progress you have made.'[118]

Even more serious matter was contained in the *Dissertation sur les raisons d'établir ou d'abroger les lois*. Frederick's obsession with law corresponded to his first attempts to establish a proper legal code for Prussia (see above, p. 182): 'A perfect body of laws would be a masterpiece of the human mind.' Frederick sought to create something which functioned as perfectly as a watch. Yet these laws should not be too many. He compared the treatment of society through law to a doctor encumbering his patient with prescriptions: 'a profusion of laws becomes a labyrinth into which stray both justice and justiciar'. Frederick considered Prussian law to lie somewhere between the light-heartedness of ancient Egypt and the severity of modern France. Small misdemeanours were but mildly punished; capital punishment was reserved for brigand, assassin and murderer.[119]

De la superstition et de la religion dates from the same productive year. It was a fashionable theme for *philosophes* wherever they lurked. Frederick turned a Voltairean glance at the history of religion in Germany: idolatry, superstition, slaughter, persecution. The Brandenburg Wends had been mistreated by their Christian conquerors: 'The niches of their absent idols were filled with all sorts of saints; and new follies followed the old.' Frederick was always scathing about monks. They were misanthropic, lazy good-for-nothings. They had their come-uppance in (the former monk) Martin Luther, who brought religion back to its primitive simplicity; even he was personally flawed, and he saw devils and even threw an ink-pot at one. Although Frederick claimed to despise all organised religion, he hated Catholicism the most. He told his readers that Protestantism was more suitable for republics and monarchies as it bows down to the temporal authority. Catholicism breeds plots and artifice and owes allegiance only to the pope.[120] More important was the message for Brandenburg-Prussia:

All the sects live in peace here, and equally contribute to the happiness of the state. From the moral point of view, there is no religion which differs much from the others, therefore they are all equal in government, which, in consequence, leaves the individual the liberty to go to Heaven by whatever route he chooses. All that is asked of him is that he should be a good citizen. False zeal is a tyrant which depopulates provinces: tolerance is a tender mother who looks after them and makes them bloom.[121]

In September he was telling Algarotti about *Coriolan*, an opera he was writing for Graun. He had taken the capacities of his singers into consideration in a short work lasting three and a quarter hours with ballets! The Italian libretto had been knocked up by the king's poet, Villati, but he passed it on to his Swan for his opinion. It needed more profundity, and Algarotti could give it the feeling of a French tragedy: 'be the Prometheus of our poet [Villati], inject him with divine fire from the Heavens ...'[122] Algarotti knew how to flatter his master: '*Coriolan* will harvest almost as many tears from the pretty eyes of Berlin as *Iphigénie* [*Ifigenia in Aulide*] at the last Carnival.' *Coriolan* was first performed on 19 December.[123]

One of Frederick's great heroes, Marshal Saxe, visited Berlin in July, and after spending a couple of days at the Hôtel Vincent (the best in Berlin), he came down to Sanssouci on the 15th to pass a night under Frederick's roof. He was the illegitimate son of Augustus the Strong and his *maîtresse en titre*, Gräfin Königsmarck, and more importantly for Frederick, the victor of Fontenoy over the army of his uncle George. Frederick had been in correspondence with Saxe since October 1745 and had excused some of his *folies de jeunesse* (possibly Mollwitz) in a long letter he sent to the marshal in November 1746. They talked so late into the night that Frederick felt he need to apologise: 'I am such a good ally of France[!] that far from wanting to ruin the health of its heroes, I should like to prolong their lives.'[124]

Algarotti was feeling the strain of being too close to his jealous master. He pleaded illness in order to get to Berlin at the very least. Frederick fussed about his health. Algarotti informed him that he was taking Selters waters, 'mixed with a little wine at lunch'. Both Frederick and his physician, Lieberkühn, thought the waters of Eger in Bohemia better. He also thought his Latin friend should stay off gassy food and confine his attention to vegetables and fruit; advice he was not wont to take himself. Algarotti replied, 'Apollo is a doctor too.'[125] Italians knew how to use

Algarotti as a means to find employment at Frederick's court. In September the great violinist Tartini was looking for a home for his 'best pupil' Pasquale Bini, who had had to leave his Roman post in a hurry.[126]

Wilhelmina and her husband visited Frederick in August and she was sorry to leave.

In my head I am still back in Potsdam ... I walk into your study and see how you work for the well-being of your country. I follow you on to the parade [ground] and see you transformed into Mars. After you return to your apartments I see you take on Apollo's form. And in the evening the melody of your flute once again fills my heart. I shall not forget your little suppers; they made too great an impression to be erased from my mind.

Meanwhile, keeping Algarotti in line was proving difficult. He was showing an interest in one of the king's dancers, Giovanna Corrini, the wife of Jean-Baptiste Denis, who played *commedia dell'arte* roles and was known as 'la Pantaloncina' as a result. Whether the interest was carnal or not is an interesting question. Frederick evidently thought it was: 'I hope that you have less need of physicians than you do pimps, from the point of view of both diet and pleasure,* and that rather than obtaining galbanum from the chemists you are drinking the wine of Aÿ,† which makes the blood circulate faster and carries happiness to the brain.'[127]

Algarotti knew how to parry this ribbing. He sent the gourmand king broccoli seeds. Frederick was delighted: 'the only way to eat decent stuff, you will have the first'. He was deep in composition in that most fruitful year: 'the legislator and the conqueror disappear to make way for the poet and wit'. Frederick was collaborating with Graun and Villati on a new opera for the carnival: *Phaeton*, which had been adapted from Quinault; and, if he refused to pose himself, one of his Italian greyhounds was sitting (or standing) for the engraver Schmidt, who presumably had to address the mutt with a formal 'Sie' or 'vous', like the rest of his household.[128]

---

* *Macquereau* is the French for both mackerel and pimp.
† Galbanum resin was used for treating venereal diseases. Aÿ is in the Marne Valley, i.e. Champagne.

CHAPTER EIGHT

Frederick and François

[1]

Frederick still desperately wanted Voltaire to be a part of his court. Ever since his abortive visit in 1743, Frederick had been trying to tempt him back with promises of a safe haven from the malicious clergy in France, honours of all sorts and money – which was far the most important lure for the leading French intellectual of his day. Voltaire's excuse was his mistress 'Venus-Newton': Emilie du Châtelet, who was surprised to find herself pregnant at the age of forty-three in 1749. The all-knowing Collé confided to his journal: 'Madame du Châtelet is with child. The last person suspected is her husband ... M. de Voltaire is not at all guilty either ... everyone has decided that it was M. de Saint Lambert who made that soul there.' Voltaire was happy to pretend that the child was his, but even far away in Prussia no one was convinced. Frederick even said as much to Algarotti.[1]

The king had an ulterior motive. Despite the stacks of poetry piling up that spring, he continued to feel that it had not come right. 'I swim in a poetic ocean with rushes and bladders under my arms.' He wanted Voltaire to teach him to be a great poet. Voltaire was flattered, and walked into the role with his eyes closed. In April, when he could still take refuge in the paternity of the unborn child, he told Frederick:

If you want to perfect your style in all the finer points of our language and poetry, in which you honour us, you will need to have the goodness to work with me for two hours a day for six weeks or two months; I will have to evaluate critically our best authors together with Your Majesty. You will enlighten me on all that appeals to [your] genius, I will not be useless to you on all that concerns the mechanics, language and above all the different styles. A profound knowledge of eloquence and poetry requires a lifetime's work. I have not limited myself just to that profession and at fifty-five, I am still learning.[2]

Frederick compared himself to a lutinist who spent half his time tuning his instrument and the other half playing it. 'Now that I see some certainty in your coming, I have redoubled the severity with which I deal with myself.' Voltaire was to be his Virgil 'in the guise of Quintilian'.* He was also redoubling his efforts to dislodge Voltaire from the court of King Stanislas in Lorraine, where he had taken refuge from the usual pack of enemies: clerical, literary and governmental. Sanssouci would be to Voltaire what Tusculum was to Cicero. At the end of August he could not resist a sly dig at Emilie: 'she hasn't given birth yet, she has more trouble bringing a child into the world than she does a book'; or, less than a week later, 'As Madame du Châtelet writes books, I think she has children to amuse herself. Tell her to hurry up; I'm dying to see you.' He signed the letter 'Possesseur de Voltaire'.[3]

Frederick gave his real opinion of Voltaire to Algarotti on 12 September.

It is a great pity that such a cowardly soul should be joined to such a great genius. He has all the lovableness and maliciousness of a monkey ... I am not going to make a fuss because I need him for the study of French elocution. You may learn pretty things from a scoundrel. I want to know his French: how important is the moral issue? This man has found the means to combine opposites. You admire his mind at the same time as despising his character.[4]

Frederick did not know yet, but it had already ended in tragedy two days before, when Madame du Châtelet died in childbirth. The infant expired not long after. The validity of Voltaire's grief is disputed: he himself admitted to Madame du Deffand that he had not been smitten with the idea of the child whose birth had caused her death.[5] Her death had the advantage of allowing him to prevaricate yet longer; even if it ultimately removed the reason for his remaining in France or Lorraine. He none the less turned on his royal fan:

I have lost a friend of twenty-five years, a great man whose only fault was being a woman, and who all Paris laments and honours. Possibly justice was not granted her during her life, and you didn't judge her as you might have done had she had the honour to have been acquainted with Your Majesty. But a woman who was capable of translating Newton and Virgil, and who had as many virtues as an honest man, you will doubtless find time to mourn.[6]

Frederick was unimpressed: he had never thought much of Madame du Châtelet's intellectual pretensions. Her death was 'irreparable for those

* Marcus Fabius Quintilianus was the most famous Roman teacher of rhetoric.

who do not command armies or govern states'; as for Voltaire, it was a question of the lady protesting too much: 'Voltaire makes too much noise about his affliction, which leads me to believe that he will be rapidly reconciled.'[7] For the time being, Frederick had the company of another Frenchman, François de Baculard d'Arnaud. Frederick had written verses to him and passed them to Thiériot, who had given them to Charles Collé. Collé was not over-impressed with these 'petits mauvais vers', which lacked the essence of poetry, or indeed any feeling for the French language.[8] Perhaps it was high time that Voltaire came to give him a lesson or two.

The great poet was clutching at straws: he said he had been maligned by d'Argens. Frederick assured him that this was not the case, and tried to work out a system that would make residence in Potsdam more tolerable: six months at Sanssouci and six months in Paris. Frederick was bored with his excuses: 'one moment domestic arrangements, King Stanislas the next; or new tittle-tattle. You know, I am as sceptical about this trip as I am the coming of the Messiah, for whom the Jews are still waiting.'[9] The next pretext for deferring the journey was Voltaire's new mistress, his niece Madame Denis. Voltaire was going to drive a hard bargain and hit Frederick where it hurt most: his pocket. 'I'm rich, even very rich for a man of letters. I have, as they say in Paris, put down roots, I live as a *philosophe* with my family [i.e. la Denis] and my friends.' Such arrangements could not be disrupted for under 4000 thalers.

Frederick was prepared to pay up: 'You will be received as the Virgil of our time, and the gentleman of the bedchamber of Louis XV will take precedence, if you like, before the great poet.' Voltaire could not resist that sort of blandishment. At the end of June he was writing from Compiègne, where he had gone to take his leave of Louis *le bien-aimé*.[10] He once again offered the king his services as a secret agent, but Louis was not interested, and nor was the foreign office in his repeated attempts to renew their relations. Madame de Pompadour was even less impressed at Voltaire's decision, and never forgave him for going to Prussia. After he left, the French king allegedly quipped, 'That's one less madman at my court and one more at his.'[11]

Even while Voltaire's bones were rattling over the hellish roads of Westphalia, there were negotiations – doubtless inspired by the poet himself – to bring him back to Paris. Madame Denis had thrown a tantrum.

I would prefer your happiness to the extreme pleasure of having you, but you are a *philosophe*; and I am one too. What is more natural, simple and orderly than the way in which *philosophes* live together, united by the same studies, the same tastes, and by a similar way of thinking ... I respect you as my master of eloquence and knowledge; I love you as a virtuous friend.

Frederick added indulgently, 'I am not mad enough to make out that Berlin is a substitute for Paris.'[12]

But Voltaire was happy to compare Sanssouci to Trianon, once he had taken a look round the king's new summer retreat.[13] There was a brief honeymoon. Voltaire, alluding to Danae, had not been showered with gold, but he had got 20,000 thalers for himself and 4000 for his niece. He had been given the *pour le mérite*, Frederick's new order, but he had not been given a county like Algarotti. Still, he felt pleased enough to sit down and write a letter to his schoolfriend d'Argental, three days after his arrival, on 24 July:

Well, here I am in a place that was once a wilderness, and which today is as embellished by the arts as it is ennobled by glory. One hundred and forty thousand victorious soldiers, no prosecuters, opera, comedy, philosophy, poetry, a hero who is at once philosopher and poet, grandeur and grace, trumpets and violins, Platonic banquets, company and liberty! Who would have believed it! It is all true, however, and none is more precious to me than our little suppers. It was worth seeing Soloman in majesty; ... I am thoroughly ashamed of having Marshal Saxe's apartment.[14]

Summer at Sanssouci was not so bad. In August there was a 'carousel' in imitation of that given by Louis XIV in Paris in 1685; the margravine was the guest of honour. At the party 46,000 Chinese lanterns were lit, and 31,000 soldiers were stationed round the park. There were little armies dressed as Romans, Carthaginians, Persians and Greeks, led by the princes William, Henry and Ferdinand and the margrave Charles of Schwedt. Warlike music was played. At the close, Princess Amalia was there to distribute the trophies. Despite his minor court appointment at Versailles, Voltaire was treated better in Prussia. He had the right to dine at the queen's table in Berlin (for all that it was worth – it might have sounded more impressive by report in Paris). He told Madame Denis that he had heard not a word of German spoken so far: 'our language and literature have made more conquests than Charlemagne'. He wanted her to join him, but she was not at all keen. She told him that she imagined Berlin was like Paris in the age of the first Capetians.[15]

Voltaire replied that the poetry in the opera performed in Berlin was indeed worthy of Hugh Capet. It was unkind of him: it was as often as not written by Frederick! 'In truth, Berlin is a little Paris. There are the same foul mouths, the same red tape, the same jealous women and authors and the same pamphlets. I am impatient to learn my destiny from both you and Versailles.'[16] Disillusion might have set in as early as mid-September, but Voltaire was not admitting as much. To Madame de Dompierre de Fontaine (his other niece) he praised both Prussian grapes and peaches. A difference of three or four degrees was no reason to run a country down. He was living for virtually nothing in Potsdam. A place was permanently set for him at the king's table.[17]

Frederick was an attractive man to an ambitious poet. Voltaire himself was not entirely tongue in cheek when he told his friend of the seductive effect of 'his big blue eyes ... his gentle smile, his siren voice, his five battles ...'[18] He wrote to his niece on 13 October:

It is true that Potsdam is inhabited by a lot of moustaches and busbies; but, thank God, I don't see them at all. I work quietly in my apartment to the beating of the drums. I have cut back on lunches with the king; there are too many generals and princes. I couldn't get used to being always face to face with a king on a formal footing, or speaking in public. I have dinner with him in a more select group. The dinner is shorter, more gay and healthy. I'd die at the end of three months of boredom and indigestion if I had to attend the king's formal lunches every day.

I have been formally granted, my dear child, to the king of Prussia. My marriage has been celebrated; will it be a happy one? I have no idea. I could not stop myself from saying *yes*. The marriage would have happened anyway, after flirting for so many years. My heart beat nervously at the altar.[19]

These passages later found their way into his posthumous *Mémoires*. It has since been shown that Voltaire tinkered with the texts in an attempt to get his revenge for his later humiliation in Frankfurt. This might explain the overtly sexual tone. 'He was accustomed to singular demonstrations of tenderness from favourites much younger than me; and he forgot for a moment that I was not the same age as them, and I didn't have a pretty hand, he took it and kissed it. I kissed his and did his bidding.'[20] This line has led one recent French writer to assert that Voltaire actually had sex with the king.[21]

Writing to d'Argental, he none the less used a less *risqué* metaphor, but

Frederick's bedroom in the
Stadtschloss in Potsdam. The
substantial ruins of the palace
were finally demolished by the
communist authorities in 1968.

Knobelsdorff's French protestant church in Potsdam. Another of the
round buildings based on the Pantheon, favoured by Frederick.

Typical buildings in Potsdam's new town, Frederick often lent a hand in their design.

A copy of Adolph Menzel's *Tafelrunde*. The painting was destroyed in 1945. The king is surrounded by his French intellectual friends in the dining hall at Sanssouci.

La Mettrie, the free-thinking intellectual who became Frederick's reader, and who was snuffed out by an indigestible pâté.

Maupertuis, head of Frederick's Academy, and the butt of Voltaire's campaign in 1752, which led to the poet's departure from Prussia.

Peter Ludwig Moreau von Maupertuis.

James, brother of the last Scottish earl Marischal, George Keith, by Menzel. James was killed at the Battle of Hochkirch in 1758 having been made a field marshal.

Hans Joachim von Zieten, Frederick's greatest cavalry general, by Menzel.

Friedrich Wilhelm von Seydlitz, whose timely charge routed the French army at the battle of Rossbach in 1757.

Wilhelmina by Pesne. Frederick's favourite sister died on the same day as the defeat at Hochkirch, 14 October 1758.

The interior of Wilhelmina's opera house in Bayreuth by Guiseppe and Carlo Galli Bibiena. The exuberant design put even Knobelsdorff's theatre on Berlin's Unter den Linden to shame.

The so-called *communs* at Potsdam's new palace, constructed after the end of the Seven Years War.

P. Haas

Ein Becker in Potsdam hatte von einen Bauer Roggen gekauft, und ihm statt Currant Münze gegeben, wodurch ein Zanck entstand, den der König, der in der Nähe ritt, hörte, Er erkundigt sich nach der Ursache des Zancks, und frägt den Bauer warum er die Münze nicht nehmen wolle, worauf dieser erwiederte, *Nimmt he' se denn.*

Frederick debased the currency during the Seven Years War. A peasant refuses one of the new coins. Frederick wants to know why. 'You take it then', says the man.

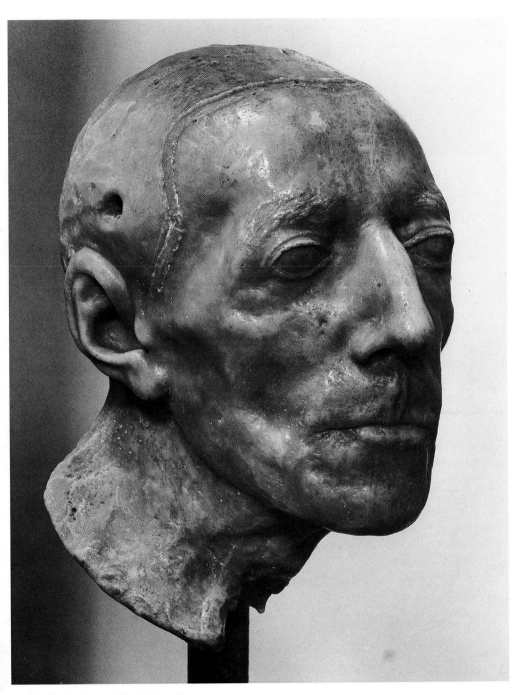

Frederick's death mask by J. Eckstein.

The obelisk at Rheinsberg. Here Prince Henry recorded the names of the heroes of the Seven Years War who had been omitted from Frederick's own memoirs. They included Prince William. The roundels were stolen by the Russians after 1945.

the message was the same: 'I couldn't nor ought I to have refused what the king of Prussia was offering me.' Voltaire enjoyed the court and its princes. Disillusion took longer to set in than was later supposed, and the famous 'but' letter of 6 November was subject to plentiful revision.

So it is known in Paris, my dear child, that we performed *La mort de César* in Potsdam, that Prince Henry is a very good actor, has no [German] accent, is very nice, and that there is pleasure to be had here? All that is true; ... but ... the king's suppers are delicious, we speak of reason, wit and science; freedom reigns; he is the soul of it all; no bad moods, no clouds, at least no storms. My life is free and busy; but ..., but ..., operas, comedies, carousels, dinners at Sanssouci, war manoeuvres, concerts, study, reading; but ..., but ..., the city of Berlin is big and better laid out than Paris, palaces, theatres, friendly widows, charming princesses, maids of honour who are beautiful and shapely, the house of Madame Tyrconnell is always full and often too much so; but ..., but ..., my dear child, it is getting a bit cold here.[22]

[11]

Voltaire did not have enough to fill his brilliant, malicious mind. His duties involved an hour a day with His Majesty, rejigging his drafts in poetry and prose.[23] Hanbury-Williams was fully *au fait* with Voltaire's mission: 'The works are printed with the largest margin I ever saw; and that margin in some places is filled up entirely with Voltaire's own handwriting.' When he was not rescanning Frederick's poems, he quarrelled with the other Frenchmen at the court. He did not always get on with La Mettrie, and d'Argens was on prolonged leave: he had gone to France. Together with d'Arnaud, Algarotti, Maupertuis, Pöllnitz and Darget, these men formed the new *Tafelrunde* of Sanssouci.[24] Hanbury-Williams called them the 'nine he-muses of the German Parnassus'. His master in London, Lord Chesterfield, thought them a rum lot: Algarotti was a 'consumate coxcomb', and d'Argens 'below mediocrity'.[25]

Voltaire described the atmosphere of those *petits soupers*. They dined at a table designed by Pesne: 'a lovely priapic. You saw young men kissing women, nymphs under satyrs, cherubs playing, sodomites and catamites, several people who stared as if dumbfounded at the different sports, doves kissing one another, billy goats leaping on nanny goats, and rams tupping ewes'. Anyone who had eavesdropped on this bizarre collection at table 'would have thought they were listening to the Seven Sages of

Greece in a brothel'.[26] That moment was perhaps the high point of Frederick's literary court between the wars, but it was not all sweetness and light. Maupertuis was a difficult customer who spoiled the evenings by his 'little jealousies'. Frederick later described him as the 'grumpiest man' he had ever seen, and brutally honest. His heart was good, however: 'the Lapp* Maupertuis was light-years away from the monkey Voltaire'.[27] Those days did not last long. Frederick was too difficult to live with, and his selection of friends not always calculated to bring him happiness. Chasot, Darget and Voltaire fled. Algarotti claimed consumption and went home to Italy. La Mettrie and Maupertuis died.

Julien Offray de La Mettrie was one of the new stars of Frederick's court. He had studied medicine, specialising in venereal disease and aphrodisiacs, and was a self-avowed atheist. His literary claim-to-fame was *l'Homme machine*, an essay on man's mechanistic nature, in which the principal object of God's creation was reduced to 'a digestive tube pierced at both ends'. It was not appreciated by the church and he had sought refuge at Frederick's court from persecution at home. While he was in Berlin he wrote two more books, though not perhaps as edifying in their content as that which made him famous: *l'Art de jouir*, exploring the orgasm, and *Le Petit Homme à grande queue* (The little man with the long tail). For once Voltaire got on reasonably well with him (even if he had no respect for his mind), and wrote home to describe this 'gay fellow, his ideas are a firework display made up entirely of rockets. The excitement lasts for about seven minutes, but is lethally boring after that.'[28]

Voltaire was not certain of the physician either: 'he would quite innocently give me some powerful acid instead of rhubarb, and then burst into laughter'. He was apparently at his happiest when he stripped himself naked and slapped his buttocks, crying 'I'm skint! I'm skint!' His role as Frederick's reader was partly to feed the monarch's prejudices towards the Catholic church: 'he is currently reading him *Histoire ecclésiastique*.† It goes on for hundreds of pages and there are places where the king and his reader practically suffocate from laughter.'[29]

There does not appear to have been too much friction between Voltaire and George Keith. The earl Marischal was packed off to Paris in August 1751 as Prussian ambassador. It did not go unnoticed in Britain that Frederick had made an exiled Jacobite his minister, just as Louis XV had

---

* Maupertuis had travelled to Lapland to study the shape of the earth.
† Almost certainly that written by Claude Fleury.

done in Tyrconnell. He carried with him a letter for Madame Denis, explaining the character of the new envoy:

You will see a rather pretty little Turk he takes with him. They caught her at the Siege of Oczakow, and made a present of her to our Scot, who does not seem to have much need of her ... He has in his retinue a sort of Tartar footman, who has the honour of being a heathen; as for him, he is, I think, Anglican, or nearly so...[30]

Voltaire particularly disliked Baculard d'Arnaud, a former protégé of his who had written some choice works with titles such as *l'Art de foutre* and *l'Epître au Cul de Manon*,* and who had replaced his friend Thiériot as Frederick's literary correspondent in June 1748. Baculard had gone so far as to describe a night of sex he had allegedly had with Madame Denis in unflattering terms. He was now receiving verses from the king. Voltaire and Darget ganged up to have Baculard exiled from the court, spreading rumours that there was a homosexual relationship between Baculard and Frederick. Collé noted: 'The dear, tender friends d'Arnaud and the king of Prussia have been split up. It is said that Voltaire had had d'Arnaud banished; he doesn't imagine that he will suffer the same fate and will be banished himself one day; and in a more dramatic way than this scamp.'[31]

Voltaire also had the knife out for a young Protestant, Angliviel de La Beaumelle, whom he thought was angling for La Mettrie's job as royal reader. He nipped any chance of a working relationship between the two men in the bud. La Beaumelle took his revenge in print with his book *Mes Pensées, ou qu'en dira-t-on*, in which he compared the writers at Frederick's court to the buffoons more usually found in the households of German princes. On Voltaire he was equally sharp. He said there had been greater poets in history, but never one better paid.[32] Voltaire was cut to the quick.

Voltaire was not only bored, he might also have been annoyed. At the beginning of September 1751, he wrote to his niece cum mistress to narrate a story he had heard from La Mettrie. Frederick had told his reader, 'I will need him for another year; you press the orange and you throw away the peel.'[33] The remark rankled. 'What should I do?' he asked his niece. 'Ignore what La Mettrie told me, confide in you alone, forget everything and wait?' He felt like a cuckold, he said. Recent research has cast some doubt on this episode, but Frederick certainly expressed the

* The Art of Fucking and An Epistle to Manon's Bum.

same sentiment to Algarotti.[34] It might have been there and then that he decided to get his revenge by fair means or foul.

Food was as unkind to La Mettrie as it had been to Charles VI. He was a great gourmand. He was finally carried off in November 1751 by a huge pheasant pâté stuffed with truffles, which he tucked into a little too liberally at Lord Tyrconnell's house. The rumour ran round Paris that it had actually been an eagle stuffed with bacon, pork and ginger. Frederick was worried, when he heard of his reader's death, that the great atheist might have received extreme unction from a priest, but 'finally it was made clear to him that the gourmand died a philosophic death'. 'I am content for the repose of his soul,' said the king. 'We began to laugh', wrote Voltaire, 'and him too.' Frederick wrote a sympathetic epitaph for his sometime reader: 'He was gay, a good devil, a good physician, but a very bad writer. If you never touched his books, however, you could be more than happy with him.'[35]

When La Mettrie died, his job was eventually awarded to the abbé de Prades, a proper heretic who had presented a doctoral thesis at the Sorbonne which denied good and evil, the existence of the soul and miracles. Not surprising, perhaps, that such a tormentor of the Catholic hierarchy should find himself knocking on Frederick's door in his search for gainful employment. Voltaire had approved the choice. He boasted to the renegade priest of the luxury of his surroundings, his apartment in the Stadtschloss – a big room on the ground floor, divided into two by a screen – and his lodgings in the town itself, which he used when the king was on his progresses. 'I scarcely go to Berlin any more, the marquis d'Argens and I spend the whole year here, except for six weeks in winter, the only time when the king establishes himself in his capital.'[36]

[III]

Almost as soon as he had unpacked his bags in Potsdam, Voltaire was looking for a means of making a little money on the side. He decided to speculate on Saxon tax bonds (which were banned in Prussia) through a certain Abraham Hirschel. The deal involved defrauding the Prussian state, but Voltaire evidently paid little heed to the idea that Frederick might find out or disapprove. Frederick did not take long to discover what he was up to. At first he was only mildly annoyed, but when the business hit the courts his attitude changed. He wrote to his sister at the end of 1750: 'Everybody is well here, my brothers are having tantrums, I am deep in politics, Voltaire is swindling Jews ...'[37] It was possibly less than exaggeration: Voltaire had loaned Hirschel 12,000 thalers, on top of which he was given letters of exchange amounting to 40,000 livres drawn on Paris. Voltaire also bought 30,000 thalers worth of diamonds from Hirschel's son, who had apparently discounted them to make the deal more attractive to Voltaire. The Frenchman was not convinced. He revoked the letter of exchange and had Hirschel arrested to get his money back. Hirschel protested that Voltaire had had the money in diamonds. Voltaire then alleged that the diamonds were substandard.[38]

Hanbury-Williams filled James Harris in on what he had gleaned; on the 'various intrigues ... the lyes they tell, the villanys they commit, the verses they make and deny afterwards'[39] all of which was chiefly applicable to Voltaire. He wrote a verse against the unwashed marquis, calling him 'that haddock more Jewish than the wandering Jew',* and promptly put it about that Algarotti was the author. To make the jest more piquant, he went to the Swan and told him that d'Argens had been abusing him.[40] Frederick was beginning to get angry about Voltaire. His tone was more bitter in the next letter he sent Wilhelmina: 'It is a case of a rogue trying to cheat a crook.'[41] Collé pointed out that Voltaire's annual income was believed to be in the region of 80,000 livres, but he still could not resist this sort of shoddy deal.

The business had blown up in Voltaire's face when he thought he had discovered that Hirschel was cheating him out of 1 per cent of the profits. Voltaire evidently tried to throttle Hirschel, telling him he did not know whom he was dealing with and that he would have him thrown into a dungeon for the rest of his days. He also attempted to rip a ring off his finger to compensate himself for what he believed were his losses in the affair. Voltaire was caught *in flagrante delicto* when Hirschel took his case to the courts and complained to the king.[42]

Now Frederick got tough. In the course of his temper tantrum, Voltaire had insulted the justice minister, Cocceji: 'he behaved like a lunatic'. The king wrote, 'I shall wait till the business has been concluded before I give him a dressing down and to see if, at the age of fifty-six, it is not possible for him to behave reasonably, and if not, at least less like a rogue.'[43] Scales were falling from his eyes. A week or so later he told his sister, 'in the end I prefer living with Maupertuis'.[44] Things were hotting up between

* D'Argens' nickname of 'Isaac' or 'the wandering Jew' derived from his successful *Lettres juives* of 1736.

the two Frenchmen. Fur was flying. Frederick was increasingly taking Maupertuis's side, much to Voltaire's consternation, as he believed it was the president who convinced the jeweller to go to law. By the end of the year Frederick was writing Voltaire off as 'a dangerous lunatic' and making it clear that he would indeed have to banish him before long.[45]

The careful monarch was also mildly annoyed that the Prussian state was supposed to compensate the French usurer to the tune of 10,000 thalers when he had bought the stock at a 35 per cent discount. He decided he would not see Voltaire until the courts had decided the matter.[46] Pöllnitz wrote to the margravine to tell her:

the head of the troop is still in exile from Augustus' court; but perhaps even better treated in his disgrace than Ovid was when he was in favour. He continues to be housed in the Berlin Schloss; he is fed; has his own carriage and his expenses are paid in everything; on top of that he has a stipend of 20,000 thalers and enjoys the liberty to plead against Israel and provide the material for a great many farces.[47]

It was actually rare that Jews had the right to pursue Gentiles before the courts, but Hirschel was a *Schutzjude* and enjoyed legal protection in Prussia. French sympathy was generally with Voltaire. The French ambassador, Valory, told Collé that 'poor' Voltaire was going through a 'disagreeable trial with a Jew', but it was noted in the French capital that 'the Jew talks about honour too'.[48] Voltaire himself was outraged: 'What! This miserable fellow whose ancestors crucified Our Lord?' 'A fugitive from the Old Testament', he called him.[49] When Voltaire won the case in February 1751, Hirschel appealed. Voltaire's victory was Pyrrhic: he won back just 2000 thalers and had to keep the diamonds that he had dismissed as mere brilliants. In the course of his undignified squabbles, he had become the laughing stock of Paris and Berlin.[50] The dramatist Lessing, employed to translate Voltaire's writ into German for the Court, sent up the proud Frenchman with the lines:

Um kurz und gut den Grund zu fassen,	*So you want to know the reason then?*
Warum die List	*Why the old Jew's*
Dem Juden nicht gelungen ist,	*Not had so much luck with his ruse?*
So heisst die Antwort ungefähr:	*Here's the answer for what it's worth:*
Herr Voltaire war ein grösserer Schelm als er.[51]	*Monsieur Voltaire was a bigger crook from birth.*

Voltaire, who had been sent to Coventry, importuned Frederick for the chance to be near him in Potsdam. He had his eye on the marquis d'Argens' house, Le Marquisat, which was virtually opposite the gates of Sanssouci, its gardens running down to the Havel. The owner was still away in France.[52] Now that he had got rid of Baculard d'Arnaud, Voltaire needed a few more projects to occupy his time and mind. Among these was the chance to destroy a budding pen-friendship between Frederick and Elie Fréron, one of Voltaire's arch-enemies. The king simply wanted a replacement for his Paris agent Thiériot, who happened to be one of Voltaire's best friends. Frederick listened to Voltaire, but regretted it. On 24 February 1751, he was on the brink of losing his temper.

First of all, in the oddest way, you demanded that I should give no employment to Fréron as my correspondent in Paris and I was weak enough to comply, despite the fact that it is not up to you whom I take into my service. D'Arnaud had offended you, a generous man would have forgiven him; a vindictive man pursues those he decides to hate. D'Arnaud did me no harm, it was for your sake that he went. You have been with the Russian ambassador [de Gross] and spoken to him about things which do not concern you and it was thought that I gave you the commission. You have meddled in the affairs of Madame de Bentinck, and it certainly wasn't your place to do so. You have had the ugliest dealings with the Jew. You have left a frightful trail throughout the town.[53]

Voltaire was banished to Berlin, but was soon allowed to return to his apartment in the Stadtschloss in Potsdam and to the Marquisat nearby. Voltaire apologised by damning Hirschel and his diamonds, but Frederick kept his distance and issued the Frenchman with stricter guidelines as to the company he was to keep: 'a bookseller [like] Gosse, a violinist at the opera [Travenol], a Jewish jeweller, in truth names which in no matter should find themselves coupled with yours. I write this letter with the coarse good sense of a German who says what he feels, without employing the flabby, equivocal and calming terms which disfigure the truth.'[54] His true feeling he expressed – in no uncertain terms – to Darget. 'Voltaire has behaved like a scoundrel, like a consummate knave; I have told him what for as he deserved. He is a base fellow, and I am ashamed for the sake of the human race that a man who possesses so much should be so stuffed with mischief.'[55]

Three months later Voltaire was soliciting the king's favour. He gave the impression of total idleness. He spent his life in bed.

I am completely alone, morning noon and night; my sole consolation lies in the necessary pleasure of taking air. I want to walk and work in your garden in Potsdam. I think that is allowed; I go there in a dream. I find great big devils, grenadiers who stick their bayonets in my belly, and shout 'Furt' [*Fort!* – go away], and 'sacrament' [?] and 'the king!', and I flee, just as the Austrians and Saxons did before them.

Voltaire mocked his own skeletal appearance. It must have been true, or the chambermaids in old Prussia must have been made of strong stuff. On one occasion as he lay in bed, one of these Junos mistook him for a heap of dirty linen and picked him up, mattress and all, and threw him on the floor.

Attention seeking, comic and otherwise, continued all summer, until the long-awaited return of the marquis d'Argens in August meant that Voltaire had to seek other lodgings, this time back in Berlin:[56]

> Chaque chose à la fin, dans sa place est remise.
> Isaac, après mille détours,
> Vient de fixer ses pas, son caprice et ses jours
> Auprès de Sans Souci, dans sa terre promise.
> Moi, je vais fixer mon destin
> Dans la chambre ou Jordan, de savante mémoire,
> Commentait à la fois Saint Paul et Aretin,
> Sans savoir des deux à qui croire.[57]

> *Everything comes to an end, is put in its place.*
> *Isaac, eagerly awaited,*
> *Has just returned, his old role is reinstated,*
> *His promised land, Sanssouci, now sees his goatish face.*
> *Me, I will seek my humble fate*
> *In the room where Jordan, by candle light would read,*
> *Aretino and Saint Paul he would annotate,*
> *Not knowing which of them to heed.*

Frederick must have been happy to see his 'Isaac', although whether the marquis was as content to be back in Potsdam is another matter. One night Frederick asked him what he would do if he were king of Prussia. 'Me Sire, ... I'd sell my kingdom as quick as a flash and buy a good estate in France.' They enjoyed one good farce together. A pastor had declaimed against the king's godlessness from his pulpit. Frederick had him brought to Potsdam, where he was tested on his orthodoxy by a jury composed of the king, 'Isaac' and Voltaire, dressed up in clerical garb.[58]

The summer frost between the two friends continued into the autumn. Voltaire was reduced to going to the opera to see the king. He heard that he had been ill with piles. Voltaire sent his best wishes for Frederick's recovery:

Que la veine hémorroïdale	*Oh that a royal person's piles*
De la personne royal	*Cease to sadden his smiles*
Cesse de troubler le repos.	*And allow him rest,* hélas!
Quand pourrai-je d'un style honnête	*Oh tell me when it can be said,*
Dire; le cul de mon héros	*That my martial hero's arse*
Va tout aussi bien que sa tête?	*Enjoys the perfect health of his head.*

Already banished for the best part of a year from the society of the king, Voltaire was spending his time with Gräfin Bentinck, a scandalous figure at the time who had lived in a lesbian relationship and had a child by a page. She had come to Berlin to petition the king over her lost property in East Friesland. Voltaire and she became close: there are some 250 letters or notes in their extant correspondence. Voltaire took up her case at court.[59] Frederick did not approve of her and told Voltaire as much.

At the queen mother's court, Voltaire heard that he was in disgrace. He wrote to the king again to ask him not to 'break the fragile reed he had brought from so far away ... You have shown a feeling of humanity which you put in your beautiful works. I demand that goodness...'

I only aspire to that permission to see and hear you. You know that it is the only consolation, and the only motive behind the renunciation of my country, my king and my dependences, my family and the friends I have had these forty years; your sacred promises are my only resource, the only thing which sustains me in the fear of having displeased you.[60]

He was told to go to Berlin, where he lodged with the father of Francheville, his secretary. Frederick cannot have been unaware that Voltaire was also enjoying one of his favourite games: circulating rumours through pamphlets published on the more liberal markets of Leipzig, Amsterdam and London. The material victims were Frederick himself and Maupertuis. Frederick's Achilles' heel was his alleged homosexuality. It is worth recalling that this was still perceived as a capital offence, although the sentence was likely to be enforced only if the delinquents were of humble origin. But only as recently as July 1750 a bogus marquis (who was in fact a cobbler) and a sausage-maker were strangled to death and burned on the place de Grève in Paris after they had been caught in the act in the rue de Beaurepaire by the captain of the watch. The pork-butcher's claim that he was simply relieving himself got him nowhere.[61]

In June 1752 there appeared in London a short text in French by 'M. M. C. F. Ecuier', entitled *Mémoires secrets pour servir à l'histoire de notre tems*, subtitled 'Idea of the person, the manner of living and the court of the king of Prussia, by M. de ...' It is a warts-and-all portrait of a king in a dirty coat. Opportunities for sex present themselves at various times of day. After the morning parade, back in his chamber, there is someone convoked to 'present his rear'. Then, again, after his post-prandial walk: 'It happens quite often that he has a few of his young boys brought to him, all those who serve him are as pretty as pictures with the loveliest faces.' If that were not enough to satisfy the ravenous king, there was another chance at nine, after his supper. Voltaire and Algarotti were there (nothing like laying a false trail) and 'one or two pathics'.[62]

The tone, language and content were remarkably similar to Voltaire's *Mémoires*, written soon after his escape from Prussia. In them Voltaire described Frederick's *lever*. His characterisation of this behaviour as 'schoolboy pleasures', might reveal something of the nature of his own schooldays:

The Stoic allowed himself a few moments for the sect of Epicurus: he had two or three favourites brought to him, either subalterns or pages; a lackey or a young cadet. They drank coffee, and the chosen one remained for half a quarter of an hour *en tête à tête*. Things didn't go all the way, seeing as during the late king's lifetime, the prince was extremely badly treated in his amorous escapades, and even more badly cured. He couldn't play the leading role; and had to make do with a secondary part.[63]

Whether or not there was any truth in these allegations is hard to say after more than two centuries. One writer has pointed out that Frederick suffered from chronic piles, which would have made the implied secondary role uncomfortable, to say the least. Evidence of a much more timid interest in his pages comes from his surviving letters to Fredersdorf, in which there is talk of a certain Carel (C. F. von Pirch). It records slights: 'Carel has been extremely impolite'; and presents: a leveret and a hussar's coat for his fifteenth birthday; but it would be hard to see such obsessive doting as a manifestation of the rapacious and tyrannical sexuality described by Voltaire or the pamphleteer.[64]

In July 1752 the already frosty relations between the king and the court poet had become even icier as a result of one of Voltaire's choicer *bon mots* coming to the attention of the king. He let slip (he was proud of the metaphor) to a General Manstein, who had brought him a French text to look through, that his role in the king's literary life was that of a ghost: 'My friend, another time. You see the king has handed me his dirty linen to launder; I'll clean yours afterwards.' Voltaire never actually denied making the remark; on the other hand, he laid the blame fairly and squarely at Maupertuis's feet for repeating it to Frederick. Maupertuis had blocked the abbé Raynal's candidature for the Academy, overriding Voltaire's favourite. Voltaire also claimed to be annoyed that Maupertuis had said to him that the post of 'court atheist' was vacant after La Mettrie's death, and that he should possibly apply. He was also convinced that Maupertuis led a cabal at court which aimed to destroy his good relations with the king. It was too much. He decided to go on the offensive.[65]

Voltaire was jealous of Maupertuis's presidency of the Academy, just as he was envious of Algarotti's county: neither had been offered to him. He thought he was on safe ground because, as he told Madame Denis, the king preferred him to 'Plato', whom he found dull company. The excuse he fabricated at the time sounded more honourable. Voltaire had come to the defence of the mathematician Johann Samuel König. Maupertuis had unfairly dismissed König from the Academy because he had put it about that Maupertuis was trying to take credit for theories more properly attributed to Leibniz. Voltaire set to work. The campaign went badly, however. With brutal frankness, Voltaire made a clean breast of it to his niece:

I have no sceptre, but I do possess a pen; and I had, I don't know how, cut that pen in such a manner that it made Plato look a trifle ridiculous with his giants, his predictions, his dissections and his impertinent quarrel with König. The ribbing was innocent enough; but I didn't know then that I was lashing out at the king's pleasures. The game has turned sour.[66]

At first, Frederick had been mildly amused by the lampoons directed at the president of his Academy, but things began to get out of control when Voltaire began publishing his attacks. Maupertuis was coughing up blood and not in the best health to defend himself. Voltaire was granted permission to return to the palace in Potsdam at the end of November, but only after he had signed an affidavit written in the king's hand:

I promise His Majesty that for all the time that he has the grace to lodge me in his palace I shall write against no man; not the government of France, against its ministers; or against other sovereigns, or against famous men of letters towards whom I shall render the respect which is due; I shall in no way abuse the letters of His Majesty; and I shall behave in a manner which is suitable for a man of letters who has the honour of being a chamberlain to His Majesty, and who lives among honest men.[67]

Voltaire was writing, and showing the off-cuts to the king. Frederick had suggested a philosophical dictionary, on the lines of Bayle's, but without the latter's cumbersome textual apparatus. This was later to grow into the *Dictionnaire philosophique*, a work that severely mocks Frederick in the article 'Guerre'.* Voltaire sent him the articles 'Atheisme', 'Ame' and 'Baptême'. These pithy little essays brought Voltaire a short respite: Frederick invited him to dinner. It was clearly a tense occasion, as both the king and Voltaire had taken up their positions and neither was prepared to budge. Voltaire called it 'Damocles' supper; after which I left with a promise to return, and with the firm intention never to see him again for the rest of my life'.[69] It is impossible to know now, whether this was a later construction. It is certain that their relations did not slump as utterly as his *Mémoires* would lead us to suppose. Voltaire now cast Frederick in the role of a tyrant: 'My friend means "my slave"; my dear friend means "you mean less than nothing to me"; you must understand by "I will make you happy", "I will put up with you until I no longer have need of you"; "Come to dinner" means "I feel like making fun of you tonight".'[70] To punish Frederick for his ingratitude, Voltaire wrote to d'Alembert to prevent him from entertaining the idea of replacing Maupertuis at the Academy when the time came. If he was not offered the job, then no one of any stature should have it either.

Although Voltaire signed Frederick's letter of 27 November, he showed little desire to abandon his feud with Maupertuis. He was busy at that very time, penning new libels against his fellow countryman, starting with a *Réponse d'un académicien de Berlin à un académicien de Paris* and culminating with the *Diatribe du docteur Akakia*, where Maupertuis's theories were

---

* 'il les habille d'un gros drap bleu à cent dix sous l'aune, borde leurs chapeaux avec du gros fil blanc, les fait tourner à droite et à gauche, et marcher à la gloire'.[68]

examined by the Holy See, which, after pointing out various borrowings from Leibniz, recommended that the president of the Prussian Academy learn to write and not restate trivial truths. The doctor Akakia* prescribed herbal teas and a little course of study at a university.

Frederick caught him out. A refutation to the *Réponse* appeared in the form of a *Lettre d'un académicien de Berlin à un académicien de Paris*. Voltaire read some sharp words describing his person: he was a 'libeller without genius'; 'a despicable enemy'; his imagination 'sterile'; his nastiness 'blind'; and he was a coward to attack a great man. He sent a page to Voltaire in the Berlin Schloss with a message: 'Your heart is more than a hundred times as dreadful as your mind is admirable.' Voltaire responded by insulting the king. The king's emissary was only fifteen or sixteen, but he had his wits about him: 'Recall and reflect that he is the king and that you are in his house, and that I am in his service and I hear what you are saying.' The page made a full report to Frederick, who commented laconically: 'He's a madman.'[71]

When *Akakia* appeared, Frederick had the brochure publicly burned before the author's windows on 24 December, but spared his friend by keeping his name out of the gazettes. He followed up, however, with his *Lettres au public*, which appeared unsigned, but emblazoned with a Prussian eagle. Voltaire seems to have admired it, and told Madame Denis that Frederick could write quite well, even without his help. By that time Voltaire was no longer asking for his old Potsdam rooms back. He had decided it was time to go. He had fled to an old royal property, the Belvedere near the Stralauer Tor, on the eastern outskirts of Berlin. There he was visited by Fredersdorf, who presumably offered him some chance to redeem himself before his ireful master. Voltaire told him that he had been insulted by Maupertuis and felt fully justified in his campaign against the president. 'All that remains for me is go away and hide myself for ever,' wrote Voltaire in his special 'pathetic' vein.[72] Fredersdorf had come, however, to ask Voltaire to return the cross of his order *pour le mérite*, as well as the ceremonial key he possessed as one of the king's chamberlains. The usurious Voltaire replied that Frederick still owed him money.[73] Voltaire's new secretary, Collini, claimed that Voltaire returned the items, but that the king gave them back to him before his departure. If this is true, it is because Voltaire agreed to return in October: no one was allowed to leave the country for good with the king's precious *Oeuvres*.

---

* Greek for 'without malice', which seems hardly appropriate.

On New Year's Day, Voltaire wrote another tear-jerker: 'I have lost everything, all there is left is the memory of having spent a happy time in your Potsdam retreat.'[74]

Throughout the affair he proved himself a consummate liar. He had denied all relations with König, who had been one of Emilie's mathematical gurus; now he admitted that he was a friend, but claimed that he was 'more attached to His Majesty'. He also told Frederick that he was in no way responsible for some of the stories of the king's homosexuality that were currently being printed in London. He had the nerve to suggest that Maupertuis was the source. 'I only write to my niece,'[75] he said. Frederick continued to display patience, and a degree of humour while Voltaire tried to halt the distribution of the libels. His new secretary, the abbé de Prades, wrote to Voltaire on the king's behalf: 'The king has consulted his consistory, and his bishops have examined the question of whether your sin was mortal or venial. In truth the churchmen recognised it as being extremely mortal ... but, however, by the power of Beelzebub's grace which resides in His Majesty, it is believed possible to absolve you...'[76]

A squirming, apparently sore-lipped, Voltaire replied to the abbé de Prades on 15 March 1753. Using his health as a pretext, he said he needed to take the waters of Plombières. The hypochondriac Frederick was unlikely to have been fooled. In truth, discretion was the better part of valour: Voltaire had decided to run for it.

I swear that I am in despair over leaving you and the king; but it is a thing I cannot avoid. Please do what you can with the dear marquis, Fredersdorf, good God, with the king himself, find out what can be done to allow me the consolation of seeing him before I leave. I really want it, I want to hug the abbé, and the marquis; the marquis shall have no bigger hug than you; nor the king either.[77]

The king replied coldly the next day.

He may quit my service whenever he chooses, he doesn't need to use the pretext of taking the waters in Plombières, but might he have the goodness to return to me before he leaves, his contract, the key, the cross, and the volume of poetry I lent him; I should have been content had he and König merely attacked my works, I am happy to offer them up to those who enjoy denigrating the reputation of others; I have none of the lunacy or vanity of authors, and the cabals of literary folk seem to me the very pinnacle of vileness...[78]

Voltaire finally left ten days later, on 26 March. In the meantime there had been a small reconciliation between the feuding friends. Voltaire had promised to return to Prussia in October, after his cure in Plombières. Frederick then left for Silesia to review his troops.

He might have been genuinely carried away by his desire to put down Maupertuis and defend König, but Voltaire gave free rein to his 'ingenuity, verve, malice, wickedness and injustice', thereby hastening his rupture with Frederick.[79] Perhaps this was his desire after all. As early as 9 September 1752, Voltaire had written to his niece to tell her that he was going 'to set sail from the island of Calypso as soon as the cargo [was] ready':[80] that is, long before the real storm had broken. It is hard to resist the interpretation that Voltaire was doing everything physically possible to make the king of Prussia angry, possibly in the hope that he would accede to Voltaire's desire to go home.

[IV]

Genuine remorse on Voltaire's part seems unlikely. As soon as he had left Prussian soil and arrived in Leipzig, he was busy reviving *Akakia*, which was now reissued as *l'Histoire du docteur Akakia*, complete with supplementary texts. It enjoyed enormous popularity. Poor Maupertuis, at death's door, but still a nobleman and a former officer, felt it incumbent on him to challenge Voltaire to a duel. Collé called it 'the best possible joke and the most biting sarcasm'.[81] Frederick was still seething, not least because Voltaire had neglected to return certain texts that he did not want taken out of the country. He wrote to his sister on 12 April:

You ask for news of Voltaire; here is the truth of the story. He behaved here like the greatest rascal in the universe ... he is distilling new poisons ... As far as you're concerned, my sister, I advise you not to write to him in your own hand: I was caught that way. He is the most treacherous rascal in the universe ... Guilty men are broken on the wheel for crimes of less importance than his.

His misdemeanours could 'fill a book as fat as a volume of Bayle'.[82]

Frederick had Voltaire's rooms redecorated after he left. They were painted yellow, the colour of envy, and the walls were decorated with grimacing monkeys, proud peacocks and venomous snakes and toads, all attributes of the departed trouble-maker.[83] Frederick made light of it, but with Voltaire's departure ended the second and the last of his golden ages, when he was surrounded by the purveyors of peace and pleasure rather than war and strife. Just five days before Voltaire's final departure from Prussia, he sent Wilhelmina a self-pitying letter: 'When I look back on my life, I see just a succession of follies. Perfect reason is not designed for us. Sensitivity is our lot; all the happy moments we experience are like so many forbidden fruits plucked from a tree by a jealous monster.'[84]

Unfortunately for Frederick, the Voltaire affair was not quite finished. He was indeed manufacturing new poisons: he spent twenty-three days in Leipzig, supervising editions of his attacks on Maupertuis. He was doing a little banking on the side, and lending money to Frederick's ward, the duke of Württemberg, no doubt at excessive rates of interest.[85] Voltaire had been pestering Wilhelmina, as they knew that she was keen to have the great intellectual grace her court too. Initially Fredersdorf had been tested out by Wilhelmina's minister, marquis d'Adhémar.[86] Frederick was warned: 'Tell Adhémar that my sister may do what she likes. If she wants to have Voltaire, then I wish her more luck with him that I had. I would only advise her not to do so, as the fellow has an ugly and infamous character.'[87]

Frederick wrote to his sister directly to warn her against Voltaire: 'You wouldn't believe to what degree these people play games; all these convulsions, illnesses, fits of despair, it's all nothing but an act. I was fooled at the beginning, but not at the end.'[88] 'Forget your domestic unhappiness' was Frederick's advice. Wilhelmina badly needed solace: not only had her husband lost interest in her, but in January the old Schloss in Bayreuth had been consumed by fire. Frederick's sister had been lucky to salvage a few small items from the flames. Frederick was on hand with relief for the homeless margrave and margravine: he sent them books, flutes and sheet-music.[89]

In Potsdam there was a change of heart. Voltaire had left the king on reasonable terms, promising to return as soon as he was summoned. For that reason, perhaps, he had been allowed to take with him the *Oeuvres de poésie*, which could not otherwise be taken out of Prussia. Possibly Voltaire's behaviour in Leipzig convinced the king that Voltaire meant to cause trouble, and use the poems with their rude remarks about his brother rulers (not to mention the bawdy text of *Palladion*) to smooth his passage back to Versailles and King Louis' grace. Certainly the French government would have been keen to see them, as it later proved when it had two editions pirated during the Seven Years War.

As head of Frederick's secret service, Fredersdorf issued instructions to Frederick's resident in Frankfurt am Main, Freytag and his assistant, the

Hofrat Schmid, to detain Voltaire and Collini on their arrival, and lighten them of the key, cross and cordon, as well as any letters or writings by the king. They were also to examine the writer's coffers and take out a book. If Voltaire refused to allow this, he was to be arrested. Only on 29 April did Fredersdorf specifically mention the *Oeuvres de poésie*.[90]

In the meantime Voltaire and Collini had arrived in Gotha, where they were entertained for a month by the philosophic duchess. They travelled on to Kassel, where the poet was alarmed to see Pöllnitz at the Landgrave's court. Voltaire expressed a fear that the elderly courtier had been sent to kill him.[91] They went on to Frankfurt, arriving on 31 May, and put up at the Goldner Löwe. Frederick's agents were ready for them. The next day they interrogated Voltaire for eight hours, reporting that the poet was 'much shaken' by this treatment. As they could not locate the book in question, Voltaire was placed under house arrest.[92]

Voltaire had been humiliated. It was not something he would forgive lightly. Freytag and Schmid were certainly heavy-handed officials, possibly they were also venial, but in Voltaire's version they have also come down to us as a brace of uneducated louts who would stop at nothing to get their hands on their master's '*Oeuvres de Poeshie*' (sic). That Freytag had no problems with the French language was clear to Varnhagen von Ense, who examined the letters a century after the events. Voltaire was now in a foul mood and lashed out at those who called on him. On 9 June, Madame Denis arrived from Strasbourg. She was no less hysterical than her uncle and wrote to the Lord Marischal in Paris, who had never taken the feud seriously ('we need Voltaires and Ariostos,' he told his brother).[93] Marischal none the less wrote a firm and realistic reply: 'The king my master has never committed a single vindictive act.[94] I defy his enemies to name one; but if some great Prussian were to be offended by the utterances of your uncle, he would punch him on the head, and crush him ... Stop your uncle from doing stupid things.'[95]

When Voltaire's more voluminous luggage arrived, Freytag was able to relieve the Frenchman of Frederick's precious poems, but the Prussian resident still refused to allow Voltaire to leave Frankfurt. On 20 July, Voltaire and Collini made a dash for it, leaving Madame Denis behind with the rest of the belongings. In a hired coach they reached the outskirts of the imperial city, but Voltaire tarried to recover a writing desk and the two men were apprehended. As they were brought back into town they were insulted by the mob.[96] After a histrionic scene involving much dissembling on the part of the poet, which Freytag dismissed as

'Contorsiones und Tartuffereien', the Bürgermeister reluctantly agreed to extend the house arrest, although he had no specific orders from the king.[97]

Madame Denis was also detained for good measure. On 23 June, Voltaire was forced to sign an assurance on behalf of himself and his niece, not to try to leave his quarters until fresh orders had come from the king. Voltaire wrote to Frederick, once again claiming to be at death's door.[98] He was furious with the king, who was compared to the illustrious tyrant, Dionysius of Syracuse.[99]

Freytag returned the book to Potsdam on 23 June, but Voltaire remained under arrest. Freytag and Schmid were clearly exceeding their instructions. When Frederick returned from Silesia, he made it clear that the party should be allowed to go as soon as the book had been recuperated.[100] Freytag even toyed with the idea of sending Voltaire back to Prussia.[101] The farce dragged on for a further two weeks before the city council allowed Voltaire, his secretary and his niece to depart for Mainz.[102] In the meantime, the claims of brutality multiplied. Collini maintains that Voltaire was guarded by twelve soldiers. Freytag's report admitted to two.[103] Madame Denis asserted that Freytag's secretary Dorn spent the night in her room, 'emptying bottle after bottle', and making attempts on her honour. Varnhagen von Ense found evidence that Voltaire's niece had asked the official into her room, presumably to protect her from the soldiers.[104] Most persistently, Voltaire claimed to have been robbed by Frederick's men. Later he aimed a pistol at Dorn, and Collini had to stand between the two. Voltaire later said it was not loaded.[105]

Voltaire had been crushed. His response was extraordinary. On the one hand, he sent letters this way and that comparing himself to Alcibiades and claiming that he had been jilted by the Socratic king of Prussia; in the others, addressed to the emperor in Vienna, for example, he cast Frederick in the role of a tyrant 'more absolute than the Great Turk', all the time stressing that he had but a few more days to live (he died a quarter of a century later).[106] The process ended with the most damaging and misleading work of all: the memoirs, with all their 'revelations' of the homosexual paradise that was Potsdam and Sanssouci.

Varnhagen von Ense summed up the Frankfurt incident as a 'lovers' quarrel'.[107] Voltaire himself talked of a 'sphinx who devoured an old maid and bathed in her blood, and they spoke of love'. He wanted his revenge to be terrible. Collini admitted in his posthumous memoirs that 'Voltaire dreamed all his life of getting his revenge for the brutality he suffered in Frankfurt.' The projected novel, *Paméla*, therefore became the 'The secret garden of nemesis'.[108] The incident was neither forgiven nor forgotten. Prussia became 'Oursie' or 'Vandalie',[109] and all those things he had so genuinely admired about its king were mocked or denigrated: 'In the "Lettres de Prusse" you will find no trace of that Soloman of the North governing his land, reforming justice, establishing wise laws, guaranteeing the liberty of conscience and looking after the happiness of the subjects who adore him. Frederick the Great is seen only through the wrong end of the telescope."[110]

· Frederick was moderately critical of Freytag's heavy-handed treatment of 'le fou et la folle', which fell short of his own standards in matters of justice. Already by the beginning of August he had had intimations of just how much trouble Voltaire could cause if he put his mind to it. Freytag's falsified letters were now in circulation:

It is sad for him that he writes as badly as the poet writes well, and that the woman Denis can use [Freytag's behaviour] to improve her stock in the eyes of the host of lovers she has in Paris in order to salvage an honour which had been exposed to the bold enterprises of Sieur d'Arnaud. For my own part, I am happy that the business is over...[111]

On 13 July, however, a moderately appeased Frederick had been able to write to his ambassador in Paris:

Well my dear Milord, I think I have finished with the business of the poet and his niece, who, as you say, could be a nice slut who is as malicious as her uncle. These people committed acts worthy of hanging against my resident Freytag in Frankfurt, and he is giving thanks to Heaven for being delivered of them. The poet has petitioned the queen of Hungary to enter into her service. She has sent an ingenious reply that there was room for Voltaire only on Mount Parnassus, and as that was not in Vienna, they couldn't receive him in the manner due. On learning this the poet wrote to the king my uncle,* asking him for a pension of £800 a year...[112]

The affair refused to die. More and more libellous writing circulated; more damaging gossip changed hands. Marischal was obliged to warn of the scurrilous pamphlet printed in London which was now doing the rounds in Paris (see above, p. 222). Frederick showed a degree of

---

* George II of Great Britain.

equanimity throughout it all: he did not want the text refuted, or the author punished. He probably suspected that Voltaire was behind it. A king should be impervious to such impertinent gossip. 'I serve the state with all the ability and all the integrity that nature has granted me; even though my talents are weak, I owe the state nothing more, because I cannot give any more than I have, and it is also incumbent on a public person to serve as a butt for satire, criticism and often calumny too.'[113]

The earl proved a solid friend. Frederick wrote hopefully:

Here is the last time that I write about the lunatic poet and his Medea. I forgive him his unpleasantnesses, his mischief, his calumnies and satires; full absolution for all sins as in a Holy Year! I should have preferred it had he unleashed his lampoons against me alone, and I should not have pursued him; but the infamous way in which he treated Maupertuis is inexcusable ... Goodbye dear Milord ... keep out of dealings with poets and arguments with harlots, it is the only way to remain happy here below.[114]

The following January a rumour blew around that Voltaire had indeed died. Frederick did not take it seriously, but he took up his pen and wrote a little obituary in verse.

Ci-gît le seigneur Arouet,	*Here lies the noble Arouet,**
Qui de friponner eut manie	*Who so loved to cheat and lie*
Ce bel espirit toujours adroit	*This cunning wit, this rogue so gay,*
N'oublie pas son intérêt	*To rob Satan found a way,*
En passant même à l'autre vie.	*When he passed to the other side.*
Lorsqu'il vit le sombre Achéron,	*When he saw the grim Acheron,†*
Il chicana le prix de passage de l'onde	*He swindled old Beelzebub out of his gold*
Si bien que le brutal Charon	*So well that the thug-like Charon‡*
D'un coup de pied au ventre appliqué sans façon	*Gave the man a kick in the guts so strong*
Nous l'a renvoyé dans le monde.[115]	*That he landed back in this world.*

* Voltaire's born name.
† River in Hades.
‡ Ferryman in Hades.

The earl was mildly critical of the style of these verses. 'Your reflexions on the subject of the epigram are apposite, my dear Milord; [but] although I make way for Voltaire the poet, I would be very annoyed if people were able to place our characters on the same footing...'[116]

Despite all the mischief-making in which Voltaire had indulged since he came to Berlin in 1750, when Wilhelmina passed through Colmar in May 1754 on her way through France to Rome, she was visited by an abject poet: 'He told me that he adored you, that he had been wrong, that he admitted his mistakes, that he was the unhappiest man in the world. His [physical] state, his words and his expression made me sorry for him. I reproached him a little over his conduct, but I didn't have the heart to go too far.'[117] Some of his remorse might have been the result of his bad behaviour in the Upper Alsatian city. Frederick had heard the news and reported it to Algarotti in Italy:

Your brother in Beelzebub has had a quarrel with the Jesuits in Colmar. It was not the most prudent thing he has done in his life. They say that he might be obliged to leave Alsace. It is astonishing that age has done nothing to wither his madness, and that this man, so admirable for his talented mind, should be so despicable in his conduct.[118]

Algarotti had been a disappointment to Frederick too. In July 1754 he even heard a rumour that he was on the point of marrying.[119] As his 'Swansong', Algarotti organised the completion of the Catholic church on Frederick's new forum in Berlin. Money for such an enterprise was not forthcoming. Frederick liked the outward show of tolerance, but Algarotti had the clever idea of selling Frederick to the pope. He was, after all, a Calvinist monarch who had declared his intention not only to allow Catholics the right to worship freely in his land, but also to grant them the same protection accorded to Protestants. The money to fill in the shell of the church was finally stumped up by Cardinal Quirini, who insisted on the *quid pro quo* of having his name on the frieze, where it still is.[120]

Frederick was grateful to the cardinal for taking the burden off his own pocket. Generally his utterances on the subject of Catholicism were not so generous. In the *Histoire de mon temps*, he recounted the story of his experience in Landeshut during the Second Silesian War when the local Protestant assembly asked permission to slaughter all the Catholics in their midst. By the sound of things there were not many: one priest ploughing a lonely furrow. Still Frederick allegedly told them to turn the other cheek and go home.[121] For the rest Frederick's fantasy world was well populated with idle, sinful monks living 'dimly in cloisters ... [spouting] in their filthy lowliness their miserable theology'. He looked forward to a better age when 'our descendants have long forgotten the puerile idiocy of faith, creed and the ceremonial of both priest and religion'.[122]

The count and royal chamberlain left a month before Voltaire to settle matters with Quirini and to see what had been dug up in the excavations at Herculaneum near Naples. Meanwhile, Algarotti tried to keep his master sweet with consignments of botargo and truffles, but Frederick none the less gave Fredersdorf instructions to withhold his salary until he returned to Potsdam.[123] Herculaneum interested Frederick, as it was the place where 'Cicero harangued [the crowd], where Virgil wrote, Tibullus sighed and Ovid crawled ...' He wanted a block of marble sent back to him 'like Jews who return from Palestine bring back earth from the former Temple for their co-religionaries'.[124] In the end Algarotti sent the marble, but it was not enough for Frederick, who wanted yellow agate for a brace of tables and chimney pieces too.

Frederick was good at living in Italy vicariously: when Wilhelmina arrived there in the spring of 1755, he was able to tell her what to see in Genoa, recommending the church of the Annunciation. 'You will find Italy like an old flirt who thinks herself as pretty as she was in her youth ...' Wrinkled Italy might have been, but Germany was still nothing to compare to her.

It will take a lot of time before our plump German peasants write verse like the Florentines, before our painters equal the likes of Paul Veronese or Titian, and before we have enough superb palaces to turn into pretty ruins when the time comes; and I think that will only happen when our sun exerts the force it does on the thirty-sixth parallel.[125]

In his boredom and disillusion he wrote to Darget, who had also made a bolt for it, claiming he would find pictures for Frederick's new gallery in France.

Our set has gone to seed; the madman is in Switzerland, the Italian has left without leaving a forwarding address, Maupertuis is at death's door, and d'Argens has hurt his little finger, which means carrying his arm in a sling, as if he'd been injured at [the Battle of] Philippsburg by cannon shot ... I live with my books, I talk to people of the century of Augustus, and soon I shall learn less of my contemporaries than the late Jordan knew of the streets of Berlin.

Two months later he was giving the hero of the *Palladion* the homely instruction: 'Goodbye my dear; piss well and be gay, that is all there is for us to do in this world...'[126]

[v]

The bickering that characterised the denizens of Sanssouci might seem a trivial pursuit for a king of Frederick's stature, but he was not idle during that short time before Germany once again went up in the smoke of the Seven Years War. In 1752 he carried on a tradition established by his father by setting down a *Testament politique* for the enlightenment of his successor, William Prince of Prussia. Much space was given over to the administration of his new province of Silesia. The pro-Austrian clergy and nobility needed to be elbowed out, but those who behaved were entitled to stay. The monasteries were taxed at 30 per cent 'in order to make them good for something'.[127] The king was 'In some way the pope of the Lutherans and Calvinists; I make priests, and I demand of them only morality and gentleness.'

It was the moment to give his views on Prussia's neighbours. To an earlier generation these were so brutal that the Hohenzollerns refused to allow the two *Testaments* to be published while they were still kings and kaisers. It is questionable to what degree these statements of Prussian interest, however, constitute a real desire to acquire or invade neighbouring provinces; more that if the opportunity arose, these areas would be of the most interest to Prussia. Saxony was 'a rudderless boat which moves according the wind and currents'. Denmark's politics were based on the desire to acquire Holstein. Frederick reiterated the interest he had in grabbing provinces of Poland, which he had first made in his letter to Natzmer (see above, pp. 78–79): the country was to be consumed like an artichoke, leaf by leaf. His aim was to link up Pomerania and East Prussia by the creation of a land bridge through Pomerelia. Danzig was to be the fulcrum of this new province: 'This acquisition will make the Poles scream a lot, who ship their corn through Danzig, and who rightly fear they will become dependent on Prussia through the taxes which it would impose on all those goods which the Poles sell in other countries and for which they use the Vistula or its estuary.'[128]

Besides setting down guidelines for his successor, Frederick continued to patronise the arts. Stocking up his new gallery at Sanssouci absorbed a deal of the time and the effort of his friends and diplomats abroad.

In the autumn of 1753 the trusted Fredersdorf was dispatched to deal with Mettra, Frederick's agent in Paris. He was told what to buy and for what prices, and that he should avoid 'ridiculous' religious themes.[129] On 1 October, he reported on a lot of 271 paintings, including many Rubens and van Dycks, valued at 273,000 livres. The king was sceptical, and minuted 'a lot of money, I must see the catalogue'. In the middle of the following year, Mettra was advised to bid for Titian, Veronese, Jordaens and Correggio. His former secretary kept him up to date on the sale of private collections. The earl marischal secured him a Battoni, and went in pursuit of a brace of Mengs and a Constanzi. The Südetenländer Mengs was doubtless promoted by Algarotti, who thought him 'il piùdotto pittore della presente età'.[130] Through Darget he made the acquisition of Correggio's *Leda and the Swan*, although the regent duke of Orleans had mutilated it, splitting it into four and cutting out Leda's head. Frederick bought what was left, and had the painter Schlesinger paint Leda a new face.

Frederick's taste was changing. The old rococo stand-bys were no longer enough. In November 1754, Darget wrote to tell him that he had put his hand on a cache of ten Lancrets. Frederick wrote back that he did not want them. 'For the time being I am happy to buy Rubens and van Dyck, in a word, pictures by the great painters of the Flemish or French schools. If you know of any for sale, you will make me happy by telling me.' In April 1755, Frederick showed his prescience once again when he wrote to his friend that war was coming between France and England and that he wanted to finish his collection before it began in earnest. Work on the building itself, a conversion of the old hothouse by Johann Gottfried Büring, only began a few months before war broke out: Frederick wrote to his sister: 'I am building a picture gallery at Sanssouci, another silliness, if you like, but the world is like that, and if you wanted to record only the reasonable things which men do, history would be very short.'

He was pleased with his collection: 'it is astonishing with what ease I was able to assemble a fairly large number of paintings which were known or famous among connoisseurs. It is going to be a little embellishment for Sanssouci, and will also be used as a promenade when bad weather prevents you from going into the garden.' It was indeed an achievement. Without borrowing any pictures from Berlin he had put together more than 100: two Veroneses, a Tintoretto, a Solimena, twelve Rubens, eleven van Dycks. In November 1755 he was telling his sister that he was still short of fifty canvases which he was expecting from Italy and Flanders. 'As soon as I have filled the space, I shall buy nothing more.' That only happened in 1770. In the meantime he had acquired three Leonardos, a Michelangelo and nine Correggios, and had brought his collection of Rubens and van Dyck up to thirty-eight and fifteen respectively and added a Poussin.[131] The building itself – 'without contradiction the most splendid in all Europe' – was finished in the year of Frederick's triumphal return.[132]

Frederick was determined to have a porcelain factory of his own. Prussia had been cheated by Böttger, who had left the country, taking his secrets to Saxony where he founded Europe's first great porcelain manufacture at Meissen. In 1751 Frederick had his first success with Wilhelm Kaspar Wegely, who brought in experts from Meissen for the factory he built in the Neue Friedrichstrasse in Berlin. In 1757 Frederick tried to get the staff at Meissen to defect *en masse*, but efforts to make something that could really challenge Meissen were hampered until a source of kaolin was found in Silesia.[133]

Frederick continued to take a close interest in his court orchestra and opera. By 1752, the former was already perceived as the best in Europe, with individual players of the calibre of C. P. E. Bach, Franz Benda, Czarth, Graun, the viola da gamba player Hesse, Quantz and Richter. Franz Benda and his family continued to live modestly in their house in Nowawes,[134] across the water from Potsdam, with the rest of their clan of Bohemian immigrants. The present house was built after lightning struck the original building on 22 July 1755. Frederick and Benda were in the middle of the Sanssouci concert, but as soon as the king had finished his *adagio* he rode over to inspect the damage. Fifty houses had been destroyed by the blaze. Frederick spent an hour and a half at this *intermezzo*, inspecting the damage and promising financial help, then rode back and finished the concert.[135]

In his libretti, Frederick continued to borrow from his favourite poets. For the carnival of 1751 he reworked Racine's *Mithridate* with the help of Graun and Villati.[136] In 1753 *Sylla* combined elements from both Racine's *Britannicus* and Corneille's *Cinna*. He had problems with his principals. On 7 November that year he wrote of his frustration to Fredersdorf: 'La Astrua and Le Carestini[137] have had a fight with one another and now they are asking for permission to leave; they are rabble, may the devil take the lot of them! You pay this scum to give you pleasure, and not to give you all this vexation.' He had problems with his instrumentalists too, who deemed their salaries too small. Frederick seriously undervalued C. P. E. Bach, paying him only 300 thalers. The musician heard that his rival, Agricola, was being paid twice as much and wrote to Fredersdorf in protest. 'Bach is lying' was Frederick's reply. 'Agricola got only 500 thalers. [Bach] played once in yesterday's concert, now it has gone to his head!'[138]

The greatest work by Frederick and Graun is deemed to be *Montezuma*: 'Graun has surpassed himself with the music', Frederick told his sister.[139] The monarch was adapting it for the carnival of 1754. Frederick worked some of his religious prejudices into a didactic text. 'What,' says the Aztec, 'shall I think of a religion which teaches you to hold all others in contempt ... Our religion is more perfect ... it commands that we should love all mortals ...' 'You are right to assume that for *Montezuma* I am interested in making Cortez into a tyrant,' he wrote to Algarotti in Padua, 'and as a result we can unleash, in the music itself, a few jibes at the Catholic religion; but I am forgetting you are in one of the countries of the Inquisition; excuse me, and I hope I shall see you soon in a land of heretics where even opera can serve to reform manners and destroy superstition.'[140] Frederick and Graun's last joint effort before the outbreak of war was Voltaire's *Mérope*, which was first produced on 27 March 1756. The text did not appeal to Voltaire: 'Without question it was the worst thing he ever wrote.' Frederick must have known: 'I have spoiled the tragedy of *Mérope* by making it into an opera,' he told Wilhelmina.[141]

[VI]

In 1755 Frederick the Great was only forty-three years old, but he was ageing rapidly. In a more sensitive mood, before he had quarrelled with both, Voltaire had sent some affectionate lines to Maupertuis about the king:

Ami, vois-tu ces cheveux blancs	*My friend, do you see that greyness*
Sur la tête que j'adore?	*On the head I adore?*
Ils resemblent à ses talents:	*It resembles his genius,*
Ils sont venus avant le temps,	*Which will grow much more and still*
Et comme eux ils croîtront	*impress,*
encore.[142]	*And like the hair was premature.*

His light brown hair was indeed turning grey, his body was bent and his teeth were falling out.[143] He suffered from palpitations, insomnia, colic and incessant gout. His correspondence with Fredersdorf gave free rein to the illnesses of both men. Frederick was obsessed with the need to improve his servant's frail constitution and at the same time keen to regale him with the minutiae of his own condition. The time they spent in one another's company seems to have been much taken up with comparing ailments. In April 1755, for instance, Frederick wrote to commiserate with his sick friend: 'You can't piss and I can't walk, we are both so useless that we are fit only for the knacker's yard.'[144]

His misanthropy became more noticeable with every day that passed. He wrote to Algarotti in 1753: 'With age I feel more and more incredulous when it comes to histories, theology and physicians. There are few known truths in the world, we look for them, and while we do so, we satisfy ourselves with the fables that are created for us, and the eloquence of charlatans.'[145] His relations with his family were as difficult as ever and were to come to a head during the Seven Years War. It was, however, a period of better relations with his sister Wilhelmina. She was busy constructing her own Sanssouci in the Neue Schloss Eremitage outside Bayreuth with the help of the architects Joseph Saint-Pierre and Carl Gontard.

In 1749 Bayreuth had received the plans of Frederick's summer residence from Potsdam. Sanssouci was the Temple of Bacchus, hers the Temple of Apollo. To this she added another rural retreat in Sanspareil, which was decorated with scenes from the adventures of *Télémaque*.[146] After the fire that destroyed the old Schloss in 1753, a site was found in another part of Bayreuth for a new palace. This would be the ultimate showplace for the rococo style that she and her brother loved so much. Frederick was able to experience the loveliness of the new Bayreuth when he visited his sister in June 1754, with his court and a retinue of twenty-five hussars. Frederick was idolised by his sister and her subjects. After he left she wrote to him, telling him that she had revisited all the places where he had dwelt in order to have the feeling of being with him: 'I am still suffering from the deepest melancholy.'[147]

William kept the peace with his brother William, but Henry, and to a much lesser extent Ferdinand, were thorns in Frederick's side. Both William and Henry sought out their quarry in the rather more sociable atmosphere of Monbijou. As Frederick himself put it: 'My mother's court is my brothers' brothel.'[148] Henry had to be confined to quarters from time to time, after his disappearances into the lower depths of Berlin. Frederick's way of dealing with his second brother was remarkably similar to that employed by his father with him: freedom was bought at the cost of a forced marriage, for which Henry never forgave his brother. On 25 June 1752 he wed Wilhelmina of Hesse-Cassel. Bielfeld enthused, 'Her appearance was that of more than mortal beauty',[149] but Henry was, as a contemporary put it, a 'Potsdamite': 'Poor princess, how you will find yourself missing out.'[150] Frederick remained true to his word, however: Henry was immediately allowed to move out. For the time being he was lodged in the Palais Schwerin in Berlin's Wilhelmstrasse, while a sumptuous palace was constructed for him on the Linden as part of the Frederician forum.[151]

As the solution had been similar to Frederick's own, so the marriage followed along the same lines. It was very unlikely that it was ever consummated, and after the Seven Years War the couple were more or less separated, their apartments being left and right of the main staircase in Berlin, and with Wilhelmina banished from Rheinsberg. As the courtier Lehndorff put it to Henry: '*Monseigneur*, the king has built a palace for you with admirable arrangements: one may spend one's life there without ever setting one's eyes on one's wife.' Like Frederick and Elisabeth, however, there was a period when they operated together as master and mistress of the same house, and it was under that very same roof: Rheinsberg. Frederick's idyll came to an end with the march into Silesia; Henry's with the Seven Years War.[152]

Ferdinand had little charm for his contemporaries. He was described as 'sly and exceedingly drunken. Everyone avoids him.'[153] Hitching him up to a suitable bride proved less difficult than it had been in Henry's case. He married the daughter of his sister Sophia of Brandenburg-Schwedt, whose father had something of the same nasty character as the groom. Frederick described the marriage as *à la juive*, as it remained in the family. Frederick was pleased to see an early pregnancy: 'Ferdinand is putting down roots; you will see a whole tribe spring from his nuptual bed,' he told Wilhelmina, emphasising the lack of productivity in their branch of the Hohenzollerns: 'It is only for the good, for we don't have so many.'[154]

Just before war clouded the horizon once again, Frederick made his second peacetime visit to a neighbouring state, the country that his father had admired so much, and in which he had toyed with the idea of laying down his bones: Holland. He had been in Emden, and Wesel inspecting a regiment, and it occurred to him to make a dash across the border and visit Amsterdam. Once again travelling incognito, he took with him just the engineer, Colonel de Balbi, and a valet, and endeavoured to pass himself off as a member of the king of Poland's court orchestra. He soon discovered that it was not always much fun to be a simple musician. He met a collector called Richard:

'Sir, I have heard that you own some lovely pictures.'

'This is true.'

'Might I be allowed to see and admire them?'

'Who are you, sir? I don't know you at all.'

'I am the leader of the king of Poland's orchestra.'

'Well then, Mr Leader ... I have no time to waste this morning. Come back this afternoon.'[55]

On a boat from Utrecht to Amsterdam he met Henri de Catt, who was returning to his native Switzerland after a course of study at the University of Utrecht. They talked Wolff and the king in disguise offered him a share of his pâté. Frederick then put him through a typical royal grilling. 'If you will permit me to say so Sir, that is an awful lot of questions for a slice of pâté.' Frederick excused himself for his rudeness, but took the young Swiss's address.[56] When Frederick was recognised in the road, the party resolved to flee. He put Balbi in the first carriage and travelled with his valet in the one behind. As they went through the streets, Balbi was saluted as the defender of the Protestant cause. Frederick had difficulty suppressing his mirth. It was only the next day that Catt learned to whom he had been speaking. Six weeks later he had a letter from Potsdam asking him to enter Frederick's service.

Frederick's reputation was ever a contradictory one. There in Holland and later in Britain, the deist was saluted as the fighting arm of the Protestant faith. Despite the seizure of Silesia, to many of Europe's intellectuals he remained an enlightened monarch, the patron of philosophers and the wise father of his people. There on the brink of the Seven Years War, however, another Frederick was also being sold to the European public: Frederick the Tyrant. Voltaire had his own reasons for comparing him to the literary-minded monster, Dionysius of Syracuse, but evidence of real tyranny at this or any other stage of his life is limited to individual cases, such as the unfortunate Trenck.

Trenck had spent the best part of a decade at large after escaping from under La Motte Fouqué's nose in Glatz. He was happily snoozing in Danzig (which was not yet part of Prussian territory) in 1754, when he woke to find his bed surrounded by two police officers and twenty militia men, bearing a signed warrant from the Bürgermeister. Frederick 'had neither forgotten nor forgiven'. He was borne off to the grim fortress of Magdeburg, festooned with chains, and thrown into a profound dungeon, where, for the next ten years of his adventurous life, he was obliged to sleep on his own tombstone, picked out with his name and a skull and crossbones.[157] How much exaggeration there is in this story, and indeed, how much Trenck was being punished for suspected espionage rather than a flimsy tale of dalliance with Princess Amalia, is hard to say. That Frederick never had the former officer formally tried, and that he personally ensured that he was kept safely under lock and key, is undeniable. There exists an instruction from Frederick to Prince Ferdinand of Brunswick, the governor of the prison, which expressly demands that Trenck 'should not be released from his chains'.[158]

One of the men keenest to brand Frederick a tyrant was the British ambassador, Hanbury-Williams, who none the less admitted that he could not find a means of being admitted into His Majesty's presence. He was to change his mind when he went to Russia, but for the present he had no time for any of the Hohenzollerns. Wilhelmina did not impress him at all: 'HRH's conversation exceeded a comedy by Molière. I never met with a woman so learnedly ignorant or so seriously foolish in all my life. She went to bed at 11 o'clock; and I came home laughing all the way to the coach by myself.' He reserved even choicer words for her brother: 'The compleatest tyrant that God sent for to scourge an offending people. I had rather been a post-horse with Sir J. Hind-Cotton* on my back, than his first minister; or his brother, or his wife.'

The lack of proper courtly distractions also annoyed Hanbury-Williams. He was used to better things in Saxony. 'There is nothing here but an absolute prince and a people, all equally miserable, all equally trembling before him, and all equally detesting his iron government.' 'Nero' had spiked Amalia's marriage to the prince of Pfalz-Zweibrücken: 'The thing His Prussian Majesty has in the greatest abhorrence is matrimony. No man, however great a favourite, must think of it. If he does, he is certain never to be preferred.' This policy Hanbury-Williams attributed to Frederick's 'unnatural tastes'. The British diplomat thought they might have learned their lesson in the late king's day; that Frederick William's behaviour 'might have taught them humanity. Instead of which they seem

---

* Sir John Hynde-Cotton, Jacobite MP and evidently a very fat or cruel baronet.

to have learnt the art of making those under them as miserable now as they themselves were formerly."[59]

Hanbury-Williams was led to exaggerate by the animus he bore the king, but one thing was true: Frederick was a menace to all those who had the misfortune to come too close.

CHAPTER NINE

I am Innocent of this War

[1]

His *Testament politique* not withstanding, after 1746 Frederick put it about that he had won his laurels, and he was no longer interested in war. He believed the best way to secure peace was to act with 'gentleness and restraint' towards his neighbours.[1] This peace-loving pose did not prevent him from thinking hard about the lessons of the Silesian Wars, and trying to use them to perfect the operation of his huge fighting force. His *Principes généraux de la guerre* of 1748 were the result of these deliberations. They contained general staff-like plans for attacking Saxony, Bohemia and Moravia,[2] and have been called 'unique' by one recent military historian: 'no other army had a similar set of guidelines for senior officers'.[3] There was a mixture of philosophy prefiguring Clausewitz, joined to a practical military handbook. As such it was translated into German by Eichel and kept top secret. The Austrians knew nothing of it until they found a copy of it in Frederick's friend La Motte Fouqué's baggage, when they took him prisoner in February 1760.[4]

Frederick saw that battles determined the destiny of states: he was a pragmatist, and neither an annihilationist nor an attritionist. He was not even a militarist in the accepted sense. War had to possess an important political objective. What Frederick had to weigh up precisely was the cost of war to a poor state such as Prussia. He filled his arsenals and re-equipped his artillery.[5] He wrestled with deployment and fire-power, and how to get the most from his cavalry. He also reformed the hussars so that he would no longer be caught out by the likes of Pandur Trenck. In all these reforms he was backed up by Hans Karl von Winterfeldt, who if not the father, was the grandfather of the Prussian General Staff, and one of the first masters of military intelligence.

Frederick created a modern officer corps with promotions based on performance and merit. The king was a devotee of sticks and carrots. The Black Eagle was handed out to those who reached the rank of lieutenant-general, and officers were decorated and promoted on the battlefield, like Prince Maurice, who was made a field marshal after Leuthen. However, Frederick was to sack his brother William and spurn his brother Ferdinand because they were inadequate. Men such as Lehwaldt, Schwerin, Keith, Prince Maurice of Anhalt-Dessau, La Motte Fouqué, Finck von Finckenstein, Ferdinand of Brunswick and Prince Henry were without fear of contradiction great generals; they were not like Charles of Lorraine, some sort of princely buggins. Frederick wanted his generals to be brave, but he also understood that there was an element of luck in war. Professionalism, however, governed only the higher ranks.

Desertion remained a problem in an army composed of anything up to 50 per cent mercenaries.[6] It was recommended to watch the troops closely, and keep them out of the woods. As far as possible, the soldiers should be provided with everything that made them happy, or brave: bread, meat, straw and brandy.[7] Discipline, however, remained ferocious. There was no question of enacting the liberal measures that existed for Prussian civilians after 1740, among those who wore the king's blue coat; or indeed among the crowds of camp followers that were a feature of armies at the time. The people needed to be protected. A female sutler who had stolen a peasant's horse was whipped. Frederick told Catt, 'If we sometimes torch or pillage it is because we are obliged to do so. You would have to be a complete barbarian to torment the gay hearts of these poor villagers who have nothing to do with our quarrels.'[8]

At the beginning of the war, Frederick told his brother William what to do with pillagers, advising him to set an example, 'by having one of those fellows hanged'.[9] The most infamous punishment was running the gauntlet, where the miscreant was beaten with rods by other members of his regiment. A Prussian soldier was required to be an automaton, functioning by 'blind obedience and steadfastness in the face of death'. Casualties and deaths were high and brutal discipline was the only known means of making sure that the soldiers did not make a dash for it.[10]

Frederick remained alert because he had to be. He knew that the Austrians had been rearming and reforming their system to cope with a future conflict too. In his *Histoire de la guerre de sept ans*, Frederick characterised Maria Theresa as 'an ambitious and vindictive enemy'.[11] He also knew that she was not content to leave Silesia in his hands and that her diplomacy was being directed towards making the right sort of friends to ensure Prussia's defeat in the coming war. Graf Wenzel von Kaunitz-Rietberg, Maria Theresa's clever chancellor, was keen to reverse previous

Austrian policy and conclude an alliance with France. Britain had proved largely useless to her last time round. Like Britain, France had guaranteed Austria's ownership of Silesia at Aachen, but the French were prepared to entertain the Austrian proposals, which were rendered all the more attractive by the fact that Madame de Pompadour and cardinal de Bernis were still angry about Frederick's perfidy during the Silesian Wars.[12] France also felt the need to protect its back while fighting a colonial war with Britain.

This Franco-Austrian alliance meant pushing Britain, Austria's traditional partner, out of the nest. Frederick was aware that his uncle's land could now be brought into his fold. The question remained whether Britain believed a European war important enough to merit its full attention. There was none the less the need to protect the vulnerable electorate of Hanover, and this decided the duke of Newcastle in favour of Prussia. The British had to be careful to keep the Russians sweet too, and in September 1755 they signed a convention with them.[13] Although Prussia and Russia were to fight a bloody war until 1761, the continuing Russo-British alliance proved something of a safety net during the years of conflict. Negotiations between Frederick and George's governments ended in January 1756 with the Convention of Westminster, formally binding Britain and Prussia.

The colonial war broke out between France and Britain in 1755. The French had still not decided whether they wanted to get into bed with the Austrians after all and made overtures towards Prussia for a renewal of their old alliance. Unaware of the deal struck between de Bernis and Kaunitz, the duc de Nivernais was actually negotiating an alliance with Frederick in Berlin. The French were in for a rude shock. Their lack of preparation might have had something to do with Tyrconnell, who proved himself a hopeless judge of Frederick's character during his period as ambassador in Berlin.[14] Frederick showed Nivernais a draft of the treaty he was concluding with the British. Louis XV's ministers were outraged and ran straight into the open arms of Kaunitz. The First Treaty of Versailles was therefore signed on 1 May 1756. It was a purely defensive agreement. The second instalment came precisely a year later when Kaunitz had managed to convince the French diplomats that Frederick had indeed been the aggressor. It required France to field 105,000 men as well as provide financial back-up.[15]

The Austrians had also excited Russian fears about the dangers of a powerful Prussia, and convinced them that it was in their interests to take action with them to recover Silesia. In reward they would receive some of Frederick's territory in the form of East Prussia. Anti-Prussian feeling was strong with both the tsarina, who resented Frederick's success, and her chancellor Count Bestuzhev-Ryumin, who saw Russian influence declining in its traditional markets, Poland and Sweden, particularly after the arrival of Frederick's sister Ulrica on the throne of the latter. Kaunitz could pretty well count on their full support. Frederick heard from the British envoy, Andrew Mitchell, that Russia had joined France and Austria on 23 June.[16]

Austria had successfully managed to make Frederick's nightmare come true. All Kaunitz had to do now was to drive Prussia into making war, thereby retaining the high moral ground for Maria Theresa. Frederick had been scrutinising the world political scene for some time. When war broke out between Britain and France, he was certain it would spread to Europe. Russia was a loose cannon. He observed Marshal Browne, then in the Russian service but soon to join the Austrian army, conferring with Kaunitz in Vienna and told Field Marshal Lehwaldt in East Prussia to be on his guard, sending him a hundred officers' patents to fill in as and when he wished.[17]

It was Russian troop movements that made Frederick aware that the heat was now on, and that the Prussian kettle was threatening to boil over. Such ganging up on a state was virtually without precedent. He wrote to his sister: 'I am in the position of a traveller who sees himself surrounded by a bunch of rogues, who are planning to murder him and divide the spoils up among themselves.' 'I am waiting for a reply from the queen of Hungary which will decide whether there is to be peace or war.'[18] For his part Frederick knew he had to attack in order to prevent the loss of the strategic and operational initiative.

'I am innocent of this war,' Frederick told William in a much quoted letter of 26 August: 'I have done what I could to avoid it. However great may be the love of peace, one may never sacrifice honour and security ... now we must think only of the means of carrying out this war which removes the pleasure our enemies derive from disrupting the peace.' Frederick was anxious to square his family. To his unlovely little brother Ferdinand he said, 'the sword must bring our enemies to reason'.[19] His sister had heard all about it on 22 June:

I have an opera which consumes my time a little more seriously. Your nasty neighbours are once again laying a plot which looks to me as if it will only be dissipated by a huge catastrophe ... We have one foot in the saddle, and I think it will soon be joined by the other. Things should come to a head in two months at the very latest ... War seems to me inevitable ... I wash my hands of what is coming, at least I am convinced that no one can accuse me of being the cause.[20]

The next day he wrote to Field Marshal Keith, calling him and his fellow officers back from the baths of Carlsbad. Similar letters went out to other general officers.[21]

Once Frederick had decided that war was unavoidable, his eyes roamed over central Europe and he began to covet areas such as Saxony and West Prussia, which would prove useful additions to his straggling lands.[22] With the pre-emptive strike against Saxony on 29 August began the prototype of all *Blitzkriege*. He told the king of Poland that he was obliged to violate his territory to maintain his supply lines to Bohemia.[23] In his memoirs, the Prussian king justified his aggression by citing Saxon relations with Austria; right, politics and war. In the carve-up that was to take place after Prussian defeat, Brühl had arranged that neutral Saxony would be compensated with the duchy of Magdeburg. 'At the same time, he was resolved to win as much territory as he could in that first campaign', he wrote in the Caesarian third person in his *Histoire de la guerre de sept ans*, 'in order better to protect the states of the [Prussian] king and push the war as far away as possible, and finally, to establish the conflict in Bohemia if that was at all possible.' It was indeed a startlingly modern approach which underlined the king's great pragmatism: he wanted to knock Saxony out of the conflict before it could do any harm, and guarantee free communications with Bohemia, which was to be the true theatre. Frederick was aware that it was not going to be an easy war, and he needed to fight with both hands.[24]

In his later account, Frederick was keen to say how well his troops behaved in Saxon territory. At the beginning of the war, at least, this might have been true. The soldier poet Ewald von Kleist told Gleim that the Prussian soldiers were popular with the Saxon population as a 'result of the good order we keep, and we are seen as protectors of religion'. On 17 September he wrote to tell him: 'We have put Leipzig, Wittenberg, Torgau, Dresden and the whole of Saxony behind us and occupied it with our troops, and Leipzig has, as they say, paid a rather large contribution.'[25] According to the king, the inhabitants of Dresden had 'nothing to complain about', even if the Prussians mauled the queen of

Poland and turned the electoral archives upside down in their desire to seize the document, signed by the detested Graf Brühl, which implicated the Saxons in Austrian plans for aggressive war; Frederick claimed he found it, already packed up to be transported to safety in Warsaw. This proof was of capital importance to Frederick: already the French and British, not to mention his own ministers, were throwing up their hands at his violation of Saxon neutrality.[26]

However, there were instances when the Prussians did not earn the instant approbation of the population: Prince Maurice of Anhalt-Dessau had the job of taking the Lutheran Holy Place of Wittenberg. He wrecked the city while he was about it. Despite all Frederick's hypocrisy about the Protestant cause (most likely uttered to please the British and the Dutch), the memory of the German theologian did not signify any more to the Alte Dessauer's son than it meant to the king.[27] Frederick was none the less incensed by the ferocity of the sermons preached by Catholic priests from their pulpits and was prepared to use the Protestant message when it was convenient. Wilhelmina had reservations: 'I'm frightened it will lead to a religious war. Were I to see the funny side of things, I'd say that you could win yourself a place of honour as the defender of the faith, and find yourself elevated, at the very least, to the status of Luther and Calvin.'[28]

At the Prussian approach, the Saxon army, all 19,000 men and eighty guns, beat a prudent retreat and established themselves in an impregnable site on the heights of Pirna. Frederick was philosophical: he determined to starve them out. He had put Schwerin in command of the army in Silesia. He wrote to Frederick on 12 September to describe the Saxon camp: their position was good, but they had no supplies, 'I hope to get them cheap in a few days' time.' A few days later he made another optimistic pronouncement to Bevern: 'The Saxons are beginning to squeal, it will probably be over tomorrow.' It was to take another month.[29]

Frederick was thinking about food too, but rather negatively: he decided to forgo dinner from now on. The idea horrified the Frenchman d'Argens: 'Put the Saxons on a diet if you must, I consent from the bottom of my heart; but don't set them a pernicious example by teaching them to go without food.' Frederick's correspondence with the marquis was one of the few wholly positive things produced by the Seven Years War: a touching record of a true friendship between two of the most extraordinary men of their century. D'Argens was virtually all he had left: 'the most loving, most faithful, the surest soul I know'.[30] Frederick suspected his reader, the heretic abbé de Prades, of espionage: d'Argens was wrongly informed and thought he had been showing excessive zeal by taking up arms; he counselled Bishop Frederick to absolve him 'if by chance he has brutalised some Austrian and run the risk of censure from Holy Mother Church'.[31]

For the time being Frederick was not telling d'Argens the whole story, informing him that Prades was being left in Saxony while he continued on to Bohemia on 13 September: he did not want to 'sully his clean hands with Catholic blood'. Later Frederick told d'Argens that Prades was a traitor, and he had the proof. De Prades had been retailing his plans all over Dresden. Frederick had him arrested, after which he told d'Argens and everything went smoothly again. The abbé did not have to languish in chains for too long. Finally Frederick's heart got the better of him in the first months of 1758 and he had him released. 'As long as he continues to behave well, I shall find some benefice to suit him, which is even more indispensable to him, as almost all Catholic doors are barred to him.' Frederick found him a sinecure in the cathedral in Breslau.[32]

On his campaigns, Frederick wrote not only the usual odes and epistles, but little satires and parodies, often to be used for propaganda purposes against the Austrians and his other enemies. In October 1756 he brought the cardinal de Richelieu back to life to comment on how the European situation had changed since the good old days of the Thirty Years War: Austria ruled by the Lorraines and bent on establishing despotism and tyranny in Germany while robbing France of its most faithful ally (Prussia!); and Sweden under the thumb of a 'cruel and bloodthirsty aristocracy'.[33] Frederick was pleased with his work, and sent it back to d'Argens to have printed. The poor marquis, not knowing enough German to deal with the typesetters, had to give the thing to Voltaire's former landlord Francheville, but only after he had toned down the passages relating to the Swedes.

In Berlin a worried d'Argens and Fredersdorf heard distant rumblings from the first battle of the war, fought at Lobositz on 1 October. The Austrians under another of their Irish commanders, Maximilian von Browne, and supported by yet another – Franz Moritz, Graf von Lacy – had detached 9000 men and sent them to Pirna in an attempt to rescue the Saxons. Some 34,000 remained to face 28,000 Prussians. It was a bloody scrap, nominally a Prussian victory. Frederick's soldiers none the less suffered marginally more casualties than the Austrians, chiefly due to the 'fierce Croats', not irregulars this time, but infantry. For a while it looked as if the Austrians would win the day. Frederick himself showed bravery at first, but later repeated his behaviour at Mollwitz and disappeared from the battlefield, leaving his brother-in-law, the duke of Bevern, in command. It was he, together with Prince Ferdinand of Brunswick and Keith, who turned the tables on the Austrians and forced them to quit the field.[34] 'They weren't the same Austrians,'[35] said Frederick. He was none the less relieved enough to write to Wilhelmina: 'May it please the Heavens to grant our valiant armies a stable peace! This must be the aim of this war.'[36]

Meanwhile the starving Saxons had failed to make contact with Browne's force and on 14 October they decided to give themselves up. Frederick allowed the officers to go free, but took the not unheard-of step of forcibly conscripting the men into the Prussian army. He was unwise enough to organise the 18,500-strong force into ten regiments commanded by inadequate Prussian officers. When the war turned against the Prussians in 1757 they deserted *en masse* and joined the Austrians, obliging Frederick to admit that he had made a mistake.[37] At the nadir of Prussia's fortunes, men were fleeing the colours at a rate of fifty or sixty a day. Saxony was now humiliated by Frederick off and on (generally on) for the rest of the war. It was forced to pay a huge contribution of between 5 and 6 million thalers a year and provide recruits for Frederick's armies. Money that had previously gone into the beautification of Dresden now went into Frederick's war machine. His vindictive treatment of his ostensibly neutral neighbour did nothing to enhance his reputation abroad as a just monarch.[38]

Yet one foreigner stoutly defended Frederick at this time: Andrew Mitchell, the British ambassador, who had taken to the field with the Prussian king and was enduring its Spartan style ('neither convenience nor luxury dwell here').[39] Frederick was something of a heart-throb in Britain even before his victories turned him into a folk hero. On 18 September 1756, the secretary of state, Lord Holdernesse, wrote to Mitchell to tell him: 'Our constant toast here now is, success to the king of Prussia: he grows vastly popular among us ...' Frederick's success with the British largely hinged on his disingenuous assumption of the Protestant cause. On 17 November, for example, Frederick informed Mitchell that the British should drop all personal interest in the war 'in order to put themselves behind the common cause, which is that of Protestantism and European liberty'.[40]

Frederick also impressed his own officers. Ewald von Kleist was a poet who felt already in April 1755 that the king's character provided more material for verse than had ever existed before. A few months before the war broke out, Kleist was telling Gleim that Prussia should annex Austria. When he received his orders to march, he was clearly delighted and directed not just his sword, but also his poetic sallies against Maria Theresa and her armies:

> Glaubest Du aber, das der Preussische Staat
> Noch gar nicht zum Kampf gerüstet hat?
> Komm nur ins Zeughaus, viel hundert Stück Kanonen und
> Wörfer, die stehen schon da.

> *You can forget the notion that our great Prussian state*
> *Will calmly submit to an inglorious fate.*
> *Come into our arsenal, hundreds of cannons and mortars*
> *are now standing by.*

He was included in the units laying siege to the Saxons at Pirna when Frederick visited the camp: 'He speaks to everyone, provides them with genial reassurances and behaves towards his soldiers as if they were children.'[41] Gleim was no less passionate in his advocacy of the Prussian cause:

> Ein Löwe schlummerte, bei Sorge für sein Reich
> Und seiner Völke Ruh liess ihn nicht ruhig schlafen;
> Er lag, wie auf den Sprung, gefasst auf jeden Streich,
> Die Feinde seines Reichs zu schrecken und zu strafen.[42]

> *Anxious for his kingdom, a lion raged and growled*
> *He couldn't sleep for worry, when an enemy lay at hand;*
> *The claws were out, and he watched them as they prowled,*
> *Ready to punish and chasten those who trespassed on his land.*

When the campaign closed for the winter, Frederick retired to Dresden and indulged a few of his more pacific interests. He went to the opera and heard La Pilaja sing badly: 'She screamed like a tooth-carpenter.' The musical scene was not wholly unaffected by the war. Hasse for one took fright and applied to leave for Italy. Frederick told him to travel via Erlangen to avoid the concentrations of soldiers.[43] In January 1757, Prussia was expelled from the Holy Roman Empire, which promptly declared war on him: 'A pack of kings and princes want to hunt me down like a stag and they are inviting their friends along to be in at the kill.'[44] Frederick went to Berlin for a few days before returning to Dresden in the middle of the month, where he was surprised to receive an affectionate letter from Voltaire, who had been rumoured dead again.[45]

When the season opened once more, Frederick went back to Bohemia and endeavoured to prevent a build-up of Austrian forces there, while uniting the two main Prussian armies. By the beginning of May, he had chased the Austrian forces to the gates of Prague. He dreamed of a battle that would beat his enemies fairly and squarely, and end the war. Mitchell dined with Frederick on 4 May 1757: 'He was very hearty and cheerful, told me in a day or two the battle of Pharsalia* between the Houses of Austria and Brandenburg would be fought.'[46] On the 6th the two armies united and prepared to do battle. The king was in a hurry.[47]

The Prussians had been excessively gung-ho: Schwerin was particularly keen to fight. The king, however, had eaten a pâté that disagreed with him the night before and spent the day of the battle throwing up.[48] Schwerin's forces were scattered by Austrian fire and Frederick's chief tactician, Winterfeldt, was struck from his horse by a bullet in the neck. As he lay bleeding, the seventy-four-year-old field marshal rode up and lent Winterfeldt his packhorse. Tearing a flag out of the staff-captain's hand in order to rally his straggling troops, he shouted 'all brave fellows follow me!' and rode to the head of his regiment. The soldiers cheered him on, calling him 'father'. He replied with an encouraging 'Heran, meine Kinder!'†

In a letter to Algarotti, Frederick painted the picture of Schwerin's dying moments, which were once familiar to every German schoolboy: 'encouraging his troops, he was hit in the head and chest and died at once; the flag he was carrying covered his body'.[49] In the usual version, his charge turned the battle. The soldiers shouted, 'Revenge for father Schwerin!', and fought like lions. In fact, the decisive action of the day was that of the 'hussar king', Zieten, and his cavalry, who scattered the enemy like 'straw in the wind'. An Austrian force of 50,000 took refuge within the walls of the Bohemian capital. Frederick began to shell the city. Artillery destroyed the bakery and reduced the garrison to a diet of horseflesh.[50]

---

* The battle of Pharsalus or Pharsalia in Thessaly, where Caesar defeated his rival Pompey decisively in 48 BC. Frederick was never to achieve his Pharsalus with Maria Theresa.

† 'Come on children!' Children was the usual way of addressing men in the Prussian army.

Whether his death was responsible for victory or not, Schwerin remained and remains the most poignant character of the fight. Mitchell described him as 'one of the greatest officers this or perhaps any country has produced and one of the best of men'. Frederick himself wrote to King George, calling him 'one of the greatest generals of the century'.[51] The British were over the moon about the victory of their allies. On 20 May, Holdernesse wrote to Mitchell:

A fishing boat dispatched by Colonel Yorke brought us last night the news of the great and glorious victory obtained by the king of Prussia near Prague on the 6th inst., which fortunate event has filled the court and the whole nation with the highest joy, and raised the admiration we already had of His Prussian Majesty's heroism to the highest pitch; women and children are singing his praises; the most frantick makers of joy appear in the publick streets. He is in short, become the idol of the people...[52]

From this time date the first of the pubs called 'The King of Prussia' that used to exist all over Britain. Less than a handful survive; most fell victim to the anti-Prussian feeling at the beginning of the First World War.[53]

Frederick's hopes of starving or shelling the Austrians out were founded on a miscalculation: there was enough food for two months, and he was short of ammunition and heavy artillery.[54] He described it as 'one of the bloodiest battles of the century'. Losses were extremely high: the Austrian figure was around 14,000 for dead, wounded and captured; the Prussian even more. Much as he vaunted his victory, the battle has been described as playing the same role in the Seven Years War as the Marne did in the First World War, and Moscow in the Second: it brought the Prussian advance to a halt and altered the war from an aggressive to a defensive one. From now on Frederick's entire task was to keep his many enemies apart.[55]

With the second Treaty of Versailles, France's defensive alliance had been scrapped in favour of an aggressive role. Frederick indulged his self-pity to Wilhelmina on 3 June: 'The new triumvirate has outlawed me; Judas sold Christ for a mere thirty pieces of gold: the king of France has sold me to the queen of Hungary for five Flemish towns, I am therefore worth more than our Saviour.'[56] Two weeks later, on 18 June, Frederick experienced his first defeat in battle at Kolin. He later claimed he had been badly advised by Prince Maurice in particular. He overestimated his own strength, and underestimated his enemy, hoping for great things from the battle and victory. He was going to knock Austria out of the war, then ride to the Rhineland to deal with the French.[57]

With 35,000 men he attacked an enemy numbering 53,000 commanded by the Austrian general Daun. The disaster might have been all the greater had it not been for the bravery of Frederick's cavalry. First the dragoons charged under Major-General Siegfried von Krosigk, who was blown off his horse by 'lethal canister shot'.[58] It was then the moment for Colonel Friedrich Wilhelm von Seydlitz to display the mettle that made him, beside Zieten, the greatest cavalry officer in the history of Prussia. At the head of his cuirassiers, Seydlitz broke the Austrian lines.

It was only a temporary reverse. The Austrians regained the initiative, and the Flemish and Saxon soldiers in the Austrian army, above all, chased Frederick's exhausted men from the battlefield; the latter screaming 'Dies ist für Striegau' (Hohenfriedberg) as they slaughtered defenceless boys and wounded men.[59] Frederick allegedly produced one of his most famous lines: 'Ihr Racker, wollt ihr denn ewig leben?' To which one fleeing grenadier uttered the realistic reply: 'Fritze, für acht Groschen ist es heute genug!'[60] He retired from the battle completely demoralised, unable to give the necessary commands. He had lost over a third of his army. To the Lord Marischal he sent a report on the battle in which he commended the Austrian grenadiers:* 'Ferdinand [of Brunswick] attacked seven times, but without success ... Henry worked wonders. I shudder for my worthy brothers, they are so brave.'[61]

For one of them the defeat was excellent news – 'Phaethon has fallen to earth,' said Henry and called for champagne. Frederick blamed his generals: Prince Maurice and C. H. von Manstein (who did not have to suffer the obloquy for long: he died of his wounds soon after), but in truth he had not listened to the advice of some others, such as Zieten, who had warned him of the overwhelming Austrian strength.[62] Even a year later Frederick was still insisting that the defeat was not his fault, and that his orders had not been heeded. Had the generals done what they were told, the war would have ended there and then.[63] He wrote to Wilhelmina: 'Had I followed my inclinations, I would have ended my life right after I lost the unfortunate battle. But I saw that as a weakness and

---

* Maria Theresa was ecstatic. She founded a new 'Maria-Theresien-Orden' and rewarded Daun with the grand cross. She also had a medal struck. It showed the goddess Pallas Athena striking a pyramid with a thunderbolt, with the inscription 'Gott zernichtet alle Hochmut' – 'God strikes all arrogance down'.

observed that it was my duty to make good the tragedy.'[64] To d'Argens he said, 'If I'd been killed at Kolin, today I'd be in a port where I'd have no more fear of squalls. I have to sail some more on that storm-tossed sea, until a little plot of earth offers me the goodness which I have not been able to locate in this world.'[65]

Frederick had lost all the advantages he had won at Prague and put the divided Prussian army at great risk.[66] On 1 July he heard that his mother had died on the 28th, and this personal tragedy added greatly to his black mood following Kolin. 'Philosophy is useful for soothing past evils or future ones, but it is vanquished by present troubles.' For two days he granted no audiences and dined alone with the princes. To d'Argens he was showing that he was low, but not yet prostrate: 'don't think I will give in. Should all the elements perish, I will see myself buried beneath their rubble with the same coolness with which I write these lines.'[67] It was Voltaire, of all people, who offered Frederick helpful advice. He reminded him that the Great Elector had been obliged to cede conquered territory. Suicide was not the solution: 'Our morals and your situation in no way require you to adopt this position; in a word, your life is very necessary.'[68]

Frederick toyed with the idea of making peace in those dark days. Wilhelmina was egging him on, trying to get him to conclude a deal with the French. Indeed, this was William and Henry's intention too: to turn the French at the time when the Franco-Austrian pact was purely defensive. William was not keen on the British, but he showed little flair for politics. One of Germany's leading authorities on the period has dismissed his complaints as those of a 'naive and ailing prince', who was already suffering from the cerebral condition that killed him.[69] By the end of June, Frederick was already more confident, telling Wilhelmina that his plans were 'disturbed but not desperate'.[70] In July he none the less opened a fund for Wilhelmina to employ the right person to promote peace between Prussia and France in Versailles by bribing the marquise de Pompadour or the duc de Richelieu. That person was comte Louis-Alexandre de Mirabeau, uncle of the revolutionary. Wilhelmina and her husband had met him in Avignon, and invited him to Bayreuth where he was made a chamberlain and privy councillor, and put in charge of the art school. He went to Paris in September. By October Frederick had changed his mind again: a 'base' deal had been suggested that he was not prepared to accept – he would have 'rather died a hundred deaths'. Nor was he convinced that the French were really in earnest.[71]

Everyone was against him and, besides Wilhelmina, his family were not helping at all. The chief problem among them was William, who was proving himself a less than brilliant general now that Frederick had been forced into a defensive position. On 20 June, Frederick had been obliged to lift the siege of Prague and retire to his stronghold at Leitmeritz. He hoped to be able to remain there, but the Swedes and French were now streaming into Germany. The former were ravaging the Uckermark just north-east of Berlin. The French were performing some quite alarming acts of barbarism on their way east. They reached Prussian territory at Halberstadt, where their army clearly celebrated with much raping and pillaging. Mitchell noted that their behaviour 'greatly exceeds for cruelty and wanton inhumanity everything that has been done since the beginning of this war on both sides'.[72]

As for William, commanding Prussian forces on the east bank of the Elbe, he was proving a sleepy cat and allowed the Austrians to capture one of Prussia's most important magazines at Zittau, which contained sustenance for 40,000 men for three weeks. He then abandoned his position altogether, putting Prussian communications at the greatest possible risk. Frederick wrote to William, telling him he had lost his head. 'You are making me pay dearly for the trust I placed in you.'[73] He relieved him of his command on 18 July. The next day he wrote again:

Command a harem, fine, but as long as I live you will have no detachment greater than ten men. When I am dead, you may commit as much folly as you like; it'll be on your head, but as long as I live you will do nothing more to damage the state. That is all I have to say to you. Let your best officers clean up the shambles you have made ... What I say is hard but true.[74]

Frederick marched back to Saxony on 21 July, leaving Keith to bring up the main army. On the way he posted an angry letter to Wilhelmina, blaming William for the volte-face: 'I hope to repair [the effects of] his idiocy, if it is humanly possible.'[75] That William was verging on nervous collapse is clear from the spelling of his letters, never good at the best of times. He none the less maintained that he had nothing to reproach himself for.[76] The brothers met in Bautzen. Frederick could not bring himself to look at William, but stood aside, and made Winterfeldt admonish him: 'he deserves to have his head chopped off,' he told the generals. Von der Goltz had to take him the message that he was to go back to Berlin and produce children – go forth and multiply.[77]

More insults followed. On the 30th, the king told his heir that he could not take advice: his ears were used only to flattery and he lacked judgement. For the time being he did not know what to do. He asked for permission to retire to Berlin. Frederick answered his letter on 7 August: 'you are soft in the head'. On the 12th: 'You want to give the army an example of cowardice.' He agreed to his brother's request, but rubbed more salt into the wound. He would hole himself up in some fort with the women: 'A fine role for the heir to the throne!' Frederick's last direct communication with his brother was sent on 30 August: 'Do what you want; I shall not concern myself any more with your circumstances.'[78] William's letters were now answered by his secretary.

William fairly wallowed in self-pity. It was a Hohenzollern failing. Another was an adamantine conviction that he had done nothing wrong and that others were to blame. After his dressing down in Bautzen, he wrote to Henry's bride to tell her:

I am as skinny as an old nag. You will surely hear much criticism of my marches and movements. Please ask people to defer judgement until they have heard me out. The king has questioned my honour. I have sacrificed my health to him and a hundred times I have thrown my life into the balance. It would be too hard to renounce my honour for his sake, in order to cover up his own mistakes ...[79]

On 9 August he wrote to Henry's wife again. He was ruminating on writing a justification of his conduct: 'I am in a very good mood and have a calm conscience and I am thinking only of preserving my reputation, for in no other army in the world is a general in danger of losing his honour as he is in ours.'[80]

William eventually went back to Oranienburg to sulk in his palace. To an enquiry from his friend Graf Viktor Amadeus von Henckell Donnersmarck in May 1758, William revealed the fact that the bitterness had in no way abated:

don't believe that I am thinking of seeing my regiment again: no, as long as the king's glorious reign persists I see myself effaced from the list of those who work to improve his military reputation. I possibly lost the opportunity to lay the keel to my own, or possibly destiny favoured him by withdrawing me before I had the chance to expose all my incapacity and stupidity[.] Interpret that as you will, here I am retired and I use my time extremely well[.] Sometimes I still think of the shame of being here uselessly in exile, but as I am convinced that I did nothing wrong, I don't give a fuck.[81]

He died in June, adding further fat to the fire. People spoke of a broken heart, and the *frondeurs* in Frederick's family, Henry, Ferdinand and Amalia, used it as a stick to beat him with. In the twentieth century, a commission was appointed to look into his death: William died from a cerebral haemorrhage or tumour possibly aggravated by an earlier fall. Frederick commented laconically in a letter to George Keith. He thought the officers should wear mourning: 'It is a theme which afflicts me greatly; but I simply don't have the time to cry.'[82]

[II]

In theory at least, Frederick was not wholly alone: he still had Brunswick, Anhalt-Dessau and the British. The duke of Cumberland landed on the continent with his 'observation army for the defence of the electorate of the British king', while the 'Circles' or *Kreise* of the German Reich raised their own forces to fight the outlaw Frederick under Prince Joseph of Saxony-Hildenburghausen and were attached to the French. The latter were making progress. They overran Cumberland's army at Hastenbeck, even if their losses were greatly in excess of the British, and they occupied the ports of Hamburg and Bremen. Much to Frederick's annoyance, the British would not use their fleet to protect Prussian interests in the Baltic from the Swedes and the Russians. On 8 September, the British and the French signed the Convention of Klosterzeven, and Cumberland ducked out of the war.[83]

The Russians had worried Frederick more than anyone. He was longing for the tsarina to die so that Prussia-loving Peter could accede to the throne. Frederick was not leaving it to chance. He had his spies everywhere. Eichel reported a Polish Jew who had volunteered for his service, but he was not keen: 'I pay up in order to keep my enemies off my back, but shall never in my life give money to Polish Jews or magnates ... Up to now it looks quite good in Russia; this winter I am certain the empress is on her deathbed and I don't think there will be any problems in the future.'[84] He also worked on Catherine's mother, Johanna of Anhalt-Zerbst, asking her to intervene with her daughter after the tsarina's death, in order to preserve the 'happy harmony between the court of Russia and myself'. He had had reassurances from Johanna, but in 1757 Zerbst had sided with the Reich, and Johanna's influence was for nought.[85]

He continued to hope for all that and delighted in every report of her illnesses. Even in March he reported with glee that the tsarina was 'in agony'. Now on 22 September he heard a rumour that she had indeed died. Mitchell understood Frederick's anxiety on this score. He wrote to Holdernesse in the middle of October: 'If the empress of Russia should die, I hope not a moment will be lost to improve the event that may save the whole, however melancholy it is to think that the fate of Europe depends on such accidents.'[86] Prussia's ultimate victory in the Seven Years War might have been achieved by the 'Miracle of the House of Brandenburg', but never was there a miracle so heavily relied upon and so often predicted.

Frederick's diplomatic contacts with Saint Petersburg were assured by the British and their envoy Hanbury-Williams. Hanbury-Williams had changed his mind about the king since Frederick had him recalled from Berlin, and he was now 'the zealous defender of the interests of Prussia'. Frederick, too, was reconciled to the Englishman and had had him provided with a fat purse. He was endeavouring to bribe Bestuzhev and working on Peter's wife Catherine at the same time. He had no luck with the former, although 'my offers were very large'. Indeed, Frederick had provided him with the princely sum of 100,000 thalers to woo the chancellor. He now shifted his attention to the generals. Despite her mother's small diplomatic role (see above, p. 172), Catherine had a cooler head than the tsarina. For the time being at least, she was relatively open-minded towards Frederick. On 20 November 1756 she wrote to Hanbury-Williams: 'I read the writings of the king of Prussia with the same avidity as those of Voltaire. You will think that I am making up to you, if I tell you today that I am a profound admirer of His Prussian Majesty.'[87]

Despite fair means and foul, Frederick had been able to do nothing to accelerate the tsarina's demise or bribe the Russian generals to march in the wrong direction at the onset of their campaign. Now the nightmare had begun and Russian soldiers under Field Marshal Apraksin had started tramping towards East Prussia in May. Their progress had been slow: bad discipline, poor supplies, poorer roads, heat and the region's voracious insects slowed them down. By August a fifth of the army was out of action. That still left around 80,000 to face Lehwaldt and the 30,000 men he had to defend Königsberg. On 30 August they gave battle at Gross Jägersdorf. The Prussians suffered casualties of 4600, the Russians 7000. Apraksin ordered a tactical retreat.[88]

Frederick badly needed a victory to restore his spirits. Alcohol would not do. 'Often I'd like to get drunk', he wrote to his sister Amalia in September, 'to drown my annoyance, but as I can't drink I distract myself by writing verses and as long as I am absorbed by this distraction, I don't feel my unhappiness any more.'[89] He dashed off odes to Henry, Wilhelmina and Amalia as well as an epistle to the marquis d'Argens. In Henry's ode he bewailed the fate of his land:

> Dans nos jours désastreux, la guerre qui vous mine
> Semble annoncer, Prussiens, la prochaine ruine
> De vos vastes États;
> L'Europe conjurée, à l'oeil brûlant de rage,
> Porte jusqu'en vos champs la flamme, le carnage,
> L'horreur et le trépas.[90]

> *A terrible war undermines our great land*
> *And seems to presage, Prussians, the imminent end*
> *Of your huge estates;*
> *Europe in concert, its eyes scorching with rage,*
> *Is strewing your fields with fire and carnage,*
> *Fear and death are your fates.*

For d'Argens there was the by now familiar talk of playing the noble Roman:

> Du bonheur de l'État la source est tarie,
> La palme a disparu, les lauriers sont fanés;
> Mon âme, de soupirs et de larmes nourrie,
> De tant de pertes attendrie,
> Pourra-t-elle survivre aux jours infortunés,
> Qui sont près d'éclairer la fin de ma patrie.[91]

> *The source has dried up of this our most happy realm,*
> *The palm has vanished and our laurels begin to fade;*
> *And my soul, the sighs and tears overwhelm,*
> *Moved by so much loss to yell,*
> *Can it outlive so many unfortunate days,*
> *Which illuminate my country's end, who can tell?*

A despair bordering on self-pity, and similar in style to William's missives, was voiced not only in her ode, but also in the letter he sent Wilhelmina:

I can't perform any good at present; there are too many enemies. Even if I manage to beat two armies the third will crush me ... I shan't be defeated by unhappiness, I have had to bear so much: the loss of the Battles of Kolin and

[Gross] Jägersdorf, the disastrous withdrawal of my brother and the loss of the magazine in Zittau, the loss of my provinces in Westphalia, the unfortunate death of Winterfeldt, the invasion of Pomerania,[92] Magdeburg and Halbestadt, the desertion of my allies.[93]

A new shock came with the brief occupation of Berlin on 16–17 October by the Hungarian general Andreas Hadik.[94] The city had been badly prepared, the governor, General von Rochow, having refused to entertain the idea of an attack. The court fled to Spandau and allowed the small Austrian force to be bought off for 250,000 thalers. Despite their danegeld, the Austrians had a little fun in the Friedrichstadt, plundering the most prosperous houses on the Linden and beating up their owners for good measure. Rochow was not popular after they left: it was discovered that there were approximately four times as many Prussian troops in Berlin as there had been invaders.[95]

When not harried by Ferdinand of Brunswick, the French were having a wonderful time. Frederick wrote to d'Argens to complain about his countrymen: 'Your Frenchmen have committed acts of cruelty worthy of the Pandurs, they are monstrous pillagers.'[96] Klosterzeven had removed the impediments to their progress and Voltaire's childhood friend, Richelieu, plundered enough in Hanover to build himself a new palace in Paris. Frederick had positioned himself in Thuringia to deal with the encroaching French. A clash was predicted as early as 6 September.[97] On the 17th, Seydlitz chased the prince de Soubise (another man with a sublime *hôtel particulier*) and Prince Joseph out of Gotha by a cunning ruse, pretending that the main Prussian army was on its way. Frederick was keen to protect the town, and his friend, the philosophic duchess, Louise Dorothea.[98] For the time being he was sending his circle gifts of porcelain, although he added, 'I dare not send Meissen, lest they accuse me of rapine.'[99]

Frederick was to have the battle, and the victory he longed for, on 5 November. He marched 170 miles in two weeks for his appointment with Soubise, a general who owed his command to his friendship with La Pompadour. The march to Rossbach has been described as 'an unheard of achievement by eighteenth century standards'. The precise size of the French and imperial army has been disputed. It has certainly come down over the years, but no one has ever questioned its numerical superiority to Frederick's. Soubise probably had around 40,000 men, of whom about a quarter were Germans from the 'Circles', and was trailing around 12,000 camp followers. Frederick's army had just 21,000 officers and men.[100]

It was the moment of glory for the 'new man', Seydlitz, another figure from the pages of the old German histories, although they left out the loucher side of his character, the wine, women and venereal disease.[101] Frederick, who had been having lunch when the French advanced, had decided to retreat, worried that the size of the Franco-Imperial army might spell another Kolin. It was Seydlitz who saw the moment.[102] He waited until the French advanced to within 1000 paces, then he pounced. He is pictured by Menzel with clay pipe in hand. When he hurled it into the air, it was the signal for the 8th Cuirassiers to charge.[103] The imperial units fought back, and Seydlitz ordered up eighteen fresh squadrons. This broke the line, which turned tail and ran; their flight turned to a total stampede when they came crashing down on to a sunken road.[104]

Frederick only realised what was going on when he climbed to the upper floor of a house and was immediately struck, not by the braveness, but by the stupidity of the enemy. He sprang into action and had his artillery deal with the advancing Mailly and Piedmont regiments. The Prussian volleys 'shredded the enemy advance'. The French began to run, but were cut down by Seydlitz's cavalry. Three Franconian regiments threw away their arms. More than 5000 of the allied soldiers were killed or wounded and another 5000 taken prisoner. The tally included eleven generals and a rumour ran round that General de Broglie had died of his wounds in Merseburg. Frederick had lost 169 dead and 379 wounded. Prisoners kept arriving in dribs and drabs. Before the battle a boy had come to Seydlitz to enlist. The cavalry commander had told him he was too young to be a trooper. 'What must I do?' asked the youth. Seydlitz told him to take a French general prisoner. After the battle the boy came in trailing a dejected Gaul: 'See, here is a French general as you ordered.' Keith commented that he had done it as 'coolly as if he had been ordered to buy a pound of biscuit'. He was promptly made an officer.[105]

Two peasant girls brought in a French soldier on the end of a lead.[106] Mitchell thought that if there had been two more hours of daylight the French would have been annihilated.[107] After the battle Seydlitz was promoted lieutenant-general and awarded the Black Eagle. Six months before he had been a humble colonel.[108] The other officers grumbled. Seydlitz rebuked them: 'I obey the king and you will obey me.'[109] 'Now I will go peaceably to my grave, since the reputation and honour of my people has been saved,'[110] Frederick wrote to Wilhelmina.

To Podewils he wrote expressing a rare piety: 'We have just totally beaten the French and the Circles ... Heaven has blessed the just cause. You must organise a few *Te Deum* with cannon salutes and infantry salvoes in Berlin, Stettin and Magdeburg.'[111] The triumph was fêted on all sides and way beyond the German borders. The poet Klopstock parodied Caesar: 'Sie kamen, sahn, flohn.'* Protestant Germany revelled in Frederick's victory over Catholic and Frenchman alike. A popular rhyme went through different versions, but the message remained unchanged:

Wenn unser grosser Friedrich kommt	*And so our great king Frederick comes,*
Und klatscht nur auf die Hosen,	*And slaps his woollen breeches.*
So läuft die ganze Reichsarmee	*Off sprints the Kaiser's army then,*
Noch mehr als die Franzosen.[113]	*E'en faster than the Frenchies.*

More significant than all these accolades was the practical result: the British renewed military activity in Germany and allowed Ferdinand of Brunswick to take command of the Hanoverian army. His combined force of Hanoverians, British, Germans and Prussians would now be used to keep the French at bay.[114]

Rossbach may have even more importance than that. It has often been described as the Agincourt of the German nation. Voltaire would settle for no less: 'It was the most unimaginable and most complete rout in history ... The defeats of Agincourt, Crécy and Poitiers were not as humiliating.'[115] Even the francophile king had to admit that, although the French spoke the same language as Louis XIV, they possessed neither Turenne nor Condés to satisfy their pretensions.[116]

Ah! Quel spectacle a plus de charmes	*Is there a sight which more joy affords*
Que le cul dodu des héros,	*Than some fleshy warrior's bum,*
Lorsque par le pouvoir des armes	*When by the power of the sword*
On leur fait tourner le dos![117]	*He turns on his heels and runs!*

The battle gave rise to the first flush of German self-awareness: language, thought and literature became respectable again, a fact that would have severely puzzled the king, who was no friend of any of them.[118] In a much quoted passage from the second book of *Dichtung und Wahrheit*, Goethe showed how a boy in imperial Frankfurt reacted to the news of

* 'They came, they saw, they scarpered.'[112]

Frederick's victories. The personality of the 'great king' had an effect on everyone. He copied out the ballads and the satires, even though the doggerel was generally pretty flat.[119]

If the outside world was stunned by Rossbach, however, the greater victory was to come at Leuthen near Breslau. Here Frederick dealt with the Austrians. They had managed to overrun half of Silesia after the destruction of Winterfeldt's corps at Moys, and capture Breslau and Schweidnitz. Frederick was furious and blamed the duke of Bevern (who had managed to get himself captured), and Generals Kyau and Lestwitz, whom he placed under arrest.[120] But he did not sulk; he went into action. Frederick showed once again his mastery of his own men in getting them to perform an incredible march. Wilhelmina gushed to Voltaire: 'the corps which the king commanded had travelled forty two German miles [over 300 kilometres] in fifteen days, they had only one day of rest before committing themselves to this memorable battle.'[121] On 28 November he arrived at Parchwitz. Here he wrote a will: 'I want to be buried at Sanssouci without crowds or ceremony and at night; I don't want my body opened, only that I should be sent to the other side without fuss ...'[122] He remained in Parchwitz until the 4th of the following month. He was nervous of the chances of victory, and wrote to Henry on the 30th about the problems he foresaw.[123]

On the 3rd he summoned his regimental and battalion commanders and delivered the 'Parchwitz Declaration', a rare instance of his using German for anything other than commands to menials. They were going to do battle:

I must take this step or all will be lost; we must beat the enemy or bury ourselves before his guns.

... think of yourselves as Prussians for all that, but you will certainly not show indignity in this advantage; if there is one or other of you who is frightened to share these dangers with me, he can take his leave today without suffering the slightest reproach.

[The officers fell into rapt silence which was broken by a Major von Billerbeck shouting, 'Imagine any cur wanting to do that!' The king continued] I already knew that none of you would desert me ... Now farewell, gentlemen, in a short while we shall have beaten the enemy or we shall never meet again.[124]

On 5 December he fought the Battle of Lissa, or Leuthen, as it later became. Frederick was facing a much larger army once again: his 39,000 men and 170 guns against the Austrians' and Saxons' 66,000 and 210.

Before the fight began, a veteran commander complained of the bitter cold; it was late in the year to be engaging armies. The king told him that things would get hot soon enough. First Frederick's cavalry scattered the enemy at Borne, but he succeeded in concealing the real point of his attack, using the rolling countryside around Breslau. For once, Frederick was to fight the battle according to his own rules. As he told Henry, 'I turned their army right round' and concealed the movements of his own forces.[125]

Frederick was enjoying himself so much at the head of his army that he would not listen to those who pleaded with him to take care: 'The king was constantly in the thickest fire,' wrote Eichel. 'It wasn't possible to hold him back, even though we made every effort to do so.'[126] The attack was led by the 26th Infantry, who swiftly dispersed the Württembergers and Bavarians. Prince Maurice told them to fall back, as they had won their laurels. 'We'd have to be yellow-bellies to fall back now!' they shouted. 'Cartridges! Cartridges!' The 26th won fourteen *pour le mérites* that day.[127]

'Thanks be to God, everything is going marvellously,' Frederick told Eichel.[128] The decisive cavalry charge was led by Lieutenant-General Georg Wilhelm von Driesen, with the Bayreuth Dragoons once again taking a large percentage of the laurels. Zieten was left to deal with the stragglers, scooping up two generals along the way. Mitchell recorded other details of the glorious battle: 'So great was the panick and consternation in the Austrian army during the pursuit that a cornet of hussars with 100 men brought in 1000 prisoners. The king of Prussia immediately gave him the *croix de mérite** [sic] and a troop of hussars.'[129] As Frederick retired for the night, the whole army sang the chorale that would be known as the 'Leuthen' ever after: *Nun danket alle Gott*. Prussia lost about a fifth of its effective force in dead and wounded, but won 55 flags and standards, 130 guns and more than 12,000 prisoners. The Austrians lost a further 10,000 in dead and wounded. A few days later, on 20 December, they abandoned the garrison at Breslau to its fate and Frederick added another 17,000 to the bag. Frederick had got Silesia back and won 'the greatest victory of the generation, and perhaps of the century...'[130]

Frederick surprised a number of exhausted and wounded Austrian officers in the manor house in Lissa. 'Good evening, gentlemen; certainly you weren't expecting me here, is there any room to spare?' Perplexed,

---

* *Pour le mérite.*

but aware that the Prussian army was not far behind, they led him up to the hall of the manor where dinner was being served. Frederick talked to them politely for a while then found himself a room and settled down to pen letters and dispatches.[131] Frederick told the story of the battle as he saw it; the poet Gleim celebrated the victory in a few verses for Maria Theresa:

Nun beschliesse deinen Krieg	*Come now, finish off this war*
Kaiser-Königin!	*Great queen and empress!*
Gib dir selbst den schönsten Sieg!	*Give us what we're waiting for!*
Werde Siegerin!...	*Be magnanimous!...*
Überwinde dich und gib	*Forget your quarrel and heed*
Menschlichkeit Gehör!	*Voices that implore!*
Habe deine Völker lieb,	*Listen to your people's needs,*
Öpfere nicht mehr!*[132]	*Sacrifice no more.*

Maria Theresa was crestfallen: 'The empress cries endlessly and is almost inconsolable.' Frederick believed she would see reason and make peace, but he soon realised that this was not to be. As he told Algarotti, 'You see it is not enough to fight, and that it is easier to make brave men concede than nasty women.'[133]

Mitchell was caught up in the euphoria that succeeded the battle and the fall of Breslau. It was Frederick's greatest victory. 'This great stroke ... will show the world that no power, and no troops, are able to resist him.' Parliament promptly voted Prussia a new subsidy. The duke of Newcastle broke the news to Mitchell in Breslau, adding that his wife was 'the strongest Prussian in England'. Frederick reminded her of her grandfather, the duke of Marlborough: 'according to our English custom, we drink the king of Prussia's health; and further success, every day'.[134]

CHAPTER TEN

The Stag at Bay

[1]

After Leuthen Frederick dreamed of peace before the spring.[1] The recapture of Breslau meant that Frederick could move into comfortable winter quarters at least. He wanted the trappings of civilisation around him. He called for his fiddlers, Benda among them,[2] and his few remaining friends. He was to be denied Fredersdorf: in April 1757 he had gone into retirement at Zernikow, where he finally succumbed to his various ailments on 12 January 1758.[3] Frederick tried to make the idea of a winter camp attractive to d'Argens on 13 December: 'We'll banish all the draughts; I'll have cotton, overcoats and skins all ready to wrap you up in. You shall see the fine Bernini mausoleum in the cathedral.'[4] On Boxing Day he tried again: 'I have said that we should order the horses, and that the rooms should be heated along the way, and that wherever you go a good hen should be dished up for you. Your room in the house is hung with tapestries and hermetically sealed; you will be troubled by no winds, draughts or noises.'[5]

With pressure of that sort, d'Argens had little choice but to come. Now that the abbé de Prades was under suspicion of treason, Frederick needed a reader. The choice fell on Henri de Catt, the Swiss he had met in Holland. He wrote to him soon after he retook Breslau, and Catt arrived in the city in March. 'Would you have recognised me?' he asked his new companion.

'Yes, Sire.'

'From what?'

'From your eyes.'

'But I have lost a lot of weight.'

After his interview with the king, Catt received some words of friendly advice from d'Argens. The king never changed his opinion of any man. The important thing was not to annoy him. He recommended the following: don't speak much; don't ask for money; don't talk to those people Frederick believes to be fools, nasty, plotters or rebels. Mitchell also gave him advice: to talk about literature, metaphysics and philosophy, and not to go too far if he asked you to comment on his verses.[6]

The cenobitic Frederick had established himself in suitable lodgings: the abbot's apartment in the huge baroque abbey of Grüssau in the Riesengebirge. The following day Frederick too gave Catt some advice. He warned him against his ADCs: Oppen was jealous; Gaudy, rebellious; and Marwitz, a grumbler.[7] Catt was not to gamble and not to lend money.[8] Frederick had established a routine in those months of winter camp. He rose at 3 a.m., occasionally earlier, and played the flute for an hour. He then dealt with the business of state until noon. He handled around forty letters a day. Most of them were nonsense, but 'I love my people'. He invited the abbot to his table at lunch: 'I ask him questions which he has difficulty answering.' After his one daily meal he wrote poetry and prose, to calm his nerves, covering himself from head to foot with Spanish snuff ('I am surely not as filthy as our good marquis?'). He went to bed at nine.[9] Writings penned at the time, such as the *Sermon sur le jour de jugement* showed that he had forgotten none of his Bible; and that he had not lost his sense of humour either.

Apart from the reluctant d'Argens (who was forever trying to think up ruses that would take him back to the delicious climate of his native Provence), Frederick had more intimate company in 'Quintus Icilius'. Charles Theophile Guichard was a former teacher at the University of Leyden, who had left in high dudgeon when they had failed to make him professor of Greek. He was born in Magdeburg, the son of Huguenot parents. His strange *nom de guerre* was the result of a question from Frederick: 'Who was Caesar's best ADC?'

Guichard replied, 'Quintus Icilius.'

'You shall be my Quintus Icilius.'[10]

Quintus was the habitual butt of Frederick's cruellest pranks and jibes. One day that spring, Quintus told him that Roman soldiers had carried more kit than the Prussians. *On verra*, said the king and made him stand in his hat for an hour carrying the full load: sabre, musket, a leather belt with sixty cartridges and haversac. The humiliation was total. Once he had been divested of his weights, Quintus was furious: 'Tiberius would not have treated me thus.' Still seething with anger, he too gave Catt some advice on his new master: 'He doesn't feel sadness or humanity, I shall strip him of his title of philosopher.'[11]

Close contact with the Catholic clergy of Silesia allowed the king to give rein to a rich seam of anti-clericalism that was built into his own nature. He had imbibed anti-Catholic sentiments with his mother's milk. The frustrations he experienced made him lash out on the one hand, and pose as the Protestant prince on the other.[12] He railed against the prince-bishop, Graf Philipp Schaffgotsch, who had fled to Austria: 'fucking Schaffgotsch ... has betrayed me in the unworthiest way'. On 22 April he was at Silesia's oldest Cistercian monastery, Heinrichau. The monks wished him good luck with his campaign. Frederick was not convinced of their sincerity and told them that if they lied he would have them all hanged. He harangued the clergy of the 'Silesian Rome', Neisse, in a similar way. He told Catt:

My dear, you have no idea about this priestly scum, they are the biggest rogues in the world. I have been incredibly good to this clerical rabble and they still haven't ceased their perfidy; they constantly provide my enemies with information, thereby committing an irreparable wrong towards me; if ever I catch a prelate, canon or priest at it, the fate he'll suffer will terrify all the other examples of that race in habits.[13]

Fortunately, these furious tirades were rarely acted upon, but there was one example: Father Andreas Faulhaber of Glatz, whom La Motte Fouqué had hanged on 30 December 1757 for allegedly inciting the garrison to desert, after previously granting them absolution for breaking their oaths. Proof was hard to glean, as Faulhaber refused to divulge the secrets of his confessional. The priest's appeal is said to have gone to Frederick, who is supposed to have replied by asking why the execution had not been already carried out.[14] Frederick was experiencing some of the problems that were later to lead to Bismarck's celebrated *Kulturkampf* with the Catholic church: how to address a papal power that came into conflict with the monarch's temporal authority in a largely Protestant land. Glatz depended on the archdiocese of Prague, which was also a thorn in Frederick's side.[15]

In those calm days before the storm broke again, Frederick opened his soul to Catt in a way that he had not done to anyone since the Rheinsberg years. He spoke of the horrors of war: 'Ah hell, lovely glory, scorched villages, towns reduced to ashes, thousands of men reduced to misery, and as many massacres and horrors of every description, let us not mention it again, my hair is standing on end.'[16] This was where philosophy was meant to help. He subscribed to his own blend of the Stoics, with their rejection of human passions, and the Epicureans who preached

ultimate peace of mind, self-sufficiency and serenity. The latter he fuelled
by frequently dipping into his 'friend' Lucretius's *De rerum natura* (which
he read in French translation).[17] He did not believe in the immortality of
the soul. He explained himself to the duchess of Saxony Gotha:

Stoicism is the last attainable effort of the human mind; but to make us happy
it renders us insensitive, and the human animal is more sensitive than reasonable;
his senses wield a powerful empire over him, which is natural, but which they
often abuse, and the war which constantly breaks out between them and reason
is a little like that between me and my enemies: one is frequently laid low by
their superiority in numbers.[18]

Of the moderns, his favourite was the Calvinist Bayle, with his mixture
of sound good sense, scepticism and firm advocacy of tolerance.[19]

I have studied all systems of philosophy and I have adopted that which seemed
to me the least unreasonable, and I have observed well, that to be happy you
must have morality, enlightenment, occupation, and live moderately without
making too much of a business of life ... [there is] humanity in certain cases,
and barbarism in others, that is how the world lies, for better or for worse you
must accept it for what it is.[20]

Frederick revealed himself the moralist in those conversations with
Catt. 'The terrible corruption of morals is everywhere I look in all ranks
and classes of society, above all at the court: virtue appeals to no one
there.' Women were some of the worst miscreants: 'vanity continually
absorbs them and pursues them to the tomb of all vanities ...' Frederick,
however, largely spared his enemy Maria Theresa from this sweeping
indictment. He even had her portrait hanging in his town palace in
Potsdam.[21] She was 'sainthood itself', and he praised 'her talent, her
courage, her goodwill and generosity and her spotless virtue'.[22] Neither
the tsarina nor the marquise de Pompadour was excluded: they were
immoral women. The former was also refusing to die, and thereby
prolonging the war.[23]

Catt's job was far from easy. He did not read as such, but listened to
Frederick reading, or reciting his favourite plays, such as Racine's *Phèdre*
or *Britannicus*, or Gresset's *La Chartreuse*. He often altered the lines to slip
Daun or La Pompadour into the roles. Once, when they had taken
lodging in a peasant cottage, Frederick was keen to show Catt that he
could still dance a bit, and promptly did five or six *entrechats*. When he
had finished he expressed curiosity as to what Daun or Prince Charles

would have made of the sight.[24] He would sit down and draw Catt the buildings of his 'Potzedam' (as the marquis said): the gallery, gardens, the Chinese pavilion, the new colonnade, the greenhouses or the statuary. He wanted his reader to show him his attempts at verse: 'I shall be your Voltaire,' he said, and literally wrote poetry for Catt's use, to help him woo a merchant's daughter. Worse still was the cavalier use of Catt's time. One day he forgot the name of Graun's best opera to date. Catt left him and eventually went to bed. A servant woke him in the middle of the night bearing a slip of paper bearing the title *Montezuma*. Catt could not get back to sleep.[25]

Frederick's appearance was a fright. A French prisoner at Rossbach took him for one of his own corporals and asked if he could go home to France. He showed Catt his coat. 'I tore it a bit at Schmirsitz ... My hat goes with the rest of my clothes: everything feels worn out and ancient, and everything is a hundred times better for me than it would be new.' He apologised for the yellow snuff stains that covered his clothes: 'Go on, tell me I'm a bit of a pig, go on.' 'When my good mother was alive I was cleaner ... or [rather] less filthy.'[26]

'There are few men like me who love their family as much as I do.'[27] Despite what he had told his Milord, Frederick found time for tears after his brother died. Catt saw him, his head collapsed into his hands. 'Ah my friend, what disastrous news I have had, my poor brother is no more.' He then began to sob. He told Catt that he regretted the tone of his last letters to William, if not the content.[28] It was unlikely that his two brothers were any more opposed to him than before, but now they thought they had cause. Ferdinand had done well commanding a battery at Leuthen,[29] but had nearly killed Frederick as he sought to pass his guns, apparently by mistake. He retired sick from the army soon after. Henry refused to take over William's command.

Henry proved an exemplary general, but took every opportunity to criticise his brother's moves. In December 1759 he vented his frustration in a celebrated note: 'I don't trust this news; it is always as uncertain and contradictory as his character. He inflicted this cruel war on us; the bravery of his generals and soldiers alone can get us out of it. Since the day he joined my army he has sowed disorder and unhappiness ... Frederick loses everything.' However unjust, it was not just Henry's view; it was well represented in the higher echelons of the officer corps.[30]

Behind the sour grapes were completely different views on tactics and politics. Henry had sought a French alliance. Shortly before the war he was making up to Madame de Pompadour, asking her for her portrait for Rheinsberg.[31] Even when the Treaty of Versailles was signed, he pointed out that it was a defensive pact. He thought the war unnecessary.[32] He had no faith in the British. In military terms he was a 'Cunctator': he sought to avoid confrontation and carry on a war of attrition. He complained too much and failed to seize the moment, which he might easily have done after Frederick was routed at Kunersdorf. At the time Henry was seen as jealous of his brother. Just before Breslau fell, Mitchell wrote to Holdernesse expressing his suspicion that Henry was anxious to conclude a separate peace with France:

I know the prince's way of thinking; ambition is his only principle. He imagined (looking on the state of the king of Prussia's affairs as desperate) that he should have the glory of making peace; for this purpose he began first to show a most enormous partiality to the French officers and to hold frequent and long conferences with Martinfort...[33]

The bitterness increased beyond measure after William's death. Frederick tried to comfort him: 'My dear brother, you mustn't become misanthropic. Any man who lives in society must try to make himself useful to it, above all a prince like you must understand that he cannot renounce the world ... You have lost a brother; but you still have a family which loves you ...'[34] Henry's reply showed little desire to forgive his brother for what he termed the 'misunderstanding' with William. An exasperated Frederick wrote back at the beginning of August. He had prescribed reason and philosophy as the only medicaments for an incurable disease: 'We have enough foreign enemies without wanting to tear ourselves apart in our own family ... The important thing for the present is to preserve the state.'[35] To add to Frederick's malaise, he was aware that Wilhelmina was sinking fast:

Consider that I was born and brought up with my Bayreuth sister, that these first bonds are indissoluble, that between us the most demonstrable tenderness has never seen the slightest alteration[!], that we have different bodies but just one soul. Reflect that having brooked so many different sorts of misfortune capable of making life disgusting to me, there remains only one which can make my life insupportable. There you are, my dear brother, I have shown you the bottom of my heart, and I have described a mere part of the black thoughts which reign there.[36]

Frederick never ceased telling Catt how great his father had been, despite all the brutality he had been subjected to in those early years: 'he was absolutely a philosopher-king in every sense of the word.' He was tormented by dreams of both his father and mother. In one he was taken off to prison in the fortress in Magdeburg (where he had sent, among others, Trenck and the abbé de Prades) because, as the voice told him, 'You did not love your father enough.'[37]

[11]

The 1758 campaign got off to a slow start. Despite the calm in Saxony and Silesia, there had been a further shock in the Baltic provinces on New Year's Eve when the East Prussian orders had sworn an oath of loyalty to the tsarina. The king took it badly, and never really forgave the local nobility. An urgent priority was now to keep them from flooding Pomerania and joining up with those Austrians remaining in Silesia, currently holed up in Schweidnitz. It became Frederick's first objective to get them out. He installed himself in Grüssau in March, which was handy not only for Schweidnitz, but also for Neisse, where he was assembling men for the next Bohemian campaign, designed to prevent the Russians and the Austrians from coming together. If he could take Olmütz, he thought the Austrians might be ready to sue for peace.[38] Schweidnitz fell on 18 April, yielding him another 5000 prisoners and large quantities of arms and ammunition, which had been lodged in a town so severely wrecked that there was nothing left bar the walls.[39]

By 3 May the Prussians were already perched above Olmütz, seven marches and a hundred miles ahead of Daun and his army.[40] The Austrian commander had been fooled. Frederick laid siege. It went badly, and Frederick looked around for a scapegoat. He found one in Colonel Balbi, the same engineer who had accompanied him to Holland, who was in charge of siege warfare.[41] He had Balbi brought before him and for an hour said all the 'harshest things imaginable'. Balbi was in despair afterwards. As he told Catt, once Frederick had made up his mind – for good or bad – he never changed it.[42] The Austrians had now caught up with him, ambushed his supply column and made off with 3000 wagons, which were on their way to Olmütz.[43] They also succeeded in creating a lifeline to the garrison in Olmütz. Frederick raised the siege.

Frederick executed a much admired retreat, keeping his men covered from the marauders who had dogged him in the Second Silesian War. At the beginning of August he was home in Glatz. He now chose to travel north up the Oder and to try to knock the Russians out of the war. The French were weary, the Austrians were losing their will to fight, and he now considered the Russians his most dangerous enemy.[44] The army made for Frankfurt an der Oder. On the night of 19–20 August, Frederick relaxed by reading Cicero's *Tusculan Disputations*. The next morning the king of Prussia headed north-east to meet Fermor's army. Since Winterfeldt's death he had communicated his master plans only to Henry. He wanted to beat the Russians, then send Dohna up to deal with the Swedes while he returned to strike at the Austrians. If he was killed in battle, Henry was naturally to take command of the army.[45]

The Russians had been shelling Küstrin since the 15th and much had burned to the ground. Kleist noted: 'Soon the harvest of death will begin; the Russian are ready, they have turned Küstrin into a heap of stones.'[46] Frederick's feelings must have been mixed when he surveyed the wreck of the town where he had been forced to watch Katte's head fall. A cavalryman shouted out to him: 'Father, take heart, we'll carve those bastards up and we'll give no quarter, we are sharpening our sabres.' The fort had survived the pillage. Frederick went to visit the 'hole' where he had been incarcerated, an experience that put him in a melancholy mood: he sat down and wrote some verse.[47]

The Battle of Zorndorf began some way to the north of Küstrin on the 25th. Frederick's army of 37,000 faced 43,000 Russians. The sound of his men chanting religious music in the woods put him in a bad temper. 'My chaps are frightened, they are singing Clement Marot's Psalms, they'll soon hear a different tune.'[48] He thought victory was in the bag and that he would cut Fermor off from the rear, but despite the bad position of the Russian army with the sun in their eyes, things began to go badly for the Prussians and Zorndorf started looking like another Kolin. Frederick himself behaved with great courage. Mitchell was there for some of the time: 'In this action His Prussian Majesty exposed himself to the greatest dangers. I was witness to some of them, and I am informed that when the infantry on the left began to give way he bravely took the colours in his own hand and led them on.'[49] Once more it was Seydlitz who provided the Prussian trump-card. Seydlitz selected his own moment for attack, supposedly discarding an order from the king with the line: 'Tell the king that after the battle my head is at his disposal, but in the meantime I hope he will permit me to use it in his service.'[50]

The battle continued with extraordinary ferocity throughout the hot, long summer day. At one stage the king was spotted sitting quite demoralised by Prince Maurice, who felt it was incumbent upon him to take over the role of rallying the exhausted soldiers. The slaughter finally ceased after nine hours at 8.30 p.m. The Russians had lost a staggering 18,000 men; the Prussians, 12,800, which was a third of their effective force.[51] It was only the next day that everyone became aware of the extent of the damage and, as the Russians retreated, the number of villages they had put to the torch after slaughtering their inhabitants. Mitchell expressed the general view: 'I have had many unpleasant moments of late. We were on the very brink of destruction. The Russians fought like devils. The king of Prussia's firmness of mind has saved all. Would to God I was out of this scene of horror and bloodshed.'[52]

Not all the atrocities had been committed by the Russians, and some felt that the battle might have gone much better for Frederick had the East Prussians not left the field to rob the Russian baggage train. Their action did not improve Frederick's dim view of this Baltic province, which had paid homage to its Russian invaders. Mitchell again thought that the Russians had set a bad example: 'Such have been the barbarities of the Russ, killing, burning and destroying, wherever they came, that the Prussian soldiers for some time gave no quarter. They are provoked to madness, and, indeed, it is no wonder; the whole country was in flames during the battle and the night after.'[53] The Russian performance had been awe-inspiring in its doggedness. Frederick told the Lord Marischal that the Russians had no generals; on the other hand, they had stout and ruthless fighting men and he would know them from now on. Contemporaries awarded the battle to Frederick, but if Zorndorf was a victory at all, it was at best Pyrrhic.[54]

Frederick thought otherwise. He was let down by his left wing, otherwise it would have been another Leuthen. He sat down and piously wrote a letter to his wife. Some Russian prisoners were led by. One was still armed. Catt brought it to Frederick's notice: 'Can you take away that rascal's sabre?'[55] His cell in the ruins of Küstrin was not the only nostalgia-provoking experience of those sad days. Frederick cast around for quarters and settled on Tamsel, the home of Frau von Wreech. The Russians had not just killed the family retainers, they had murdered peasants for miles around and raped their women. Catt noted, 'I can still see before the house an unfortunate woman whom the Cossacks had raped, stripped and pierced in several places with their pikes.' Frederick had also noticed the dead woman: 'Is that what war is about? Princes who employ such troops should blush for shame. They are guilty and responsible to God for all the horrors they commit.' An old peasant came to see him at Tamsel to solicit a place for his son. 'How can I give you a job when I am not certain of keeping my own?'[56]

He wrote to his old *flirt* to reassure her that he would make good the damage which the Russians had made to the Schloss, and the despoliations committed by his own hussars in their need to find supplies of food. Frau von Wreech does not seem to have been placated. The letter was minuted: 'Received 30 August 1758, the year when I lost everything I had in the world to live on.' She still managed to scrape together enough money to marry her daughter in March the following year. She went like mutton dressed as lamb: Lehndorff noted in his diary that she had made herself 'exaggeratedly young and pretty, which ended up making her look absurd'.[57]

In September, Frederick's sister Amalia visited him at Müllrose as he marched south to face the Austrians in Saxony. She had been at William's bedside and related his last moments. Frederick came to the conclusion that he had been killed by his inadequate surgeons – 'Esculapian executioners', he called them. The marquis d'Argens had taken refuge in Hamburg. Frederick speculated on his life there: 'He is scoffing oysters and crabs, he is clearing the pharmacies of pills and the apothecaries of enemas, and I bet that as we speak he is hermetically sealed into his bedroom.'[58]

In thirteen days Frederick penned four new works: *Lettre de la marquise de Pompadour à la reine de Hongrie*; *Lettre d'un secrétaire du comte Kaunitz à un secrétaire du comte Cobenzl*; *Lettre d'un Suisse à un noble Vénitien*; and the *Relation de Phihihu, émissaire de l'empereur de la Chine en Europe. Traduit du Chinois*.[59]

These writings show that Frederick was developing the art of writing propaganda. In the first, Frederick lays the flattery on with a trowel; in the second, the king exposed Austria's alleged desire to scrap German liberties. The secretary writes that they will 'totally destroy the king of Prussia, so that the imperial court finds no power in Germany capable of stopping it from establishing a solid dominion'. Frederick also worked on the fears of the Silesian gentry, that they would be ultimately dispossessed, and the Bavarians, stressing the indubitable truth that the Austrians had been trying to annex them for half a century.[60]

Frederick was trying to be a tough general. It showed in his language. Whores and buggers abounded; Voltaire was a bugger, Maria Theresa had become the 'Apostolic carcass', and the tsarina the 'Greek harlot'. The pose was less than wholly convincing. A few days before the disaster of Hochkirch, he showed the polite, more delicate side of his nature in an epistle to his ailing sister: 'Vous goûtiez mon bonheur, vous pleuriez mes revers.' [You tasted my happiness,/You will lament my setbacks]. She was to die on the very day of the second of Frederick's military defeats.

Frederick was trying to dislodge the Austrians from Saxony. He had selected Hochkirch as a temporary resting place for his 30,000-strong army until supplies arrived from the magazine at Bautzen. Keith had told Frederick not to camp there, as the position was too exposed and dominated by a hill known to be alive with Croats: 'If the Austrian generals let us stay quiet in this position, they deserve to be hanged,' said Keith. Frederick seemed unaware of the danger, yet replied: 'Let us hope they fear us more than they fear the gallows.'[61] Daun, now advised by Lacy, had 80,000 men under his command. Frederick's army was so badly positioned that Daun's men were able to make it all the way to the village of Hochkirch under the cover only of a murky dawn. Even when the disaster was clear, Frederick was still not ready to believe the enormity of the crisis.[62]

The Prussians were literally caught napping. The Austrians cut the ropes of their tents and bayoneted the soldiers through the canvas.[63] One of the first prominent victims was Keith, who was wounded twice before being thrown from his horse by a cannon ball in his stomach as he tried to hold on to Hochkirch village. He died in the arms of his English servant, Tibay. His stripped and plundered body was later recognised by Lacy, who had fought with him in the Russian army: 'he was my father's best friend,' he said. He had him buried with full honours. The Austrians fired three salvoes from twelve cannons.[64] The Austrians cut a bloody swathe through the rest of Frederick's military circle: Elisabeth's youngest brother, Prince Francis of Bevern was beheaded by a cannon ball and Prince Maurice of Anhalt-Dessau was wounded and captured. Prussian soldiers were packed so close in the so-called Blutgasse that they remained standing in death. Under Major Simon von Langen, an understrength battalion continued to hold the churchyard in Hochkirch against seven regiments until there was no ammunition left. He died of eleven wounds. At the close of play, Prussian losses were over 9000: just under a third of the army.[65]

Frederick himself did not lack courage that day. He was seen under heavy fire by Major Paul Sigismond von Schmelinski:

'Your Majesty, I beg of you, for all the world, save your royal person, and at the very least, ride out of the musket fire. Look people are falling beside you.'

'I only want to see how this battalion in front of us is going to be driven away.'

'For God's sake, I beg you ... save your royal person, Hochkirch is lost, and the enemy will eventually catch us in the rear ... Your Majesty, your horse is wounded.'

'Me?'

'The horse will lose blood and fall over.'

'Where are my horses? Bring me a horse there!'

The horse did just as predicted: the little brown 'Engländer' keeled over and died.[66]

Once again Frederick would not take responsibility for his own failure: 'I tell you, I still can't make out how we were surprised. It was only possible if the watches were negligent.' To Lord Marischal, whose brother had died so bravely that day, he accused the 'wickedness and ambition of a few rulers who sacrifice everything to their boundless passions'.[67] He mourned the Jacobite field marshal honestly enough. His death spawned another poem. To Algarotti it was a 'loss for the army and society'. His diplomat brother was admirably philosophic about the loss. He had just received a letter from James expressing his weariness with the war. Lord Marischal wrote to Madame Geoffrin in Paris: 'My brother has left a fine inheritance! At the head of a great army he has just levied a contribution in all Bohemia; and in his purse I found just seventy ducats.'[68]

The loss of Prince Maurice was almost as bad; but he was suffering from cancer of the mouth and would die before long. The Alte Dessauer shared Frederick William's views on learning and had given his son no formal education whatsoever. He was as crude an individual as you were ever likely to find. Frederick had told Catt to wash his face once when Maurice had kissed him: 'He is very strange, good old Maurice, but he is as brave as his sword, there is no greater fun for him than fighting, he sees everything through rose-tinted spectacles; what a man he might have become had his education not been neglected, but he is exactly as nature made him.'[69]

Although Catt missed the battle, he had a ring-side seat afterwards, to study the king in defeat. Frederick adapted *Mithridate*:

> Je suis vaincu. Daunus a saisi l'avantage
> D'une nuit qui laissait peu de place au courage...[70]

I'm beaten, now Daun has seized the advantage
Of one night which left us little room for courage...

'My friend, I am a poor, beaten man,' he told his reader.

Catt tried to comfort the despairing monarch: 'Sire, your mind is needed, to prevent the shipwreck of the state ... you must look after it.'

'My friend, so many great men [lost], and how I detest this profession to which the blind accident of my birth has condemned me; but I have about me the stuff to finish the play, when it becomes unbearable.'

Frederick undid the neck of his tunic. On his chest a little oval box hung from a ribbon. Together Frederick and Catt counted out eighteen pills. 'These pills ... are opium, the dose is more than sufficient to send me to the shadows whence I shall never return ...' He explained that he used to keep the box in his pocket, but he had been afraid that a servant might remove it. So he had decided to tie it round his neck. Once again Frederick was frightened of the humiliation of capture. 'I shall tell you plainly, if a new misfortune comes, I shall certainly not survive the ruin and desolation of my country.'[71]

To cap it all, a letter from marquis d'Adhémar was brought in: 'Ah my dear, the letter is to prepare me; for certain my dear sister is no more ...' The letter spoke of a worsening condition, but confirmation was not slow in coming. Catt found Frederick sobbing. Years later he could not quite rid himself of a superstition that Wilhelmina's death had been somehow caused by his defeat at Hochkirch.[72] Shortly before Christmas that year, Frederick poured out his gloom and despondency to d'Argens:

I have lost all I loved and respected in the world ... I can still see the ruins of our loveliest provinces and the horrors that a horde of brutes, rather than men, have committed in them. In my old age I am almost reduced to a pantomime king. You will agree with me that such a situation lacks the charm which would endear it to a philosophic soul. I am buckling under the weight of work and worries and I lead the life of a hermit ... don't forget a poor fellow damned and cursed by God.[73]

He survived Hochkirch as he had survived Kolin. Daun failed to capitalise on his victory, and Frederick went into winter quarters in Breslau. At the end of November, and not before time, the campaign drew to a close. Mitchell thought Frederick had had a creditable innings 'notwithstanding the most unhappy 14th of October. He has not lost one inch of ground.' Frederick saw things differently. Mitchell had never seen him 'so much afflicted and depressed'. The behaviour of the Russians in the Neumark, and the Saxon royal family, still rankled. Mitchell himself was 'dreading the next campaign ... and I think I see in him, who knows what fear is, an eager desire for peace, which I never observed so strong before'.[74]

He found one small way of cheering himself up, involving old Seckendorff, who was presumably still ensconced in his Thuringian Schloss at Meuselwitz. He was the man who had made Frederick's adolescence so grim, and who had saddled him with his unwanted wife. On the 12th he wrote a mischievous letter to his brother Henry: 'My dear brother, I forgot to say, that it would be good to abduct old Seckendorff, we could take him straight to Magdeburg. He is the creator of all our enemies' dangerous projects; he is currently in their service, if it does nothing else it will make it easier to redeem Prince Maurice.' It paid off: in May the following year, Prince Maurice was exchanged for Seckendorff.[75]

The routine was re-established. Frederick lived 'like a Carthusian',* rising early, reading the dispatches and casting the unwanted ones into the fire. He played the flute; he saw his ministers and dictated his letters; he composed poetry and prose until eleven; he lunched with the generals and Mitchell; after lunch he went back to his flute playing and composition. Catt came to him at five and stayed for a couple of hours. Quantz was there to help with the concert. He read until ten: the classical histories were his favourites now – Sallust, Tacitus and Cornelius Nepos – but after his sister's death he became interested in the question of immortality, which made him turn to Christian writings. He wanted to see her and his mother again.[76]

Naturally there were writings from this time. The fact that Pope Clement XIII had rewarded Daun for Hochkirch with an anointed sword and helmet was nothing short of an obsession. He decided to follow it up with a spoof letter from the pontiff to the general. The purpose was clear: Frederick wanted to frighten German – and other – Protestants.

May this sword we send you serve between your hands to forever extirpate those heresies of which the foul smell issues from the abyss ... That it might be washed in rebel blood, that a blow should be delivered to the roots of that tree which bore such cursed fruits, and that by the example of Saint Charlemagne, the north of Germany be converted by sword, flame and blood.

---

* The Carthusians are a silent order. We would probably say 'like a Trappist'.

D'Argens congratulated Frederick on his style, but pointed out that the pope did not write in French. He translated it into Latin, leaving a column for the king's French version. Now Frederick could not be restrained: he followed it up with a bogus letter of congratulations from Soubise to Daun, and a letter from Daun himself to the pope. The message was much the same.[77]

Frederick's correspondence with Voltaire was also in full flood. The poet had written some verses for Wilhelmina and sent him *Candide* ('Job in modern dress'),[78] which, despite his resemblance to the character of the king of the Bulgarians,* Frederick claimed to love. This puzzling dialectic had in no way dried up. 'I love your poetry and prose, your wit, your robust and manly philosophy. I can't live with or without you. I am not talking to the king, to the hero, that is the business of sovereigns; I am talking to the man who enchanted me, whom I loved, and with whom I am still cross.'[79] Strange as it may sound, they needed one another. Catt described Frederick devouring Voltaire's letters with his eyes, muttering that he would not try to harm him again, he was sure of it. He was a fool to believe it. Voltaire literally hounded Maupertuis into the grave in July that year. Frederick was *bon prince*: 'Because of your genius I forgive all the vexations you gave me in Berlin, all the things you have said or had printed against me, which have been strong, hard and in great quantity, without harbouring the slightest grudge.'[80]

Voltaire was worried lest his correspondence with Frederick be discovered by some Austrian hussar plundering the post. He was nervous of his position with Louis XV now that Madame Denis had turned patriot by publicly burning Frederick's poems.[81] Frederick told him not to be so vain:

I can assure you they are keener on schnapps than they are on pretty poetry or famous authors ... The most civilised nations make war like wild beasts. I am ashamed of humanity. Let us face the truth; the arts and philosophy affect only a tiny number; the great mass of the people, and the common nobility, remain as nature made them: nasty animals.[82]

Three months later he returned to the theme:

Do you believe that there is any pleasure in this dog's life, witnessing and having unknown men slaughtered, daily losing friends and acquaintances, to see your

---

* The French word *bougre* in its original sense of 'bugger', was derived from the Bulgarians, who were supposed to favour such practices.

reputation constantly exposed to the caprices of chance, to spend the whole year in worry and uncertainty, risking life and fortune?

Despite schools of philosophy, man will remain the vilest beast in the universe: superstition, self-interest, revenge, treason, ingratitude will produce until the end of time, bloody, tragic scenes because passion, rather than reason, governs us.[83]

At the beginning of the 1759 campaign Frederick was ill again; but 'I must finish the campaign and obtain a good peace and for that it is worthwhile sacrificing my health to the good of the state.'[84] Frederick examined his resources as he did at the start of every military year. He had 50,000 men, Henry 30,000, Dohna 28,000 and Fouqué 13,000, while another 5000 were being used to keep the Swedes at bay: a total of 126,000, not including Ferdinand's army in the west. The enemy under the 'three whores' numbered 100,000 with Daun, 35,000 in the combined Austrian and imperial army, 40,000 in Russian and Swedish forces active in Pomerania and Brandenburg, and 70,000 in Saltykov's force: a figure of 245,000, without the French forces being held back by Ferdinand. Frederick's recruiting officers had scoured Saxony and Mecklenburg as well as the rest of the Reich, which was theoretically at war with him, but it was a time when everyone who had wanted to put on a uniform had already done so. Frederick even allowed the middle classes to enter the officer corps, so short was he of the decent noble material he preferred. Half the original corps had been lost since 1756.[85]

He told Catt on 1 April:

I don't know how I'm going to get out of this; who would not be afraid to see the number of enemies I have clinging to my back, and the strength they make up: but it is no use being amazed, I must act and scatter them; there is something diabolical about my position, in order to keep myself afloat, I am continually forced to undertake difficult, deeply hazardous things...[86]

What made 1759 different was that the enemy showed every desire to act in concert. Frederick wrote to d'Argens to express his misgivings. 'If they manage it, you will have nothing left but to write my epitaph and to charge your vessel for Jamaica.'[87] On 28 May he told his French friend that he thought the name Sanssouci now singularly inappropriate, even if he was anxious for a report on the progress of the gallery, garden and Chinese tea-house. Mitchell reported to Holderness that Frederick's health was deteriorating fast. Frederick concurred: the marquis would hardly recognise the king, 'an old man with greying hair, lacking half his teeth, without gaiety or spark, or imagination; less than the vestiges of Tusculum, of which architects have made so many imaginary plans, lacking the ruins to indicate the house of Cicero'.[88]

D'Argens was still working on propaganda, a deist putting the fear of God into the Protestants, admittedly a little hampered by his lack of German. He came up with the bright idea of making the archbishop of Canterbury offer a sword to Prince Ferdinand of Brunswick, a pendant to that presented to Daun by the pope.[89] Henry was doing sterling work too, mopping up enemy magazines and interrupting the supply lines, thereby causing 700,000 thalers worth of damage. Frederick was as ever fulsome in his praise for his brother: 'You sweep away our enemies like dust in the wind.'[90] More worrying was that Prince Ferdinand's luck seemed to be coming to an end. He had been repulsed by the duc de Broglie at Bergen.[91] Much worse was the Battle of Kay on 23 July. It announced the re-emergence of the Russian bear after its long hibernation, its strength fully restored. The royal favourite Kurt Heinrich von Wedell temporarily fell from grace when he lost a staggering 8000 men to Saltykov's 4800. 'Those buggers there are losing their heads...'[92]

[III]

Ferdinand more than redeemed himself when he soundly beat the French at Minden on 1 August, but news of the victory failed to lift Frederick's spirits when he received it on the 5th: he thought Saltykov a tougher nut than Marshal duc de Contades.[93] After Kay there was nothing to stop the Russian general achieving the planned merger with Daun's Austrians in the Neumark, on the right bank of the Oder, and some 24,000 Austrians promptly came up to join the 40,000 Russians. Anointed sword or not, Frederick's respect for Daun had also increased, and he was wont to refer to him as 'le grand Daun' in his private conversations. Together with the remnants of Wedell's army and Dohna's force, the king of Prussia had mustered around 49,000 men and marched them up the Oder at breakneck speed. He claimed that he had not slept for six nights when he arrived at Beeskow on the 3rd.[94] Frederick's pessimistic analysis of his fortunes was correct. The Battle of Kunersdorf that year was to prove the nadir.[95]

Kunersdorf was not a great distance to the south of Zorndorf, where the bloody battle of the summer had been fought the year before. It was on the far side of the Oder from the old Prussian university town of

Frankfurt. The Prussian army marched before dawn to take up their positions. Some soldiers passed the king, who asked them in their own *Platt* or dialect, 'Morning, children. Would you like to eat some beans soon?' The soldiers cried, 'Yes!' Frederick replied in the best of moods: 'Well, be a little patient then.' Frederick had badly positioned his assault, but the first stages of the battle went well for him with the capture of many enemy cannon, in the course of which the Prussians committed an unusual number of atrocities. Some of his generals advised him to stop there, as the Russians would probably abandon their camp. Frederick was determined to press on.[96]

The next stage of the battle proved the end of the soldier-poet Ewald Christian von Kleist. His last letter to Gleim had been sent from the camp at Rothhauslitz on 23 July: 'Terrible marches, appalling heat and sleepless nights ... There must be something for us this year ... just to beat Daun once, then I will happily die.'[97] Sleep had caught up with him on 11 August, when friends in Finck's corps woke him from a dream of battles and victory. Kleist fought with great bravery. He helped take three batteries, receiving twelve contusions and wounding two fingers on his right hand. He was obliged now to carry his sword in his left. While he attempted to take a fourth battery, he was shot through the left arm and one of his legs was shattered by three bullets.[98]

Kleist could no longer move, but he tried to rally the troops for all that. He shouted to his men: 'Children, don't abandon your king!' The rest of Kleist's story reveals some interesting details of the savagery and sensibility of eighteenth-century warfare. As he attempted to dress his wounds, he was shot in the head. Cossacks stripped him of all his clothes, but he mustered the strength to address them in Polish, a language spoken by many a Pomeranian landlord. They decided he was a Pole and tossed him into a marsh rather than killing him there and then. Some Russian hussars took pity on him and gave him some clothes, straw and money; but the Cossacks robbed him once more. He was finally found by a German officer in the Russian army called von Stackelberg, who had him put in his carriage and brought to the house of Professor Nicolai in Frankfurt. He died of his wounds on the 24th.[99]

Another officer who was put out of the fight by a wound was Seydlitz, a general whom the king could not easily do without. Frederick's armies might have dislodged the Russians, but Daun's men were counter-attacking. Once Frederick's soldiers saw eight fresh battalions of grenadiers coming towards them, nothing could hold them back. The king remained in the van, encouraging his men. He cried out, 'Children, don't leave me!' Two horses were shot from under him and a bullet was stopped in his pocket by a gold snuff box. Finally he grabbed the flag of Prince Henry's regiment and exclaimed, 'All brave soldiers follow me!' As he later told his minister Finckenstein, he would have stayed on the battlefield had he had any more resources, but Frederick would have fallen into the hands of the pitiless Cossacks had he not been sighted and collected by a squadron of Zieten hussars commanded by Captain von Prittwitz.[100]

'The Prussian army had not been defeated. It had been routed.'[101] Only 4000 soldiers remained. The rest had been killed or injured, or had fled from the battlefield. Luckily for Frederick there was a little 'miracle' at Kunersdorf: the Russians refused to advance. The Croats and Cossacks were too busy slitting the throats of the wounded and robbing the corpses. Saltykov had lost 13,000 to the Austrians' 2000 and he drew his own conclusions.[102] 'Another victory like that and I shall take the news back to Saint Petersburg all alone, baton in hand. The Prussian king sells his defeats dearly.'[103] A division was revealed between the allies: Maria Theresa was for *Endsieg*, unconditional surrender; the tsarina had told Saltykov to avoid pitched battles. Had they gone for the jugular then, as the Austrian general Loudon wanted, there would have been little to stop them.[104]

Frederick underwent a minor mental collapse after the battle. He shook the musket balls from his clothes – others picked them from their hats – and he wrote his famous letter to his minister, Graf Finckenstein in Berlin using Prittwitz's back as a desk.

I attacked the enemy at three o'clock this morning. We pushed them as far as the Jewish cemetery near Frankfurt. All my soldiers performed prodigiously well, but that cemetery made us lose a considerable number. Our people panicked; three times I rallied them, at the end I was nearly taken prisoner myself and I was forced to leave the battlefield. My coat is shot full of holes, two of my horses were killed; I am unhappy to be still alive. Our losses are very great. Of an army of 48,000 I have 3000 left for the time being. At the moment I write everyone is fleeing. I am no longer master of my people. In Berlin they would be best advised to think of their own safety. It has been a cruel change of fortune, I shall not survive it. The consequences are going to be worse than the battle itself. I have no more means of helping, and, if I am honest, I believe that all is lost. I shall not survive the loss of my country. Goodbye for ever.[105]

For the first time, he briefly renounced his command, handing it over to General Finck. By the 16th Frederick had recovered and was looking for someone to blame. 'The battle would have been won had it not been for the infantry suddenly collapsing,' he told his brother Henry:

our dead was not above 2500 [it was nearer 6000], but there are 10,000 wounded, of whom 6000 will come back in a little while ... The moment I reported our disaster to you, everything looked desperate; the danger is still great, but be assured that as long as I keep my eyes open, I will uphold the state as is my duty ... The dead are happy, they are sheltered from worry and chagrin.[106]

He wrote to d'Argens too:

We had bad luck, my dear marquis, but it was not my fault. Victory was ours, it would even have been complete, had the infantry not grown impatient, and done the wrong thing by abandoning the battlefield. Today the enemy is marching towards Müllrose to join up with [the army of] Hadik. The Russian infantry is almost wholly ruined. All that I have been able to reassemble from the debris has been 32,000 men. I am going to follow them, cut my throat or save the capital. I don't think I lack constancy. I would not be able to answer for the event. If I had more than [just] one life, I would sacrifice it for my country; but, if I don't succeed, I think that I have done my best for it, and that I am allowed to think of myself. There are always limits.[107]

D'Argens proved to be the fine friend he was, and wrote the most moving reply. He reminded him that Caesar, Turenne and the great Condé had all suffered defeats.

I am mortified at not being by your side ... In the name of your people, in the name of your glory, which will live for ever despite the annoying events which might affect you [now.] Do not do anything which, by damaging your health, will cause more suffering to your people than the loss of a hundred battles. Reflect that Louis XIV put up with far greater reverses, and that his reputation is all the more substantial for his having known how to deal with them, than it is for conquering a handful of provinces. What is your aim? To defend the state; and, if you are lost to that state, it is doomed for ever and without resource. Peace made in certain conditions is neither a disgrace nor prejudicial; where is the prince, where the hero, who has not been obliged on occasion to give in to the crushing weight of events? Finally, Sire, I adore you, and you know that, if you perish, your people will never cease to accuse you of their misfortune; if you live, in whatever way events may lead, they will adore you [too], because you alone can save them from the disaster they will undergo by losing you.

Excuse me Sire, for the liberty I am taking; but it is excusable in a man who, if he had a hundred lives instead of one, would give them all to see you happy.[108]

D'Argens might have had no great reputation for his physical courage, but moral courage he did not lack. On the 18th he wrote again to say that he would not leave Berlin until he knew that the king was well. He offered, despite his obvious loathing for army camps and the physical discomfort they represented, to come with the first escort leaving Berlin, adding that they left every day, 'and I will do the rest of the campaign. I am reasonably well and am in a [fit] state to ride a horse; like that I shall cause no embarrassment to Your Majesty'.[109]

Frederick wrote back to his friend on 20 August. He was in Fürstenwalde, on the heights dominating the left bank of the Oder. His people had abandoned him at Kunersdorf and he had nearly fallen into the hands of the barbarians. His was still in his Roman mode:

'I have my way of looking at things. I am not imitating either Cato or Sertorius;[110] I am in no way thinking of glory, but of the state, and if it succumbs, despite all I have done and after my having sacrificed everything to it, I must shed this burden of life, which has already bothered and weighed heavily upon me for a long time now.[111]

The next day Frederick had his first indication that the Russians were not going to exploit their great victory. He sent to d'Argens in a much more light-hearted mood. 'If you want to do me the pleasure of coming here, you may do so in all safety. Bring your bed with you and take along my chef Noël, I will have a little room made up for you. You will be my consolation and my hope.'[112]

He spoke too soon. The enemy was still in the vines above Frankfurt. Frederick told d'Argens to flee. He did not need too much encouragement. In his next letter he announced his intention of going to Tangermünde in the Altmark. He got even farther: on 9 September he reached Wolfenbüttel. Yet the panic was over in a moment. Three weeks later Frederick's mental health was restored and he was calling the aftermath of Kunersdorf the 'Miracle of the House of Brandenburg' (there were to be two; it was the second that brought the war grinding to a close): 'The moment when, crossing the Oder, the enemy might have chanced a second battle and ended the war, it marched off from Müllrose to Lieberose' – that is, towards Saxony. Henry had also done sterling work, once again proving himself an excellent tactician. He cut the Austrian supply lines, thereby obliging Loudon's force to retreat in the wake of the Russians.[113] Frederick was nearly safe: 'My martyrdom will last another two months, then frost and snow will finish it.'[114]

D'Argens had evidently taken over as the head of Frederick's secret service. The wife of the dead poet Gerolamo Tagliazucchi claimed to possess the Austrian code books. Possibly as a result of this precious information, d'Argens was able to unmask the spy Giovanni Renazzi, who was considered an important catch: he had been working for Daun, and was going off to join Frederick's armies. He languished in Spandau until after Frederick's death. Frederick was not too worried about spies, for the simple reason that he was not in the habit of confiding in anyone: 'In order to know my secrets, you need to corrupt me personally, and that isn't easy.'[115]

The end of the campaigning season was calm. Frederick was attempting to clear Saxony of Austrians by a war of attrition. 'I am making our blessed friend's [Daun] retreat as difficult as possible,' he told Voltaire on 19 November. 'I hope he'll have a few nasty adventures over the next few days.'[116] News of the British victory in Canada at the end of October brought him fresh hopes of peace for the spring: 'we will go and see the gallery at Sanssouci, which is, according to what my inspector of paint-ings[117] told me today (he arrived from Potsdam yesterday), the loveliest thing he has seen in all the world, and he has been six years in Italy'. 'Oh Sanssouci! Oh Sanssouci! Why can't I give my prickly heat to the queen [of Hungary] ... my diarrhoea to the tsarina and my indigestion to Louis!'[118]

Frederick was reunited with Catt on 11 November, after three months without seeing his confidant. The king showed Catt his flattened snuff box, and the place in his tails where the musket ball had gone in, crudely stitched up with thread.[119] The relative calm was interrupted by the third shock of 1759, the defeat of General Friedrich August von Finck at Maxen on 20 November. Finck had been sent to defend an isolated plateau. The Austrians had attacked with an overwhelming force of 32,000 and the Prussian cavalry had stood by and not lifted a finger to help. Surrender was unconditional. Finck had told the men to lay down their arms: a disaster in purely numerical terms exceeded only by Kolin. The Austrians bagged 9 generals, 549 officers, 12,500 men and 70 cannons; and exchanges of prisoners between the two sides had now dried up. The disappointment in Finck was all the greater since Frederick had placed his trust in him after the rout at Kunersdorf in August.[120]

Finck wrote to excuse his conduct the next day, but the king was ice cold in his reply: 'I have received your letter of the 21st. Until now there has never been an example of a Prussian corps laying down its arms before the enemy.' He told Finck he would defer judgement until the events had been examined by the appropriate commission. Two days later Frederick was still 'dizzy' from the disaster. D'Argens reminded him of the wider world: the destruction of the French fleet, the taking of Münster by Imhof and Ferdinand's victory over the Württembergers at Fulda. Henry found in Maxen another pretext for criticising his brother's leadership. This time he was quite open in his attacks, threatening to quit the army. Mitchell believed he saw signs of discouragement everywhere, but Catt claimed that the mood of the army was still with Frederick. Even William's former ADC, Henckell von Donnersmarck, put it thus: 'We must have our revenge, vanquish or die for our Fritz!'[121]

[IV]

As the campaign drifted on into the winter snows, the war of attrition continued. D'Argens tried to divert the monarch with amusing stories. The French had been sending their old spoons to the mint to help the war effort. When they had finished, thought the Provencal, they might make war with their stew and saucepans, and pay their subsidies to the Russians and Swedes in coppers.[122] Frederick wanted Bayle, and he wanted d'Argens in person. He had lost Dresden in the débâcle following Kunersdorf. Now he settled in Wilsdruff a few miles to the west. There was an apartment right next to his: 'you can come without a coat or a handkerchief in front of your nose ... There is a Catholic church opposite where they play excellent music.'[123]

Recruits were brought in to restock Frederick's depleted forces, but their quality was poor. A tenth of the officer corps had gone into captivity at Maxen. Mere boys were brought in to take their places. At the end of April, Frederick ran into a very fresh-faced officer: 'You are young ... are you quite dry behind the ears?' The youth was unabashed and replied, 'Sire, I admit I'm young, but my courage is antique.' Later the king was surprised to see a gang of these infantile subalterns playing leap-frog under his window.[124] D'Argens found a French nobleman named de Foresta who was looking for a commission. He was about thirty-two and had a 'handsome face'. D'Argens added in a characteristic vein that de Foresta had fought in Canada, 'against people who, while singing Iroquois verses, scalp you and sometimes cook you alive, then eat you afterwards. I should be as happy preaching Judaism in Lisbon as fighting a war in America.'[125]

Frederick was happy to take d'Argens' 'Iroquois', as he called him, 'from today we can even kill, without being accused of homicide, as many Austrians as it pleases him'. But it ended badly for d'Argens' protégé. He died in the siege of Dresden that spring: 'it was a useless sacrifice', noted Frederick.[126]

There had been a proposal from Britain to institute a peace conference in the Hague. Voltaire had once more got the idea that he might play a starring role, and Frederick encouraged him: 'It is high time we brought these horrors to a close.'[127] But an exchange between Mitchell and Holdernesse at the end of January shows how powerless the British were to bring about the peace that Frederick longed for. Moreover, Parliament was about to scrap Frederick's annual subsidy of £670,000. Mitchell believed that France could be detached from the alliance and Russia subdued by Britain. This had to happen, else 'the king of Prussia will, I fear, be irretrievably lost'. Holdernesse could hold out no great hope: 'We cannot efficaciously defend him ... The court of Vienna moves Heaven and earth to prevent a pacification; and you see by [Robert] Keith's last despatch how little we have to hope for from Russia...'[128]

Frederick had been informed. His enemies were still the Austrians and the 'Barbarian Empress': one of Frederick's politer names for the tsarina. Frederick tried his own brand of diplomacy. He wrote to Henry, who must have been happy to hear his brother talking what he considered sense. He thought the Austrians could be bought off with some canton of Bavaria, and the Saxons would have to be compensated too, possibly with the Prussian Thuringian city of Erfurt. His mind ranged this way and that. He was still trying to find someone to bribe at the Russian court. Henry had suggested Peter Shuvalov, the tsarina's all-powerful minister, but he was already too rich to have need of Frederick's money. He grabbed at the Turkish straw: if he could interest them in the war, it would expose the Austrian rear.[129] To his blue-stocking friend, the duchess of Saxony-Gotha, Frederick expressed the sentiment that 'the best-informed politician knows no more about the future than the stupidest of men'.[130]

Like his father, Frederick spoke of abdication. He told Catt that he would take one province out of his large portfolio, enough to yield 100,000 thalers, and there he would build himself a house to lodge a band of friends, but no ambitious people or plotters. A modest 12,000 would be spent on food, 20,000 on 'fantasies' and the rest on his companions. He promptly drew his reader a plan of the house. The comparative peace was shattered by the intelligence that two pirated editions of his poems were circulating in France. They were the king's 'Achilles' heel'. He gave a copy to Mitchell, claiming that several things had been omitted, altered or mangled. It was not just that he did not believe the poems good enough to be published for general consumption; they also contained embarrassing jibes at foreign courts, including the British. Shortly afterwards his correspondence with Voltaire was also released. He suspected the former ambassador to Berlin, the duc de Nivernois, Darget and others, but chiefly Voltaire: 'I know that rascal like the back of my hand.'[131]

Frederick faced Voltaire with his well-founded suspicions. The poet writhed, hissed and spat. He had in fact leaked the papers to Versailles, but he had not been responsible for their publication, which was ordered by the French government. He even went so far as to try to put the blame on the dead Maupertuis. His method was to turn the attack on the warrior-king:

You have hurt me quite badly; you have caused a permanent rupture between me and the king of France; you have made me lose my offices and pensions; you mistreated me in Frankfurt, me and an innocent woman, who was dragged through the mud and thrown into prison; and next, while honouring me with your letters, you poison the sweetness of that consolation with bitter reproaches.[132]

Voltaire's attack on Frederick's personality touched in places the bitter core of the king's double-sided character. Frederick's reserves of wisdom were

distorted by the passions inseparable from a great imagination; a little by moodiness; and by thorny situations which inject a little bile into your soul; and finally by the malicious pleasure you have always taken in wanting to humiliate other men, in wanting to say and write cutting things[.] It is a pleasure which is unworthy of you, all the more so because you are on a higher level than them by virtue of your blood and your unique talents.[133]

Frederick took this rebuke in reasonably good heart: 'I know very well I have great faults. I assure you that I don't treat myself with kid gloves. I forgive nothing, when I speak to myself.'

I am not looking at the past at all. Without doubt you committed grave wrongs against me. No philosopher would have put up with your behaviour. I have forgiven you everything, and I would like to forget everything too. But, if you had not been dealing with a lunatic who was besotted with your fine genius, you would not have got away with it that easily ... Take it as read, therefore, that I don't want to hear any more about that boring niece, who is no better than her uncle when it comes to covering up her imperfections...[134]

Voltaire once again claimed to be dying. He had tried that trick too often: Frederick told him that he would survive long enough to write a malicious couplet on his tombstone. He also mentioned another suspicion that Voltaire had sent off their correspondence for publication. Voltaire again claimed innocence:

1. I never go out. I never go to Geneva.
2. In Geneva there are only people who would be hacked to death for Your Majesty. We have a cobbler who beats his wife every time you suffer a set-back and a locksmith, who is a German, and who would strangle his wife and three children for your well-being.[135]

There was a rupture in the correspondence, which lasted more than four years. Frederick was now happiest with d'Argens, who was able to keep him abreast of developments in intellectual Europe without annoying him like Voltaire. Frederick had been included in a *Freydenker Lexikon* published in Leipzig that year; but while it did not disturb him to be classed an atheist together with the marquis, he did not take to being included in the same category as 'that scoundrel Beaumelle'.[136] On 12 March his pirated *Oeuvres du Philosophe de Sanssouci* were placed on the Papal Index. D'Argens had had to warn him against using such rough language to describe the church and its doctrines: it was not calculated to win over the Protestants either.[137] Samuel Formey was commissioned to write *L'Anti-Sans-Souci, ou la folie des Nouveaux philosophes*, which denied Frederick's authorship of the *Oeuvres* and stressed the king's piety.

D'Argens had some news from His Majesty's kitchens:

Your cook Champion won't make you any more *ragoûts* which are either too salty or too peppery. The thing which served the first man to generate the human race was cut right off; he died three days later. All over town they are saying that the surgeon who performed the operation, and who is some sort of lunatic (he is called Coste), put the thing he had chopped off between two plates and sent it to Champion's mistress, a woman called Le Gras. This nasty prank is making all the women's and the prigs' tongues wag.[138]

Champion was guilty not only of overseasoning his sauces. He had been mixing with French prisoners and talking treason: 'You see, Sire, that Heaven punished him more severely than your judges might have done, for they certainly would not have castrated him.' Frederick was very unsentimental about Champion's macabre fate. He had been reading some high-faluting verse when d'Argens' letter arrived. 'I made a terrible descent from all those glories to Champion's balls. I have lost a very bad cook ... I have given Noël the job of fetching me the best he knows.'[139]

When Frederick shifted his quarters to Meissen he was delighted by the porcelain he saw all around him. He made presents of services to his friends. D'Argens received one with symbols of philosophy and scepticism.[140] Gotzkowsky was offering him new pictures: a Correggio, a Carlo Maratto, a Ciro Ferri, a Titian and what was billed as a Raphael, but which was in reality by Frans de Vrient. The latter had been smuggled out of Rome. It represented Lot being inebriated by his daughters. He was not satisfied. Gotzkowsky was also to find him a Giulio Romano and a Luca Giordano. Art was better than war. He was thinking of Sanssouci and his gallery. 'I tell you, in the end, these thoughts are more pleasant than carnage, murder and all the misery that has to be planned, and which would make Hercules shiver. Rabelais' quarter of an hour is about to ring...'[141]

[v]

'The king of Prussia is reduced to the fatal necessity of depending upon the faults of others,' wrote Mitchell to Holdernesse in February.[142] The problem was that the Austrians and Russians were now making fewer mistakes. Even if, under the aegis of Prince Henry, some wings of the army were openly grumbling, there was a loyal brand of officer who was never likely to abandon his king. One of these was Zieten, who despite his diminutive stature was a lovable thug, with a remarkable fondness for punch-ups of all sorts. When the sixty-one-year-old cavalry general was told that the fighting was going to start again, he grabbed another general's hand and began to jump up and down: 'Long live our good, our dear, our great king!'[143]

To make it abundantly clear to Frederick that he was no longer master of the game, the campaign opened with another disaster: the capture of his friend La Motte Fouqué and his 8000-strong force at Landeshut on 23 June. General Loudon (who had been rejected for service in Frederick's almost exclusively noble officer corps) faced him with a force three times as big. La Motte Fouqué was not going to bow out like Finck. He made a desperate charge and succeeded in capturing two flags. He formed a square where his horse was killed under him. The Austrians broke the square, the Loewenstein Dragoons slaughtering the soldiers as they fell back. La Motte Fouqué received three sabre strokes and would have perished there and then had it not been for his ostler, Trautschke, who threw himself across the general's wounded body: 'Do you want to kill the commanding general?' Hearing Trautschke, Colonel Voit of the Loewensteins ran over to La Motte Fouqué, pushing his men aside, and picked him up in his arms. He offered the Prussian his horse: 'I might soil the fine saddle with my blood.' Voit replied: 'My saddle can only gain from being stained by the blood of a hero.'[144] When Frederick heard the news he said, 'Fouqué behaved like a Roman.'

A month later began one of Frederick's most controversial sieges: Dresden, where the garrison was commanded by yet another Austrian Irishman: General Maguire or Macquire. Frederick might really have wanted to lure Daun into a pitched battle, but he claimed that Maguire had given him the impression that he would yield up the city after a token fight. That was not to be. The Austrians set fire to some of the suburbs to make the city easier to defend. The Prussians moved up their artillery to punish the 'Florence of Elbe' for daring to defy them. Fire destroyed the roof of the Kreuzkirche and spread throughout the city, destroying 416 buildings and damaging 115 more in this baroque gem. A night-time raid scattered the Bernburg Infantry Regiment and took their guns. Frederick was appalled and pettily had the braid cut from the uniforms of officers and NCOs, while soldiers had to yield up their swords. Munition was too short for a long siege, and Frederick was forced to abandon it. 'It was apparently written in the book of destiny that the Prussians would not retake Dresden.'[145]

The shelling of Dresden was not good for Frederick's reputation. Mitchell wrote that he could 'not think of it without horror'. The same envoy wrote with disgust at Frederick's plundering of Brühl's house in Leipzig and sacking of Schloss Hubertusburg, which demonstrated a 'meanness that I am really ashamed to narrate'.[146] 'Meanness' was the *mot juste*. Soon after Prussia descended on Saxony, there had already been a correspondence with Gräfin Brühl on the return of her furniture, no doubt plundered from her house in town. Frederick had answered the countess's enquiries with a courtesy that had earned him the title of 'the most polite man of the century',[147] yet a year later he was writing to Field Marshal Keith, 'I'd be much obliged if you'd detach Lieutenant-Colonel de May. Although under his own authority, with a few of his free companies to make a bit of noise [at Brühl's country estate], I don't want to hear about it.'[148]

Regular army officers would not touch the job of sacking Hubertusburg. It was meant to be Frederick's revenge for the destruction of Charlottenburg, which seems to have been chiefly the work of the Austrians (see below, p. 298). Marwitz sought a means to leave the army rather than sully his hands with it (see above, p. 269), and the man credited with taking up the commission was Frederick's stooge, Quintus Icilius, who called his squad of misfits the 'Free Roman Legion'. Even here, Frederick was mean: he took every opportunity to rub it in that Quintus was a pillager.[149] Meanwhile, Frederick posed as the innocent. Just before Frederick started shelling Dresden, he wrote a letter to Algarotti lamenting the damage that the war was doing to Saxony. The Italian had spent some splendid moments in Saxony himself: 'I have saved this lovely country as much as chance has allowed me.'[150] In reality, Frederick bled Saxony white: in January 1762 alone, the Leipzigers had to drum up three and a half million thalers in war contributions.[151]

He was under a lot of strain. The next heartache was the fall of Liegnitz, Parchwitz and the siege of Breslau, Glatz and Neisse at the end of July. Henry was able to relieve the Silesian capital, but the province had been opened up to the Austrians again. Frederick found to his frustration that wherever he turned on his Silesian marches, Daun's armies kept pace with him along the Katzbach, as if they were just a fourth column of his own infantry, except there were only 30,000 Prussians, with 80,000 Austrians dogging their steps. On 15 August, Loudon saw that the Prussians were hemmed in on three sides. He thought he had another Hochkirch on his hands, and decided to attack under cover of darkness. Frederick was awoken at 3 a.m. by Major von Hundt, who was directed to Frederick's tent by Major General Saldern.

'Where is the king?'

'What's up?'

'The enemy has arrived! They have beaten back all my advance guards and they are four hundred paces away.'

'Keep them back as long as possible.'

Hundt gave just enough warning. It was the Bernburgers who fought hardest, joining in the counterattack: 'one of the few occasions in military history in which the infantry have ever taken the offensive against cavalry'.[152] They were so determined to redeem themselves that they attacked without orders. General von Bülow went to the regimental commander to ask him what the devil was happening: 'For God's sake keep your people in order!' However, an ensign replied, 'They won't obey calls or orders any more.' With a cry of 'Honour or death!' they broke the Austrian line. Frederick took the hint. After the victory at Liegnitz, Frederick gave them back their braid and side arms.[153]

Saldern offered ten thalers to the first man to silence the Austrian battery. A well-aimed cannon shot hit the enemy powder-wagon. Frederick himself was constantly in the thick of it. He 'exposed his person to the greatest of dangers. A grape shot pierced the skirts of his coat; the horse he rode was wounded by a musket ball; one of his pages had his horse killed by a cannon shot; and his ecuyer, and one of the grooms, were both mortally wounded.' He was chuffed: He told d'Argens that he was 'invulnerable for the time being'.[154]

Frederick badly needed a victory to restore confidence in the army: Liegnitz was the first real one for a year and half. The Austrians lost 8400, as well as 80 guns and 23 flags and standards. The Prussian total was a modest 3000. Daun arrived late, thereby incurring the wrath of Loudon, who blamed him for the defeat. He could do nothing against Zieten and his horsemen.[155] After the battle, Frederick promoted Zieten general of cavalry and sat down and announced the victory to his wife. This hypocritical connubial piety did not go unnoticed in Berlin.[156]

After Liegnitz, Frederick drove his army up to Breslau, where Tauentzien had held out despite the Austrians' heavy bombardment of the city, which had destroyed the king's house among others. Loudon had tried to frighten the garrison by telling them that no one in the city would be spared, not even children in the womb. Tauentzien sent word that he was 'not pregnant, and my men are not either'. The sight of the city gave rise to another flood of dejection: 'I don't know if I shall survive this war; but I am wholly resolved, if that happens, to spend the rest of my days in retirement, in a world of philosophy and friendship.'[157]

Berlin had laid open since the beginning of the war; Hadik's shameful occupation had not changed much. Now a joint Austrian-Russian expedition was planned under General Gottlob Kurt Heinrich von Tottleben, a German 'wastrel and adventurer' serving in the Russian army. Like Loudon, he had been denied a commission by Frederick.[158] The combined force was made up of 15,000 Austrians, 18,000 Russians and 5600 Cossacks. They started menacing the city on 3 October, demanding a ransom of 2 million thalers. Generals Seydlitz and Lehwaldt,[159] who were living as invalids in Berlin, saw them off, manning the city's defences throughout the night. The court was already safe in Magdeburg.

The city was shelled from the Hasenheide, and three attempts were made to blow up the city gates. Things looked bad for Seydlitz and Lehwaldt until they heard that they were to be relieved by a small force led by the prince of Württemberg. The Berliners were banking on the prince, and slaughtered a large number of oxen and brought bread and beer to the Opera House to welcome him to the city. Württemberg chased Tottleben and his 15,000 Russians all the way to Köpenick.[160] But it was to be only a short pause. Lacy's corps arrived and it was decided to yield up the capital. The force entered Berlin on the 7th and celebrated with a march through the streets. They stayed for four days and renewed their ultimatum for a contribution or they would pillage the city. The sum had gone up: Tottleben had new instructions from Fermor and was demanding *four* million.[161]

Lacy was decent enough to want to protect the royal palaces in Potsdam, and sent Fürst Emeric Esterházy to make sure no damage was done. Esterházy snatched a portrait and a couple of flutes.[162] The prince de Ligne supervised the collection of the captured trophies from the last wars. While he was there he too took a memento from Sanssouci, a pen from the great man's desk, but d'Argens reported impeccable behaviour, and not the slightest damage. Others behaved less well. Before the Berliners could muster the levy, Cossacks and Austrian hussars wrecked the royal palaces of Niederschönhausen and Charlottenburg. The Cossacks beat up Elisabeth's *castellan* and turned her palace upside down. In general, however, the Russians under Tottleben received a better press than the Austrians, who damaged the Polignac marbles and waded knee-deep in porcelain and crystal. Frederick unkindly (or politically) blamed the Saxons for the destruction. Algarotti dutifully commiserated: 'I was sad to learn that your enemies, Sire, unable to beat your soldiers, took out their revenge on your statues.'[163]

D'Argens was quick to reassure the king that the damage to Charlottenburg was not that great:

they stole the tapestries and the paintings, but, by some strange twist of fate, they left the three nicest ones, the two Watteau panels and the portrait of a woman which Pesne painted in Venice. As regards the marbles, they simply knocked them over; a few heads and arms are broken, but as they are still lying next to the sculptures, it will be very easy to repair them. They didn't damage the ceilings or the gilding.[164]

They also kidnapped about 130 eleven- or twelve-year-old cadets, who were taken to Königsberg and only released at the end of the war. There were attempts to steal the 'Mollwitzer Schimmel', but the nag proved its mettle and stood its ground. Some of their mischief was sensible enough. They destroyed a cannon foundry and the powdermills, but did not manage to locate other places of strategic importance, generally contenting themselves with minor acts of vandalism.[165] The allies failed to exploit their possession of the Prussian capital. They should have used their presence to lure Frederick up to the city and into abandoning his positions in Silesia. They simply departed with their loot.[166]

Frederick still feared the Russians like no other enemy. He coined a word for them, calling them 'les oursomanes' with manic, ursine connotations. The Berlin experience had not made things any better. Voltaire recommended that Frederick read his book on Peter the Great. Frederick snapped back, 'I am not going to read any history of these barbarians; I should even like to forget that they inhabit our hemisphere.'

Human intelligence is feeble; more than three-quarters of mankind is made for slavery or the most absurd fanaticism. The fear of the devil or hell fascinates them, and they detest the wise man who attempts to enlighten them. The lion's share of our species is stupid and vicious. In vain I search for that image of God of which theologians assure us they carry the impression. In every man is a wild beast; most of them don't know how to hold it back and the majority give it full rein when they are not restrained by terror of the law.[167]

The hero of the second brief Berlin occupation was the silk merchant Gotzkowsky. As one of the city's leading employers (1500 worked in his factory), he had visited Frederick in his quarters near Lebus after the Battle of Kunersdorf. Frederick had informed him that there was no way of protecting the capital, and that all the rich merchants should think about means of safeguarding their money and resources. After Gotzkowsky revealed the depth of his patriotism, Frederick had 'appointed' him to look after the interests of the capital.[168] Gotzkowsky assembled the leading merchants and much of their gold under his roof. He had also invited Tottleben's brigadier von Brinck to stay with him so that they could convince him that there were not 4 million thalers in the city. When the Russians set about the business of destroying the war industries, they also tried to abduct the leading Jewish businessmen, Ephraim and Itzig. Gotzkowsky put his head together with the other Berlin plutocrats: he could raise 1.5 million, and offer 200,000 thalers more as a 'sweetener',[169] but had to stand as a guarantor for the money. This meant accompanying the Russians back to their winter quarters in Königsberg. Here Fermor got tough with him. He reminded him of the sums Frederick was exacting from the Leipzigers. Fortunately, Gotzkowsky was able to escape back to Berlin when a troop of Cossacks who were accompanying him were ambushed by the Prussian General Werner and his men.[170]

A free man again, he went to see Frederick in Meissen, who told him to inform the merchants not to honour the letters of change they had written out to the Russians. Frederick would pay the debt.[171] Frederick showed Gotzkowsky some porcelain, and told him to produce something similar in Berlin. Frederick had found an artist in Gotha who knew the secrets of porcelain production.[172] Gotzkowsky might have felt put upon by both Frederick and the Russians, but he made a decent profit out of the business for the time being at least, especially when he was left to deal with the Leipzigers and cheated them by paying his debts in Frederick's now debased coinage.[173]

At the end of October, Frederick hatched plans to retake Leipzig, Wittenberg, Torgau and Meissen, and the Silesian Mountains. That would leave the Austrians in Dresden, but he would be master of the rest of Saxony.[174] On 2 November, Frederick told his generals he was going to engage Daun's army, which for once was only slightly bigger than his own: 'This war is lasting too long for me. It must be boring for you too. We are therefore going to end it tomorrow.' It was not so simple on the 3rd. The order to attack was given too early. Frederick's grenadiers were slaughtered in droves and a musket ball went through his fur coat and penetrated his tunic, grazing his chest.[175] The victory was Zieten's: 'For the old hussar tension was best dispelled by action.'[176] He charged. As a cannonball ripped off the head of one of his hussars, Zieten commented wrily: 'He has had a gentle death.' The last attack, which secured the king's victory, was mounted by

General Hülsen, who, being too old and infirm to ride up to the plateau, had himself carried up on a cannon.[177]

Frederick spent the night in a church, believing the battle was lost. When he heard the good news, he collapsed in Zieten's arms. Despite the bloodbath, the survivors were happy enough. 'Long live the king! Long live our Fritz! Long live Zieten, the king of the hussars!'[178] Frederick had lost 17,000 men, a third of his army and a thousand more than the Austrians, although Daun was wounded and that counted for a good deal.[179] He announced his Pyrrhic victory to d'Argens, but was careful not to conceal his losses or to overrate its strategic importance:

We have just beaten the Austrians; we both lost a great many people. Perhaps this victory will afford us some peace and quiet during the winter, and that is about it.

I received a shot which tore up the top of my chest; but it is just a contusion, a bit of pain but no danger; and it won't stop me from going about my business.

The news caused great joy in Britain, where Frederick had lost none of his popularity. Frederick's Milord was visiting the old country, now that the king of Prussia had successfully had his attainder lifted. He wrote to Colonel Chaillot on the 15th: 'Yesterday guns were fired for the king's [of Prussia] victory, which has never been done till now, not even for the defeat of the French at Rossbach; they are only fired for English victories.'[180]

The British were behind further peace moves that autumn. Uncle George died the same month as Torgau and the new administration was not so keen on supporting Prussia with huge subsidies, stopping them altogether in 1761. Frederick was sceptical. He liked Mitchell and admired the 'truly Roman' Pitt, but he was wary of perfidious Albion and attempts to make peace with France. 'What have they done for me?' he once exclaimed in desperation. Mitchell was aware of the one-sidedness of the operation. He even suggested to Holdenesse that the British should send the king of Prussia horses: 'trifles, your lordship knows, sometimes operate on the greatest of minds'.[181]

Frederick was still missing East Prussia, large amounts of Pomerania, the duchy of Cleves and the county of Mark. If the allies had agreed to peace then, he would have lost more than he had gained in the First and Second Silesian Wars. To d'Argens he voiced his concern: 'I will never see the moment to make a disadvantageous peace ... Having sacrificed my youth to my father [and] my riper years to my country, I think I have the right to do what I want in my old age. I have told you and I repeat, my hand will never sign a humiliating peace.'[182]

Frederick spent the first few weeks of the winter lull in Meissen. Catt was no longer with him, but he was still looking after his literary needs. He sent Frederick picture catalogues, but the king told him that he was in no situation to think of paintings. Instead he wanted books: a complete Cicero in French, Voltaire's *Tancrède* and *Pucelle*, Xenaphon and a few other books by minor French writers of the time. He thought *Tancrède* 'badly written'. In the preface Voltaire said he was not responsible for the slightly obscene and irreligious *La Pucelle*, which led Frederick to make a few comments on Voltaire's intellectual dishonesty: 'It is a tissue of lies, ... in another letter to the Académie française he owns up to being the author ...' Voltaire was trying to pass himself off as a good son of the church:

Him, who wrote me letters which exuded incredulity and might have had him burned at the stake. He is a great scoundrel. I say it with regret, it is a pity that such a great genius should have such a perverse, base and cowardly soul. I shall abandon him to his turpitude and I shall no longer mix in his business.[183]

The same problems obsessed him as he recharged his batteries. He needed recruits. He wanted Seydlitz back, for obvious reasons. On 16 January he wrote to tell the newly married general that the 'air was healthier' in Saxony than it was in Berlin.[184] His old friend Chasot was working for the city of Lübeck and making money on the side. He was busy drumming up as many men in Mecklenburg as he could find. Frederick would pay up to ten thalers a head. In the course of pressing men into the king's service, Chasot had a son and asked Frederick to be his godfather. He was baptised Friedrich Ulrich. 'We are killing men', wrote Frederick light-heartedly, 'while you make them.'[185]

From 1 December, Frederick took a house in Leipzig. He amused himself by meeting the professors at the university, and although his intention had clearly been more to bait them than learn from them, he ended up admiring Johann Christoph Gottsched, the professor of Greek, whom he thought had more judgement than he generally found among German scholars.[186] He was anxious to have d'Argens there. 'I have had a connection made with the [apartment] next door so that you can come to see me with no discomfort.' 'I shall be like a Carthusian whose superior has accorded him the right to speak.' As usual the Frenchman dwelled on his poor health: 'if I can't get there in a carriage, I shall be carried on a stretcher ...' He wanted to be back in Berlin before March, when he had an appointment with a recurrent ailment to attend to.[187]

CHAPTER ELEVEN

Expecting a Miracle

[I]

As the 1761 campaign opened, the enemies were the same and their war aims were the same too: the 'total destruction'[1] of Prussia. The itineraries were also similar: those same roads of Saxony, Silesia, Bohemia and Moravia. Frederick had not only trudged them for four and a half years, but he also knew them from the first two Silesian Wars. It was becoming second nature to him. As he had told Voltaire a few months before, 'The ox must plough its furrow, the nightingale must sing, the porpoise swim, and I must go to war.'[2] The problem was that the king of Prussia was turning around in ever diminishing circles, pursued, or sometimes pursuing, an enemy which both was larger and had better reserves than he did. Sooner or later the Austrians and Russians would unite, strike decisively and dismember the Prussian state. Silesia, East Prussia, Magdeburg and Pomerania were the carrots dangled before Austrians, Russians, Saxons and Swedes. Frederick needed a miracle; but that could come about only through what he termed 'the divine asininity of my enemies'.[3] Which of them was going to play the donkey and sue for peace?

March saw the departure of D'Argens and the beginnings of Frederick's preparation for the new campaign. Frederick had moved back to Meissen and was buying porcelain for all and sundry. The manufacturers clearly valued their royal customer. At one point they went so far as to serenade him: 'they have a band which plays prettily'.[4] When D'Argens got back to Potsdam he was able to report on the progress of the royal picture gallery: 'after Saint Peter in Rome, it is without doubt the most beautiful thing in the world. I was extremely surprised, and I had never believed that the gallery would produce half the effect that it does; it is completely finished.'[5] Later he wrote in praise of the colonnade that had been built on the reverse side of the little palace. D'Argens' letters made Frederick home-sick for Sanssouci.

'I am beginning this campaign like a man who jumps head first into the flood.'[6] In fact, the war picked up a bit more like a woman dabbling her feet in a swimming pool. The slowness of it all allowed Frederick to return to some of the teachings of his childhood, especially predestination:

Everyone must fulfil his destiny and submit to the fatality which holds events in check and forces man to suffer what he may not avoid. I don't know whether there is predestination or not. I can hardly believe that Providence takes an interest in our miseries; but I know for certain from experience, that circumstances force men into taking certain positions, that they don't influence the future at all [but] they lay schemes which are tossed about in the wind and often the very opposite happens to that which they imagined and determined.[7]

It was not going to be the Austrians who gave in first. Maria Theresa had proved impressively stubborn in her desire to get her province back. For years Frederick had been looking hopefully at the Russians, desperate for the unhealthy tsarina to die. There had been so many false alarms that he must have felt that fate was against him. He was in a poor physical condition too, but it was probably no more than fatigue and the usual hypochondria. He could still joke about it. Frederick wrote to one of his few women friends, Gräfin Camas, to tell her what he looked like after four years of campaigning: 'On the right-hand side of my head, my hair has gone completely grey; my teeth break and fall out; my face is wrinkled like the pleats of a skirt, my back is bent like a bow and my thoughts are sad and low-spirited like a Trappist monk.' He was subsisting, in the evenings at least, on just a cup of chocolate.[8]

He was having the usual problems with Henry. His brother wanted to avoid the pitched battle, to whittle down the enemy by a war of attrition. Frederick wanted to concentrate his forces and fight.[9] Henry's hatred for Frederick emerges chiefly in the letters between him and his brother Ferdinand. Frederick was a 'tyrant' and a 'scoundrel'. A year later Henry was able to write: 'If only it had pleased God to give our dead mother a miscarriage on 24 January 1712.'[10] Deserted by the British, Frederick looked around for other allies. His eyes fell on the Danes and the Turks, either or both of whom might be convinced to cause the necessary diversion.[11] The Turks were quizzed once more as to whether they wanted to have a go at the Austrians or not. In June, Prussian officers were drinking to the health of Mustapha III, their new ally, but despite Frederick's hoping against hope, it was not a military alliance: Turkey was too weak. His new friends were considerate enough, however, to send him a brace of camels in September 1762.[12]

On 20 May, Frederick heard that the 'Oursomanes' were on the move again. Three weeks later they were approaching the Prussian borders. The thought disturbed the attention he was giving Lucian, Racine and Voltaire. The latter was in disgrace for sucking up to the French court. He had played the Catholic card so well, and fawned over Madame de Pompadour so much, that he had been allowed to return to Paris.[13] The campaign of 1761 now consisted of endless marching aimed at preventing the fatal merger between the two main enemy armies. The only military bravado was happening in west Germany, where Prince Ferdinand continued his streak of successes by beating the French at Vellinghausen. Frederick was not expecting much: a year of manoeuvring before he could go into winter quarters again in November. On 9 July he wrote: 'It adds up to a hundred and ten days until November; I must be firm and show an heroic indifference.'[14]

He did this by plunging his head into Gassendi. Once again he was defeated by the Latin, which his father had so adamantly expunged from his curriculum. He wrote to d'Argens: 'you people, you read Latin, Greek and Hebrew, etc., while I just know a little French and when that fails me I remain mired in deepest ignorance'.[15] Despite Gassendi, the war came home to Frederick. The Russians plundered Silesia and proceeded to the habitual atrocities. They surpassed themselves this year: 'They might have stirred emotions in Busiris and Phalaris.'*

The Russians and the Austrians merged in Silesia on 19 August, fielding a joint army of 72,000 Austrians and 47,000 Russians. Frederick had just 55,000 men. He dug in at Bunzelwitz with 450 guns, Voltaire's *Oedipe* and Cicero's *Philippics*,[17] and waited for the attack. Loudon was keen to break Frederick's well-constructed earthwork; Buturlin, the new commander of the Russian army, rather less so, as he was running out of provisions – a situation aggravated by the fact that Frederick's men were plundering his magazines. The allies gave up, the Russians leaving only 20,000 men with the Austrians. The rest of their army went north to the Vistula again.[18] According to a modern writer, Bunzelwitz was 'a tactical victory ranking with Leuthen and Liegnitz'.[19]

The allies fell on Schweidnitz and Glatz. Major-General Seers had been told to defend Schweidnitz at all cost. The stronghold fell in two hours with 4 generals, 194 officers and 6000 men going into captivity.[20] Glatz

---

* Two ancient tyrants. The first slaughtered strangers, the second roasted his enemies in a brazen bull.[16]

took all of four hours. In Schweidnitz, Frederick must also have lost the phenomenon he had written about to his brother Henry:

the eleven-year-old Italian-born son of an Austrian officer ... He has a long beard and they say that Priapus was nothing likened to him, and he has all the force and vigour of a fully grown man. This astonishing reputation made Schweidnitz a place for pilgrimage for all the women of the neighbourhood, who came to see the prodigy and might well have had a taste of him had not the regimen of mother and father been opposed to it. For the rest, the prodigalities of nature are confined to the male organs of this young man, and those who know him say that his head is as disappointing as his virility is impressive.[21]

The Russians continued to besiege the Pomeranian port of Kolberg, which was proving a very tough nut. With Kolberg they could land their supplies by sea, which meant that they could begin their campaigns more quickly and prevent Frederick from torching their magazines. They had originally been repulsed by a tiny force of pensioners and townsfolk under Major von der Heyde before being scattered by General Werner and a few regiments of hussars, who also drove off the Swedish navy. In their gratitude the Pomeranians had a medal struck with the heads of Werner and Heyde on one side, and Kolberg on the other. It bore the legend 'Res similis fictae' (just like a fairy tale).[22] They spoke too soon, however. The next siege was led by General Rumyantsev, who had served in Frederick's army. Kolberg finally fell on 16 December, and half of Pomerania with it.[23]

[11]

The detested Tsarina Elisabeth had a series of small strokes about the same time as Kolberg was preparing to yield. She died on the penultimate day of Christmas 1762 (5 January) and her nephew came to power as Peter III. Frederick was slow to receive accurate reports of what was happening in Saint Petersburg. The news came as a complete surprise. It was sent to him by Benoît, his envoy in Warsaw. Frederick replied on 19 January, describing it as a 'great event'.[24] 'Finally confined to Pluto's empire, one who will never return to fan the flames of discord' was Frederick's epitaph.[25]

On 31 January he wrote to Henry: 'Bless Heaven for what has happened, which promises even better consequences.' Peter's admiration for the enlightened warrior-king of Prussia had been well known for some time, but since the war began it was obviously not clear to Frederick whether he had undergone a change of heart. He wrote to Finckenstein: 'we don't know what the grand duke thinks about us [or] if the ruses and flattering insinuations that our enemies are making over there have not altered his mind and convinced him to continue the war against us'.[26]

For a while Frederick had no idea what the consequences of Elisabeth's death would be. Still he allowed himself a slightly stronger dose of euphoria with every day that passed. To his cousin George III of Britain he recalled 'the grand duke has always shown me friendship'. 'The emperor of Russia is as much in our favour as the stoutest Berlin burgher,' he told d'Argens.[27] To Ferdinand of Brunswick, he was more optimistic, writing 'the sky is beginning to clear ... *bon courage*'. To Knyphausen, his envoy in London, he wholly dropped the masque of politeness: 'morta la bestia, morto in veleno'.[28]

Since the publication of Catherine the Great's memoirs, Russian historiography has cast Peter as an idiot, a retarded adolescent who liked playing with soldiers and who was bribed with baubles and parade uniforms by the king of Prussia.[29] But his stupidity has been wildly exaggerated. The new tsar, like a number of his courtiers, saw that the war with Prussia was not actually in their interests.[30] Apart from the possibility of using East Prussia to exchange with Poland for some choice chunk east of the Bug, Russia had no clear war aims. The struggle had caused untold bloodshed, with Russian casualties on the battlefield always gruesomely high. His views had been obscured by the fact that his aunt had given him no power whatsoever, but now he was in control, a ray of light in the east was observed throughout Prussia and Europe. The poet Sulzer wrote to Bodmer in Switzerland: 'The new tsar seems to have a strong liking for the king, and to show an unshakeable dislike for the French.'[31]

On 27 January, Finckenstein was able to confirm some of Frederick's wildest dreams. The story had also got out among the Berliners, who emptied fifty barrels of wine in their enthusiasm.[32] He reported the arrival in Berlin of Brigadier Andrei Gudowitsch from Peter, bringing a message for Frederick. Mitchell, also in Berlin, sent the king a transcript of a letter he had had from the British envoy in Saint Petersburg, Robert Keith. Peter had already halted the Russian advance and told his generals to cease hostilities. Chernychev had orders to leave the Austrians with his 20,000 men. The new tsar was keen on a scrap with the Danes in order to win back the province of Holstein, his ancestral duchy. The suggestion was made to Frederick that he should be kind to the people of Zerbst, and also to the Russian POWs.[33]

On 6 February, Frederick wrote from his winter quarters in Breslau to congratulate Peter on his accession to the throne and to offer his 'precious friendship'.[34] In the meantime he sent his diplomats across the wintry landscape to do what they could to make the new tsar happy. Graf Hordt reported back: 'The emperor speaks only of you, Sire, of your troops and your strategy.'[35] Peter did indeed want peace. When Ambassador von der Goltz arrived on 18 February he was authorised to give Peter the Order of the Black Eagle. The jeweller Ephraim was also setting some gems for him.[36] Frederick wrote to Henry: 'We may flatter ourselves that come March we shall be rid of the Russians and Swedes.'[37] To Lord Marischal, now his governor in Swiss Neufchâtel, he spoke of the obligations he owed Peter, who was capable of 'forcing the obstinate people to peace'. 'I have no one on my side except God, my just cause and the emperor of Russia.' He wrote yet again on 11 May, using Peter as a stick to beat the British with: 'There is only my divine emperor of Russia; whose praises I shall never cease to chant so long as I live. I believe Heaven caused him to be born in order to prove that virtue is quite compatible with qualities which belong to the throne. It is not so among your fellow countrymen...'[38]

Brigadier Gudowitsch finally tracked the king of Prussia down in Breslau on 22 February and gave him official notification of the alliance between the two courts. The 20,000 men under Chernychev who had been with the Austrians were now attached to the Prussian army. They came in handy at the 'skirmish' of Burkersdorf, where the Prussians were able to claim a victory.[39] Frederick was probably not exaggerating *too* much when he told the Russian soldier, 'My dear sir, I look on you as the dove which brought the olive branch to the Ark. You are the first instrument that Providence has employed to cement the happy alliance with that dear and admirable emperor.'[40]

Peter was now Frederick's 'best friend in the world'. He was invested with the Order of the Black Eagle on 23 March. There was a big feast where toasts were drunk to Frederick's health and 150 cannon were fired for him in Saint Petersburg. The hero-worship was apparently mutual. 'If I were a pagan,' wrote Frederick, 'I'd set up altars to Your Imperial Majesty.' In his private correspondence, Frederick was a little more cautious, but d'Argens continued to display a brand of Panglossian optimism for which he was often teased. At the suggestion that Peter might die, he replied, 'Why should he? He is young, he is healthy, and we are no longer in the century of the Medicis.'[41]

[III]

The carnival was dull compared to Leipzig, but Frederick enjoyed his winter quarters in Breslau in the usual way, busying himself with reading and writing and hearing the gossip from the marquis, among others. D'Argens had a particularly juicy snippet for him in December:

A prostitute has accused Porporino of siring her child; the courts declared the child to be his, sentenced him to pay the prostitute 100 thalers and to feed the infant. There was no question of appealing against the verdict, Porporino paid the 100 thalers at once and admitted paternity of the child, which he took away and is having brought up in his house; and he thanked the judges for making good the loss inflicted on him by the Venetian surgeons. This story has spread mirth throughout the city.[42]

Henry was still seething with jealousy and anger towards his elder brother, who had been dipping into his regiments to replenish his own forces. The news from Russia seemed to be the right moment to offer his resignation from the army. On 26 March he wrote to Eichel to warn him of his intentions. Something of the bitterness comes through in his note to Frederick of 18 April: 'Do you believe that I am giving up my command without good reason? And what better will I have for the rest of my life? What career do I have to look forward to? What happiness, what pleasure to hope for? Nothing. Mediocrity is my lot ...'[43] Frederick succeeded in convincing him to remain with the army, but he never managed to cure the bile.

On 8 May, Frederick was putting the final touches to his army and preparing to start a campaign that he hoped would be his last. He fantasised about d'Argens, who had gone to take the waters at Sanssouci, and taken with him his bride, Marianne Cochois's sister Babet.[44]

I shall follow you in the house and the alleys of the garden and out into the park. I'll say to myself, at the moment the marquis is playing the viol; now he is making a commentary on the Greek New Testament; here he is muttering sweet nothings to Babet; in this alleyway he is making policy decisions, and, seeing my apartment, he is thinking of me. Then, I will have some little exchange of ideas with you; but some news of Daun will butt in and scatter that pleasant illusion, gone with the wind.

There was still not enough war about to occupy Frederick's mind. During the siege of Schweidnitz he plunged his head into the pages of Fleury's *Histoire ecclésiastique*: 'I am tempted to believe that the entire universe was imbecilic from the time of Constantine to Luther, arguing in an incomprehensible jargon about absurd visions, with bishops establishing temporal authority with the help of the credulity and stupidness of princes and nations.'[45] The Russian alliance led d'Argens to believe that peace was just a few days off. He invited the Bürgermeister and a few more of his sort to lunch at Sanssouci, and borrowed a few cannon and shot from the town hall. While they ate from twelve to seven, they fired twenty-four salvoes from the terrace to celebrate the king's alliance with the tsar.[46]

In June the Swedes also abandoned their rather dismal attempts at war, thereby releasing a body of battle-fresh soldiery for Frederick's wider use. Frederick was unkind to the Swedish plenipotentiaries, claiming he was unaware that he had been at war with their country: 'Oh yes, I remember now, my Colonel Belling had some dealings with them.'[47] With the Russian withdrawal, Frederick could also recruit in Pomerania and East Prussia again, and lost not a moment in doing so.[48] D'Argens regaled His Majesty with the contents of a French colonel's knapsack, captured at the Battle of Wilhelmsthal. Instead of Caesar and Turenne, the officer's reading consisted of Gervaise de Latouche's *Portier de la chartreuse*, La Morlière's *Campagnes de l'Abbé de ...* and Galli de Bibiena's *La Poupée*, all scabrous novels. Of course, d'Argens was hardly being honest. To him is attributed one of the raciest of the lot: *Thérèse philosophe*.[49]

Then, on 18 July, Frederick was informed that Peter had been deposed by his wife on 28 June and murdered, possibly with her connivance, on 6 July. Peter died, allegedly from a severe colic brought on by piles![50] Frederick later made a wry comment in his *Testament politique*: 'we know how dangerous that illness is in Russia'.[51] Events may have taken Frederick by surprise. His intelligence from Robert Keith via Mitchell would have told him that the tsarina had little power at the time of her accession. She had acted quickly, playing to those elements who were outraged by the westernising policies being put through by her husband. When Keith wrote to Grenville on 1 July, he attributed Peter's downfall to his reform programme: his nationalisation of church lands, his introduction of severe discipline in the elite guards regiment, the promotion of a Danish war after he had 'sacrificed the conquests made by Russian arms' and, last but not least, his friendship with the king of Prussia. Finally Keith put paid to the reputation for barbarism later retailed by Catherine: Peter 'had many excellent qualities' and 'never did a violent or cruel action in the course of his short reign'.[52]

On 2 July, Robert Keith reported that the Russians now intended to hang on to some of their conquests 'notwithstanding the late peace'. Saltykov retook possession of East Prussia, which he had given up to a Prussian regency some days before. Catherine was courting those who had been angry with Peter for riding roughshod over Russian dignities. There were fears in Britain that the whole peace process might be at an end.[53] On 18 July, Chernychev received the order to take his troops away from Frederick's army. Frederick, however, seems to have seduced him into keeping his troops in his line until he had won the small-scale but important psychological victory at Burkersdorf.

There were further rumours that the Russians were moving in on an undefended Stettin.[54] Frederick was worried, wrote to Catherine and was reassured. Catherine would continue to work for peace.[55] It is possible that the English had stayed her hand. They had abandoned their one-time Prussian ally, but they were not anxious to see Russia make gains at its expense. Catherine wrote to Saltykov with a 'sharp reprimand for this rash and unwarranted step, and with orders forthwith to restore everything to its former state ...'[56] Twelve days after Peter's death, Frederick's sources reassured him that there was unlikely to be a change in Russian policy under the 'Prussophobic' Catherine.[57]

What lay behind Catherine's volte-face is not wholly clear; she had assumed power with the support of the prominent anti-German lobby among the nobility and clergy. She needed to play the Russian card to overthrow her Germanocentric husband and occupy the throne herself. Before the war started, Hanbury-Williams had written to Holdernesse to report that Catherine believed Frederick to be 'the formidable and natural enemy of Russia'. He also found that 'she hates him personally'.[58] That being said, at the beginning of the war, she had been suspected of using her influence on Marshal Apraksin to delay the Russian advance in East Prussia.[59] She might simply have wished to end the war, but that did not prevent her from hanging on to East Prussia; after all, Frederick did not possess the means to take it back. Frederick thought he did, and surmised that she was simply too poor to continue.[60] Possibly she looked at the map of Europe in a statesmanlike way, and realised that Prussia would be useful later, in order to realise her territorial ambitions in Poland.[61]

The earl Marischal alerted Frederick to Jean-Jacques Rousseau, who was seeking asylum in Prussian Neufchâtel. Frederick was willing. 'His only sin is having peculiar opinions, which he thinks are good.' He sent him 100 thalers. 'If we were not at war, if we were not ruined, I would have a hermitage built for him, with a garden where he could dwell as he thinks our forefathers lived ... He will never persuade me to graze on herbs and to go on all fours.' He did not actually read *Émile* until the following spring, when he reported back to the duchess of Saxony-Gotha. He did not think the book contained much that was new, but it was written in an elegant style.[62]

Frederick's defeat of the Austrians at Burkersdorf finally decided Daun to abandon Silesia. The Austrian garrison in Schweidnitz gave up after a long siege on 9 October. When the news hit Berlin on the 14th, the moment proved the last for a pullet and a turkey cock which had been quietly munching in D'Argens' *basse cour*, they were going to join a ham at a table composed of Frederick's academicians.[63] Frederick was still uncertain which way Russia would jump that winter. He wrote to Gräfin Camas from Peterswaldau on 19 October, 'If our dear emperor were still alive, we would have peace this winter.' His worries about Russia were at an end, however, and he was interested to note the sales of his *Poésies divers* among the officer corps. They had ordered 900 copies: half the print run. He was philosophic about the popularity of his poetry in Russia: 'It is probably only in that country that they take me for a good French poet.'[64]

There were no roses to make crowns, and no falernian for the libations, but D'Argens had some excellent 'Pontac'* to celebrate the last victory of the war, which occurred at Freiberg on 29 October. It was Henry's swansong and Austrian casualties were almost double Prussian ones. Frederick was no less enthusiastic than his philosophic friend in Berlin. He told Henry that the news had taken years off his life: 'Yesterday I was sixty, now I am eighteen.' He gave Henry a rare distinction: from now on he was to have a permanent escort of twenty-five hussars.[65] Austria was exhausted and more and more convinced by Henry's performance

---

* Originally Château Haut Brion in the Graves region near Bordeaux, and by extension wines from the whole region. Falernian was Ancient Rome's best wine, it came from near Pompey.

along with minor victories at Leutmannsdorf and Burkersdorf that there
was little point in going on. Its remaining allies were at best unenthusiastic
about continuing the war. Maria Theresa's emissary arrived on 29 November. Peace negotiations opened on 30 December.[66]

Frederick did not go home. He went back to Meissen, where he bought
more porcelain. Gräfin Camas got a snuff box decorated with a dog –
the symbol of fidelity. Sets of china were ordered for Niederschönhausen
and for his sisters-in-law.[67] The indefatigable king was already laying plans
to rebuild his wasted provinces and restock his much depleted army.[68]
Egged on by the philosophic duchess, he turned his mind to the human
condition again and came to the conclusion that 'enlightenment' was a
waste of time:

There is no more extravagant idea than wanting to destroy superstition. Prejudice
is the reason of the people, and does this imbecile people deserve enlightenment?
Don't we see that superstition is one of the ingredients that nature has put into
man's nature? How should we fight nature, how should we go about destroying
an instinct which is so universal? Everyone is entitled to his opinions, if he
respects those of others. This is the only way of living in peace during the little
pilgrimage that we make on this earth, and peace, madame, is possibly the only
piece of happiness which has any effect on us.[69]

He was just as hard on his soldiers: the men he had sent to their
deaths, and the epigones who had replaced them. There was a dearth of
good generals. The best senior officers had perished, the subalterns lacked
experience. The soldiery was largely made up of former deserters who
were 'incapable of putting up with the strain of a hard campaign'. The
long war had had an effect on the officers' morality too: the Prussians
were beginning to behave like the Russians. One of his old officers,
Möllendorf, summed it up when he said, 'I was not frightened of the
enemy, but I was frightened for the state.'[70]

Daun's men were still in control of Glatz, and there was much arguing
over who was to retain that chunk of Silesia. Frederick clinched the deal
at Hubertusburg on 15 February 1763. He agreed to withdraw from
Saxony in return for Glatz. The warring factions returned to the *status
quo ante bellum*. On 5 March, d'Argens saw a herald under his window in
Berlin's Brüderstrasse, proclaiming the peace. He was followed by four
or five thousand people 'whose shouts and cries of joy seemed to me
more touching than the most harmonious music'. Frederick was less
enthusiastic. He was still laid low by a strong dose of misanthropy. When

an adjutant asked him if it was not the greatest day in his life, Frederick replied that 'The best day in your life is the one on which you leave it.'[71] An ailing Algarotti was possibly saying nothing less than the truth in a letter that none the less reeked of Latin flattery: 'For six years Your Majesty has been assailed front and back by practically all Europe, been surrounded by armies which were always superior in numbers and often equal in discipline. There is only Your Majesty who was capable of fighting the war which you have just concluded with a glorious peace.'[72]

CHAPTER TWELVE

Picking up the Pieces

[1]

Frederick made his way slowly back to Berlin via Silesia and the Neumark. There was plenty of wreckage lying about to cause him to reflect on whether it had all been worthwhile: 'the majority of fields remained fallow, provisions were rare and sold for excessive prices, and the countryside was barren of man and beast so that throughout the [Prussian] provinces you saw just the atrocious scars of war, and the precursors of an even greater calamity in the future'. In human terms the losses had been terrible indeed: estimates of dead Prussian soldiers range between 160,000 and 180,000. Frederick had lost thirty-three generals and two field marshals even by the end of the 1759 campaign, including Schwerin, Winterfeldt and Keith. Arguably, the only generals of that stature who survived the war were Seydlitz, Prince Henry and Zieten.[1]

As he travelled north, he could see such things with his own eyes. He was profoundly depressed. In Greiffenberg in Silesia the people thanked him profusely for promising them the money to rebuild their farms and houses: 'You don't need to thank me,' he said. 'It is my responsibility to put my people back on their feet after this misfortune, that is what I am here for.'[2] He stopped again in Grünberg, Silesia's great wine town, although the product itself was a by-word for nastiness.* Frederick leant out of his carriage and asked Senator Schander, 'How is the wine going to be this year? Last year it all froze.' 'It is looking good. We lost the whole vintage last year.' A merchant chipped in: 'Wine is the only source of revenue for us. The loss was therefore very important to us.' It was Frederick's bedside-manner of kingship, in which he excelled.[3]

Frederick approached Berlin on 30 March. The people had erected triumphal arches, hung up inscriptions along the way,[4] and prepared a

---

* Since 1945 the Poles have discontinued production in Zielona Góra. The town is now famous for its vodka distillery.

splendid reception, but it was a day for false alarms. At seven or so, the vast majority of the citizens had given up hope and gone home. Gotzkowsky noted the enthusiasm and the disappointment:

From half a [German] mile [3.5 kilometres] outside the city walls [right] up to the royal palace, everyone was milling around the streets. Loyal subjects in their Sunday best had lined the way which they assumed the king would take, from early that morning until late that night. Fate decreed, however, that His Majesty could only make his entry very late and in the dead of night, and thereby all the longed for jubilation proved in vain [and] the reception and procession could not take place as prepared. A large body of citizens [none the less] equipped themselves with torches, and when they finally heard the rattle of the carriage announcing the king's arrival there was a general cry of joy – 'Long live the king!'[5]

It was nine when Frederick arrived. He was greeted by the city's magistrates at the gates, but refused to mount the horse provided for him, and took a back route to the Schloss. Only about 3000 people remained before the palace to welcome him. An estimated 50,000 Berliners had given up. He had convoked his friends. D'Argens was to meet him in his bedroom,[6] and the courtiers in the public rooms had to wait another three-quarters of an hour before the king was prepared to pass in revue of his court. He embraced his brothers as well as the Dutch consul, who had behaved bravely during the occupation. He ignored his Danish counterpart, who had not. His only words to his long-suffering wife were to tell her that she had put on weight.[7]

Frederick could not find it in his heart to celebrate, any more than he could properly thank those who had bled for him. He remained obsessed with the need to make his land fit to live in. The next day a delegation came to him with a petition for their area. The spokesman cleared his throat, but Frederick cut him short. 'Let him be quiet and let me speak. Does he have a pencil? Now let him write down: the gentlemen need to sow so much rye for bread, so much summer corn, and how many horses, oxen and cows their area is in need of. Think hard about it, and come back and see me tomorrow morning.'[8]

There was a lot on his conscience. If all three Silesian Wars are taken together, the losses begin to look dramatic: 1530 officers were killed, including sixty generals. Certain noble families seem to have borne the brunt of it: the Kleists counted sixty deaths in the male line; the Münchows fourteen; while the Seydlitz, Schenkendorf, Winterfeldt, Krosigk, Arnim,

Bredow, Schulenburg, Sydow and Puttkamer families lost seven or eight each.[9] Civilian casualties in the Seven Years War were much worse: East Prussia, 90,410; Pomerania, 72,216; the western provinces, 65,000; the Neumark, 57,028; the Kurmack, 56,993; Silesia, 46,088; and central Germany, 7186.[10] More than half a million men and women had been wiped off the map of Prussia: a tenth of the prewar population. Frederick's officials estimated the loss of habitations at 12,360.[11] As many as 60,000 horses were dead, and 'the nobility and peasantry had been pillaged, plundered and held to ransom by so many armies, in such a way that they possessed only their lives, and a few miserable rags to cover their nudity'.[12]

Frederick's debasement of the coinage at the end of the war had led to terrible inflation with many businesses going to the wall. They were still dying like flies in 1767. Cottage industry was also affected: the number of looms declined by as much as a third. One of the king's first tasks was to create new colony villages for weavers. One of these which is still reasonably well preserved was created around the ruins of the old Cistercian monastery at Kloster Zinna in the Mark. It is recognisable from its neat, single-storey houses laid out around a central square, on a grid plan that once again goes back to Knobelsdorff's design for Rheinsberg.[13]

There had been a terrible loss in revenue to the crown. The king's provinces in Westphalia, East Friesland and the Rhineland had given him nothing since the beginning of the war, as they had been permanently under enemy control. Frederick estimated his loss of income at 3,400,000 thalers. He had not earned much from Pomerania and Silesia either.[14]

There was a certain amount of clutching at straws. Frederick was taken in by Antonio di Calzabrigi, an adventurer from Leghorn who specialised in lotteries, and who turned out to be a friend of Casanova. He proposed setting up a bank, based on the ill-fated Banque de France, in its first incarnation created by the Scotsman Law. Quintus was involved, and the Hamburg trader Wurmb. It was not long before it closed its doors. In 1765 Frederick vented his spleen in a verse against the 'écornifleurs et philocopros',* citing Wurmb and his friends as 'brigands puked up by hell' and promising himself a ritual bath to purify himself after their attentions.[15] He also briefly toyed with the idea of creating a wool monopoly.[16] The next attempt at money making in this way was to import

---

* Parasites and lovers of excrement.

some *fermiers généraux* from France in 1766 and create a French-style Régie by farming out tax collection. The move led to protest, and when the king attempted to lower taxes on essential foodstuffs, the promised reductions were absorbed by the foreign moneymen. The criticism mounted, and Frederick commissioned an investigation from one of his civil servants, Erhard Ursinus. When Ursinus produced his warts-and-all report, Frederick was so outraged that he had the poor bureaucrat tyrannically imprisoned in Spandau fort. In general, Frederick's get-rich-quick schemes left him with a bitter taste in his mouth.[17]

Several old chief ministers had been carried off by old age during the conflict, and Frederick had to look to his officials too, replacing those at the heads of the five departments. A whiff of corruption was *mal vu*: Friedrich Christoph von Görne, a departmental head, was sent to Spandau for embezzlement in 1782.[18] The war-torn provinces were granted tax exemptions – Silesia for six months, Pomerania and the Neumark for two years – while 20,399,000 thalers were raised for the second *réta-blissement*. Within a year, the king said he had satisfied his creditors. He set about rebuilding the towns and cities of his land. Königsberg in Prussia, for example, had been burned down twice. Grants were made to the towns deemed to have suffered. The largest went to Landeshut, which had been the victim of a long siege; but sizeable amounts were also doled out to Halle, Minden and Halbestadt, which had all suffered in their way.[19]

Frederick was remarkably quick in rebuilding his shattered land. In September 1766 he was able to boast that he had already constructed 8000 houses in Silesia alone; 14,500 including Pomerania and the Neumark.[20] He needed people, and that meant bringing them in from elsewhere. He did not care where, but they generally came from west Germany. In the last quarter-century of Frederick's life, more people emigrated to Prussia than to the United States of America. After 1773 he even toyed with the idea of settling some Islamic Tartars in West Prussia, perhaps to dilute the 'slovenly Polish stuff' which made up a large part of the population. In reality, however, he was not even that antipathetic towards the Poles, who populated some of his new villages in the Oderbruch.[21]

Agriculture was also of capital importance. East Prussia and Prussian Lithuania were famous for cows and pigs; and the Electoral Mark and Pomerania for sheep. After 1763 Frederick was keen to see potatoes planted as widely as possible, especially after a famine in 1771 led to a shortage of grain. Fruit trees were also encouraged, especially in more temperate Magdeburg, and civil servants were sent to England to learn new agricultural techniques at first hand. Less popular with the peasantry was the progressive enclosure of common land, a trick the king learned from the British.[22] There was more draining of soil in the Warthe and, after 1773, in the Netze district, which prepared both for settlement and agriculture.

[II]

Frederick's rude treatment of his Berliners rankled. Elisabeth might have felt the same – she was used to it after all – but the Berliners never forgave the slight occasioned by his less than triumphant return, and remained largely indifferent to their king for the remaining quarter-century of his reign; even if, as the British envoy Hugh Elliot noted in 1777, they were still ready to cheer his rare apparitions on the Berlin streets.[23] Frederick's capital had suffered badly, not just from two brief occupations, but also for want of trade. Grass was growing in the lanes, there were no coaches to be seen and food was scarce. Frederick had never liked Berlin. Now he found it all foreign to him. He sat down and wrote a letter to Ulrica. Now that Wilhelmina was dead, she and Charlotte were the closest to him of his sisters.

I find myself here in a city where I recognise the walls, but where I can no longer locate the people who used to be the objects of my respect or friendship. Dear sister, I am a stranger here; these seven years of war have changed the city totally, there are now few people I know, and if it weren't for the buildings, I'd feel myself as much a stranger here as I would in London.[24]

Mitchell's hero-worship for the king of Prussia had come to an end. He saw qualities, but he saw many more faults than he had in the campaigning years of the Seven Years War, especially his 'vanity, fraud and avarice'. He reported to Lord Halifax that people were carrying placards saying that Frederick should suffer the same fate as Peter III.[25] Berlin had been bled white, and the Berliners were apt to blame a handful of louche Jewish financiers who had got rich on the debasement of the coinage and supplying the king's armies. The jeweller Veitel Ephraim, for example, is rumoured to have made 10 million thalers out of the war, and commissioned Diterichs to build him the prettiest house in Berlin on the proceeds.[26]

'It is the king of Prussia's peculiar misfortune to have no minister able enough, or honest enough, to represent to him the fatal effects of the repeated breaches of public faith in the coinage of money, by which his subjects are already drained, and must inevitably be ruined, if the same false system goes on much farther [sic].'[27] The crisis of confidence in the regime was great; even ministers' salaries were reduced to nothing.[28] The courtier Lehndorff wrote in his diary of the total confusion, which was now 'greater than ever ... at the same time the Jews are coining it from our misery and living off the fat of the land'.[29]

In the circumstances, the Berliners cannot have been that impressed that Frederick was spending so much money building palaces for himself and his brother. He took positive pride that he alone of all the belligerent princes had some money in his treasury at the end of the war.[30] On 20 May 1763, Frederick told Henry, 'I have had 66,000 thalers paid out for your palace, so that all the interior panelling and the ironwork grille will be finished.' He had used another 26,700 thalers to buy his brother furniture, but admitted owing another 3000. Two months later he reported to his brother that he had engaged the painter Labile to do the ceilings of the hall and gallery. Henry was supposed to come up with the themes, but either did not want to, or thought Frederick was happiest doing it himself. Once again the king had made the initial designs for the building on the Linden.[31]

As you don't want to decide on the ceilings for your drawing room, I shall attempt to do the job as best I can; we'll have a few godly suppers in the hall, and for the ceiling of the gallery we'll put Apollo driving his chariot accompanied by the hours, preceded by Aurora, with the genies strewing flowers. The painter who should do the work is called Guglielmi.[32] He did the ceilings at Schönbrunn, and according to connoisseurs, he is the most talented in Italy at the moment.[33]

Henry himself was up in Rheinsberg sulking, but still prepared to communicate with his brother. His bad mood this time might have something to do with his wife, who was believed to be having an *Effie Briest*[34]-style affair with Friedrich Adolf von Kalkreuth. Whether it was true or not, the rumour led to a total separation between the two.[35] Henry had just heard Graun's *Te Deum*, which he thought a rare work. He compared it to Pergolesi's *Stabat Mater*, 'which strikes me as a perfect piece of music. However, those who have heard the *Miserere*[36] sung in Rome prefer that music to all others.'[37] Henry made an effort to answer Frederick's letters only when he had a favour to ask. In this case it was a young Paléologue, who needed a place. Frederick was prepared to go along with his brother: 'If he is stupid, he must be pushed into the Silesian clergy and made a canon.'[38]

The Seven Years War had left Frederick with some unfinished business. After 1760, the Austrians had refused to exchange prisoners, leading Frederick to some petty acts of vengeance when he locked up a number of enemy generals in the fortress at Magdeburg. Now his own officers were coming home. Some of them were accused of cowardice or dereliction of duty, and Frederick had them committed for trial. The highest-ranking officer arraigned before the courts martial was General Finck, who had capitulated with his corps at Maxen. Frederick had never forgiven Finck, but he was careful to make the court as impartial as possible: Generals Finck, Gersdorff and Rebentisch were to be tried before their peers Zieten and Wedell. The latter had also gone through the bitter experience of defeat at Kay, but Frederick had pardoned him.[39]

Zieten formed a jury composed of twelve generals and staff officers. On 26 May, Finck and Rebentisch[40] were sentenced to one year of fortress detention and dismissal from the army. There was a suggestion of cowardice, but the sentence was hardly draconian considering the time. Only six years before, the British had shot Admiral Byng for losing a battle. Gersdorff got one year more than the others and his regiment was dissolved. The next trial was for those who yielded up Breslau to the Austrians in February 1758: Generals Kyau, Katte and Lestwitz. Prince Maurice was put in charge. The sentences ranged from six months for Kyau to two years for Lestwitz. At Schweidnitz, General Seers had capitulated despite orders to defend it 'à toute extremité'. He was cashiered.[41]

Further trials cashiered and briefly imprisoned General Horn for relinquishing Wittenberg and Field Marshal Schmettau for capitulating at Dresden. Frederick commented, 'I couldn't say to him that I was happy with his conduct.' By far the most draconian sentence was that meted out to Lieutenant-Colonel d'O and his fellow officers Quadt, Knobelsdorf and Wrede, who had been responsible for defending Glatz. The court decided on a firing squad for d'O, and sentences ranging from four years to a year for the three others. D'O was not shot, but led to the post and reprieved on the spot with a two-year sentence. Knobelsdorf was banished.[42] Frederick's behaviour towards his own brother seems to have been justified in the eyes of his contemporaries. After the war, many people asked why Prince Charles of Lorraine was allowed to remain in command for so long, despite his incompetence as a general.

There was still a good deal of turmoil, with regiments disbanded and impoverished officers and men on the streets looking for some means of keeping body and soul together. The most famous case was Major von Tellheim in Lessing's comedy *Minna von Barnhelm* of 1763. The landlord of a Berlin inn has become impatient with an impecunious officer who has been lodging under his roof since the end of the war: 'during the war the gentlemen lived as if it would go on for ever; as if we would go on paying our contributions until kingdom come. Now all the inns and taverns are full of them; and a landlord has really to beware.'[43] All Berlin had to watch out for the human driftwood washed up by the war. One breed was the crooked French soldier posing as an aristocrat, and pocketing anything he could get in the process. In Lessing's play the role is performed by the so-called 'Chevalier Riccaut de la Marlinière, seigneur du Pret-au-val, de la branche de Prensd'Or'.

Frederick had struck up a new intellectual correspondence, one which would survive until 1783, with the philosopher Jean le Rond d'Alembert, whom he had had elected to his Academy and granted a state pension of 1200 thalers in 1746. After Maupertuis's death, Frederick unsuccessfully tried to lure him to Berlin as its president. The Frenchman could claim his work on the vast *Encyclopédie* as an excuse. D'Alembert always maintained a prudent distance. Writing once the conclusions of the combat were clear, he was careful to praise Frederick's achievements in the Seven Years War, although he added that he thought His Majesty himself 'would have forbidden him to rejoice at Rossbach'.[44]

Frederick arranged to meet d'Alembert in Cleves on the first of his postwar progresses to his western provinces. D'Alembert later described that first meeting. They spoke for two and a half hours at lunch, and later Frederick reappeared, regretting that they had not had the chance to talk alone. He took him into his study, where they had another long session. 'He spoke of his reputation and his fame, with unaffected modesty,' d'Alembert told Julie de Lespinasse. Frederick fetched him up to Potsdam when he returned to the east. Here d'Alembert was able to experience the life of Sanssouci: the library was 'not extensive but [well] chosen' and the king 'played the flute splendidly'. He marvelled at his *oeuvre* of 200 concertos: 'What a man! Where does he find the time for all this?'[45]

While d'Alembert was resident at Sanssouci, the Paris Parlement decided to outlaw inoculation. It was something of a sacred cow among enlightened monarchs. Catherine of Russia had herself inoculated against smallpox by an English physician in 1768.[46] Frederick was incensed. The Lord Marischal replied that they would ban shaving next. D'Alembert wrote back to his mistress:

You would be enchanted by the clarity of his judgement, his good taste and actually by the way he talks about his enemies. He apologises for their mistakes and seeks to find a way of attributing their black judgements to respectable reasons. Last night we walked up and down in his picture gallery. We spent nearly two hours there and it seemed to me that he spoke as well about painting as he does about war and politics.[47]

D'Alembert was clearly enraptured by the king, but he knew enough from Voltaire to believe the period of grace would not last. Frederick told him that he would rather have written *Athalie* than fought a war. On 16 July, d'Alembert wrote to Julie de Lespinasse from Charlottenburg. He had refused the offer of the presidency once again. Frederick was no longer charm itself:

Our meals are rather frosty, as the king has lots of ministers, counsellors and generals around his table. Dinner is a gayer affair, at least the conversation is livelier, and the king doesn't seem to get bored with it. For all that, apart from the Lord Marischal and myself (d'Argens has stayed behind in Potsdam), silence reigns; as one might imagine at a tableful of Trappists; as all the others are dumb and only occasionally listen to our stories...[48]

D'Alembert tried to put his finger on what he believed to be the king's misfortune: 'he stands too high above his people, and has no one who can support him in his unstinting work and allow him to relax with conversation'. The Frenchman thought Frederick's influence was for the good: 'God maintain him, for the well-being of his land and as a model for Europe.' He disagreed with Voltaire. He thought that the elimination of the king of Prussia would have been nefarious for both literature and philosophy.[49] Frederick must have known that he could not hope to hang on to the Frenchman. He wrote to his brother in July, 'd'Alembert is here, I don't know if he'll stay; he is a clever man who knows a good deal'.[50] It was not long before d'Alembert was suing for permission to return to France or travel to Italy. Frederick could hardly conceal his disappointment: 'I was happier than Diogenes, for I thought I had found the man I had been looking for for so long, but he is leaving, he is off.'[51]

Frederick gave d'Alembert a gold snuff box decorated with his picture when he left. D'Alembert tried to do the done thing: 'I bowed and following custom, attempted to kiss the pans of his coat. He pulled me up, however, held me in his arms and kissed me.'[2] Frederick never gave up in his attempts to get d'Alembert back. He even went so far as to recommend the famous 'Berliner Luft', and tell the reluctant philosopher that French *émigrés* lived to great ages in the city, sometimes as old as ninety.

Frederick was still anxious to fill his academic stable. A geometer, Monsieur de la Grange, was on his way, and already in position were the astronomers Messieurs Castillon, *père et fils*. Euler had been lost. 'He is mad about *Ursus* Major and Minor, and has gone north, to be able to study them more easily.'[3]

Winckelmann being German, there was less enthusiasm about making him a member of the Prussian Academy. Winckelmann's support for the king had wavered. He was born in Stendal in the Prussian Altmark, but had received rather more patronage from the Saxons than he ever had at home: the king of Poland even paid him a pension. If he called Frederick a 'divine monarch' in 1752, he changed his mind soon after, when the king went into Saxony, guns blazing, and demolished a fair part of the lovely city of Dresden. He would not make up his mind, however. In October 1759, when Frederick's fortunes were at their lowest ebb, Winckelmann was telling Cardinal Alessandro Albani 'benedetto il re di Prussia'. In January 1763, when it was all over bar the shouting, the tone had changed. Now Winckelmann said, 'meglio farsi Turco circonciso che Prussiano' (better a circumcised Turk than a Prussian). He explained this contradictory opinion a month later: 'My hatred is only personally directed against the king, and this on grounds of humanity and love for Saxony.'[4]

Winckelmann had no faith in Frederick's ability to create a real artistic climate in Prussia: 'In a land like Sparta the arts couldn't take root. Once planted, they get out of control.' Yet, on 30 November 1763, Winckelmann showed a desire to become a member of Frederick's Academy. Frederick, however, displayed his customary meanness. He thought a stipend of 1000 thalers was quite sufficient for a mere German, and that was not enough to tempt Winckelmann to leave his Roman bolthole. Two years later, after the unsuccessful attempt to get the great Prussian to come home, Winckelmann expressed his contempt for the offer in a letter to one of the sons of the Silesian minister Schlabrendorff: 'I can say with equal justification what a castrato said in a similar situation in Berlin –

"Eh bene! faccia cantar i sue generale!"' (If that's the case, get your generals to sing).''

Another who failed to be elected to the Academy was Moses Mendelssohn, the remarkable Jewish merchant and philosopher who is best remembered today for being the grandfather of Felix and the model for Lessing's *Nathan der Weise*. That Moses was one of the very cleverest men in Frederick's Prussia was never disputed. Soon after he returned from the war, Frederick received a petition for a trading privilege from Mendelssohn with an endorsement from the marquis: 'A *philosophe*, who is a bad Catholic, bids a *philosophe*, who is a bad Protestant, to grant the privilege to a *philosophe*, who is a bad Jew. There is all in all too little religion in this that reason should not be taken into account.' Mendelssohn had his privilege.'⁶

The reason why Moses was rejected by the Academy had less to do with his religion than bad timing. Frederick had Catherine the Great made a member of the body, for all the obvious reasons. It just so happened that Moses's was the next name that came up. Frederick 'was revolted by the idea that the first Academician elected after the acceptance of Her Imperial Majesty should be a Jew'. Thiébault hastens to add that Moses was perfectly admissible, just that it would have looked 'sarcastic' in the circumstances, to elect one of his faith.'⁷

[III]

The real excitement that November 1763 was the arrival on the 3rd of the Turkish envoy, Ahmet Effendi, bearing gifts. The appearance of the promissory Ottoman might have led Frederick to make one of his most famous outbursts on the subject of tolerance: that he was prepared to see a mosque built in Berlin. The Turk had brought with him twelve ells of muslin, a dozen of cloth or gold, another of silk and a horse for Henry. He came to Potsdam, where he met the king and enjoyed some hunting. Despite that largesse, the Turkish envoy cost Frederick money, which was almost a capital offence. Lodging him required fully 7000 thalers a month: 'The Turks are even more miserly than the Jews,' sniffed Frederick.

In Berlin he was lodged at the sumptuous Palais Verzenobre, built for a French merchant. It was bought by Frederick's sister Amalia in 1772 and later became the Prinz Albrechts Palais,'⁸ the residence of Frederick's great-great nephew. Effendi's arrival heralded a fashion for all things

Turkish in Berlin, but the need to maintain a certain degree of etiquette did not go down well with the king:

We are obliged to observe a strange ceremonial with the Turks, which both upsets and angers me; but it has to be done, and I can console myself if it leads to a good defensive alliance with the circumcised gentlemen. It is now the fashion in Berlin to eat dates; and any moment now the *petits maîtres* will be wrapping turbans round their heads and those with enough money will set up harems. To be fashionable you have to have seen the Turk, everyone is telling stories which would make you fall asleep on your feet, but it will pass...'[59]

It was Henry's thirty-eighth birthday on 18 January 1764 and, as was now the practice, a big party was thrown for him, including a full-dress dinner with the gold service. The most prestigious members of the bourgeoisie were invited. The two brothers took it in turns to entertain one another. Frederick's birthday was held at Henry's palace. There was a masked ball for 4000 and anyone in silk could come in. The brothers' anniversaries fitted in with the short carnival, which still offered two operas and two masked balls a week, the latter held behind the stage at the Opera House. Frederick was as bored as ever, and quit the ball straight after supper.[60]

In February 1764 there was a scene at lunch in Potsdam, which showed how irritable Frederick could be; indeed, just as difficult as his father had been before him. Graf Borck, who was in charge of the young prince of Prussia's* court, made the mistake of saying that peace was superior to war. The king heard him, but asked him to repeat his contention. 'Had I known you thought like that, I would not have entrusted you with my nephew.' When Borck appeared at the table two days later, Frederick exclaimed, 'Get rid of that man, or I'll have him thrown out.' Wylich turned to Borck and said, 'You are not needed here, get out as quickly as you can.' He was sacked, but on full pay.[61]

Frederick was well rid of most of the family. The only one he really loved was William's younger son Henry, 'my other self', who died in June 1767, causing him what was possibly the greatest pain since the loss of Caesarion and Jordan.[62] The only one left unmarried was Amalia, who hated him, but did not adhere to the Henry–Ferdinand alliance because she loathed Henry too. As she told the prince of Prussia's second wife when she prepared to take the Hohenzollerns on board: 'The whole gang

* The later Frederick William II.

is worthless.'[63] She had very little contact with them. She had her own world, and her own position within it. She was abbess of Quedlinburg, and as such an imperial princess. Frederick took some pleasure in the visits he received from his sisters or their children in later years: Charlotte in 1764, who had always been one of his favourites, Prince Charles of Sweden in 1770, and his mother Ulrica in 1772.

Prince Charles came in October. They talked about his mother. Frederick had not seen Ulrica since she had left for Sweden twenty-six years before, during the Second Silesian War: 'I don't think I have seen a more beautiful woman than my sister.' Frederick sat his nephew next to him at the concert: 'You will tell my sister that you have heard Porporino and Paolino sing, old servants of the House whom she knows, also Quantz, who taught me to play the flute; the two others, Concialini[64] and Coli, she doesn't know.'[65] Frederick did not have to wait too long until Charles's mother arrived for an extended stay. Frederick felt rejuvenated, and they sat down and talked, a good deal about Voltaire, who had had the nerve to make indecent advances to the future queen.[66]

Leaving Frederick behind, Ulrica, Amalia, Charlotte and Elisabeth made a pilgrimage to Wusterhausen. The house was now empty, and barren of furniture. The thought stirred up bitter-sweet memories in the king. He speculated as to whether they had taken old Pöllnitz along:

I can imagine what he said: it was here that Frau von Kameke always ate so much that she damaged her stomach; ... this is where the late king liked to sit and puff ... In this hall the Feast of Saint Hubert was celebrated until everything was foggy with smoke; on the table there were jugs and sausages. There the oboists stood who played bits of old operas which Buononcini had composed for Queen Sophia Charlotte in Charlottenburg. Here the dogs were given their prizes. Grumbkow and Seckendorff stayed in these rooms, and in this place the Prince of Dessau and Grumbkow nearly came to blows.[67]

Despite the sentiment expressed at the time, there was a rumour that Frederick sacked his chef in order to get Ulrica to cut short her visit to Berlin.

[IV]

Frederick was a famous man after 1763 and foreigners came to gawp at the increasingly crotchety king of Prussia.[68] As Voltaire had had cause to observe, the whole of Protestant Switzerland was Prussian to a man.

During the war in Venice, the public had divided into rival camps of *Teresiani* and *Prussiani,* the latter asserting 'Chi non è buon Prussiano, non è buon Veneziano'. (No one who is not a good Prussian, may be a good Venetian.) Another Venetian, Casanova, had composed a poem about the conquest of Silesia which he thought would be a suitable metaphor for a seduction: he was Frederick's army, she Silesia. A cardinal who read the poem was tickled pink: 'I see ... Silesia is a woman ... The king of Prussia is ... Oh really! It is a marvellous idea.' 'We had to wait ten minutes for His Excellency's laughter to subside.'[69]

Later Casanova was to have a couple of interviews with his hero when he visited Berlin looking for work in 1764. He had met Lord Marischal in London, and he told him to write to Frederick. The king wrote back, giving him an appointment the next day in the garden at Sanssouci. Casanova found no one and went into the picture gallery, where he was told to wait outside until the king had finished playing his flute. He appeared soon after, followed by Catt and a 'pretty spaniel'.* Frederick asked the Venetian what he wanted. Casanova was struck dumb. When he recovered his voice the king quizzed him about gardening, hydraulics, the Venetian armed forces and finance. The last worked best: 'I thought I was called upon to play a scene of Italian improvised comedy, where, if the actor is at a loss, the groundlings hiss at him.'[70]

Frederick established Casanova's connections with Calzabrigi: they had been involved with the lottery in Paris seven years before. Frederick was already suspicious of Calzabrigi, but had not given up on the idea of a lottery, which continued to function at a profit for the king for a few years yet. The king dismissed his visitor, telling him he was a 'very fine figure of a man'. Marischal told him that he had made a good impression on the king, but they did not meet again until 18 July and the festivities occasioned by the engagement of the duchess of Brunswick's daughter to the prince of Prussia at Charlottenburg. The king appeared stiffly in mufti at the palace opera, 'wearing a coat of lustrine with gold braid on all the seams and black stockings ... only the very old could remember seeing him appear in public except in uniform and boots'. The pleasure for Frederick was seeing his sister 'Sans Souci' again after a lapse of years. The marriage was not to be a happy one, and Prince William was already unenthusiastic about his destiny.[71]

The next time the Italian saw Frederick was at the parade of the First

* Unlikely, Frederick liked only Italian greyhounds.

Battalion beside the Havel in Potsdam: 'every soldier ... had a gold watch in the fob of his breeches. It was thus that the king rewarded the courage with which they had subjugated him as Caesar subjugated Nicomedes in Bithynia.[72] No secret was made of it.'[73] Frederick had a well-attested mania for doling out cheap presents. Casanova developed the theme of the king's sexuality yet further: Frederick was a catamite. Frederick was most unlikely to have corroborated the fact. He showed an interest, however, in the writings of Bartolomé de Las Casas, a tolerant Dominican who was a sixteenth-century bishop of Chiapas in Mexico and who excused the practice of sodomy: 'However bizarre the opinion, there is always someone who becomes its zealous defender. The bishop of Las Casas [sic] declared himself the protector of Socratic love. He argued that nature had created two ovens, and occasionally one is too preoccupied to use the right one.'[74]

Casanova made the improbable claim that Frederick had gone off women after his 'affair' with La Barberina, and that once, passing the inn where Casanova stayed, he had seen a female dancer naked at an open window, and ordered that the windows be shut ever after; but the liaison with La Barberina was probably no more than a handy fiction, like hanging his bedchamber with her portrait, and those of La Cochois and Maria Theresa.[76] Casanova saw those portraits, and the rest of the king's room, with the small bed behind a screen, and the absence of slippers and dressing gown, when he was given a guided tour; he also learned that he occasionally slept in his hat, 'which must have been awkward'. Five or six weeks after the brief conversation between Frederick and the Italian, Casanova was offered a job teaching army cadets, but he thought better of it when he saw his pupils and the way the king treated the other tutors.[75]

It was not just an amateur poet like Casanova who was excited by the feats and letters of Frederick the Great. Goethe had not yet lost his initial enthusiasm, and could not imagine a more 'godless' court in the whole of Europe than Frederick's in Prussia. Lessing had yet to suffer the disappointment that came – in part at least – from his neglect at the hands of the king:

Wer kennt ihn nicht.	*Who knows him not.*
Die hohe Miene spricht	*The lofty forehead speaks*
Dem Denkenden, der Den-	*To the thinking man, the thinker*
kende allein	*alone*
Kann Philosoph, kann Held,	*Can be a sage and a hero*
kann beides sein.[76]	*all in one.*

By the end of the decade he had changed his mind. He was never considered for the Academy, and was passed over for the job as the king's librarian. Nor were any of the other Prussian luminaries of the German enlightenment, such as Herder and Hamann, patronised by Frederick. Lessing concluded there was no true liberty in Prussia. Nicolai had to remind him that he would have found far less in Vienna.[77]

James Boswell came in July 1764, hoping to meet the great man. Like other Britons, he had an introduction to his compatriot, the earl Marischal: 'It was fine to see the old Scots nobleman lodged in the palace of Prussia, just as if he had been in the Palace of Holyroodhouse.' Through him, Boswell was able to meet Frederick's nephew, since William's death the prince of Prussia, and Catt, whom he found 'dry and insipid'. He had a guided tour of the town palace in Potsdam. The Scotsman admired the concert room, the king's bedroom and the 'neat, little library', where he saw books by Voltaire and the *Oeuvres du philosophe de Sanssouci*. The next day he was taken to see Sanssouci itself:

The king has apartments here for himself and four friends. The building is light and elegant. But the gallery is truly superb. It is long, very lofty and very richly furnished. The collection of pictures is not as yet very numerous, but they are all fine pieces, and I was told by Lord Marischal that there is not a better collection in one place, even in Italy.[78]

Marischal was very attentive and took Boswell to see the foundations of the new palace as well. He had his first view of the king on the parade ground by the Stadtschloss.

I saw the king. It was a glorious sight. He was dressed in a suit of plain blue, with a star and a plain hat with a white feather. He had in his hand a cane. The sun shone bright. He stood before his palace, with an air of iron confidence that could not be opposed. As a loadstone moves needles, or a storm bows the lofty oaks, did Frederick the Great make the Prussian officers submissive bend as he walked majestic in the midst of them ... I beheld the king who had astonished Europe by his warlike ideas. I beheld (pleasant conceit!) the great defender of the Protestant cause, who was prayed for in all the Scots kirks. I beheld the 'philosophe de Sanssouci'.[79]

Boswell did not get the chance to meet his idol. He returned in August when he met Gotzkowsky ('a gallant German, stupid, comely, cordial'). He saw some of the nastier side of Prussian discipline when he witnessed a regiment being drilled in the Tiergarten.

The soldiers seemed in terror. For the least fault they were beaten like dogs. I am, however, doubtful if such fellows don't make the best soldiers. Machines are surer instruments than men. Were I to knock down a scoundrel, I would rather take a stick than take a child by the heels to give him a blow with. I saw a deserter pass the *baguette** twelve times. He was much cut. It made me sick to see it.[80]

Lord Marischal took him back to Sanssouci before he left. There was poetry lying unfinished on the desk in Frederick's bedroom. Boswell wrote to Frederick about Paoli and Corsica, and had an answer, but the man eluded him. It remained the 'major social defeat of his life'.[81]

Through the duke of Saxony Weimar, Goethe had the chance that Boswell lacked. In August 1776 he wrote to his friend Merck that he had 'been really close to Old Fritz, I have seen the way he lives, his gold, silver, marble, monkeys, parrots and torn curtains, and I have seen a great man reasoning with his own dumb dogs'.[82] Foreigners kept arriving in dribs and drabs. Only a year after Boswell's visit the scandalous and bigamously married Mrs Chudleigh tried to gain an audience with Frederick. She made the mistake of going through Elisabeth. Frederick wrote to his wife: 'If the Chudleigh woman wants to be presented, she must address herself to the English minister, so that it might be known in which name;[83] but the best thing would be not to see her at all.'[84] In 1772 she attempted to woo him with an English plough. She was rewarded with some lines of poetry 'Pour mademoiselle Schidley'.[85]

In 1775, Lord Dalrymple,[86] 'A mylord with a baroque name and a likable nature', bearded him in his lair,[87] but in general he preferred French noblemen, or philosophers. Helvétius came in 1765, but Diderot avoided him on his way to join Catherine in Russia.[88] In that same year, Voltaire recommended a marquis de Saint-Aulaire, who was apparently on his way. Frederick waited, and told his old bugbear that there were plenty of foreigners, but no marquis. Three years later he reported to Voltaire that he had been much taken with his visitors, M. de Laval-Montmorency and a Clermont-Gallerande: 'the latter above all has a lively wit'. De Laval-Montmorency put him off by telling him he wanted to learn German. He came again in 1775, bringing with him the duc de Lauzun.

In the summer of 1773, Frederick had a visit from comte Jacques

---

* The stick. Boswell witnessed a man running the gauntlet. See above, p. 245.

Antoine de Guibert, the author of an *Essai général de la tactique*, which had been sent him by d'Alembert. Frederick thought receiving a book on tactics from a philosopher was like getting a work on tolerance from the pope. He took umbrage at certain lines in the preface which denied the bravery of Prussian soldiers, on which he personally based his own success.[89] Guibert left a lively description of the shabby old king in his threadbare uniform covered in Spanish snuff, darned and washed out, covering his patched breeches, over boots so old that they had changed colour from black to yellow.[90]

Not all visitors left Prussia pleased with what they had seen. The Tuscan poet Vittorio Alfieri came in 1769 and heartily detested Potsdam and its author. Frederick asked him why he was in mufti: 'Because there seem to be enough uniforms at this court.' He looked the king in the eyes and thanked God he had not been born his slave. He left 'the great barracks that was Prussia' in the autumn, apparently without regret.[91]

Frederick had spent the winter months of 1764 writing his history of the Seven Years War. Once he had finished, he wrote to Lord Marischal, who had not yet returned from a long overdue visit to Scotland.

The memoirs ... which I have just finished, convince me more and more that to write history is to compile the follies of man and the blows of fate. Everything runs on these two lines, and so the world has gone on for eternity. We are a poor race, which is very restless during the little time it vegetates on this atom of mud called the earth. Whoever passes his days in quietness and repose until his machine decomposes, is perhaps more sensible than they who, by so many tortuous circles, spiked with thorns, descend to the grave. In spite of that, I am obliged to go round like the wheel of a water mill, because one is dragged by one's fate, and one is no longer master to do or to leave undone what one wishes.[92]

Frederick was being a fatalist again, returning to that doctrine of pre-destination that had so troubled his father.

Lord Marischal came back to Potsdam. He would rather have retired to some more clement latitude, but, he maintained, the king of Prussia had given him a love potion, like Isolde did to Tristan.

Were I in Spain I should feel it on my conscience to denounce Frederick to the Holy Inquisition, because the king has given me philtres to make [me] love him, as Hal did to Falstaff. If he had not bewitched me, why do I stay here, where I only see the spectre of the sun, when I might live and die in the happy clime of Valencia.[93]

Before the war, Frederick had granted the old Jacobite a small plot of land on the edge of the park at Sanssouci and allowed him to build himself a house and lay out a garden at the king's expense. Frederick had a part in the design, and neglected to install adequate sewage disposal facilities, albeit spending 16,000 thalers of his own money. On 11 September 1764, Milord wrote to David Hume in Paris to describe what is still one of the loveliest houses in Potsdam.

It is not going to be that small, having a façade 89 feet long and two 45 foot wings; the garden is small, big enough for me, however[.] I have a key to let me into the gardens of Sanssouci. There will be a good room with a vestibule, and a *cabinet* big enough to fit a bed, quite apart from the other apartments, if d'Alembert came he could stay there and take the waters...

There was also a larder where the old peer could smoke meat for his table, and the many English and above all Scottish guests he entertained there.[94]

The house was finished the following year, when Marischal moved in his library: Montaigne, Ariosto, Voltaire and Swift, and his big dog, 'Schnell'. He had no German books because, as he was happy to tell Rousseau, he did not understand the language. Guests were treated to Spanish food, and a glass of sherry.[95] Marischal had a motto composed, possibly by Hume: 'Fridericus II, nobis haec otia fecit'.[96] A place was permanently laid at Frederick's table for the last hereditary marshal of the Scottish court. Frederick would help him to food. With time the old Jacobite went less and less as he could not manage to get up the hill. Sometimes Frederick would dine with him in his Chinese Tea House, which was less of an effort for Marischal. He quarrelled with d'Argens: 'I cannot be the friend of anyone who goes every day at the king's table and collects gall there in order to distil it.'[97]

Lord Marischal was about the same age as Pöllnitz, who had the small job of reminding Frederick of court ceremonial from time to time. Frederick needed to know who was who, and how much fuss to make of them, but he was indifferent to the rest. As he told one of his diplomats, Graf Solms Sonnenwalde:

We don't have any differences of rank here and we don't recognise any either. I don't intend to introduce any. You wear my Order [the Black Eagle] therefore you have the same position as my ministers and the others who have received it.

When Charles V was in Milan a storm blew up between two of the first ladies of the court as to which of the two walked before and which behind the other. The quarrel reached his ears and he decided that the stupidest came first. That decision removed all distinction and the women came in in whatever order they chose. I don't want to know about any ceremonial either, when you get to the door first, you enter first; when another reaches it before you, he precedes you.[98]

Pöllnitz had retained a small place in Frederick's affections immediately after the war. He sent him a melon, and later a turkey cock he had fed on nuts. Frederick was impressed: 'It was taken for an ostrich, it was so big and pompous; and the flavour was found to be admirable.' He sent him an ox in return.[99] Later, age seems to have been the only thing which recommended him to the king. He died in 1775, a little younger than the oldest man Frederick saw, Pastor Le Cointe. Frederick's epitaph was churlish: 'He died as he lived, that is, playing roguish tricks the very day before he expired. The only people who will mourn him will be his creditors.'[100]

D'Alembert would not come himself, but he was happy to send others. It was he who dispatched the professor of grammar, Dieudonné Thiébault, to Frederick as his new French secretary and teacher at the cadet school.[101] He arrived on 16 March 1765, and Frederick received him with his customary lack of formality: 'Good evening, *Monsieur*, I am very pleased to meet you.' There followed the standard two-hour grilling, where Thiébault had to supply him with the minutest details of his past. The final question was: how had he managed in a land where no one spoke French? Thiébault had bought a grammar in Strasbourg, and said he fully intended to learn German. 'I strongly suggest you never learn it, it is a pleasure that you don't know it.' Frederick believed that he would blemish the purity of his French that way, and that he had been summoned for another purpose.[102]

Frederick was still fulminating against Rousseau. He did not like his philosophy much, but he wanted him as a part of his intellectual *ménage*. 'I think his is unfortunate and we should pity him. I don't like his paradoxes, or his cynical tone,' he told Voltaire.[103] After he had given him money and asylum in Neufchâtel during the war, he had followed up his munificence with an invitation to live in Pankow,* where he would have 2000 thalers a year and meadow for his cows

* On the River Panke, then north of, now in Berlin.

and chickens. Lord Marischal had put all to his philosophic friend, but Rousseau had simply replied with an insulting letter. 'That one is a madman,' concluded Frederick.[104]

In those days Frederick's circle was composed of the epigones who had settled in Potsdam since the end of the war. D'Argens was out of favour; the new luminaries were Quintus, François-Vincent Toussaint and Panage. Frederick was rarely alone. Soon after Thiébault arrived, he saw Frederick ill: he was stretched out on a camp bed with his boots on and a white handkerchief tied round his head. He was using his greatcoat as a blanket. When he was well they had plenty to talk about. Frederick needed Thiébault to correct his French texts. Like Catt he discovered that it could be hard work. Frederick read some of his own poems and laughed out loud. When Thiébault also laughed, the king grew serious again: '*Monsieur*, what are you laughing at?'[105]

After the Seven Years War, Frederick maintained a small circle of female friends. The flypaper was his 'petite mère', Gräfin Camas; for the rest there was Frau von Kanneberg, Frau von Kameke and Frau von Morien, the wife of an infamously stupid courtier who had been attached to Frederick's mother's court, Fräulein von Zerbst, Fräulein von Podewils, Fräulein von Knesebeck and Madame de Maupertuis (née von Borke). From 1763 to 1766, Frederick spent his New Year's Eves with this little coterie. His sister Amalia was also invited, on one occasion in verse, to a 'soupé [sic]/Très simple et même un peu rustique'.[106] After Frau von Camas died there were no more parties of this sort.

Another woman Frederick admired was the Polish countess Skorzewska, who came to Berlin in 1764. She spoke Latin, Greek, French, Italian and English (Frederick does not mention whether she spoke either German or Polish!). 'I recommend her example to all women, who might have other talents than this Polish woman has for educating herself; but they don't know the happiness of those who cultivate letters; and because it isn't a physical pleasure, they don't recognise it to be one at all.' Frederick agreed to be godfather to one of Madame Skorzewska's sons. After she died in 1773, he wrote to her children to commiserate: 'She was someone of merit whose talents and personal qualities will always be a precious memory.'[107]

Thiébault gives us an insight into Frederick's obsessive love of order. He divided books into two broad categories: those to be read, reread and studied; and those to be skimmed, once. The books in the first category were read, over and over again, always in the same order. He possessed five sets of each: at Sanssouci, in the Potsdam Stadtschloss, in the Berlin Schloss, in Charlottenburg and at his palace in Breslau. This dispensed with the need to lug his books around with him.[108] He travelled always in the same old carriage, which served him for the entirety of his 46-year reign. It was pulled by a dozen horses, which meant the king could cover a phenomenal distance on his progresses. When he stopped for the night, he demanded nothing more than a roof, a table, a chair and a bed. On one occasion his coach tipped over and the king of Prussia was landed in a ditch. He went for the coachman with his cane. The driver shouted at him, 'Don't believe that I am not a thousand times angrier than you?' Frederick laughed, and forgot his temper.[109]

Relations were beginning to sour with the marquis d'Argens. First there was the question of his wife. Some have maintained that Frederick could not bear the sight of Babet Cochois. Thiébault says that the marquis married secretly during the Seven Years War, and that Lord Marischal had to play a trick to get Frederick to recognise her when they crossed the park at Sanssouci together after the war had ended: 'Who is that woman?' 'The marquise d'Argens.' 'What!' the king allegedly replied. 'Has the marquis married?' According to the story, Marischal was obliged to tell Frederick that it had happened several years before, but that he had not thought to bother him with such 'trifles'. Thiébault claimed that Frederick never spoke to the marquis about his wife.[110]

This is clearly untrue. For a start the marriage took place in 1749, legitimising a daughter, who had been made earlier. That was seven years before the Seven Years War and Frederick must have known Babet for some time as part of the French theatre troupe and as the sister to the famous La Cochois. During the war he told the marquis to bring her to Leipzig, and Catt records Frederick uttering quite sympathetically on the subject: she was a 'delicious wife for the marquis, she is filled to the brim with wit and knowledge, talents and attentions for him, you meet few women as educated as her ...'[111] The marquis' marriage was not the problem; it was the increasing sickness of the sexagenarian Provencal, who was now longing to return to a warmer land to shuffle off his coil, and the bitterness that provoked in Frederick.

D'Argens spent the winter of 1764 in his homeland, staying at the family's country house at Éguilles, or their baroque town palace in Aix. He prolonged his stay until the summer of 1766, and was in contact with his Prussian master by letter. The taunts were often cruel. When he made slow progress towards Aix: 'I think the Colossus of Rhodes would be easier to move than you are.' In another letter the king accused his friend of being the real 'beast of Gevaudan', a wolf that was then savaging sheep in the south of France. Frederick repeated this assertion to d'Alembert: 'You will see that it is the marquis in his cloak that people have taken for a monster. They say that it eats children and is very nimble, jumping from branch to branch, [but] that doesn't sound like him, if the monster slept, it couldn't be anyone else.'[112]

D'Argens had not been back in Prussia two years when he wrote to the king to say that he was too ill to go on, and needed to return to Provence where wine and meat were cheaper, and where the sun shone for most of the year, thereby dispensing with the need to buy costly fuel. Frederick let him go, but called him an 'ingrat', and was increasingly cold in his very occasional letters. It was from Babet that Frederick eventually learned of d'Argens' death, which occurred at Toulon on 12 January 1771. She wrote to him on 6 February, asking the king for instructions as to what to do with their voluminous correspondence.[113] Frederick's most considerate epitaph was written in reply to one of Voltaire's letters: 'poor d'Argens has stopped talking, thinking and writing. He is my quartermaster, and he has gone to find me lodgings in the land of hollow dreams, where we will probably all be meeting up.'[114] Frederick proved a considerate master in the end: he had a monument set up in the church of the Minims[115] in Aix to the man who had sustained him throughout the miseries of the last war.[116]

[V]

One year after the end of the war, Algarotti died in Pisa. The author of *Newtonisme pour les dames* and *Le Congrès de Cythère* wanted to leave his royal master his portrait by Pesne, to compensate him for the loss of his company, and the little consignments of botargo he knew the king liked. Frederick offered to pay for the picture, but his old friend would not hear of it. Once again Frederick dipped into his pocket for a suitable monument. It was set up in Pisa cathedral: 'Hic jacet Ovidii aemulus et Neutoni discipulus.' (Here lies Ovid's equal and Newton's disciple).[117] With friends disappearing at this rate, Frederick was on the look-out for replacements. He met Graf Hoditz-Roswald in Moravia during the Seven Years War, the husband of the dowager margravine of Bayreuth – Wilhelmina's stepmother-in-law. Roswald's gardens were renowned: they were full of concealed fountains that took promenaders by surprise.

Behind a wall in a park, Hoditz kept a brothel for his sole use.[118]

Frederick visited Hoditz and on that occasion refused to reveal his identity. He came again in 1769, this time in majesty, if that was the word. Hoditz was charmed, and gave a magnificent feast for the king of Prussia. Hoditz had his own little opera at his Schloss and the local peasants acted in his plays. The women also stocked his private brothel. If they so much as looked at another man, he had them locked up and put on a diet of bread and water. Frederick loved Hoditz's conversation, and built a little frigate to bring him up the Oder to Berlin and Potsdam. When he was not in Prussia, the two men sent one another gifts: Brinza cheese, prunes, Istrian wine, champagne, even swans. In later years Hoditz took the place of the earl Marischal.[119]

Gifts of food and drink also figured in the correspondence between Frederick and his Rheinsberg friend La Motte Fouqué. The gallant general was released from captivity at the end of the war, wheelchair bound, and believing himself to be in disgrace after his defeat at Landeshut. At the end of July that year, Frederick wrote to reassure him that his love was undiminished. He was offered his old job back as governor of Glatz, but he soon retired from the army and went to live off his prebend in Brandenburg. Here he was the recipient of the king's largesse: coffee brought by Ahmet Effendi and porcelain in April 1764 (the first Königliche Porzellan-Manufaktur, or Royal Porcelain Factory, products were not yet ready). Like many men of his time, Frederick believed in the therapeutic qualities of old wine. He offered Fouqué not only old tokay, but also a 1684 hock, which he had in the royal cellars. It was not in perfect condition – Frederick calls it 'vin vinaigre' – but Fouqué took it for all that.[120]

In June 1764, Frederick paid a call on his old friend at his home in Brandenburg. 'I don't need much to eat; I ask for just a good soup and a dish of spinach, a smile from my host and to find you in good health.' The visit seems to have gone off well. In October, La Motte Fouqué was sending the king delicacies: 'a pâté de Périgord de Brandebourg' arrived in Potsdam. The old general was aware that Frederick ordered a pâté from Perigord[121] every year, possibly because his chef, Noël, was from Périgord himself.[122] He had obtained some truffle hounds in Croatia and had set them to work in the oak forests around Magdeburg and Halbestadt. The truffles they unearthed 'were in no way inferior to those of Italy'.[123] Fouqué had a terrine made up in the manner of Périgord. The king found it very good.[124]

Fouqué must have followed up the pâté with a few loose truffles, for at the end of October (too early for the *melanosporum*), Frederick was dispatching a pâté made up in Noël's kitchen to the old general in Brandenburg. When the king sent a real *Périgourdin* in February, the king's good subject told him that he found Noël's superior. Frederick visited his friend again that summer. Once again he wanted only the simplest food: 'a stew, and nothing more', and no black diamonds were to be unearthed for his royal person. The flirtation flared up again that winter, when Frederick had some Italian truffles delivered from Vienna and promptly sent some or all of them to Fouqué.[125]

Frederick had not tired of writing his works of philosophy and poetry. Tolerance remained a central tenet. In the summer of 1766, Frederick wrote to his friend d'Alembert after he had heard news of the destruction of new literature in France:

They tell me that they are still burning books in France. It is a resource in a cold winter if there is a lack of wood, providing you burn the writings alone, and not the writer, which might be a little too drastic and it would put me in a bad mood if they piled up the faggots for certain philosophers in whom I continue to take an interest.[126]

Frederick was also in the process of reforming the Prussian legal system, which meant burying his nose in the writings of Beccaria. A good code was what he was after: 'society can live without religion, but not without laws'.[127] Voltaire was anxious to know the reason behind his sentencing policy. Frederick enlightened him: 'If you smash a statue, I sentence you to put it back together again; you neglected to doff your cap for the parish priest, who was wearing you know what, I sentence you to appear for fifteen days on the trot, bare-headed in church...'[128]

As the codification of the Prussian legal system continued, the king became more and more wrapped up in the business of making good laws. In August 1777 he noted that the Swiss were reforming theirs and making them less severe. Their action had given him food for thought and he had set down his ideas in writing.[129] In another letter to Voltaire, Frederick showed how mild Prussian laws could be. Voltaire wanted to know about capital crimes. In an ordinary year only fourteen or fifteen people were sentenced to death. They were mostly whores who had killed their own children, a few murderers and the odd highwayman. Even then not all the prostitutes found guilty actually went to the gallows. To discourage abortion and child murder, Frederick had encouraged the denunciation of servants who got pregnant. Public penitence had been scrapped. Instead he had created hospices where the children could be born and brought up.

There was still torture in cases of treason, but Frederick assured Voltaire that it existed only to 'cut the roots of the conspiracy'. 'In civil cases you should adhere to the maxim that would save a guilty man rather than letting an innocent one perish.' Frederick believed in the efficacy of a good police force, which could be as useful as gentle laws: 'If people don't steal or commit murder, it is because they are certain to be quickly discovered and arrested.' Frederick was quick to add that there was no such thing as arbitrary arrest in Prussia. It was not like France with its infamous *lettres de cachet*: 'No one may be arrested without my signature, nor anyone sentenced without my having ratified the verdict.'[130]

There was a hiatus in Frederick's correspondence with Voltaire between 1767 and 1769 occasioned possibly by the latter's feelings of guilt after the theft of his yet unpublished *Mémoires*. When the ink began to flow again, both the writer and the king were much taken up with the need to refute godlessness. 'Atheism can never do any good and superstition has done an infinite amount of harm', wrote Voltaire in February 1770, 'save us from these two abysses.'[131] As it turned out, Frederick was busy with a refutation. He kept returning to the theme that year. In September he told Voltaire: 'My principal occupation is combating ignorance and prejudice in a country where an accident of birth has brought me to power, [I have to] enlighten minds, cultivate morality, and make the people as happy as it suits human nature, and as the means at my disposal permit.'[132]

Frederick was frightened that *philosophes* would turn against the tolerance which he held so dear. This would indeed be the case only three years after his death, and would carry at least one of his correspondents – Condorcet – to the scaffold. 'We know the crimes which religious fanaticism has engendered. Let us take care to keep philosophy free of fanaticism; it should be characterised by moderation,' he told Voltaire. 'Socrates did not adore the *deos majorum et minorum gentium* (the gods of the common people); he none the less took part in public sacrifices. Gassendi attended Mass, and Newton heeded the homily.'

In society tolerance should allow everyone the liberty to believe in what he wants; but tolerance would not be extended to authorising outrageous behaviour or licensing young scatterbrains to rudely insult the things that others revere.

These are my views, which suit the maintenance of liberty and public security, which is the first object behind all legislation.[133]

Controversial is Frederick's attitude to serfdom. As an enlightened monarch, the mere mention of serfdom or slavery was an abomination to him. Frederick was also good at dealing with the common man, especially the simple soldier, whose rough dialect he spoke and at whose fires he warmed his rump. He expressed a fondness for the peasant – the 'père nourricier' he called him. In May 1763 in Kolberg, Frederick made his advanced views on serfdom clear to the Pomeranian nobility: 'Without further ado, there must be from this hour forward a total abolition of serfdom and indeed any royal, noble, or civic ownership of villages.'[134]

The nobles fought back, however. In Stettin that December they imposed conditions, claiming that they could not survive without their serfs. To cap it all, there was the odd Hodge revolt, notably in Silesia in 1766 when peasants refused to bring in Graf August Wilhelm Leopold Gesler zu Odersch's crop. The unrest spread to other Kreise, and troops were sent in under Seydlitz, who turned out to be a model law enforcer: convincing the peasants to return to the farms without violence.[135] The difference between the old and the new ways was to be largely semantic: the services they performed in Pomerania and in East (and later West) Prussia were redefined; serfdom became hereditary subjection; serfs could not be bought and sold, but they did much the same work.

Another barrier to abolition was Frederick's consciousness of the need to retain the love of his nobility. His affection for them was well known: they were 'the first and most brilliant order of the state'. After the war he paid off the debts of those whose land had been destroyed by passing armies.[136] When Stein did finally manage to scrap serfdom in the first years of the nineteenth century, it was as a result of a crushing defeat. But after victory bought at the price of so much noble blood, it was not feasible for Frederick to deprive them of their cheap labour force.

Frederick's nobility also preserved their almost exclusive control of the officer corps[137] (bourgeois commissions were pretty well limited to the artillery and the hussars), but he also restricted the nobility's activities to allow the middle classes to flourish in their own way: they were forbidden to practise trade and the king was anxious to prevent them from wallowing in luxury; rather they should cultivate 'German virtues'.[138] The middle classes were in turn exempt from military service to allow them to get on with mercantile activities from which the state was ultimately likely to benefit. The same reasoning made the king place obstacles in the way of their acquiring noble estates.[139]

In the army, the noble officer corps was very largely Prussian, or culled from Prussia's traditional allies and satellites, such as Anhalt-Dessau and Brunswick. The officers had a strict code of honour, which was noticeable in the behaviour of von der Marwitz, say, over the order to sack Schloss Hubertusburg. On the other hand, their was no *esprit de corps* among the men: they were checked by fear of discipline alone.[140] Nobles were obliged to seek the king's permission to marry or travel outside Prussia. This caused much discontent at the time, and the marriage restrictions led to a certain wildness of sexual morality in noble circles during the Frederician years, which had the king himself railing against the lapsed mores of his court.[141]

Middle-class Prussians must have suffered disappointment after the end of the Seven Years War. The dearth of officers had meant that many of them had been able to achieve temporary commissions, which were then revoked once the war came to an end. In the *Testament politique*, Frederick returned to this theme: 'commoners think ignobly and make bad officers'. There were rare exceptions, and Frederick thought no barrier should be erected against them; only against those who thought they were noble for being rich.[142] Once again Frederick was not anxious to cause waves within his officer corps, and he has been criticised for this. Other armies, such as the Austrian, were far less rigorous about noble birth, and double-defeat for Prussia at Jena and Auerstedt in 1806 has often been attributed to its failure to introduce a system based on merit. It should be said, however, that the noble officer corps served Frederick well enough in the Silesian Wars.[143] The problem with the armies facing Bonaparte was perhaps a too powerful notion of invincibility rather than over-reliance on the upper class.

There were areas where middle-class Prussians could prosper in state service. The higher ranks of the bureaucracy were open to them, with the nobility being squeezed out of all but the top ministerial posts by the time of Frederick's death. In this Frederick carried on his father's policy, but he was less open handed with patents of nobility than Frederick William had been. The classic instance was Eichel, who served Frederick's predecessor for ten years, and Frederick himself for twenty-eight. Bismarck's bourgeois grandfather, A.L. Mencken, proved something of a replacement for Eichel in the latter years of Frederick's reign. Neither, however, was ennobled for his pains, which he would almost certainly have been under Frederick's father. In 1768, Frederick told his heir to be sparing with ennoblements. He had handed out a few in the army and the law, but that was all. He did not mention cronies like Algarotti and Bielfeld.[144]

[VI]

Despite Frederick's determination to provide Prussia with just laws and display his love of tolerance at all times, there were those (even outside his own family circle) who were wont to accuse him of tyranny. His habit of sticking his nose into everything, his desire to control his nobility, as well as Prussia's rigid customs policy, sometimes gave the country the image of a police state. Once again his old friend Mitchell was critical of Frederick:

The ministers have not the courage to report to their master what is told them, and much less dare they insinuate what may be the consequences of a rash or false step. He is impatient of contradiction, and receives too easily impressions that flatter or coincide with his present passion; and experience has shown to me how difficult it is for a monarch to vanquish even his ill-grounded prejudices.[145]

Something of the feel of Prussian life is given by the experience of the candidate Linsenbarth, who came to Berlin from the university of Jena in 1766 and was promptly lightened of his purse containing 400 thalers by officious Prussian customs men. The coins were *Batzen* minted in Nuremberg, and the king had issued a decree that they were not legal tender in Prussia. The officers therefore decided that the theology student was a smuggler, and ignorance of the law was certainly not an excuse. When Linsenbarth asked what he was to live on, now that they had taken away his entire means, the inspector said that he would have to see. In the meantime he was lodged at the Weisse Schwan, where the landlord accepted his books and linen as security for board and lodging.[146]

Linsenbarth lived on at the Weisse Schwan for eight weeks until someone gave him the advice to take his case to the king. He wrote a *short* petition and, without so much as a penny in his pocket, he walked to Potsdam. There, on the Schlossplatz, he saw Frederick drilling his soldiers. When the parade was finished, Frederick disappeared into the garden, but some officers told Linsenbarth that the king was in a good mood, and that he should go to him with his petition. Linsenbarth was frightened, but the officers literally took him by the arms and carried him into the garden where the king was squatting on his haunches, conferring with a gardener about a shrub.

The officers then rehearsed him in the correct posture: 'Hat under the left arm! Right foot forward! Chest out! Letters out of the pocket! Chin up! Raised right hand! Stand like that!'[147] Linsenbarth was aware that the officers had been having fun at his expense. The king, however, noticed the student, and sent the gardener to take the papers out of his hand. He then took them off down an alleyway. He returned having looked at the papers and signalled Linsenbarth to come to him. The king affirmed that the *Batzen* were invalid in Prussia, but condemned the customs officials, who should have told him to go home and bring other thalers that were legal tender in Frederick's lands. The king decided that Linsenbarth should have his purse back, and with interest.

'Now I must go, lunch is waiting,' said the king. Linsenbarth reflected that he had had nothing to eat for twenty-seven hours and had walked 28 miles in sand and sun to present his petition. Suddenly a servant appeared before the Schloss and asked where the man was who had just been with the king. Linsenbarth presented himself. He was taken into the palace and a big room full of lackeys where a small table had been set up. Here was a bowl of soup, a dish of beef, a portion of carp with a green salad, another of game with a cucumber salad, bread, knife, fork, spoon; 'nothing was missing'. A lackey pulled up a chair and told him that the king had commanded that he should eat his fill, and that he was to serve him, heating up the meat and fish and pouring him wine and beer. When Linsenbarth left, the servant packed up cherries and pears to refresh him on his return journey.

That was not all. The king's secretary brought the student's papers back, together with a sealed envelope containing instructions for the customs and a small purse filled with five ducats and a gold Friedrichsdor. Linsenbarth might have believed that he was going back on foot, but no: the secretary escorted him out on to the Schlossplatz and hailed a supply wagon, instructing the driver to take Linsenbarth back to Berlin, and not to demand a tip. When he got to Berlin, he went straight to the customs office. The first officer blushed when he read the letter, passed it to another and again to a third. They were to repay the Nuremberg coin in Brandenburg currency. More, the customs officers were to go round to the Jüdenstrasse and settle the 24 thalers owing at the Weisse Schwan, 'and so the vexatious story came to its desired end'.[148]

[VII]

Naturally the years of peace meant Frederick could put down his reflections on virtually every subject that sprang to mind, practical and philosophical. The most important of his works was the second *Testament politique* of 1768, which was addressed to his new successor, Frederick William, prince of Prussia. Much of it is familiar from his other writings: the duty of a monarch to serve his country, for example. Frederick states that it is no longer possible for a king to administer justice, but he must keep an eye on it and make sure that everybody obeys the law, even the monarch himself.[149]

Frederick was keen to make his state as profitable as possible. The customs system, seen as so onerous for visitors to his country, had to tax luxury goods. On the other hand, what was made in Prussia paid no excise. He was confident that the KPM porcelain would yield a small profit at export which could be spent on French wine. Flour and small beer paid no tax. Frederick came down hard on coffee abuse, as he had himself suffered enough from that commodity. Prussia would never be a great trading power and had no need of a fleet, which merely encouraged wars; what Prussia needed as a land power was a good and powerful army. The army stood at 154,000 men, but Frederick thought it could be increased to 163,000 with provision for expansion to 210,000 in time of war.

Frederick William was to continue the methods ordained by his grandfather where possible. Frederick had every confidence in the cantonal system of recruitment, 'which rendered regiments immortal by constantly repairing their losses'.[150] He had learned a few lessons from war, however. He now recognised the importance of the artillery and the cavalry. By the end of the Seven Years War, the infantry, which had been his father's creation, were behaving poorly, while his cavalry was still on top form. Frederick William was to continue the annual revues in Potsdam, Berlin, Stargard, Magdeburg and Silesia: 'The proverb is true which holds that the eye of the master fattens the horse.'[151] His successor did not listen, however, only attending the parades with the greatest reluctance.[152]

Frederick warned against unjust wars: 'War is like the other arts: helpful when used well and pernicious when abused; the prince who goes to war because he is worried, frivolous, disorganised or ambitious is as damnable as a judge who uses the sword of justice to stab an innocent.'[153] The Seven Years War had been prolonged by poor strategy at Prague and

Kolin. He recommended a number of officers to his nephew, chief among them Henry and Seydlitz, and hinted at the need to create a general staff with proper maps and studies. 'Policy is the art of reading the future, and deducing from a given principle the consequences that will be played out.'[154]

Frederick's strategy remained the same. Saxony needed to be taken first.[155] While he was on the subject of Saxony, his old enemy Brühl got a mention. A monarch, he told his heir, should relieve poverty, not fatten a favourite. He passed his provinces in review, as he had done in his previous *Testament politique*. He was still cross with the East Prussians for yielding and paying homage to their Russian conquerors. He accused the nobility of idleness and said that in the last war they had been more 'Russian than Prussian', and as vile as the Poles. The ordinary folk were not so bad, even if the girls were prone to abort their children and the men enjoyed sexual congress with their cows![156]

The Pomeranians were good tough soldiers; those from the Mark, frivolous and spendthrift. Something of the same criticism was levelled at the Altmärker and Halberstädter, but they were more urbane, and had even dipped into their pockets to relieve the Pomeranians. The people of Minden were free of faults: 'the best in the world', hard working and faithful. Their neighbours in Cleves had in no way improved since 1752: the nobility was too fond of its wine and had gone almost mad as a result. He had no faith in the Upper Silesians, as the nobility was wholly Austrian in its loyalties. This extended to the canons of Breslau too: 'As soon as it looks as if we are slipping into war again, we must arrest the most suspicious people and send them to Magdeburg or Stettin until the peace, to stop them from betraying us and to spare us the annoying necessity of using more rigorous punishments on them.'[157]

He was keen to deal with the problem of the Jews, after a wave of anti-Semitism had been provoked by the (Frederick-backed) schemes of Veitel Ephraim and others during the war years.

We have too many Jews in the towns. They are needed on the Polish border because in these areas Hebrews alone perform trade. As soon as you get away from the frontier, the Jews become a disadvantage, they form cliques, they deal in contraband and get up to all manner of rascally tricks which are detrimental to Christian burghers and merchants. I have never persecuted anyone from this or any other sect [sic]; I think, however, it would be prudent to pay attention, so that their numbers do not increase.[158]

In 1769 Frederick wrote his will. The document contains the famous instructions for his burial, which were only carried out (with modifications) on 17 August 1991: 'I have lived as a *philosophe* and I want to be buried as one, without finery, without ceremony, without fanfares; I don't want to be dissected or embalmed; bury me at Sanssouci, at the top of the terraces, in the sepulchre that I have prepared.' He looked after the queen in his way: according her an apartment in the Berlin Schloss and another in Stettin (where wicked Elisabeth had been confined after her sexual misconduct had led to a divorce from Frederick William). The bequests are remarkable only for the minute consideration given to all of his siblings: snuff boxes, KPM porcelain, horses, chandeliers, diamonds and tokay.[159]

Frederick was anxious to give his officers (and by extension, his nobility) the best possible education. He had observed during the Seven Years War that the younger officers were not capable of making decisions for themselves. The result was the Académie des nobles in Berlin, and another cadet school in Pomerania. In order to set down the principles for teaching at the former, Frederick wrote his *Instruction pour la direction de l'Académie des nobles à Berlin*: he wanted to create a school so that no more than fifteen noblemen of genius could be true to their vocation of arms or politics. Lesser luminaries could go to the new school in Stolp or the other academy in Silesian Liegnitz, but even they were given a weighty reading list, including Casper Abel on the history of Brandenburg, and Feuquière on war. Frederick wanted all officers to have mastered French. Those serving in Silesia or East Prussia should have had some Polish too.[160]

At the elite school as many as three tutors were to be assigned to each cadet. It was the school that Frederick envisaged for Casanova. The first classes for religion and Latin were to be seconded to the Joachimsthal Gymnasium. French rhetoric was to be taught by Thiébault and Toussaint. Metaphysics would combine French teaching with the study of Locke and Leibniz. Cicero would be used to learn the law. Frederick had clear ideas for the teaching of history too: it should instil a loathing for fanaticism: they were to hear all about the Massacre of Saint Bartholomew's Day. There was to be *no* corporal punishment: 'it is a criminal offence for the tutors to strike their pupils: they are gentlefolk, and it is the object to inspire nobility of the soul; the only punishments permitted are those which excite ambition, and not those which make it appear vile'.[161]

More writings on education followed in the form of a *Dialogue de morale à l'usage de la jeune noblesse*, and a *Lettre sur l'Education d'un Génevois à M. Burlamqui, Professeur à Genéve.*[162] The first was in the form of a catechism, which would have served Frederick well in his teens. Children should honour their parents, and obey them. They should do everything possible for their country. Nobles should be conscious of their lineage, and continue to work for the glory of their race. War was evidently one way of doing this. One should never give in to passion. Debauchery, idleness, ineptitude, ignorance and bad conduct render man despicable. The highest good is service to the greater family, which is the state.[163]

The letter to Burlamqui was another attempt to present Frederick's views on education. He sketched the system at present in force in Prussia: the Joachimsthal Gymnasium (he omits the Graue Kloster), the Académie des nobles, the Ritterakademie in Brandenburg and the Klosterschule Rossleben in Magdeburg presented the first possibilities for a young nobleman, then the choice was between university (Halle or Frankfurt an der Oder: noblemen were not encouraged to leave Prussia) or the army. The former had been reformed; the latter was obviously preferable for a noble: 'a true school of manners'. In general, schooling was to be improved after the Seven Years War: ignorance turned people into beasts and rendered them lazy.[164]

Frederick deals with noblewomen too. Idleness was their worst enemy: 'spending two or three hours in front of a mirror to ponder on, refine and admire their charms, tell stories all afternoon, then the theatre, spending the evening by the fire, then dinner and gaming'. Can such a life do anything other than lead them to want pleasures of another sort? Frederick asks. Frederick proposes an education of a more masculine sort: economics, literature, music, even dancing. His views are advanced for his day. From his own bitter experience he was opposed to marrying women against their will.[165]

He was much concerned with morality, in his *Essai sur l'Amour propre* of 1770, Frederick extolled the need to cultivate virtue, without which man was just a wild beast, and more ferocious than a lion. Self-love is an antidote if properly governed, if it can teach you to love life and your own preservation; glory and honour. The *Examen de l'Essai sur les préjugés* of the same year is one of his most important essays, as it deals with his almost obsessive interest in tolerance, which went back to his first reading of Bayle and Voltaire's *Henriade*. In it he repeats many of the more misanthropic ideas that he had developed during the Seven Years War: 'prejudice is the reason of the people'; 'truth is not designed for man'.

Frederick reckoned on a very small number of people who were capable of higher understanding. Out of 16 million Frenchmen, he thought only 200,000 possessed of intellects: 1.25 per cent. In *Thérèse philosophe*, the erotic novel attributed to d'Argens, the philosophic abbé T*** gives his own calculation as one in 5000, with only one in 20,000 immune to dangerous passions.[166]

Frederick returned to fighting the bigotry he saw emerging among the *philosophes*, the baron d'Holbach in particular, which would end up by destroying the liberties they were calling into existence. He was outraged to find in his riper years that essays were being written to encourage intolerance: 'The world would have been happier if these scribes had lived in total idleness and not been hard-working writers. It is therefore demonstrated that activity is the mother of all crime ...'[167] There had to be a tolerance of religion, even if it struck the intellectual mind as folly. Frederick defended the existence of hereditary nobilities because it created a desire to emulate one's ancestors and to serve the state. He defended the just war, citing his heroes Marcus Aurelius, Trajan and Julian. The military upholds the state: 'do I need to remind you that the arts are cultivated in peacetime only under the protection afforded by arms?' Frederick also defended the monarchy, but stripped it of its mystic powers: 'Kings are men like any other; they do not enjoy the privilege of being perfect in a world where nothing is...'[168]

Frederick returned to his attacks on the mechanism of d'Holbach in his *Examen critique du système de la nature* of 1770. Man possesses a free will that is proven by his ability to correct himself. D'Holbach had attacked religion as the source of all evil. Frederick defended it on the basis of the precept in the Gospels: 'Do unto others as you would be done by.' D'Holbach should not confuse the law with its abuse. Frederick above all insisted that d'Holbach was wrong to adhere to the *tabula rasa* school: crime is not simply caused by poverty and necessity; there is no such thing as perfection in man, and no earthly use in striving to find it.[169]

In 1772 Frederick wrote an attack on Rousseau in the form of a *Discours de l'Utilité des sciences et des arts dans une société* to present the difference between a civilised and a barbarous people. The former can boast arts and science, and cultivates them: 'the biggest mind, deprived of knowledge, is nothing more than a rough diamond which will only acquire a price once it has been shaped by the hands of a talented jeweller'. Frederick was not taken in by noble savages. He returned to

the theme that emerged often in his letters to Voltaire: the art and science
of war. Voltaire had poured scorn on the intellectual warrior; Frederick
came to his rescue. He pointed out the different sciences that the good
general had to master: geometry, hydraulics, fortification, mechanics,
history and geography.[170]

Besides these philosophic writings there was the usual heap of poetry
produced in those first dozen years of peace. One poem was ostensibly
written by his dog Diane to 'wicked Elisabeth', the first wife of the future
Frederick William II. Frederick's purpose is clear:

> Une chienne en ce jour vous donne un grand exemple.
>
> J'ai mis au monde deux petits;
>
> Tout curieux qui les contemple
>
> Les trouve comme moi beaux, bien-faits et gentils.
>
> Soyez marraine à leur baptême,
>
> Et mes voeux seront accomplis,
>
> Si, madame, dans peu vous en faites de même.[171]

> *Today a lowly bitch sets a grand example.*
>
> *I delivered my puppies two;*
>
> *The curious come and marvel*
>
> *They're as pretty as me, kind and tough too.*
>
> *Be godmother and bring them fame,*
>
> *And all my wishes would come true,*
>
> *If, Madam, in a while, you did the same.*

[VIII]

Frederick inaugurated his new palace, 3 kilometres to the south of
Sanssouci, in the summer of 1768. It is a favourite story that Frederick
constructed the vast building to show that he had not been ruined by the
Seven Years War, but it is not true. The palace had been vastly expensive:
almost 3 million thalers, a fact that had not gone unnoticed in the lean
years following the Seven Years War. Frederick had commissioned the
work in 1755, before the war broke out. Heinrich Ludwig Manger and
Johann Gottfried Büring used designs by an unknown architect which
Frederick had brought back with him after his short trip to Amsterdam,
but the palace was clearly influenced by the elevations of Sir John
Vanbrugh's Castle Howard, which Frederick knew from *Vitruvius Britannicus*. In 1764, Wilhelmina's architect, Carl von Gontard, took over the

work, designing the individual apartments that were to house friends and visitors, who were not deemed important enough to stay at Sanssouci or in the Neue Kammern.[172]

It was Gontard who designed the theatrical 'Communs' opposite the new palace.[173] The last pieces of architecture Frederick had Gontard design at this time were the Freundschafts and Antikentempel in the park at Sanssouci. The temple of friendship was to be his monument to Wilhelmina, and he sent the plans to Voltaire – the author of the poem 'Temple de l'Amitié' – for his approval.[174] It was round and open, a last incarnation of the idea that went back to Knobelsdorff's Amalthea. The Antikentempel was built to house Frederick's growing collection of antiquities, before it was adopted by later Hohenzollerns as a mausoleum.[175]

In Berlin, Frederick was active too. He developed a fondness for an old Fischer von Erlach design for the Kohlmarkt façade of the Vienna Hofburg, which was not erected in full until the years immediately before the First World War. It was out of date even when Frederick handed it to the younger Boumann to turn into a new royal library to face the Opera House across the Opernplatz. With its gentle curvaceous façade, the Berliners thought it looked like a chest of drawers, and christened it the 'Kommode'. Frederick wrote to Voltaire in November 1777 to describe his new building, and flattered the old poet: 'The works of Voltaire were too meanly lodged beforehand.'[176]

Henry stayed away from the ceremony at the New Palace on 18 July 1768, but Amalia was there to enjoy an oratorio commissioned from Hasse with words by Maria Antonia of Saxony: *La Conversione di Sant' Agostino*. Frederick was not pleased with the subject matter – he thought Saint Augustine of Hippo a 'bad dialectician' – but 'the music was beautiful, and that is enough for me'.[177] The margravine of Saxony was a pianist. Two years later she performed at a royal concert in Potsdam at which Frederick and Quantz played the flute roles, the hereditary prince of Brunswick the first violin and the prince of Prussia the cello. This remarkable occasion was immortalised in the woodcut by Adolph Menzel as the 'flute concert at Sanssouci'.[178] In October 1771, Johann Gottlieb Graun died and Franz Benda finally took up the baton of royal *Konzertmeister*.

Frederick's talents as a musician were affirmed by the testimony of Dr Burney, who arrived in Berlin from Leipzig in 1772, but the Englishman none the less thought the sixty-year-old king was now past his best as a performer. Burney stayed in Berlin before making his pilgrimage to Potsdam. He met many members of the court orchestra, then made up of two composers, two concert masters, eleven violins, five cellos, two keyboard players, a harpist, four viola players, four flutes, four oboes, four bassoons and four horns. He was able to glean from Agricola, Kirnberger, Nicolai and others that music was 'truly stationary' in Prussia, 'His Majesty allowing no more liberty in music than he does in civil matters of government'. Everywhere he found the offerings 'second rate and out of date', with the names of Graun and Quantz invoked as if they were Luther and Calvin. C.P.E. Bach had had enough. Never appreciated by his royal master, he had decided to migrate to Hamburg, but retained close contact with Amalia, Frederick's no less musical sister.[179]

Like Boswell, Burney had an introduction to Lord Marischal, which he had obtained from the ambassador, Harris. He received Burney on the last day of September 1772 in his nightgown. A discussion of music ensued, in the course of which Marischal proved himself most knowledgeable. He also had a trick up his sleeve: he was able to call on his own bagpiper to illustrate some themes on the pipes, but sent him out into the garden so that he would not offend Burney's Italianate ears. Burney lunched with Marischal the next day, then had a tour of the New Palace where he admired the concert rooms, one for Frederick, one for Amalia and another for the prince of Prussia;[180] the Silbermann piano; and the collection of flute scores by the king himself, together with fingering and breathing exercises that he had had copied and distributed to each of his palaces.[181] Marischal had arranged for Burney to hear the king that evening. He met Franz Benda and Quantz in the anteroom as the musicians prepared to accompany the king.

The concert began by a German flute concerto, in which His Majesty executed the solo parts with great precision; his *embouchure* was clear and even, his finger brilliant and his taste pure and simple. I was much pleased, and even surprised with the neatness of his execution in the *allegros*, as well as by his expression and feeling in the *adagio*; in short, his performance surpassed, in many particulars, any thing I ever heard among *Dilettanti*, or even professors. His Majesty played three long and difficult concertos successively and all with equal perfection…

M. Quantz bore no other part in the performance of the concertos of to-night than to give the time with the motion of his hand, at the beginning of each movement, except now and then to cry out *bravo!* to his royal scholar, at the end of the solo parts and closes; which seems to be a privilege allowed to no other musician of the band. The cadences which His Majesty made, were good, but very long and studied. It is easy to discover that these concertos were composed at a time when he did not so frequently require an opportunity of breathing as at present; for in some of the divisions, which were very long and difficult, as well as in the closes, he was obliged to take his breath, contrary to rule, before the passages were finished.[182]

Burney observed Quantz's gigantic size, but he might have felt that the flautist was already past his best. In the course of their conversation, Quantz told Burney that Frederick adhered to his usual order, and played his collection of concertos by rota. Quantz died a year later, in 1773, leaving his 300th concerto unfinished. Frederick completed it, telling Benda, 'You can see that Quantz quit this world with some very good ideas.'[183] The following year it was the turn of the court *Kapellmeister* Agricola. The twenty-three-year-old Königsberger Johann Friedrich Reichardt was anxious to be named his successor and sent the king the score of his opera *Le feste galanti*. Frederick wrote to ask how much he wanted to be paid. When Reichardt named 1200 thalers,[184] the job was his.[185]

He arrived for the carnival of 1775. Frederick was ill, and Reichardt whiled away the time in Novawes with the Bendas, falling in love with and marrying Franz's daughter. His thoughts on Berlin music were published in Hamburg that year. He did not disagree with Burney. Prussian music was 'dry and hard', and he went out of his way to praise the now absent C.P.E. Bach and his 'fabulous technique'.[186] Frederick's musical world might have been past its peak, but in the immediate period before Mozart it represented some of the best operatic music the European stage had to offer, and Graun's works, increasingly rediscovered today, were in no way inferior to the body of mid-eighteenth-century musical theatre, with the exception of Gluck. On a personal front, Frederick's incipient toothlessness gave him increasing problems in his old age. He blew the odd wrong note, and other musicians had to cover for him or suffer a reproach.[187] Frederick finally put his flute into storage after the War of the Bavarian Succession, announcing to Benda that he had 'lost his best friend'. It was Reichardt who composed the poignant *Trauerkantate* after the king's death.[188]

The Königliche Porzellan Manufaktur (KPM) was up and running in September 1764 with twelve ovens to turn out objects that Frederick hoped would be more beautiful even than Meissen, which he banned the following year along with all other imported porcelain. At first the factory combined Silesian kaolin with Passau brown earth to give the china a creamy colour, but it was only from 1771 that the winning formula was hit upon, and KPM started using the characteristic blue and white designs. It was the object of the king's particular pride now that he had bought it from the bankrupt Gotzkowsky.[189] Frederick was anxious that the factory on the Mühlendamm, which employed around 400 people, should pay its own way, and he forced the Jewish merchants to offer pieces as part of their lists. He could also now send gifts of his own porcelain to his various friends, and he commissioned twenty-four services for that purpose.[190]

Voltaire received a set in November 1772, as did Catherine of Russia. Voltaire was complimentary: 'The king my master [i.e. Louis XV of France], has none more beautiful, and he hasn't sent me any either.'[191] Three years later KPM was issuing busts of Voltaire, 'which resemble you in the old days, perhaps even now', said Frederick. Voltaire peevishly acknowledged the gift of an 'old man in porcelain'.[192] The king thought it a very good likeness and told d'Alembert it lacked only the power to speak. He recommended that the best effects could be had by reciting the *Henriade* to it and watching it at the same time.[193] Voltaire wanted revenge in the form of a Frederick, but the king of Prussia still adhered to his policy of keeping portrait painters at arm's length, deeming them as adept at flattery as the most refined courtiers. He allowed Anna Dorothea Therbusch, however, to make the familiar bust of him that served as the KPM's model, injecting a little youthful grace into his raddled face. Voltaire received one in good time. Frederick decided that the bust would be more likely to 'ruin an apartment than to decorate it'. The king joked that the sculptress had refused to clothe him in the garb of an anchorite.[194]

All Frederick's friends played a role in augmenting the royal painting collection. In 1765 Catt located a Correggio that was the property of the duke of Parma, but the duke's death ended negotiations for eight years, by which time it was being touted by the monastery that had obtained it from the duke. They wanted 14,000 thalers for it. Frederick must have agreed, although he was only prepared to go to 12,000, for in May 1773 a Correggio 'of great beauty and a wholly excellent state of preservation' arrived in Potsdam from Italy via Vienna. Voltaire was still one of Frederick's buyers when it came to paintings. In May 1770 he was offering the king van Loo's *Three Graces*, once the property of King Stanislas and more recently of the French resident in Geneva, for 11,000 livres.[195]

Frederick had retained his interest in theatre, but after the Seven Years War it had lost its lustre. In January 1771 he was telling Voltaire 'we have a good Opera but, with the exception of one actress, a bad comedy'. There was a rare treat occasioned by the arrival of some passing player. The actor Aufresne* paid a call and appeared as Coucy in Voltaire's *Adelaide du Guesclin* and in Racine's *Mithridate*, and in the summer of 1775 it was the turn of Le Kain,† who performed Orosmane in Voltaire's *Zaïre* to divert various members of the growing family. 'The whole of my household is full of nieces and nephews and great nephews; you have to give them theatre which removes the tedium of being in the company of an old man.' Amalia was there, and Princess Ferdinand, the landgravine of Hesse and the princess of Württemberg. Le Kain he admired: he thought him 'Very talented, he has a good voice, presents himself with dignity [and] has noble gestures', even if he thought his playing a little too mannered.[196]

Frederick might have learned a little from *Candide*: at least to cultivate his garden – Prussia. That being said, it was not the easiest soil to work. No lesser expert on gardening than Voltaire himself teased Frederick on his infertile sandpit. Frederick took up the challenge in the spirit of his correspondent's creation:

I will own, that with the exception of Libya, few states can claim to be our equals in sand; however, this year we are turning 76,000 arpents[203] [38,000 hectares] of prairies into arable land; these prairies will feed 7000 cows, their manure will enrich and correct our soil and the harvests will get better. I now it is not given to man to alter the nature of things; but I think that from industry and [hard] work it will be possible to correct a sterile soil and transform it into a mediocre one; and we must be happy with that.[197]

---

* The Swiss-born actor Jean Rival, or 'Aufresne', 1728–1804.
† Henri Kaïn, or 'Le Kain', was one of the greatest actors of his day. As a pupil of Voltaire, Orosmane was one of his star roles.

CHAPTER THIRTEEN

Dividing up the Pudding

[1]

By the time Frederick and his family sat down to watch Le Kain, Prussia had once again grown in size, but this time not a shot had been fired, and the king had acquired his territory by smooth negotiation. Frederick disliked Poland and the Poles. As a state with an elected monarchy, Frederick saw Poland as weak and a danger to its neighbours. He thought the nobility a bunch of idle wastrels; the first Pole an 'orang-utan'.[1] As he told Voltaire in 1771, Poland would be carved up and it would be all the fault of the 'stupidity of the Potockis, Krasińskis, Oginskis and that whole imbecile crowd whose names end in -ki'.[2]

Frederick's interest in West or Polish Prussia went back to the Natzmer letter or before. The usefulness of this 'corridor', as it was dubbed two centuries later, was undeniable. East Prussia lay beyond Poland, and had done since the Peace of Thorn had halved the extent of the duchy of Prussia in 1460. Frederick wanted a bridge to connect Pomerania with East Prussia. West Prussia and the Netze district was that bridge. It was not particularly important to him that the area contained large numbers of *Hauländer*, peasants of Germanic stock; as well as German-speaking merchants and noblemen; or that the towns and cities were almost all more German (or Jewish) than they were Polish: the fact was not even raised in the course of the negotiations that ended with the First Partition. He saw the area as a poorly administered part of a moribund state which was useful to him; and therefore ripe for the picking.[3] 'That acquisition was one of the most important we could have made because it attached Pomerania to East Prussia, and because, in making us masters of the Vistula, we gained the double advantage of being able to defend our kingdom and charge large tolls on the Vistula, because all Polish commerce uses that river.'[4]

'I have never misled anyone during my life; even less will I fool posterity.' So Frederick concluded the above passage in his *Mémoires depuis la paix de Hubertsbourg jusqu'à la paix de Teschen.* In his *Testament politique*, Frederick goes even further in his frank expression of Prussian interests in north-eastern Poland. Danzig and the Vistula were the keys, and they should be acquired like the last leaves of an artichoke, the rest having been consumed first.[5] These are statements which have, however, caused a great deal of confusion, and will continue to do so; for they have obscured the other parties who played a primary role in the First Partition, and whose immediate influence was stronger than Frederick's: Joseph II, Catherine of Russia and her minister Nikita Panin, and lastly, Frederick's own brother Henry.

Frederick's frustration with the Polish situation had been growing since the end of the Seven Years War. As he put it to Voltaire, 'You need an angelic patience to see a way out.'[6] In January 1763, the last Saxon king of Poland fell ill. He died in October, and Catherine took the opportunity to foist her ex-lover, Stanislas Poniatowski, on the Polish diet when it met in the following spring. Frederick saw the chance to revive the short-lived Prusso–Russian alliance if he consented to Catherine's ploy. That was signed on 11 April, with the two powers concluding a defensive bond that guaranteed one another's territories. It contained several secret clauses, among which was one safeguarding the interests of various minorities in Poland: Orthodox Christians and Protestants. Stanislas was elected king in September.[7]

Panin was keen to secure peace by a system of alliances with the northern powers which allowed for a reconciliation with Prussia. The puppet in Poland, however, proved less tractable than Catherine had wished: he started demanding reforms of Poland's constitution and moves were made in Saint Petersburg to oust him, leading to an extraordinary diet that autumn while the country was crawling with Russian troops. Frederick feared a Russo–Austrian war, and was relieved that trouble died down when the diet reconvened the following year. Peace was, however, short-lived. As the Russian forces withdrew, the Poles announced an anti-Russian Confederation in Bar in Podolia. Poland descended into a bloody civil war and, to celebrate, Frederick amused himself with a long satire about the Poles: *La Guerre des Confédérés.*

Frederick had always seen the possibilities of expansion in the east. In April 1767, d'Alembert had tried to coax an answer out of him on the subject of Danzig and Poland.[8] The first Frederick heard of a clear plan for the partition of Poland came from a Prussian in the Danish service, Graf Lynar, who visited him as a private individual at the beginning of

1769. He proposed that Prussia should take Ermland and a protectorate over Danzig; that Austria should have Galicia; and that Russia could help itself to the rest. All three could then launch an attack on the Porte. Frederick called the plan 'seductive', but the Russians were at that time more interested in a collective campaign against the Turks.[9]

In Vienna, Joseph II had also come of age and showed his desire to become an enlightened ruler like his hero Frederick of Prussia. His mother was naturally against it, and managed to scrap a planned meeting between the two princes. 'This hero that everyone talks about, this conqueror, does he have a single friend? Must he not distrust the entire world?'[10] Frederick and Joseph did finally meet, however, in Neisse in Silesia on 25 August 1769. Joseph wanted Prussia to declare its neutrality. Frederick refused: he was still allied to Russia. He none the less tried to alert Joseph to the dangers of Russia: 'In time either I, or all Europe will need to hold these people back. The Turks are nothing compared to them.'[11] Joseph did not believe the Russian alliance was of interest to him, and refused to join Frederick, who renewed the bond in the autumn of that year. He gave a fulsome report to d'Alembert for all that: 'He showed me the most cordial friendship. He is gay, and in no way shy, hard on himself and tender towards others. In a word, he is a prince from whom one may expect only great things, and Europe will talk of him as soon as he gets some elbow room.'[12]

Frederick was sympathetic towards the Habsburg prince and evidently far more anxious to strike a deal with him than the Russians, whom he continued to see as barbarians. He wrote to Voltaire on 18 August 1770:

I am leaving for Silesia to meet the emperor who had invited me to his camp in Moravia, not to fight as in the old days, but to live together as good neighbours. The prince is nice and has many merits. He likes your books and reads as much as he can ... He is an emperor who is like no other that we have had for a long time in Germany. Neither one of us likes stupid or barbarous people; but that is no reason for exterminating them. If it were necessary to wipe them out, the Turks wouldn't be the only ones.[13]

The second conference took place on 3 September 1770 at Neustadt. Frederick stayed at Roswald, with his friend Hoditz.[14] Both men were nervous of one another, and Joseph placed the prince de Ligne at their table to work his charm on the Prussian king.[15] Frederick was none the less impressed: here was something (just something) of the young Frederick himself, burning with ambition and anxious to reform his land.

He noted, however, that Joseph had 'the desire to learn, but not the patience to teach himself'.[16] Writing again to Voltaire, he showed an understanding of the special circumstances of the young man's upbringing:

Born in a bigoted court, he has shaken off superstition; brought up in luxury, he has adopted simple ways; fed with incense, he is modest; swollen with the desire for glory, he sacrifices his ambition to filial duty, which he carries out scrupulously; and, having had but pedantic masters, he has enough taste to read Voltaire and to esteem him of merit.[17]

Voltaire was sceptical of Frederick's description of the emperor: 'A master painting his disciple,' he called it.[18]

The poet Klopstock was pleased to hear of the meetings between Frederick and Joseph. He wrote to Gleim in September 1769 to express the hope that their discussions were 'more about ploughshares than swords'.[19] He was almost certainly disappointed. The scramble for Poland was launched by Joseph, who marched into Zips, claiming it was a part of the Hungarians' ancestral lands. In 1770 Austrian troops occupied yet more starosties of an electoral monarchy turned upside down by the civil war. Polish noble families were fleeing in all directions; 120 of them even came and begged hospitality from Frederick in Potsdam. Once again Europe's intelligentsia was anxious to know which way the king of Prussia would leap. He contented himself with telling d'Alembert that he thought the Polish system of government the worst there was, with the exception of the Turks'.[20]

After a decade of discord and revolt, Frederick was more impatient with the Poles than ever. He too must have been anxious to see what would happen next in the political vacuum that was Poland. He had set up an armed cordon to ensure his communications with East Prussia, using an outbreak of plague as an excuse to move his troops into Polish Prussia. He put his views to Voltaire: 'Montesquieu would have wasted his time looking at them for the principles of republic or even a sovereign government. Self-interest, haughty pride, baseness and pusillanimity seem to be the fruits of their anarchic system. Instead of intellectuals you will find there minds rendered dumb by the stupidest superstition, and men committing all the crimes of which cowards are capable.'[21]

Now Henry was finally given the chance to show his mettle: Catherine was asking for him. He went to Sweden first to visit his sister. There was a little diplomacy to be effected there, reconciling Ulrica to the tsarina. He spent the winter of 1770–1 in Russia as Frederick's plenipotentiary, revelling in the splendour of everything he saw around him.[22] Henry was much keener on the idea of territorial expansion than his brother. He had his eyes on Swedish Pomerania (which fell to Prussia in 1815), believing that Sweden could be compensated in Finland; Mecklenburg (the duke would be offered Prussian Westphalia and Gelderland); Lusatia in exchange for Bayreuth and Ansbach; a bit of Bohemia on the right-hand side of the Elbe; Danzig, Thorn and Elbing. Thiébault observed, 'Clearly the First Partition of Poland was his invention.'[23]

Frederick did not wholly see eye to eye with his brother. He thought the Russians were unpleasant neighbours, to say the very least, and he did not want them to have any more land than they already had. The immediate cause of the partition was Frederick's feeling that the Russians should be kept sweet, which was why he had dispatched Catherine's childhood friend Henry in the first place. She was evidently pleased to see him. Henry told his brother on 8 January that Catherine the Great had made a suggestion:

'Why shouldn't everyone tuck in?' I replied that you, dear brother, had imposed a *cordon sanitaire* [against the plague] in Poland, but had not occupied a single starosty. 'But why shouldn't you occupy [one]?' said a laughing tsarina. A little while later Count Czernichev came up to me and brought the subject up again, concluding, 'Why don't you annex the bishopric of Ermland [i.e. Warmia]? After all, in the end, everyone should get something.[24]

The ball was in the Prussian court. Frederick was not overly impressed by the suggestion of taking the small Polish enclave around Frauenburg, which dug into his East Prussian land on the Frische Haff. He wrote back to Henry at the end of January:

As to the question of occupying the duchy of Warmia, I ruled that out, as the whole operation is not worth tuppence. The portion is so small that it fails to compensate for the song and dance it will necessarily drum up. On the other hand, Polish Prussia would be worth the trouble, even without Danzig, as then we would have the Vistula and what would be very important, free access to the kingdom [of Prussia] ... If you are too eager to snatch at trifles, it gives you a reputation for greed and insatiability which I don't want to have any more than I do already in Europe.[25]

It was Henry who convinced Frederick that an equal aggrandisement on the part of all Poland's neighbours would not upset the balance of power in Europe, while maintaining the alliance with Russia that he believed was in Prussia's interests. Now it was over to Panin and Kaunitz to make objections. The latter insisted that, if any redrawing were to be done to the map, it should be in Glatz and Silesia. He then pointed at Turkey and suggested that there was booty for all three in the Ottoman Empire. Next he decided that the huge lump of Poland being proposed for Austria was not big enough. Joseph was more of Frederick's way of thinking, though temporarily restrained by his mother, who did not like the idea of so many Catholics being condemned to Frederick's Protestant rule. Eventually even she relented. As Frederick put it sharply, 'She cried, but she grabbed.'[26]

Once it became clear that the partition was going ahead, Frederick decided which cuts of the turkey he would like best: Pomerelia, south of Danzig, the part of Great Poland that lay beyond the Netze, the bishopric of Warmia and the palatinates of Marienburg and Culm. He was also anxious to get his hands on Danzig and Thorn. The Russians, he alleged, had offered him the former, and then had withdrawn the offer, citing their 'guarantees' of Polish liberties. Frederick believed that the 'base perfidious' British had scuttled the acquisition because they did not want to see him master of the Vistula.[27] Frederick reconciled himself with the idea that he would get it in the long run,[28] possibly starving it out by transferring the port trade to Elbing. His sentiments closely followed those he had expressed in the 1768 *Testament politique*. In September 1773, he acquired 36,300 square kilometres. It was the smallest chunk: the Austrians had taken 81,900 and the Russians, 92,000.[29] He thanked Henry for (West) Prussia, 'which I have in some ways as a result of you'.[30]

Frederick had gained half a million inhabitants, of whom a third or so were of pure, Polish, Catholic stock, and the rest were made up of Germans, both Protestant and Catholic, Jews, Cassubians and Autochtones. The area around the confluence of the Vistula and the Nogat near the old Teutonic Knights' headquarters at Marienburg, as well as the more waterlogged Netze district, provided him with good fertile soils. Pomerelia and Culm's sandy earth interested him far less. Frederick felt he now had enough corn to eradicate the risk of famine in his lands. In his enlightened way, he felt he could offer the inhabitants of his new lands a more civilised existence than they had enjoyed under Polish rule. There was to be some compensation for the gentry, posts were to be established and there was to be justice, 'the name of which was scarcely known in these lands'. He planned and laid a canal to connect the Netze and Bromberg with the Vistula and the Oder; and he rebuilt the towns, which were 'in a most pitiful state. Culm had good walls and big churches; but instead of roads, you just saw the cellars of the houses which used to exist. The main square was made up of forty houses, of which twenty-eight had no doors, roofs, windows, or owners.'[31]

Frederick might not have been completely honest about the dilapidated state of West Prussia in his memoirs and letters. To Henry he wrote a letter expressing a sort of gratitude:

It is a very good and advantageous acquisition, both from a financial and a political point of view. In order to excite less jealousy I tell everyone that on my travels I have seen just sand, pine trees, heath land and Jews. Despite that there is a lot of work to be done; there is no order, and no planning and the towns are in a lamentable condition.[32]

One problem that Frederick had not fully evaluated before the partition was that he was about to increase substantially the number of Catholics in his kingdom: not just Germans, but antipathetic Poles too. Despite all he said, Frederick disliked Catholicism, which he believed to be more superstitious than the Reformed Church.[33] At the head of his new subjects was a clergy at best unwilling to serve their new temporal ruler. Frederick was undismayed. He thought he had a sympathetic ear in Voltaire. He wrote to him on 29 February 1773:

We are clearing up the chaos here, and our bishops will keep 24,000 thalers of income [and] the abbots seven thousand. The Apostles didn't have that much. It has been arranged in such a way as to alleviate them of their earthly cares, so that they might seek to gain that celestial Jerusalem which is their real home without distraction.[34]

He made a little concession to the clergy in his new provinces: he invited Ignaz Krasicki, the prince-bishop of Warmia, to open the long delayed Catholic church of Saint Hedwig in Berlin. Krasicki performed the inauguration on 1 November 1773, and stayed the night with Frederick in Potsdam. He was one '-ki' whom the king treated well.[35]

Voltaire was interested in Thorn, where, egged on by the Jesuits, Catholic Poles had beheaded ten Protestants in the so-called *Thorner Blutgericht* of 1724. Frederick had to explain that Thorn had not been in his portion, but that he was keen to honour the memory of the region's most famous son, Copernicus, who was buried in the cathedral at Frauenburg. Voltaire was pleased at Frederick's interest in the astronomer: 'Put up a little man on his ashes so that the sun, which he put in its proper place, should come and salute him every day at noon, its rays coupled with your own.'[36]

Copernicus was to be used as a metaphor for the introduction of the Enlightenment into Prussian Poland. Frederick contended (to Voltaire again) that Polish grandees had gone so far as to abolish schools in order to exercise their power without the slightest restriction. Frederick boasted to d'Alembert that he had founded twenty-four schools for Protestants and Catholics, 'and I regard myself as the Lycurgus and the Solon to these barbarians'. 'The Polish provinces may be compared to no state in Europe, they may only be likened to Canada [he persisted in likening his new subjects to Iroquois]. As a result we will need time and work to allow them to regain what bad administration has left in neglect for so many centuries.' It was important to reap what profits he might as quickly as possible. There were to be tolls for Danzig. Salt and tobacco monopolies were started and maps worked out of the different sectors.[37]

[11]

Frederick had already inherited a few Jesuits when he seized Silesia; now, with Ermland, West Prussia and the Netze, he had grabbed a few more. The Order of Jesus was the *bête noire* of enlightened thinkers, and its gradual eclipse in the different states of Europe, leading to its eventual banishment by order of Pope Clement XIV on 16 August 1773, was hailed as a triumph.[38] Ever contrary, Frederick the Great was in two minds. In May 1767 he celebrated the news that the order had been banned in Spain by writing to d'Alembert, 'Vivent les philosophes!' By February 1768 he was beginning to change his mind. He told the musical Maria Antonia of Saxony that he intended to keep his Jesuits. He even changed his tune with d'Alembert: 'I shall tolerate them as long as they stay quiet and don't try to murder anyone.'[39]

Frederick began to boast in April 1769 that anyone wanting to set eyes on one of the breed would have to come to Silesia. Elsewhere they had all been 'despotically' banished. D'Alembert enjoyed the joke too. He wrote to the king in June that year: 'It is going to be odd, Sire, that whereas Their Very Christian, Very Catholic, Very Apostolic and Very Faithful Majesties* are destroying the grenadiers of the Holy See, Your Most Heretical Majesty is the only one to preserve them.'[40] In October

---

* The kings and emperors of France, Spain, Austria and Portugal.

1773, only two months after the ban, Frederick felt he could boast a little of his achievements in his letter to Voltaire:

I have been in Prussia abolishing serfdom, reforming barbarous laws and promulgating more reasonable ones[. I have] opened a canal which joins up the Vistula, the Netze, the Warthe, the Oder and the Elbe, [started to] rebuild towns destroyed by the 1709 plague, drain the marshes and establish an administration in a land where my name was still unknown. From there I went to Silesia to console my poor Ignatians* for the rigours [imposed by] the court of Rome, to corroborate their order and form them into a corps in various provinces where I shall protect them and make them useful to their country by directing their schools and making them wholly responsible for training youth. On top of that I have arranged for the building of sixty villages in Upper Silesia, where there was nothing left but fallow land. Each village has twenty families. I have had some main roads laid in the mountains to help trade and rebuilt two towns which had been burned; they had been wood, now they will be [made of] brick and even ashlars quarried in the mountains.[41]

Voltaire was clearly incredulous. In December, Frederick wrote him a disingenuous letter further explaining his reasons for not publishing the Papal Bull in Prussia: 'I promised at the Peace of Dresden that as far as religion was concerned I would preserve the status quo in my provinces. Now, I had Jesuits, so I must keep them.' Unlike the Catholic princes, he continued, no one could absolve him of his pledge.[42] In reality he must have enjoyed the fun of annoying the pope, especially after his predecessor had given Daun a blessed sword and mitre. D'Alembert was given the comparison with 'men of letters': they were not exterminated because a few individuals 'had committed murders two hundred leagues from my country'. 'You accuse me of being too tolerant,' he told d'Alembert in one of his most famous statements. 'I glory in this failing, would it were so that one could only reproach sovereigns for such faults.'[43] Frederick, however, felt himself required to submit to at least some of the pope's rulings in 1776, in consultation with von Strachwitz, the prince-bishop of Breslau, who had been placed in an invidious position by the king's stance. He abolished the order, but retained them in their teaching roles.[44]

When the dust had settled in 1777, Frederick gave his old friend some

* Jesuits, after their founder, Saint Ignatius of Loyola.

more cogent reasons why he, the 'heretic and unbeliever', had preserved the Jesuits:

In our land there are no literate Catholics with the exception of the Jesuits; we have no one capable of taking classes, we have no Oratorians, no Piarists [and] the other monks are crassly stupid: it was therefore necessary to keep the Jesuits or allow all the schools to perish ... More, the priests who filled the positions of parish priests were trained at the Jesuit University...

Had they closed the seminary, the latter would have been obliged to study in Austrian Moravia.[45]

[III]

In 1774 Louis XV died. 'He was an honest man, who had no faults other than being king.'[46] Frederick was outliving not only all his friends, but also his enemies. The Tsarina Elisabeth was long gone, and Frederick was Russia's ally. Maria Theresa was to last until 1780.

He had greeted the death of Madame de Pompadour with an excess of bile. In his *Testament politique* he gave vent several times to his hatred of Louis' mistress. He even referred to his dogs as his 'marquises de Pompadour', adding that they cost him far less than his mistress had cost the king of France.[47] He had had cause to warn William against women; now he renewed his preaching for William's son, adding that wine was not good for him either. Henry IV and Louis XV had been brought low by the one; Good King Wenceslas and Alexander the Great by the other.[48]

Voltaire was in trouble again. His attempts at reconciliation with the Catholic church had provoked a mixture of mirth and disappointment in Prussia, where it might not have been fully appreciated that the old man was trying to square his welcome in Paris and at the court. Frederick had seized on some digs at him in *La Tactique*, and he tried to make amends in his *Voyage de la Raison et de la liberté* by showing what trouble Frederick had taken to treat the injured French soldiers after Rossbach, buying the linen from a neighbouring Schloss to dress their wounds: 'I can't get used to shedding French blood,' Frederick is alleged to have said.[49] Frederick got wind of a rumour that Voltaire had been ennobled as the *marquis* de Ferney. D'Alembert was quick to disillusion him, but Frederick used it to bait the old man and his pretensions to nobility. It would not have escaped Frederick's attention that Voltaire had followed the well-trodden path and bought himself a *charge* of *secrétaire du roi*, which allowed him to call himself monsieur *de* Voltaire.[50]

When he was not teasing him about his pretensions, Frederick liked to regale Voltaire with his achievements in his various provinces. In September 1777, Frederick returned from a trip to Silesia and shook the sand off his boots before writing to the sage of Ferney:

I was very pleased: agriculture has made very considerable progress; industry is prospering, we have exported five million thalers worth of linen and 1,200,000 worth of woollen cloth. A cobalt mine has been created in the mountains [Querbach]. We make vitriol which is as good as the foreign product [in Schreiberhau]. A very industrious man [Jacobi] in Nieder [Lobendau] makes indigo like the stuff from India [and] has turned iron into steel [Schawentzitz] with the advantage of being a lot easier than the method proposed by Réamur.

The epic correspondence was drawing to a close. On 25 January 1778, Frederick wrote to Voltaire: 'The pitiless gazettes have announced your death ... we were struck with terror.' Voltaire wrote from Paris on 1 April to reassure him: 'may Frederick the Great be the Immortal Frederick'. Voltaire was not; he died on 30 May. It was d'Alembert writing on 29 June who filled Frederick in on the involved circumstances of Voltaire's death. Despite all his flirting, the church had refused the application to bury him in the city and had decided that he must be buried in the monastery of his nephew, abbé Mignot, thirty leagues away at the abbaye de Scellières. To cap it all, the Académie française had refused a service for him. D'Alembert poured scorn on the 'stupid and ridiculous joy [expressed] by all fanatics about this death'.[51]

D'Alembert had told the old bedridden sage to feign Christianity. Voltaire had a horror of his body being cast into the open sewer, as that of his friend, the actress Adrienne Le Couvreur, had been. An abbé Gaultier had been with him for an hour and finished by demanding a written profession of faith. However, Voltaire recovered and, forgetting his promises to the church, went to the Académie française and presided over a session, then went to see his *Irène* at the Comédie. Here he was crowned with laurels by the actors, and his bust was brought on in the interval. He fell ill again at the end of April. Now the curé of the parish of Saint Sulpice demanded 'solemn and public repentance for the scandal he had caused', otherwise he would be denied consecrated ground. Voltaire gave him 25 Louis for the poor, but that was not enough. The dying Voltaire lost patience with the priest and waved him aside: 'Let me die in peace,' he said.[52]

D'Alembert thought Frederick should show up the Académie française by giving Voltaire a proper farewell in Berlin.[53] Frederick was now campaigning, but in the *longueurs* of his phoney war, Frederick penned an *Éloge de Voltaire* to be read in his Academy, in which he glossed over Voltaire's dreadful behaviour in Berlin. It was in the Academy that Frederick intended to put Voltaire's bust by Houdon and make a sort of shrine to his friend. D'Alembert had been keen for Frederick to buy the marble and set it up in the Catholic church of Saint Hedwig, doubtless as a provocation for the church that had behaved so narrow-mindedly at the time of the philosopher's death. Frederick went so far as to have a Mass said for Voltaire (how his friend would have laughed; and how the church authorities scowled), but he thought the Saint Hedwig unsuitable for a monument: it 'is modelled on the Pantheon in Rome, and it would not be possible to create a mausoleum without disfiguring it'.[54]

[IV]

Before he died, Voltaire had given his fullest support to Frederick's mounting attack on the German language and its literature. Whether he was quite the man to express a view is another matter: in nearly three years in Germany, Voltaire had made no attempt to learn German, and had restricted his circle entirely to Frenchmen (and women) and Germans who spoke French. Frederick would hardly have held that against him. He was consistent with all his visitors from abroad, and told them under pain of his displeasure not to undertake to learn the local language. Now, in the twilight of his existence, Frederick was observing a growing pride in their language among Germans and an equally strong desire to make something of German literature.

On 24 July 1775, Frederick had written to Voltaire:

Our Germans are ambitious to have their turn at playing with the advantages of the arts; and they are making their bid to equal Athens, Rome, Florence and Paris. Much as I love my country, I cannot say that they have succeeded up till now; two things are lacking, language and taste. The language is extremely verbose; proper society speaks French, and a few vain pedants and professors are not able to lend it the politeness or the turns of phrase which can only acquire in proper company. As regards philosophy, since the genius Leibniz and that great monad Wolff, no one has touched it.'[55]

In the circumstances, it was hardly surprising that Voltaire was sympathetic to Frederick, but his consolation contained a bitter truth: 'I think you judge German very well, and that cluster of words which goes into a sentence and that multitude of syllables which goes into a word, and a taste which is no better formed than the language; the Germans are at the dawn; they would have been at high noon, had you deigned to write German verse.'[56] Voltaire was almost certainly twisting the king's tail, but the point had been made as long before as 1760 by Moses Mendelssohn, who was moved to lament the loss to the German language caused by Frederick's affection for French. Frederick took Voltaire's point in his reply: 'I should have liked to have contributed to their birth; but what could a being do who was bogged down in war for two-thirds of his span, and obliged to make good the evils that they have caused and without the talent for such grand projects.'[57]

Frederick felt that German culture had been nipped in the bud by the Thirty Years War. 'Taste will only be disseminated in Germany by a reflective study of the classical authors, Greek, Roman and French, Two or three geniuses will correct the language, will render it less barbarous and will bring home the masterpieces made by foreigners.'[58] Frederick seemed to be calling for a Goethe – who was later to domesticate Greek tragedy with *Iphigenie auf Tauris* – and a Schiller; but he had the chance to read and judge both, and reject them out of hand: two more prophets who found no royal recognition in their own land.

Frederick was enjoying his black thoughts about the German language when he saw his minister Graf Hertzberg. Frederick told him that he thought it doubtful that Tacitus could be as well translated into German as French. Hertzberg took that as a challenge. On 29 April 1779, he wrote to the king: 'I take the liberty of presenting a chapter of Tacitus's *Germania* to Your Majesty, which I have translated into German and French. It strikes me that the German version is in no way inferior to the French either in purity or precision.'[59] Frederick being Frederick, he started to put his thoughts down on paper. The result was *De la littérature allemande, des défauts qu'on peut lui reprocher, quelles en sont les causes, et par quelles moyens on peut les corriger* of 1780. He had rehearsed some of his arguments with Voltaire. He attacked the language itself first, and the multiplicity of its dialects, which meant that a Swabian could not understand a Hamburger, and that Austrian style seemed obscure in Saxony: 'It is therefore physically impossible for an author, with a gift of fine genius, to work this rough language into a superior product.'[60]

It was a pity that the crusty old king could find no one at the time who was able to point out a few authors who were writing in a language that was intelligible to educated Germans. For all the king's claims, he had not been looking in the right place. Frederick persisted: 'I am undertaking research to establish our Homers, Virgils, Anacreons, Horaces, Demostheneses, Thucydides and Livys; I can find nothing, all my labours are lost.' He opened his hand: there were three names: Gellert, Canitz and Gessner.[61] 'I shall not speak of German theatre. Melpomene has been courted only by rough lovers, either hoisted on stilts, or crawling in mud, both of whom, ignorant of her laws, know neither how to interest her nor how to touch her and have been rejected from her altars.'[62]

Frederick put his finger on some of the genuine drawbacks of the German language. Authors 'pile parenthesis upon parenthesis, and often you find only at the end of an entire page the verb on which depends the meaning of the whole sentence'.[63] English was no better: 'The sharp sounds in their language shock foreign ears. Other languages lose something in translation; English alone gains.' He had seen some Shakespeare. His judgement was even more jaundiced than Voltaire's had been: 'Ridiculous farces worthy of Canadian savages ... How can this bizarre mix of baseness and grandeur, of tragedy and burlesque, be attractive to anyone?' The one work of Goethe he knew, *Götz von Berlichingen*, was just a 'hateful imitation of a bad English play'.[64]

He was not calling for a Marot, a Rabelais or a Montaigne: Germany needed Corneille and Racine. The basic sounds of German would not do. You could do nothing with *sagen, geben* or *nehmen*. Frederick's suggestion was to add an 'a' at the end to give them a down beat: 'sagena', 'gebena', 'nehmena'. The ancients had to be translated into correct German. But for all his criticism, Frederick was not wholly negative. 'The fine days of our literature have not yet come; but they are approaching.'[65]

Hertzberg stuck to his guns. He followed up with another translation into German from Tacitus and flanked it with the standard French text by Amelot de la Houssaye, 'which strikes me as a paraphrase which has been totally frenchified without the translator coming to terms with the real meaning of the Latin'. Hertzberg was prepared to agree, however, that 'the German language still has great need of purification and enrichment'.[66] Frederick replied within a quarter of an hour. He was kind to his minister: 'This is some good German, one of the best bits I have ever seen.' There were some small objections: he preferred the Latin *Exempel* to the Teutonic *Beispiel*. 'It is certain that if people of your capacity became involved in forming the German language, there would be no question of success.'[67]

Hertzberg had done well. He now convinced the king to read some German fiction: Ludwig Heinrich Nicolai's *Das Schöne*. Frederick picked up one or two stylistic mistakes. 'Brennende Wangen' (burning cheeks), he thought an 'impertinent hyperbole'. It could be an angry or a drunken man, but not a happy prince. Eventually Frederick declared he had had enough of this game: he had been mild in his criticism of the German language; he could have gone far further.[68] He was rather proud of his essay and it was well distributed. Naturally, many German intellectuals, even then at the beginning of the first great literary flowering of the language, took Frederick's words ill. For many it must have seemed like a form of betrayal.

[v]

Frederick's last philosophical writing dates from the late 1770s. The *Exposé du Gouvernement prussien, des principes sur lequel il roule, avec quelques refléxions politiques* was written for Henry's edification. Frederick was keen to stress the importance of finance, which was like 'the nerves of the human body'. Frederick's simple mercantilism has often come under attack. Some have asserted that he stuck with the wisdom of Hille, and the training he received in Küstrin, but this is now disputed. Frederick left nothing to chance: he was 'one of the most active and effective economic politicians of the eighteenth century'. This fact was proved, perhaps, by his ability to put Prussia back on track after 1763. Austria could not manage it; nor, notably, could France.[69]

Many of his decisions in financial matters were taken with a view to a contractual relationship between the monarch and his people, an idea gleaned from reading Locke and Wolff. He could not abolish serfdom because that would lead to a serious loss of income among the poor provincial nobility in areas of sandy steppes such as Pomerania.[70] He scrapped his father's, and indeed Hille's, teaching when he created the fifth department of the Generaldirektorium, with responsibility for trade and manufacture, under Samuel von Marschall. As he grew older, his interest in economic theory developed too, and he read the latest outpourings of the French economists who immediately prefigured the physiocrats, such as Jean-François Melon's *Essai politique sur le commerce.* This gave him the idea of introducing a free trade in grain, while limiting the import of foreign manufactured goods, and banning the export of raw materials.[71]

The *Exposé* contained the usual instructions to keep the army strong and to beware of idleness. Frederick was aware of his successor's limited interest in military matters. He explained the Russian alliance on the basis that it was necessary to form pacts with those states that could do you the greatest harm. Russia protected Prussia's back in the east, and prevented the Swedes from attacking in Pomerania. Henry was told where future conquests might lie: Saxony again, or Bohemia and Moravia, which could be swopped for Prussia's west German provinces. His thoughts on Saxony were governed by the need to protect Berlin: 'a village on the frontier is worth more than a distant principality'.[72]

Different forms of administration also interested the old king. The *Essai sur les Formes de gouvernement et sur les devoirs des souverains* was written in 1777. Frederick put monarchy under the microscope: 'the best and the worst [system] of all, depending on how it is administered'. The worst was elective monarchy; the unique Polish example (Frederick had forgotten about Venice) 'abominable'.[73] Frederick repeats his austere conception of kingship:

the first magistrate, the first general, the first financier, the first minister of the society, he is not there to represent, but in order to fulfil his duties. He is no more than the first servant of the state, obliged to act with probity, wisdom and disinterest, as if he had to give a report on the conduct of his administration to his citizens.[74]

It was the organic relationship of the head to the body. He comes down hard on mistresses: their power serves 'to commit injustices, to protect immoral people, to sell offices and other similar infamies'.[75]

[VI]

In April 1778 an old man went to war. Goethe was in Berlin, delighting in the feeling of sitting in the kettle as it was about to boil over. All around him he saw men ready to sacrifice their lives in fresh battles, while horses, carriages and cannons plied the city's majestic streets.[76] Frederick's disciple Joseph II had learned his lessons well. The Austrian wanted to redesign his land and make it look more like a state than a loose collection of territories. The immediate pretext was the death of the last of the Bavarian Wittelsbachs at the end of 1777. It was not just that Bavaria struck him as the best piece to round off Austrian territory to the north; he thought he had a made a more than generous offer in proposing that the Wittelsbachs receive the Austrian Low Countries in return.

Frederick thought Joseph had been toying with territorial expansion ever since his father died from smallpox in 1765. Not content with his chunk of Poland, he was prepared to move in on Bavaria. 'From then on war became almost inevitable; as we were informed of the unbounded ambition of the imperial court and the cupidity of the young emperor ...'[77] Joseph had manifested no desire to fight Prussia. He tried to keep Frederick away with promises of Bayreuth and Ansbach when those dynasties died out. Henry took that idea at face value. The Bavarian Wittelsbachs could simply accept what they were being offered. Frederick, however, decided to come to the aid of the Empire: he did not want further Habsburg encroachment in Germany. He might have realised that there was a growing fear of Prussian involvement in southern Germany, now that a Protestant line had been established in Baden, and it looked likely that both Bayreuth and Ansbach would fall to Frederick before long. His own interests were at stake: in January 1778 he began to mobilise.[78]

Frederick did not reach his usual stations in Bohemia until July. He was the poacher turned gamekeeper. His allies were the Russians and the Reich, and his 140,000 troops made their way to their usual positions in Bohemia and Moravia in the company of 21,000 Saxons. The Russians stood by and watched, but their commitment worried the Austrians.[79] On 11 August, Frederick wrote to Henry, who was leading Prussia's second army: 'The empress-queen has written to me ... she made a strange proposal, she would restore the entirety of Bavaria on condition that we renounce for ever our claims to Ansbach. We need to beat these buggers in order to inspire a few more reasonable sentiments in them.'[80]

They called it the 'Kartoffelkrieg' and the 'Zwetschgenrummelkrieg' in Austria because the idle Prussian troops foraged for potatoes and the Austrians ate stewed plums.[81] The war is supposed to have greatly advanced the cause of the potato in central Europe.[82] Frederick wrote to Catt in August: 'may the Holy stomach of His Imperial Majesty return this Bavaria which he has swallowed too quickly; and which is giving him indigestion'.[83] Most of the losses were caused by freak weather in the summer of 1778, desertion and dysentery: the Prussian army went home depleted by 30,000 men. Frederick suffered from constant ill-health too. There were no battles to raise his spirits, just a sad little skirmish at Habelschwerdt in January, where the Prussians got the worst of it.[84]

Despite his diplomatic triumph in Russia at the beginning of the decade, when he brought home West Prussia and the Netze, Henry was no better prepared to serve his brother than he had been during the second half of the Seven Years War. He would no longer heed Frederick's entreaties that he should stay in command until Prussia could at least dictate terms; he claimed he could not face the hardships of war any more, and retired.[85] In December 1778 he was replaced by the hereditary prince Charles William Ferdinand of Brunswick.

Frederick was still relying on the Russians in Moravia, so that he could push the war down to the Danube.[86] In February 1779, the Austrians were retreating: they had been chased out of all but a tiny portion of the county of Glatz, and Frederick was able to report with pleasure that the Austrians had abandoned Braunau on the Inn.[87] They were to win it as part of their concessions in the peace treaty. Braunau's most famous son, Adolf Hitler, would therefore be born an Austrian, not a Bavarian, 110 years later.

Much to Joseph's annoyance, his mother started peace negotiations behind his back. On 13 May 1779 the Peace of Teschen was signed on Maria Theresa's sixty-second birthday. Frederick gained his right to succeed in the two west German Hohenzollern margravates of Bayreuth and Ansbach, and the Austrians won 2000 square kilometres on the Inn, with 60,000 inhabitants.[88] It proved a diplomatic victory if nothing else. Frederick found himself in a new, but not unattractive role as Europe's elder statesman.

Russia had won a seat for itself at the top table, despite offering no material assistance to Prussia in the course of the war. The following year, the Russians switched horses and allied themselves to Austria. They had business in common in the outlying territories of the Ottoman Empire, which were certainly not worth the bones of a Prussian grenadier. Not only were Frederick's armies depleted, but he came back to Berlin to find that yet another of his cronies had gone the way of all flesh: the last hereditary earl Marischal. As the campaign got under way, Milord had seized the moment to die, but not without wit. He summoned the British envoy, Elliot, on 23 May 1778: 'I called you, because I find pleasure in emitting the last sighs of a Jacobite to a minister of King George.'[89]

Frederick's problems with Austria did not end there. Frederick had never had much time for the Holy Roman Empire. It was an 'ancient folly', its envoys dogs barking at the moon, its bishops drunks, he told Voltaire.[90] He was content to allow it to continue, but took no notice of those, like the Alte Dessauer and Podewils, who thought he should make a bid to have himself elected emperor. There was also an attempt to have Prussia made permanent head of the imperial armed forces, which Frederick pushed away with contempt. He was ably served in Regensburg by his ambassador there, Erich Christoph von Plotho, who did nothing to tone down Frederick's scornful messages.[91] Joseph's behaviour during the War of the Bavarian Succession, however, changed Frederick's thinking on the Reich. He was upset that Austria had decided to pick the remaining flesh off the imperial carcass, and decided to make himself the champion of imperial law. As he put it in a deathbed conversation with his doctor, Zimmermann, 'Germany is a sort of republic; it is in danger of losing its republican form, and it is a real pleasure for me to re-establish it.'[92]

Frederick did control a sort of block vote in Regensburg. Since Saxony had gone over to Catholicism, Frederick had become the head of the *Corpus Evangelicorum*, as he put it; he was to some extent the pope of all German Lutherans. At the time of the short-lived, ill-fated Emperor Charles VII, Frederick had shown some interest in forming an organisation for the defence of the Reich against Habsburg encroachments. In 1784 he returned to the idea with his *Fürstenbund*, or league of princes. The pact was signed on 23 July 1785, uniting Prussia, Saxony, Brandenburg and Hanover, together with an impressive clutch of secondary German powers. It was strength in numbers, a defensive alliance against Habsburg attack. It was also the beginning of a German national consciousness, and all the more important in that it already excluded the multi-ethnic Habsburg Empire. The first German nationalists were not slow to seize on it, and misinterpret its creator, turning him into the founding father of a country that could not have been further from his thoughts.[93]

CHAPTER FOURTEEN

Twilight

[1]

At the end of his life, Frederick had problems with the law. The case of a miller called Johannes Arnold was brought to his attention. Arnold lived near Küstrin, on the right bank of the Oder. Although he owned his mill, his status as a peasant meant that he had to pay dues to the local lord of the manor, Graf von Schmettau. Next door to Schmettau lived Frederick's local representative, a *Landrat*, von Gersdorff. The stream that fed Arnold's mill ran into the Oder. It passed through both Schmettau's and Gersdorff's estates. Gersdorff dug a carp pond, and Arnold claimed that he could no longer make enough money to pay Schmettau his feudal dues, because he was not getting any water. Schmettau's manorial court dismissed Arnold's excuses. Arnold took it to the local administration in Küstrin, which told him that he might bring a case against Gersdorff. This he neglected to do. He also persisted in refusing to pay Schmettau the 300 thalers he owed. As a result, Schmettau put the mill up for auction to recover the money.[1]

The mill was eventually bought by Gersdorff, who sold it on to a widow. Arnold and his wife (the leading spirit in the affair) started petitioning the king. Through the son of Frederick's minister, Graf Finck von Finckenstein, they succeeded in drawing Frederick's attention to their plight: 'The miller shall have justice!'[2] exclaimed the king and appointed a two-man commission to examine the case. The two judges failed to come to an agreement. One wanted to look at the pond; the other thought that a case should be brought against Gersdorff. Frederick now got it into his head that the nobility were abusing the local peasantry. His wrath was terrible. He ordered the local administration to re-examine the case. They came to the same conclusion. 'That this case be brought before the higher court, and great care is to be taken that justice will be pronounced in the autumn,'[3] said Frederick, transferring it to the supreme jurisdiction: the Kammergericht in Berlin.

In the meantime Frederick sent an officer to Küstrin to inspect the pond and the mill. He reported that the Arnolds had spoken the truth.

The Kammergericht, on the other hand, came down on the side of the Küstrin authorities: Arnold should bring a civil action against Gersdorff. Frederick was furious and rounded on his judges with a succession of choice epithets. When Frederick showed an imperfect knowledge of the nomenclature of the Prussian courts, his chancellor, Carl Joseph Maximilian von Fürst, corrected him. That was the final straw: 'Get out, I've already filled your position.' He allegedly chased the whole pack of them out of his study, calling them scum and kicking them in the backs of their legs.[4] The Arnolds got their mill back. Fürst got the sack, along with Finck von Finckenstein and Gersdorff. The seven judges involved in the case were sent to Spandau for a year. One of them, Neumann, whiled away the time writing an amusing diary. Frederick wrote to Finck's father to explain his imprisonment of the judges: 'The blindfold of justice has closed the eyes of these gentlemen, they can see only prevarications.'[5]

Frederick was not a believer in an independent judiciary. As he told his minister Zedlitz when none of the courts would revise their judgements, despite the king's fury, 'If you are not going to pronounce, I will do it, and my verdict is the following: I am firing these judicial bastards and I am sending them to prison.'[6] What the local authorities almost certainly knew, and Frederick did not, was that Arnold was no 'capable miller', simply a liar. There was another mill between his and Gersdorff's pond, and that had never ceased to function. The judges were not put on trial, but were arbitrarily arrested and imprisoned. In the interests of protecting his peasantry, Frederick had behaved like a common tyrant.

His behaviour incensed his nobles, but made him the hero of the little people all over Europe. He had the following published on 14 December 1779 in the official *Berlinsche Nachrichten von Staats- und gelehrten Sachen*:

The courts must know that the most humble peasant, a beggar even, is just as much a man as the king. All men are equal before the law, whether it happens to be a prince pleading against a peasant or vice versa. A bench which arrives at a false judgement is worse and more dangerous than a bunch of thieves: from the one you can protect yourself; but no man may take refuge from rogues who use the cloak of justice to indulge their evil passions.[7]

Frederick cannot have known what he was starting. While the nobles sulked with him, peasants congregated before the Berlin Schloss that carnival, some armed with petitions, and shouted, 'Long live our king, who helps the poor peasant to get justice!' The story travelled far and wide. Catherine the Great had Frederick's pronouncement translated into Russian and distributed to the courts. Later Frederick admitted that he had over-reacted. In his *injustice*, Frederick reaped a reputation as the most just prince in Europe, however, and the effect was noticeable in Prussia too: it speeded up the process of judicial reform. After long deliberation, Frederick went forward with his codification of the law in 1780. More enlightened jurists such as Johann-Heinrich von Carmer replaced Fürst, and together with Carl Gottlieb Svarez, they put the final touches to the *Allgemeine Landrecht*, which was, in some ways, Frederick's abiding monument.

Although it was not published until 1794, eight years after Frederick's death, and was softened and bent in the light of fear caused by the French Revolution, the new code represented the sum total of Frederick's attempts to create an advanced body of law – 'a faithful mirror image of Frederick's Prussia', one historian has called it.[8] Some minor reforms were contained in its clauses. There was a small modification of the position on nobles and trade, possibly because the king had seen how successful the Silesian nobility had been, possibly because Frederick could no longer justify his pronouncements on human equality and maintain the laws on derogation. Serfdom was only partially abolished in Silesia and East and West Prussia, and then only on crown land. But even then there were loud cries of protest from the provincial nobility. It was defeat in 1806 that finally silenced most of the feudal critics.

[II]

Frederick was not just the elder statesman, he was the grand old man of Europe: visitors never stopped their pilgrimages to Prussia and Potsdam to see the 'alte Fritz'. On 11 July 1780, the Austrian general Prince Charles de Ligne was presented to Frederick once again. Frederick invited Ligne, his son Charles and the poet Jacques Delille to lunch during his stay. The chief interest in Delille was that Voltaire had died in his arms. Ligne's celebrated charm seems to have worked on the king again. They had not seen one another since Neustadt in 1770. Together they relived the campaigns of the Seven Years War, but Frederick stayed off the subject of the conflict that had ended a year before. Ligne rightly took this to mean that he was not proud of Prussia's performance. He wisely kept quiet about his last visit to Sanssouci while Austrian hussars smashed Frederick's marbles in Charlottenburg.

They were on safer ground with art, strategy, medicine, literature,

religion, philosophy, history and the law. The banter continued for a full
five hours. They fell out over Virgil's talents as a gardener. Frederick had
planned the park at Sanssouci with a volume of the *Georgics* in his hand,
'But my gardener said to me, "You are mad, and that book too."' At
another meal, Ligne showed a tactful interest in Frederick's porcelain,
and must have pleased him by taking it for Meissen. If Ligne was
unimpressed by Prussia, where everything was done by force, down to
the growing of oranges and lemons, he was captivated by the 'old wizard',
as he called him.[9]

In September, Charlotte called to see him. There was a family lunch in
Potsdam, at which Amalia was present. Frederick was still busy with the
inferiority of German literature. His sisters defended it. Charlotte knew
better what she was talking about: she had taken Lessing in and given him
the position of her court librarian.[10] From May that year Frederick had had
the companionship of the marchese Girolamo Lucchesini, who was made a
chamberlain, but whose real job was keeping him company at the dining
table. That meant anything from one hour to three, while the old king put
literature, politics, the economy and strategy to rights.[11]

Frederick continued to keep regular hours, rising astonishingly early: in
summer just after three, and rarely later than four. Another fact that gives
the lie to the various tales of his sexual wantonness is his extreme prudery.
His servant Schöning, who occupied a position of great trust at the end
of Frederick's life, maintained that he could not suffer anyone to see him
without his clothes on, and would not even attend to a call of nature in
their presence. He relaxed at the concert at 6 p.m., after which Quintus,
or another member of his literary circle, would be called upon to talk to
him until he retired. Since he no longer dined, he could be certain of
being in bed by ten.[12]

He enjoyed his food, curious as it was. Breakfast consisted of cold
meats and fruit in season: cherries, strawberries or melons; as well as sweet
things, such as meringues. For 'dinner' – that is, the meal corresponding to
our lunch – there were seven to ten dishes laid out in the old French
service, and often no dessert other than his favoured fruit, which sat
about his palaces in bowls ready for his needs. Schöning later denied that
Frederick had added spoonfuls of spices to his meals to make them
hotter, but others dispute this and the dishes betrayed a heavy hand
wherever pepper, nutmeg or ginger were concerned. Zimmermann saw
him eat an eel pâté which was so hot that one of His Majesty's dining
companions claimed it looked as if 'it had been cooked in Hell'. Thiébault

tells the story of his chef Noël, who was asked if he really had to put so much spice in the soup. The chef replied, '*Parbleu* ... if you made me eat it all up by myself there would be less.'[13]

Frederick ate on impulse, generally too much and too fast, giving himself colic or indigestion. He told Catt that 'Like a pregnant woman, I have disorderly cravings.' The dishes were a blend of French and Italian: broth inflamed with ginger and nutmeg, boiled beef with vodka, polenta with an inch-thick crust of parmesan cheese and more spices, noodle pasties, savoury puddings and macaroni with parmesan cheese, butter and garlic; as well as a few of the doughtier German foods beloved of his father – cabbage or sauerkraut, eel pâtés and yellow peas. He loved cheeses and had them brought to him from all over Europe.[14] One of the jobs of his French correspondent Thiériot was to send him regular consignments of brie[15] from Meaux.[16]

He maintained a lifelong fondness for tokay and champagne, and avoided hock, which he claimed to have been responsible for his gout. As far as he was concerned, his father's favourite wine was 'a foretaste of hanging'.[17] German wines in general, and that meant the infamous Grünberger, were to be avoided. He was no great drinker, and although he liked to ape French courtly manners and be served only sparkling champagne, he added water to it. For dinner he had just a cup of chocolate and some fruit. The years of experimenting with coffee were over, when he thought he could use it to rid him of the need for sleep. Now he had just six to eight cups laced with mustard and peppercorns.[18] We know the complete menu for one of his last meals, on 5 August 1786: broccoli soup *à la Fouqué*,[19] beef in breadcrumbs with carrots, chicken with cinnamon and stuffed cucumbers in the English style (Frederick crossed it out and asked for cutlets), little pasties *à la Romaine*, young roast hake, salmon *à la Dessau*, chicken fillet *à la Pompadour* with ox tongues and croquettes, Portuguese cake, green peas, fresh herrings and gherkins.[20]

[III]

The *Rétablissement* continued after the hiccough of the war, although Frederick claimed to have no money, even to the degree of having to save up to buy the Houdon bust of Voltaire. He was still issuing rescue packages in the last years of his life. There was a bad harvest in 1782, and he distributed 200,000 thalers in aid. That year he built over fifty houses in Berlin and established weavers' colonies in Luckenwalde and

Treuenbrietzen, as well as factories making watches and Dutch-style paper. In the Neumark he built dykes on the Warthe. The investments made in his various provinces that year amounted to 2,118,000 thalers. Surprisingly enough, the lion's share went to Magdeburg, but substantial amounts were still going to war-torn Pomerania, and Frederick's largest province, East Prussia.[21] In January 1783, Freiherr Friedrich Anton von Heinitz reported that Frederick continued to 'govern without counsel and to carry out his own plans'.[22]

Frederick could survey the scene with a certain smugness: *il a echappé belle*. He watched France's reaction to the fundamentalist Christophe de Beaumont, the new archbishop of Paris who had been responsible for having the abbé de Prades' thesis burned. It was an appointment that had raised Louis XVI's eyebrows; Frederick agreed (but for different reasons): he was 'worthy of being the archbishop of the devil'.[23] He was amused to watch his old disciple and adversary, Joseph II, setting to work abolishing the minor and mendicant orders in his lands. He wrote to d'Alembert: 'All is calm. We are creating nothing. We limit ourselves to enjoying what we already have; and while the emperor is squabbling with the pope, and you lot with the English, I am rolling my barrel like Diogenes in order not to be the only person with nothing to do.'[24] In September 1783 he was boasting that he was rebuilding Catholic churches while Joseph was destroying them: 'I leave everyone the liberty to think as they will.'[25] Ironically, there was now talk of nuns fleeing Joseph's lands and seeking asylum in Silesia.[26]

D'Alembert died later that year. The news was broken by Grimm on 31 October. The German baron later proved his worth by snaffling up Frederick's voluminous correspondence and preventing its publication. Despite the fidelity of d'Alembert, and the calm relations they had enjoyed for nearly thirty years, Frederick did not intend to set up a monument to him, as he had previously done for Algarotti, d'Argens, Copernicus and (of a sort) Voltaire.[27] The transition was smooth, and slightly heartless. Before the year was out, d'Alembert's place had been taken by the marquis Antoine de Condorcet, who also took over one of d'Alembert's most important functions: finding new talent for Frederick's Academy.[28]

The king's pleasures were those of an old man: his few surviving friends, reliving the past and moderate eating and drinking. In February 1784 he had a visit from the last of the Rheinsberg circle, Chasot, who still lived in Lübeck. 'He speaks only of the edible, champagne, hock, madeira, tokay and the high-living gentlemen who operate the stock exchange in Lübeck, of that great river, the Trave, the port, and of his garden, of which he made an exact count of the trees, shrubs, plants, vegetables and herbs which make it as beautiful as it is.'[29] His favourite was the Graf Friedrich Albrecht von Schwerin. He was amazed by the evenness of Schwerin's temper. Schwerin attributed it to the influence of his two good friends: 'Who are they?' Frederick wanted to know. 'The first is the Good Lord, who has always been kind to me, although last year he let my barn in Silesia go up in smoke; the second is Your Majesty, even if you are sometimes cross with me, you are often good to me with it.' The next day Frederick saw Schwerin: 'Your first friend has given me the job of making reparations for the damage caused by the fire. Here are 2000 thalers.' Schwerin replied, 'Amen!'[30]

Voltaire's modest monument might have had something to do with his *Mémoires*, which began to circulate in 1784. Goethe obtained a copy and wrote to Frau von Stein that Voltaire spoke of Frederick 'like Suetonius on the *scandalosa* of the emperors': 'a lovely paliative', he called them. Later he heard an unfounded rumour that Frederick was trying to have the memoirs suppressed.[31] That Frederick never undertook such a thing is greatly to his credit (see above, p. 272). In November 1785, to the French ambassador, comte Antoine d'Esterno, who in the circumstances might have been the first to feel his wrath, he reiterated his indifference to this sort of defamatory literature. Frederick read it if it was well-written and asked the booksellers how well it was selling.[32]

But the moments of good will were brief. Frederick was an irritable old man, unstinting, unsleeping, never content with those around him. He was literally a fright to behold. Gräfin Henriette Egloffstein caught sight of the king from her carriage. He was on horseback, riding at the head of his troops. He wore a shabby uniform and a big feather hat pulled down over his face. His nose was huge, his mouth a little slit. The most noticeable feature, however, were his big blue eyes, which promptly turned upon the young countess, 'giving her a piercing stare, so that I pulled back my head in horror'.[33]

He could still impress some of the younger generation of *philosophes* with his ideas of justice and tolerance. Condorcet wanted to hear about his legal system. He learned that Frederick had abolished torture almost fifty years earlier. It was simply not an efficient way of discovering the truth. The death sentence was carried out only for 'atrocious crimes', such as patricide. It was seen as a deterrent, nothing more. Frederick believed life imprisonment to be worse than death, although the threat of execution was necessary to intimidate malefactors. Condorcet, whose life and body were cut short by the Terror, revealed himself to be an enemy of capital punishment too. In November 1785 he saw a hope that the old soldier would now become the guarantor of peace: 'The whole of Europe expects only that Your Majesty maintain the calm we currently enjoy. It is a glory which was reserved for you, and which no warrior hero has ever deserved before.'[34]

Three days before Christmas, Frederick had his last visit from General Zieten. As the 'Hussar King' came into the room, Frederick got to his feet and hugged him: 'There is my good old Zieten!' And then turning to his servants, 'Quickly, bring up an armchair.' The old Spartan objected: stools were more his thing. He liked hard chairs, did not possess a dressing gown and never wore anything but uniform. Neither tea nor coffee ever passed his lips. Frederick, however, insisted: 'Let him sit, old father, sit down, my dear Zieten, else I shall go away, for the last thing I want is to be a burden to him.'[35]

There were still frequent callers, chiefly Frenchmen. Lafayette came in the summer of 1785, and observed the manoeuvres in Silesia; Frederick was soaked to the skin one day, and the chill he caught then was never to leave him. Mirabeau – the nephew of Frederick's Bayreuth plenipotentiary – was the most famous of those who hung about the king in his dying months. He was left in peace to damn all and sundry, even Frederick, without anyone calling him to order.[36] It was he who concocted the famous line about Prussia being an army in control of a state. It might have been true of Frederick's father, but it was not really true of Frederick. The marquis de Bouillé saw him then, a little man who stooped and walked with a cane. He might have been debilitated, but he paused for no one. In the last years of his life, Frederick was immensely busy. He told the all-licensed Lucchesini he would die at his desk. Floods that spring had destroyed the dykes on the Warthe, Vistula and Oder; he was importing merino lambs, and wanted to see the beasts at Sanssouci before dispatching them to their new homes.[37]

On 6 June 1786, Frederick was suffering from serious asthma. He wrote to the duke of York's physician, Johann Georg Zimmermann, who had treated him once before in 1771.[38] Zimmermann arrived on the 24th and found the king sitting in a chair, wearing an old hat, a stained overcoat and boots, with one badly swollen leg propped up on a stool. He was suffering from gout, asthma and wind, possibly chronic malaria too; more seriously, he was coughing up blood: 'I'm nothing more than an old carcass, good only for throwing in the gutter.' There was a fear of dropsy, but Zimmermann thought he had bronchial catarrh. Frederick proved a difficult patient; the amateur physician was all too happy to countermand the proposed cure. He might, however, have been right about its inefficacy: it was composed chiefly of dandelion syrup, which, being a diuretic, was intended to shed some of the king's excess water. He continued to torture himself with gassy foods and as medicine advocated rhubarb and fresh herrings. Zimmermann was frustrated with his patient to the degree that he allowed himself to say, 'The only dangerous enemies Your Majesty has are his cooks.'[39]

Zimmermann left Potsdam and Frederick on 10 July. About this time, the marquis Hipplyte de Toulongeon came to Potsdam, expecting an audience with the king. Frederick was too ill to see him, but Toulongeon was able to bribe the porter at Sanssouci, who concealed him behind a fence. After a wait, the door opened and Frederick was brought out by two valets. 'He was sitting in an armchair; I saw this old hero who had made his enemies shake with fear so much, struck down, crushed by disease, his face was white and totally transformed by suffering...'[40] Frederick was crawling ineluctably towards death. There were no more distractions, no more concerts. In a last letter to Henry, he made him a loan of Franz Benda.[41]

Ministers and members of his family began to gather in Sanssouci from 9 July: Hertzberg, Lucchesini and Schwerin were now permanently in residence. Apart from the heir apparent, the rest of the family kept their distance. His poor, forgotten queen, Elisabeth, heard about his illness. Frederick wrote her a cold note in answer to her solicitations: 'Madame, I am most obliged to you for the good wishes you deign to send, but the massive fever which I have prevents me from giving you an answer.'[42] In his last letters to Charlotte and Amalia on 6 and 10 August, the philosophic Frederick was still apparent. Seventy-four was a good age after all: 'The old must make room for the young,' he said.[43]

He was confined to a chair; but he did not cease working. He still got up between 4 and 5 a.m. and received his cabinet secretaries with the morning's business. At eight he was dressed and then worked further on state papers. For nourishment in the evening his reader fed him his favourite extracts from Cicero and Plutarch. This slightly truncated royal regime continued until 15 August. The next day he was unable to work. He died at 2.20 on the morning of the 17th in the arms of his *valet de chambre* Strützki. His last words were 'La montagne est passée, nous irons mieux.'[44]

[IV]

Frederick's death was anti-climactic. He had outlived his friends, outlived most of his family, outlived his fashions, his music, his art, his philosophy and his literature. Mirabeau rather conceitedly noted that his death made little of a splash in Berlin. Prussia was indifferent: 'no regrets, no sighs, no epitaphs'.[45] Frederick's call for a philosopher's funeral and a simple burial on the terrace beside his dogs was ignored. He lay in state in the Stadtschloss before being taken over to the Garrison Church and laid to rest in the crypt, alongside the father who had so effectively broken and remoulded him. His successor, Frederick William II, feared the summer heat, and the whole burial process took place in an indecently hasty forty-two hours. An official funeral with a dummy coffin followed on 9 September. It was for this occasion that Reichardt composed his manly Latin *Trauerkantate*. The notes were spare, as Reichardt was no Graun. There were no rococo frills at the great man's passing.[46]

Up in Rheinsberg Henry must have breathed a sigh of relief. He could go ahead with building an obelisk in the park, on which he intended to commemorate all those whose memories had been poorly served by his brother the king; 'about whom his fucking memoirs say nothing'. Chief among them was his brother William.[47]

They were not all so black hearted as his brothers. Eight months after the king's death, Goethe was in Sicily, enjoying an *al fresco* dinner in Caltanisetta and answering the enquiries of locals who had gathered around his table *à l'antique*: 'We had to tell stories of Frederick II, and their interest in the great king was so great that we kept quiet about his death, so as not to incur the hatred of our hosts as the harbingers of bad tidings.'[48]

They had forgotten the 'rape' of Silesia. Neither Goethe nor the Sicilians thought Frederick had 'doomed Europe to generations of bloody strife'.[49] They did not enjoy the benefit of hindsight that allows a modern writer to lay all the misfortunes of modern Europe at the Prussian king's feet.[50] To Goethe and the Sicilians, Frederick was still the hero who had pitted his inferior numbers against the combined mights of Europe and not lost an inch of land; he was the ruler who had sacrificed his little pleasures for the good of his people and the sage administration of his country; he had abolished torture and reformed the law from top to bottom; most recently he had taken the side of the little peasants against the great lords. This man who had sparred nightly with the greatest intellectuals of his day had, they heard, found relaxation in writing poetry.

When they looked at the rest of Europe, they could see little to rival the Prussian king: neither George III of Britain nor Louis XVI of France had anything like his charisma. Their own Bourbon rulers were a byword for cruelty. Frederick's 'pupil' Joseph II was well-intentioned, but the dice were loaded against him. Only in far-away Russia was there a monarch who was his equal in stature, and she too had instigated many of her reforms in imitation of his.

The best epitaphs were written before his death. Voltaire, who had sought to use posterity to destroy his friend and correspondent, once sent him some lines he had adapted from his own play *Mahomet*:

> Chaque peuple à son tour a regné sur la terre,
> Par les lois, par les arts, et surtout par la guerre;
> Le siècle de la Prusse est à la fin venu.[51]

> *In their turn every land has reigned over this world,*
> *By laws, through the arts, and above all by the sword.*
> *The Prussian century has finally arrived.*

Voltaire was not exaggerating when he described Frederick in 1772 as a 'man who gives battle as readily as he writes an opera; who takes advantage of all the hours that other kings waste following a dog chasing after a stag; he has written more books than any of his contemporary princes has sired bastards; and he has won more victories than he has written books ...'[52] Even Gleim, who performed the difficult role of being at once the unofficial poet to Frederick's campaigns and the magnet to the literary renaissance in eighteenth-century Germany, was able to turn a decent line for an imaginary tomb:

> Auf Ihm die Grabschrift? – kurz und klug? –
> 'Hier liegt der Einzige!' das, mein' ich, ist genug![53]

> *An epitaph then? Short and sweet,*
> *He was quite unique. That I think, will fit a treat.*

Fewer than three years after his death the French Revolution broke out, and a new Frederick was about to be born. With time he would cede his place to a whole panoply: Frederick of Germany, Frederick the Hero, Frederick Hitler and Frederick the Militarist; while the real Frederick lay there mouldering in an unquiet grave.

Notes

INTRODUCTION

1 The first lives of Frederick were largely anecdotal: Nicolai's *Anekdoten von König Friedrich II von Preussen* was published between 1788 and 1792. More powerful by far were the images of the king by Adolph Menzel, which appeared in Franz Kugler's immensely popular *Geschichte Friedrichs des Grossen* of 1842. Scholarly biography was initiated by the royal archivist J.D.E. Preuss, who also edited the first, French, edition of the king's *Oeuvres* from 1846 to 1857.

2 Thomas Babington Macaulay, *Biographical Essays*, Leipzig, 1857, 71. Macaulay none the less admitted that Frederick was 'the greatest king that has in modern times, succeeded by right of birth to a throne'.

3 The Ahnenallee, nicknamed 'Puppen-' or 'Dolls'-allee was unveiled in 1901, presenting an idealised sculptural portrait of the kaiser's favourite ancestors and their minions.

4 Robert Reinhold Ergang, *The Potsdam Führer: Frederick William I, Father of Prussian Militarism*, New York 1941.

5 G.P. Gooch's *Frederick the Great: The Ruler, The Writer, The Man* (London, New York, Toronto, 1947) is a testament to the postwar mood. See Preface, v–vi.

6 Bürgermeister Frank Letz, speech made on the main square of Kloster Zinna, 8 April 1996.

7 Interview with Friedrich Wilhelm Fürst von Hohenzollern, 14 May 1996; 'Vichy's last stand: a prince's story', *Financial Times*, 5 October 1996; conversation between Professor Curt Elwensbock and F.W.

Fürst von Hohenzollern, communicated to the author by the prince.

8 For Prussia's rehabilitation, see Giles MacDonogh, *Prussia: the Perversion of an Idea*, London, 1994, 1–11.

CHAPTER ONE: THE FATHER

1 Voltaire, *Histoire de la guerre de 1741*, Paris, 1971, 5 n. a.; *Mémoires pour servir à la vie de M. de Voltaire écrits par lui-même, suivis de lettres à Frédéric II*, ed. Jacques Brenner, Paris 1988, 32.

2 *Mémoire pour servir à l'Histoire de la Maison de Brandebourg*, in *Oeuvres*, I, 96 n. a. J.D.E. Preuss affirms the truth of Frederick's statement; there were documents in the Venetian archives to back it up.

3 Pöllnitz, *Mémoires pour servir à l'Histoire des quatre derniers souverains de la Maison de Brandebourg Royale de Prusse*, 2 vols, Berlin 1791 (hereafter *Mémoires*), I, 207–9.

4 Frederick I's patent is illustrated in Sebastian Haffner, *Preussen ohne Legende*, Hamburg, 1982, 78.

5 Dieudonné Thiébault, *Mes souveniers de vingt ans de séjour à Berlin, ou Frédéric le Grand: sa famille, sa cour, son gouvernement, son académie, ses écoles, et ses amis littérateurs et philosophes*, 5 vols, Paris, 1804, II, 4.

6 Id., 6.

7 *Lettres et Mémoires du baron de Pöllnitz contenant les observations qu'il a faites (sic) dans ses voyages*, 3rd edn, 5 vols, Amsterdam, 1737 (hereafter *Lettres*), I, 16.

8 Theodor Schieder, *Friedrich der Grosse: Ein Königtum der Widersprüche*, Frankfurt am Main, 1983, 16.

9 *Mémoires*, in *Oeuvres*, I, 110, quoted in Giles MacDonogh, *Prussia* 29.

10 Gerd Heinrich, *Geschichte Preussens*,

Staat und Dynastie, Frankfurt am Main, Vienna, Berlin, 1984, 127.
11 *Oeuvres*, II, 38.
12 *Histoire de Brandebourg*, in *Oeuvres*, I, 107.
13 Gerhard Oestreich, *Friedrich Wilhelm I: Preussischer Absolutismus, Merkantilismus, Militarismus*, Göttingen, Zurich, Frankfurt am Main, 1977, 9.
14 Pöllnitz, *Mémoires*, I, 219.
15 Oestreich, 17.
16 Pöllnitz, *Lettres*, I, 29; Hans-Joachim Neumann, 'Friedrich der Grosse: Ein medizinhistorisch Beitrag über seine Krankheiten und seine Ärzte', in *Mitteilungen des Vereins für die Geschichte Berlins*, July 1997, 237.
17 Pöllnitz, *Mémoires*, II, 10.
18 Oestreich, 26.
19 Id., 28.
20 Id., 91.
21 Giles MacDonogh, *Berlin*, London, 1997, 21.
22 *Mémoires de Frédérique Sophie, Wilhelmine, Margrave de Bayreuth, soeur de Frédéric le Grand, depuis l'année 1706 jusqu'à 1742, écrits de sa main:* Préface de Pierre Gaxotte, notes de Gérard Doscot, Paris, 1967 (hereafter Wilhelmina), 23.
23 *Histoire de Brandebourg*, in *Oeuvres*, I, 137.
24 Ernst Lavisse, *La Jeunesse du grand Frédéric*, Paris, 1899, 5; Pöllnitz, *Mémoires*, II, 6; Oestreich, 42.
25 Johann Michael von Loen, *Kleine Schriften*, I, 3, 22ff.
26 Schieder, 17.
27 Loen, op. cit.
28 Thiébault, II, 18–19.
29 Thiébault, II, 20.
30 Roland Vocke, *Friedrich der Grosse: Person, Zeit, Nachwelt*, Gütersloh, 1977, 22; Wolfgang Venohr, *Fridericus Rex, Friedrich der Grosse: Porträt einer Doppelnatur*, Bergisch Gladbach, 1988, 45.
31 Oestreich, 45.
32 Charlotte Pangels, *Königskinder im Rokoko: Die Geschwister Friedrichs des Grossen*, Munich, 1976, 14.
33 Pöllnitz, *Lettres*, 17.
34 Gerd Bartoschek *et al.*, *Der Soldatenkönig als Maler*, Potsdam, 1990, 21, 61.
35 Thiébault, II, 17.
36 Oestreich, 52.

37 Id., 44.
38 Id.; Schieder 18–20.
39 Thiébault, II, 22.
40 Pöllnitz, *Mémoires*, II, 140.
41 Frederick William is alleged to have paid out 12 million thalers for tall soldiers between 1713 and 1735. One batch of forty-three recruits cost him as much as 43,000 thalers, and the later Field Marshal von Schmettau received 5000 thalers for one particularly good specimen alone, and was granted a place in a noble charitable foundation for his sister (see Seckendorff, II, 164, n. 1).
42 Id., 26; Pöllnitz, *Lettres*, I, 49; *Du militaire*, in *Oeuvres*, I, 193.
43 Vocke, 30; Oestreich, 74.
44 Ingrid Mittenzwei, *Friedrich II. von Preussen*, Berlin [East], 1979, 14.
45 Loen, op. cit.
46 *Du militaire*, in *Oeuvres*, I, 186–93.
47 Loen, op. cit; Georg Holmsten, *Friedrich II in Selbstzeugnisse und Bilddokumenten*, Reinbek, 1969, 17.
48 Oestreich, 71.
49 Oestreich, 70.
50 *Lettres*, I, 46.
51 Loen, op. cit.
52 Id., 108.
53 Pöllnitz, *Mémoires*, II, 12–13.
54 Carl Hinrichs, *Preussentum und Pietismus: Der Pietismus als religiös-soziale Reformbewegung*, Göttingen, 1971, 93; *Oeuvres*, I, 211.
55 Id., 20.
56 Id., 14.
57 Id., 16.
58 Id., 60.
59 Id., 93.
60 For a discussion of the 'Prussian virtues', see MacDonogh, *Prussia*, 109–37, 273–8.
61 Hinrichs, *Pietismus*, 126.
62 Id., 152, 165–6.
63 Oestreich, 84.
64 Id., 111.

CHAPTER TWO: THE GROWING BOY

1 Carl Hinrichs, *Friedrich Wilhelm I, König in Preussen: Eine Biographie – Jugend und Aufstieg*, Hamburg, 1941, 600.
2 Gustav Berthold Volz, *Friedrich der Grosse im Spiegel seiner Zeit*, 3 vols, Berlin 1925, I, 3.
3 Hinrichs, *Friedrich Wilhelm*, 600.

4 Id., 4; Hans Jessen (ed.), *Friedrich der Grosse und Maria-Theresia in Augenzeugenberichten*, Düsseldolf, 1965, 24; Hinrichs, *Friedrich Wilhelm*, 601–2.

5 Reinhold Koser, *Geschichte Friedrichs des Grossen*, 4 vols, Darmstadt, 1963, I, 3.

6 Jessen, 25.

7 Loen, op. cit; Pöllnitz, *Lettres*, I, 34.

8 Id.

9 Pangels, *Königskinder*, 15.

10 See Giles MacDonogh, *Prussia*, 32 n. 1.

11 Pöllnitz, *Lettres*, I, 43.

12 Wilhelmina, 29.

13 Id., 28.

14 For the reliability of Wilhelmina's *Mémoires*, see G.P. Gooch, *Courts and Cabinets*, London, 1944, 118–148. Gooch cites Carlyle, who thought that the account was only between 25 and 75 per cent trustworthy. J.D.E. Preuss, the royal archivist who edited the *Oeuvres*, noted that Wilhelmina had 'disfigured' Frederick's letters in quoting them. The reason for this, he suggests, is that the memoirs were put down between 1744 and 1746, at the time when she was most unhappy about her husband's infidelity, and her brother's lack of sympathy for her cause (*Oeuvres*, XXVII, xvi–xvii); also Wilhelm Oncken (see below, Oncken, II, 174) talks of 'the whole novel which she serves up to her readers'.

15 Venohr, 40.

16 Holmsten, 18.

17 Two others were the Habsburg emperor Charles VI, and the elector of Hanover, later George I of Great Britain.

18 Wilhelmina, 43.

19 Id., 44.

20 Id., 45.

21 Id., 33.

22 Loen, op. cit.

23 Schieder, 21.

24 Id.

25 Frank Schumann, (ed.), *Allergnädigster Vater: Die Verkrüppelung eines Charakters zu Wusterhausen – Dokumente aus der Jugendzeit Friedrichs II*, Berlin, 1986, Introduction, 12.

26 Carl Hinrichs, *Der Kronprinzenprozess: Friedrich und Katte*, Hamburg, 1936, 9.

27 Id., 17; Reinhold Koser (ed.), *Unterhaltungen mit Friedrich den Grossen:*

Memoiren und Tagebücher von Heinrich de Catt, Leipzig, 1884 (hereafter Catt), 34.

28 Hinrichs, *Kronprinzenprozess*, 10.

29 Schieder, 27.

30 Eugene Helm, 'Frederick II', in Stanley Sadie (ed.), *The New Grove Dictionary of Music and Musicians*, London 1980, VI, 811–12; Schumann, op. cit. 23–4.

31 Id.

32 Quoted in id.

33 Id.

34 Id.

35 Id., 26.

36 Koser, I, 24, 10.

37 Catt, 71.

38 Schieder, 28.

39 Fénelon, *Les Aventures de Télémaque*, Paris, 1994, introduction by Jeanne-Lydie Goré, 45.

40 Hinrichs, *Kronprinzenprozess*, 5; Alfred Cobban, *A History of Modern France*, 3 vols, Harmondsworth, 1963, I, 20–1; Fénelon, 137.

41 Schieder, 23.

42 *Télémaque*, 124.

43 Id., 143.

44 Id., 167.

45 Id., 195–7.

46 Id., 325–6.

47 Id., 383.

48 Schieder, 29.

49 Koser, I, 8.

50 Mittenzwei, 17.

51 Schieder, 28.

52 Hinrichs, *Kronprinzenprozess*, 11.

53 Koser, I, 10–11.

54 Wilhelmina, 73–4.

55 Jessen, 23.

56 Koser, I, 18.

57 Id., 17–18.

58 *Allergnädigster Vater.*

59 Macaulay did not mince words: 'Oliver Twist in the parish workhouse, Smike at Dotheboys Hall, were petted children when compared with this wretched heir-apparent to the crown.' *Biographical Essays*, 5.

60 Hinrichs, *Kronprinzenprozess*, 12; Schieder, 30.

61 To Duhan, 20 June 1727, in *Oeuvres*, XVII, 269.

62 *Grove*, op. cit.; Schieder, 46.

63 Koser, I, 20.

64 Jeremy Black, *The Collapse of the Anglo-*

French Alliance, 1727–1732, Gloucester and New York, 1987, 61, 140.

65 *Mémoires,* II, 172.

66 Wilhelmina, 76.

67 Vocke, 47.

68 Koser, I, 20, Lavisse, *Jeunesse,* 101.

69 Id.

70 Id., 83; Vocke, 46.

71 Seckendorff, II, 33.

72 Koser, I, 21.

73 Pangels, 181–2.

74 Wilhelmina, 84.

75 A system of the same sort was used at the Café Mécanique in Paris's Palais Royal during the French Revolutionary years: the *limonadière* communicated with the kitchens through a speaking tube. This was revived by the gastronomic writer Grimod de La Reynière at the sessions of his 'Jury dégustateur': meals were brought up by a dumbwaiter that came through the floor, and instructions to the kitchen were delivered through a tube decorated with the head of a cook. See Giles MacDonogh, *A Palate in Revolution: Grimod de La Reynière and the Almanach des Gourmands,* London, 1987, 53, 69.

76 Wilhelmina, 84–5.

77 Albert Quantz, *Leben und Werke des Flötisten Johann Joachim Quantz, Lehrers Friedrich des Grossen,* Berlin, 1877, 18–19.

78 Wilhelmina, 86.

79 Koser, I, 24.

80 Holmsten, 24.

81 Hinrichs, *Kronprinzenprozess,* 10, 7.

82 Id., 8.

83 Black, *Collapse,* 8.

84 Hinrichs, *Friedrich Wilhelm,* 606.

85 *Histoire de Brandenburg,* in *Oeuvres,* I, 125.

86 Heinrich, *Geschichte Preussens,* 175.

87 *Mémoires,* II, 117.

88 Karl Baedecker, *Northern Germany,* Leipzig, 1897, 217.

89 Author's visit to Szczecin, August 1992.

90 'Gerd Heinrich, Friedrich der Grosse: Jugend, Hof, Dynastie', in Wilhelm Treue, (ed.) *Preussens grosser König,* Freiburg and Würzburg, 1986, 25; Hinrichs, *Kronprinzenprozess,* 16.

91 Hinrichs, *Kronprinzenprozess,* 16.

92 Id.

93 Lavisse, *Jeunesse,* 90; Ernst Poseck, *Die Kronprinzessin: Elisabeth Christine Gemahlin*

Friedrichs des Grossen, geborene Prinzessin von Braunschweig-Bevern, Berlin, 1940, 36.

94 Koser, I, 14, 16.

95 Black, *Collapse,* 39.

96 K. Seckendorff, *Versuch einer Lebensbeschreibung des Feldmarschalls Graf von Seckendorff meist aus ungedruckten Nachrichten bearbeitet,* 2 vols, 1792, II, 16; Pöllnitz, *Mémoires,* II, 162–3.

97 Id., 178.

98 Skalweit, in O. Busch and W. Neugebauer, *Moderne Preussische Geschichte 1648–1947. Eine Anthologie.* 3 vols, Berlin and New York, 1981 I, 106.

99 Oestreich, 111.

100 Pöllnitz, *Lettres,* I, 53.

101 Id., 61.

102 Id., 110; Lavisse, *Jeunesse,* 163.

103 Seckendorff, II, 211–12.

104 One of the Schulenburgs was in a particularly advantageous position: she was George I's mistress. Gräfin Ehrengard Melusina von der Schulenburg had been showered with titles as baroness of Dundalk, countess and marchioness of Dungannon, and duchess of Munster, all in the Irish peerage; baroness of Glastonbury, countess of Feversham and duchess of Kendall, in the English peerage; as well as princess of Eberstein in the imperial nobility. Her influence was eclipsed when King George died in 1727. Wilhelmina thought her 'good for nothing. She had neither vices nor virtues and all her art consisted in keeping herself in favour and stopping anyone else from taking her place.' *Mémoires,* 57.

105 Koser, I, 16–17.

106 Venohr, 57.

107 Seckendorff, II, 10.

108 Wilhelmina, 72–3.

109 *Histoire de Brandebourg,* II, 137, quoted in Seckendorff, I, 15–16.

110 Seckendorff, II, 12.

111 Id., I, 2, 4–5.

112 Id., II, 9 n. 3; Pöllnitz, *Lettres,* IV, 418.

113 *Mémoires,* II, 210.

114 Koser, I, 25.

115 Seckendorff, II, 6–7.

116 Pöllnitz, *Lettres,* I, 48.

117 Author's visit to Stern, 11 August 1996.

118 The Schloss was in a dreadful state

in August 1996, but the author was told in the local museum that there were plans to restore it before the end of the millennium. From the outside it looks like two simple houses with gable ends. The only 'feature' is the oldest part of the house: the staircase tower. It is astonishing to think that it predates Sanssouci by less than thirty years.

119 Thiébault, III, 69–70.
120 Hinrichs, *Kronprinzenprozess*, 93.
121 Koser, I, 22–4.
122 Hinrichs, *Kronprinzenprozess*, 10.
123 Id., 14.
124 Schieder, 29.
125 *Allergnädigster Vater*, 28–9.
126 Koser, I, 17.
127 Id., 26–7.
128 Wilhelmina claims that Seckendorff tried to stop him from approaching the king.
129 *Allergnädigster Vater*, 30–1.
130 Wilhelmina, 89–90.
131 Koser, I, 21, 23.
132 Wilhelmina, 102.
133 Roger Peyrefitte, *Voltaire et Frédéric II*, 2 vols, Paris, 1992, I, 70. It has to be said, however, that Peyrefitte is not particularly reliable, and assumes Frederick's circle was exclusively homosexual from the beginning.
134 Hinrichs, *Kronprinzenprozess*, 69.
135 Holmsten, 18.
136 Wilhelmina, 90.
137 Hinrichs, *Kronprinzenprozess*, 25 n. 2; *Deutsche biographische Enzyklopädie*, Munich, 1997, 5, 488; *Neue Deutsche Biographe*, 11, 413.
138 Hinrichs, *Kronprinzenprozess*, 26 n. 3.
139 Koser, I, 32.
140 *Mémoires*, II, 209.
141 Wilhelmina, 105.
142 Theodor Fontane, *Wanderungen durch die Mark Brandenburg*, 3 vols, Munich and Vienna, 1991 (hereafter *Wanderungen*), I, 859; II, 373.
143 Wilhelmina, 97–104.
144 Hinrichs, *Kronprinzenprozess*, 18; Lavisse, *Jeunesse*, 173–5.
145 Hinrichs, *Kronprinzenprozess*, 14.
146 Pöllnitz, *Mémoires*, II, 189.
147 Poseck, 19, 31, 33–4.
148 Black, *Collapse*, 39; Poseck, 54–5.
149 Koser, I, 28; Black, *Collapse*, 154.
150 Poseck, 43, 46–7.

151 Schieder, 44; Poseck, 50.
152 Seckendorff, II, 10.
153 Wilhelmina, 105.
154 Hinrichs, *Kronprinzenprozess*, 21.
155 Wilhelm Oncken, 'Sir Charles Hotham und Friedrich Wilhelm I im Jahre 1730: urkundliche Aufschlüsse aus den Archiven zu London und Wien', in Albert Naudé (ed.), *Forschungen zur Brandenburgischen und Preussischen Geschichte*, Leipzig, 1894 (hereafter Oncken, I), 81–2; Black, *Collapse*, 95–6.
156 Wilhelm Oncken, 'Sir Charles Hotham und Friedrich Wilhelm I im Jahre 1730, II: der Sturmlauf wider Reichenbach und Grumbkow', in *Forschung zur Brandenburgischen und Preussischen Geschichte*, Leipzig, 1895 (hereafter Oncken, II), 169–70; Black, *Collapse*, 96.
157 Oncken, I, 173–4.
158 Hinrichs, *Kronprinzenprozess*, 21.
159 Oncken, I, 180.
160 Id., 185.
161 Id., II, 186.
162 Id., I, 85; Lavisse, *Jeunesse*, 214.
163 Oncken, I, 92.
164 Pöllnitz, *Mémoires*, II, 203, 208.
165 Oncken, I, 94.
166 Id., 95–6.
167 Id., 97.
168 Id., 99.
169 Id., 30.
170 Id.
171 Id., II, 186–7.
172 Id., I, 101–3.
173 Id., 104.
174 Id., 105.
175 Id.
176 Id., 106–7.
177 Id., 106.
178 Id.
179 Pöllnitz, *Mémoires*, II, 210–11; Oncken, I, 107.
180 Oncken, I, 109. There is an anti-English tone throughout Oncken's essays, which may have something to do with the time in which he was writing.
181 Id., II, 199.
182 Id., 31.
183 Id., 201.
184 Poseck, 62–4.
185 Wilhelmina, 120.
186 Koser, I, 33.
187 Pöllnitz, *Mémoires*, II, 222.
188 Seckendorff, II, 231–2; Koser, I, 34–5.

189 Koser, 32.
190 Pöllnitz, *Mémoires*, II, 226.
191 Koser, I, 35.
192 Hinrichs, *Kronprinzenprozess*, 67.
193 Koser, I, 37.
194 Lord Townshend had sent the intercepted correspondence to Hotham to show to Knyphausen. See Black, *Collapse*, 182.
195 Pöllnitz, *Mémoires*, II, 211.
196 Koser, I, 36; Black, *Collapse*, 182.
197 Pöllnitz, *Mémoires*, II, 215.
198 Oncken, II, 204.
199 Wilhelmina, 133.
200 Poseck, 71.
201 Poseck, 60.
202 Hinrichs, *Kronprinzenprozess*, 22; Koser, I, 38.
203 Koser, I, 39.
204 Id.; Hinrichs, *Kronprinzenprozess*, 23.
205 Seckendorff, II, 234.
206 G.M. Trevelyan, *Blenheim*, London and Glasgow, 1965, 376.
207 Hinrichs, *Kronprinzenprozess*, 77.
208 Koser, I, 40–1.
209 Id., 41.
210 Hinrichs, *Kronprinzenprozess*, 73.
211 Koser, I, 41–2.
212 Id., 43.
213 Pöllnitz, *Mémoires*, II, 230–1; Wilhelmina, 148. The story crops up in all the early biographies: see, for example, Franz Kugler, *Geschichte Friedrichs des Grossen*, Leipzig, 1936 (a reprint of the original 1842 edn), 64.
214 Koser, I, 43.
215 Hinrichs, *Kronprinzenprozess*, 25–6, 33.
216 Id., 27.
217 Id., 31.
218 Wilhelmina, 140; Pangels, 32.
219 Koser, I, 43; Pöllnitz, *Mémoires*, II, 235.
220 Hinrichs, *Kronprinzenprozess*, 36.
221 Koser, I, 44; Hinrichs, *Kronprinzenprozess*, 37–8.
222 Id., 38.
223 Koser, I, 44.

CHAPTER THREE: NO TWO MEN QUITE LIKE THEM
1 Hinrichs, *Kronprinzenprozess*, 38–9; *Allergnädigster Vater*, 46; *Wanderungen*, I, 835.
2 *Allergnädigster Vater*, 56.
3 Wilhelmina, 145.

4 Wilhelmina, 152, attributes the line to Grumbkow.
5 Pöllnitz, *Mémoires*, II, 238.
6 Voltaire, *Mémoires*, 25.
7 Pangels, 33–9.
8 *Allergnädigster Vater*, 49.
9 *Wanderungen*, I, 837.
10 Wilhelmina, 138–9.
11 Pöllnitz, *Mémoires*, II, 233.
12 Wilhelmina, 141; Pöllnitz, *Mémoires*, II, 235; Fontane points out that Wilhelmina might be untrustworthy here too: that the reason why Katte was caught is that he had simply too much to do – destroying papers – before he left (*Wanderungen*, I, 837).
13 Wilhelmina, 142.
14 Id., 34.
15 Hinrichs, *Kronprinzenprozess*, 69–70 and n. 1.
16 Id., 88–9.
17 Id., 91.
18 Id., 105.
19 Hinrichs, *Pietismus*, 170.
20 Hinrichs, *Kronprinzenprozess*, 105.
21 Id., 115.
22 Pangels, 321–3.
23 *Allergnädigster Vater*, 40.
24 Id., 58; *Oeuvres*, XXVII, 3.
25 Schieder, 39.
26 Schulenburg's house survives, much altered in the village of Beetzendorf in the Altmark. The East Germans turned it into a boarding school. More interesting is the village church, which he had built to imitate the now vanished garrison church in Berlin (author's visit to Beetzendorf, 12 May 1996).
27 Hinrichs, *Kronprinzenprozess*, 116.
28 Id., 119, 120, 121, 124–6, 129, 130.
29 Id., 119, 120, 129, 130.
30 Id., 120, 130, 132.
31 *Oeuvres*, XVII, 206.
32 Hinrichs, *Kronprinzenprozess*, 117, 121, 124–6, 128–9, 130.
33 Id., 118, 119–20, 122, 124–26, 129, 130.
34 Hinrichs, *Kronprinzenprozess*, 131–2.
35 Id., 134–5.
36 Wilhelmina, 154; Pöllnitz, *Mémoires*, II, 242.
37 Volz (ed.), I, 32.
38 Hinrichs, *Kronprinzenprozess*, 137; *Wanderungen*, I, 843; MacDonogh, *Prussia*, 32 and n. 2.

39 Pöllnitz, *Mémoires*, II, 246.
40 Hinrichs, *Kronprinzenprozess*, 143.
Katte's father later successfully sued the king to have the body reburied in the family vault at Wust.
41 *Wanderungen*, I, 848.
42 Hinrichs, *Kronprinzenprozess*, 114–50; *Wanderungen*, I, 851.
43 Schieder, 40.
44 It was not the first time that Frederick William had insisted on this. In 1718, the wife of the concierge Runck, who had been found guilty of robbing the Berlin Schloss with the locksmith Stief, was obliged to witness her husband's beheading. Pöllnitz, *Mémoires*, II, 71.
45 Catt, 35.
46 Wilhelmina records a rather longer dialogue in which the prince offered to abdicate his right to the succession if Katte's execution could be halted.
47 Hinrichs, *Kronprinzenprozess*, 143, 160. There are several versions of the exchange. See also *Wanderungen*, I, 852–3, where Friedrich blew his friend a kiss.
48 Hinrichs, *Kronprinzenprozess*, 159.
49 Wilhelmina, 167.
50 Schieder, 40; the letter and the king's reply are given in Seckendorff, II, 288–90.
51 Seckendorff, II, 237.
52 Schieder, 43; Wilhelmina, 166.
53 *Allergnädigster Vater*, 62.
54 Id., 64–5.
55 Id., 66.
56 Id., 61.
57 Jessen, 44; Hinrichs, *Kronprinzenprozess*, 184.
58 Schieder, 41.
59 Id., 45.
60 *Allegnädigster Vater*, 42.
61 Volz (ed.), I, 14.
62 Holmsten, 22.
63 Schieder, 42.
64 Venohr, 36.
65 Id., 74.
66 Volz (ed.), I, 32.
67 Id., 13.
68 Id., 13–14.
69 Id., 14.
70 Id., 14.
71 Volz (ed.), I, 17–20, 22.
72 Id., 22–3.
73 'mit meinem Latein am Ende'.

74 Volz (ed.), I, 20–1.
75 Jessen, 50.
76 *Allergnädigster Vater*, 78.
77 Volz (ed.), I, 21.
78 'Frédéric se croyait poète et cette illusion embellissait sa vie.' Christiane Mervaud, *Voltaire et Frédéric II: Une dramaturgie des lumières*, 1736–1778, Voltaire Foundation, Oxford, 1985, 75.
79 Jessen, 43.
80 Volz (ed.), I, 22–3.
81 Thiébault later claimed that this had been Frederick William's idea (*Souvenirs*, I, 194).
82 Volz (ed.), I, 29.
83 Jessen, 46; Poseck, 91.
84 Jessen, 46–7.
85 Volz (ed.), I, 31.
86 *Oeuvres*, XVI, 3–5.
87 Heinrich in Treue (ed.), 27; Volz (ed.), I, 62.
88 The king's fool, Gundling, had just been buried in a barrel of wine at Bornstedt cemetery, near Potsdam.
89 Volz (ed.), I, 26.
90 Id., 32.
91 Id., 33.
92 Id.
93 Frederick William uses the word 'Quark', or curd cheese. It can also mean filth or nonsense.
94 Quoted in full in Poseck, 89–90.
95 Poseck, 102.
96 Volz (ed.), I, 40.
97 Jessen, 48.
98 Id.
99 Volz (ed.), I, 39.
100 *Allergnädigster Vater*, 80–4.
101 Poseck, 74.
102 Id., 75.
103 Id., 79, 86.
104 Id., 91; Volz (ed.), I, 13 contains a similar outburst.
105 *Allergnädigster Vater*, 75.
106 Poseck, 97; Volz (ed.), I, 36.
107 Volz (ed.), I, 36.
108 Frederick William was in no hurry to pay the 400,000 thalers due to the margrave. See Volz (ed.), I, 45.
109 Poseck, 96.
110 Volz (ed.), I, 33.
111 Poseck, 100–1.
112 *Allergnädigster Vater*, 79.
113 Poseck, 113.
114 Id., 107–10.

115 *Allergnädigster Vater*, 85.

116 Poseck, 110–11.

117 For a discussion of Prussian beer, see MacDonogh, *Berlin*, 267–74.

118 *Allergnädigster Vater*, 94.

119 Volz (ed.), I, 45; *Oeuvres*, XVI, 17.

120 Volz (ed.), I, 46.

121 G.A. Buettner (ed.), *Mémoires du Baron de la Motte Fouqué, Général d'Infanterie prussienne*, 2 vols, Berlin, 1788, 4–5.

122 *Wanderungen*, I, 896.

123 Volz (ed.), I, 54.

124 *Vers* in French means 'worms' and 'verses'.

125 *Oeuvres*, XVI, 10; *Wanderungen*, I, 899.

126 A fertile part of the Ukraine; one presumes the beasts were fat.

127 *Oeuvres*, XVI, 15–16.

128 *Wanderungen*, I, 898; *Oeuvres*, XVI, 151.

129 *Wanderungen*, I, 903.

130 Volz (ed.), I, 46.

131 Id., 48.

132 Poseck, 110.

133 *Allergnädigster Vater*, 85.

134 Id., 90–1.

135 Johannes Richter (ed.), *Die Briefe Friedrichs des Grossen an seinen vormaligen Kammerdiener Fredersdorf*, Moers, 1979 (hereafter *Fredersdorf*), 19.

136 Volz (ed.), I, 51.

137 *Allergnädigster Vater*, 93; Volz (ed.), I, 46.

138 *Oeuvres*, XXVI, 65.

139 Elisabeth Christine was passionate about music, and the Beverns had Graun at their court, who had succeeded the great Hasse. The Berlin court could boast nothing in comparison. See Poseck, 27–8.

140 *Oeuvres*, XVI, 38.

141 Volz (ed.), I, 51.

142 *Allergnädigster Vater*, 96.

143 *Oeuvres*, XVI, 41; *Allergnädigster Vater*, 98–9. The last reference is to his sister, the margravine of Ansbach. See *Oeuvres*, XVI, 42.

144 *Oeuvres*, XVI, 43.

145 Volz (ed.), I, 56–7.

146 *Oeuvres*, XVI, 44.

147 *Allergnädigster Vater*, 100; *Oeuvres*, XVI, 45.

148 *Oeuvres*, XVI, 44.

149 Volz (ed.), I, 59.

150 Poseck, 127, 130.

151 Id., 131–2.

152 Id., 138.

153 Id.

154 *Allergnädigster Vater*, 101, n. 1.

155 Id., 101; *Oeuvres*, XXVI, 4.

156 Wilhelmina, 255–72.

157 *Oeuvres*, XXVII, 5.

158 Poseck, 139, 144.

159 Id., 172–86 *passim*.

160 Jessen, 54; Poseck, 188.

161 Poseck, 190.

162 *Wanderungen*, I, 83.

163 Id., 85 and n. 1. Fontane was born in Neuruppin.

164 *Oeuvres*, XVI, 52.

165 Id., 54.

166 Poseck, 198.

167 *Oeuvres*, XVI, 64.

168 Id., XVI, 68.

169 Id., 65.

170 Id., 69–70.

171 Id., 70.

172 Schieder, 56.

173 Quoted in *Wanderungen*, I, 92–3.

174 Id., 94.

175 Id., 87, n. 1; *Letters of Baron Bielfeld*, tr. by Mr Hooper, 5 vols, London, 1768–70 (hereafter Bielfeld), III, 112.

176 Hans-Joachim Kadatz, *Georg-Wenzeslaus von Knobelsdorff, Baumeister Friedrichs II*, Leipzig, 1983, 33–4.

177 Kadatz, 38–9.

178 Hans-Joachim Giersberg, 'Die Bauten Friedrichs des Grossen', in Johann Georg Prinz von Hohenzollern (ed.), *Friedrich der Grosse: Sammler und Mäzen*, Munich, 1992, 58; *Wanderungen*, I, 88–9; *Oeuvres*, XVI, 329.

179 Franz Lorenz, *Die Musikerfamilie Benda: Franz Benda und seine Nachkommen*, Berlin, 1967, 148. Lorenz reprints Benda's short autobiography.

180 Id., 15–16.

181 *Oeuvres*, XXVII, 37.

182 Lorenz, *Benda*, 16–18.

183 *Oeuvres*, XVI, 99.

184 Id., 27–34.

185 Jessen, 105.

186 *Oeuvres*, XVI, 55.

187 Seckendorff, II, 49.

188 *Oeuvres*, XVI, 78.

189 Id., 79–80.

CHAPTER FOUR: RHEINSBERG

1 Jessen, 56.

2 Poseck, 206–7; Max Braubach, *Prinz*

Eugen von Savoyen, 1965, V, 250–1.

3 *Oeuvres*, XVII, 9; Poseck, 208–11.

4 Jessen, 57.

5 Poseck, 231, 235.

6 Christian Graf von Krockow, *Die preussischen Brüder: Prinz Heinrich und Friedrich der Grosse – Ein Doppelportrait*, Stuttgart, 1996, 106; *Oeuvres*, XXVII, 12.

7 Poseck, 254–60.

8 Dietrich Rohmer, *Vom Werdegang Friedrich des Grossens: Die politische Entwicklung des Kronprinzens*, Greifswald, 1924, 38–40; Catt, 41–2.

9 *Oeuvres*, XXV, 461.

10 Id., XXVII, 12.

11 Wilhelmina, 311.

12 Volz (ed.), I, 82.

13 *Oeuvres*, XVI, 131.

14 Jessen, 58.

15 Id., 59.

16 *Oeuvres*, XXVII, 17.

17 *Allergnädigster Vater*, 117–19.

18 Poseck, 282.

19 *Oeuvres*, XXVII, 25.

20 Poseck, 289.

21 *Allergnädigster Vater*, 130, 133–4.

22 Id., 142.

23 Pangels, 61.

24 Wilhelmina treats them no more kindly earlier in her own narrative.

25 Wilhelmina, 318–19.

26 Wilhelmina, 358.

27 *Allergnädigster Vater*, 142.

28 *Oeuvres*, XXVII, 53–9.

29 Id., XVII, 270.

30 It is not clear if these dots are Fredericks, or those of J.D.E. Preuss, the editor of the *Oeuvres*.

31 *Oeuvres*, XVII, 271.

32 *Oeuvres*, XVI, 107.

33 Andrew Hamilton, Rheinsberg: *Das Schloss, der Park, Kronprinz Fritz und Bruder Heinrich*, Berlin 1996. This is an abridged German translation of the remarkable two-volume English work published by John Murray in London in 1880. Nothing is known of the Scotsman who spent the summer of 1872 studying Rheinsberg. There is a suggestion that Hamilton might have been a pseudonym: see the 'Nachwort' by Franz Fabian, 250–1; Holmsten, 35; Poseck, 359.

34 Poseck, 355–9.

35 Id., 380.

36 See 'Apologie des bontés de Dieu' of 1737, or his 'Ode sur l'amour de Dieu' composed the following year. *Oeuvres*, XIV, 7–14.

37 Schieder, 49.

38 Id., 47.

39 See *Oeuvres*, XXVI. The letters are brief and generally uncontroversial.

40 Schieder, 48; Poseck, 360.

41 Poseck, 362.

42 Holmsten, 26–7.

43 Elisabeth later claimed to have had a miscarriage. See Thiébault, I, 194.

44 Hans Leuschner, *Friedrich der Grosse: Zeit – Person – Wirkung, mit einem Essay von Karl Erich Born*, Gütersloh, 1986, 76.

45 Thiébault, I, 194.

46 Gerhard Ritter, *Friedrich der Grosse: Ein historisches Profil*, 3rd edn, Düsseldorf, 1978, 38; Hans-Joachim Neumann in *Mitteilungen*, 235.

47 Venohr, 90: 'Sie hat einen wunderschönen Leib und ein zuckersüsses Vötzchen.' The line is even more suspicious in that Frederick is expressing himself in German dialect, which he rarely did to his intimate friends. It is clearly not a translation from French.

48 Peyrefitte, I, 112.

49 *Oeuvres*, XXV, 478.

50 Poseck, 365.

51 Id., 333–5.

52 Bielfeld, III, 75.

53 Friedrich Nicolai, *Beschreibung des Lustschlosses und Gartens Sr. Königl. Hoheit des Prinzen Heinrich Bruder des Königs zu Reinsberg* (sic), Berlin, 1778 (facsimile 1991), 7–12; Hamilton, 48 and n.

54 Kadatz, 40, 48.

55 Hamilton, 77.

56 Giersberg in Hohenzollern (ed.), 58.

57 Such as survive: the Russians stripped what was left of Rheinsberg after 1945. The movable furniture was already scattered by the time Hamilton looked round the house. The last kaiser sold off more of the inventory at the turn of the century to pay for Achilléon: the villa on Corfu where he indulged his archaeological yearnings. See MacDonogh, *Prussia*, 84.

58 Hamilton, 48; Poseck, 401.

59 *Oeuvres*, XXVII, 75.

60 Id., XXI, 242.

61 Krockow, *Brüder*, 111.

62 *Oeuvres*, XIV, 22.

63 *Allergnädigster Vater*, 150.
64 Jessen, 72.
65 *Oeuvres*, XVI, 142.
66 *Allergnädigster Vater*, 155, 168, 170.
67 Pangels, 184. See also A.A. Löwenthal, 'Braunschweiger Mumme: Bier für Könige und Kranke', in *Gesammelte Schriften*, Tübingen and Stuttgart, 1963, VIII, 67–75.
68 *Oeuvres*, XVI, 141.
69 Id., 148.
70 Id., 169.
71 Poseck, 374.
72 *Oeuvres*, XVI, 250, 271.
73 Id., XVI, 249.
74 C.B.A. Behrens, *Society, Government and the Enlightenment: The Experiences of Eighteenth Century France and Prussia*, London, 1985, 25–6.
75 *Oeuvres*, XVI, 312–13.
76 Id., 301–2.
77 Id., 319–320, 324, 325.
78 *Oeuvres*, XVI, 367, 384–5, 388.
79 Poseck, 351.
80 Id., 397.
81 Id., 370.
82 *Oeuvres*, XVII, 52; Koser, I, 107; Mervaud, *Voltaire et Frédéric*, 22.
83 *Oeuvres*, XVII, 271; Koser, I, 107; Mervaud, *Voltaire et Frédéric*, 22.
84 *Oeuvres*, XVII, 274.
85 Id., XVI, 140.
86 Id., 154.
87 Bielfeld, III, 15–16.
88 *Oeuvres*, XVI, 204.
89 Bielfeld, III, 29–30.
90 Id., 32–38.
91 *Oeuvres*, XVI, 204–11.
92 Id., 216.
93 Bielfeld, III, 38–9.
94 Id., 75.
95 Id., 81–91.
96 Id., 86–7.
97 Id., 91–5.
98 Id., 100–2.
99 'Cato, the austere Cato, occasionally enlivened his wisdom with the nectar of Falernian.' *Oeuvres*, XVI, 167.
100 Bielfeld, III, 104.
101 *Oeuvres*, XVII, 6.
102 Id., XVI, 196–7.
103 Id., 234, 238–9.
104 Id., XXI, 206.
105 Id., XXI, XXII, XXIII.
106 Id., XXI, 4.

107 Christiane Mervaud, *Voltaire et Frédéric*, 20; *Oeuvres*, XXI, 7.
108 *Oeuvres*, XXI, 9–10.
109 Peyrefitte, I, 26.
110 Jacques Brenner in Voltaire, *Mémoires*, 11.
111 *Oeuvres*, XXI, 18.
112 Peyrefitte, I, 56.
113 *Oeuvres*, XXI, 23.
114 Id., 26.
115 Id., 41.
116 Helmut Eisenlohr, 'Wie sah Friedrich der Grosse aus?' in the catalogue to *Friedrich der Grosse: Sein Bild im Wandel der Zeiten*, exhibition, 12 November 1986 to 15 February 1987 in Frankfurt am Main's Historisches Museum, 27–8. Eisenlohr maintains that Knobelsdorff did the best likeness, but that both the portraits of Franke and Graff have their merits, even if the king refused to sit for the artists.
117 *Oeuvres*, XXI, 51–2.
118 Id., 52. The story was not made up by Frederick. It was first aired by Eilhardus Labinus (d. 1621) and was given further credence by Berkmann's *Historische Beschreibung des Chur und Mark Brandenburg* of 1751, 422–32.
119 *Oeuvres*, XXI, 68.
120 Id., 79–80.
121 Voltaire, *Mémoires*, 27.
122 *Oeuvres*, XXI, 263.
123 Id., 211.
124 Id., 123.
125 Id., 135–9.
126 Id., 147.
127 Id., 233.
128 Emil Jacobs (ed.), 'Briefe Friedrichs des Grossen an Thiériot', in *Mitteilungen aus der Königlichen Bibliothek*, I, Berlin, 1912, 7; Peyrefitte, I, 43, 51, 92.
129 Corneille, *Cinna*, II, 1.
130 *Bérénice*, IV, 5.
131 *Mithridate*, II, 6.
132 *Phèdre*, III, 3.
133 *Alexandre le Grand*, V, 1.
134 *Oeuvres*, XVII, 29.
135 Id., XXI, 224.
136 Id., 233, 237.
137 D. Michelessi, *Mémoires concernant la Vie et les écrits du comte François Algarotti*, Berlin, 1772, 20.
138 Robert Halsband, *Lord Hervey, Eighteenth Century Courtier*, Oxford, 1973, 192.

139 *Oeuvres*, XVIII, 4; XXI, 326–7; Poseck, 455.
140 *Oeuvres*, XVIII, 8.
141 Id., 6; similar sentiments are expressed in *L'Antimachiavel*, *Oeuvres*, VII, 61–2; Bielfeld, III, 92.
142 *Oeuvres*, XXI, 253.
143 Niccolò Machiavelli, *The Prince*, translated with an introduction by George Bull, Harmondsworth, 1995, 7, 16, 17, 51; *Oeuvres*, VIII, 67, 72.
144 *Oeuvres*, VII, 160.
145 *The Prince*, 8, 38, 47, 70, 80.
146 Id., 46.
147 Venohr, 94.
148 *Oeuvres*, VII, 161.
149 Voltaire, *Mémoires*, 32.
150 *Oeuvres*, VIII, 1, 21.
151 Id., 43.
152 Id., XXI, 356–7.
153 Ritter, 39.
154 *Oeuvres*, XXI, 149, 172.
155 Id., XVI, 208–10.
156 Id., XXI, 305; MacDonogh, *Prussia*, 33.
157 *Oeuvres*, XVI, 134–5; XXI, 305; Pöllnitz, *Mémoires*, II, 261.
158 *Oeuvres*, XVI, 166.
159 Id.
160 Bielfeld, III, 65–6.
161 Id., 69–73.
162 *Oeuvres*, XVI, 157.
163 Id., 164.
164 Lorenz, *Benda*, 20, 149.
165 Nicolai, *Rheinsberg*, 41–2.
166 Kadatz, *Knobelsdorff*, 72; *Oeuvres*, XVI, 223; Poseck, 477; Hamilton, 195–9.
167 *Oeuvres*, XXVII, 80.
168 Id., XVI, 145.
169 *Allergnädigster Vater*, 159–61.
170 Poseck, 373.
171 Jessen, 79.
172 Carl Hinrichs, *Der allgegenwärtige König: Friedrich der Grosse im Kabinett und auf Inspektionsreisen*, 3rd ed, Berlin, 1943, 41; Jessen, 80.

CHAPTER FIVE: THE NEW KING
1 *Oeuvres*, XVI, 184; *Allergnädigster Vater*, 177.
2 *Oeuvres*, XVI, 183; XXI, 379.
3 Id., XXI, 379.
4 Venohr, 99.
5 Pöllnitz, *Mémoires*, II, 367–70; Volz (ed.), I, 86–87; *Oeuvres*, XXII, 12.

6 Venohr, 100.
7 Bielfeld, III, 118.
8 *Mémoires pour servir à l'Histoire de la maison de Brandebourg*, in *Oeuvres*, I, 174; *Allergnädigster Vater*, 181; *Oeuvres*, XXII, 12.
9 Bielfeld, III, 124–5, quoted in Poseck, 487, 491.
10 *Oeuvres*, XXII, 8 n. a.
11 Kadatz, *Knobelsdorff*, 119; Bielfeld, III, 144–5.
12 Bielfeld, III, 162–3.
13 Venohr, 98–9.
14 Bielfeld, III, 122.
15 *Oeuvres*, XVIII, 15.
16 Volz, (ed.), I, 116.
17 Buettner, *La Motte Fouqué*, 7.
18 *Oeuvres*, XVII, 283.
19 Id., XXII, 3.
20 Id., XVI, 391.
21 Bielfeld, III, 69.
22 Id., 37.
23 Pöllnitz, *Lettres*, I, 35; M.M.C.F., Ecuier, *Mémoires secrets pour servir à l'Histoire de notre tems*, London, n. d. [1752], 3–4; Peyrefitte, I, 158–9.
24 *Oeuvres*, XVI, 396 and n. a.; XXVII, 335; XXII, 13.
25 Holmsten, 44.
26 *Oeuvres*, XVII, 283.
27 Michelessi, *Algarotti*, 130.
28 Pangels, 74.
29 Id., 194.
30 Holmsten, 44.
31 Pangels, 330.
32 *Oeuvres*, XVI, 67; MacDonogh, *Berlin*, 206.
33 Five of these were vacant at his death.
34 Thiébault, III, 4–7.
35 Id., 9.
36 M.M.C.F., *Mémoires*, 13.
37 Schieder, 50–1; Richter (ed.), *Fredersdorf*, 20.
38 It survived both the Red Army and the DDR.
39 Richter (ed.), *Fredersdorf*, 20–1; Hamilton, *Rheinsberg*, 237–241; Dehio, *Handbuch der Deutschen Kunstdenkmäler*, Berlin/DDR, Potsdam, Berlin [East], 1983, 474; Leuschner, 79–80; *Wanderungen*, I, 322–5.
40 Schieder, 51.
41 Thiébault, II, 60–3.
42 Id., III, 3–4.
43 Kadatz, *Knobelsdorff*, 120.

44 In the boulevard Saint Germain; since 1840 the ministère des travaux publics. Carl von Lork, *Preussisches Rokoko*, Oldenburg, Hamburg, 1964, 6, 7, 13, 14.

45 Hans-Joachim Giersberg, 'Die Bauten Friedrichs des Grossen', in Hohenzollern (ed.), 63.

46 These were destroyed in the Second World War, but the rococo panelling has been sensitively restored.

47 Volz (ed.), I, 101.

48 Voltaire, *Mémoires*, 35.

49 Lork, *Rokoko*, 19.

50 Volz (ed.), I, 103.

51 Id., 106–7.

52 Kadatz, *Knobelsdorff*, 119; *Oeuvres*, VII, 35.

53 *Oeuvres*, XXII, 13.

54 Volz (ed.), I, 106–7.

55 Bielfeld, III, 137–42.

56 Volz (ed.), I, 119–20.

57 Bielfeld, III, 143; Volz (ed.), I, 108.

58 Seckendorff, I, 282–4.

59 Volz (ed.), I, 113.

60 Id., 133.

61 Id., 110–11.

62 Venohr, 19.

63 Volz (ed.), I, 96.

64 Holmsten, 40; Mittenzwei, 45; *Oeuvres*, IX, 28–9.

65 *Oeuvres*, XXII, 12–13.

66 Volz (ed.), I, 101; *Oeuvres*, XXII, 6; Koser, I, 203.

67 *Oeuvres*, XXII, 13.

68 Id., XVII, 66; Vocke, 108.

69 *Oeuvres*, XXII, 4–5.

70 Id., 9.

71 Volz (ed.), I, 98.

72 Id., 129.

73 Id., 136.

74 Jessen, 83; *Oeuvres*, XXII, 7, 13.

75 Id., XXVII, 87.

76 Venohr, 26.

77 Lorenz Seelig, *Friedrich und Wilhelmine von Bayreuth: Die Kunst am Bayreuther Hof, 1732–1763*, Munich and Zurich, 1982, 29.

78 Wilhelmina, 369.

79 Pangels, 146, 157.

80 Wilhelmina, 370–1.

81 Thiébault, I, 203.

82 Voltaire, *Mémoires*, 29n; *Oeuvres*, XIV, 156. Koser, I, 221–2.

83 Lork, *Rokoko*, 14.

84 Quoted in Peyrefitte, I, 156.

85 Id., 157.

86 Id., 154–8.

87 *Oeuvres*, XXII, 26.

88 Mervaud, *Voltaire et Frédéric*, 113; Peyrefitte, I, 163; *Oeuvres*, XVII, 67.

89 Voltaire, *Mémoires*, 30–1; Peyrefitte, I, 163–5.

90 Raymond Trousson, Jeroom Vercruysse and Jacques Lemaire (eds), *Dictionnaire Voltaire*, Brussels, 1994, 9; *Oeuvres*, XVII, 70.

91 Christopher Duffy, *Frederick the Great: A Military Life*, London, 1985, 21; *Politische Correspondenz Friedrichs des Grossen*, 46 vols (hereafter 'PC'), I, 7; *Oeuvres*, XVII, 67.

92 Duffy, 22; PC, I, 39.

93 *Oeuvres*, II, 54.

94 Bielfeld, IV, 14–18.

95 *Oeuvres*, XXII, 48–9.

96 Id., XVIII, 20.

97 Id., XXVII, 36.

98 PC, I, 86.

99 Id., 7–8; *Oeuvres*, XVIII, 20.

100 PC, I, 62.

101 Id., 159; Chester Easum, *Prince Henry of Prussia, Brother of Frederick the Great*, Madison, 1942, 13.

102 Volz (ed.), I, 138.

103 *Oeuvres*, XVIII, 20.

104 Id., 17.

105 Halsband, *Hervey*, 272.

106 Peyrefitte, I, 185.

107 *Oeuvres*, XXII, 56.

108 *Oeuvres*, XVIII, 18–19.

109 Volz (ed.), I, 139.

110 Wilhelmina, 371.

111 *Oeuvres*, XVI, 403–4.

112 Id., XVIII, 25.

113 Frederick stood as ward for Suhm's children. He also educated those of his friend La Motte Fouqué, who died of old age.

114 Jacques Maurens in Voltaire, *Histoire de la guerre de 1741*, introduction, x.

115 Algarotti's origins changed from time to time: Mantua, Padua, Venice or Florence.

116 *Oeuvres*, XVII, 25–6.

117 Peyrefitte, I, 200.

118 *Oeuvres*, XVII, 72.

CHAPTER SIX: CHASING CLOUDS OF GLORY

1 PC, I, 74; Schieder, 138; Franz Herre, *Maria Theresia: Die Grosse Habsburgerin*,

Cologne, 1994, 54; Dennis Showalter, *The Wars of Frederick the Great*, London and New York, 1996, 41.

2 M.S. Anderson, *The War of the Austrian Succession*, London and New York, 1995, 59.

3 Holmsten, 54; Schieder, 137–8.

4 Schieder, 141.

5 Voltaire, *Histoire de la guerre de 1741*, 9.

6 'et prenez du meilleur orviétan et du bon or pour dorer vos pillules'. The literal translation is ungainly. PC, I, 94, 131–2.

7 *Oeuvres*, II, 54–5.

8 PC, I, 100, 146.

9 Herre, 55.

10 Volz (ed.), I, 140.

11 *Oeuvres*, XVII, 73.

12 Kadatz, *Knobelsdorff*, 126.

13 *Oeuvres*, II, 58; Duffy, 24.

14 Quoted in Emil Ludwig, *Wilhelm der Zweite*, Frankfurt am Main, Hamburg, 1968, 52; Volz (ed.), I, 102.

15 *Oeuvres*, XVII, 91.

16 PC, I, 147–8.

17 *Oeuvres*, XXVII, 97.

18 PC, I, 169; Volz (ed.), I, 163–8.

19 *Oeuvres*, , XVII, 84.

20 Id., XVIII, 28.

21 Id., XXVII, 99.

22 Id., II, 58–74.

23 Voltaire, *Mémoires*, 109–11.

24 Jessen, 134–5.

25 *Oeuvres*, I, 82; Mittenzwei, 60–1; Venohr, 103.

26 Jessen, 137.

27 *Oeuvres*, XVII, 91. Jordan quotes a Dutch gazette.

28 Venohr, 117; Herre, 59.

29 *Oeuvres*, XVII, 74–7, 79, 87.

30 Herre, 56.

31 C.A.Macartney, *Maria Theresa and The House of Austria*, London, 1969, 34.

32 *Oeuvres*, XVIII, 29.

33 Jessen, 96.

34 Voltaire, *Histoire de la guerre de 1741*, 17.

35 *Oeuvres*, XVII, 100.

36 Id., XXVI, 85.

37 PC, I, 201; Jessen, 140.

38 Showalter, 45.

39 They managed to capture Maupertuis and lead him – apparently stark naked – into captivity. Frederick later implied that the mathematician had brought his fate on himself.

40 Showalter, 50.

41 Id.

42 *Oeuvres*, XVII, 99; XXVII, 101.

43 Duffy, 34.

44 *Histoire de mon temps*, in *Oeuvres*, I, 75–6.

45 *Oeuvres*, XVII, 98.

46 Jessen, 18.

47 *Oeuvres*, XIX, 4; Bielfeld, I, 131–2.

48 *Oeuvres*, XVII, 114–15.

49 Id., II, 93.

50 Id., XVII, 127; PC, I, 298, 319.

51 Voltaire, *Histoire de la guerre de 1741*, 20.

52 Anderson, *Austrian Succession*, 82.

53 Bielfeld, I, 9–12.

54 MacDonogh, *Prussia*, 233–4; Venohr, 121.

55 K.A. Varnhagen von Ense, *Leben des Feldmarschalls Grafen von Schwerin*, Berlin, 1847, 87, 98–9; Jessen, 175; *Oeuvres*, XVII, 191.

56 Anderson, *Austrian Succession*, 88–9; Duffy, 36.

57 Venohr, 119.

58 Kadatz, *Knobelsdorff*, 134.

59 Bielfeld, I, 104; *Oeuvres*, XVII, 135, 82.

60 Reed Browning, *The War of the Austrian Succession*, Stroud, 1994, 87–8.

61 Anon., *Hans Joachim von Zieten*, Berlin, 1865, 12.

62 *Oeuvres*, XVII, 151; XVIII, 30–1; Bielfeld, I, 116–17.

63 *Oeuvres*, XX, 3.

64 Id., XXII, 93.

65 Lorenz, *Benda*, 8.

66 *Oeuvres*, XVII, 159, 167, 170, 198.

67 Algarotti suggested that he had only fought the battle there because the word rhymed with Mollwitz. When Voltaire complained of the prosaic name – 'comment parler de Chotosits [sic] en vers?' – Frederick was quick to remind him of Algarotti's argument.

68 For example, Showalter, 59.

69 Jessen, 175; *Oeuvres*, XVII, 209, 213.

70 Duffy, 44–5; Venohr, 128; *Oeuvres*, XVII, 213.

71 *Oeuvres*, II, 129.

72 *Oeuvres*, XVIII, 34.

73 *Oeuvres*, III, 72; PC, II, 179, 183; quote from Anderson, *Austrian Succession*, 221–2.

74 Peyrefitte, I, 229, 236.
75 *Oeuvres*, XVIII, 35–9.
76 Id., XVII, 216, 242 n. a.
77 Id., 223.
78 Venohr, 125.
79 Voltaire, *Histoire de la guerre de 1741*, 28.
80 *Oeuvres*, XVII, 110.
81 PC, II, 187, 191, 194, 215, 224, 238.
82 *Oeuvres*, XXII, 100–1, 105; Peyrefitte, I, 246.
83 Kadatz, *Knobelsdorff*, 131.
84 *Oeuvres*, XXV, 527.
85 Id., XVIII, 48–9.
86 Id., XVII, 224, 234, 235, 249.
87 Id., 242.
88 Id., II, 141; III, 28.
89 Mervaud, *Voltaire et Frédéric*, 2, 133, 137; *Oeuvres*, XXII, 109.
90 Id., XVIII, 50.
91 Keyserlingk married in the last years of his life and had a daughter, who was Frederick's ward. Id., XXV, 523.
92 Id., XXII, 126.
93 Id., XXVII, 113.
94 Lorenz, *Benda*, 23.
95 Pangels, 273–4; PC, II, 375.
96 The name 'Ane de Mirepoix' was a play on the fact the bishop signed himself 'anc. de Mirepoix', or 'anciennement de Mirepoix'.
97 *Oeuvres*, XXII, 138; Peyrefitte, I, 264–5.
98 *Oeuvres*, XXII, 131–2; III, 23–4; Peyrefitte, I, 267; Mervaud, *Voltaire et Frédéric*, 148.
99 Peyrefitte, I, 248; Jessen, 186.
100 *Oeuvres*, XXII, 143–4; Peyrefitte, I, 274.
101 Peyrefitte, I, 277.
102 Pangels, 148–50.
103 Mervaud, *Voltaire et Frédéric*, 155; Peyrefitte, I, 279.
104 *Oeuvres*, XXII, 157.
105 Id., XIV, 89.
106 Id., 92.
107 Pangels, 275–6.
108 *Oeuvres*, XXII, 154.
109 Id., 156.
110 Bielfeld, I, 183.
111 *Oeuvres*, XXV, 528.
112 Friedrich Freyherr von der Trenck, *Merkwürdige Lebensgeschichte*, 4 vols, Berlin, 1787, 30–1, 42; vicomte E. du Jeu, *Trenck: Un aventurier prussien au dix-huitième siècle*, Paris, 1928, 28–9.

113 The literature on Trenck is enormous. The following is by no means exhaustive: Thiébault, IV, 203–7; *Wahrhafte Beleuchtung der Lebensgeschichte des Freiherrn von der Trenck wider die Beschuldigungen gegen Friedrich den Grossen, von einen Brandenburgischen Patrioten*, Lausanne 1787, is a defence of Frederick against Trenck's accusations; Theodor Wahrmann, *Friedrich Freiherr von der Trenck: Leben, Kerker, Tod*, Leipzig, 1837, 55; possibly the most useful is the sage Friedrich von Oppeln-Bronikowski, *Abenteurer am Preussischen Hofe, 1700–1800*, Berlin, Leipzig, 1927, 98.
114 On the other hand Voltaire might still have been fantasising about Ulrica.
115 *Candide*, chapter I; du Jeu, *Trenck*, 182–3.
116 Formey, *Choix des mémoires et abrégé de l'Histoire de l'academie de Berlin*, 4 vols, Berlin, 1767, I, 10–11.
117 Bielfeld, I, 161–6.
118 Showalter, 65.
119 Isabel de Madariaga, *Russia in the Age of Catherine the Great*, London, 1981, 5; Vincent Cronin, *Catherine, Empress of All the Russias*, London, 1989, 43.
120 *Oeuvres*, XXVI, 77.
121 Jessen, 187.
122 PC, III, 357.
123 Id., 63, 128, 133.
124 Id., 153.
125 Id., 261.
126 *Oeuvres*, III, 58.
127 Holmsten, 68.
128 Showalter, 76.
129 PC, IV, 7, 14.
130 Id., 24, 31, 101.
131 Holmsten, 69; *Oeuvres*, XVII, 288.
132 Holmsten, 69.
133 Showalter, 81.
134 PC, IV, 181–2; Jessen, 201, 205; Jacobs (ed.), *Briefe an Thieriot*, 44; *Oeuvres*, XVII, 287.
135 Oppeln-Bronikowski, *Abenteurer*, 97; du Jeu, *Trenck*, 40.
136 Fouqué had taken over the job from Winterfeldt, who was badly needed elsewhere.
137 K.A. Varnhagen von Ense, *General Hans Karl von Winterfeldt*, Berlin, 1836, 29; Buettner, *La Motte Fouqué*, 8, 18, 23, 28n.
138 PC, IV, 218; *Oeuvres*, XXV, 530–7, 543–5; Richter (ed.), *Fredersdorf*, 51.

139 Richter (ed.), *Fredersdorf*, 58.
140 *Oeuvres*, III, 140; XXVII, 137; PC, IV, 290, Showalter, 84.
141 PC, IV, 291, 293, 307, 320; *Oeuvres*, III, 70; XVII, 289; *Koser*, II, 227; Richter (ed.), *Fredersdorf*, 57.
142 Richter (ed.), *Fredersdorf*, 56.
143 *Oeuvres*, XVII, 290.
144 Richter (ed.), *Fredersdorf*, 67.
145 Christian Graf von Krockow, *Friedrich der Grosse: Ein Lebensbild*, Bergisch Gladbach, 1987, 61, quoted in MacDonogh, *Prussia*, 35.
146 Duffy, 74.
147 Holmsten, 69; Showalter, 87.
148 Voltaire, *Histoire de la guerre de 1741*, 173.
149 Joseph Gregor, *Kulturgeschichte der Oper: Ihre Verbindung mit dem Leben, den Werken des Geistes und der Politik*, 2nd edn, Vienna and Zurich, 1950, 148; Lorenz, *Benda*, 23; Richter (ed.), *Fredersdorf*, 82.
150 Richter (ed.), *Fredersdorf*, 86.
151 Schieder, 170; Holmsten, 70; Jessen, 220.
152 Bielfeld, I, 244.
153 Id., II, 4–6.
154 Voltaire, *Histoire de la guerre de 1741*, 174; Holmsten, 70; Volz (ed.), I, 213–15; Jessen, 221.

CHAPTER SEVEN: FREDERICK THE GREAT
1 *Oeuvres*, XVII, 297; Bielfeld, II, 10–11.
2 Bielfeld, II, 21–2.
3 Schieder, 72; Richter (ed.), *Fredersdorf*, 65–6.
4 Splitgerber had bought him French books and lent him money as crown prince.
5 Showalter, 95, 97–8, 102–3; Hubert Johnson, *Frederick the Great and his Officials*, Newhaven and London, 1975, 84.
6 Johnson, 134.
7 Walther Hubatsch, *Frederick the Great of Prussia: Absolutism and Administration*, tr. Patrick Doran, London, 1975, 75, 78.
8 Schieder, 72; Bielfeld, II, 36–7.
9 Carl Brinitzer, *Die Geschichte des Daniel Ch.: Ein Sittenbild des 18. Jahrhunderts*, Stuttgart, 1973, 9–10.
10 Holmsten, 72–3.
11 *Oeuvres*, XVII, 321, 329.
12 Id., XXVII, 193; Pangels, 91; Venohr, 242.

13 Voltaire, *Mémoires*, 44; Johnson, 69, 16–17.
14 *Oeuvres*, XXVII, 150; Johnson, 84.
15 Hubatsch, 83–4.
16 Id., 90, 94–5.
17 Frederick's work was undone by the terrible floods of the spring and summer of 1997.
18 Hubatsch, 101–2; Mittenzwei; 87, 92.
19 Hubatsch, 102–3; Venohr, 177; Fontane, 'Meine Kinderjahre', in *Fontanes Werke in fünf Bänden*, Berlin and Weimar, 1986, I, 119.
20 Hubatsch, 105–7; Lorenz, *Benda*, 9.
21 Schieder, 72.
22 Johnson, 125–8; Schieder, 89; Bielfeld, II, 40, 107, 125–30.
23 Venohr, 206; Detlef Martin, 'Allgemeines Landrecht', in Treue (ed.), 69; Koser, II, 45.
24 Voltaire, *Mémoires*, 45.
25 Jessen, 249; Venohr, 187, 225.
26 Schieder, 104–11.
27 Duffy, 255.
28 Jessen, 250–4.
29 Id., 254–5.
30 The earl of Ilchester and Mrs Langford-Brooke, *The Life of Sir Charles Hanbury-Williams, Poet, Wit and Diplomatist*, Bristol, 1928, 169.
31 *Oeuvres*, XXII, 137.
32 Holmsten, 80.
33 *Oeuvres*, XVII, 244.
34 Brinitzer, *Daniel Ch.*, 9, 14, 16.
35 Paul Dehnert, *Daniel Chodowiecki*, Berlin (West), 1977, 6.
36 Frederick William had made his fool president of the Academy.
37 Schieder, 74.
38 *Oeuvres*, XVII, 336; A le Sueur, *Maupertuis et ses correspondents*, Montreuil-sur-Mer, 1856, 17; Schieder, 57.
39 Richter (ed.), *Fredersdorf*, 76.
40 Gregor, *Kulturgeschichte*, 144–5.
41 Richter (ed.), *Fredersdorf*, 84; Lorenz, *Benda*, 21–3; Quantz, 13.
42 Lorenz, *Benda*, 28; Charles Sandford Terry, *John Christian Bach*, Westport, Conn., 2nd edn, 1967, 7.
43 Volz (ed.), I, 106–7.
44 Terry, *J.C. Bach*, 4–7.
45 Id., 5.
46 Darrell Berg, 'C.P.E. Bach's character pieces and his friendship circle', in

Stephen Clark (ed.), *C.P.E. Bach Studies*, Oxford, 1988, 25–31.

47 Volz (ed.), I, 112; Terry, *J.C. Bach*, 7.

48 Lork, *Rokoko*, 18; Kadatz, *Knobelsdorff*, 20.

49 Lork, *Rokoko*, 15.

50 Id., 19; Koser, II, 227.

51 Kadatz, *Knobelsdorff*, 120.

52 The house, which survived until the 1930s when it was pulled down by the Nazis, had served as a residence to the theatre people, Gustav Gründgens and Max Reinhardt, among others. Id., 124.

53 H.J. Giersberg, *Friedrich als Bauherr: Studien zur Architektur des 18 Jahrhunderts in Berlin und Potsdam*, Berlin, 1986, 15; Kadatz, *Knobelsdorff*, 133, 135–6, 179–81; *Oeuvres*, XXVII, 158, 176; Bielfeld, II, 119.

54 Lork, *Rokoko*, 19.

55 Kadatz, *Knobelsdorff*, 190–1; Bielfeld, II, 132–3.

56 Lork, *Rokoko*, 20; Dehio, *Berlin/DDR und Potsdam*, 352; Kadatz, *Knobelsdorff*, 211.

57 *Oeuvres*, XXII, 80.

58 Thiébault, I, 82–3; IV, 230.

59 *Oeuvres*, XIX, 12–13.

60 Frederick Pottle (ed.), *Boswell on the Grand Tour: Germany and Switzerland, 1764*, London, 1953, 16.

61 *Oeuvres*, XXVII, 169; XIX, 17–19, 24, 35 n. 2.

62 Id., XXVII, 155, 158; Koser, II, 237; Seelig, *Friedrich und Wilhelmine*, 33; Kadatz, *Knobelsdorff*, 211.

63 Kadatz, *Knobelsdorff*, 225–7.

64 Id., 214–15; Bielfeld, II, 116.

65 Friedrich Nicolai, *Beschreibung der königlichen Residenzstadt Potsdam und der umliegenden Gegend*, Leipzig, 1993, 36; Bielfeld, II, 116–18.

66 I.e. Am Kanal 3, General Wade's house in London came down in 1935, the house it inspired on the Blücherplatz in Potsdam, ten years later.

67 *Oeuvres*, XVIII, 57–9, 79–81; Howard Colvin, *A Biographical Dictionary of English Architects, 1660–1840*, 3rd edn, London, 1995, 149–151, 210; Pamela Kingsbury, *Lord Burlington's Town Architecture*, London, 1995, 59–72; Giersberg, *Friedrich als Bauherr*, 144–5; Giersberg in Hohenzollern (ed.), 81, reproduces Frederick's sketch for Am Kanal 3.

68 Holmsten, 90.

69 Bielfeld, II, 53.

70 Holmsten, 89.

71 *A Fragment of a Memoir of Fieldmarshal James Keith, written by himself, 1714–1734*, Edinburgh, 1843, ix.

72 Edith Cuthell, *The Scottish Friend of Frederick the Great: The Last Earl Marischal*, 2 vols, London, 1915, I, 231.

73 Id., 233.

74 Krockow, *Brüder*, 70.

75 Schieder, 56.

76 Ilchester and Mrs Langford Brooke, *Hanbury-Williams*, 187.

77 Bielfeld, I, 199; *Oeuvres*, XXVI, 106.

78 *Oeuvres*, XVI, 84.

79 Pangels, 421.

80 *Oeuvres*, XXVI, 149; Schieder, 54–5.

81 PC, II, 312.

82 *Oeuvres*, XXVI, 153.

83 Id., 154.

84 Pangels, 342.

85 Bielfeld, I, 219; *Oeuvres*, XXVII, 147.

86 *Oeuvres*, XXVII, 140, 145.

87 Bielfeld, II, 21–3.

88 *Oeuvres*, XXVII, 145; XXVI, 89.

89 Id., IX, 5–6.

90 Id., I, 123.

91 Id., XXVI, 90–1.

92 Id., 93, 91; XXVII, 147.

93 Marianne Cochois was married to the ballet master Desplaces, and was the subject of a portrait painted by Pesne in 1745, a pendant to his portrait of La Barberina. Her sister Babet married the marquis d'Argens; Madame de Hauteville had been recruited by d'Argens in 1743. Id., XXII, 161; Giacomo Casanova, *Chevalier de Seingalt: History of My Life*, 12 vols, tr. Willard Trask, Baltimore and London, 1997, X, 341 n. 36; Helmut Börsch Supan, 'Friedrich der Grosse als Sammler von Gemälden', in Hohenzollern (ed.), 166.

94 Pangels, 333–4; Casanova, *My Life*, X, 78; Henry Lionnet, *Dictionnaire des Comédiens Français*, Geneva, 1908, II, 192; Voltaire, *Mémoires*, 48.

95 Casanova, *My Life*, X, 341 n. 34.

96 *Oeuvres*, XI, 120; XXII, 164; Richter (ed.), *Fredersdorf*, 95, 103, 116.

97 Richter (ed.), *Fredersdorf*, 118, 120.

98 Lorenz, *Benda*, 24.

99 Albert Schweizer, *J.S. Bach*, Wiesbaden, 1954, 366. Schieder, 434, citing Philip

Spittas, gives the date of Bach's meeting with the king as the 11th.

100 Schweizer, *Bach*, 366–7.

101 Jessen, 238; Pangels, 165.

102 Ilchester and Mrs Langford-Brooke, *Hanbury-Williams*, 205, 212–13.

103 Schieder, 85; Bielfeld, II, 28.

104 *Oeuvres*, XXVI, 98.

105 Id., I, 224–30.

106 Id., XXVII, 171.

107 The painting is thought to have been destroyed in the Russian invasion, but there are prints and copies.

108 Schieder, 57.

109 Seelig, *Friedrich und Wilhelmine*, 52–3; Pangels, 340.

110 *Oeuvres*, XXVII, 187.

111 Id., XXII, 223.

112 Id., XI, 130–1.

113 Id., 139–40; Pierre Gaxotte (ed.), *Frédéric II roi de Prusse*, Paris, 1967, aperçu bibliographique, 399–400.

114 *Oeuvres*, XI, 165, 173.

115 Id., 205.

116 *Oeuvres*, XI, 211–12.

117 Id., xii–xiii; XVII, 313–15.

118 Id., X, 250, 278, 296, 284.

119 Id., IX, 24–5, 27.

120 Id., I, 200–11.

121 Id., 212.

122 Id., XVIII, 63–4.

123 Id., 64; XXII, 223.

124 Id., XV, 309.

125 Id., XVIII, 59–62.

126 Id., 67.

127 *Oeuvres*, XVIII, 70–71; Casanova, *My Life*, X, 338 n. 12.

128 *Oeuvres*, XVIII, 71–3; Venohr, 183.

CHAPTER EIGHT: FREDERICK AND FRANÇOIS

1 Peyrefitte, II, 50, 60.

2 *Oeuvres*, XXII, 197, 194–5.

3 *Oeuvres*, XXII, 207, 211–12, 214–15.

4 Id., XXVIII, 65–6.

5 Voltaire, *Mémoires*, 123–4.

6 *Oeuvres*, XXII, 215–16.

7 Id., XVIII, 68–9.

8 Charles Collé, *Journal et Mémoires sur les hommes de lettres, 1748–1772, nouvelle édition*, ed. Honoré Bonhomme, 3 vols, Paris 1868, I, 184–6.

9 *Oeuvres*, XXII, 219, 221, 222, 222–3.

10 Id., XXII, 246, 249, 253.

11 Mervaud, *Voltaire et Frédéric*, 173; Peyrefitte, II, 134.

12 *Oeuvres*, XXII, 255.

13 Peyrefitte, II, 130.

14 Voltaire, *Mémoires*, 127–8.

15 Bielfeld, II, 61–3; Peyrefitte, II, 137–43.

16 Voltaire had not abandoned the idea of doing a little spying for his country. Louis, however, had responded to his departure by abolishing his offices. He retained only his court pension.

17 Peyrefitte, II, 143–9.

18 Voltaire, *Mémoires*, 139–40.

19 Id., 129.

20 André Magnan, *Dossier Voltaire en Prusse (1750–1753)*, Voltaire Foundation, Oxford, 1986, has shown that Voltaire intended to use the correspondence with his niece as a basis for a novel called *Paméla* 1, 2; 54–5. The letters were reworked and shortened, and a quantity suppressed so that now there are only 38 of the 50-odd written in the original correspondence. *Paméla* has been reconstructed by Edouard Guitton, *Voltaire: Romans et Contes*, Paris, 1994, see notes pp. 894–6. Voltaire, *Mémoires*, 56.

21 Peyrefitte, II, 356–7.

22 Voltaire, *Mémoires*, 129.

23 Peyrefitte, II, 149.

24 Menzel's painting shows Frederick with Voltaire, the brothers Keith and d'Argens drinking flutes of champagne. Others left out of Hanbury-Williams' list were the Germans, Stille, Winterfeldt, La Motte Fouqué and Gotter.

25 Ilchester and Mrs Langford-Brooke, *Hanbury-Williams*, 202–5; Helmut Eisenlohr in *Friedrich der Grosse: Sein Bild im Wandel der Zeiten*, Frankfurt am Main, 1986, 73.

26 Voltaire, *Mémoires*, 45.

27 Catt, 66.

28 Voltaire, *Mémoires*, 133.

29 Voltaire, *Mémoires*, 133.

30 Cuthell, *Earl Marischal*, I, 245.

31 Mervaud, *Voltaire et Frédéric*, 70 n. 1, 186 n. 76; *Oeuvres*, XXII, 255; Peyrefitte, II, 109, 151–5, 157; Collé, *Journal*, I, 261. Peyrefitte quotes Collé talking of Frederick's 'amours' with Baculard d'Arnaud; Collé's text gives 'amis', which is another thing altogether.

32 Come Alexandre Collini, *Mon Séjour*

auprès de Voltaire et lettres inédites, Paris, 1807, 38; Mervaud; *Voltaire et Frédéric*, 209 n. 204. Peyrefitte, II, 204.

33 Voltaire, *Mémoires*, 141.

34 Peyrefitte, II, 197.

35 Peyrefitte, II, 200–1; Holmsten, 91; Voltaire, *Mémoires*, 143; *Oeuvres*, XXVII, 203.

36 Collini, *Mon Séjour*, 30; Peyrefitte, II, 235.

37 Magnan, *Dossier Voltaire*, 276. Magnan quotes Hirschel's petition; Oeuvres, XXVII, 198.

38 Ilchester and Mrs Langford-Brooke, *Hanbury-Williams*, 207; Collé, *Journal*, I, 288–90. Mervaud, *Voltaire et Frédéric*, 193–5.

39 Ilchester and Mrs Langford-Brooke, *Hanbury-Williams*, 205.

40 Catt, 70.

41 *Oeuvres*, XXVII, 199.

42 Collé, *Journal*, I, 290; Peyrefitte, II, 158, 166–7; Mervaud, *Voltaire et Frédéric*, 199 n. 154, 200 n. 156.

43 *Oeuvres*, XXVII, 200.

44 Id., 201.

45 Magnan, *Dossier Voltaire*, 96; *Oeuvres*, XXVII, 204–5; Mervaud, *Voltaire et Frédéric*, suggests that Baculard might have encouraged Hirschel: 197 n. 136.

46 Collé, *Journal*, I, 291.

47 Peyrefitte, II, 169.

48 Collé, *Journal*, I, 287–8.

49 Peyrefitte, II, 158, 162, 167.

50 Id., II, 171.

51 Koser, II, 269; Venohr, 214.

52 *Oeuvres*, XXII, 261.

53 Id., 262–3.

54 Id., 265.

55 Id., XX, 32.

56 Id., XXII, 273–4; Thiébault, IV, 282.

57 *Oeuvres*, XXII, 278.

58 Peyrefitte, II, 197.

59 Cronin, *Catherine: Empress of all the Russias*, 29; Magnan, *Dossier Voltaire*, 87, 83, 95.

60 *Oeuvres*, XXII, 286–8.

61 Peyrefitte, II, 126–7.

62 M.M.C.F., 5–7. *Voltaire et Frédéric*, 255, suggests Beaumelle was the author.

63 Voltaire, *Mémoires*, 43.

64 Richter (ed.), *Fredersdorf*, 315, 337.

65 M.M.C.F., 10; Voltaire, *Mémoires*, 58, 147; Le Sueur, *Maupertuis*, 27.

66 *Dictionnaire Voltaire*, 104; Voltaire, *Mémoires*, 152.

67 K.A. Varnhagen von Ense, *Voltaire in Frankfurt am Main, 1753*, Leipzig, 1859, 6; *Oeuvres*, XXII, 302.

68 Voltaire, *Dictionnaire philosophique*, Paris, 1967, 228–32.

69 *Oeuvres*, XXII, 297; Voltaire, *Mémoires*, 60.

70 Voltaire, *Mémoires*, 153. The same caveat applies.

71 Thiébault, IV, 271–3; *Oeuvres*, XV, 60–3.

72 Collini, *Mon Séjour*, 45; *Dictionnaire Voltaire*, 104; *Oeuvres*, XXII, 305; Peyrefitte, II, 258–73; Mervaud, *Voltaire et Frédéric*, 225.

73 Richter (ed.), *Fredersdorf*, 207–8.

74 Collini, *Mon Séjour*, 49; *Oeuvres*, XXII, 306; Mervaud, *Voltaire et Frédéric*, 211, 232.

75 *Oeuvres*, XXII, 288, 304, 307.

76 Mervaud, *Voltaire et Frédéric*, 226. Madame Mervaud allows her fondness for Voltaire to get the better of her. Frederick was unreasonable and made 'aucune démarche aimable', id., 236. *Oeuvres*, XXII, 308.

77 *Oeuvres*, XXII, 308.

78 Id., 308–9.

79 *Dictionnaire Voltaire*, 104. For Frederick's brief reconciliation see d'Alembert's letter to Madame de Deffand of 16 February 1753 published in Benedetta Craveri, *Madame du Deffand and her World*, London 1994, 108.

80 Peyrefitte, II, 246.

81 *Dictionnaire Voltaire*, 104; Collé, *Journal*, II, 189.

82 *Oeuvres*, XXVII, 226–7, 230.

83 The Blumenkammer at Sanssouci is often confused with the Voltairezimmer in the Berlin Schloss. Hoppenhaupt's decoration included birds, but none of the other beasts associated with Voltaire.

84 Nicolai, *Potsdam*, 102; PC, IX, 365.

85 Collini, *Mon Séjour*, 64; *Oeuvres*, XXVII, 236 n. a.

86 From the ancient Provencal family.

87 Richter (ed.), *Fredersdorf*, 256.

88 *Oeuvres*, XXVII, 235.

89 PC, IX, 365; *Oeuvres*, XXVII, 193, 234; Pangels, 91.

90 Varnhagen von Ense, *Voltaire in Frankfurt*, 8–9, 12.

91 Collini, *Mon Séjour*, 67.

92 Varnhagen von Ense, *Voltaire in Frankfurt*, 14–16. Anton Schindling, 'Friedrich der Grosse und das Reichische Deutschland, in *Friedrich der Grosse: Sein Bild im Wandel der Zeiten*, Frankfurt am Main, 1986, 9.

93 Cuthell, *Earl Marischal*, I, 263.

94 Peyrefitte, II, 327.

95 Id., 328.

96 Collini, *Mon Séjour*, 80.

97 Varnhagen von Ense, *Voltaire in Frankfurt*, 47, 52.

98 Déclaration de M de **** detenu en prison à Frankfort par le roi de Prusse, n. d., 22.

99 Lettre de M. de *** à M. D*** à Maience le 9 juillet 1753, 25–6.

100 Varnhagen von Ense, *Voltaire in Frankfurt*, 58; Mervaud, *Voltaire et Frédéric*, 243.

101 Id., 243.

102 Peyrefitte, II, 330–50.

103 Collini, *Mon Séjour*, 87; Varnhagen von Ense, *Voltaire in Frankfurt*, 55.

104 Varnhagen von Ense, *Voltaire in Frankfurt*, 56.

105 Id., 72, 82–4; Collini, *Mon Séjour*, 91.

106 Voltaire, *Mémoires*, 59, 156–7.

107 Varnhagen von Ense, *Voltaire in Frankfurt*, 3–4.

108 Collini, *Mon Séjour*, 94; Mervaud, *Voltaire et Frédéric*, 254.

109 Jean Goulemot, André Magnan and Didier Masseau, *Inventaire Voltaire*, Paris, 1995, 1118.

110 André Magnan, *Dossier Voltaire*, 58.

111 PC, X, 31–2.

112 PC, X, 14.

113 Id., 135.

114 Id., 39–40.

115 PC, X, 216–17.

116 Id., 250.

117 She granted him another audience in Avignon in December that year.

118 Quoted in Wilhelmina, Préface de Pierre Gaxotte, 19; *Oeuvres*, XVIII, 97.

119 Id., XX, 47.

120 Id., XVIII, 77–9, 85; MacDonogh, *Berlin*, 71.

121 Id., III, 118.

122 Id., XXI, 222.

123 Richter (ed.), *Fredersdorf*, 292.

124 *Oeuvres*, XVIII, 86–9.

125 Id., XXVII, 264.

126 Id., XX, 43.

127 *Testament politique 1752*, in Gaxotte, 295.

128 Id., 335.

129 Brinitzer, *Daniel Ch.*, 76.

130 *Oeuvres*, XX, 264; Steffi Roettgen, *Anton Raphael Mengs 1728–1779 and his British Patrons*, London, 1993, 18.

131 Only sixty pictures from the original collection of 172 are still hung in the gallery. The majority never made their way back from Russia after the war.

132 Richter (ed.), *Fredersdorf*, 233, 309, 353, 373; *Oeuvres*, XX, 54, 55, 57, 60, 65, 66; XXVII, 262–3, 277, 281; Kadatz, *Knobelsdorff*, 211; Gerd Bartoscheck, *Bildergalerie Sanssouci: Die Gemälde* (catalogue), 1996; Matthias Oesterreich, *Beschreibung aller Gemälde, Antiquitäten, und anderer kostbarer und merkwürdiger Sachen, so in Beyden Schlössern von Sans-Souci wie auch in dem Schlosse zu Potsdam und Charlottenburg enthalten sind*, Berlin, 1773 [reprint 1990], 71, 75–6.

133 Winfried Baer, *Berliner Porzellan vom Rokoko zum Biedermeier*, Berlin-Charlottenburg, 1969, 5.

134 That house still existed in 1967, at least; it was at Karl-Liebknecht-Strasse 10, the former Priesterstrasse.

135 Lorenz, *Benda*, 28–30.

136 *Oeuvres*, XXVII, 200.

137 Giovanna Astrua sang at the Berlin Opera from 1747 to 1756; Giovanni Carestini from 1750 to 1754. He excelled in *Orfio* and *Mithridate*.

138 Richter (ed.), *Fredersdorf*, 243, 376–7.

139 *Oeuvres*, XXVII, 257.

140 *Montezuma*, II, 7; Capriccio, *Königsdorf*, 1992; *Oeuvres*, XVIII, 90; Terry, *J.C. Bach*, 12 n. 3.

141 Terry, *J.C. Bach*, 13; Voltaire, *Mémoires*, 66; *Oeuvres*, XXVII, 284.

142 *Oeuvres*, XXVII, 188 n. a.

143 Id., 274.

144 Richter (ed.), *Fredersdorf*, 373.

145 *Oeuvres*, XVIII, 89.

146 Seelig, *Friedrich und Wilhelmine*, 40, 49.

147 Pangels, 94–6.

148 Ilchester and Mrs Langford-Brooke, *Hanbury-Williams*, 217.

149 Bielfeld, II, 85–6.

150 M.M.C.F., 20; Voltaire uses the term 'Potsdamite' for sodomite: see Mervaud, *Voltaire et Frédéric*, 361.

151 This is now the Humboldt University.

152 Holmsten, 84; Thiébault, II, 139–46, 178; Krockow, *Brüder*, 74, 76.

153 M.M.C.F., 21.

154 *Oeuvres*, XXVII, 264, 275–6.

155 Catt, 4.

156 Thiébault, I, 218.

157 Du Jeu, *Trenck*, 130, 99; Trenck, *Merkwürdige Lebensgeschichte*, I, 297–8.

158 *Oeuvres*, XXX, 195.

159 Ilchester and Mrs Langford-Brooke, *Hanbury-Williams*, 211, 215–17.

CHAPTER NINE: I AM INNOCENT OF THIS WAR

1 Venohr, 131.

2 *Oeuvres*, XXVIII, 9.

3 Showalter, 106; Schieder, 161.

4 *Oeuvres*, XXVIII, xiv–xv.

5 Id., IV, 7.

6 Wolfgang Lotz, *Kriegsgerichtsprozesse des Siebenjährigen Krieges in Preussen: Untersuchungen zur Beurteilung militärischer Leistung durch Friedrich II*, Frankfurt am Main, 1981, 11, 58, 62, 84–5.

7 *Oeuvres*, XXVIII, 5–6.

8 Catt, 56.

9 *Oeuvres*, XXVI, 116; PC, XV, 215.

10 C.B.A. Behrens, *Society, Government and Enlightenment*, 182–3.

11 He had been warned by Wilhelmina. See B.P.H. Rep. 46 W 17, vol 1 fol. 10–11, illustrated in Peter Krückmann, ed., *Galli Bibiena und ver Musenhof der Wilhelmine von Bayreuth*, Munich, New York, 1998, 151; *Oeuvres*, IV, 7.

12 The marquise was also thought to be upset by Frederick's verses about her and Louis:

> Quoi! Votre faible monarque,
> Jouet de la Pompadour,
> Flétri par plus d'une marque
> Des opprobes de l'amour…

These were leaked to the court by Voltaire. Choiseul commissioned a reply from the poet Palissot:

> Jusque-là, censeur moins sauvage,
> Souffre l'innocent badinage
> De la nature et des amours.
> Peux-tu condamner la tendresse,
> Toi qui n'en as connu l'ivresse
> Que dans les bras de tes tambours?

Voltaire slightly adapted Palissot's lines in his *Mémoires*.

13 PC, XII, 327.

14 R. Koser, 'Aus der Korrespondenz der französischen Gesandschaft 1746–1756', in *Forschungen zur Brandenburgischen und Preussischen Geschichte*, Leipzig, 1894, 88–9.

15 M.S. Anderson, *Europe in the Eighteenth Century, 1713–1783*, 2nd edn, London, 1976, 257; Schieder, 175, 183.

16 Johannes Kunisch, *Das Mirakel des Hauses Brandenburg: Studien zum Verhältnis von Kabinettspolitik und Kriegsführung im Zeitalter des Siebenjährigen Krieges*, Munich and Vienna, 1978, 31–3; Schieder, 176–7; PC, XI, 446–8.

17 PC, XI 199, 234–5; XIII, 37.

18 Schieder, 177; Holmsten, 119; Jessen, 290; *Oeuvres*, XXVII, 290.

19 *Oeuvres*, XXVI, 116; PC, XIII, 283; quoted endlessly: Holmsten, 108; Jessen, 262; Pangels, 350–1. The letter to Ferdinand is in Pangels, 488.

20 PC, XI, 445–6.

21 Id., 457, 459.

22 Schieder, 203, and Ritter, 130, offered balanced views; the Marxist Ingrid Mittenzwei is keen to put the blame on Frederick, see 111–16.

23 PC, XIII, 309, 344.

24 *Oeuvres*, IV, 39, 40–1, 80; PC, XI, 466–7; XIII, 75.

25 Jessen, 274; *Ewald von Kleist: Werke*, ed. August Sauer, 2 vols, Berlin, 1880–2, II, 335.

26 K.A. Varnhagen von Ense, *Leben des Feldmarschalls Jacob Keith*, 117; Ritter, 128–9; Kleist, *Werke*, II, 337.

27 *Oeuvres*, IV, 81–3; author's visit to Wittenberg, 18 August 1991.

28 Jessen, 276.

29 PC, XIII, 371, 386.

30 Catt, 87.

31 *Oeuvres*, XIX, 40–1.

32 Id., 41, 45, 47, 49.

33 Id., XV, 82.

34 Showalter, 136–42; Duffy, 102–7; Andrew Bisset (ed.), *Memoirs and Papers of Sir Andrew Mitchell KB*, 2 vols, London, 1850, I, 208.

35 Edith Kotasek, *Feldmarschall Graf Lacy: Ein Leben für Österreichs Heer*, Horn, 1956, 19.

36 PC, XIII, 487.

37 *Oeuvres*, IV, 97; Alfred Graf Schlieffen,

Friedrich der Grosse, Berlin, 1912, 19; Duffy, 108–9.

38 Schieder, 188; Showalter, 145.

39 Mitchell, I, 220.

40 Id., 218.

41 Volz (ed.), II, 3.

42 Id., 4.

43 PC, XIV, 123–4.

44 Id., 254.

45 Id., 185, 187, 201, 213.

46 Mitchell, I, 325.

47 Duffy, 115.

48 Catt, 236.

49 Varnhagen von Ense, *Schwerin*, 212–13; *Oeuvres*, IV, 118; XVIII, 107; Mitchell, I, 330; Volz (ed.), II, 20.

50 *Oeuvres*, IV, 122; Venohr, 249; Showalter, 155; PC, XV, 9.

51 Mitchell, I, 247; PC, XV, 9.

52 Mitchell, I, 249; the information on pubs comes from the late Mr Jimmy Young.

53 In central London, there was one in Leather Lane and Lower John Street in Holborn and another in Smithfield; on the periphery there were Fredericks in Anchor Street, Bethnal Green; in Sadlers Wells; and in Church Street, Deptford.

54 PC, XV, 101.

55 *Oeuvres*, IV, 119; Schieder, 190–1.

56 PC, XV, 121.

57 Schlieffen, *Friedrich der Grosse*, 57; Catt, 236–7.

58 Duffy, 127–8.

59 Id., 129.

60 'Scoundrels, do you want to live for ever then?'; 'Fred, for eight pence we have done enough for today!'; Venohr, 252.

61 *Oeuvres*, XX, 267.

62 Anon., *Hans Joachim von Zieten*, Berlin, 1865, 25.

63 Catt, 100.

64 Jessen, 295.

65 *Oeuvres*, XIX, 43.

66 Mitchell, I, 353–4.

67 *Oeuvres*, XIX, 44–5.

68 Id., XXIII, 11–12.

69 Gerd Heinrich, in Treue (ed.), 39.

70 PC, XV, 187, 195.

71 PC, XV, 218, 434, 441; Showalter, 178. Louis de Loménie, *Les Mirabeau, nouvelles études sur la société française au XVIIIe siècle*, 5 vols, Paris 1879, 1, 133–

135. In 1759, Mirabeau had an hour's talk with Choiseul in Marly.

72 Mitchell, I, 388.

73 Pangels, 354.

74 Id., 355.

75 Duffy, 133; PC, XV, 261.

76 Pangels, 356.

77 *Wanderungen*, II, 150; Catt, 105.

78 Pangels, 357–8.

79 Volz (ed.), II, 30.

80 Pangels, 398.

81 Leo Amadeus Graf Henckell Donnersmarck, *Briefe der Brüder Friedrich des Grossen an meine Grosseltern*, Berlin, 1877, 43–4.

82 *Oeuvres*, XX, 270; Pangels, 360–7; PC, XVII, 74.

83 Showalter, 176–7; Mitchell, I, 140–1, 241.

84 PC, XIV, 105.

85 Id., 15–16, 99.

86 Id., 347; Mitchell, I, 373, 278.

87 Earl of Ilchester and Mrs Langford-Brooke, *Correspondence of Catherine the Great when Grand Duchess, with Sir Charles Hanbury-Williams. And letters of Count Poniatowski*, Bristol, 1928, 16, 50, 116, 134, 235.

88 Showalter, 178–9.

89 Pangels, 398.

90 *Oeuvres*, XII, 3.

91 Id., XII, 52.

92 Id., XII, 52. Pomerania had been attacked by the Swedes. The population put up a lively resistance. Winterfeldt had recovered of the wounds sustained at Prague, but died in September after he and his escort were attacked by the Austrians at Moys. His body was found with a bullet in the back. It has been suggested that he might have been killed by one of his own Catholic, Upper Silesian, soldiers.

93 *Oeuvres*, XXVII, 304–5; for Winterfeldt's death, see Christopher Duffy, *The Army of Frederick the Great*, Newton Abbot, 1974, 176.

94 There is a monument to the Hussar Hadik on Castle Hill in Buda. Traditionally, students from the nearby hall of residence touch his horse's testicles for luck in their exams. The organs in question are notably shiny.

95 MacDonogh, *Berlin*, 444; Mitchell, I, 282.

96 *Oeuvres*, XVIII, 45.
97 Kleist, *Werke*, II, 434.
98 *Oeuvres*, XVIII, 161.
99 Id., XVII, 344.
100 Showalter, 182–3; Duffy, 140.
101 Catt, 83.
102 Volz (ed.), II, 42.
103 Kugler, 298.
104 Showalter, 186–7.
105 Cuthell, *Earl Marischal*, II, 286.
106 Catt, 83.
107 Volz (ed.), I, 48; Mitchell, I, 289; Kleist, *Werke*, II, 449.
108 K.A. Varnhagen von Ense, *Leben des Generals Freiherrn von Seydlitz*, Johann Balthazar von Kurtbach-Seydlitz, Sammlung einiger, *Schriften dem Andenken Se. Excellenz Herr Friedrich Wilhelm Frey-Herr von Seydlitz*, n. p., 1776, 31.
109 Showalter, 187–90.
110 *Oeuvres*, XXVII, 310; PC, XVI, 8; Jessen, 300.
111 PC, XVI, 7.
112 Volz (ed.), I, 48.
113 Id., I, 44; Jessen, 301.
114 Duffy, 145.
115 Voltaire, *Mémoires*, 73.
116 PC, XVII, 20.
117 *Oeuvres*, XII, 71.
118 Venohr, 261–2.
119 Erich Schmidt (ed.), *Goethes Werke in sechs Bänden*, Leipzig, 1914, III, 35.
120 Duffy, 176; Robert Asprey, *Frederick the Great: The Magnificent Enigma*, New York, 1986, 474.
121 B.P.H. Rep. 46 Nr. 77. Quoted in MacDonogh, *Prussia*, 37.
122 PC, XVI, 70.
123 Id., 60.
124 *Oeuvres*, XXVII, pt 2, 262 (both Duffy, 147, and Showalter, 195, use a different version of the speech as set down by Prince Ferdinand. The meaning is much the same).
125 PC, XVI, 75.
126 Id., 77.
127 Showalter, 196–201.
128 PC, XVI, 74.
129 Mitchell, I, 302.
130 Showalter, 205; Duffy, 153.
131 Showalter, 203; Asprey, 481; Friedrich der Grosse, *Gedanken und Erinnerungen*, reprint (n. d.) of the original edition of 1910, Essen, 539.
132 Volz (ed.), II, 59.

133 Herre, *Maria-Theresia*, 237; *Oeuvres*, XVIII, 112–13; Jessen, 325.
134 Mitchell, I, 292–3, 296.

CHAPTER TEN: THE STAG AT BAY

1 PC, XVI, 78.
2 Lorenz, *Benda*, 30.
3 Richter (ed.), *Fredersdorf*, 24.
4 Frederick meant by the Bernini mausoleum the Elisabethkapelle built by Giacomo Szianci from 1680 to 1686. *Oeuvres*, XVIII, 46; Klaus Ullmann, *Schlesien Lexikon*, 4th edn, Mannheim, 1985, 54.
5 *Oeuvres*, XVIII, 48.
6 Catt, introduction by Koser, v, 7–9.
7 Colonel Johann Friedrich Adolf von der Marwitz of the Gensd'armes is chiefly remembered for his refusal to pillage Brühl's palace at Hubertusburg: 'one might use a mercenary officer, but not the commander of his majesty's Gensd'armes'. On his grave Marwitz had written 'Wählte Ungnade, wo Gehorsam nicht Ehre brachte' (Chose disfavour where obedience brought no honour). The sacking was performed by Quintus Icilius.
8 Catt, 10; MacDonogh, *Prussia*, 131.
9 Catt, 12, 58.
10 Thiébault, V, 377–8.
11 Catt, 26–8.
12 See *Oeuvres*, XXVII, 294. There are countless examples.
13 Catt, 33.
14 Buettner, *La Motte Fouqué*, I, 28n; Duffy, 47.
15 Hubatsch, 191.
16 Catt, 38.
17 Id., 168.
18 *Oeuvres*, XVIII, 181–2.
19 Mittenzwei, 177; Lucretius, *On the Nature of the Universe*, Harmondsworth, 1994, contains a useful introduction on the Epicureans by John Godwin.
20 Catt, 44.
21 Lehndorff observed a tailor's boy's reaction when he espied it in the middle of the war: 'I always thought she was nasty and had big ears!'
22 Karl Edouard Schmidt-Lötzen (ed.), *Dreissig Jahre am Hofe Friedrichs des Grossen: Aus dem Tagebüchern des Reichsgrafen Ernst Ahasverus Heinrich Lehndorff*, Gotha, 1910, I, 191; Catt, 39, 45, 49, 50.

23 PC, XVI, 247; Kunisch, *Mirakel,* 13.
24 Catt, 61.
25 Id., 51–5.
26 Id., 88.
27 Id., 104.
28 Id., 102–3.
29 Mitchell, I, 389.
30 Scheider, 210; *Oeuvres,* XXVI, 203 n. b.
31 Koser, *Französische Gesandschaft,* 79, 80.
32 Easum, *Prince Henry,* 36 n. 6.
33 Martinfort was the Commissaire des vivres in Soubise's army. Schieder, 210–11; Mitchell, I, 110, 306.
34 *Oeuvres,* XXVI, 176.
35 PC, XVII, 79–80; *Oeuvres,* XXVI, 178.
36 *Oeuvres,* XXVI, 189.
37 Catt, 33, 76.
38 PC, XVII, 96.
39 Duffy 157; Mitchell, II, 15.
40 PC, XVII, 2.
41 Id., XVII, 60.
42 Catt, 119–20.
43 Showalter, 211.
44 PC, XVII, 53.
45 Id., 158.
46 Kleist, *Werke,* II, 509.
47 Catt, 149–54.
48 Id., 158.
49 Mitchell, I, 430–31.
50 Varnhagen von Ense, *Seydlitz,* 79; Duffy, 167.
51 Duffy, 170.
52 Mitchell, I, 433.
53 Koser, III, 197; Mitchell, I, 438.
54 *Oeuvres,* IV, 205; XX, 270; PC, XVII, 188; Schieder, 194; Showalter, 219, calls it a draw.
55 Catt, 161.
56 Id., 165–6.
57 *Oeuvres,* XVI, 20–1, Mitchell, II, 46–7; Schmidt-Lötzen (ed.), *Lehndorff,* 201.
58 Catt, 172.
59 Id., 175.
60 *Oeuvres,* XV, 2, n. x., 89, 92.
61 Varnhagen von Ense, *Keith,* 247; Cuthell, *Earl Marischal,* II, 56.
62 Duffy, 174–5.
63 Showalter, 223; Duffy, 184.
64 A monument was later set up to the Jacobite field marshal. Varnhagen von Ense, *Keith,* 252–3, 258–9; Cuthell, *Earl Marischal,* II, 59–60. Information from Douglas Graf O'Donnel in Vienna.

65 Duffy, 175–7; Showalter, 226–7; Asprey, 504.
66 Volz (ed.), II, 69.
67 Catt, 191–3; Jessen, 34 .
68 *Oeuvres,* XVIII, 117; Cuthell, *Earl Marischal,* II, 57; *A Fragment of a Memoir of Fieldmarshal James Keith Written by Himself, 1714-1734,* Edinburgh, 1843, vii.
69 Catt, 129–30.
70 Act II, Scene 3.
71 Catt, 184–92; Christiane Mervaud (*Voltaire et Frédéric,* 274) points out that the king has plenty of examples of noble suicides in the pages of Corneille.
72 Catt, 195; *Oeuvres,* IV, 223.
73 *Oeuvres,* XVIII, 54.
74 Mitchell, I, 470, 475; II, 48.
75 *Oeuvres,* XXVI, 195.
76 *Oeuvres,* XVIII, 56–7; Catt, 223; Ritter, 144.
77 *Oeuvres,* XV, 122–3; XVIII, 72.
78 Id., XXIII, 39.
79 *Oeuvres,* XXIII, 33.
80 Id., 37.
81 Id., 50, 58.
82 Id., 35.
83 Id., 53–4.
84 Id., 61–2.
85 Showalter, 231–6.
86 Catt, 228–9.
87 *Oeuvres,* XVIII, 64.
88 Mitchell, II, 63; *Oeuvres,* XVIII, 73.
89 *Oeuvres,* XVIII, 65–6.
90 PC, XVIII, 179, 185, 189, 250, 327.
91 *Oeuvres,* XX, 279–80; Asprey, 511.
92 Showalter, 241; Duffy, 182.
93 Contades had a more positive legacy: as governor of Alsace he was the recipient of the first *pâté de foie gras,* prepared for his table by his chef, Jean-Pierre Clause, sometime between 1779 and 1783. *Oeuvres,* XXV, 305; for de Contades pâté, see Henri Gault and Christian Millau, *Guide gourmand de la France,* Paris, 1970, 245.
94 *Oeuvres,* XXV, 305.
95 Catt, 242–3; Duffy, 182–3.
96 Volz (ed.), II, 89; Duffy, 185–6; Showalter, 244–5.
97 Kleist, *Werke,* II, 572.
98 Ewald Christian von Kleist, *Sämmtliche Werke nebst des Dichters Leben aus seinen Briefen am Gleim,* ed. Wilhelm Korte, Berlin, 1803, 146–9.
99 Id., 150–3.

100 Volz (ed.), II, 88; PC, XVIII, 483; Showalter, 248; Duffy, 188.

101 Showalter, 248.

102 The situation is reminiscent of the Second World War: again the Russians felt they had unjustly borne the brunt of the fighting. No wonder Goebbels was so fond of reading Hitler passages from Carlyle's Frederick the Great.

103 Venohr, 292.

104 Oeuvres, V, 20; Schieder, 197; Showalter, 250.

105 Oeuvres, XXV, 306; PC, XVIII, 481.

106 Oeuvres, XXVI, 199–200.

107 Id., XVIII, 78–9.

108 Id., 79–80.

109 Id., 81.

110 Cato of Utica, the great grandson of the famous Cato, who committed suicide after hearing of Caesar's victory over Pompey. Quintus Sertorius at one stage held most of Spain against Pompey; he was killed by his own lieutenant.

111 Oeuvres, XVIII, 82.

112 Id., 83.

113 Lotz, Kriegsgerichtsprozesse, 93.

114 Oeuvres, XVIII, 86; Holmsten, 121.

115 Oeuvres, XVIII, 91–3.

116 Id., XXIII, 66.

117 Matthias Oesterreich, author of a description of the king's paintings published in Berlin in 1773.

118 Oeuvres, XVIII, 98, 103.

119 Catt, 253.

120 Lotz, Kriegsgerichtsprozesse, 97–9; Duffy, 189; Showalter, 253.

121 Lotz, Kriegsgerichtsprozesse, 99; Oeuvres, XVIII, 106; Catt, 258–66.

122 During Louis XIV's wars it had become patriotic to eat off faïence instead of gold or silver. This encouraged production. D'Argens must have known the faïence of Moustiers. See Paul Clappier, Chroniques de Moustiers, 1700–1750, Saint-Cénéré, 1976.

123 Oeuvres, XVIII, 109.

124 Catt, 310.

125 Oeuvres, XIX, 124–6.

126 Id., 137, 189.

127 Id., XXIII, 67.

128 Mitchell, II, 127–9.

129 PC, XIX, 65, 171–2, 343.

130 Oeuvres, XVIII, 174.

131 Id., XIX, 168; Mervaud, Voltaire et Frédéric, 354.

132 Oeuvres, XXIII, 76; Mervaud, Voltaire et Frédéric, 308, 309, 353–4.

133 Oeuvres, XXIII, 77.

134 Id., 82.

135 Id., 84.

136 Id., XIX, 135.

137 Id., 148 and n. a.; D.C.R.A. [Samuel Formey] L'Anti-Sans-Souci, ou la folie des nouveaux philosophes, naturistes, déistes et autres Impies dépeintes au naturel, Bouillon, 1760.

138 Oeuvres, XIX, 136.

139 Id., 137, 140–1.

140 The dishes were inscribed with the motto 'dubium sapientiae initium': 'doubt is the first step towards knowledge'.

141 Oeuvres, XIX, 144, 151.

142 Mitchell, II, 131.

143 Venohr, 300.

144 Buettner, La Motte Fouqué, II, 99–100.

145 Wanderungen, I, 209; Oeuvres, V, 53–4.

146 Mitchell, II, 184; I, 165, 283.

147 Voltaire, Histoire de la guerre de 1741, 173.

148 PC, XIV, 95; XVI, 89.

149 'Quintus is here, he talks about books in German, which I don't know and I don't want to know. I have promised him the annals of all the famous pillagers from Charles V to our own times, and usum legionum franquum.' Frederick to Catt, Meissen, 18 November 1762. Thiébault, V, 393; Oeuvres, XXIV, 18.

150 Oeuvres, XVIII, 120.

151 Johann Gotzkowsky, Geschichte eines patriotischen Kaufmanns, Berlin, 1873, 76.

152 Duffy, 204.

153 Wanderungen, I, 209; Venohr, 301.

154 Mitchell, II, 201; Oeuvres, XIX, 189.

155 Showalter, 276–80.

156 Lehndorff, I, 255.

157 Oeuvres, XIX, 192; Venohr, 299.

158 Lehndorff, 270.

159 D'Argens gives Lehwaldt's role to General Knobloch – a Provencal prejudice perhaps.

160 MacDonogh, Berlin, 444; Lehndorff, I, 268; Gotzkowsky, 16.

161 Gotzkowsky, 19.

162 Duffy, 208.

163 Philip Mansel, Charles-Joseph de Ligne, 1735–1814: le charmeur de l'Europe, Paris, 1992,

36–7; *Oeuvres*, V, 80–1; XVIII, 121;
Lehndorff, I, 276.

164 *Oeuvres*, XIX, 198.

165 Lehndorff, I, 270, 273; Schieder, 197;
Duffy, 209.

166 Showalter, 283–4.

167 *Oeuvres*, XXIII, 89.

168 Gotzkowsky, 12–15.

169 Id., 19–25.

170 Id., 28–39.

171 *Oeuvres*, XIX, 222, n. a.

172 Gotzkowsky, 42–9.

173 Mittenzwei, 135.

174 *Oeuvres*, XIX, 199.

175 Id., 204.

176 Showalter, 292.

177 Venohr, 302; Duffy, 216.

178 Venohr, 307.

179 PC, XX, 46–7.

180 Cuthell, *Earl Marischal*, II, 99.

181 Schieder, 201; Mitchell, I, 402–3, 408.

182 Schieder, 199–200; *Oeuvres*, XIX,
202.

183 *Oeuvres*, XXIV, 3–6.

184 *Ein deutscher Reiter Offizier, Friedrich
Wilhelm von Seydlitz, königl. Preussischer
General der Cavallerie*, Kassel, 1882, 163.

185 *Oeuvres*, XXV, 290–1.

186 Id., XVIII, 193–4.

187 Id., XIX, 205–12.

CHAPTER ELEVEN: EXPECTING A
MIRACLE

1 Herre, *Maria-Theresia*, 228.

2 *Oeuvres*, XXIII, 89.

3 PC, XVIII, 516.

4 *Oeuvres*, XIX, 213.

5 Id., 214.

6 Id., 220.

7 Id., 226–7.

8 Id., XVIII, 145.

9 Duffy, 219.

10 Pangels, 490–2.

11 PC, XIX, 343, 373.

12 Volz (ed.), II, 93; *Oeuvres*, XXVI, 252,
253.

13 *Oeuvres*, XIX, 227, 229, 230, 231.

14 Id., 243.

15 Id., 246.

16 Id., 249.

17 Id., XXIV, 6.

18 Id., XIX, 252.

19 Duffy, 221; Showalter, 306.

20 *Oeuvres*, XIX, 256.

21 Id., XXVI, 225–6.

22 *Wanderungen*, I, 558, 680; Venohr, 284,
302.

23 *Oeuvres*, XIX, 275.

24 PC, XXI, 189.

25 *Oeuvres*, XIX, 284.

26 PC, XXI, 189.

27 *Oeuvres*, XIX, 288.

28 PC, XXI, 191, 192, 194.

29 For a reiteration of this view, see
Vincent Cronin, *Catherine: Empress of all
the Russias*, London, 1989, 131–43.

30 On 10 August, Frederick wrote to
Henry: 'Le sang du petit-fils de Pierre Ier
crie contre elle et ce prince avait en Russie
un plus grand parti qu'elle n'avait
presumé.'

31 *Oeuvres*, XXVI, 237; Volz (ed.), II,
138.

32 *Oeuvres*, XIX, 292.

33 PC, XXI, 211.

34 Id., 233.

35 Id., 254 n. 3.

36 Id., 277 and n. 3, 284.

37 *Oeuvres*, XXVI, 239.

38 Cuthell, *Earl Marischal*, II, 122–4.

39 Showalter, 319.

40 *Oeuvres*, XVII, 365–6.

41 Id., XIX, 306; PC, XXI, 339; Jessen,
395.

42 *Oeuvres*, XIX, 270–1.

43 Id., XXVI, 243.

44 Voltaire bitchily maintained that Babet
was ugly. She does not appear so in
Pesne's picture of her sister dancing, in
which she is portrayed among the
spectators. She is described in one account
as 'a pretty brunette with big dark eyes'.
After she married d'Argens she deserted
acting for scholarship. Lyonnet,
Dictionnaire des Comédiens, I, 367.

45 *Oeuvres*, XIX, 317; XIV, 17.

46 Id., XIX, 325.

47 Duffy, 228.

48 Showalter, 316.

49 *Oeuvres*, XIX, 331.

50 Frederick was as incredulous as
everyone else: 'Il était mort d'une violente
colique qui l'avait emporté. Il ne sera pas
difficile, je crois, à pénéter de quelle
espèce a été cette colique.'

51 *Testament politique*, 221.

52 *Snoshenie s russkim istoricheskim
obshchestrom*, Saint Petersburg, 1873, I, 9.

53 Id., 11, 13.

54 *Oeuvres*, XIX, 336.

55 PC, XXII, 42.
56 *Snoshenie*, 27.
57 *Oeuvres*, XXVI, 250, 251.
58 Ilchester and Mrs Langford-Brooke, *Hanbury-Williams*, 326, 336.
59 Madariaga, *Catherine*, 15.
60 PC, XXIII, 93; Madariaga, *Catherine*, 187.
61 *Snoshenie*, 68.
62 Cuthell, *Earl Marischal*, II, 132; *Oeuvres*, XVIII, 216.
63 *Oeuvres*, XIX, 355–6.
64 Id., XVIII, 148; XIX, 348.
65 Pangels, 450.
66 Showalter, 320.
67 *Oeuvres*, XVIII, 149.
68 Id., XIX, 381.
69 Id., XVIII, 215.
70 Id., V, 219.
71 Venohr, 320.
72 *Oeuvres*, XVIII, 127.

CHAPTER TWELVE: PICKING UP THE PIECES

1 Schieder, 184; S.B. Hermann, *Hans Joachim von Zieten*, Leipzig, n. d., 129–30.
2 Holmsten, 135–6.
3 Hinrichs, *Der allgegenwärtige König*, 115.
4 Thiébault, III, 20.
5 Gotzkowsky, 88.
6 Koser, III, 173; Nicolai, 'Anekdoten', quoted in Friedrich von Oppeln-Bronikowski, *Der grosse König*, Leipzig 1935, 149; *Oeuvres*, XIX, 385.
7 Lehndorff, 456–7; MacDonogh, *Berlin*, 54–5.
8 Ritter, 157.
9 Schieder, 65.
10 Hubatsch, 148; Venohr, 329, gives slightly different figures. Frederick, in his history of the Seven Years War, says that only 20,000 civilians were killed: *Oeuvres*, V, 230.
11 *Oeuvres*, XXIV, 102.
12 Id., VI, 74.
13 Information from Oliver Schmidt, Kloster Zinna, April 1996.
14 *Oeuvres*, VI, 73.
15 *Oeuvres*, XIII, 23–4.
16 Mittenzwei, 147–8.
17 *Oeuvres*, XXIII, 301.
18 Hubatsch, 149, 154.
19 *Oeuvres*, VI, 75–6, 82.
20 Id., XXIII, 107, 108.
21 Ritter, 218–19.

22 Hubatsch, 170.
23 Thiébault, III, 20; Volz (ed.), II, 223.
24 Pangels, 297, 360.
25 Schieder, 213.
26 Thiébault, IV, 120; MacDonogh, *Berlin*, 22.
27 Mitchell, II, 343–4.
28 Lorenz, *Benda*, 31.
29 Lehndorff, I, 369.
30 *Oeuvres*, VI, 9.
31 Giersberg, *Friedrich als Bauherr*, 246–8; *Oeuvres*, XXVI, 274, 277.
32 Gregorio Guglielmi, born Rome 1714, died Saint Petersburg 1773.
33 *Oeuvres*, XXVI, 278.
34 Novel by Theodore Fontane of 1895, in which Effie Briest has an adulterous affair with a man of inferior class.
35 Easum, *Prince Henry*, 245.
36 Henry possibly means the work by Gregorio Allegri, which was an exclusivity of the Sistine Chapel until Mozart transcribed the notes from memory.
37 *Oeuvres*, XXVI, 280.
38 Id., 284.
39 Lotz, *Kriegsgerichtsprozesse*, 100–3.
40 Despite their dishonourable dismissals from the Prussian army, Finck continued his military vocation under the Danish flag and Rebentisch found employment in the Portuguese service.
41 Lotz, *Kriegsgerichtsprozesse*, 107–9, 116–17, 127, 136–7, 145.
42 Id., 150, 162, 167, 174–5.
43 Gotthold Ephraim Lessing, 'Minna von Barnhelm', II, ii, in Lessing, *Dramen*, Frankfurt am Main and Hamburg, 1962, 49.
44 *Oeuvres*, XXIV, 367.
45 Volz (ed.), III, 130–1.
46 Cronin, *Catherine*, 168. It had first been used in Boston in the American colonies in 1721, and became increasingly popular in the New World in the first half of the century. See W.J. Fraser, *Charleston! Charleston! The History of the Southern City*, Columbia, 1989, 65.
47 Volz (ed.), III, 131.
48 Id., 132–3.
49 Id., 134–5.
50 *Oeuvres*, XXVI, 278.
51 Id., XXIV, 377–8, 380, 381.
52 Volz (ed.), III, 135.
53 *Oeuvres*, XXIV, 398, 407.
54 Volz (ed.), III, 31–4.

55 Id., 38.
56 *Oeuvres*, XVIII, 385; Brinitzer, *Daniel Ch.*, 208–9.
57 Thiébault, IV, 114–17.
58 It was part of Gestapo headquarters during the Third Reich. As such, the substantial ruins were blown up by the Americans after the war.
59 *Oeuvres*, XXVI, 293, 295, 296.
60 Thiébault, III, 14–17.
61 Lehndorff, I, 369, 389, 393.
62 Pangels, 299–300; Thiébault, I, 83.
63 Pangels, 409.
64 Giovanni Carlo Concialini, 1742–1812.
65 Pangels, 303–4.
66 *Oeuvres*, XXIII, 209.
67 Pangels, 301–2.
68 C.B.A. Behrens, *Society, Government and the Enlightenment*, 10–11, maintains the opposite.
69 Volz (ed.), II, 140, 113; Casanova, *My Life*, I, 299.
70 Casanova, *My Life*, X, 68.
71 Id., 70, 71; Lehndorff, I, 404; *Oeuvres*, XVIII, 154–5.
72 Caesar's bisexuality was a well-aired theme in eighteenth-century Europe. One notes that Casanova's description of Frederick's tastes is similar to Voltaire's, which would have been current in the *philosophic* salons of Europe frequented by the Venetian. Casanova affirms that he later learned much from d'Argens when he visited him near Aix, but neglected to put it down. Thiébault (I, 195) swears blindly that there was no evidence to support the Voltaire-Casanova position: 'J'ai interrogé autant que je l'ai pu, les sages, et même les hommes les plus enclins à tout dire. Or, personne, absolument personne ne m'a donné sur ce point la preuve aucun fait ...' Blanchot, the secretary at the Swedish legation, told Boswell that Frederick was impotent.
73 Casanova, *My Life*, X, 77.
74 *Oeuvres*, XV, 15.
75 Casanova, *My Life*, X, 78, 316.
76 Id., 79–80.
77 Volz (ed.), III, 3, 19–20.
78 Pottle (ed.), *Boswell*, 17–18.
79 Id., 23–4.
80 Pottle (ed.), *Boswell*, 80.
81 Id., 80, 100 n. 1; *Oeuvres*, XVIII, 265.
82 Jessen, 456.
83 She was in fact at that time married

to Augustus Hervey, later earl of Bristol. She later wed the duke of Kingston without bothering to divorce her first husband.
84 *Oeuvres*, XXVI, 37–8.
85 Id., XXIII, 360 n. c, 90.
86 Later the sixth earl of Stair and minister plenipotentiary to Berlin in the last year of Frederick's life.
87 *Oeuvres*, XXV, 21.
88 Id., XVIII, 252; XXIV, 395; Thiébault, III, 143.
89 *Oeuvres*, XXIII, 217; XXIV, 570, 602, 605; XXV, 7.
90 Mittenzwei, 173.
91 Volz (ed.), II, 223.
92 Cuthell, *Earl Marischal*, II, 194.
93 Id., 201.
94 Id., 248.
95 Marischal was unfortunate with his wine. He preferred sweet, white Bergerac, which refermented in the hot summer. 'The common drink here is called Pontac, red, nasty, stuff, about 12 pence French a bottle, buying it at Stetin [sic], where I suppose it is made ...' (see above, p. 000).
96 Cuthell, *Earl Marischal*, II, 204, 206, 207.
97 Id., 210.
98 *Oeuvres*, XXIV, 323.
99 Id., XX, 93, 95.
100 Id., XXIII, 321, 341, 344.
101 Id., XXIV, 392.
102 Thiébault, I, 6–7, 9.
103 *Oeuvres*, XXIII, 116.
104 Thiébault, I, 11–16.
105 Id., 23, 111.
106 *Oeuvres*, XIII, 16.
107 Id., XXIII, 124–5; XX, 21–2.
108 Thiébault, I, 147.
109 Id., 200–2.
110 Id., V, 352–6.
111 Catt, 87.
112 *Oeuvres*, XVIII, 390–1, 396; XXIV, 397.
113 Id., XVIII, 421, 423, 427.
114 Id., XXIII, 187, 192.
115 *Oeuvres*, XVIII, x; Jean Paul Coste, *Aix en Provence et le pays d'Aix*, Aix, 1981, 19, 78, 132.
116 The church survived the French Revolution, but the monument has been transferred to the Musée Granet.
117 Michelessi, *Algarotti*, 172.
118 Thiébault, I, 220–37.

119 Id., 238–51; Catt, 39; *Oeuvres*, XX, 221–8.

120 *Oeuvres*, XX, 122, 124.

121 These were unlikely to have been made from foie gras at the time; rather partridge, chicken livers and truffles.

122 *Oeuvres*, XIII, 85.

123 The author asked the head of the truffle hunters' union in Tricastin (which yields 60 per cent of French truffles) whether German truffles could really be this good. He characterised them as 'brumales', which have a strong, musky flavour that is generally seen as inferior to the black *tuber melanosporum*.

124 *Oeuvres*, XX, 133.

125 Id., 133–46.

126 Id., XXIV, 408.

127 Id., XXIII, 115.

128 Id., 102.

129 Id., 405.

130 Id., 409–12.

131 Mervaud, *Voltaire et Frédéric*, 385; *Oeuvres*, XXIII, 150.

132 *Oeuvres*, XXIII, 169.

133 *Oeuvres*, XXIII, 103–4.

134 Schieder, 80–3.

135 Hubatsch, 178.

136 *Oeuvres*, VI, 81.

137 Frederick was prepared to accept pretty flimsy evidence of nobility if he felt that the candidate had the right qualities.

138 Except in Silesia where a Graf Colonna was the biggest iron manufacturer by the end of the century.

139 Behrens, *Society, Government and the Enlightenment*, 64; Schieder, 59–61; *Testament politique*, 180–1.

140 Schieder, 212.

141 Id., 52.

142 *Testament politique*, 130.

143 See, for example, Gordon Craig, *The Politics of the Prussian Army, 1640–1945*, London, Oxford, New York, 1964, 16–17.

144 Behrens, *Society, Government and the Enlightenment*, 62–5; *Testament politique*, 130.

145 Mitchell, II, 369–70.

146 The story has been told many times. I have taken Linsenbarth's own account from Inge Hoeftmann and Waltraud Noack, *Potsdam in alten und neuen Reisebeschreibungen*, Düsseldorf, 1992, 64–9.

147 Id., 66.

148 Id., 69.

149 *Testament politique*, 110–11.

150 Id., 140.

151 Id., 149.

152 [Mirabeau], *Histoire sécrète de la cour de Berlin*, II, Rotterdam, 1789, 136, quoted in MacDonogh, *Prussia*, 41.

153 *Testament politique*, 160.

154 Id., 177.

155 Id., 115–25.

156 Id., 178.

157 Id., 179.

158 Id., 133.

159 *Oeuvres*, VI, 215–17.

160 Id., XXX, 5, 295.

161 Id., VI, 99; IX, 77–80, 83.

162 Jean-Jacques Burlamqui (1696–1748) was a Swiss jurist.

163 *Oeuvres*, IX, 101–12.

164 *Testament politique*, 132–3.

165 *Oeuvres*, IX, 120–6.

166 J.P. Savage, 'Fredrich der Grosse und die französische Kultur', in Oswald Hauser (ed.), *Friedrich der Grosse in Seiner Zeit*, Cologne, Vienna, 1987, 22; *Oeuvres*, IX, 136; Boyer d'Argens, 'Thérèse philosophe', in Raymond Trousson (ed.), *Roman libertins du XVIIIe siècle*, Paris, 1993, 622–3.

167 *Oeuvres*, XV, 17.

168 Id., IX, 132–51.

169 Id., 160–7.

170 Id., 171–9.

171 *Oeuvres*, XIII, 11.

172 Johnson, 190; Hans Huth, 'Chambers and Potsdam' in Fraser, Hibberd and Lewine (eds), *Essays in the History of Architecture presented to Rudolf Wittkower*, London, 1967, 214.

173 Giersberg in Hohenzollern (ed.), 68–9.

174 *Oeuvres*, XXIII, 258; Dehio, *Bezirke Berlin/DDR und Potsdam*, Berlin, 1983, 362.

175 It appears ruinous today. The bones of the last kaiser's widow 'Dona' and her eldest son William were clearly an embarrassment to the old regime.

176 *Oeuvres*, XXIII, 414; MacDonogh, *Berlin*, 72–3.

177 *Oeuvres*, XXVI, 311.

178 For Franz Kugler's *Friedrich der Grosse*, of 1839–42. This is not to be confused with the painting in the National Gallery, which recreates an earlier concert in honour of a visit from Wilhelmina.

179 Percy Scholes, *The Great Dr Burney*, 2 vols, Oxford, 1958, I, 230; Lorenz, *Benda*, 38.

180 Lorenz, *Benda*, 35.

181 Hoeftmann and Noack, *Potsdam*, 70–83, gives extracts from Burney's diary translated into German. See p. 75.

182 Quoted in Scholes, *Burney*, I, 233.

183 Lorenz, *Benda*, 33.

184 It was under a tenth of what the singers Porporino and Conciolini received.

185 Lorenz, *Benda*, 40–1.

186 Johann Friedrich Reichardt, *Schreiben über die Berlinische Musik an den Herrn L v Sch in M.*, Hamburg 1775, 10–13.

187 Thiébault, I, 271.

188 Lorenz, *Benda*, 42; there is a recording of the *Trauerkantate* coupled with E.T.A. Hoffmann's *Miserere*, Koch, 1988.

189 Winfried Baer, *Berliner Porzellan*, 6; *Oeuvres*, XX, 124; XXVI, 284–5.

190 Christiane Keisch, 'Friedrich der Grosse und sein Porzellan: die königlichen Tafelservice', in Hohenzollern (ed.), 299.

191 *Oeuvres*, XXIII, 218, 223, 226, 238.

192 Id., 304–5.

193 Id., XXV, 11–12.

194 Id., XXIII, 322, 329.

195 Id., 150; XXIV, 19, 24; Oesterreicher, *Beschreibung*, 104, footnote to the index entry for Correggio.

196 *Oeuvres*, XXIII, 184, 284, 335–6; Lyonnet, *Dictionnaire des Comédiens*, I, 58; II, 333–6.

197 *Oeuvres*, XXIII, 365.

CHAPTER THIRTEEN: DIVIDING UP THE PUDDING

1 Thiébault, I, 110.

2 *Oeuvres*, XXIII, 205; William Hagen, *Germans, Poles and Jews: The Nationality Conflict in the Prussian East, 1772–1914*, Chicago, London, 1980, 36, quoted in MacDonogh, *Prussia*, 315.

3 For a discussion of this fraught issue, see MacDonogh, *Prussia*, 314–17.

4 *Oeuvres*, VI, 7.

5 *Die Politischen Testamente Friedrichs des Grossen: Ergänzungsband zur Politischen Correspondenz Friedrichs des Grossen*, Berlin, 1920, 213, 219.

6 *Oeuvres*, XXIII, 120.

7 Madariaga, *Catherine*, 191.

8 *Oeuvres*, XXIV, 419.

9 Schieder, 244–5.

10 Herre, *Maria-Theresia*, 294; Holmsten, 156.

11 Schieder, 246.

12 *Oeuvres*, XXIV, 461.

13 Id., XXIII, 165–6.

14 Id., XIII, 57.

15 Mansel, *Ligne*, 65.

16 *Oeuvres*, VI, 25.

17 Id., XXIII, 169.

18 Id., 171.

19 Volz (ed.), III, 23.

20 Schieder, 248; Holmsten, 146; *Oeuvres*, XXIII, 173; XXIV, 557.

21 *Oeuvres*, XXIII, 208; Schieder, 248.

22 *Oeuvres*, XXVI, 320–32.

23 Thiébault, II, 179–80.

24 *Oeuvres*, XXVI, 345; Schieder, 249; Jessen, 444; Easum, *Prince Henry*, 269–71.

25 *Oeuvres*, XXVI, 349–50; Jessen, 444.

26 Walther Mediger, 'Friedrich der Grosse und Russland', in Hauser (ed.), 132; Schieder, 250–5; T.C.W. Blanning, *Joseph II*, London, New York, 1994, 48; Herre, *Maria-Theresia*, 335.

27 He was probably right: see Madariaga, *Catherine*, 231.

28 It came with the Second Partition of 1793.

29 *Oeuvres*, VI, 38–47, 89; Holmsten, 147.

30 *Oeuvres*, XXVI, 358.

31 Id., VI, 88–9.

32 Id., XXVI, 358; Holmsten, 147–8.

33 See, for instance, *Oeuvres*, XVIII, 239.

34 Id., XXIII, 242.

35 Id., XX, 179–80.

36 Id., XXIII, 250.

37 Id., 267; XXVI, 363.

38 John Kelly, *The Oxford Dictionary of Popes*, Oxford, 1986, 300.

39 *Oeuvres*, XXIV, 422, 429.

40 *Oeuvres*, XXIV, 453.

41 *Oeuvres*, XXIII, 258.

42 Id., 268.

43 Id., 629–30.

44 Id., XXIV, 616, n. b.

45 Id., XXIII, 414–15.

46 Id., 281.

47 Thiébault, I, 276.

48 *Testament politique*, 221.

49 *Oeuvres*, XXIII, 308.

50 Id., 370 and n. a.; Behrens, *Society, Government and the Enlightenment*, 52.

51 *Oeuvres*, XXV, 101.

52 Id., 103–11.

53 Id., 110.
54 Id., 159.
55 Id., 337.
56 Id., XXIII, 342.
57 Id., 350.
58 Id., 350.
59 Id., XXIV, 342; the translations are in *Huit dissertations lues dans les séances publiques de l'Académie royale des sciences et belle-lettres de Berlin, pour l'anniversaire du roi dans les années 1780, 1781, 1782, 1783 à 1787, par M. de Hertzberg*, Berlin, 1783 etc., 19–20.
60 *Oeuvres*, VII, 92.
61 Christian Fürchtegott Gellert, 1715–69, professor at Leipzig, and minor Enlightenment poet, novelist and playwright; Salomon Gessner, 1730–88, Swiss writer and artist. For the Prussian Canitz, see above, p. 200.
62 *Oeuvres*, VII, 94.
63 Id., XXIII, 97.
64 Id., VII, 105–7.
65 Id., 122.
66 Id., XXIV, 344.
67 Id., 343.
68 Id., 344.
69 Karl Erich Born, *Wirtschaft und Gesellschaft im Denken Friedrichs des Grossen*, Wiesbaden, 1979, 4–5.
70 Id., 11.
71 Id., 15–16.
72 *Oeuvres*, IX, 188.
73 Id., 198.
74 Id., 208.
75 Id., 199.
76 Volz (ed.), III, 176.
77 *Oeuvres*, VI, 137.
78 Schieder, 273–4; Blanning, *Joseph*, 132.
79 Holmsten, 150; Showalter, 349.
80 *Oeuvres*, XXVI, 439.
81 Herre, *Maria-Theresia*, 345.
82 Showalter, 345.
83 *Oeuvres*, XXIV, 25.
84 Showalter, 348; Duffy, 275.
85 *Oeuvres*, XXVI, 466, 468.
86 Id., XXIX, 126.
87 Id., XXIV, 25; XXVI, 472.
88 Herre, *Maria-Theresia*, 346–7.
89 Keith, *Fragment*, xiv.
90 Anton Schindling, in *Friedrich der Grosse: Sein Bild im Wandel der Zeiten*, 17.
91 Schieder, 262–5.
92 Zimmermann, in Gaxotte (ed.), 232.

93 *Oeuvres*, VI, 210; Schindling in *Friedrich der Grosse: Sein Bild im Wandel der Zeiten*, 20–2; Schieder, 278–82.

CHAPTER FOURTEEN: TWILIGHT
1 Behrens, *Society, Government and the Enlightenment*, 110–15, contains an excellent analysis of this famous case.
2 Thiébault, IV, 19.
3 Id.
4 Id., 21.
5 *Oeuvres*, XXV, 312–13; J.E. Neumann, *Aus der Festungszeit preussischer Kammergericht- und Regierungsräte auf Spandau 1780*, Tagebuch, Berlin, 1910.
6 Volz (ed.), III, 177–8; Venohr, 366–7.
7 Born, *Wirtschaft*, 10, quoting the gazette no. 149; Venohr, 367.
8 Schieder, 293.
9 Günther Elbin (ed.), *Literat und Feldmarshall: Briefe und Erinnerungen des Fürsten Charles Joseph de Ligne, 1735–1814*, Stuttgart, 1979, 48–51; Mansel, *Ligne*, 90–2.
10 Pangels, 213.
11 Volz (ed.), III, 191.
12 Id., 204–6; Holmsten, 154.
13 Thiébault, III, 155; Zimmermann, in Gaxotte (ed.), 223.
14 Thiébault, I, 266.
15 In those days it did not sport a mould. Frederick's cheeses were delivered fresh (like *fromage frais*) or in pots.
16 Jacobs (ed.), *Briefe an Thieriot*, 24, 37.
17 Volz (ed.), III, 204–6.
18 Hans-Joachim Neumann, 'Friedrich der Grosse: ein medizinhistorischer Beitrag über seine Krankheiten und seine Ärzte', in *Mitteilungen des Vereins für die Geschichte Berlins*, July 1997, 236; Thiébault, I, 266.
19 One is tempted to believe that this was with truffles.
20 Neumann, in *Mitteilungen*, 236.
21 Hertzberg, *Dissertations*, 35–42.
22 Volz (ed.), III, 196.
23 *Oeuvres*, XXV, 188.
24 Id., 219.
25 Id., 237.
26 Id., 244.
27 Id., 348, 351.
28 Id., 369.
29 Id., XXVI, 501.
30 Volz (ed.), III, 189.
31 Id., 5.

32 Volz (ed.), III, 216.

33 Id., 198.

34 *Oeuvres*, XXV, 375–83.

35 Anon, *Hans-Joachim von Zieten*, Berlin, 1865, 37, 45.

36 Volz (ed.), III, 216.

37 Graf Hertzberg, *Mémoire historique sur la dernière année de la vie de Frédéric II, roi de Prusse*, Berlin, 1787, 3–7.

38 Zimmermann, in Pierre Gaxotte (ed.), *Frédéric II, roi de Prusse*, Paris, 1967, 213.

39 Ragnhild Hatton, 'Frederick the Great and the House of Hanover', in Hauser (ed.), 158 n. 21. Zimmermann, in Gaxotte (ed.), 231.

40 Toulongeon, in id., 240.

41 *Oeuvres*, XXVI, 532.

42 Id., 62.

43 Pangels, 219; Oppeln-Bronikowski, *Grosse König*, 249.

44 Hertzberg, *Mémoire historique*, 9–10.

45 Gaxotte, 110.

46 Werner Schwipps, *Die Königl. Hof- und Garnisonkirche zu Potsdam*, Berlin, 1991, 47–50.

47 Henckel Donnersmarck, *Briefe*, 54.

48 J. W. von Goethe, *Italienische Reise*, Frankfurt am Main, 1976, 366.

49 Gooch, *Frederick the Great*, V.

50 'The spirit of Potsdam expired in Potsdam.' Rudolf Augstein, *Preussens Friedrich und die Deutschen*, Frankfurt am Main, Vienna, Zurich, 1970, 357.

51 It does not seem to have been Voltaire's wish to publish the *Mémoires* which began to circulate six years after his death. *Paméla* was abandoned. *Oeuvres*, XXIII, 326.

52 Id., 447.

53 Volz (ed.), III, 47.

Index